P9-CLC-274

SHOWING AND JUDGING DOGS

The Author

SHOWING AND JUDGING DOGS

By

HILARY HARMAR

ARCO PUBLISHING COMPANY, INC.
NEW YORK

By the same author

CHIHUAHUAS
THE POMERANIAN
THE CHIHUAHUA GUIDE
THE COCKER SPANIEL GUIDE
THE BLOODHOUND
THE DOBERMANN
THE JACK RUSSELL TERRIER
DOGS AND HOW TO BREED THEM
DOGS AND HOW TO GROOM THEM
THE COMPLETE CHIHUAHUA ENCYCLOPEDIA

In preparation

THE SHIH TZU
BREEDING BETTER DOGS

Published by Arco Publishing Company, Inc.
219 Park Avenue South, New York, N.Y. 10003

Library of Congress Catalog Card Number 75–795
ISBN 0–668–03793–8

Photographs by Anne Cumbers
Drawings by Leslie C. Benenson

Printed in Great Britain

WIN WITH HUMILITY AND
LOSE WITHOUT
MALICE

JUDGE WITHOUT FEAR OR FAVOUR

"This above all things, To thine own self be true. And it shall follow as the night the day, thou canst not then be false to any man."

William Shakespeare—Hamlet

FOR MUFFY

Contents

Foreword

Frankly, I'm not much interested in Pedigree Certificates that look like a genealogical tree of the Romanovs. They remind me of that rather repetitious chapter in the Old Testament where Seth begat Enos who begat Cainan who begat Mahalaleel; until Enoch begat Methuselah, who lived 969 years: *and he died.*

Once I bought a miniature Dachshund from an awfully nice woman in Norfolk. He was sired by Jacko of the Abbeys out of Shandy of Norwich. Grand Sire Swifty of Attlebridge and Grand Dam Drayton Helga . . . all the way to Grand Sire No. 13, who was Antway Andy, and Grand Dam No. 14, Jennifer of the Abbeys.

Which was, I suppose, all very splendid. But I called the little chap Small. It was probably betraying his birthright; but it didn't seem to put him off his food.

A year later someone gave me a Dalmatian puppy, eight weeks old and, improbably, smaller than Small. The Dalmatian, christened Justin, was also impeccably bred; but, being the new boy, was patronized outrageously by Small, who swanked around the place like mad, knowing where all the best bones were buried and which local tom could be chased with impunity and which should be treated with caution.

Everything went well until Justin started to grow. It was a traumatic time for Small, diminishing in stature day by day beside this gallomping plum-pudding of a dog. If there were dog-psychiatrists Small would have spent more time on the couch than in his kennel. But it worked out in the end because each came to terms with his own limitations. Justin, for example, could outrun Small; but Small could chase rabbits down very narrow tunnels. They forgot their differences, forgot their pedigrees and became inseparable friends.

Coming to terms with things is nothing to do with compromise. Compromise is often a kind of retreat, whereas, in my opinion, coming to terms with a situation is an awareness, forged upon the anvil of tolerance, understanding and generosity. It is also a question of communication—and this is where Hilary Harmar, the author of this book, comes in.

There is, in bookshops and libraries, a wealth of reading matter available to the dog-expert: volumes crammed with esoteric information about feeding theories and in-breeding. However, Hilary Harmar has already written with great experience and scholarship excellent books on the many facets of dogs. Her world-renowned book on *Dogs and How to Breed Them* which is the bible of all serious breeders, is in language that a layman can easily absorb and understand.

Hilary Harmar's most recent tour de force is, one might almost say, the dog book to end all dog books. The author, who has written that 'There is no such thing as the perfect dog', would no doubt admonish me by retaliating that there is no such thing as the perfect dog book.

I have made no secret—in fact I seem to have broadcast it quite blatantly—of my own ignorance about the more specialist aspects of dog showing. I simply like dogs. I enjoy going to dog shows; I delight in walking with a dog at my heel; I like tossing them bones; I, not infrequently, enjoy their conversation in preference to that of many of my two-legged acquaintances. In this respect, then, I am an Ordinary Dog Lover, as opposed to a Very Earnest Dog Fancier. And Hilary Harmar has, for the most part, written about dogs in a way that even I can understand. Her latest book is both for dog lovers and dog experts; and it also bears out the enormous importance of exhibiting only top-bred, sound dogs and the importance too of expertise and integrity in judging. People like me can then derive full enjoyment from our strong, healthy and intelligent pets.

Tarston Hall
Needham Market
Suffolk

Michael Watkins

Author's Preface

It has been quite a challenge to write a book on such controversial subjects as showing, handling and judging dogs. It has taken me years to accomplish and I have learnt much in the process. Rules and regulations and certain judging procedures vary slightly in different countries. I have chosen to take the Kennel Club rules and regulations as the basis, since this was the first Kennel Club in the world, and all the others have been based on this original club. I have written this book to help the keen, aspiring, novice exhibitor and judge, so that the basic principles may be understood regardless of individual kennel-club rules and regulations. Every kennel club's rules and regulations are changed frequently, and it is therefore important to keep up to date in whichever country and under whichever kennel-club regulations the dogs may be registered and exhibited.

There are many techniques of handling dogs. These vary enormously from breed to breed, and from dog to dog. What may be considered as 'over handling' in one country is considered correct for the breed in another. I have taken the methods used for most breeds in the United States, where the majority of breeds are handled with the same lead control and technique. In Britain some of these techniques might be considered as 'over handling'. It is easier, however, to modify these methods for individual judges' preferences than it would be the other way round.

My grateful thanks must go to the Kennel Club for all the assistance and courtesy that I have received, for the use of their splendid library, for permission to print the breed standards and various interesting lists from the Kennel Gazette, and for permission to reproduce some of the Kennel Club paintings. I must also thank Mr Alfred M. Dick, the late President of the American Kennel Club, for so kindly granting me permission to print the American Kennel Club Rules in full, their breed standards and their list of breeds in order of popularity, and also for the assistance of M. J. A. Lafore Jnr, President of the American Kennel Club. My sincere thanks and tremendous appreciation must go to Anne Cumbers for all the work and patience she put into the exacting work of obtaining the photographs of all the breeds at numerous championship shows. This has been no mean accomplishment. There is no such thing as the perfect dog but her beautiful photographs have certainly made this book more explicit and helpful to the novice breeder and judge. My sincere thanks must go to Leslie C. Benenson for her illustrations and diagrams.

My appreciation extends to all owners and breeders of dogs whose photographs appear in the book. To all authors past and present, whose books I have enjoyed reading, and in the process of which I have gained useful knowledge to pass on to others; to my long-suffering husband who has had to wade through my book and give helpful advice; to our daughter Muffy, for her part in the dog game; to Hilde Brookfield for so kindly taking my dictation and encouraging me to go on; and last but by no means least to all my dogs, wherever they are, who have never let me down.

Hilary Harmar

HIS APOLOGIES

Master, this is Thy Servant. He is rising eight weeks old.
He is mainly Head and Tummy. His legs are uncontrolled.
But thou has forgiven his ugliness, and settled him on Thy knee . . .
Art thou content with Thy Servant? He is *very* comfy with Thee.

Master, behold a sinner? He hath done grievous wrong.
He hath defiled Thy Premises through being kept in too long.
Wherefore his nose has been rubbed in the dirt, and his self respect has been bruiséd.
Master, pardon Thy Sinner, and see he is properly looséd.

Master—again Thy Sinner! This that was once Thy Shoe,
He hath found and taken and carried aside, as fitting matter to chew
Now there is neither blacking or tongue, and the Housemaid has us in tow
Master, remember Thy Servant is young, and tell her to let him go!

Master, extol Thy Servant! He hath met a most worthy Foe!
There has been fighting all over the Shop—and into the Shop also!
Till cruel umbrellas parted the strife (or I might have been choking him yet).
But Thy Servant has had the Time of his Life—and now shall we call on the vet?

Master, behold Thy Servant! Strange children came to play,
And because they fought to caress him, Thy servant wentedst away.
But now that the Little Beasts have gone, he has returned to see
(Brushed—with his Sunday collàr on—) what they left over for tea

Master, pity Thy Servant! He is deaf and three parts blind,
He cannot catch Thy Commandments, He cannot read Thy mind.
Oh, leave him not in his loneliness, nor make him that kittens scorn
He has none other God than Thee since the year that he was born!

Lord, look down on Thy Servant! Bad things have come to pass,
There is no heat in the midday sun nor health in the wayside grass.
His bones are full of an old disease—his torments run and increase
Lord, make haste with Thy Lightning and grant him a quick release.

Rudyard Kipling

PART 1

Showing and Judging

CHAPTER I

The History of Dog Shows

DOGS

The dog has, of course, long been recognized as man's best friend, but unfortunately man has not always returned the compliment. However, wherever man chooses to live in the world, there to accompany him will always be found his dog. It is interesting that there are only two animals out of all the millions on earth that have ever entered man's home on their own initiative and not as prisoners. They are, of course, the dog and the cat. No animal has changed his original role and his way of living or his shape and size to the extent that the dog has done in order to adapt himself to man's way of life and particularly to man's interests. There is no animal that treats man so undeservedly as his god. The dog's loyalty, friendship and trust are such that no one can claim to have lived who has never known the love and companionship of a dog.

Primarily, dogs hunted and worked for man and also guarded his property. They became his companions and provided man with his sport. Over the centuries dogs were slowly developed and bred in the ways most suited to man, and so started the divisions of dogs into breeds for their particular uses.

Gradually, as man became more civilized and affluent, he found himself with more time. No longer were his days occupied with his daily living and search for food: he had time for sport and other activities. Over the centuries the deviations between the types of dogs to be found grew and grew, until our present time when there are probably some eight hundred and fifty different breeds to be found throughout the world.

It is about two hundred years since Lord Orford founded the first dog club in 1776. It was not, however, until the affluent society of the middle of the nineteenth century, finding themselves with more time to spare, required entertainments with which to occupy their leisure. There were the small social gatherings at taverns, where the customers brought their dogs. There were tea parties, where the rich took their fat and often spoilt pets. Small exhibitions were held in the larger towns and, when diplomats, missionaries, soldiers and sailors returned home, many of them brought back dogs from far distant shores where they had been serving. Exhibitions became more and more popular and at first they were not confined to one subject, but would include not only dogs but all manner of things.

THE EARLY EXHIBITIONS

Gradually, the early exhibitions became more selective until they turned into small shows just for dogs. To start with there was no governing body such as the Kennel Club as we know it today. There were few rules to be adhered to, and these were made by the promoters, who ran the shows entirely for their own personal gain and profit. There are, of course, no longer any privately organized dog shows in Britain, since all shows come under the strict jurisdiction of the Kennel Club.

Without some form of governing body, it was not surprising to find in those early days that there were a tremendous number of what might be generously termed as 'irregularities', not to mention some really scandalous behaviour. It will be seen, therefore, that the early dog shows bore little resemblance to those held at the present day!

Many of the early shows were small friendly affairs held in the local taverns mostly for the smaller sporting breeds, of which the terriers were the most popular.

One of the earliest recorded canine exhibitions was held in the bar of a public-house in Denmark Street in London. This was called 'A Fancy Dog Show' which was organized by a Charles Aistrop, a most notorious character. He had previously been the proprietor of the infamous Westminster Pit in Duck Lane, near Westminster Abbey. This was the place where bears and badgers were baited and where dog fights and ratting took place against the clock, before these cruel sports were abolished by law in 1835. Charles Aistrop, therefore, had many old connections from the bad old days, whom he persuaded with great plausibility to join his newly-formed club. This club was the second club for dog fanciers to be formed, and it consisted mostly of breeders of the smaller breeds. Amongst the exhibits were Blenheim Spaniels, Italian Greyhounds, Skye Terriers and King Charles Spaniels. There were also quite a number of unspecified breeds. Many of the dogs were for sale on the premises and some were sold for exceedingly high prices, which obviously the gullible public were prepared to pay.

As an example the owner of a dog called Prince is said to have been offered £250 for him. This is equivalent to well over £2000 today, and the owner apparently refused it. At Cruft's in 1971 a Poodle was for sale for £10,000. It was not, however, sold. £10,000 was once refused for a well-known Pekingese. £1500 is by no means unknown today or even $7500 in the United States. Charles Aistrop advertised well in order to entice the public to visit his exhibition, for which they paid an entrance fee of sixpence. It was at this exhibition that Billy, who had been the well-known champion of the Westminster Pit, and who had made the phenomenal record of killing one hundred rats in seven minutes ten seconds was to be seen there stuffed, standing in a glass cage.

This exhibition must certainly have been a tremendous success, because not long afterwards other exhibitions were held and were equally popular.

The first recorded specialist show was rather an illustrious one, and somewhat surprisingly was organized for a Toy breed. Few people would probably guess that of all the Toy dogs it is the Pug who can lay claim to being the first for which a specialist show was held. This show took place on 30 May, 1850. It was described as being 'A Great Exhibition of the Pugs of All Nations'. In reality, it was a social gathering for charity. All the exhibitors were titled, and Mr Davenport Bromley organized the show, which was an amusing affair and most successful. There is a charming illustration of this event, in which the élite Pug aristocracy are seated round a tea table where they are being served by deferential servants, with their adoring owners looking on. One of the Pugs, however, it not particularly well mannered as he has just leapt on to the middle of the table. The picture first appeared in the *Illustrated London News* on 8 February, 1851. Pugs indeed seem to have been well to the fore in the early days of dog exhibitions as some of the earliest lady judges seem to have been judges of Pug classes. A Pug too, must have been one of the first dogs to have been smothered in a show travelling box. His name was Lord Salisbury and he died in April 1891. These early shows went from strength to strength, and some of them might perhaps have been better called 'dog markets', because this was really what many of them were, since most of the buying and selling of dogs took place at them. As can be imagined, the tall stories about the prowess of each dog were often grossly exaggerated. Undoubtedly the gullible public were often taken in and consequently the prices of dogs soon rocketed.

Jemmy Shaw, another publican and a prize fighter, who managed the Blue Anchor, Bunhill Row at St Luke's, also organized small shows and ran the Toy Dog Club. He used to advertise his rat-killing terriers. His most famous was a splendid little English Toy Terrier weighing 5½ lbs, whom he called Tiny-the-Wonder. In 1884 he took on a wager that Tiny could kill two hundred rats in three hours. Jemmy won his wager easily, Tiny managed to kill the two hundred rats in fifty-four minutes, much to the admiration of his customers. Jem Burn, the proprietor of the Queen's Head Tavern, Windmill Street, Haymarket, London, was another dog fancier and was well known as a breeder of Bulldogs. In his younger days he too had been a prize fighter. After Burn's death Jemmy Shaw took over the Queen's Head in 1852. Here he ran dog shows, 'lead' or matches which became extremely popular in the area. He had been running such dog shows from 1835, when an Act of Parliament was passed prohibiting 'blood sports', and modern dog shows took their place.

The first known oil painting of a dog show which now hangs in the Kennel Club was painted by R. Marshall in 1855 nearly twenty-two years before the Kennel Club was founded. This shows Jemmy Shaw standing by the fire place in shirt sleeves amongst his customers and exhibitors seated round the room with at least eight different breeds. Most of the men are wearing high-crowned top hats and smoking very long stemmed clay pipes. Obviously, a happy relaxed evening was being enjoyed by all including the dogs. It is interesting that amongst the dogs in the painting is the now extinct English White Terrier.

To keep the public interest up, Jemmy advertised that foreign dogs were to be exhibited at his shows. Breeders were also permitted to bring along their stud dogs, and pet owners and exhibitors frequently brought their bitches to be mated on the premises.

It was not surprising that these small shows were so popular, since there were no cinemas, radio or television to entertain the public. From these early beginnings other clubs and shows were soon founded.

The Great Exhibition of 1851, which was held in Hyde Park, was the forerunner of very many large exhibitions organized in the nineteenth century. The leisured and often prosperous Victorians delighted in this new form of entertainment.

The British have always been renowned for their love of dogs and in particular for all rare things, so that when such shows exhibited rare breeds, the Victorian crowds flocked to see them. Within a comparatively short period many buildings suitable for exhibitions were built all over the country.

THE FIRST ORGANIZED DOG SHOW

Within a decade the first officially organized dog show was held in the Town Hall of Newcastle upon Tyne on 28 and 29 June, 1859. This show was organized by Messrs Shorthose and Pape at the suggestion of Mr R. Brailsford. There were sixty entries of Pointers and Setters. There were three judges allocated to each class. One of the judges of the Setters succeeded in winning a first prize with his Pointers, whilst the judge of the Pointer class took the first prize in the Setters. One cannot help wondering if this was a precedent set for all time!

This highly successful show was soon followed by more ambitious shows and by larger exhibitions at which dog classes were held. The formation of the Birmingham Dog Show Society was soon underway, and they held their first exhibition in 1860 at Cheapside, in Birmingham. This was the first general dog show ever to be held, and it is interesting to realize that this Society is the oldest dog show society in the world, and it is still one of the leading societies today.

The Dachshund Club, founded in 1881, is the second oldest dog society in the world. The Club held a splendid dinner at Painters Hall in the City of London on 30 March, 1971, to commemorate their 90th anniversary. Guests came from many countries and Princess Antoinette of Monaco was to have been the guest of honour, but unfortunately she was indisposed at the last moment, and was unable to attend. Her place was taken, however, at a moment's notice by the Very Reverend Martin Sullivan, the Dean of St Pauls. This great orator from New Zealand kept the assembled guests in continual laughter with his many amusing stories. One of the anecdotes he told us was that, although dogs were not officially allowed into St Paul's Cathedral, some were occasionally admitted and the Dean said, 'What more marvellous place for a dog with all those beautiful columns!'

The first all-breed dog show held at Cheapside, in Birmingham, included classes for Mastiffs, Newfoundlands, Bulldogs, Sheepdogs, Dalmatians, Terriers, Toy Spaniels and Toy Terriers (under five pounds in weight) and there were also a few foreign dogs, the most popular being Pugs and Italian Greyhounds. It is interesting that only one class was held in each breed at these shows. The dogs were unidentified, since there was no form as yet for registration, so that the dogs were quite simply named by their kennel name. As can be imagined, there was soon a conglomeration of 'Spots', 'Beautys', 'Princes', 'Nettles', 'Vics', etc, which were the popular names of the day. So, it quickly became obvious that some form of identification would have to be worked out. But this somewhat naturally took a considerable time.

At one of the early shows a Mr Murrell's 'Spot', was priced at the astronomical figure of £5000, he was competing against a Mr Brown's 'Venus' priced at only £1·50. Unfortunately, this catalogue is not marked, so that the winner of Spot versus Venus is not known, but one cannot help having a sneaking hope that perhaps it might have been the glamorous little Venus.

The Show Game was progressing rapidly. By 1861 the number of different breeds to be seen at the shows was increasing by leaps and bounds, and shows were held at Leeds, Birmingham and Manchester. London was well behind the Midlands by some two years, the first show there was held at Islington at the Agricultural Hall. This was for very many years the site of the world-renowned Cruft's International Show. This first show organized in London drew nearly one thousand entries. The following year, 1864, saw two more London shows, one at Islington and the other at the Cremorne Gardens in Chelsea. There was also another show in Birmingham that year. The Islington show increased its previous entry by two hundred dogs to a total of nearly 1200 entries. His Royal Highness, the Prince of Wales, later King Edward VII, had a popular win with one of his Harriers. 1870 saw the continuation of shows for the sporting breeds mostly for Pointers, Setters and Terriers.

It soon became obvious that an organizing body was required to handle the growing boom in dogs and particularly dog shows. Many ill practices had crept in, and dishonest breeders and exhibitors were bringing the dog game into bad repute. It had become increasingly impossible to keep track of all the dogs and their owners, not to mention changes of ownership, or even of the breeds that were exhibited. Very often dogs were not thoroughbred and were entered in classes for the breed which they most resembled!

It was essential that the chaos that reigned should be organized with some form of order and that an attempt should be made to try to make dog breeding and exhibiting a sport to be enjoyed and one in which people of integrity would take part.

The dishonest breeders somewhat naturally disliked the idea of the tyranny of a possible Kennel Club, but clearly something had to be done to prevent a dog being given the name of a famous prize winner, or from being exhibited under several aliases, not to mention all the other unscrupulous practices which then went on.

THE KENNEL CLUB

A number of excellent dog shows were held at the Crystal Palace which were run by Mr S. E. Shirley, who was the Member of Parliament for Ettrington, and his committee of twelve. It was after the second show at the Crystal Palace which was held in April 1873, that it was decided to form a Kennel Club. The meeting for this took place in a tiny three-roomed flat at 2, Albert Mansions, Victoria Street in London. Rules and regulations were drawn up and subsequently Mr Shirley became the Kennel Club's first chairman for 1873–99, he then became its first President. Besides organizing legislation on canine matters, it was decided to form a stud book to bridge the gap of fourteen years since dog shows had started in 1859. Up to this date extremely few breeders kept accurate records, and pedigrees were for the most part only memorised.

THE KENNEL CLUB STUD BOOK

The origin of the Kennel Club Stud Book is a remarkable story of perseverance. Mr Frank C. S. Pearce, who was the son of the Reverend Thomas Pearce, the well known Idestone of 'The Field'. Mr Pearce was asked by the Committee of the Kennel Club if he would be willing to compile a comprehensive list of pedigrees on all breeds. The amount of work involved was obviously tremendous. Mr Pearce wrote to over 3500 people—no typewriters in those days—and, as can be imagined, the same results occurred then as they would today. Many people did not bother to reply, some had died, whilst others had left their residences and their addresses were not known. However, after a great deal of work the first Kennel Club Stud Book was at last compiled. Some of the pedigrees in it went back as far as 1859, and they covered the period from then until 1874, when it was first published. The names of the dogs were registered in strict alphabetical order and in breeds. The order had nothing to do with the dates when the dogs were born or registered.

As an example of how the first stud book was compiled for Bloodhounds, I have chosen three famous names; Abeille, Druid and Welcome, and they appear (by kind permission of the Kennel Club) in the following order:

'No. 1 ABEILLE—Mr. G. T. Rushtons, Hale, Cheshire (bitch); breeder Prince Napoleon, born in 1865; colour black and tan. Pedigree: By Jenning's Old Druid (No. 17) out of Welcome, bred by Mr. Attwood (see Welcome I). No. 69 Abeille once belonged to M. Leone Claverie and M. Paul Garuzaz.

'No. 17 OLD DRUID—Mr. T. A. Jennings, Kirby Moorside, Yorkshire (dog); breeder owner, born in September 1857 (Mr. Jennings is dead). Pedigree: By Jennings' Raglan out of his Fury; Raglan (bred by Lord Faversham) was by Sir O. Wombwell's Forester (bred by the Duke of Leeds) out of Lord Faversham's Countess; Countess was by Royal out of the Duke of Hamilton's bitch; Royal was by Earl Carlisle's Warr out of a bitch of Lord Faversham's (bred by the Duke of Marlboro'); Fury was bred by Baron Rothschild. Chief performances: Birmingham 1st prize 1860, 1862, Leeds 1st prize 1861, Islington Agricultural Hall, 1st prize 1862; 1st prize Championship class, 1863 (never beaten); Old Druid was the sire of Abeille, Beldam.

'No. 69 WELCOME—Owner Mr. Jennings sold to Napoleon bred by Mr. Attwood of Durham, born 1858. No record of pedigree, probably Lord Bagot's blood.'

It is interesting to find that this first stud book listed forty breeds and over 4027 dogs. There were only two classifications, which were divided into Sporting Dogs and Non-Sporting Dogs.

The stud book was an immediate success and was naturally much appreciated by all serious breeders. This stud book was soon followed by others until it became an annual publication, which was much looked forward to by its subscribers. The stud book also contained a section for a 'Code of Rules for the Guidance of Dog Shows' and a section for the 'Conduct of Field Trials'.

The Kennel Club arranged to hear objections raised at shows and were able to punish culprits guilty of malpractices.

THE FIRST KENNEL CLUB LIST OF BREEDS

Sporting Dogs

i. Bloodhounds
ii. Deerhounds
iii. Greyhounds
iv. Foxhounds
v. Otterhounds
vi. Harriers
vii. Beagles
viii. Fox Terriers
ix. Pointers
x. Setters (English)
xi. Setters (Black and Tan)
xii. Setters (Irish)
xiii. Retrievers
xiv. Clumber Spaniels
xv. Irish Water Spaniels
xvi. Spaniels (Field Cocker and Sussex)
xvii. Water Spaniels (other than Irish)
xviii. Dachshunds (or German Badger Hounds)

Non-Sporting Dogs

xix. Mastiffs
xx. St. Bernards (Rough and Smooth)
xxi. Newfoundlands
xxii. Dalmatians (or Carriage Dogs)
xxiii. Bulldogs
xxiv. Bull Terriers (all sizes)
xxv. Sheepdogs and Scotch Collies
xxvi. Black and Tan Terriers (except Toys)

xxvii. Dandie Dinmonts
xxviii. Bedlington Terriers
xxix. Skye Terriers
xxx. Wire-haired Terriers and Irish Terriers
xxxi. English and other Smooth-haired Terriers
xxxii. Broken-haired Scotch and Yorkshire Terriers
xxxiii. Pomeranians
xxxiv. Italian Greyhounds
xxxv. Pugs
xxxvi. Maltese
xxxvii. Blenheim Spaniels
xxxviii. King Charles Spaniels
xxxix. Toy Terriers (Smooth-coated)
xl. Toy Terriers (Rough and Broken-haired)

Much of the support for the Kennel Club emanated from the Midlands, so that it is not surprising that the Kennel Club held its first Annual General Meeting at the Western Hotel in Birmingham in December 1874.

The Committee formulated a code of ten rules which applied to dog shows in general. The rules were straightforward and simple. Societies were encouraged to accept the rules and to abide by them. Provided that the societies conformed, the winners at these shows were then eligible to be entered in the Stud Book. The Committee endeavoured to strengthen their position by disqualifying dogs which were entered at unrecognized shows, but in actual fact this was not enforced for a number of years.

Eight years after the inauguration of the Kennel Club it was found necessary to enforce rules and to penalize exhibitors for faking, dyeing or for having surgery performed upon their dogs. All dogs had to be officially registered at the Kennel Club before they could be exhibited. A Kennel Club Gazette was published in 1880, in which were recorded all the newly registered dogs and puppies. Pedigrees were still unimportant except for identification purposes. The Gazette was naturally taken by all serious breeders, so that any false registrations were likely to be spotted by some ardent breeder. The latter could then report the incident to the Kennel Club, just as can still be done to this day.

It is obviously not possible for the Kennel Club to be responsible for the accuracy of all registrations, but breeders even today keep a wary eye on all registrations in their particular breeds and are quick to report any mistakes. This keeps dog breeding as accurate as is humanly possible. Nevertheless no one can stop a crooked breeder from falsifying a pedigree, nor prevent breeders from inadvertently muddling up a number of large litters in a breed, where all the puppies look as like as two peas. However, the great majority of breeders love their dogs and have their breed at heart, so that such malpractises seldom occur.

In 1900, the Kennel Club was making such great progress that a Council of Representatives was formed. Delegates represented clubs registered with the Kennel Club, in order to keep the Kennel Club in touch with the exhibitors. By this time there were nearly thirty championship shows being held, whilst the small informal shows were becoming extremely popular. The Kennel Club wisely kept their rules and regulations to a minimum. Shows were 'recognized', 'licensed' or 'sanctioned', provided that the guarantors of the show signed a strict undertaking to conduct the show under, and in accordance with, the rules and regulations of the Kennel Club, just as they do to this day. So much had dog showing improved by the end of the century, that over half the exhibitors were women. In spite of this, the Kennel Club refused to have women judges at their shows in 1899. However, the new Kennel Club constitution permits twenty-five per cent Ladies from the Ladies Branch to sit on the sub-committees of Show Regulations, Judges, Breed Standards, Stud Book and Breed Registrations, and Cruft's Dog Show. This undoubtedly is a small step forward, but it is unlikely to satisfy the Ladies Branch Members for long, as it is really a blatant discrimination against the female sex, and Dog Women's Lib will surely take action.

The trend of more and more women exhibitors taking up dog breeding increased so much over the years that today in many breeds almost ninety per cent of exhibitors are women. Within a very few years I predict that women will be on the committee of the Kennel Club with equal standing.

The Kennel Club insisted that all dogs exhibited at their shows must be registered and the shows licensed. The Club was not strong enough to enforce its rules on all clubs. However, it was not long before the exhibitors realized that the Kennel Club had been formed for their benefit, especially when many of the disgraceful practices in other clubs were witnessed. Not infrequently, the organizers of shows welshed with the entry money and failed to distribute prize money, amongst many other iniquities which can all too easily be imagined.

All dogs exhibited at Kennel Club shows have to be registered, and this came into force on 31 July, 1904. Only four months later it was passed at an extraordinary general meeting that all dog shows must come under the jurisdiction of the Kennel Club. A rival club was started in Lancashire. By this time, however, the Kennel Club was strong enough to suspend all exhibitors who attended other shows, and the Kennel Club quickly dominated, ruled and monopolized the dog scene as they still do. His Royal Highness the Prince of Wales, who was later King Edward VII, was Patron of the Club from the time of its institution, and His Majesty King George V was the second Patron, followed in turn by their Majesties King George VI and Queen Elizabeth II. Her Majesty Queen Victoria, His Royal Highness the Prince Consort, Their Royal Highnesses Princess Alexandra and the Duke of Windsor have all had their dogs exhibited.

Mr S. E. Shirley became the first President of the all-male Kennel Club in 1899, and held the position until his sudden death in 1904. In 1902, he had been presented with his portrait at the Kennel club Annual Dinner.

In 1874 the membership of the club was one hundred. Later the numbers increased although for a time it never exceeded two hundred and eighty members, whereas today membership is restricted to five hundred.

Mr R. J. Lloyd Price, with the help of the committee, designed the first Kennel Club Uniform. This consisted of a frock coat in dark green with eau-de-nil facings, breeches and two-toned top boots. There are several portraits of the Reverend John Russell, of Jack Russell Terrier fame, wearing the Kennel Club Uniform. Since those early days the uniform has undergone a number of fashion changes, and today it consists of tails and dinner jacket made up in the original colours, the latter being the most recent innovation. In the early days regular house dinners were held monthly. Probably these dinners were for the Committee only, but later a Kennel Club dinner was held annually. In recent years a cocktail/buffet has been held in February or March for members both of the Kennel Club and the Ladies Branch.

THE LADIES BRANCH OF THE KENNEL CLUB

That there should be a Ladies Branch of the Kennel Club was first mooted as early as the 7 October, 1897. Fifty ladies' names were approved including a committee of fifteen. The first meeting of the Ladies Branch was held on 19 July, 1899. Her Grace the Duchess of Newcastle was the first President, and her Committee included, amongst others, the Countess of Darnley, the Countess of Limerick, Lady Aukland, Lady Eveleyn Ewart and Lady Lewis. The meeting was held in the Club House in Old Burlington Street, London.

Probably the first lady judges were a Miss Holdsworth, who judged Pugs at Scarborough in 1887, and a Mrs Forster who judged the same breed in 1891 and 1892.

In 1903, the Ladies Kennel Association (LKA) and the Ladies Branch of the Kennel Club were refused permission by the Kennel Club to be amalgamated. The Ladies Branch held their first show in 1905 in conjunction with the Kennel Club's Jubilee Show. It is interesting that the Kennel Club refused to allow Challenge Certificates to be awarded at the Ladies Branch Show, since it was restricted to members and not an open show.

PERMISSIVE REGULATIONS

On 18 February, 1902, the Kennel Club passed a regulation permitting the shortening of tails. Another regulation was adopted regarding permission for Poodles to have their coats clipped, and all breeds could have dew claws removed if necessary. The same year the word 'Spaniel' was dropped from both the Pekingese and Japanese. In 1903 the word 'Terrier' was dropped from Maltese.

Ear cropping was finally abolished by the Kennel Club on 1 July, 1903. There is an interesting letter written from Marlborough House, dated 22 January, 1895, by Francis Knollys, regarding the Prince of Wales' feelings on the barbaric custom of ear cropping. 'Sir, I am desired by the Prince of Wales to acknowledge receipt of your communication . . . but that he never allowed any dog belonging to him to be "mutilated". His Royal Highness has always been opposed to the practice which he considers causes unnecessary suffering, and it would give him much pleasure to hear that owners of dogs had agreed to abandon such an objectionable fashion.'

I feel it would be a wonderful gesture on the part of our present Prince of Wales, if he could adopt the same attitude towards tail docking as his great-great-grandfather did towards ear cropping.

It is terrible to think that civilized people still restort to mutilating many breeds by docking their tails. Surely public opinion and strong-minded dog lovers could do something about this horror in the very near future.

THE KENNEL CLUB TODAY

Since 1957 the Kennel Club has been housed at 1–4 Clarges Street, Piccadilly, London, W1Y 8AB. Telephone Number 01-493 6651. It is a small, valuable, unobtrusive, centrally situated, modern building.

The Kennel Club has had numerous homes since 1873. Before moving to Clarges Street it was housed at 84 Piccadilly, which was on the corner of Clarges Street, almost next door. There is an excellent well-appointed council chamber and there are committee rooms where meetings are held throughout the year. Over the years, members have presented the Kennel Club with a number of very fine and interesting paintings of dogs, which adorn the walls of all the rooms. There is also an excellent library, containing over 12,000 books.

THE REGISTRATION OFFICE

The large office on the second floor of the Kennel Club deals with nearly 200,000 registrations annually. The incredible filing system is well worth visiting and is under the keen supervision of Mr D. Chiverton. All the registration cards are kept in banks. The files of individual breeds are kept in what might be described as oblong trays 31 inches by 6 inches, each previously holding 2500 cards. Every prefix or affix has its allotted alphabetical space in the breed section. The registration cards measure approximately 6 inches by 4 inches. Each tray holds 4300 cards, because the Kennel Club have now reduced the thickness of the cards from 0·012 of an inch to 0·007 of an inch. After ten years a dog's registration card is removed to a drawer below, and after a further period the card is eventually removed down to the cellars for safe-keeping and these registration cards are never destroyed (nor are the Kennel Club transfer forms). The registration cards of dogs in the stud book remain in their original trays. To become eligible for entry in the stud book a dog must win a limit class or above. (See page 28.)

MEMBERSHIP

Membership of the Kennel Club is still strictly limited owing to the small size of the accommodation. No more than 500 male members and 250 members of the Ladies Branch may be enrolled. Luncheon is served daily but no table bookings are accepted. The Club closes early, at 6-30 pm. Once a year, generally in February or March, a popular cocktail-buffet party is held for members and their guests. The Ladies Branch hold an annual Christmas tea party in December.

THE KENNEL CLUB HOUND

This is the famous hound which now stands on the outside porch of the Kennel Club. The original was cast nearly half a century ago in 1925 from a sculpture by Captain Adrian Jones, who took as his model a Foxhound from the Old Berkeley pack. Adrian Jones did most of his work in the latter part of the eighteenth century, and he is best known for his famous quadriga, which consists of four horses and chariot and charioteer and was erected in 1912 as a Victory Arch at the top of Constitution Hill at Hyde Park Corner. Owing to the recent alterations there the quadriga had to be moved slightly and it is now situated on the centre island.

The Kennel Club hound was presented to the Kennel Club in 1928 by one of the members and it resided in great splendour in the bay window of the smoking room of the old Kennel Club, which was then just round the corner from the present Club, at 84 Piccadilly. The story goes that rather a stupid custom grew, whereby the Club members wrote rude comments on various personalities in the dog world and then attached these to different parts of the hound's anatomy. A year later, however, the hound was moved to the side entrance in Clarges Street where he remained for twenty-seven years watching the changing face of the Piccadilly traffic and patiently waiting for a fox to break cover across the open spaces of Green Park just opposite.

The Berkeley foxhound was moved once again in September 1957, when the new Kennel Club premises were opened, and there he remains to this day outside the main doors. He can no longer see Green Park but many a member of the Kennel Club has given him a friendly pat in consolation when passing.

CHARLES CRUFT

There can be no one in the world of dogs who has not heard of Mr Charles Cruft, the founder of the largest and best known dog show in the world.

Charles Cruft was born in 1852. He was the son of a jeweller, who, like many a fond parent, had hoped that his son would follow him in the family business. Charles, however, had other ideas. He left Birbeck College in 1876, and was first employed by James Spratt, who had recently returned from the United States. Mr Spratt had discovered that the Americans were selling a consignment of ship's biscuits as dog food. This had been such a success that soon the Americans were manufacturing 'dog cakes' from similar biscuits and these were selling like the proverbial 'hot cakes'. On his return to England James Spratt started manufacturing similar dog cakes. It was at this time that Charles Cruft started his career with a short apprenticeship as an office messenger boy. It was not long before his ability was recognized and he was soon promoted to sales traveller in 'dog cakes'. This entailed visiting most of the counties of England selling Spratts dog cakes to the large estates, where packs of hounds were bred and kept for hunting. The dog cake business flourished, and in no time at all Spratt was exporting his wares. In 1878 when Charles was twenty-six he was sent to Paris by his firm to visit the local dog breeders and hunt kennels in the area.

While he was in Paris, the French breeders asked Cruft if he would be prepared to organize a canine exhibition for them at the famous Paris Exhibition. This he did with tremendous success. It was not, therefore, surprising that on his return to England, British breeders asked him if he would organize their shows too. He accepted with alacrity and these shows were equally successful. It was not long before he wanted more limelight being a born showman, and he soon started organizing his own shows. His first show was held for the Allied Terrier Club Show, which was held at the Royal Aquarium, Westminster, in 1886. In 1891 Charles Cruft hired the Royal Agricultural Hall at Islington for the first of his long and successful series of Cruft's Dog Shows.

It was as early as 1886 that Charles Cruft realized and appreciated how much the general public at the time were interested in rare breeds. Being a first-rate business man, he set about obtaining rare breeds to entice the general public to his shows, and he soon started calling his shows 'Cruft's Shows'.

By 1900 there were no less than 76 breeds and varieties of dogs registered at the Kennel Club. The British Commonwealth, stretching across the world so that the sun never set on her domains, was administered by her soldiers, sailors, diplomats, explorers and missionaries. It was, therefore, not surprising that rare and new breeds were frequently introduced into Britain when her colonial administrators returned home for their well earned leave.

Many of our rare and interesting breeds have been brought over here by members of our forces. Admiral Lord John Hay, for instance, brought back a brindle dog Pekingese and a little black and white bitch from the sacking of the Imperial Palace in Peking in 1860. Her Majesty Queen Victoria's famous little Pekingese 'Looty' was brought to Britain by General Dunne. General and Lady Brownrigge again introduced the charming little Shih Tzus in 1930, Colonel V. D'Oyly Harmar Mexican Hairless dogs, and Major General Adam Block and Mrs Block the Pharoah hounds from Malta. Afghans, Salukis and numerous other breeds have all been brought in by members of our forces during the last one hundred years or so.

To return to Charles Cruft and his enterprises. The rare breeds which he introduced at his shows over the years included Afghans, Salukis, Basenjis, Borzois, Rhodesian Ridgebacks, Finnish Spitz, German Short-haired pointers, Weimaraners, Shih Tzus, Boxers, Schnauzers, Tibetan Mastiffs, Japanese Akitas, several Bear hounds and quite a number of other breeds, which failed for some reason or other to become popular. On one occasion, a wit entered a dog for one of Crufts Shows as a 'Siberian Eelhound'. Luckily for Charles Cruft, he realized, before it was too late, that his leg was being well and truly pulled, and he was able at the last moment to substitute another breed without losing face.

Perhaps one of his most magnificent displays of rare breeds was the occasion when he procured teams of Russian Wolfhounds (or Borzois as we know them today). These were most impressively handled by Russian moujiks, and belonged to the Russian aristocracy. Prince Constantine of Oldenburg, Prince Dimitroff and Grand Duke Nicholas, later Tzar of all the Russias also sent their dogs. After the show a number of these beautiful borzois were presented to Her Royal Highness Princess Alexandra and other members of the Royal Family.

Cruft's Dog Shows went from strength to strength as did the Kennel Club registrations which in 1913 were 19,846, and which rose to 57,762 in 1938 and to 183,784 in 1974. In 1936 Cruft's famous Jubilee Show had an all time record for those days with an entry of 10,650 and 4397 dogs. Sadly two years later this great showman died. After her husband's death, his widow organized one Cruft's Show which was held in 1939. The project became too much for her, however, and she decided in 1942 to hand over the show to the Kennel Club so that they could continue his shows and perpetuate his name. The Kennel Club gladly accepted and they held their first Cruft's Show at Olympia in 1948. This show was a tremendous success and has been held at Olympia ever since. The 75th Show was held there in 1971 and in spite of restriction on entries by merit, there were 8430 dogs, almost double the number of the Jubilee Show. The 1974 figure with even more restrictions was 7877 dogs and 11,824 entries. The popularity and prestige of Cruft's, and the magic of the name, draw breeders and dog lovers from the ends of the earth. Every dog breeder aims at exhibiting his dogs at Cruft's. Although many breeders scoff at the prestige involved, they are the first to advertise that they were there! This is even more so since the entries have been curtailed even further. The number of dogs entered was becoming so out of hand that in 1973 only Champions were exhibited at Cruft's, or dogs which have won a first prize at a Championship show during the previous year. Each year the Kennel Club Committee alter the necessary qualifications for Cruft's.

CRUFT'S QUALIFICATIONS FOR 1974

First or Second in Puppy Class
First or Second in Junior Class
First in Novice Class
First in Post Graduate Class
First or Second in Limit Class
First, Second or Third in Open Class

The scramble to get dogs qualified for Cruft's has become almost a bitter battle, and the be-all and end-all of the whole year's championship shows, sadly to the detriment of the open shows. The 1971 two day Cruft's Show with its entry of 8430 dogs in 1200 classes, 100 judges, and an estimated gate of 50,000 people was a world record. The number of foreigners who charter planes to visit Cruft's increases yearly, and so the export of dogs continues to rise. Before the Kennel Club took over Cruft's, the export figure was only 577 dogs. In 1948 the export figure increased to 1281, in 1966 it was 7567, in 1967 8327, and in 1968 it increased to 12,791. In 1969 14,764 dogs were exported, being the record year. In 1970 the exports dropped to 11,864 dogs and they rose again in 1973 to 13,399. The total of exported dogs is around 126,500. One only hopes they all end up in good kind loving homes.

The magnitude of the work of the Kennel Club can seldom be realized when one considers that there are 20,000 affixes, 750,000 dogs registered, 58,733 dogs transferred and 11,641 dogs exported. There are also 2577 dog shows licensed with 1500 matches and exemption shows, 302 championship shows and 350 breed shows. There are also 1500 clubs and societies, and agreements with 38 countries. All this is run with a staff of 70, a General Committee, and 9 permanent sub-committees. There were over 65,000 transfer applications in 1969. Beside all this the Kennel Club also cater for the Field Trials for Gun Dogs when during the shooting season there is an average of almost one trial a day. There are also the Working Trials, which include the practical training of dogs for police work.

Popularity in breeds change with the fashions prevailing at the time. The 1969, 1970 and 1973 Export List is interesting.

TOP EXPORT COUNTRIES

	1969	**1970**	**1973**
USA	5699	5906	2333
Canada	915	1445	1697
France	671	737	1094
W. Germany	434	637	1660
Italy	363	554	2398
Switzerland	324	449	446
Netherlands	272	288	416
Belgium	195	262	215
Spain	124	213	643
South Africa	160	184	152

TOP EXPORT DOGS 1970

	Exports	**Registrations**	**% Exports**	**1973 exports**
Yorkshire Terriers	2,265	11,016	20·6	2395
Toy Poodles	1,224	7,926	15·5	946
Old English Sheepdogs	786	2,343	33·6	469
West Highland White Terriers	573	4,933	11·6	492
Shih-Tzus	544	1,526	35·7	268
Pekingese	350	4,243	8·3	513
Cocker Spaniels	345	7,121	4·8	618
Cairn Terriers	333	3,860	8·6	225
Min. Poodles	304	5,291	5·7	276
Scottish Terriers	295	1,614	18·3	210
Labradors	256	14,827	1·7	302
Basset Hounds	252	2,642	9·5	491
Afghan Hounds	242	2,853	8·5	274
Bulldogs	233	1,021	22·8	266
14 Breeds	8,002	71,216	11·2	
Other breeds	3,862	103,858	3·7	
Total	11,864	175,074	6·8	

KENNEL CLUB REGISTRATIONS

The 1970 figure of registrations rose to the then highest record 175,074 dogs of which there were no less than 156 different breeds, with 112 being eligible for the stud book. Since the

Second World War 2,932,296 dogs have been registered. The growth of registrations is nearly double that between 1903 and 1946. 1971 figures dropped to 161,065 but rose again in 1972 to 183,722.

TOTAL REGISTRATIONS

Year	Registrations
1966	133,585
1967	146,046
1968	157,229
1969	169,918
1970	175,074
1971	161,065
1972	183,722

It is interesting that the American Kennel Club registered 1,056,225 dogs in 1970 but this figure includes whole litters as well as the individual parents.

It has been estimated that there are probably 850 breeds of dog throughout the world. Some of the European shows list 400 breeds. In Britain, however, in 1950 the Kennel Club recognized 97 breeds. At the present time, 1973, 156 breeds and varieties are recognized and registered by the Kennel Club. This number includes some rare breeds which have not yet reached sufficient annual registrations to be allocated challenge certificates. The total registrations of each breed from 1966 to 1972 is shown in the appendix.

BREEDS WITHOUT CHALLENGE CERTIFICATES

Breed	
Hound Group	
Bassets Griffon Vendeen	6
Dachsbrake	13
Ibizan Hounds	151
Pharaoh Hounds	110
Portuguese Warren Hounds	9
Swedish Foxhounds	19
Swiss Laufhunds (Jura)	3
Gundog Group	
Chesapeake Bay Retrievers	24
German Wirehaired Pointers	5
Large Munsterlanders	14
Terrier Group	
Glen of Imaal Terriers	10
Soft Coated Wheaten Terriers	69
Utility Group	
Canaan Dogs	6
Iceland Dogs	40
Mexican Hairless	13
Working Group	
Alaskan Malamutes	173
American Eskimo Dogs	2
Anatolian Sheepdogs (Karabash)	37
Australian Kelpies	2
Beaucerons	10
Bernese Mountain Dogs	25
Hungarian Kuvasz	1
Hungarian Pulis	36
Huskies	88
Maremma Italian Sheepdogs	173
Siberian Huskies	25
Toy Group	
Affenpinschers	5

Chinese Crested Dogs	61
Lowchens	48
Silky Terriers	21

The Kennel Club list 112 breeds for separate registration and stud book entries, whilst the American Kennel Club list 116 breeds. The top three breeds in Great Britain in 1970–72 were the Alsatian (German Shepherd dog) 16,834 and 15,078, the Labrador Retriever 14,827 and 13,880, and the Yorkshire Terrier 11,016 and 12,832. In the United States the three top breeds in 1970 were Poodles 265,879, German Shepherd Dogs (Alsatians) 109,198 and Dachshunds 61,042. The comparative figures are not really quite fair as the Poodles are counted as three distinct breeds in England. If they were all counted as one breed in England the equivalent figure would be 13,957 Poodles, and so they would lie in third place. Dachshunds in the United States are also counted as one breed. In England the total figure would be 7650 for the six varieties which would have made them fifth. Beagles came fourth in the American list with 61,007 registrations whilst they came 15th on the English list with 3445 registrations. In 1969 Smoothcoat Chihuahuas were 20th with 2714 registrations. The American Kennel Club listed the breed for that year as sixth on the list with 28,801, but this figure included the Longcoat Chihuahuas. If the English figure included the longcoats too it would have been listed as thirteenth on the list with 4149. You can of course prove anything by mathematics it seems! The most popular breeds in Japan are the Pomeranian and Maltese. The interesting point, however, is the eye-opening fact of sheer numbers: in the United States in 1970 1,056,225 dogs were registered as compared with 175,074 in England. The mind boggles at the number of dogs. How many of these dogs live a happy life, and how many are destroyed by the RSPCA and similar organizations, when the owners are bored with their dogs?

CHAIRMAN OF THE KENNEL CLUB

It is interesting that out of the first hundred years of the existence of the Kennel Club three of the chairmen held office for a total of seventy-two years. Mr S. E. Shirley, the Club's founder, was chairman for a record twenty-six years, from 1873 to 1899. Air Commodore J. A. C. Cecil-Wright, the eighth chairman, held office for twenty-five years from 1948 to 1973, Mr. J. Sidney Turner, who followed Mr Shirley, was chairman for a mere twenty-one years, from 1899 to 1920. The present chairman, the ninth, is Sir Richard Glyn, who took office in 1973.

The first chairman Mr S. E. Shirley, Air Comodore J. A. C. Cecil-Wright, AFC, TD, and the present chairman, were all members of Parliament.

It is now over one hundred years since Mr S. E. Shirley the first chairman of the Kennel Club took office and the 'Ten Commandments' of the Canine world formed the code of rules for dogdom. Dr Sidney Turner took office from 1899 to 1920. The first quarter of the Kennel Club history was spent in transforming dogdom to a more respectable pastime. Mr Mark Beauoy was chairman from 1920 to 1922, followed by Mr Francis Redmond from 1922 to 1925, and Mr W. L. McCandish from 1925 to 1935. Mr C. D. Howlett was chairman from 1935 to 1937 and Mr Arthur Croxton Smith was chairman from 1937 to 1948. This was a period of expansion and the semi-professional breeders took the stage. These people had to sell dogs to help pay the expenses of exhibiting, and so it was that pedigree dogs became the vogue amongst the general public. The Kennel Club by this time had been organizing dogdom for three quarters of a century.

AIR COMMODORE J. A. C. CECIL-WRIGHT AFC, TD, DL

He was elected chairman in 1948 to 1973 and it is during his tenure of office that perhaps the greatest changes have taken place. Cruft's Show was taken over by the Kennel Club in 1948. Breeders from being semi-professional changed for the most part to hard-headed business breeders, almost reverting to the business breeders of 1873. There are, of course, still numbers of breeders who come into the game as a hobby. Sadly many of the nicest people do not last long in the tough competition of the dog world, although the clever ones may enjoy breeding outstanding stock in a small way often for others to handle and win with. The Kennel Club have a tremendous job to cope with the many problems set before them. As the late Chairman said: 'The Kennel Club have always borne in mind that the pedigree dog world consists of widely different interests, and the common link between breeders, show promoters, exhibitors, owners, judges, trainers, handlers and journalists, whether professional or amateur, is a very slender one.' 'A frame work is provided within which the varied interests of a multitude of people can flourish, and they give no particular privileges to any section of the canine world at the expense of any other.'

The Air Commodore showed his brilliance as an active chairman and he also sat on all the sub-committees. His intuitive choice of the right man for the right job helped him completely to re-organize the Kennel Club during his twenty five years of tenure. One of his many projects was to have the constitution of the Kennel Club redrafted. It was he, who was largely responsible for the purchase of the enormously valuable site and the building of the present Kennel Club. He brought the club to the greatest heights that the world of dogs has ever known, a club which is respected wherever there is a pedigree dog. His canine particular interests were Alsatians.

COLONEL SIR RICHARD GLYN, BART, OBE, TD, DL CHAIRMAN OF THE KENNEL CLUB

Sir Richard was born in 1907, and came from an old Dorset family. He is a barrister and farms on an extensive scale. He was a member of Parliament for North Dorset from 1957 to 1970. He had a political career and was also active in the Territorial Army. Amongst other appointments he was ADC to her Majesty the Queen from 1958 to 1962. Sir Richard obtained his law degree at Oxford University, which he represented at boxing and fencing. His canine interests included his kennel of Bull Terriers, and he is well known in the dog world for his book *Champion Dogs of the World*. He became the ninth Chairman of the Kennel Club on July 9, 1973. He became a member of the Club in 1934 and has sat on committees since 1938.

KENNEL CLUB REVISED REGISTRATION SYSTEM

The revised registration system came into force on 1 April, 1976, and comprises three main stages:

(a) Recording of each litter
(b) Basic registration
(c) Advancement to an 'Active Register'.

(a) Recording of each litter

This must be done within one month of the puppies being whelped. It requires the names of the sire and dam, the date of birth and the number of male and female puppies. The sire's owner will be required to certify on the form that the mating took place. The breeder is then sent a special litter number and a 'Litter Pack'. The pack contains application forms for each puppy, so that it may be entered in the basic register at a later date, if required. The litter number is also recorded on the sire's card at the Kennel Club

(b) Basic Registration

This requires further details of sex, colour and name. Puppies may be registered either by the breeder or the owner, and the names may be chosen by either party. These details are sent to the Kennel Club on forms provided in the 'Litter Pack'. This record of registration i then returned to the owner of the puppy or puppies

(c) Active Register

This is only for dogs that have been bred from, exhibited or entered for competition, or are to be exported. All dogs on the Active Register will be published in the monthly *Kennel Gazette*.

CHAPTER II

International Kennel Clubs and their Shows

KENNEL CLUBS

The tremendous success of the first Kennel Club, founded in 1873, aroused great interest throughout the civilized world. The Scottish Kennel Club was formed in 1881, and the American Kennel Club was founded three years later in 1884. In France La Société d'Acclimation was formed in 1882 and did excellent work for a number of years, until a more specialized organization was required. This resulted in the formation in 1884 of La Société Centrale pour l'Amélioration des Races de Chien en France. Later on this body split up into more specialized clubs. Soon many more clubs were formed. The Kennel Club is always called the Kennel Club and never the English Kennel Club.

In 1911, the Austrian, Belgian, Dutch, French and German Societies formed the Fédération Cynologique Internationale which is now the recognized European authority. This club which has its headquarters at Thuin, Belgium, has a special agreement with the Kennel Club. There are at the present time thirty-eight Kennel Clubs throughout the world which have reciprocal agreements with the Kennel Club.

LIST OF CLUBS WITH WHICH THE KENNEL CLUB HAS RECIPROCAL AGREEMENTS

AUSTRALIA	Australian National Kennel Council—Royal Show Grounds, Ascot Vale, Victoria (Incorporating: The Canine Association of Western Australia N. Australian Canine Association The Canine Control Council (Queensland) Canberra Kennel Association The Kennel Control Council Kennel Control Council of Tasmania The RAS Kennel Club South Australian Canine Association)
BARBADOS	Barbados Kennel Club, Everton, Dash Valley, St George, Barbados, WI
BELGIUM	Société Royale Saint Hubert, Avenue de l'Armée 25, B-1040, Brussels, Belgium
BERMUDA	The Bermuda Kennel Club, Inc. PO Box 1455, Hamilton, Bermuda
BRAZIL	Brazil Kennel Club—Caixa Postal, 1468, Rio de Janeiro
BURMA	Burma Kennel Club, Room No. 10, 342 Maha Bandoola Street, Rangoon, Burma
CANADA	Canadian Kennel Club—111 Eglinton Ave. East, Toronto, 12, Ontario
CARIBBEAN	The Caribbean Kennel Club, PO Box 737, Port of Spain, Trinidad
CHILE	Kennel Club de Chile—Casilla 1704, Valparaiso
COLOMBIA	Club Canino Colombiano, Carrera 7a, No. 84–61, Apto. 101, Bogota, DE, Colombia
DENMARK	Dansk Kennelklub, Norrebrogade 40, 2200 Copenhagen
EAST AFRICA	East Africa Kennel Club—PO Box 40 511, Nairobi, Kenya, East Africa
FINLAND	Suomen Kennelliitto-Finska Kennelklubben, Bulevardi 14A, Helsinki
FRANCE	Société Centrale Canine—215 Rue St Denis, 75083, Paris Cedex 02
GERMANY	Verband für das Deutsche Hundewesen (VDH)—Schwanenstrasse 30, Dortmund
GUERNSEY	Guernsey Dog Club—Myrtle Grove, St Jacques, Guernsey, CI
HOLLAND	Raad van Beheer op Kynologisch Gebied in Nederland—Emmalaan 16, Amsterdam, Z
HONG KONG	Hong Kong Kennel Club—3rd Floor, 28B Stanley Street, Hong Kong
INDIA	Kennel Club of India—Kenhope, Coonoor I, Nilgiris, S. India
IRELAND	Irish Kennel Club—23 Earlsfort Terrace, Dublin 2
ITALY	Ente Nazionale Della Cinofilia Italiana—Viale Premuda, 21, Milan
JAMAICA	The Jamaican Kennel Club, 8 Orchard Street, Kingston 5, Jamaica, WI

JERSEY	Jersey Dog Club—'La Huppe', Birches Avenue, St Saviour, Jersey, CI
MALAYSIA	Malaysian Kennel Association—PO Box No 559, Kuala Lumpur, Malaya
MALTA GC	Malta Kennel Club, 12 Our Saviour Street, Sliema, Malta GC
MONACO	Société Canine de Monaco—Palais des Congrès, Avenue d'Ostende, Monte Carlo
NEW ZEALAND	New Zealand Kennel Club—PO Box 19–101 Aro Street, Wellington
NORWAY	Norsk Kennelklub—Teglverksgt 8, Rodelokka, Postboks 6598, Oslo, 5
PAKISTAN	The Kennel Club of Pakistan, Fortress Stadium, Lahore, West Pakistan
PORTUGAL	Cluba Portuguese de Canicultura—Praca D. Joao da Camara 4–3°, Lisbon 2
SINGAPORE	The Singapore Kennel Club, Suite 544, Tanglin Shopping Centre, 19 Tanglin Road, Singapore 10
SOUTH AFRICA	Kennel Union of Southern Africa, PO Box 562, Colonial Mutual Buildings, 106 Adderley Street, Cape Town
SPAIN	Real Sociedad Central de Fomento de las Razas en España—Los Madrazos 20, Madrid
SWEDEN	Svenska Kennelklubben, Luntmakargatan 40, Box 1308, 1183 Stockholm
SWITZERLAND	Schweizerische Kynologische Gesellschaft—Falkenplatz 11, 3012 Bern, Switzerland
URUGUAY	Kennel Club Uruguayo—Avda, Uruguay 864, Montevideo, South America
USA	American Kennel Club—51 Madison Avenue, New York NY 10010

THE SCOTTISH KENNEL CLUB, the delegated Authority of the Kennel Club in Scotland—Secretary, W. N. K. M. Crawford, CA, 18 Ainslie Place, Edinburgh, EH3 6AX

A Special Agreement has been made with the FÉDÉRATION CYNOLOGIQUE INTERNATIONALE, Rue Léopold II, B-6530, Thuin, Belgium

In some countries the dogs are judged as they are in England. Other countries have copied the American Kennel Club method by which the dogs become champions by a point system. There are some Kennel Clubs which organize their shows by a compromise: they use some of the British methods but adopt the American point system. The variations of method are not particularly important except that in some countries it is very much easier to make up a champion than in others. It is even easier to make up a champion in some breeds than it is in others.

The different methods and the various point systems are, however, not too complicated for a foreign judge visiting another country to be able to adapt from one system to another. What may be more difficult is that not all standards are the same, and a judge in England who prefers a dog weighing, say, about eight or ten pounds may find that in the USA the breed is preferred to be a little larger. Some countries consider the number of teeth to be more important almost than the dog. Therefore, a judge, for example, in Germany, must judge according to the standard of the country and must remember to count the dog's teeth.

INTERNATIONAL STANDARDS

The idea of International Standards for pedigree dogs would be a great step forward; particularly now that there are so many international judges. It becomes quite complicated when, for example, the American Kennel Club have the nomenclature of all their breeds in the plural and in the United Kingdom the nomenclature is in the singular and often the names are quite different. Further complications ensue when both countries have their pedigree dogs divided into six groups, but the groups do not necessarily have the same breeds in them. In the United States a Shih Tzu is considered as a Toy breed, whilst in the United Kingdom the Shih Tzu is in the Utility Group amongst the Non-Sporting dogs. In the United States the Japanese Chin is known as a 'Japanese Spaniel', the Dobermann is known as the 'Doberman Pinscher' (note the second 'n' being left off Dobermann), the King Charles Spaniel is known as the 'English Toy Spaniel'. The Elkhound has the prefix 'Norwegian'. The Pyrenean Mountain Dog is known as the 'Great Pyrenean'. The Keeshond is called 'Keeshonden', whilst the Staffordshire Bull Terrier is simply the 'Staffordshire Terrier'; to mention just a few breeds.

Some people may well feel that the nomenclature of the breeds is really so similar that why should the Kennel Clubs bother to come to an agreement on the names of the breeds and their groups? I remember the fuss that some English breeders created when I wrote to them for photographs for a Doberman Pinscher book, I was well aware that they were called Dobermann in the United Kingdom, but the book was also to be sold in the United States. It seems so unnecessary, when writing 'Alsatian', to have to put in brackets after it 'German Shepherd Dog', or vice versa.

BREED STANDARDS

Breeders and judges are ruled by the breed standards. It is the standard that people are endeavouring to interpret. It therefore stands to reason that all standards should be clear, concise and explicit, but at the same time they should not be too rigid. Unfortunately, not all standards are perfectly worded, nor are they written in good English. If these standards could become internationally standardized, they could be drawn up by the leading experts in the breed and top-ranking veterinary surgeons. The latter could perhaps recommend skeletal alterations to some standards, where over-exaggeration is causing distress or problems in certain breeds. For example it might be considered that some breeds have a dangerously exaggerated length of back, causing problems of paralysis in some lines. Too short a muzzle, too deep a stop, or too narrow a pelvis are causing trouble in other breeds.

It seems strange that in some standards where docked tails are required there is no mention even that the tail should be docked. Other standards mention that the tail should not be docked too short. But how short is 'short'? There are many similar anomalies which really should be altered. The standard should say: 'The tail should be docked to the third or fourth joint,' or whatever length is considered to be the correct length. Should a judge put a dog 'down' because his tail has been left too long or docked too short?

In some countries the standards are probably too rigid and precise, so that there is little leeway for a judge's interpretation. Many European countries go so far as to make exact measurements, or stipulate the precise number of teeth a dog must have. In so doing judges and breeders so often cannot see the wood for the trees. After all, there is a definite limitation in descriptive words suitable for a breed standard. Quality and type can be seen through very different eyes. Then there is that word 'sound', so imperative in the dog game, and yet which few breeders understand, and on which fewer judges agree. There is also the eternal 'dog game' argument as to whether presentation and soundness should come before type. This is similar to which came first, the chicken or the egg?

Type should conform to the standard of the country of origin provided that the country has a Kennel Club standard. It is interesting that in the USA the Pekingese has a weight limit of 14 lbs with a medium-weight dog preferred. In the United Kingdom the smaller type of Pekingese is preferred, that is, one weighing in the region of eight to ten pounds although in fact there is no weight restriction in the standard.

The world is becoming smaller daily, as air travel becomes faster and faster. More and more pedigree dogs are being exported to distant lands where they are exhibited under judges with international reputations. Surely, the time has come when height restrictions should also be universal. It is quite astonishing to think that the world popular Toy Poodle has a different height restriction in the United Kingdom from that in the United States. How complicated for a judge doing a judging tour round the world, to remember the different standards in each breed!

Size is often a matter of comparison. If, for example, all the American Cocker Spaniels in a class are too small and there is only one of the correct size, that one dog more often than not, would be considered to be too large, or vice versa, unless a measure was used.

In the United Kingdom the standard is set by the breeders, and the type by the specialist judges, which often comes to the same thing; whereas, in the United States the standard is ruled by points, the shows dominated by the professional handlers, and type is controlled by the all-rounders. It is an interesting fact, however, that regardless of the wording of a breed standard, a good dog shines out above the others, and generally judges continue to put up the same dogs. A person with no knowledge of a breed can pick out a really outstanding dog from the ringside, even knowing nothing about dogs or the breed standard. There is something special about a really outstanding dog enjoying his own performance.

AMERICAN SHOWS

The first dog show in the USA was held in Chicago on 4 June, 1874, with an entry of twenty-one dogs. The first show catalogue was printed in November, 1877, which was seven years before the American Kennel Club was founded in 1884. In those early days, dog shows were becoming more and more popular and were held in the chief large cities of New York, Chicago, Philadelphia, Boston and elsewhere.

AMERICAN KENNEL CLUBS

Monopolies are not permitted in the United States of America, and there are therefore two national Kennel clubs. The American Kennel Club was founded on 17 September, 1884, and was one of the first of the early dog clubs. At the present time it is situated at 51 Madison Avenue, New York, New York 10010. This is the club with reciprocal agreements with the Kennel Club. Mr John A. Lafore, Jr, is the President. The other club is the United Kennel Club Inc 321 West Cedar Street, Kalamazoo, Michigan, 49006. The latter also registers pedigree dogs and issues its own rules and regulations for dog shows and field trials. The United Kennel Club publishes a magazine every two months, called *Bloodlines Journal.* Champions are made up by a points system, but this is worked out in a different manner from that of the American Kennel Club. The United Kennel Club caters for special breeds, including the American Bull Terrier, six varieties of Coonhounds, the English Shepherd Dog, the Toy Foxterrier and other breeds.

The American Kennel Club has 394 member clubs and 500 licensed clubs. Each group of clubs sends a member to the American Kennel Club meetings to organize the dates of the shows throughout the year. The American Kennel Club recognizes 116 breeds for registration and dog shows. It issues licences for handlers and judges and approves dates for shows, sanction matches, field trials. Its monthly magazine is called *Pure Bred Dogs—American Kennel Gazette,* and it functions in a similar manner to other kennel clubs. Fines of $25 may be imposed on exhibitors for breaking rules and regulations.

In 1972, the American Kennel Club held 2823 shows, of which 1296 were championship shows, with 705,117 dogs competing. 8369 dogs became champions, and no less than 1,101,943 dogs were registered, but this includes whole litters. The total enrolment of dogs is 16,000,000. There are 1700 show judges, and 1100 licensed handlers. The Club has an excellent library of over 9750 books and it also has a fine collection of paintings, most of which have been presented by past and present members of the Club. The American Kennel Club also publishes an excellent book called *The Complete Dog Book.*

The Westminster Show, which is held in February, is a most spectacular affair, and is not in the least like Cruft's Dog Show in London. Dogs do, however, have to qualify before they may be entered at Westminster. They must be champions, or they must have won major points. The number of dogs entered is restricted to 2500, with 30 to 40 judges. In 1974, there were 7877 dogs entered at Cruft's. In 1971, the two-day show was also restricted in numbers, but 8431 dogs were exhibited and there were about one hundred judges.

One of the early American Kennel Club innovations was that individual clubs should hold their shows during a specified period and that there should be a circuit of shows. This was an excellent plan, because the distances between great cities was so enormous. Some of the shows were three-day shows, some were two-day shows, whilst others were held on one day only. Dog showing soon became a serious business, and professional handlers spent days and weeks on various circuits held throughout the country. Some were held in one area in the spring, another area in the summer, and so on. Most of the handlers travelled by train. Nowadays, a great many fly to the shows with their dogs, and a tremendous number go by car.

The United States is divided into four zones. Division 1 is East and North, Division 2 West and South, Division 3 State of California, and Division 4 Pacific North West. There are three special divisions for Alaska, Hawaii and Puerto Rico. The Schedule of Points are brought up to date and published in *Pure Bred Dogs—The American Kennel Gazette.* But every show catalogue

Above: Newfoundland with his Sash of Honour.

Left: I must see who is winning 'Best in Show'!

Below: The judge examining an English setter from the front. The handler, having dropped the lead, controls the dog from the rear and is well out of the way of the judge.

Above: The world renowned judge Mr. W. G. Siggers.

Above right: The judge examining the mouth of a Cocker Spaniel, correctly set up at the edge of the table. The handler has kept contact with the dog from the rear so that he is out of the judge's way, but it would have looked better if he had kept the lead in his hand. Stray lead ends are untidy.

Right: Mrs. Catherine Sutton judging a Lowchen at Cruft's. This was the first occasion on which the breed was awarded challenge certificates.

Below: In England a Pekingese class is normally judged on a table. In the United States not more than two dogs of any breed may be placed on a table at the same time.

must have the schedule of points for their particular section printed in full. The number of points that any breed is awarded depends entirely on the show popularity of the breed in each particular division. The points are regulated according to the number of dogs registered each year in a particular breed and the number exhibited in one area. The final points are calculated on the number of dogs and number of bitches which are exhibited and competing against each other at a particular show.

For a dog to become champion he requires a total of fifteen points—awarded only in the winners class—and these points must have been won at at least two major shows and under not less than three different judges. The lowest award is a one-point win and the highest a five-point win. A major show is one where three, four, or five points are awarded. An outstanding dog could thus become a champion in three shows. Under this complicated system the dog rating and bitch rating in a breed are not necessarily the same. The dog may have won 'winners dog' with five points whilst the bitch may win 'winners bitch' with only three points. If the bitch then beats the winners dog she automatically takes the winners dog's points, if these are higher than her own winner's bitch points; but no dog loses the points that he has already won. The dog or bitch that becomes best of breed is called best of winners. If the winning dog has gained its fifteen necessary points to become a champion, this may not be announced until the American Kennel Club issues the certificate. As can be imagined, with such a complicated point system errors can easily be made owing to absentees, disqualifications or place ribbons withheld, and it may take weeks for the AKC to announce the official results in *Pure Bred Dogs—The American Kennel Gazette.*

It is, however, very much easier to make up a champion in America than in Britain, since once a dog becomes a champion he is generally entered only in the winners class. American classes consist of puppy, novice, bred-by-exhibitor, American-bred, open and winners. The winners of each class are given a blue ribbon, the second a red, the third a yellow, and the fourth a white ribbon. The blue ribbon winners all compete in winners class and these compete against each other for the purple ribbon and championship points. The judge picks the winners dog or bitch and a reserve of winners dog or bitch. If the dog or bitch placed second in the earlier class won by the winners dog or winners bitch has not been beaten by any dog other than the winner, he or she is called into the ring to compete amongst the other exhibits for the title of reserve winner. In the event of a disqualification at a later date the reserve winners would be moved up to winners. Group and show winners can obtain extra points, if dogs they beat have won higher points than they have.

American, Canadian, Mexican and many other kennel clubs divide the breeds into six groups; Group I—Sporting Dogs; Group II—Hounds; Group III—Working Dogs; Group IV—Terriers; Group V—Toys; and Group VI—Non-Sporting Dogs. Unfortunately, the breeds included in these groups are not the same in each country. The best of breed winners compete in group judging. The best of each group is then selected by the judge, together with the second, third and fourth places. The winners of each group then go forward to compete for best in show. The best in group, provided that he is not a champion, is awarded the highest number of points already won on that day by any of the dogs that he has defeated in the group, provided that these points are higher than those that he has already won himself at that show. The elimination process from perhaps three or four thousand dogs ends with the excitement for the owner, handler and/or breeder of one single winning dog.

There are other interesting classes which are non-regular classes, such as local classes, for which the exhibits must come from within a certain area; brace and team class; miscellaneous class, for breeds registered at the American Kennel Club with more than 600 registrations. A veterans class generally stipulates that dogs must have reached five, six or seven years of age, and there are the interesting stud dog and brood bitch classes which includes the stud dog and his get and the brood bitch and her offspring.

As with all dog shows there is a great deal of luck in making up a champion. An outstanding dog may be unlucky in that he is doing the circuit with another dog who just has the edge on him at every show, whilst a few shows later a much inferior dog may be made up in three shows entirely from lack of good competition. An outstanding dog can become a champion in three shows with three major five-point wins. A poor specimen can go on winning one point wins, with two three-point majors. Good handlers can choose the dogs they handle and know where to exhibit the dogs, so that any reasonably good dog can be made up in the USA and Canada, but this is not so in Britain, where there is no elimination of champions enabling new comers to gain points without having to compete against the champions.

The point system is sometimes unsportingly utilized to advance the number of points awarded by what is known as 'fillers'. This is when an exhibitor enters a number of inferior dogs in a class, in order to be able to gain the maximum number of points towards a dog's championship. Fillers for a class is an expensive pursuit, particularly if the idea backfires, and a rival's dog beats the dog whose owner provided the fillers. The rival would have thus gained the maximum number of points towards his championship.

An outstanding dog should be able to win his championship in three majors. Sometimes, as explained above, a dog may be unlucky and will be on the same circuit as another very outstanding dog. In three shows, however, the dog becomes a champion and the way is then made clear for another dog. In England, an outstandingly good dog can be kept out for ever by being unlucky, and always coming reserve to a fabulous champion. I have seen several pedigrees where a dog has had fourteen reserve best of sex's (reserve cc's), and has never been 'made up'. By the time the famous champion has been retired, the other dog was too old to compete against the younger dogs coming on. But this is the luck of the dog "game". Shows in the United States of America are extremely highly organized. They are generally run by professional superintendents, who not only own their own printing presses but also make their prize ribbons with their own special ribbon machines. The efficiency is so great that the printing of show catalogues can be made up in as little as ten days.

Professional handlers generally prepare, condition and train dogs, transport them to the shows and board them between shows. Handlers may exhibit nearly two dozen dogs at weekend shows and perhaps attend six or seven shows in ten days. The circuits are the money makers for the professional handlers when many amateur dog owners cannot attend shows during the week. The handling fees are high for a top professional, but all handlers must be licensed and the top handlers can choose the dogs they handle. Many owners now show their own dogs and become as proficient as the handlers. If they did not become so proficient, their dogs would not win against the expert handling of the professionals. This is why the handling in the USA is, on the whole, much better than it is in England, where the majority of exhibitors are novices and handle their own dogs. Handling in England is bound to improve tremendously in the near future, since the cost of showing a dog has increased so enormously in recent years that showing dogs has become too expensive just to play at it. Everyone is going to have to become as good as the professionals. An American judge does not necessarily have to go over every dog in the class as a judge has to in England. An American judge need only examine the dogs which he wishes to place. In a large class it is perfectly permissible for the judge to dismiss the rest of the class, while he makes his final placings. There is no limit to the number of dogs that an English judge may go over in one day. The judge, however, is obliged to examine individually every dog in the breed. In the United States no judge is permitted to judge more than 175 dogs on one day; but he does not necessarily have to go over that number individually. The judge is not required to write a critique or show report on the first three dogs placed in each class as is expected in the United Kingdom.

I myself have had an entry of over 220 dogs of one breed. A judge can easily manage to go over each dog thoroughly provided that he is given sufficient time to judge his classes. It is recommended, however, that he should not be required to judge more than twenty dogs an hour.

CANADIAN SHOWS

Shows in Canada are very strict and are run on similar lines to the American Kennel Club. American dogs exhibited in Canada require a health certificate, an anti-rabies vaccination within a year and a temporary entrance permit. The dog must also be registered by the Canadian

National Live Stock Records, Ottawa, Ontario. This requires the American Kennel Club registration certificate, and a nose print or tattoo form and two dollars for registration. A dog may be listed for one dollar and can be shown indefinitely, but he cannot become a Canadian champion until he is registered.

THE CANADIAN KENNEL CLUB

The Canadian Kennel Club has its offices in Toronto. Although their shows are run on similar lines to the American Kennel Club, a judge may withold winners points, if he does not consider the dog to be of high enough standard at the particular show. The dogs are also divided into six groups.

The Canadian Kennel Club institute a system of tattooing. All imported dogs are allotted individual numbers and a serial number, and are generally tattooed on the ear.

Breeders may apply to the Canadian Kennel Club for letters for their own exclusive use. Capital letters indicate the year of the dog's birth. The letters I O Q are not used as these are too easily faked. The tattoo markings may be made on the right or left ear, the lip, belly, or flank. If a breeder goes five years without using his registered tattoo markings, the letters may then be allotted to another breeder. The breeder or owner may, if he wishes, send two nose prints to the Club with the dog's registered number. The nose print must be a good clear specimen with no smudge marks.

Tattoo equipment can be obtained from Ketchum Manufacturing Co, PO Box 388, Westboro, Ontario, Canada, and nose print material from Canadian Kennel Club, 677 Yonge Street, Toronto, Ontario, Canada. The cost of the latter is one dollar.

There are differences regarding the recognition of breeds, and additional rules concerning 'doctoring of dogs' with drugs. All dogs are examined by veterinarians. There is also a different points system, but the shows are run in circuits similar to the system in the USA.

A dog requires ten points to become a champion but the scale of points is lower than in America, and does not vary with sex. Points are gained by a class-winning dog which then goes best of opposite sex and takes the highest rating of its sex.

The best-in-show judge must be licensed to judge all breeds. A non-champion winning a show automatically takes the highest points made at the show. Ten points are required to become a champion under at least three different judges. The dog must defeat at least one of its breed or be placed in its group, with five or more competing breeds.

One excellent rule of the Canadian Kennel Club is that the handler must open the dog's mouth and never the judge. This is a great help in preventing infection being passed from one dog to another. On the other hand, a clever handler may possibly try to conceal a tooth fault by sly manipulation.

The size of shows in both countries varies between 200 entries with 50 breeds and 3500 with 100 breeds. The proportion of professional handlers would be one handler to every twenty-five dogs.

MEXICAN KENNEL CLUB

La Associación Canófila Mexicana has its offices in Mexico City. The shows are run on American lines. In order to become a champion a dog must win three best of breeds at three different shows. Many American and Canadian dogs are exhibited at the Mexican Shows in order to make the dogs up into international champions. Officially, there is no such title. It merely means that the dogs are champions in more than one country.

EUROPEAN AND SOUTH AMERICAN SHOWS

The supreme control in Europe and South America is the Fédération Cynologique Internationale, the 'FCI' as it is called, which has its headquarters in Belgium. It is an international club on which every national kennel club in Europe and South America is represented. It controls every aspect of breeding in every country in Europe and South America except Britain. The Kennel Club is, nevertheless, on friendly relations with the FCI. The FCI issues all breed standards and uses those of the country of origin of each breed and, where possible, in the language of that country. There are two major types of FCI show: there is the national show with national certificates, called CAC's, and the international show which awards international certificates called CACIB's, which are open to dogs of all countries.

Some Overseas International Shows at which CACIB's are awarded:

Coimbra	Portugal	Ljublijana	Yugoslavia
Nova Friburgo	Brazil	Ludwigsburg	Germany
Porto	Portugal	St Domingue	Dominican Republic
Pirmasens	Germany	Algarve	Portugal
Caparica	Portugal	Poznan	Poland
Estoril	Portugal	Wiesbaden	Germany
Panama City	Panama	Amsterdam	Holland

DUTCH SHOWS

There are less than a dozen international shows in Holland each year. The most important of these is the Winner at Amsterdam, which corresponds to Cruft's. A certificate at the Winner counts as two. A CACIB cannot be awarded to a dog before it is eighteen months old, though a dog may receive the CACIB if the judge considers him really outstanding, provided that he is over the age of fifteen months. In Holland the open classes are judged first. There are no class cash prizes and entries are very expensive. The wins are graded as 'excellent', 'very good', 'good' and 'indifferent'. Each dog has to be graded and placed in order of merit; and if there are several 'excellents', they are graded 'excellent 1, 2 and 3', etc. All Dutch judges have to pass a stiff written and oral examination, so that most Dutch judges are professionals. Breeding is taken seriously and there is a committee which advises on suitable matings.

GERMAN SHOWS

The national dog authority in Germany is called 'Der Verband für das Deutsche Hundewesen'. It controls shows under the jurisdiction of the FCI. The breed clubs in Germany have great authority. Dogs under eighteen months and entered in the junior classes may not be given the grade of 'excellent' as in Holland. The number of awards in each grade is not limited and is left to the judges' discretion. There are no cash prizes and the entry fees are very high. Dogs are normally only entered in one class. Breeding is strictly controlled in Germany and only approved animals may be used for breeding. The breed clubs are responsible for seeing that this is carried out. Only six puppies are retained in any litter. Germans are convinced that the absence of even one of the premolar teeth present in most dogs is a sign of degeneration, and judges do not award first prizes to any dog without his full complement of teeth, however good the dog may be. These dogs are also barred from breeding. Switzerland too, is very strict on teeth, but it is the only other country to hold these views.

SWEDISH SHOWS

Swedish shows are judged partly on the Continental system and partly on the British system. All shows are controlled by the Swedish Kennel Club. The number of classes is again four to each breed, namely, junior and open classes for each sex. The junior class, which is open to dogs up to 22 months of age, is judged first. An eligible dog may be entered in a youth class, in both youth and open classes, or in the open class alone, as the exhibitor wishes. The grading is numerical, first, second and third, and as many dogs may be placed in each grade as the judge considers worthy. In the first part of the judging the dogs are graded and the placing is not competitive. It is judged to the ideal of the breed and no dog who is untypical may be graded. All the grade I puppies take part in the final decision, for the competitive grading. The best four are chosen and may go forward to the open class. The CAC may only be awarded to the winner of an open class. Progeny and breeder classes are for stud dogs and brood bitches respectively with not fewer than five of their progeny, and at least three of these must have won a first prize in an open class.

AUSTRALIAN AND NEW ZEALAND SHOWS

The Australian National Kennel Council has no less than eight member bodies. The role of the council is an advisory body rather than a controlling body. The Council was first envisaged in April, 1949. The object is the improvement of dog showing and breeding throughout Australia, a uniform system for allocating points towards the title of Australian Champion, agreement on breed standards, clearance of judges, export certificates, etc. The member bodies are: the Canine Association of Western Australia, the North Australian Canine Association, the Canine Control Council (Queensland), the Canberra Kennel Association, the Kennel Control Council of Tasmania, the RAS Kennel Club, the South Australian Canine Association and the Kennel Control Council, Victoria.

The Kennel Control Council Rules are similar to those of most other Kennel Clubs with the usual variations. Dogs are not permitted to be exhibited in a harness and no dog shall enter a ring wearing a collar on which the name of the dog or owner appears. Classes consist of baby puppy, minor puppy, puppy, junior, intermediate, novice, graduate, limit, state-bred, Australian-bred and open. Championship shows eliminate the baby puppy class. There are also classes of brace, team and litter. The latter has to be all progeny from the same litter, and there is also a local class for dogs over three months of age. A dog must win not fewer than four challenge certificates under four different judges to gain a total of 100 points, before he is awarded the title of Australian champion.

Points are allotted to dogs and bitches over the age of six months. Challenge certificate winners gain 5 points plus one point for each dog exhibited in the class for the breed. Each winner in the six recognized groups also wins 5 points plus one for each dog and bitch exhibited in the group. Best in show wins 25 points. The points are not accumulative and no dog can win more than 25 points at any one show. An imported champion may have its title recognized by the KCC on application with proper verification from the country of origin.

New Zealand shows have slightly different classes from English shows and no point system. A dog must win eight challenge certificates to become a champion.

Both Australian and New Zealand shows have an excellent feature which consists of a small marshalling ring set beside each judging ring. This ring is supervised by a special marshalling steward, so that all dogs are assembled and ready to go straight into the judging ring with no time wasted between classes. The other steward supervises the handlers in the judging ring only.

Many judges like to have the dogs placed on the table straight from the marshalling ring, without seeing them lined up first and then moved round the ring. This is a pity since the whole class are not evaluated together and then moved together before finer inspection on the table. The marshalling ring is an idea that show committees might well decide to incorporate since it is a most efficient procedure.

With large entries the classes are timed in the catalogue, and the judge is expected to adhere to this minute by minute schedule. He is permitted to finish judging a class a little early, but he may on no account start the next class before the time stated in the catalogue.

CHAPTER III

Shows and Class Classification

The main object and purpose of the Kennel Club is the registration of pedigree dogs for exhibition and for the promotion and improvement of pedigree dogs in general. This includes all aspects of dogdom: shows, field trials, working trials and obedience tests and everything that these entail. The Kennel Club are not interested in legal matters or disagreements between breeders.

In Britain there are 302 championship shows held annually for registered pedigree dogs, which include championship shows for individual breeds, and also those held for field trials and obedience. There are also about 2275 other shows held throughout the country which are recognized by the Kennel Club and come under their jurisdiction.

There are six types of show. Starting with the least important these are called exemption, matches, sanction, limited, open and championship shows. The Kennel Club show regulations overlap in some instances, which is possibly a little confusing to the novice. It is also extremely confusing for anyone looking up Kennel Club regulations for shows in their annual year book, because the show regulations are not in chronological order, but are dotted about throughout the book. There is, however, an excellent index, provided that one remembers to look for this at the front of the book.

Exemption shows and matches are permitted by the Committee; sanction shows, as the name implies, are sanctioned by the Committee; whilst limited, open and championship shows are licensed. Sanction and limited shows may be held on Sundays and are similar to each other, except that limited shows have four senior classes, but no dog who has won a challenge certificate may be entered. The licensed shows are regular shows and must have a printed schedule in accordance with the Kennel Club regulations, and prize cards must be given. The prize cards are in different colours and sizes according to the specification of the show. There are also individual regulations regarding times, days of the week, number of classes and the amount of prize money and number of prize cards allocated to each show.

EXEMPTION SHOWS

These are normally held in conjunction with agricultural shows, garden fêtes and similar functions. Application must be made to the Kennel Club twenty-eight days before the proposed date of a show on the official writing paper of the organizers, enclosing a fee of £1 and giving a copy of the proposed classification, the time and place of the show and the name of the judge. Only four pedigree classes are permitted, but the dogs need not be registered at the Kennel Club. There are often additional classes for 'the dog most like its owner', 'the dog with the longest tail', 'the best conditioned dog', 'the best child handler', 'the dog with the most beautiful eyes', 'the dog with the saddest eyes', 'the dog the judge would most like to take home', and so forth. Prize money at exemption shows must not exceed 50p. These shows are really intended only for amusement and it is extremely bad form for seasoned exhibitors to attend with their already show-winning dogs with the object of 'trophy hunting'.

MATCHES

A match may be arranged within one breed or variety, or it may be between two breeds or more. The exhibits, however, must be pedigree dogs.

A registered canine club or society may not hold more than twelve matches in any one year. The fee for each match is a nominal £1 paid by the society to the Kennel Club, and a prior notice of at least fourteen days must be given to the Kennel Club before a match may be held. The number of dogs competing must not exceed thirty-two. Should more than thirty-two dogs be present at a match, then a ballot must be taken to decide which dogs may compete. However, to obviate this complication it would be much simpler if the first thirty-two dogs to arrive at the venue were those which were permitted to take part in the match. The complication and waste of time of taking a ballot in a hall which is often very small, and which is probably overflowing with hopeful exhibitors and their frequently partially trained dogs and puppies, can only create more frustration and added disappointment. Most matches provide some small trophy for the best dog in match and a smaller prize for the runner-up. The judges are not paid for their services but they are generally presented with a small gift in kind, very often a bottle of wine or perhaps even a chicken.

A match is really a social affair and it is often held in a pub, or in conjunction with a breed club garden party. It is an excellent opportunity for a novice to get the opinion of a knowledgeable judge under much more relaxed circumstances than at a serious show. There is also more time for a judge to talk to and help the exhibitor. Matches are also extremely useful as training experience for a young puppy. Normally, an entry fee of 10p is made and each exhibitor receives a number for his dog. As soon as the match starts, the numbers are drawn two at a time and each pair of dogs then compete against each other. The judge generally requires the dogs to be walked round the ring one behind the other. Then each dog is gone over in turn, with the dog standing either on the table or on the floor, according to the size of the breed. After each dog has been examined, he will be required to move up and down the ring, and then the dogs will be moved together, the judge nominating the better specimen the winner. The winner of each heat must be ready to compete again against another dog when his number is called. If there are thirty-two dogs at the match, the first round consists of sixteen pairs, the second of eight pairs and the third round of four pairs, and this continues until the final pair compete for best in match. In cases where there are less than thirty-two dogs or where there happens to be an uneven number of dogs, then bye rounds must be organized. Variations in matches may be arranged by colours, ages, etc. There is an enormous variety of ways of organizing competitions of this type but probably the 'knock-out' form of competition is most appreciated, since all breeds compete against each other, and a judge may find that he has to decide between a Shih Tzu and a Great Dane. It is also very good training for dogs to compete against other breeds of varying sizes and shapes. This is excellent experience for the day when a dog may be competing in variety classes or even in the best in show ring.

LICENSED REGULAR SHOWS

SANCTIONS SHOWS

Sanction shows, as the name implies, are sanctioned by the Kennel Club Committee.

The secretary of a breed club or canine society must obtain permission from the Kennel Club and pay the fee of £2 at least three months before the proposed date of the show. The application must be signed by both the chairman and the show secretary. These shows may not commence earlier than 5 p.m. except on Saturdays and on the official early-closing day of the district, when they may commence at 12.30 p.m. They must conclude the same evening. The dogs, however, need not be benched. Only fully paid-up members of the society or club may enter and the prize money may not be less than 50p for a first prize if one is offered. Only members of the club, association or society may compete. A show confined to one breed or variety must not comprise more than ten classes. There may be twenty-five classes for a show of more than one breed or variety. Only classes below post-graduate may be offered. In other words, the highest class will be post-graduate. A schedule must be published in accordance with Kennel Club regulations.

LIMITED SHOWS

A limited show is a licensed show and is limited to members of clubs and societies, or to exhibitors within a specified area, unless stated otherwise. A limited show is considerably higher in standard than a sanction show, although no dog is eligible who has won a challenge certificate. These shows may or may not be benched. There must be a minimum of thirteen classes, if only one breed is scheduled, and twenty-one classes, if there is more than one breed. Unbenched limited or open shows are limited to fifty classes. A limited show of thirty-five classes or less must commence before 6 p.m., but if there should be more than thirty-five classes scheduled, then the show must start before 3 p.m. At limited shows there are four senior classes, which are not permitted at Sanction Shows. These are minor-limit, mid-limit, limit and open. The licence fee is £2. There must be at least three award cards for each class, and the money for first prize, if offered, must not be less than 50p.

OPEN SHOWS

Open shows, as the name implies, are open to all dogs irrespective of whether or not they are champions. Open shows are generally benched, and the definition for classes is identical to those for championship shows. The show must commence before 3 p.m. and the prize money is not permitted to be less than £1 for a first prize. The exceptions are in brace, team, stud dog, brood bitch, veteran and breeder classes. Breed clubs hold open shows, but it is not necessary for exhibitors to be members of the club. The licence fee is £3.

ALL-BREED CHAMPIONSHIP SHOWS

Championship shows are open shows. They may be held for one or more breeds and are unrestricted and may be held on Sundays. The exceptions are Cruft's and Blackpool. For Cruft's, a dog must have won a first prize at a championship show during the previous year, and Blackpool Championship Show requires a dog to have won at an open show within the year. These new regulations have had to be made in order to try to restrict the number of dogs at the shows. The licence fee is £5. There is an extra fee of £2 at both open and championship shows for each 500 exhibits or part of 500 exhibits. No less than three award cards must be presented as prizes for each class. If money prizes are offered, the first prize must not be less than £1.

There are twenty-four all-breed championship shows held every year. Most of these are held during the same month year after year, and generally at the same venue. More than half of these shows are held out of doors and provided that the weather is fine, those are probably the ones that both exhibitors and dogs enjoy most. The championship show year opens with Cruft's, the world-famous championship show held in London in the first or second week in February. January is the only month without an all-breeds championship show. The other championship shows are scheduled for individual breeds or groups. Challenge certificates are awarded to most of the scheduled breeds, provided that their registrations at the Kennel Club are more than one hundred and fifty. The Kennel Club allocate the number of challenge certificates for each breed. The number is regulated for each breed each year and this is based on the number of registrations during the three years ending the year previous to that in which challenge certificates are to be offered. In many breeds there was a large increase in the number of challenge certificates, and so the Kennel Club then decided to spread these increases gradually over a five-year period. The first five-year period ended in 1972.

GENERAL AND GROUP CHAMPIONSHIP SHOWS 1974

***Denotes with Obedience Certificates**

Cruft's Dog Show Society	Feb.
Manchester Dog Show Society	March
United Kingdom Toy Dog Society	March
National Terrier Club	April
*West of England Ladies' Kennel Society	May

*BATH CANINE SOCIETY	May	NATIONAL GUNDOG ASSOCIATION	Aug.
BIRMINGHAM DOG SHOW SOCIETY	May	WELSH KENNEL CLUB	Aug.
*SCOTTISH KENNEL CLUB (GLASGOW)	May	SOUTHERN COUNTIES CANINE ASSOCIATION	Aug.
LEEDS CITY AND DISTRICT CANINE ASSOCIATION	May	SCOTTISH KENNEL CLUB (EDINBURGH)	Aug.
CHESHIRE AGRICULTURAL SOCIETY	June	LEICESTER CITY CANINE SOCIETY	Aug.
THREE COUNTIES AGRICULTURAL SOCIETY	June	*CITY OF BIRMINGHAM CANINE ASSOCIATION	Aug.
*BLACKPOOL AND DISTRICT CANINE SOCIETY	June	DARLINGTON SHOW SOCIETY	Sept.
WINDSOR DOG SHOW SOCIETY	June	BOURNEMOUTH CANINE ASSOCIATION	Sept.
*PAIGNTON AND DISTRICT FANCIERS' ASSOCIATION	July	NATIONAL WORKING BREEDS DOG SOCIETY	Sept.
*SOUTH WALES KENNEL ASSOCIATION	July	*BELFAST DOG SHOW SOCIETY	Sept.
EAST OF ENGLAND AGRICULTURAL SOCIETY	July	LADIES' KENNEL ASSOCIATION	Nov.
HOUND ASSOCIATION	July	DRIFFIELD AGRICULTURAL SOCIETY	Nov.
		RICHMOND DOG SHOW SOCIETY	Dec.
		BRITISH UTILITY BREEDS ASSOCIATION	Dec.

CHALLENGE CERTIFICATES

Two challenge certificates are awarded by the Kennel Club at each championship show, one for dogs and one for bitches, where breeds are qualified. In order that a dog may become a champion —or to be 'made up' in dog parlance—the dog must win three challenge certificates under three different judges. Gun dogs require a qualifying certificate at a field trial in order to be eligible for the title of full champion, which includes both field trial and show. Toy breeds must win one of their three qualifying challenge certificates after the age of twelve months.

REGULATIONS FOR THE DEFINITIONS OF CLASSES AT CHAMPIONSHIP AND OTHER OPEN SHOWS

(Reprinted by kind permission of the Kennel Club)

Wins in Variety Classes do not count for entry in Breed Classes, but when entering for Variety Classes, wins in both Breed and Variety Classes must be counted. A Variety Class is one in which more than one Breed can compete. A First Prize does not include a Special Prize of whatever value.

In estimating the number of prizes won, all wins previous to the midnight preceding the day specified in the schedule for closing entries shall be counted when entering for any class.

Note.—In the following Definitions, a Challenge Certificate includes any Show award that counts towards the title of Champion under the rules of any governing body recognised by the Kennel Club.

With these provisos the following are the Definitions of certain Classes:—

PUPPY. For dogs of six and not exceeding twelve calendar months of age on the first day of the Show.

JUNIOR. For dogs of six and not exceeding eighteen calendar months of age on the first day of the Show.

MAIDEN For dogs which have not won a Challenge Certificate or a First Prize at an Open Show (Puppy and Minor Puppy Classes excepted).

NOVICE. For dogs which have not won a Challenge Certificate or three or more First Prizes at Open and Championship Shows (Puppy and Minor Puppy Classes excepted).

TYRO. For dogs which have not won a Challenge Certificate or five or more First Prizes at Open and Championship Shows (Puppy and Minor Puppy Classes excepted).

DEBUTANT. For dogs which have not won a Challenge Certificate or a First Prize at a Championship Show (Puppy and Minor Puppy Classes excepted).

UNDERGRADUATE. For dogs which have not won a Challenge Certificate or three or more First Prizes at Championship Shows (Puppy and Minor Puppy Classes excepted).

GRADUATE. For dogs which have not won a Challenge Certificate or four or more First Prizes at Championship Shows in Graduate, Post Graduate, Minor Limit, Limit and Open Classes, whether restricted or not.

POST GRADUATE. For dogs which have won a Challenge Certificate or five or more First Prizes at Championship Shows in Post Graduate, Minor Limit, Mid Limit, Limit and Open Classes, whether restricted or not.

MINOR LIMIT. For dogs which have not won two Challenge Certificates or three or more First Prizes in all, at Championship Shows in Minor Limit, Mid Limit, Limit and Open Classes, confined to the breed, whether restricted or not, at shows where Challenge Certificates were offered for the breed.

MID LIMIT. For dogs which have not won three Challenge Certificates or five or more First Prizes in all, at Championship Shows in Mid Limit, Limit and Open Classes, confined to the breed, whether restricted or not, at shows where Challenge Certificates were offered for the breed.

LIMIT.	For dogs which have not won three Challenge Certificates under three different judges or seven or more First Prizes in all, at Championship Shows, in Limit and Open Classes, confined to the breed, whether restricted or not, at shows where Challenge Certificates were offered for the breed.
OPEN.	For all dogs of the breeds for which the class is provided and eligible for entry at the Show.
VETERAN.	For dogs of an age specified in the schedule but not less than five years on the first day of the Show.
FIELD TRIAL.	For dogs which have won prizes, Awards of Honour, Diplomas of Merit, or Certificates of Merit in actual competition at a Field Trial under Kennel Club or Irish Kennel Club Field Trial Rules and Regulations.
BRACE.	For two exhibits (either sex or mixed) of one breed belonging to the same exhibitor, each exhibit having been entered in some class other than Brace or Team.
TEAM.	For three or more exhibits (either sex or mixed) of one breed belonging to the same exhibitor, each exhibit having been entered in some class other than Brace or Team.
SWEEPSTAKE CLASS.	For Brace, Team, Stud Dog, Brood Bitch, Veteran and Breeders Classes only, in which the entry fees may be given as prize money in such proportion as the Committee of the Show may determine.

CLASSES AT LIMITED AND SANCTION SHOWS

(Reprinted by kind permission of the Kennel Club)

Wins in Variety Classes do not count for entry in Breed Classes, but when entering for Variety Classes, wins in both Breed and Variety Classes must be counted. A Variety Class is one in which more than one Breed can compete. A First Prize does not include a Special Prize of whatever value.

In estimating the number of prizes won, all wins previous to the midnight preceding the day specified in the schedule for closing entries shall be counted when entering for any class.

NOTE.—No Class higher than Post Graduate may be offered at a Sanction Show. Minor Limit, Mid Limit, Limit and Open Classes must not be offered at Sanction Shows.

No dog is eligible for exhibition at a Limited or Sanction Show which has won a Challenge Certificate or obtained any Show award that counts towards the title of Champion under the rules of any governing body recognised by the Kennel Club.

With these provisos the following are the Definitions of certain Classes:—

PUPPY.	For dogs of six and not exceeding twelve calendar months of age on the first day of the Show.
JUNIOR.	For dogs of six and not exceeding eighteen calendar months of age on the first day of the Show.
MAIDEN.	For dogs which have not won a First Prize at any Show (Puppy and Special Puppy Classes excepted).
NOVICE.	For dogs which have not won three or more First Prizes at any Show or Shows (Puppy and Special Puppy Classes excepted).
TYRO	For dogs which have not won five or more First Prizes at any Show or Shows (Puppy and Special Puppy Classes excepted).
DEBUTANT.	For dogs which have not won a First Prize at an Open or Championship Show (Puppy and Minor Puppy Classes excepted).
UNDERGRADUATE.	For dogs which have not won three or more First Prizes, at Open Championship Shows (Puppy and Minor Puppy Classes excepted).
GRADUATE.	For dogs which have not won four or more First Prizes, at Open Championship Shows in Graduate, Post Graduate, Minor Limit, Mid Limit, Limit and Open Classes, whether restricted or not.
POST GRADUATE.	For dogs which have not won five or more First Prizes at Open and Championship Shows in Post Graduate, Minor Limit, Mid Limit, Limit and Open Classes, whether restricted or not.
MINOR LIMIT.	For dogs which have not won three or more First Prizes at Open or Championship Shows in Minor Limit, Mid Limit, Limit and Open Classes, confined to the breed, whether restricted or not.
MID LIMIT.	For dogs which have not won five or more First Prizes in all at Open and Championship Shows in Mid Limit, Limit and Open Classes, confined to the breed, whether restricted or not.
LIMIT.	For dogs which have not won seven or more First Prizes in all at Open or Championship Shows, in Limit and Open Classes confined to the breed, whether restricted or not.
OPEN.	For all dogs of the breeds for which the class is provided and eligible for entry at the Show.
VETERAN.	For dogs of any age specified in the schedule but not less than five years on the first day of the Show.
FIELD TRIAL.	For dogs which have won Prizes, Awards of Honour, Diplomas of Merit or Certificates of Merit, in actual competition at a Field Trial held under Kennel Club or Irish Kennel Club Field Trial Rules and Regulations.
BRACE.	For two exhibits (either sex or mixed) of one breed belonging to the same exhibitor, each exhibit having been entered in some class other than Brace or Team.

TEAM.	For three or more exhibits (either sex or mixed) of one breed belonging to the same exhibitor, each exhibit having been entered in some class other than Brace or Team.
SWEEPSTAKE CLASS.	For Brace, Team, Stud Dog, Brood Bitch, Veteran and Breeders Classes only, in which the entry fees are given as the prize money in such proportion as the Committee of the Show may determine.

SHOW RECORDS

A regular exhibitor, particularly one who is also a keen breeder and has good dogs, should keep a show book. These can be bought at dog shows, but it is often better to make a scrap-book into a show record book; or an even better way is to use a loose-leaf folder. One or more pages should be allotted to each dog. The pages can be ruled off into ten columns. At the top of the page should appear the name of the dog, its Kennel Club registration number, its date of birth, its sire and dam and their registered numbers, the variety of dog, and relevant colour, weight and height, the name of the breeder and the stud book number if qualified. The date of the last booster injection should also be entered.

In the first column should be entered the date of each show, in the second the name of the show, and in the third column the type of each show. The following column is for the classes entered, followed by a column for the number of entries in each class. The next column should be for prizes, and these should include the amount of money won. The seventh column might be for classes for which the dog is not eligible, followed by a column for the judge's name, and the next column could be for notes and the name of the handler. The final column should be as wide as possible, so that the judging critiques may be cut out from *Our Dogs* and *Dog World* and stuck in for future reference. The following pages may be used for photographs of the winning dogs.

It is also useful to keep the judge's critiques at shows attended, even though the dog has not been successful under that particular judge. It is good to record what the judge's fetishes are; for example, one judge may come down heavily on bad mouths, or light eyes, and therefore, even if these are not considered serious faults within a breed, it would be pointless, and a waste of money and time, to exhibit a dog with these faults under that judge again. It is also quite useful to record your opinion at the time whether a judge seemed prejudiced in favour of 'the other end of the lead'. It may be considered heresy to say this, but, human nature being what it is, all things are possible. It is worth noting such a judge's placings over a period of time. Enter under the judge again, but take another dog.

For exhibitors who do not wish to keep such elaborate records, it is an excellent idea to keep just a small note book for each show dog. This should be kept permanently with the show equipment and should be entered up after each show.

CHAPTER IV

Shows, Entries and Prizes

SHOW ENTRIES

For an owner wishing to start showing his dog, it is probably a good idea to gain experience by attending some of the smaller shows in his area. The best way of discovering where shows are due to be held is by taking one or both of the weekly dog papers. These are *Dog World* and *Our Dogs.* Both these papers advertise the forthcoming shows in all areas, and they give details of the venue and very often of the judges, the classes and the breed classifications.

When a novice has selected a suitable show—it would be wise to choose a sanctioned, limited or small open show—he should write to the show secretary and ask for a schedule. When the schedule arrives, he should read it all through carefully, particularly the classes scheduled for the breed intended for exhibition. Select the class or classes suitable for the dog or dogs to be entered and write the names against the classes on the schedule, because this is a useful reference, especially if entries are made for a number of shows during the following few weeks. It is astonishing, if one has a number of dogs, how easy it is to forget which dogs have been entered for which shows. Although the clubs send out entry passes, they sometimes do not arrive in time, and a harassed exhibitor may find that he has brought the wrong dog. This can be particularly annoying in the case of a breed which takes a great deal of preparation, not to mention its being a waste of the expense of entry fees, and the cost of a journey to the show.

ENTRY FORM

Entry forms vary in size, but they vary little in the essential lay out. It is important to read the entry form carefully, taking care to note the date when the entries have to be in. This will generally be found printed in a prominent place on the form as well as in the schedule. Most UK entries must be in four weeks before a show. In the USA entries are made 7–12 days before a show. Entries must be filled in correctly, in legible, bold print, written with either a ball-point pen or in ink. The first column is for the full registered name of the dog. The exhibitor must be the sole owner of the dog at the time of entry (unless in partnership). If the transfer of ownership for any reason has not been completed, then the letters TAF (transfer applied for) must be written immediately after the name of the dog; or if the registration of a puppy has not come through from the Kennel Club before an entry is to be made, then the letters NAF (name applied for) must be printed after the registered name that has been applied for. The next column is for the breed. If there is a variety in the breed, for example Long Coat or Smooth Coat Chihuahuas this must also be printed in the breed column. The full date of birth must be printed in the next column. The column after that is for the sex, and this is filled in with 'D' for dog or 'B' for bitch. In some countries sex is inserted as Male or Female. The next column is for the full date of birth, and after that the breeder. The breeder of a dog is the owner of the bitch at the time of the birth of the puppies. The next column is for the sire, and his name must be printed in full; this applies also to the next column which is for the dam. If the dog is a champion, the prefix 'Ch' must be added. The next column is for the price of the dog, if he is for sale, and this may be filled in or not as desired. Some clubs take ten per cent on the sale of a dog sold through the club schedule, but most clubs do not bother about this. The last column is headed 'To be entered in classes numbered: ' ' It is important to write the class numbers clearly, and probably the most difficult decision of all is the choice of which class or classes to enter. More mistakes are made and more prize money is lost through ill-considered entries than from any other cause. At the same time, choosing the correct class or classes is a lottery, because you do not know in which classes possible rivals will be entered.

It is not a good idea to enter a young dog in too many classes, especially if they are likely to be large entries. A promising dog can soon get bored with long waits, particularly if the show is unbenched.

VARIETY CLASSES

It is good experience for a novice exhibitor to enter a dog in the variety classes. It is here that the dogs will be gone over by all-rounders, who are judges of great experience and have a knowledge of a tremendous number of breeds. Specialist judges are often uneven judges, prejudiced towards particular breed points and often under pressure of friends and enemies. Sometimes breed clubs may be 'closed shops'. In this case, unless the dog is outstanding, it may take a long time for his worth to be recognized. However, it is almost impossible for a really first-class dog to be kept down for ever, although this may sometimes seem to be so to the novice.

DECLARATION BY EXHIBITOR

This must be read carefully and signed and dated accordingly; in the case of co-owned dogs, both owners must sign the declaration. The owner(s) is signing that he 'will abide by the Rules and Regulations of the Kennel Club'. Therefore he may not exhibit a dog that is totally blind, defective in hearing, or prevented from breeding as a result of a surgical operation, except as provided for in Regulations for the Preparation of Dogs for Exhibition. This regulation does not apply to a spayed bitch, which already has progeny registered at the Kennel Club.

The Kennel Club altered the rule on cryptorchidism in December, 1970, and a dog may now be exhibited even if it is not 'entire'. A judge should now consider this a fault in the same way as any other external defect. The Kennel Club Committee felt that the mode of transmission of cryptorchidism has not been firmly identified, and they were of the opinion that the condition would not be eliminated by attempted control through show regulations.

In my humble opinion, whether or not the exact mode of transmission is known, every time that a cryptorchid dog (a 'monorchid') is used at stud constitutes one more chance of passing on this defect to the whole or part of one more litter, either directly or as carriers. There is no shortage of good stud dogs practically speaking in any breed, and, therefore, the fewer dogs with faults that are used, whether it is hip dysplasia, progressive retinal atrophy, patella luxation, or cryptorchidism, the better for dogdom. Obviously, if a 'monorchid' dog becomes a champion, the temptation to use him at stud would probably be too great for some breeders. Moreover, if cryptorchid dogs can be exhibited, then there should be no reason why deaf dogs or spayed bitches should not also be shown. A cryptorchid dog should not be used at public stud, unless the owner of a bitch is informed about the fault.

The exhibitor in the Declaration is also signing 'that the dogs entered have not suffered from or been knowingly exposed to the risk of distemper or any contagious disease including any reaction to immunisation during the six weeks prior to exhibition and will not show them if they incur such risks between now and the day of the show or if they have been immunised within fourteen days prior to the show'.

Finally the name and address of the exhibitor must be filled in clearly and in block letters. The entry fees must be worked out according to the number of classes entered. These fees may vary according to whether the exhibitor is a member or a non-member of the club. In a brace class, two dogs count as one entry. Added to this may be a benching fee for each dog and a car park fee.

It is important to add up these items correctly, and it is often a good idea to have someone to check the arithmetic and, indeed, the whole schedule. It creates a great deal of unnecessary work for a busy show secretary to have to return entry forms and incorrectly filled-in cheques or postal orders. Where confirmation of receipt of entry by the secretary of the club is required, then a stamped addressed post card should be enclosed. It is an excellent idea to take this step, particularly if a show is a great distance away or if it is an exceptionally important show, such as Cruft's. Nothing can be more disappointing, not to mention the wasted expense, than to have travelled an enormous distance and to have prepared dogs for a show, where the entry form was not received owing to postal delays.

SELECTION OF ENTRIES

The majority of classes are really handicapped, since they have qualifying conditions, and this gives every dog a reasonably fair chance. The most junior class that may be in a schedule, but which seldom is, is 'special puppy'. This is for puppies between the ages of six and nine months. The normal puppy class is for puppies between the ages of six and twelve months. Naturally, a six-month-old puppy is not so mature, and probably not so well trained, as a puppy of almost exactly a year, and therefore, unless a very young puppy is extremely outstanding, it is unlikely to take precedence over a maturer puppy. This also applies to the junior class, which has an even greater age span, since this class caters for puppies and dogs between the ages of six and eighteen months. A dog of nearly eighteen months, particularly in the smaller breeds, may be fully mature and absolutely in his prime, so that an immature puppy would have little chance of winning such a class. It is better in the junior class to enter a dog who is nearer eighteen months than a much younger one.

The maiden class is probably considered the class with least competition, because the handicap for this class is that a dog must not have won a challenge certificate or a first prize at any show. The novice class is also a good class to enter, because no dog may have won a challenge certificate or three or more first prizes at open and championship shows (puppy and minor puppy classes excepted). Owing to the handicapping, these classes are often large and in novice there is no age restriction.

There are several other classes which are excellent for the novice. The wording for these may be 'For owner, handler or dog never having won a first prize.' Sometimes the wording may be 'For dogs and bitches shown by an exhibitor who has never won a first prize in the breed at a show'. It is the exhibitor who has to qualify to enter such a class and not the dog. The exhibitor could in fact be a seasoned top breeder who has never exhibited at that particular show before. The dog being handled could well be a top winning dog. The sort of person who is a seasoned exhibitor, who enters such a class for the glory of a cheap victory at the expense of novices, is really to be deplored.

It very much depends on the breed, as to what age a dog should be entered for any particular class. Obviously, most puppies are best shown between the ages of eleven and twelve months. In the long-coated breeds some dogs are slow in developing a good coat, whilst some puppies are very forward in this respect. The dice are often heavily weighted in favour of dogs with outstanding coats. In the larger breeds, which take longer to mature, it is important to take this into consideration when choosing the class in which to enter a dog. Sometimes, it may be a wise decision to keep a dog out of the ring for a few months, and bring him in to compete in the maiden and novice or even higher classes, as soon as he is mature enough. Very often a bitch will improve after a litter, just as a stud dog will, after being used at stud. On the whole it is not a good policy to enter a dog in classes which are too advanced. There are, of course, exceptions to this, and a really outstanding dog could well win in an open class after very little experience in the ring.

BRACE, TEAM AND PROGENY CLASSES

These classes are interesting for the experienced breeders and also for the ringside onlookers. Unfortunately, they are held at the end of a show and, since at championship shows they do not qualify the winning dogs for Cruft's, many exhibitors do not enter these classes after a tiring day's showing. The brace and team classes require a great deal of training. The dogs entered for them should be identical in colour, size and marking, and they should also be trained to move together in step. Such training obviously takes a considerable time, but entries trained to a high standard are very spectacular.

The progeny class is also of great interest, particularly to breeders looking for a good stud dog. The sire or the dam is brought into the ring with his/her respective progeny. Usually, but not always the progeny are judged on their own, with the sire and/or dam standing to one side, or behind. Last but not least is the veteran class. This is a fascinating class and one can often see dogs of ten, twelve or even more years of age, parading in wonderful condition and looking extraordinarily young for their age. These dogs have probably been the stalwarts of their breed a decade or so previously. It is extremely interesting for the novice, who has never had the opportunity of seeing a particular, well-known dog in the flesh, but who has seen the dog's name recurring over and over again in well-known pedigrees.

PRIZE CARDS, CUPS AND CERTIFICATES

PRIZE CARDS

At the regular shows not less than three printed award cards are given for each class. Prize money is optional and additional brace, stud dog, brood bitch, veteran, breeders and selling classes are not included. Prize cards are generally oblong and are approximately $6\frac{1}{2}'' \times 4''$. Cruft's prize cards are diamond-shaped, the Three Counties Agricultural Society cards are square, whilst those issued at the Windsor Championship Show are distinguished by the addition of a picture of Windsor Castle. There are also one or two other shows whose cards are of distinctive shape and size. All cards, however, have the name of the show, the venue and the date printed on them, in addition there are two spaces, one for the class number, which is stamped on, and the other for the exhibit number, which must be inserted later, this being done by the exhibitor. Generally first prize cards are always red, second prize blue and third yellow. The fourth prize, which is called 'reserve', is a green card, and the remaining three prize cards, if awarded, are usually white. The white cards are for 'very highly commended', which in dog parlance is known as 'VHC', 'highly commended' and 'commended'. Where a 'special prize' is offered, which may be a gift, a donation or a trophy, a pink card is awarded. This may be given, for instance, for best puppy. Winning cards are placed on the pens or benches of the dogs which have been successful; it is most important that the money voucher must be torn off first.

Prize money may be attached to the back of the prize card, but usually there is a detachable strip on the side of the card. This strip must be detatched from the card immediately and filled in with the class number, and the number of the exhibit and it must be signed by the exhibitor or handler and taken to the secretary's or treasurer's office to claim the prize money. Probably the most prized cards at any show are the cards for best of breed (BoB), and best opposite sex (BoS); and at a championship show the 'CC' (standing for challenge certificate), and reserve best of sex (the latter is often incorrectly known as the reserve CC). The top honours are best in show, reserve best in show. These cards are red-and-white-striped or green-and-white-striped. Sanction and exemption shows are allowed to award white prize cards printed in black. They may, however, be permitted to have a coloured stripe across the top left-hand corner to signify a first, second or third prize.

CHALLENGE CERTIFICATE

A challenge certificate is awarded at a championship show in breeds which are numerically strong enough. This means that they must have a registration of over one hundred and fifty dogs. From 1975 onwards the number of challenge certificates awarded will be as follows:

Three Years Registrations	Total CCs	Specialist Club CCs
200 and below	Maximum 8 at discretion of the Committee	0
201–300	11	1
301–500	13	1
501–800	16	2
801–1,000	18	2
1,001–1,200	20	2
1,201–1,500	20	2
1,501–1,800	22	2
1,801–2,500	24	2
2,501–3,500	26	3
3,501–4,500	28	4
4,501–6,000	30	5
6,001–8,000	32	5
8,001–10,000	34	6
10,001–12,500	36	7
12,501–16,000	38	8
16,001–20,000	40	9
20,001–30,000	42	10
30,001–40,000	43	11
40,001–50,000	44	12

One certificate is awarded to each sex. The challenge certificate, or 'ticket' as it is known in dog parlance, is a card measuring $8\frac{3}{4}'' \times 7\frac{1}{2}''$. It is white with a green border and green printing. The name of the show, the date, the breed, and the sex are filled in at the top of the card. The name of the dog and the owner of the dog must be filled in on the card, and the judge then signs to the effect that the dog 'is of such outstanding merit as to be worthy of the title of champion'. Later the winner of the Challenge Certificate receives another Kennel Club document almost $12'' \times 7''$, which is a white certificate printed and decorated in black, with the words 'Challenge Certificate' in red, with a large red Kennel Club seal on the right and a printed signature of the Kennel Club Secretary.

RESERVE BEST OF SEX

This is a green and white striped card $6'' \times 4\frac{1}{2}''$ which is awarded to the second best dog in the relevant sex.

BEST OF BREED

This card is red and white, and is $8'' \times 5''$ in size and awarded to the best of breed, which is judged between the best dog and the best bitch. The winner of this then goes forward to be judged with all the other bests of breed, which may be for the group system or for the final best in show award.

When a dog attains champion status, by winning the three necessary challenge certificates under three different judges, he or she may provisionally be called 'Champion' subject to Kennel Club confirmation. When the Kennel Club have verified that the dog has qualified as a champion, the owner of the dog will be sent the Kennel Club champion certificate and from then on the dog or bitch bears the title 'Champion'. Reserve best of sex cards, unfortunately, do not count towards the title of champion, so that there are often many cases of an outstanding dog being kept down by a reigning champion, and it is not uncommon to find a beautiful dog with as many as ten or more reserve best of sex certificates.

A Golden Retriever lying patiently on his bench.

Above: The beautiful setting of W.E.L.K.S. (West of England Ladies Kennel Society) Championship Show at Boddington Manor, near Cheltenham.

Above right: A Pyrenean Mountain dog is first off the coach. Coaches bring exhibitors and their dogs from many parts of the country.

Right: Basset Hounds disembarking from a small caravan.

Below right: A useful method of conveying toy breeds to their benches.

Below: Trundling their exhibits to the show entrance at Boddington Manor.

Above: Airedale Terriers ready to be loaded into a car in their strong wooden crate.

Above left: A toy dog (Griffon Bruxellois) in his box ready to leave for the show.

Left: Sealyham Terriers in show trim, in their cool wire travelling cages.

Below: In they come thick and fast. Many exhibitors travel all night.

BENCHED DOGS

Right: A young Afghan guarding his owner's picnic flask and waiting to be secured by his bench chain.

Right: A young Beagle at his first show being comforted by his best friend.

Above: An anxious Beagle watching his master disappear into the crowd.

Right: A well trained Rough Collie sitting quietly on his bench. Regulations require however that he should be secured by a bench chain.

Below: Basset Hounds well used to Show benches.

CUPS AND TROPHIES

All canine show societies have a considerable number of cups and trophies. These are generally donated by leading breeders in the club, by large firms, or by anyone who has at any time had a particular interest in the breed or society. These cups and trophies may be given to the society outright, or they may be given on indefinite loan. The latter is usually the case where a points system is in operation, the reason for this being that the donor might wish later to alter the points system or to take back the cup. If the cup is given outright to the society, then the society can alter the system, against the donor's wishes.

The clubs keep a trophy and cup register. After a cup has been presented, the exhibitor must sign a declaration in the book that he/she has accepted the cup and his/her name and address must be entered clearly. The exhibitor will be told when the cup is due to be returned to the club. This is generally at the next show, but sometimes the cups are kept for one year. The club should insure all its cups, and a trophy secretary, responsible for knowing the whereabouts of each cup, should be appointed. The secretary should arrange for any inscriptions to be put on a cup, and it should be made clear at this stage who is responsible for payment for the inscription. Many clubs arrange for a small replica of the trophy to be given to the winner as a memento of his/her win. Some trophies may become the property of the winner after they have been won by him/her for the requisite number of times in succession. Some clubs require a small token payment to cover the cost of the insurance of each cup and trophy.

The winner of any cup or trophy is responsible for its safe keeping and its condition. It is extremely important that the cup should be returned to the club or society at the appropriate time, well polished, and if it is sent by post it should be registered, insured and suitably packed. It is extremely disappointing for an exhibitor to have won, perhaps, his/her first cup, only to find that it has not been returned by the previous winner. Being sent a cup many months later is by no means the same and all the gilt is then taken off the gingerbread when there are no claps or congratulations.

POINTS CUPS

Many breed clubs have perpetual cups for specialist club stakes, which are won on a points basis. The rules naturally vary enormously. They may, for instance, be given for the 'best stud dog' on his progeny's wins. This can also apply to bitches. Other points systems can be arranged for colours, heights, weights and other variations.

ROSETTES AND SASHES OF HONOUR

Rosettes are a popular and cheap form of prize, and are always popular with exhibitors. They are made of pleated nylon or satin ribbon, surrounding a cardboard disc, bearing the name of the show, and very often the date, in gold lettering. The grander rosettes have a second row of pleated ribbon which is very often in another colour. The rosette is finished off with two flowing streamers and it may be presented for best in show and best of breed. Rosettes are always presented for these at championship shows. Rosettes, however, may be given by kind donors or breed clubs for all wins up to fifth place, and an extra rosette for Best Puppy.

The sash of honour is an exciting presentation and is usually won outright, although some canine societies present the sash annually. A sash of honour is a highly decorative wide ribbon which is given for best in show, and is draped across the shoulders or back of the dog or bitch who wins this distinction.

OTHER TROPHIES

Some breed clubs offer special prizes, which are generally donated by a breeder who may wish that the trophy should go to the dog with the best head, or of a special size, or to that day's top winning breeder. It is usual to stipulate that a dog must have won first, second or third prize, in order to compete for this special trophy. Plaques and medallions may also be presented for various wins, and club spoons and salvers and silver ornaments are sometimes awarded. Cruft's Dog Show Society offer special prizes for best dog and best bitch, and a spoon for the dog reserve best of sex winner and the same for the bitch reserve best of sex winner.

JUNIOR WARRANT

This is a Kennel Club award which must be applied for. A dog must win twenty-five points before the age of eighteen months. The points are awarded for first prizes at open or championship shows in a breed class. One point is gained for each win at an open show and three points are gained at championship shows, regardless of whether there are challenge certificates or not. A dog must be an outstanding one to win this award, because his best chances to win the puppy classes are probably not until he is between eleven and twelve months old, which then allows only six or seven months in which to gain the necessary twenty-four more points, that is, probably twenty-four more first prize cards. A dog must be in excellent show condition both mentally and physically, in order to go to so many shows without becoming stale.

The Kennel Club will, upon application with the relevant details of the first prizes which have been won by the particular dog, issue the owner with a junior warrant certificate.

STUD BOOK

Entry in the Kennel Club Stud Book is only by merit. At one time the sire or dam of a winning dog or bitch could be nominated for the stud book for the payment of 50p. The stud book entry consists of the registered name of the dog, sex, colour, date of birth, owner, breeder and a three-generation pedigree. The owner is the person in whose name the dog is registered at the time of qualification. Dogs and bitches eligible for entry in the stud book are those winning challenge certificates, reserve best of sex, or first, second or third prizes in open, limit, or field trial classes. These prizes must be won at a championship show and there must be no limitation as to weight, colour or any other classification. There are other regulations for field trials and working trials. There is no monetary advantage, but it does ensure that the dog has won high honours. The Kennel Club issue an eligible dog with a stud book number, which usually consists of one or two letters and several figures, and the appointment appears in the *Kennel Gazette*. When filling in pedigrees, it is quite usual to see these short numbers beneath the dog's name, thus denoting that he is in the stud book.

BREED CLUBS

Numerically strong breeds often have several breed clubs in existence in various parts of the country. A newcomer to the breed can write to the Kennel Club for a list of the breed clubs and societies, and a stamped addressed envelope should be included. All exhibitors should support at least one of their breed clubs, and most exhibitors belong to several clubs. There are many interesting club activities, such as lectures, teach-ins and judge-ins; social activities include garden parties and dinners; and every year there is the excitement of the annual general meetings, which can be quite lively and a great eye-opener in some breeds!

The numerically strong and popular breeds often have a great number of clubs. For example, there are no less than forty-four Alsatian clubs of all kinds; there are as many as forty Spaniel clubs, covering all varieties and colours; whilst another popular breed, Retrievers, are catered for by twenty-three clubs.

SPECIALIST CLUBS

Specialist clubs are often unfortunately notoriously tendentious, and may well become completely controlled for years by a strong-minded chairman, or by a group forming a committee. The power that they wield is often directed towards their own ends and not for the good of the breed. Tears and tantrums at committee meetings are by no means unknown. Like children, members are easily led and are liable to gang up. How members get on to or off judging lists is often suspect. Postal ballots can all too easily be rigged, for instance by issuing many extra ballot papers. These situations occur in the money-making breeds. There are undoubtedly, however, many well run and happy clubs too, but anywhere where money and prestige are involved base human nature too often rears its ugly head.

CHAPTER V

Show Regulations

REGULATIONS FOR THE EXHIBITION OF DOGS

Showing animals has frequently been described as the 'art of deception'. That this is the case with some dogs is too obviously true. It applies particularly to the breeds which are plucked, stripped, clipped or trimmed. Both the Poodle and the American Cocker Spaniel are excellent examples, not to mention the Kerry Blue and the Airedale Terrier. If these breeds and many others were presented in the ring untouched, except for bathing and brushing, they would be completely unrecognizable. Ironically there is nothing in the standard for any of these breeds which prescribes how the individual dog should be presented. Any tampering with a dog's coat is, therefore, an unauthorized whim of fashion. But woe betide any exhibitor who does not conform!

The Kennel Club lays down strict regulations for the preparation of dogs for exhibition and their infringement could lead to disqualification. It is highly probable that some exhibitors are unaware that such regulations in fact exist. Regulation No. 4 must be just such a one: 'No oil, greasy or sticky substance which has been used in the preparation of a dog for exhibition shall be allowed to remain in the coat of the dog at the time of exhibition.' When one thinks of the numerous lotions, potions, powders and sprays that are sold at almost every dog show, and which are used extensively on many breeds, particularly the long-coated varieties, one cannot help wondering how many dogs could be technically disqualified. No dyeing, colouring, tinting, darkening, bleaching or other matter may be used to alter or improve the markings of a dog. Dry white chalk may be used for cleaning, provided that it is removed from the coat before the dog enters the ring. There are also regulations about artificially altering the setting of a dog's teeth and also on altering a dog's ears in any way; but strangely, there is nothing laid down against altering the set of a dog's tail, except that approval *is* granted for shortening the tail in the following breeds: German Short-Haired Pointers, Spaniels (except Irish Water), Weimaraners, Airedale Terriers, Australian Terriers, Fox Terriers, Irish Terriers, Kerry Blue Terriers, Lakeland Terriers, Norfolk Terriers, Sealyham Terriers, Welsh Terriers, Boxers, Dobermanns, Old English Sheepdogs, Poodles, Schipperkes, Schnauzers, Miniature Schnauzers, Welsh Corgis (Pembroke), Griffons, Bruxellois, King Charles Spaniels, Cavalier King Charles Spaniels, Miniature Pinschers, Yorkshire Terriers and Soft-Coated Wheaten Terriers.

As I have said so many times previously in other books, it is high time that the barbaric practice of docking tails was stopped.

The Kennel Club Committee may at any time order the examination of any dog or dogs at a show. Such an examination, however, must be performed by a veterinary surgeon, and it is essential that he should be in possession of written authority from the Kennel Club. Armed with this authority, the veterinary surgeon may take samples from any dogs for further analysis and examination.

There does not, however, appear to be any specific rule or regulation regarding drugs. It is not unknown for some difficult dogs in some breeds to be given either tranquillizers or pep pills. This form of cheating is not done very frequently in Britain, but undoubtedly it does often occur in some other countries. Happy pills such as Largactil Chlorpromazene are used on a number of breeds, and some people even resort to giving their dog a nip of whisky.

CONTAGIOUS DISEASES

The exhibitor is required to sign an entry form for all shows declaring that the dog to be exhibited has not been exposed to the risk of distemper, any contagious disease, including any reaction to immunisation during the six weeks prior to exhibiting, nor must a dog be immunised against distemper within fourteen days of a show. I personally would like a rule to include that all dogs exhibited have to have been immunised against distemper and the other common canine viruses.

UNWRITTEN LAWS

There are one or two unwritten laws made up by the dog fraternity. One of these is that a dog should not be exhibited under a judge who has already awarded that dog a challenge certificate. Many breeders, however, feel strongly that Cruft's is the exception to this unwritten law, because it is here that the best dogs in the country are supposed to be seen, and it would seem unjust that an outstanding dog should be denied the honour of being exhibited at Cruft's because he had won under that judge on another occasion. After all, the dog is unlikely to have met many of his opponents previously. Serious breeders and the general public naturally wish to see all outstanding dogs. The Kennel Club have no objection whatsoever to such a dog being exhibited. Some exhibitors feel strongly that it is unfair to exhibit champions at open shows, but this really depends on the breed.

Another often broken unwritten law made by breeders, is that it is extremely unfair to show a bitch in season, as this obviously must affect the showmanship of stud dogs.

BENCHING REGULATIONS

The Kennel Club lay down that all breeds at a show must be benched in the catalogue order. No bench numbers may be changed from one pen to another, and, of course, no dog must be in any pen other than its own. Under no circumstances, too, must the partitions be tampered with. All dogs must wear a collar and chain whilst benched; the exceptions are the toy breeds which are penned. Only exhibited dogs may enter the show precincts unless written permission has been granted by the Kennel Club prior to the show.

No dog may be removed from its bench except for preparation before being exhibited, whilst being judged or exercised, or by order of a veterinary surgeon or a member of the show committee. A dog may leave its bench for not more than fifteen minutes whilst being exercised, and the person in charge of the dog can be fined £2 if the dog should foul any part of the show open to the public. Fines may also be incurred for a similar offence in the streets. There are numerous other Kennel Club rules regarding such items as the cleaning of dogs, the obstruction of gangways and the mating of bitches within the precincts of the show.

PRINTED CARDS

Exhibitors may display a card or board over their benches. This must not exceed 10″ × 5″, and the lettering must be black on a white ground and not larger than one inch. Only the prefix, the name and the address of the owner, and the telephone number, may be printed.

Cards 'For Sale' and 'Not for Competition' may also be placed over the benches. A dog entered 'Not for Competition' may have his name displayed, but the lettering may not be larger than one inch.

DISPLAY OF PRIZE CARDS

Certain prize cards may be displayed on benches, but, before doing so, the counterfoil of money-winning cards should be filled in and torn off to prevent theft. The card may then be placed above the bench of the appropriate dog. Where rosettes are awarded, these may be worn by the exhibitor, but they must under no circumstances be worn in the ring, except for the best of breed rosette. This may be worn in the ring for the judging of a group or best in show, but on no account may they be worn in a variety class.

SHOW CURTAINS AND SHOW EQUIPMENT

The Kennel Club have no objection to blankets and cushions being placed on the bench for the comfort of the dog. There is no objection if such rugs have a kennel name embroidered on them. Many toy exhibitors cover the interior of the dog pens with decorative curtains, primarily to keep out draughts, and to prevent dogs from seeing through the bars the exhibits in the immediately adjoining pens. Curtains also help to prevent dogs from yapping and making a noise and generally creating a disturbance. The Kennel Club do not object to exhibitors locking the pen doors with padlocks. It is not unusual in extremely cold weather to find that exhibitors have placed Perspex show travelling boxes inside the pens. The dogs can be seen, kept warm, and yet cannot be touched by the inquisitive public.

COLLARS AND LEADS

Throughout the duration of the show, all dogs must wear a secure collar, and be tethered to one of the two rings on the benches by a strong chain lead. When being exhibited, the dog may, however, wear a show lead. Obviously, these rules do not apply to the Toy breeds, when penned. When off their benches, all dogs must be kept on a lead throughout the duration of the show. The only two exceptions are in the exercising area, if one is provided, and for dogs that are entered in obedience tests. However, if a judge has granted permission to an exhibitor to handle his dog without a lead, then this may be done.

ATTRACTING A DOG'S ATTENTION IN THE RING

No exhibit must have its attention attracted whilst in the ring by any means to which the judge objects.

WITHDRAWAL FROM COMPETITION

A dog is liable to be disqualified, if it is not brought into the ring for the classes for which it has been entered. The only way in which a dog may be withdrawn from competition is through illness. However, application must be made to the show secretary immediately, and, if necessary, to the show committee. The dog must be examined by the veterinary surgeon of the show, and all cases must be reported to the Kennel Club by the show secretary. It is not infrequent for a dog suddenly to go lame for some reason, and in such cases the judge often asks the exhibitor if he would like to withdraw from the class. The exhibitor is probably only too pleased to do this, but in actual fact reporting the exhibit to the secretary is seldom done. Imagine what would happen if a dog suddenly went lame in a large class. The judging must cease, and a report must be made to the show secretary. The latter might well be at the opposite end of two great halls and he would then have to get the veterinary surgeon. In the meantime, all the other exhibitors would be waiting for the judging to continue.

FRAUDULENT AND DISCREDITABLE CONDUCT AND OBJECTIONS

Any discreditable conduct must be reported to the show secretary, for example, if an exhibitor knowingly takes the wrong black poodle into the ring, such as taking a champion dog into a junior or novice class in substitution for the correct junior or novice dog. Poodles can look as like one another as two peas in a pod.

OBJECTIONS

Anyone may make an objection against a dog, provided that he is not under a term of suspension from the Kennel Club. The objection must be made in writing, with all relevant details, and must be delivered to the show secretary at the show with a deposit of £5. The deposit will be returned provided that the objection is sustained.

EXHIBITING DISQUALIFICATIONS

A dog or puppy may not be exhibited, if it has been bred by the judge or handled in the ring by the judge, or boarded or given attention by the judge within the preceding twelve months. The only exception would be if the judge were appointed in an emergency, after the closing of entries for the show.

FINES

The Kennel Club may inflict fines upon exhibitors who have made errors in their entry forms, or for breaches of show regulations. There must be few exhibitors indeed who have not at some time or other made genuine mistakes on their entry forms; for example, leaving out the date of the dog's birth, or in the case where a dog has been bought in by a breeder, entering on the form in error, that they, themselves, were the breeders.

EARLY REMOVALS

No dog is permitted to leave a show before a specified time. There is no point in an exhibitor going to the show secretary and asking if he may leave a show early as he has a bitch due to whelp. The secretary cannot give permission for an exhibitor to leave the show ground, however genuine or sincere the reason is. It is a Kennel Club rule, and rules are rules. If, however, you do leave, and should a malicious exhibitor report you, the fine would be £2.

CLASS ELIGIBILITY

When calculating the number of wins a dog has had, it is important to remember that wins in variety classes do not count for entry in breed classes, nor therefore towards junior warrant points. All wins are estimated from midnight preceding the closing date for entry as shown on the schedule. A puppy is eligible for entry in a puppy class provided that it is at least six but does not exceed twelve calender months on the first day of the show. It is useful to remember this when entering at a two- or three-day show. A puppy may not be exhibited if its date of birth is six calendar months prior to the last day of the show, because it would be one or two days too young. It is the date of the first day of the show which is the official date and all calculations must be made from then.

A dog is not eligible for an entry in an any variety class, unless it has also been entered and exhibited in a breed class, provided that the breed is classified at the show. A puppy, however, may be entered only in a variety puppy class if there is no breed puppy class scheduled. Field trial exhibits and veterans are also exempt from this regulation.

ELIGIBILITY TO COMPETE FOR BEST IN SHOW

Any dog that has been awarded best of breed at that particular show may compete for best in show, provided that it has not been beaten in a variety class. Any other unbeaten dog is eligible. Any unbeaten dog, where no breed classes have been scheduled, may go forward after winning a variety class.

All the reserve best of sex in each group and variety should remain in a line at the side of the ring behind their respective best of breed winners. The best in show winner is chosen, and its respective best opposite sex is then eligible to be judged with the remaining group. This is because that dog has now only been beaten by the dog which is best in show, and it is therefore eligible to be judged for reserve best in show.

MISTAKES IN CLASS ENTRIES

If an exhibitor finds that inadvertently a dog has been entered in a class for which it is ineligible, for example, if a male dog has been entered in a bitch class, or if a dog just over a year old has been entered in a puppy class, or in any other class for which it is ineligible then, provided that the exhibitor reports the mistake to the secretary of the show before the judging of the class or classes takes place, the show secretary may transfer it to the equivalent class for the correct breed, colour, sex, weight or height. In the event of there being no such equivalent class, the dog must compete in the open class.

WITHDRAWAL FROM COMPETITION

A dog is liable to be disqualified by the Committee of the Kennel Club if, once it has been admitted to a show, it is not then exhibited in all the classes in which is has been entered, or if it is not brought into the ring when required by the judge. There are three exceptions to this regulation. One is if a judge is substituted at the last moment, in which case notice must be given to the show secretary in writing if the dog is to be withdrawn from competition. An application must also be made to the show secretary if it is desired to withdraw a dog from competition owing to illness during the show. It may be necessary in this case for the dog to be given a veterinary examination. Finally, a dog may be permitted to miss its class, if the class is judged after the authorised time for the removal of the exhibit.

ENTRIES FOR SHOWS NOT RECEIVED

Frequently an exhibitor will telephone the secretary of a show a day or two before the show, or will report at the show, that he has not received passes or removal cards and that his entries do not appear in the catalogue. The following procedure laid down by the Shows Regulation Committee should be carried out in such circumstances. The exhibitor should be allowed to show his dogs after completing an entry form and paying the appropriate fees. The show secretary must submit a full report to the Kennel Club immediately after the show and the Kennel Club will then write to the exhibitor asking him to provide proof of posting and to say how the entry fees were paid, whether by cheque, postal order or cash. Where entries are paid by cheque, the exhibitor is required to forward the cheque book stub for the cheque presented with the original entry which has been lost and the cheque book stub for the cheques immediately preceding and following. The Shows Regulation Committee then examines the information and decides whether the entries shall stand or be disqualified.

'The Catalogue must contain:
On the front outside cover or on the first inside page the names and addresses of the Guarantors of the Show, except in the case of shows where classes are provided for exhibits other than dogs, where the names and addresses need only be printed at the head of the dog section.
The names of the judges of each breed and other classes.
The Catalogue must be arranged so that at the beginning of each breed classification an alphabetical index containing the names of exhibitors, the name and number of each exhibit and the numbers of the Classes in which it is entered, giving a separate line to the name of each exhibitor, and full particulars of each exhibit in the first class in which it is entered.
The addresses of all exhibitors must appear either in the index referred to above, or elsewhere in the Catalogue.
The number of the ring in which each Judge will act must be given together with information regarding wet weather arrangements. When a breed is to be judged in a ring other than that intimated in the catalogue, a notice of the change must be prominently posted in the original ring.

The numbering and order of the Classes in the Catalogue and Judging Book must follow that of the Schedule.
The Show Secretary must apply for the approval of all judges who are to award Challenge Certificates and to judge all forms of competition at the Show with the exception of breeds which are scheduled without Challenge Certificates. The Judge of a Group at a Show shall not judge any breed within that Group at the Show, except when acting in the capacity of appointed Referee. The Judge of Best in Show shall not judge any breed at that Show, except when acting in the capacity of appointed Referee. There must be an interval of not less than six calandar months between the appointments of a judge to award Challenge Certificates to the same sex of the same breed and to judge the same Group and Best in Show. The names of Judges submitted for approval must be selected by a properly constituted Meeting of the Show Committee, and, if required evidence of this must be forwarded.'

KENNEL CLUB REGULATIONS FOR REGISTERING AND MAINTENANCE OF TITLE OF A REGISTERED SOCIETY

In order to start and found a new canine society, application must be made by letter to the Kennel Club, giving the proposed title and two alternatives, the objects of the society, and relevant information, together with a fee of £3. A form of application will be sent for signature of twenty-five founder members, and each must contribute not less than two pounds towards the establishment of the society. There must be a chairman, secretary and treasurer. There are also rules regarding a sponsor from another breed society; and also regarding shows which it is proposed to hold within a twenty-five mile radius of a similar society; and about annual subscriptions, annual general meetings, disposal of assets, maintenance of title and other relevant matters. All these are subject to Kennel Club ruling.

GUARANTORS

To enable many more classes to be scheduled at an all-breeds show, registered breed societies will offer to guarantee the classification of its particular breed. They do this by either paying a hundred per cent or perhaps fifty per cent of the prize money, should there be insufficient entries to make the extra classes a paying proposition. Unless there is an average of seven dogs or more a class, there will be insufficient funds to cover the prize money. A breed club which has guaranteed an extra number of classes will naturally try to persuade its club members to make good entries, in order to back up the extra classes. The breed club often offer special prizes for members only. This is an excellent arrangement, particularly in breeds which are not numerically strong. The names of guarantors must be printed in the schedule.

CHAPTER VI

Show Training and Handling

GENERAL TRAINING

There are of course innumerable methods of training dogs for shows, and much depends on the size of the breed and the individual dogs' temperament as to which is the best method to adopt. Most methods produce good results, provided that the dog has certain natural aptitudes, and certain methods produce quicker results than others. There are some dogs who are born natural show dogs and with very little training can be put down in the ring, where they will go through their show stance and movement without ever putting a foot wrong. Perhaps, what is even more important, the dog shows that he is enjoying his performance in the ring. Few judges can resist a good dog who is obviously enjoying himself. The dog knows instinctively that he is pleasing his handler and what more could an intelligent dog wish to do? Lucky indeed is the handler of such a dog. Unfortunately, there are some really outstanding dogs, perhaps even better in conformation than the natural showman who will never make the grade in the ring, simply because for some reason or other they hate every moment of it and, even with many hours of training, they will never be able to give of their best. The chances are that something went wrong during the 'critical period' of their young lives and, try as the handler may, the dog will never quite make the grade.

EARLY TRAINING

It is an undisputed fact, that dogs are most receptive to all forms of learning between the ages of three and sixteen weeks. This period is known as the 'critical period', and it is therefore essential that, if the most is to be made out of a dog's full natural potential, he must have as much human companionship and handling during this period as is possible. This is the time when he is socialized.

During this vital period the puppy should become accustomed to as many situations and experiences as possible. It is equally important that, during this critical period, he should not become frightened. Each new phase must be taken slowly, and the puppy given unending encouragement. He must learn to be handled, to stand and lie on a table, to walk on a lead, and to accept children. He must become accustomed to all sorts of noises and bangs, road traffic, crowds, cars, buses and trains. He must learn to go to bed, to lie in a dog crate or box and to sit quietly on his show bench and put up with the admiring public at a show.

The puppy will be only too pleased to do all that is within his power to please his owner or handler. For this he must be truly loved, well fed and exercised.

Preliminary show training can, in fact, start as early as the age of three or four weeks, when the puppy can be made to stand in a show position on a table. His forelegs should be lifted off the ground by lifting him up slightly under the ribcage and dropping both feet together on to the table. His hindlegs can be raised together by lifting him gently under the crutch and allowing the legs to drop on to the table both at the same time. The puppy must be encouraged by being stroked under the chin to keep his head up, whilst at the same time his tail should be positioned. If he is nervous, then gently scratch him behind his ears and then stroke his back. Obviously, it may take a little time before the puppy learns what is expected of him, and to begin with the lessons should only last a few seconds. As the puppy learns, the time of each lesson can be extended. Immediately after the puppy has done what was required, he must be given a titbit and encouraged in a suitable tone of voice. Never stop a lesson until the puppy is doing what is right and always stop before he becomes bored. End the session with a titbit and then play with him for a few seconds before giving him his meal.

The puppy must learn to wear a collar and this should be light and should be put on just before he is to have his meal. When the puppy is older, he must learn to walk on a lead on the handler's left-hand side. He must learn to be handled by strangers, and to have his body felt and touched, his legs moved and lifted, and his mouth examined. The puppy should also learn half a dozen words of command. 'Come', 'Bed', 'Walk', 'Stand', 'Turn', 'Head Up', 'Good', or any other similar useful commands.

The better trained a dog is, the more pleasure the owner or handler has from such a dog, particularly if he is one of the larger more boisterous breeds. The best trained dogs also have a far better chance of winning, because they may often just win their top prizes on showmanship, and showmanship quite rightly is very evident in top awards.

TRAINING TO STAND AND TO LIE ON A TABLE

Every puppy should be taught first to stand and then to lie on a table. This is important, particularly for grooming, and it is useful too when the dog has to visit the veterinary surgeon.

Teaching a puppy to stand on a table is easy when training is started at three or four weeks. It is a little more difficult when the puppy is older, because he will try to jump off the table, and his collar must therefore be held securely. When he discovers that he cannot jump off because of the trainer's restrictive hands, he will automatically try another manoeuvre and will back away, but as his hind feet begin to slip off the table he will try to struggle on again. Gently assist him. Make him stand again and immediately praise him. He should learn to stand on a table in one short lesson.

Next he must learn to lie down on the table. Young puppies can be put in a lying position by taking all four feet into one hand and lying him on his side. Do not frighten him in any way but talk to him soothingly. Older puppies can be trained by just taking the two fore paws in the hand and pushing him into a lying position from a sitting position. Difficult dogs might require the assistance of a member of the family. It is extremely important that the dog be always rewarded and praised for obedience and never frightened.

Another easy method to train a puppy to lie on a table is to start grooming him from a very early age whilst he is lying on your lap, brushing him very gently on his tummy, chest and neck. If he is restless, massage the base of his ears. After a day or two repeat the training on a table covered with a soft rug. After each session reward, praise and play.

TRAINING A PUPPY TO 'COME'

A puppy can easily be taught to come when he is called. At every meal place his food bowl on the ground at some distance from him and call 'Come'. The puppy soon learns that 'Come' means food. Increase the distance as he becomes proficient and later call him when the food is out of sight. The puppy quickly associates the word 'come' with going to his handler; and probably the most important lesson has been learnt with little effort. It is as simple as that.

TRAINING A PUPPY TO STAND

Every successful breeder has his own particular methods of training his dogs for the ring. Some people prefer to train their dogs at 9–10 weeks, others at 6 months. It much depends on the size of the breed and the individual character of each dog. One well-known breeder of a large and often difficult breed has tremendous success with her dogs. They are all reared in the kitchen, and as soon as they are a few months old, each puppy has two minutes individual training each day. The puppy is taught to stand alone in the middle of the kitchen floor amongst all his brothers and sisters running round him. The puppy learns to concentrate on his trainer and he quickly learns to concentrate so much that he becomes oblivious to his boisterous brothers and sisters who may even bump into him. No wonder this breeder's dogs stand so perfectly in the ring and for the photographers. Two minutes each day on each puppy is not long to spend to obtain such wonderful results. At the end of each training period the puppy must of course be well rewarded and played with. The lesson will be driven home by the association of ideas.

CONTINUATION OF TRAINING

As soon as the puppy is old enough, he should continue his show training for the ring at home or in familiar surroundings. If this is not possible, choose some suitable quiet area where there is nothing to distract his attention. The training place should always be the same one and with the same collar and lead, or slip lead. Training should be as near as possible to the same time so that the dog associates the place, equipment and time as one which means business, followed by titbits and games somewhere within a few yards of the training area.

As soon as possible, the dog must learn to become part of the two partnership team, and to walk on a slack lead by the trainer's side. He must also learn to walk in a straight line and to stand and turn on instructions. The idea when standing is that the judge should be able to see the dog standing on all four legs, not just the two nearest him. In some breeds it is much wiser not to over-handle and, instead of the legs being manipulated by hand into the required position, the dog may be lifted gently into position by raising his feet off the ground with a taut lead, so that the forelegs drop into position. Then, attracting the dog's attention with the aid of bait held in the handler's right hand, he can gently manoeuvre the hindquarters into position with his foot. The dog will be so interested in the bait that he will not notice what the handler's foot is doing jockeying his hindquarters into position. The dog must learn to stand still with head up and neck well arched. The show stance must never be held for long however. Next, move the dog in a straight line by a word of command for about twenty yards, then pause slightly to give him time to turn. Never drag or pull him as he turns, because this would throw him off balance and it would take him several yards of precious ring space before he got moving smoothly again. Once the dog has mastered his short enjoyable lessons and associates them with fun, he can progress to a different training area and may perhaps be joined with a friend's unruly dog and with the addition of more noise and distractions. These the dog must learn to ignore completely. All that exists for him must be his handler and the bait. Neither the dog's attention nor the handler's must wander for one instant during a training session, and there should be no unnecessary talking—this must come later when playing. All sorts of noise must be introduced, bands, trains, whistles, children, busy thoroughfares, shops and even pub-crawling are excellent training grounds, so that when the dog enters his first show he will accept the atmosphere of the show ground and enjoy his day to the full.

Whether he wins or loses, both he and his handler will have enjoyed the experience of a first-class partnership in the show ring.

OTHER SUCCESSFUL TRAINING METHODS

The puppy is first taught in the normal way to accept the collar and lead, and the simple basic training. Later, he is taught to stand on a small platform or table, depending on the size of the breed. As soon as the puppy has learnt to hold his stance on the table, with all four legs correctly placed, the trainer marks a circle round each foot. Every time that the dog has a lesson he is made to jump up on to the platform and is made to stand with his four legs always in the exact position marked on it. After each short period the lesson is reinforced by reward and praise. It is not long before the puppy will automatically stand in the correct show position almost anywhere. Grooming a dog on a table in his show stance is also a good idea and the height of the table acts as a deterrent to the puppy jumping off.

There are, of course, many methods of training dogs, but whatever method is used it is essential to keep all lessons short, use the same equipment and the same venue, reinforced with a titbit and association of ideas. Never lose your temper, stop before the dog becomes bored and above all remember that the more quickly a dog learns a lesson the more quickly will he forget it, unless it is repeated over and over and over again. Some breeds are more difficult to train than others, and there are some dogs which are too intelligent to train. And some handlers are too stupid to train dogs. The dog knows very quickly who is dominant and the trainer must make this clear from the start.

One of the methods used to train dogs with rapid results is the method adopted whereby the dog is starved for a period of thirty-six hours before training commences. The training is immediately reinforced by food as the reward and no lesson lasts more than fifteen minutes. No two dogs will require the same time spent on any particular lesson. The time to stop is when the dog has just accomplished what was required and well before there are any signs that he might become bored with his lesson.

COMFORTABLE HUNGER TRAINING

Doctor Leon Witney DVM, the well-known American dog authority and author of many books, has found that training can be cut down considerably if the dogs are made to feel what he describes as 'comfortable hunger' before each training period.

Most dogs are fed once a day. Doctor Witney has found that a dog that is thirty-six hours hungry will train more quickly than at any other period. It is interesting that it applies to the training of all animals too.

There seems to be something magical about the thirty-six hour hunger period as opposed to twenty-four hours or forty-eight hours. Nobody really knows the reason for this, but it certainly seems to be true.

As an example, if a dog to be trained is normally fed on a Friday morning, it will be found that he is most receptive for his lesson if his Saturday morning meal is postponed until Saturday evening. Saturday, then, is when his fifteen-minute lesson should start. The dog's meal should be placed in a bowl and the quantity should be his normal ration which must include the period of his fast. His reinforced training titbits come from his ration, but as soon as the lesson is terminated make a great fuss of the dog and give him the rest of his well earned meal. Thirty-six hours later, which would be Monday morning, the dog is ready for his lesson and his next meal. His following lesson and meal would be on Tuesday evening. It is important that the dog must have his correct ration of food during the period of training, so that he neither gets too much with titbits or too little owing to the delay of his meal.

I have never tried these methods of training, but they might be useful for training the more difficult and boisterous breeds, though possibly unnecessary for the easily trained breeds. This method of thirty-six hours' 'comfortable hunger' might be useful for training adult breeds for brace and team classes, where dogs should be taught to move in step together and to turn as a team, thus making an impressive performance.

TRAINING WITH THE AID OF A MIRROR

A large ground-to-ceiling mirror is an excellent aid to training. The handler can observe exactly the correct stance for his dog. He can also observe how much the forelegs incline in towards a longitudinal central line when the dog gaits, and at what speed the dog single-tracks. Most important of all when viewed from the front, the handler can see if the alignment of the bones from the centre of the shoulder to the pad is in one straight line; except in terriers and other breeds, where the standard actually demands that the forelegs must move straight forward, or the wide-slung breeds. The inclination inwards of the legs is correct for true kinetic balance and thereby obtains maximum proficiency with the minimum of effort, regardless of speed. It is easy to see if the column of bones is really in a straight line, so that neither the pasterns nor the elbows break the line. The imaginary line is not of course, except in certain breeds, in a vertical plane, but it will incline in the faster the dog moves. The handler moving his dog across the front of the mirror will be able to see the position of the top line as he passes and all the other details of head, neck, croup and tail.

When stacking a dog or posing him, the handler cannot only observe any faults in the position of the legs, body and head, but he will also be able to see if he himself is making any mistakes, and whether, for instance, he is being careless and slack regarding the stray end of his lead. This latter is a fault in handling seen far too often in England, but it is seldom seen in America. Even a small mirror can be quite effective and helpful, particularly for the smaller breeds.

HELP FROM AN EXPERIENCED HANDLER

It is frequently an excellent idea to get two handlers together so that they may watch and handle each other's dogs. Even dogs of the same breed and from the same kennel will move better at different speeds. One speed will suit one dog's conformation and temperament better than another. An observant bystander can help the handler considerably. The surface of the ground will effect a dog's movement. A slippery surface may make some dogs toe-in, when in fact there is nothing amiss with their conformation, and correct speeds over different surfaces may make all the difference to a dog getting placed.

TRAINING A DOG TO TURN

A dog must learn to turn well at the end of the ring when he is being moved individually for the judge. Most judges only require a dog to be turned to the right. The procedure is to walk the dog up the centre of the ring, in a straight line, and just before the end the handler should alert the dog so that he knows he is about to be made to turn. The first part of alerting the dog is for the handler to take smaller steps, then to exert a slight pressure on the lead at the same time making a clicking noise with the tongue. As the handler pivots on his right foot he should drop his arm slightly releasing the pressure on the lead, so that the dog turns naturally without altering his pace. At the same time the handler should swing his left foot round, pause so that the dog has time to turn, and dog and handler should then again continue on one flowing movement down the ring. It is quite a good exercise to practise turning to the left. This is somewhat easier, because instead of pivoting on the right foot the handler pivots on the left foot, and as the right foot swings round he can nudge the dog with the foot or leg to encourage him to turn too. This method would not apply to the small or toy breeds, nor is it necessary for fully trained dogs. Some handlers move the dog to the end of the ring, and, instead of making the dog turn with them, they change the lead to the other hand. In so doing, the dog returns down the ring on the handler's right side instead of the left. The only time that this method is advantageous is when the dog is moved in the letter 'T', and it is necessary to keep the dog on the same side as the judge at each turn.

TRAINING A DOG NOT TO CRAB

Dogs who crab generally do so owing to a constructional fault. The body may be too short, and the stride too long. Sometimes it may be caused by a lack of balance between the stride of the forelegs and the drive from the hindlegs. On the other hand well-constructed dogs may crab owing to a fault in timing. Whatever the cause the dog must learn to re-adjust either his stride or his timing. When a dog crabs the hindlegs are not travelling in the same line as his forelegs. They may be travelling to the right or to the left like a crab. The younger a dog is trained not to crab the easier it is. However, most dogs can be stopped crabbing by simply walking them along the edge of a pavement or sidewalk so that the forefeet are on the edge or curb. If the dog crabs to the left his hindlegs will be in the gutter so that he will try and straighten out and will walk with all four legs moving forward in the same plane. If he crabs to the right, reverse the proceedings. Training a dog not to crab may take some time, if he has been permitted to get into this bad habit. But once trained he can be helped in the ring by gaiting the dog along the edge of the rubber mat at an indoor show. The dog will remember his lesson on the pavement (sidewalk) and will respond to the matting in the same way.

KENNEL DOG PROBLEMS

Unfortunately, the majority of kennel dogs cannot receive the same amount of individual handling and loving as a single dog, or one which has been kept specifically for the show ring. But, with sufficient time spent daily on each puppy's training, it is often hard to tell in the ring which dog has had the most attention. It often occurs that puppies in a large kennel have tremendous temperaments at six or seven months and attend their first shows with no problems. Suddenly, and often with no warning, at about the age of eight months the owner will go out to the kennel one day and be confronted with a dog who for no apparent reason appears apprehensive.

The dog requires to know his importance as an individual, and it is imperative for the handler or owner to work on a dog whose temperament seems to change almost overnight, because unless he regains his full self-confidence he will never become a first-class showman again. Many a show dog has been classed as having been bred with a bad and timid temperament, when there has been nothing wrong with his breeding. The fault has lain with the owner who has not realized this crucial teenage period which some dogs seem to go through. Breeders of Great Danes, American Cocker Spaniels and many other breeds have had the misfortune not to have noticed early enough the first signs of apprehension in a promising dog, and to have failed to have dealt with the problem immediately. The dog has lost his self-confidence either by being bullied by a kennel mate or by something frightening him. He cannot explain his association of ideas. But forewarned is forearmed, and with a little common sense the owner of such a dog can prevent the situation even occurring. Perhaps this is the moment to stress the importance of never permitting a kennel to become too large. Good kennel staff are not always easy to come by, unforeseen illness amongst the staff and breeder are unforeseen occurrences that do happen. Tragedies occur sometimes when extra staff are taken on for holidays and perhaps they may be inexperienced in spite of their glowing references. If a problem arises they may be incapable of coping and when frightened of responsibility and the results of an unknown infection they may panic before the owner returns with disastrous results for the dogs.

WATCH THE GOOD HANDLERS

A novice can learn a tremendous number of excellent tips about handling dogs by simply standing at the ringside and watching. He will realize that there is no relaxing for the successful handler whilst exhibiting. Some people are more adept than others in being able to observe the way a dog is being handled, and can copy a good handler extremely quickly. Other people whose observation is not so acute, can watch the very same handler, but could not take in exactly what the handler does, and is therefore incapable of copying him. However, it should always be possible to get someone who is good at handling a particular breed to give the novice a few lessons, and some words of advice.

BASIC HANDLING ROUTINES

It is absolutely essential that the handler should know what he should be doing. A beautifully trained dog with a novice handler is just lost without the commands he is used to. The best way for any amateur to learn to handle any particular breed, is to spend time watching either professional handlers or experts actually showing their dogs in the ring. It is an excellent idea not only to watch one breed of dog being exhibited but to watch the methods used for all the breeds. It will then be noticed that the basic rules of handling apply to all breeds, although there may be variations in gait and in how any particular breed is made to stand in a certain position, the handler either being in front of the dog, behind the dog, or at the side of the dog. Apart from the Alsatian (the German Shepherd Dog) with its particular stance, all breeds should stand with the

Methods of arranging long leads in showing

Dog stands so that judge sees all four legs

Lead over knee. The end of the lead should be concealed behind the knee

hindlegs spread apart, so that the bones, from the hock down, are parallel with each other, and so that, when viewed from the side, the leg from the hock to the foot is perpendicular to the ground. The forelegs should be parallel with each other and well under the dog, keeping in mind, however, that they should also be perpendicular to the ground. Breeds which do not have straight forelegs should have the legs placed as straight as possible for the breed. Pekingese, however, are expected to have their forefeet turning outwards.

The method of making a dog stand in the correct show pose depends very largely on the size of the breed. The position of the head may vary, as will the position of the tail. It will be noticed that some breeds are expected to look alert with their ears pricked; other breeds must look more relaxed with pendant ears and tails down, whilst yet others must look relaxed with their tail up. In a breed like Chihuahuas, it is difficult to have an alert-looking dog still maintaining the correctly flaring ears.

In some breeds, especially in the spaniels, it is the custom to remove the show lead to empha-

Handling

Good stance - shown naturally with loose lead

Tight lead spoiling stance

Overhandled; thus spoiling outline

Top: Mr. Stanley Dangerfield judging a notable progeny class at Windsor.

Above: A class of well-stacked Whippets.

Left: Experienced judge, dog and handler. Note the neatly held lead with no stray ends. Another good method of concealing the lead when the dog is on the table is for the handler to place the lead round his/her neck holding it in one hand a few inches above the dog's collar. The other hand is then free to control the dog's tail.

Right: The judge measuring a poodle on the table.

Below right: Showing is thirsty work!

Bottom left: The judge Mrs. Judy de Casembroot with her 'Best in Show' Whippet.

Below left: Cruft's 'Best in Show' 1971 Champion Ramacon Swashbuckler.

size the dog's length of neck. The handler may draw the ears forward, if he wishes to show this off, or in some breeds the judge may wish to see if the ear leathers meet in front of the dog's nose. With American Cocker Spaniels the top lips are often drawn together under the lower jaw to see if they will meet, to prove that the dog has sufficient lip and a square enough muzzle.

It is important when holding the head not to draw in the beautiful lip on the near side. A handler can enhance the lip by holding the dew lap giving the appearance of a dry throat.

When the judge is going over the head and front of the dog, the handler should move to the rear, and, if necessary, could deal with any correcting of the rear stance. When the judge goes over the side or rear of the dog the handler should automatically move to the front of the dog. At all times the dog must be under complete lead control. The dog will obviously feel more at ease when he can see his handler, particularly if the handler keeps his attention with a piece of bait. The handler may have to remain at the dog's head if he is highly strung and likely to get out of control. The judge may very often throw something to make a dog use his ears, or to see his expression. Occasionally a dog will show no interest in the judge's antics or he may lose interest even before the judge has had time to blink. The handler should have something else ready to interest the dog. A piece of a horse's frog or baked pork-liver or even a crackly piece of cellophane paper may do the trick. The majority of breeds look their best when they are permitted to stand so that the neck is slightly up and arched, with the line of the muzzle slightly down, although there are exceptions as with pointers. Large prick-eared breeds are better when standing a short distance from their handler so that the handler can make them look up towards some bait held in the hand.

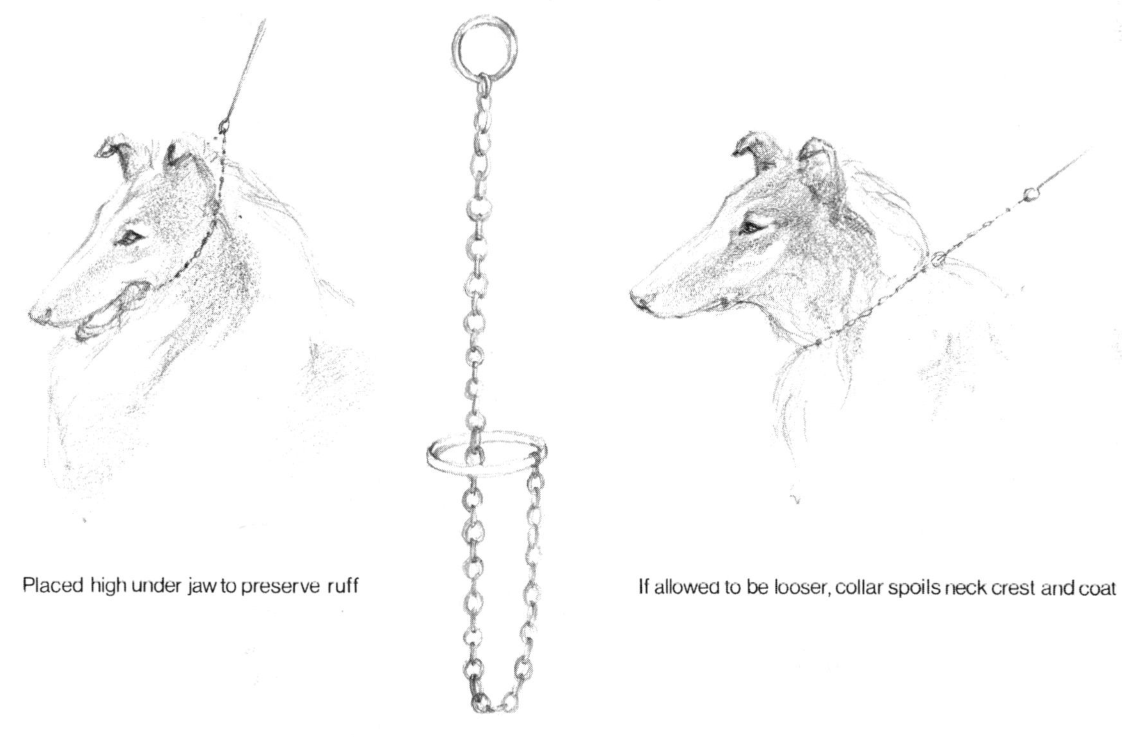

Placed high under jaw to preserve ruff

If allowed to be looser, collar spoils neck crest and coat

How to manipulate a choke-collar

THE CORRECT USE OF A LEAD

The type of lead used varies from breed to breed and from handler to handler, and country to country. Some exhibitors prefer fine, one-piece slip leads made of leather or nylon. Some handlers prefer a roll-collar and a swivel-ended lead. Others use a choke chain with a soft leather snap-on lead attached to it, whilst some breeds are traditionally shown in leather collars of varying widths and leads. Whatever the breed being handled it is best to use the type of collar and lead in fashion for that particular breed. However, whatever the breed, other than those exhibited on a loose lead, the method and use of the lead is identical. Only the strength and force exerted varies according to the size and strength of the dog.

When moving the dog the lead must always be held in the left hand only. The length of the lead is decided according to the size of the dog being exhibited, and the comparative size of the handler to the dog. In other words the smaller the dog the longer the lead required, and vice versa. The shorter the lead the better. This does not mean that the dog must be strung up. It simply means that no trailing end should be seen, because this spoils the complete picture. The remaining, unrequired length of lead must be either folded up in the palm of the hand, or, in the case of fine leads, rolled up tightly. Equally effectively, the lead may be looped around the fingers or the hand, or for small breeds the lead may be wound round the first finger only. The lead, however, should never be held in two hands. The right hand must be free, in order to balance the handler when moving. The right hand being free may also be used to advantage to pat a dog of a larger breed, if he requires encouraging or if he is lagging a little when turning at the far end of the ring, or to steady him if necessary. The right hand is the hand in which the bait should be held.

BREEDS SHOWN ON A LOOSE LEAD

Some breeds are traditionally exhibited on a loose lead and these generally wear a collar. The lead should be as fine as possible for the breed and should have a swivel attachment. Some handlers keep the swivel at the top of the collar so that the lead is only just loose. Others, for example for the Pekingese, prefer a fine round collar which should not be tighter than one finger between the collar and the neck. Owing to the profuse mane the collar must be placed next to the skin with the mane hanging over it. The swivel end of the lead should be beneath the dog's chin and the dog is moved with the lead loose and slightly looped. Part of the looped lead should be hidden beneath the mane. The dog then walks on a loose lead, but not so loose that it would get in the way of the feet. The other end of the lead should be concealed as usual in the hand.

THE CORRECT POSITION OF THE SLIP LEAD

The slip lead should first be opened up to allow the dog's head to be put through easily. It is extremely important that the lead should remain well up under the angulation of the jaw bones. It should be drawn slightly forward so that it comes up behind the base of the ears. The clip should then be adjusted according to whether a large or a small opening is required when moving the dog. The slip lead correctly placed gives the handler tremendous control of the dog. A turn of the wrist can control not only the gait but also the direction in which the dog should move. If the slip lead is incorrectly put on, so that instead of being under the jaw it is half way up the neck, there will be little control of the dog and no control over the position of his head, and at the same time it will give the appearance of shortening the neck. In the case of breeds with thick or long coats, the hair may be drawn up untidily at the top of the lead, completely ruining the appearance of an arched, extended neck.

Having put the slip lead on the dog in the correct manner, the handler should flex his left arm so that it is at right angles to his body with his thumb uppermost. He should then adjust the length of lead required, so that the lead becomes just taut enough to control the dog. From this initial position the complete control of a trained dog is maintained. Should the judge require the dog to move on a loose lead, all that is necessary for the handler to do is to lower his arm slightly. If the dog moves too close to the handler or deviates to one side, a quick turn of the wrist will bring the dog back into the correct position. A forward movement of the wrist will make the dog quicken his gait, whilst an upward movement of the wrist will make the dog hold his head up. Sometimes a dog may gait too close to the handler, and this can be rectified by the handler letting out a loop or two of the lead from the palm of the hand. If the handler wishes to draw the dog closer to heel, the lead may be twisted quickly round the fingers without altering the gait. A sharp jerk on the lead is infinitely preferable to a steady, hard pull. A dog never responds to such treatment well, and it can turn into an undignified tug-of-war between handler and dog. This can become quite comical if the dog is large and the handler small and fat.

A novice will find it surprisingly easy to control a dog, once he has practised a few times the first principles of lead control. Most of these are applied by a sharp twist of the wrist, making the quick pull or jerk come from the main joint of the little finger.

Ways of holding leads

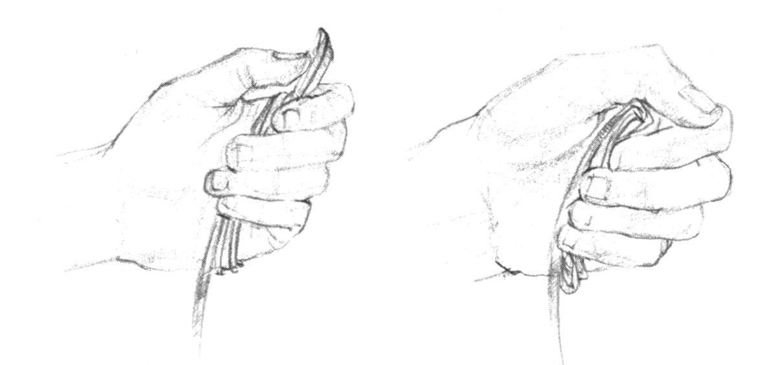

LEAD CONTROL FOR THE SHOW POSE

When the dog is in a show stance, it is important to keep the end of the lead out of sight or in a tidy position. The majority of handlers secrete the superfluous length of the lead in their hand. But there are other methods which are also quite sensible. For breeds which are exhibited on the table, the handler controls the dog with the lead held a short distance above the top of the dog's neck. The handler may place the remainder of the lead around the back of his own neck, so that the lead hangs down on his left-hand side. If he is wearing a jacket, the end can be pushed neatly inside the jacket. Another method, which some handlers favour when stacking a small- or medium-sized breed on the ground, is to kneel on the ground on one knee, and to drape the surplus end of lead over the other knee, hiding the remainder within the flexed joint. The less of the unrequired end of the lead that is seen the better.

Many handlers prefer to change the lead to the right hand when the dog is set up, whether on the table or on the ground. This is often done too for photographers for 'best-in-show' awards, when the judge is also required to be in the photograph, or where 'best-in-show' placards are required to appear in the photograph. It is only when moving that the lead must always be retained in the left hand, and certainly never held in both hands.

GAIT

The handler is expected to move his dog in the ring at the correct speed for the breed being handled. The dog must not lag behind the handler, pull forward nor veer to one side. The majority of novices move their dogs too slowly, and also use small mincing steps themselves. This combination does not give the dog a chance of showing off its outstanding qualities. Very many handlers are incapable of walking up and down the ring in a straight line, which makes it extremely difficult for a judge to assess the dog's movement. A dog is best moved at the fastest gait that he can manage (that is a fast trot), without breaking into a gallop. Some breeds, however, are better handled at a slow trot, while the handler himself is running, whilst other breeds go better with the handler moving at a fast walk. Even the toy breeds should be able to keep up with the handlers' normal walking speed. The actual speed must always be adjusted to each individual dog's advantage. Regardless of the speed chosen to suit the dog, the handler's own movement is important. His steps must be long enough and his own movement must be flowing. It is quite surprising how a handler with a relaxed, balanced, flowing movement helps the overall picture of a perfectly gaiting dog.

Whilst the judge is watching the dog's gait, he is noting exactly how sound the dog is in movement. Clever handlers can disguise their dog's cow hocks and badly angulated shoulders when it is standing, but when the dog gaits these faults cannot be hidden. Bad handling by perhaps jerking the lead at the wrong moment may, however, throw a dog slightly off balance. In so doing it may look as if the dog is throwing an elbow or has weak hind movement. In this case the wise judge will ask the handler to move the dog again.

ADVANTAGEOUS HANDLING

Handlers must know which type of handling a judge prefers and wisely should conform to this. Over-handling is generally disliked as it is often considered an insult to the judge. The dog's finest points should be shown off to best advantage. Some handlers seem to have overtrained their dogs and they stand like statues and are then perhaps more like puppets on a string, instead of dogs full of brains and character raring to go. Such dogs look dull and bored and lack the sparkle so necessary in high awards.

METHODS OF HANDLING

There are probably a dozen or more distinctive methods of handling the various breeds. The majority of breeds, however, as presented naturally. This means that the handlers have their dogs trained in such a way that, when they give the command to stand, the dogs will stand in their own natural, correct, show stance with all four feet on the ground, holding their head and tail in the correct position for the particular breed, without any further assistance. The handler concentrates on making the dog look alert, keen and interested.

THE HANDLER

The handler of quite a number of breeds is expected to walk, trot and run gracefully and with ease. Besides knowing the correct show stance for the particular breeds which are being exhibited the handler should also know when leads are removed and when they are to be replaced. The handler should be acquainted with the breeds which are exhibited on show cases (Yorkshire terriers), which are normally examined on the ground, and which breeds are shown standing facing the centre of the ring (Bulldogs, Staffordshire Bull Terriers etc.), and which breeds are placed on the table for the judge to go over.

The handler must stand when handling some breeds, whilst with others it is necessary for the handler to kneel on one knee. It is never a good idea for a handler to go down on both knees to a dog, and it is certainly not good to kneel and then sit back on the legs. The handler will find that it is extremely difficult to rise from a complete kneeling position to a standing position without looking extremely awkward and ungainly. When kneeling, the handler should try to keep his back as straight as possible, and when moving, his right arm should be free to swing naturally so that he too, looks well balanced and also moves in co-ordination with his dog. The left arm should be kept at right angles to the body, moving the arm up or down according to how much extra lead the dog requires from time to time in the ring. The slip lead must be clean and supple so that it can be easily manipulated in the palm of the hand or twined round the fingers if preferred.

When the handler moves with the dog he should start off with the left leg. In other words he should start with the leg nearest the dog taking normal, good-sized steps, and keeping abreast of the dog's forelegs.

It is worth the handler remembering that when a sound dog is nervous or apprehensive, he may often stand as though he were unsound. The dog may sag and will often stand with cow-hocks or with his forelegs slightly extended, instead of being well under him. Apprehensive dogs will often spread out the toes, just as they do when they are afraid of having their nails clipped. Some dogs are frightened of a slippery floor and, unless they have sufficient practice on such surfaces, are unlikely to move well. A little resin on the pads can help the dog not to slip about.

There are unfortunately always some handlers who are prepared to take unfair advantages and liberties with their competitors in the ring, particularly against the novices. But novices do not remain novices for long. Sometimes they may get away with it, but the judge might well ask the offender to go to the bottom of the class and even consider not placing the dog at all. It would, of course, depend on the severity of the misdemeanour.

NEVER DRAW ATTENTION TO A FAULT

The handler should never draw attention to a fault by touching the area with his hand. It is infinitely better to draw attention to an outstandingly good point instead. I remember once watching the final line-up for best in show at an important show. The handler of a Scottish Terrier kept touching it's tail, the strong electric light shining on the white hand, against the black coat, drew the attention of the spectators as well as probably the judge, until one realized that the tail was not quite correct.

Once a dog is perfectly set up in his show stance, the less he is handled the better, but he should never be kept in one position for too long. It is easy to criticise a handler from the ringside. No one knows better perhaps than the handler, how difficult dogs can be on an off day, particularly if they have become stale and bored with shows. Great effort and concentration are needed to keep the dog on his toes right up to the last minute. There is also the extreme tension and strain for the handler where top honours are being fought out in the centre ring and his anxiety can be communicated to the dog all too easily.

TO OVER TAKE OR NOT

Sometimes when moving in the ring a handler is confronted with another handler and dog moving too slowly in front of him. This is a difficult situation. It is generally considered bad manners to overtake the dog in front. The handler has the choice of trying to make a larger circle or slowing his dog up, hoping that the judge will be looking at the other exhibits. As he once again comes under the eye of the judge he will endeavour to increase his dog's speed again. A world-renowned judge once informed me, when held up by a slower exhibit, that I should definitely have overtaken the dog so as not to have checked the lovely movement of my own dog. One needs to know what a particular judge will allow or penalize. It is, however, extremely important that, whatever the handler decides to do, it is absolutely imperative that his dog must under no circumstances touch the other exhibit or put him off in any way during the manoeuvre.

It might perhaps be worth mentioning that handlers should wear soft shoes which do not make a noise particularly on wooden floors at indoor shows. A handler making a great clatter on the floor behind some unfortunate exhibit can have a deleterious effect on that dog, and such behaviour shows up the handler as a novice or as a seasoned, unsporting veteran. Many a handler knows all too well whom not to stand next to in the ring, if it can possibly be avoided. The novice invariably has to learn the hard way! It never pays a handler to try to play a fast one and to stand in a higher position than he was told to.

CHAPTER VII

Show Preparations

PRE-SHOW PREPARATIONS

There is always a tremendous amount of work and organization required before setting off for a show. Amongst all the work is the decision of what the handler should wear and whether the dog or dogs should travel in a show crate or box.

EXHIBITORS' CLOTHES

Exhibitors and handlers should pay special attention to their own groomed appearance in the ring. The handler should be as immaculately turned out as his dog because he too is contributing to the overall picture, particularly when he is moving his dog. Unsuitable clothes may even take the judge's eye off the dog or they could perhaps camouflage the exhibit, particularly if the handler is wearing white and is exhibiting a white dog; a long flapping coat which blows in front of the dog when he is moving may even obscure him from the judge's view. Women handlers perhaps have a slight advantage over the opposite sex in so much as they can choose the colour of their apparel to contrast, and enhance the appearance of their dog to the best advantage.

It is not normally considered correct for a man to wear a hat in the ring, but he would be wise to make certain that his tie is secure as a flapping tie may blow across his dog's head and obscure the judge's view at the crucial moment.

Women exhibitors and handlers should wear comfortable neat clothes. Skirts should not be too tight as it is impossible to gait a dog with mincing steps. On the other hand skirts should not be too full as the wind can play artful tricks. Low necklines are not a good idea either, where there is a great deal of bending to be done. Materials should be chosen so that dog hairs do not show, but above all the handler must feel comfortable so that she can run, bend, stretch, and walk with ease. Shoes should naturally be reasonably flat-heeled, clean, comfortable and well polished. It is not a good idea to wear large, chunky jewellery, long beads and dangling ear rings. Their place is not in the show ring.

Trouser suits which are now in fashion are excellent for show purposes. They are smart, tailored and comfortable and the drip dry variety are excellent. Tights are really a necessity and they are comfortable and sensible. It is almost essential to wear a garment which has at least one pocket for holding the bait, and this may conveniently be lined with plastic. It is quite a good idea to wear a nylon overall whilst grooming and preparing the dog, so that one's clothes remain clean and free from chalk, powder and dog hairs. Some handlers like to wear a special show apron, which has a series of pockets to hold brushes, combs and bait. These aprons can look very attractive.

Weather in some countries can be most unpredictable, and exhibitors and handlers should take a mackintosh and a spare pair of shoes. In wet weather boots should be the order of the day. Head scarves are useful against the wind and can be lined with plastic if wet, although some of the modern rain head-gear can be most attractive and sensible. The importance of some form of head gear is that the handler should not look as if she has just come through a hurricane in contrast to her immaculately prepared dog. Wigs at the moment are much in vogue and the short, neat variety are splendid for outdoor shows particularly in blustery weather, because they remain tidy. Large fancy hats are not appropriate in the show ring.

TRAVELLING BOXES

It is always safer for show dogs to travel in cars in their dog boxes, crates or show cases. Unruly dogs jumping about in a car may make the driver take his eyes off the road, and could, therefore, be the indirect cause of an accident. Dogs in their enclosed boxes seldom suffer severe injuries in car accidents, but all too frequently they are seriously injured or killed when loose in a car. Travelling boxes are also essential if the owners intend to stay with friends or in a hotel before or after a show.

PREPARATION OF SHOW CRATES

The show case must be disinfected thoroughly after each show, and, before a show, the bottom should be lined with layers of thick newspaper. On top of this, newspaper should be torn or cut in three-inch-wide strips with a knife and laid on top of the other newspaper. It will be found that in the event of a dog drooling or being sick, or of any other likely contingency liable to take place, the loose strips of paper move about and will cover up and absorb any moisture so that the dog will be kept clean. Strips of paper are very much better than several solid pages. Newspaper, however, is not suitable for white or light-coloured dogs, because the print comes off and the coat becomes a dirty grey. It is better to use white paper for these breeds.

DANGERS TO DOGS

It is unwise to tie a dog up with a lead when he is in a car. It is so easy for the lead to become entangled with the dog's legs and it has been known for a dog to hang himself, when left alone in a car. It seems quite incomprehensible, that any one could contemplate leaving a dog either shut up in a car on a very hot summer's day with all the car windows shut, or, worse still, leaving small dogs shut up in a perspex show case, and leaving them inside a car in the sun. This dangerous practice has been done by intelligent top breeders on more than one occasion, with disastrous results. The Windsor Dog Show Committee year after year have to warn owners over the loudspeakers at the show that the temperature in the cars is over 120°F (49°C). Even with these warnings dogs are still left in cars and the RSPCA inspectors have had to break the windows in order to save the dogs from suffocation and heat stroke. Will dog people never learn?

TIMING AND MODE OF TRANSPORT

It is extremely important for both exhibitor and dog to arrive at the show in a cool, calm and collected manner. This obviously entails a tremendous amount of orderly preparation the day prior to the show. Show requirements can be divided under two headings, those for the dog and those for the exhibitor. It is useful to keep a list of these requirements from show to show. Regardless of the mode of travel, it is essential to allow at least half an hour more time than is thought to be necessary. It is a good idea to set two alarm clocks in case one should fail, or, in place of the second alarm clock, arrange with the telephone exchange for an alarm call.

Organize all the work which has to be done for the rest of the kennel and household before leaving for the show. It is an excellent plan to check the times of coaches and trains, and, if the means of travel is to be by car, it is a useful form of reference to mark up the proposed route on a map or in an Automobile Association book in red ball-point pen, because this stands out and will be easy to follow. The Automobile Association or Royal Automobile Club will make out a good route on request. Part of the enjoyment of showing, particularly at the summer shows, is often a cross-country drive in the very early hours of the morning. It is always more interesting if the return journey can be made via a different route. If time permits and arrangements can be made, it is interesting to pay a visit to kennels in another part of the country. It is an excellent idea to keep a record of the length of time it takes to reach the venue of any given show. This should include the length of time spent on stops for breakfast or coffee, and also to let the dogs relieve themselves.

ORGANIZED SHOW COACHES

Many coaches from all parts of the country are booked to convey exhibitors and their dogs to the major shows. Each exhibitor or handler is allocated a double seat, one for himself and the other for his dog. Sometimes coaches are only permitted to carry one handler to a maximum of five dogs.

Many of the dogs travel in small crates or show cases. The majority, however, travel on the seat beside their owner. The coaches travelling long distances may travel all night. Frequent stops are arranged for dogs and exhibitors and many have meals at the stopping places. Coach travel is much cheaper than by rail and, since the same people generally join the coaches from the same area, friendships develop and conversation is always interesting. There is so much to learn from an experienced breeder in another breed, that one never leaves a coach journey without having learnt something interesting and new, and probably made a lasting friend, especially when there is no breed jealousy or rivalry involved.

CHECKING THE VENUE OF THE SHOW

The nomenclature of a show is not necessarily the place where the show is to be held, as I once nearly discovered to my cost, and this is also true of many shows in other parts of the world. Richmond Show is not held at Richmond but at Olympia in the centre of London. How nearly I once set off for Richmond, deciding that I would enquire about the actual place of the venue when I got to Richmond! Many of the great shows are not held anywhere near the centre of a large city, but often several miles from the outskirts. It may often take longer to find the venue on reaching a city than the long drive from your home to that city. Advanced planning, therefore, always pays dividends.

CAR PREPARATION

Obviously, the car should be checked to ensure that it is roadworthy. Pay particular attention to petrol, oil, water and tyre pressures and other essentials. All car users should carry a first-aid box, and a card should be put in a conspicuous place in the car with the name and address and telephone number of the driver, and indicating that there are animals and dependants at home in case of a serious accident.

The car should be loaded with all the necessary show equipment the evening before, and the car park ticket should be stuck on to the windscreen. Seats should be covered with paper or cellophane or other form of protection to prevent damage, and plenty of newpaper and rolls of tissue can be stored under the seats in case of emergencies, for car sickness and other unfortunate contingencies that are liable to occur en route.

EXHIBITOR'S EQUIPMENT

Suitable clothes and flat-heeled shoes.
Mackintosh and head scarf.
A spare pair of shoes or boots.
Camp chair or folding stool.

A shoulder hand-bag containing:
Show pass.
Car park ticket, or rail or coach ticket.
Cheque book and money, including small coinage for telephone calls and parking meters.
Make up, comb, sponge bag, soap and damp flannel.
Small hand towel.
Tissues.

Bottle of TCP.
Scent.
Aspirin.
Clothes brush.
Travel sickness pills.
Ring clip or safety pin (which would, however, be better worn).
Diary and note book.
Two biros.
Stud cards (two or three).
Ring numbers if applicable. Write the ring numbers on the back of the hand or on a piece of paper, putting it in some accessible place.
Schedule, to check the classes entered.

A picnic bag containing:
Sandwiches, cake, biscuits, fruit, strong coffee, thirst quencher, bottle opener, knife and spare plastic bags for rubbish. Coca Cola is very reviving, and hot soup is excellent on a cold day.

DOG REQUIREMENTS

Travelling box, lined with paper and blankets and complete with padlock and chain.
Grooming table.
Collar and bench chain and spare leather lead.
Show lead.
Dog coat, mackintosh and boots.
Bench rugs.
Pen curtains (for Toy breeds).
Newspaper for lining benches.
Trolley, two-wheeler or four-wheeler.
Dog food in plastic bags, and dog biscuits.
Water bowls, and plastic bottle of water.
Bait, such as baked liver diced.
Drool bib, if necessary.
Stud cards and advertisement pulls.

A grooming bag containing:
Brush and comb.
Hand glove or velvet pad.
Boracic powder for eye stains.
Small towel.
Scissors and thinning shears if necessary.
Johnson's Baby Powder.
Mink oil.
Water spray bottle or other sprays.
Resin block or powdered resin.
Cotton wool for eyes.
Damp Spontex cloth for wiping feet.
Chalk block or starch.
Ribbons, elastic bands and curl papers, if necessary.
Betsolan drops in case of eye injuries.

IMMEDIATE PRE-SHOW PREPARATION

DAY OF THE SHOW

Always keep an extra half hour in hand before departure. There is always some unexpected contingency which is liable to cause delay. An hour before leaving, give all the show dogs a glycerine suppository to ensure that they relieve themselves before starting. There is no excuse whatsoever for dogs to foul the pavement or the ring if they have been properly treated beforehand.

The wise exhibitor will fortify himself for a long hard day by leaving enough time for a good substantial breakfast before starting on the journey. This is the time to re-check the route to the show and to deal with any last minute problems or instructions to kennel staff.

ARRIVAL AT THE SHOW

Whether this is an indoor show or an outdoor show, the procedures are the same: the car must be parked, and the dogs and equipment must be unloaded and the dogs benched. In the event of torrential rain, it is important, particularly in the long-coated breeds, that they should be kept dry, especially the feet and legs of Afghans, American Cockers and Old English Sheepdogs, because it is almost impossible to get them dry if they are first in the ring. Therefore, each dog may have to be carried to its bench, unless they are clad in dog mackintoshes, or have their legs covered in plastic bags secured with elastic bands.

At the entrance to the venue, the dogs are taken in at the exhibitors entrance, where the entry passes will be required to be shown. These should be readily at hand. They are probably best kept in an outside pocket. Unless there are extra free passes, it may be necessary to pay for the extra ticket for a kennelmaid and it is helpful to have this money at hand.

Catalogues can usually be obtained just inside the entrance. Catalogues are important, because it is here that the benching numbers of the dogs will be found under the appropriate breed, not to mention the classes which have been entered, in case the exhibitor has forgotten. It is imperative that the exhibitor's name should be written in large letters across the top of the catalogue, as these are frequently stolen. It is a good idea, too, to tear off the top outer corner of the pages containing the entries in the required breed, for quick and easy reference. It is also useful to mark the classes entered.

BENCHING THE DOG

PENS

Toy breeds are penned. If a toy breed is involved, newspaper should be placed on the floor of each pen, in order to minimize the risk of infection. Lay a blanket on top of the newspaper and arrange the pen curtains round three sides. The latter may be hung either by means of small clothes pegs or with curtain hooks and elastic. A water bowl and a food bowl may be placed in the pen if desired. All equipment must be stored neatly beneath the pen and grooming tables and chairs must not obstruct the gangways. At unbenched shows crate and boxes should be placed on level ground away from draughts and out of the hot sun.

BENCHES

The larger breeds are benched, and all benches have to be disinfected thoroughly, according to Kennel Club regulations. Nevertheless, it is a good idea to cover the bench with thick newspaper or plastic sheeting before putting down a benching rug. Two rings are provided at the back of each bench to enable the dog to be chained securely. It is imperative that the chain should be regulated so that the dog cannot reach to within a foot of the edge of the bench. This prevents him from falling over the edge and strangling himself. It also stops the dogs on adjoining benches fighting and, in the case of nervous dogs, it prevents them from taking a nip at passers-by. The general public are less likely to touch a dog which is lying at the back of a bench, and in that way there is less chance of infections being passed on.

BENCH CARDS

Only the regulation-size bench cards with the correct wording may be placed on the benches or, where applicable, cards denoting dogs 'Not for Competition'. Advertisement pulls may be placed on top of pens or on the benches. There are strict Kennel Club regulations regarding benching, and each dog may only be chained on his allotted bench. It is also important never to obstruct gangways.

EXERCISING

The dog should then be exercised in the allocated area. Dogs will usually oblige quickly, particularly if there is a convenient scenting post. If not, screw up a large piece of newspaper so that the dog will cock his leg against that. Bitches are much more difficult and they will often not relieve themselves until after the show, and sometimes not even until they are on home ground again. This might be an appropriate moment to mention again the penalties for allowing a dog to foul pavements or show premises. In case such an accident occurs, and occur they undoubtedly will, unless the dogs have been adequately suppositorized, the person in charge of the dog should carry something with which to mop up or pick up the offending excreta, and it should be placed in a plastic bag and put into the nearest litter box. This is where plastic bags are useful as all odour is prevented from escaping. There is no excuse for dogs fouling premises when it is so easy to prevent.

The dog is only permitted to be off his show bench for fifteen minutes at a time. Provided that there is sufficient time after the dog has relieved himself, it is often an excellent idea to walk the dog round the benches and ring, so that he may become accustomed to the noise and other exhibits. In the case of an inexperienced dog, a few practice runs in an empty ring will help to give him confidence.

FINDING THE RING

In the rush and bustle of arrival at the show, with innumerable dogs and harassed exhibitors and with all the 'hellos' and 'good mornings', the exhibitor may forget to find out the exact location of the appropriate ring, and to ascertain the approximate time of judging. Whilst making these preliminary investigations, it is useful to make a note of where the entrance to the ring is, because sometimes this may be difficult to find when it is surrounded by spectators watching the judging of a popular breed. Toy exhibitors will often take their dogs to the ringside in their travelling boxes. If this is done, it is essential that the boxes should not encroach on to the ring, and perhaps even more important that the dogs in the boxes should not be allowed to bark and distract the attention of the dogs in the ring. The regulation concerning the fifteen-minute absence from benches is frequently broken, because sometimes, when the ring and the pen are a great distance apart, there is literally not sufficient time for an exhibitor to fetch, carry back to the ring and prepare five separate dogs for five consecutive classes. Consequently, he brings all five dogs to the ring at the same time and gets a kennelmaid or friend to prepare the dog to be shown. It is a much greater offence when large dogs are kept at the ringside and are permitted to sprawl and encroach on the ring whilst judging is in progress. The former is an offence against the public, who pay to enter the show in order to see the dogs. The latter is an offence against other exhibitors, who are trying to show their dogs to their best advantage.

INTERIM BEFORE JUDGING

The beginning of the day at any dog show is always exciting, and one can feel the excitement of the busy exhibitors getting their dogs to the benches and preparing and grooming their dogs ready for the big event. This is the time when exhibitors are at their best. Hope still springs eternal and there are smiles and cheery greetings for long lost friends, who may all too soon become bitter rivals. Often at the end of the show one sees to one's astonishment these very same people cutting one another, passing forced and insincere congratulations and derogatory remarks about each others' dogs, and criticizing the judge and the judging. The judge, of course, has only one friend in each class: the winner. Nevertheless, it is a great pastime and doubtless many people enjoy it. If possible, before starting to show, it is an excellent idea to watch the judge at work, so that the novice exhibitor will know what to expect.

PREPARING THE BREEDS

Some breeds require very little preparation before actually entering the ring, whilst some of the longer-coated breeds require at least half an hour's work spent on them, before they are fit for the show ring. Especially complicated breeds are those like the Maltese, which may require their forelocks replaited and neatly bowed, Yorkshire Terriers, which will require their paper strips removed, American Cockers, Afghans, Poodles, not to mention all the paraphernalia demanded for the complicated Terrier breeds. Full pre-show grooming preparations may be found in my book *Dogs—Modern Grooming Techniques,* (John Gifford Ltd).

CHAPTER VIII

Ringcraft

GENERAL RINGCRAFT

The use of the show lead, and correct setting up of a dog, play a tremendous role in successful showmanship. This combined with good technique in presentation and knowledge of the finer points of the dog game all go to make the outstanding handler. The handler must also understand his dog and get his full co-operation so that the judge sees the dog giving of his best.

A dog cannot win high honours unless he is fit, sound and in perfect condition, and also beautifully presented and trained. A dog cannot be in tip-top condition unless he is fed, kenneled and exercised correctly for his breed. All this requires knowledge, time, experience and money. One of the best ways a novice can learn how to handle a show dog is to attend show training classes. In some countries handling is largely done by professional handlers, so that unless the amateurs can handle as well as the professionals they have little hope of winning top successes. Of course, some breeds are more difficult to handle than others and this applies also to certain dogs within a breed. The genuine flair and love of handling dogs goes hand in hand with practice, patience and determination. Children brought up in dog-showing families usually master the techniques of handling from a very early age and are often better than their parents. It is not unknown for parents of attractive children to send them into the ring hoping that a child handler may possibly influence a judge, particularly a judge who is known to play to the gallery.

RINGCRAFT

There is no doubt about it, that one of the best ways for a novice to train a young dog is to attend organized ringcraft classes. These classes are held in very many areas all the year round. The fees are cheap and the instructors are generally highly trained. The dogs get excellent experience of meeting breeds in all stages of their training, and of all sizes. No dog should attend classes, go to shows, mix with other dogs, or go into towns unless he has been fully immunized against distemper and leptospirosis. Dogs which go to shows regularly would probably benefit from the precaution of having a yearly booster injection.

The ringcraft class can best be described as a 'mock-up' of a dog show. The dogs learn to walk one behind the other in line, to be gone over on the table and/or on the floor depending on the breed. The dogs learn to walk up and down the centre of the ring, and to move in a triangle and sometimes in the letter 'T'. The dogs become used to both male and female judges, and very often the dogs are switched from handler to handler, which is excellent training for people and dogs. The dogs also become accustomed to hand-clapping, and in all probability to a number of small children, who are sometimes much in evidence at these occasions.

TRAINING FOR GOOD CITIZENSHIP

These are run by Adult Further Education Classes and often are held in schools, and these sessions can also be helpful towards show-training a dog, if there are no show-training classes in the area. It is not always a good idea for show dogs to learn to sit at every halt, because they are apt to carry this part of their training into the show ring, where a dog is required to stand when halted and certainly not to sit. However, the training at these citizenship classes can very often be adapted to meet the needs of any show dogs being trained.

AMATEUR RINGCRAFT CLASSES

In areas where there are no official ringcraft classes held, it is reasonably easy for a number of enthusiastic dog lovers to organize a small training session once a week in somebody's garden or large garage. These classes might not be quite so efficient as the organized ringcraft classes, but this would very much depend on the experience of the organizer of the class. Such a person might even be highly experienced, and the training of the dogs could then be above that of an overcrowded, organized, ringcraft class. Small exemption shows are also good training grounds for potential show dogs.

GETTING A DOG FIT

Regardless of how well trained a dog may be for the show ring, he will seldom win the top honours unless he is really fit and in outstanding condition. This is not difficult to accomplish with the toy and small breeds. However, the larger the breed, the more exercise he will need to keep him well muscled up, and this may be difficult during the winter months especially with breeds with long coats which are difficult to maintain.

Regular walking is probably the best exercise of all. But unfortunately, very few show dogs are adequately exercised and many show dogs spend much of their lives in small quarters and on concrete runs. One of the quickest methods of getting a dog fit is to walk him up and down a fairly steep hill every day. This exercises opposite muscles, and is excellent for tightening up the shoulders and strengthening the hocks. Dogs who will retrieve a ball can be given a tremendous amount of exercise with the minimum effort on the part of the trainer. Digging for a bone buried a couple of feet is quite effective for some breeds. Swimming is an excellent exercise, provided the weather is not too cold. If the dog swims in the sea, he should be bathed afterwards, because salt water is not good for the skin or the coat. Some dogs will gain sufficient exercise, if two or more play together. Tugs-of-war are excellent for strengthening some of the muscles. Regular hard road exercise is difficult to beat, but the emphasis must be on the word 'regular'. A ten-mile walk on Sundays only, is not as good as one mile each day.

Breeds which require well-arched, cat-like feet can be helped, if the dogs can be exercised on a cinder run or a pebble beach. The hard, rough cinders or pebbles encourage the dog to use the ligaments of the feet and toes.

CORRECT USE OF THE SHOW LEAD

Nothing perhaps shows up the amateur handler so much as his use or misuse, of the show lead. The show slip lead is as important as the reins are to horse and rider. This does not apply to breeds exhibited on a loose lead. Correctly held and manipulated the lead directs the dog exactly in the path that he must follow. A firm hand is required. A dog cannot respond to a rough hand, or too tight a hold. The handler should have the elbow bent at right angles to his body and the lead concealed in the palm of the hand or wound round the hand and fingers. The lead must be well up and under the angle of the dog's jaw with the sides of the lead coming up under the base of the ears. The length of the lead depends on the size of the dog and the comparative size of the handler. The distance from the lead to the hand, when the arm is flexed and at right angles to the body, should be long enough for it to be just taut. To control the dog, a turn of the wrist to one side or the other will draw the dog nearer the handler or allow him to move further away. When the handler's elbow is flexed more tightly the dog's head will be drawn upwards, and when the elbow is relaxed the dog will automatically be given more lead. This obviates the necessity of taking in or letting out more lead. However, when this is necessary, the lead is either wound or unwound round the hand or fingers, or, in the case of fine leads, it may just be gathered up in the palm of the hand, and a little lead let out at a time, or vice versa.

There is nothing that looks so unprofessional and untidy as a handler with the stray end of a lead dangling down above his dog or lying untidily round his legs. Animal photographers are all too aware of untidy leads spoiling a photograph of a dog, because the handler was completely unaware of the importance of holding the lead in the correct manner. Large breeds look better, and are more easily controlled wearing a choke-chain collar, with just a short strong nylon lead with a swivel end clipped on to it. Some breeds are shown on leather collars of varying widths. The colour of the lead is probably best if it matches the colour of the dog or what the handler is wearing.

LEARNING TO POSE A DOG IN A SHOW STANCE

A dog must be trained to stand in the perfect show stance for his breed. Before a handler can set up a dog correctly, he must know what he is setting out to achieve. All dogs should face in the same direction. In the majority of breeds this would be facing in an anti-clockwise direction: in other words, the dog's head would be towards the handler's right hand and his tail towards his left. Dogs which are absolutely sound are easy to show pose, because their legs will automatically go into the correct positions. However, dogs whose fronts are not quite perfect, require to have some help to achieve the correct stance. There are several methods of setting up a dog in show pose, and it largely depends on the size of the breed as to how the pose is best achieved. Except for the Alsatian (German Shepherd Dog), all breeds are expected to stand four square, with their weight equally placed on all four legs. Some breeds may have the hindlegs extended more than other breeds, (as an example, the American Cocker Spaniel), whilst Bulldogs have their forelegs set really well apart, and Pekingese feet face outwards. Regardless of the breed, however, the legs from the hocks downwards are expected to be perpendicular to the ground, and they must be parallel to each other.

SETTING UP THE LARGE BREEDS

A well trained, sound dog can be led round the area where he is required to stop, and slowly brought forward so that he stops in the exact spot, with all four legs in a perfect show stance. If this is not achieved the first time, or the dog moves a leg out of place, he may be moved round again slowly until he is back to the required position.

ALTERING THE POSITION OF A FORE LIMB

If the position of a foreleg requires improving, the elbow should be grasped firmly in one hand, and the foot then directed to the correct place. The direction of the foot should be turned just before it makes contact with the ground, the handler using his right hand when manipulating the right leg and his left hand when altering the left fore limb. It is extremely important that the dog's head should be kept up and facing straight ahead, while any leg adjustment is being made. Otherwise the dog may be slightly off balance, and he may therefore move into an awkward position again.

ALTERING THE POSITION OF A HIND LIMB

After making certain that the dog is standing correctly on his forelegs, without losing manual contact with the dog, slide the left hand over his back and down the hindleg until the left-hand stifle joint is reached. Grasp the stifle joint in the palm of the hand with the little finger nearest the ground and direct the leg into the correct position. As soon as the hind foot is above the required spot, let it down gently, and remember not to lose contact with the dog. If the other hindleg required adjusting, it should be done in a similar manner. Only, this time grasp the stifle joint in the palm of the hand with the little finger nearest the top of the leg.

It is important to remember that any re-positioning of the hindlegs must be done by placing the palm of the hand over the stifle joint. Novices may try and move the leg by gripping the limb either above or below the stifle joint. The leg cannot be manipulated easily or quickly into the desired position unless the actual joint is grasped in the palm of the hand. Never try to adjust a position by touching the dog's foot. He will immediately move it again if it is touched. If a dog is standing crookedly tapping him on the side of his ribs will make him straighten himself.

THE STANCE

When the dog has all four legs correctly positioned, and is standing straight, the handler must then concentrate on the dog's head and tail. Many of the large breeds are shown naturally with the handler standing in front of the dog. The handler should concentrate on keeping the dog's attention, so that he is presenting the correct overall picture for the breed. He should position his dog so that the judge can see all four legs, and not just the two nearest him.

The large breeds are generally exhibited with strong leather leads. It is a good idea for these to be made as short as possible, because they are difficult to conceal in the hand. Many handlers prefer to have just a strap handle clipped on to the collar, but this gives a bulky outline. A choke-chain collar with a strong narrow lead, which is easily wound round the fingers, is probably the neatest and easiest to manage. Each breed has its own particular fashion and it is best if the handlers conform to the fashion of their particular breed and country.

SETTING UP THE MEDIUM-SIZED BREEDS

In many ways this may be easier than trying to alter the position of the individual legs in the heavier breeds. This is because the forelegs can be correctly manipulated in one operation, and so can the hindlegs, provided that the dog is sound. The dog's head should be kept up and facing directly forward. The handler should place the fingers and palm of one hand underneath the brisket just behind the dog's elbows and then gently lift his weight off the ground. The other hand must keep the dog's head absolutely straight, and, as soon as the forelegs are seen to be parallel with each other, the feet should be dropped and manoeuvred into position. The handler should then concentrate on setting up the rear end. One method is to place the left arm under the loins and to drop the hindlegs into position. An alternative way is to lift the dog by its crutch with the one hand, and to drop the hind legs rather sharply so that they fall 'true' or extended according to the breed. The legs from the hock down should be perpendicular to the ground and parallel to each other. Some handlers with the lighter breeds almost see-saw the dog into position, lifting the dog for a fraction of a second up under the jaw or by the collar and as they drop the front the rear end is lifted up by the base of the tail or the crutch with the other hand, and dropped quickly. Whichever method is adopted, the forelegs require to be dropped well under the dog, with the elbows into the sides; while the hindlegs can be made to drop either four square or extended. The see-saw method is quite good for breeds like the American Cocker Spaniel or Terriers. Some judges, particularly in the United States, like to see a dog being 'dropped' into position, since this is a great indication as to its soundness. Some handlers manipulate their dogs into position by lifting the lead up and dropping the forelegs into position. The hindlegs are nudged gently into position with a foot. The dog's attention is kept on a piece of bait so that he is oblivious to what is happening.

As soon as the dog is standing correctly, the handler should keep the dog's head facing straight forward, and make certain that it is at the correct angle to the ground for the breed. This is the moment that any help necessary should be given to the tail. The tail may have to be extended in line with the body, or held up.

As with the larger breeds, great control can be achieved with the show slip-lead. This should be kept as far up under the angle of the jaw as it will go, with the sides of the lead well up at the base of the ears. The dog is thus encouraged to extend and slightly arch its neck. If the judge happens to object to this smarter type of handling, then the wise handler should conform to a more natural method, by lowering his arm slightly.

The procedure of standing at the rear of the dog whilst the judge is going over the head, and vice versa when the judge is at the rear of the dog, is the same with most breeds.

Above: A Bloodhound on his bench.

Right: A benched Borzoi, covered with his owner's coat.

Above: A Bearded Collie on his bench.

Left: A Dalmation head study.

Right: A Rough Collie settled down for a long wait.

Below: An Afghan Hound head study.

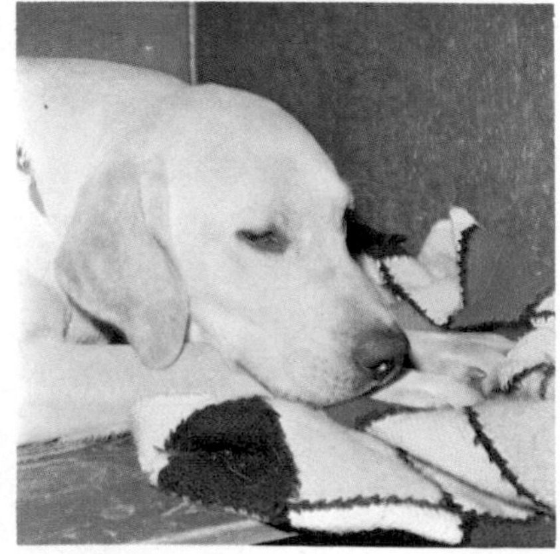

Above: A superb head study of an Airedale Terrier. Note the ear set and the trimmed beard and whiskers.

Left: A Labrador Retriever resting on his favourite rug, which makes him feel at home at the show.

SETTING UP THE TERRIERS

Most terriers are comparatively light in weight with elegant neck and straight forelegs. The majority of handlers will, therefore, position their dogs by the see-saw method of lifting the dog by the collar and tail. The lead is kept high under the angulation of the jaw with the sides coming well up to the base of the ears. The lead is held bunched up in the palm of the hand and is held either straight up or slightly forward so that the terrier looks as if he is 'strung up', showing to full advantage his lovely length of neck, and his straight forelegs with the elbows well into the sides and practically no 'give' at the pasterns. The tail is supported, or lightly stroked into position, so that it falls exactly at the slight tilt required.

SETTING UP THE SMALL OR TOY BREEDS

The smaller breeds are naturally easier to manipulate, especially when they are being posed on a table. The dog should be set up with his forelegs a few inches from the end of the table. The head should be kept facing straight forward with the right hand, whilst the left hand lifts the front of the dog up under the brisket and just behind the elbows and directs the forelegs into position just before they reach the ground. The legs should come down well under the dog, and, as with the other breeds, should be parallel with each other. The same position can be acquired by lifting the dog up with two hands on either side of the jaw. The hindlegs can easily be guided into position by lifting the rear end slightly off the ground, by placing two fingers between the top of the legs in the crutch, and gently dropping them into position.

The same use and control of the slip lead is required as for the larger breeds. The lead should be held reasonably short and kept just taut enough not to sag, particularly whilst the dog is on the table. On no account should the lead be dropped on to the table. The superfluous part of the lead should be held neatly rolled up in the palm of the hand or it may equally well be slung round the handler's neck, with the end hanging down or tucked in on his left side. Whilst the dog is on the table being show posed, the lead as with the terriers should be in the right hand.

SETTING UP THE BREEDS WITH BOWED FORELEGS AND NARROW HIND QUARTERS

There are some breeds where it is almost normal for the breed to have slightly bowed legs. The fore feet should, however, be placed into position on the ground as if the legs were straight. The exception is the Pekingese where the feet naturally splay outwards. Well trained dogs may be walked slowly and carefully towards the position required, and then stopped. The stance will often be better than a manipulated one. The hindlegs, if they require adjustments, should be set up as for other breeds. However, with Pekingese and Bulldogs, where the hindquarters are required to be narrower than the fore hand, the hindlegs may have to be positioned a little closer together.

SETTING UP THE TUCKED-UP BREEDS

Greyhounds, Whippets, Italian Greyhounds and Bedlington Terriers are amongst the breeds where a good tuck-up is desired. The legs are dropped into a four square position as with the other breeds and a hand is placed under the abdomen lifting it up slightly, so that the back curves from the loins forward, but it must not curve too much. The head must be kept facing straight forward. It is usual to show these breeds in wide leather collars. One of the other breeds which is exhibited in exceptionally wide collars is the Staffordshire Bull Terrier.

SETTING UP THE SETTERS

Setters and similar breeds may be shown in two distinctive ways and both have their own particular merits. The dog may be handled naturally on a loose lead, or the handler may prefer to assist the dog by handling him in show pose. To do this, the handler kneels on one knee and extends both arms. The right hand supports the lower jaw, extending and slightly arching the neck. It is better if the muzzle is kept parallel to the ground, although quite a number of handlers raise the muzzle a little. The hindlegs are slightly extended, so that the back gently slopes down and the flag, as the tail is referred to in this breed, is held with the left hand generally with the palm of the hand facing downwards, the slope of the flag continuing in the same line as the slightly sloping back. A few handlers hide the hand behind the flag and this in many ways looks more natural. Care is required when using the arm-stretching method, not to pull the head sideways towards the handler, nor to pull the flag out of perfect alignment. Some handlers have little idea what they are doing, with the result that they look as if they are selling the dog by the yard. Handlers who are rather short sometimes prefer to stand and to bend over the dog with arms outstretched. On the whole, kneeling on one knee probably looks more professional.

SETTING UP THE ALSATIAN (GERMAN SHEPHERD DOG)

The Alsatian is handled in a distinctive manner and is also stacked in a unique way. There are two methods of handling: one is on a tight lead, with the hand held above the back of the dog's head; in the other the dog is handled on a loose lead giving him free range and the lead drops down beneath his chin in a loop. The latter is often considered the better method, particularly if the dog has a free gait, because it shows the movement off and the lovely drive to full advantage. Alsatians are expected to move at two speeds, up and down the ring slowly and then round the ring at a fast gait, so that the dog really strides out. It is quite a test for the fitness of the handler. The gait should be typical and absolutely smooth. Occasionally, an Alsatian may start to amble or pace, particularly at the faster speed, that is when the dog moves both legs forward on the same side. The handler can correct the pacing by quickly lifting the dog by the collar and dropping him so that he changes legs and diagonal legs co-ordinate once again.

The dog must be carefully trained so that he can be brought in to stand in his natural stance, with the hindleg nearest the judge extended. In actual fact it is not a natural stance at all, but a trained 'natural stance'. The dog is eased forward on his forelegs, with the hindleg nearest the judge extended, so that the hock is at right angles to the ground, and the other hindleg remains flexed and forward, enabling the dog to balance. It is important that the weight be distributed evenly. Over-extension of the hindleg makes the dog put too much weight on his forelegs. If the leg is not extended sufficiently, the dog loses the beautiful sloping top line. This fetish of the sloping top-line and the extended hindleg is an abnormal stance, and throws added strain on the hindquarters. It is this show stance that might possibly be a contributary reason for there being so much hip dysplasia in the breed.

SETTING UP THE DOBERMANN (DOBERMAN PINSCHER)

The dog is stacked in the normal manner. In some countries the show lead or choke-chain collar is kept taut and well up under the angulation of the jaw. In other countries the choke chain is allowed to run loose, so that it hangs over the shoulders and shows off the beautiful line of neck.

SETTING UP THE AMERICAN COCKER SPANIEL

The American Cocker Spaniel is generally stacked with the handler kneeling on one knee, unless the dog is on the table. The show lead is removed and placed neatly nearby or put in the handler's pocket. The forelegs should be kept well under the dog, and these must be straight and parallel to each other. The top-line is sloped by slightly extending the hindlegs, so that the hocks are perpendicular and are parallel to each other. The head is held up under the lower jaw, so that the neck is slightly extended and arched, the muzzle being kept parallel to the ground. The tail is lightly supported with the fingers, and to make the slightly sloping top-line, which is required for the show stance, the whole body can be pushed forward by pulling the tail back, and then by pressing the finger and thumb of the left hand into the hip joint on either side of the tail. This pushes the dog forward so that the weight is towards the front, but the dog remains balanced with the hindlegs extended.

Some dogs will automatically go into the show stance the moment the handler pulls slightly on the tail. It is important to make the back look as short as possible and the neck as long and arched as possible. Whilst the dog is on the table, the handler may wish to draw the judge's attention to the beautiful reach of neck by drawing the ear leathers forward over the nose. The right hand supporting the jaw may catch in the loose skin beneath, so that the neckline is accentuated, but care must be taken that the beautiful full top lip is not caught up at the same time. All the procedures should be practised in front of a mirror. It is so easy to over-do the handling and, instead of the dog being made to look as short and compact as possible, he may look as if he is being sold 'by the yard'.

SETTING UP THE PEKINGESE

Pekingese are shown in a slightly different way from other breeds. They are not placed on the judging table until after they have gaited individually for the judge. The handler offers the dog to the judge to hold and to look at, after which the handler then places the dog on the table until the whole class are assembled on the table together. All the dogs must face forward. The swivel end of the lead or the slip lead should hang down beneath the dog's chin and it should be hidden by the mane, the collar being close to the skin.

The dogs are set up with the forelegs placed far apart and the feet turning outwards, thus accentuating the required width of front. The hindquarters are narrow and this is helped by placing the hindlegs close together. The coat is arranged carefully, first the ears and mane, the feathering, breeches and finally the extremely important arrangement of the tail. Once this is done the handler should refrain from using the brush again, until after the judge has finished examining the dog. So many Pekingese handlers seem to have a sort of 'brushing tick' and on no account should the handler brush the dog whilst the judge is going over him. The judge does not normally examine the mouth as it is taken for granted that it will be bad.

SETTING UP THE YORKSHIRE TERRIER

Yorkshire Terriers are handled in the normal method for Toy breeds, except that they are placed in show pose on their individual show cases. These show cases are generally covered in frilled velvet or some other attractive material, usually in some gay colour. This very attractive breed looks most distinctive in the ring, with the handlers standing behind the boxes and all the dogs facing in the same direction. The dogs require patient training and handling, in order to attain the perfect show pose when standing on their individual show cases.

OBTAINING THE BEST FROM THE DOG IN THE RING

However perfectly trained a dog may be, he can be encouraged to give of his best by tone of voice. A low, flowing conversation with him, either alerting or soothing him will assuredly pay dividends. A gentle stroke under the chin and the offer of a suitable bait will gain the dog's full attention at the right moment, when he has been allowed to relax during the judging of a large class. The concentration of the handler and an unhurried and orderly entry into the ring, after allowing sufficient time for the dog to relieve himself, also help to give the dog confidence. A dog should never be fed immediately before entering the ring. The only breed where this is done is Pugs, which are required to look a little portly compared with other breeds, and they are given something dry and starchy, followed by a drink of water; but I personally do not agree with this practice.

Many professional handlers do not feed their dogs the day before a show, so that the dogs go into the ring hungry. The use of the titbit in these cases is extremely important. The sight and the smell of a piece of baked pork will keep a dog's attention and alert expression for a considerable time, particularly if the dog has been trained to react to the titbit. The titbit is held at the right height and angle, so that the head is kept in the perfect position. A great many handlers hold the bait too high, especially for the small breeds. Every now and then the dog is permitted to taste a little of the titbit without being allowed to have a large chunk of it to chew, because the dog will automatically lower his head to eat the tasty morsel and in so doing will ruin the object of the exercise. As soon as the judging is over the dog is given the whole piece of the titbit. He quickly learns that to begin with he may only be permitted a lick or a quick taste of the delicacy, but he soon realizes that when all is over he can claim and will be given the whole delicious bait, which will have been well worth his while waiting for. The dog must never be disappointed in the bait at this stage.

Sometimes important points may be lost when the judge looks up to compare a dog only to find that the dog and handler appear to have gone to sleep or that the handler is discussing trivial topics with another exhibitor. Handlers must concentrate all the time, one eye on the judge the other on the dog. On the other hand the dog must not be permitted to become bored so that when the judge does finally look, the dog has sagged and relaxed and is standing badly. This is not the way to win top awards. The experienced handler knows what to do and when to do it and what's more does it, and does it at the right moment.

THE STRAIGHT RUN UP AND DOWN THE RING

Both dog and handler must move forward in a straight line. At the end of the ring the handler should turn at the same time as the dog, who should be encouraged verbally and allowed out on a longer lead during the actual turn, so that he is not jerked in any way and can continue the full flowing movement. The handler keeps the lead always in the same hand and as the dog starts to come down the line towards the judge, the handler draws the dog in towards him again. Dog and handler should stop about a yard from the judge and the dog should be commanded to stand, so that he freezes for a few seconds for the judge to have a final picture of him. The handler should praise the dog verbally and give him an encouraging pat. In small breeds a pat may be difficult, but as soon as the dog returns to the line of other exhibits the handler can praise him immediately.

In England, dogs are not permitted to be attracted in any way from the outside of the ring. In the United States it is frowned upon both by the American Kennel Club and the handlers, although such action may not disqualify the dog. It is known in the United States as 'double-handling'. The handler actually handles the dog in the ring, whilst the owner stands outside the ring at some vantage point, so that the dog hears his master's voice and sees him and continues to watch him with a typical, alert, interested expression.

Some handlers resort to squeeky toys, balls on string and other gimmicks, but this distracts other dogs and is not really a sporting practice and will be heavily penalized by some judges.

The handler who finds it difficult to walk in a straight line should fix his eye on a point at the end of the ring and refrain from looking down at his dog after he has started to gait.

CHAPTER IX

Exhibiting

WIN WITH MODESTY AND LOSE WITH DIGNITY

The exhibitor will find that there are many excitements, heartbreaks and disappointments in exhibiting dogs. Jealousies come in the wake of success and no one who has reached the top will not have encountered all these. However, it is worth remembering that few people will bother to spend time running down a bad dog or a bad kennel. It is generally the successful dogs and and kennels that come in for this treatment.

Nevertheless, exhibiting a beautiful, typical, well-trained dog under a first-class judge can be an exhilarating and rewarding experience, especially if the dog has been bred by the handler. It is important for the novice to be conversant with the etiquette of ring procedure and the idiosyncrasies of individual judges.

A novice exhibitor can learn a great deal from exhibiting even a comparatively poor specimen under a good judge. He will learn to look at his dog in a more critical way and he will appreciate his faults and virtues and from this experience he will know the type of dog he must breed or buy in order to have success in the show ring. Many a successful exhibitor has had to discard his original stock and start again before he became successful.

There are numbers of exhibitors who never breed their own dogs but who enjoy exhibiting and winning with dogs bred by other people. On the other hand, there are keen successful breeders who have little use for the show game and prefer to concentrate on breeding beautiful stock for other people to win with. Undoubtedly, the people who both breed and exhibit enjoy the best of both worlds.

There is certainly a great deal for the novice to learn about exhibiting and the first thing to learn is observation and the next is to keep the eyes and ears open and the mouth shut before it is too late! Observation of dogs, handlers, techniques, exhibitors, breeders and judges cannot be over-stressed. The more a novice observes, the faster he will learn and the quicker he will reach his goal. The path to the top is hard, and full of unforeseen snags. Bad luck is often to be found in bad judgement. Whether an exhibitor wins or loses is not really too important. The importance is that the exhibitor should enjoy showing.

The object of exhibiting should be to improve the breed and not just the winning of a few cups, and cards. Unless an exhibitor truly loves dogs he should turn to another hobby. Too many people hope to make money in showing and breeding dogs. There is no real money in dogs. If someone wants to make money, there are many easier and less time-consuming ways of doing so. However, if you do enjoy the dog game, and very many people do, there is the tremendous pleasure in meeting many people interested in dogs, not only the ones in your chosen breed but all the others in other breeds too. There is always the excitement and anticipation of winning with a really first-class dog at a worth-while show.

Exhibitors can choose their judges, but judges of course cannot choose their exhibitors. A novice should enter under all judges several times, regardless of whether their dogs were placed or not. In this way a novice can observe for himself whether the judge is a good judge or not. It is particularly useful to watch the judge at work in the ring and it soon becomes apparent what particular fetishes a judge may have regarding certain breeds.

Specialist judges are generally breeders and may know only one or two breeds really well. These judges will often judge the dogs on their finer breed points and are frequently a little unbalanced in their judging. The specialist judge is often judging under pressure. He probably knows most of the exhibitors amongst whom he will have enemies and friends. Even if the judge is completely unbiased, if he knows his breed well, he can probably recognize the breeding of certain dogs. Well known kennels with a good strong strain breed dogs with certain dominant traits. One kennel may have dogs with particularly beautiful eyes, or rather small ears or short muzzles and the progeny of these strains are easily recognizable to the expert.

The all-rounder or variety judge started his judging career first as a specialist judge, then progressed to group judging and eventually became promoted to an all-breed judge at championship shows. No judge can know the finer points of all breeds, so that generally speaking the variety judge has a more balanced attitude to judging and probably prefers a typey, sound dog with character. The aim of all exhibitors and breeders is to be able to win with a dog under both the all-rounders and the specialist judges.

The novice will soon learn by experience which judges will not tolerate a bad mouth or small eyes, which judges like large dogs, which pick out the tinies. If a judge puts down a dog which the novice feels should have been placed higher, go under that judge again; but, if the judge does not like that type of dog next time, enter another dog under him. There are many honest judges with differences of opinion, and the exhibitor is showing his dog for a particular judge's honest opinion on the day. Opinion is a matter of interpretation and may be the fly in the ointment. There are dogs which have won toy groups at Cruft's with bad mouths, yet these same dogs would not be placed by another judge at a small open show, simply because of a bad mouth. Unfortunately, there is a great deal of breed politics in exhibiting dogs. The novice has to learn the hard way, just as the well known breeders had to learn in their day. This is the dog game, and everyone in the game was once a novice. Judges often have a difficult time making a decision, when there are several dogs of equal merit in the class. Final decisions are often made on showmanship, when perhaps one dog let up and became bored with the proceedings.

The exhibitor should become familiar with the judge's ring procedure, so that once in the ring he can concentrate on his dog.

ENCOUNTERS WITH THE JUDGE BEFORE JUDGING

Exhibitors often feel embarrassed if they are friends of the judge, and wonder whether to cut the judge, if they pass him in the show before judging. Obviously, it is not a good thing to go up to such a judge, and to carry on an unnecessarily long conversation; but it would be completely in order to pass the time of day, such as saying 'good morning, what a glorious day it is', or perhaps 'I hope the rain will stop', and pass on. Under no circumstances thrust the dog in front of the judge, as if to make certain that he will be able to recognize him when it is in the ring. This behaviour is exceedingly embarrassing for the judge and, if you are friends, he probably knows all your dogs anyhow. A good, honest judge will not be biased one way or the other but such action might possibly rebound, and the judge might give the dog a lower placing than he deserved or no placing at all, which would certainly not be good judging, but might be due to the judge feeling imposed upon.

RING ETIQUETTE

It is obviously extremely bad manners to keep a judge waiting. Ring etiquette demands that exhibitors must not speak to the judge or carry on a conversation with him unless he speaks to them. Unnecessary conversations with a judge can be misconstrued by the spectators and the judge himself. Nervous exhibitors are apt to chatter to the judge. The exhibitors must be polite and considerate to other handlers and their dogs and should not make disparaging remarks about other dogs in the ring. Handlers should not crowd or edge out other exhibitors, or allow their dogs to be aggressive to other exhibits, or to touch another dog. They should not attempt to distract the attention of other exhibits whilst trying to draw the attention of their own dog. Inexcusable examples of this are: by the use of squeaky toys, dropping pieces of paper or food on the floor, stepping back on a dog, letting a dog out on an excessively long lead and in so doing allowing it to embarrass or touch another dog, in mixed classes permitting dogs to sniff bitches, or crowding into the centre of the ring and thus obscuring the judge's view of another exhibit.

It is never done to thank the judge for his placing as he is only doing his duty, but it is much appreciated by the judge if exhibitors thank him for an enjoyable day. Judges should never be thanked when advertising a dog's wins either.

OBSERVE THE JUDGE'S PROCEDURES

No two judges adopt identical methods or judging procedures. Some judges give curt orders such as 'Mouth Please'. This is an order to the handler to show the dog's teeth. 'Age' means the age of the dog which may be given in years or months. It does not mean the age of the handler (as one embarrassed lady thought when I enquired the age of her dog, and was told: 'Forty-seven next birthday'). 'Move' means that the judge requires that the dog should be moved in the same directions that the previous dog was moved. 'Table' means that the judge wishes the dog to be placed on the table to be examined. 'Heads' means that the judge wishes the dogs to be lifted up so that he may examine the heads at close quarters for comparison with the other exhibits. He is not comparing the handlers, but then who knows!

PRIOR TO ENTERING THE RING

As soon as the final show grooming is completed, the dog should be taken for a preliminary warm-up exercise, so that he may relieve himself if necessary, get his bearings and at the same time loosen up his muscles. There should be no excuse for a dog to soil the ring if he has been adequately prepared beforehand. The handler must convey to the dog that the big moment is about to commence; therefore, he must not be allowed to relax too much, nor on the other hand should he be permitted to become over-excited. The handler should call the dog by name and 'collect him up', so that he will be ready to enter the ring in all his glory and raring to go. Toy breeds and a few others are probably better off if they are carried into the ring, particularly if there are a great many spectators hovering around the ring entrance. There is nothing that will put a dog off showing more than being frightened by being stepped on or by getting lost between the spectator's feet. There is also the chance that he will make an unexpected encounter with a rival, which could upset a young, promising and inexperienced dog.

The handler should also take the opportunity to study the lay out of the ring and to pay special attention to any joins or rucks in the matting if it is used. If the ring is on grass, it is useful to notice where the ground is not quite level, so that the dog can be placed to the best advantage. The handler may observe that other dogs perhaps stop to smell an area where another dog may have previously relieved himself. The wise handler will try and avoid the area, and make his run just to one side. The handler will soon learn to stand next to other handlers who do not try to edge their opponents out of line, or deal in underhand, mean and unsporting methods of gaining advantage for their own dog.

THE JUDGING RING

The ring is normally oblong in shape, and its size is determined very often by the size of the breed and the number of the exhibits. It is enclosed by rope and poles. Across one corner there is usually a trestle table and behind this are two chairs, one for the judge and one for a steward. On the front of the table is attached a poster, announcing the name of the judge, for one or each of the dog papers, *Dog World* and *Our Dogs*, depending on whether the judge is writing a report for one or both of the papers. On one corner of the table there may be a bowl of water containing disinfectant and a towel, to enable a judge to wash his hands should he so wish or should he suspect an infection. There will be the judge's judging book, a ball point pen and envelopes containing the prize cards, rosettes and challenge certificates, if there are any to be awarded. Behind and to one side of the table and the two chairs is a blackboard, on which the senior steward must write up the class and the awards and to which he also attaches the judge's initialed award slips. These are used by exhibitors for checking and marking up their catalogues.

RING CARDS

The ring numbers may have been sent to the exhibitors prior to the show or in lieu of entry passes. They are more usually, however, handed out in the ring. All exhibitors must wear the appropriate ring number for the dog which they are handling, and they must remember to change numbers when necessary. Much loss of time and confusion is caused by handlers who forget to change cards, since the judge will enter up the wrong dog in his judging book.

Places to wear numbers

The ring numbers are generally worn securely fixed on the lapel on the left-hand side. It is most important that the card should be visible to the judge and the spectators. Occasionally, cards are worn as arm bands on the left arm. Many Terrier men prefer to sport the ring number in their hat, although in all other breeds it is not normally done for men to wear hats in the ring except the judge. It is much easier for the judge if all the handlers wear their ring numbers in the same place. Some people fix the numbers on to a button on a dress or coat. This is not really a good idea since the cards are often not secure enough and may blow off at a crucial moment. It is therefore wiser to buy a special card clip. The ring number belonging to the winning dogs must be kept, because the handler will be required to wear the dog's number in the variety classes and in the competitions for best of breed, group judging and for best in show, should the exhibit reach such dizzy heights.

On entering the ring, the exhibitor normally goes up to the steward who is handing out the ring numbers. If the classes are large, there is often a queue of handlers waiting to receive their ring numbers. The handler should know the ring number of his exhibit and ask the steward for the corresponding ring card. When he receives this, he must thank the steward, and secure it on his left-hand side in a position easily visible both to the judge and to the spectators.

DOGS EXAMINED ON THE GROUND

If the dogs are to be examined on the ground, they should all be standing facing anti-clockwise round the ring; with the exception of Bulldogs and some other breeds, which are placed facing inwards, whilst Yorkshire Terriers are made to stand on their show cases. In some of the larger breeds it is customary for the handler to stand at the rear of his dog whilst the judge goes over his head and front. The handler changes to the dog's head, when the judge goes over the hindquarters and tail. In breeds where it is the accepted custom to remove leads, this should be done and the leads left tidily and easily accessible, or better still placed in a pocket, so that they can be replaced quickly, ready to gait the dog for the judge.

BREEDS WHICH ARE JUDGED ON THE TABLE

The handler may make his own choice regarding which side of the table he wishes to stand when the judge is going over his dog, and this often depends on whether or not there is already a bowl of water on the table. It is certainly more advantageous for the handler to stand on the inside of the table facing the ring. The dog should be set up so that his forelegs are almost on the edge of the table. This enables the judge to take a good look at the dog as a whole and then to advance towards him from the front, so that he can take the dog's head in both hands and from then on continue to go over him in detail. If the judge and handler are on the same side of the table, it is more complicated for the handler to keep out of the judge's way, particularly if the judge and handler are inclined to be stout. When the judge examines the head, the handler should move to the dog's rear and vice versa. If the handler is on the inside of the table he is at an advantage, since there will be no need for him to move while the judge is going over his dog. When the latter is placed on the ground, he will already be on the handler's left-hand side ready to move off.

Whilst the dog is on the table, the handler should keep his dog under lead control and in full show pose. The slip lead should be well under the jaw, with the end concealed in the hand or slung round the handler's neck. Exceptions to this are breeds exhibited on a loose lead, and the Pekingese, where the swivel lead is kept just under the chin. The dog should not be set up until the judge has told the previous handler to gait his dog for the last time. It is imperative that the handler should keep his hands well out of the way of the judge. He must keep his dog still and never brush him whilst the judge is going over him.

If the handler decides to stand behind the table, it is better for the slip lead to be changed to the right hand. The handler then has the left hand free to support the tail, if necessary, or to deal with an alteration to a hindleg. The lead must never be dropped on the table whilst the judge is going over the dog; it looks untidy, the handler loses control of the dog, and the lead also gets in the way of the dog's feet. When judging any-variety toys, some judges like to have not more than three breeds on a table together. Pekingese classes are judged with all the dogs on the table at the same time, in large classes two or three tables may have to be put end to end. The ends of the table are obviously the two best positions to have, but obviously only two handlers can be clever enough or lucky enough to get these positions. Many toy judges like to pick up the dogs so that they can estimate their weight. If a dog is to be measured or weighed, then this is done when the dog is first placed on the table.

STANDARD OF HANDLING

Dogs must be presented cleanly, and must be correctly handled. Over-handling is considered by some judges to be an insult. The wise handler knows exactly how much handling a judge will tolerate and he will not overstep the mark, as he knows that this would be penalized. The clever, experienced handler also knows which judges penalize brushes and titbits and squeaky toys in the ring. Some judges seem to tolerate anything, whilst other judges are much more severe, and contravention might result in the loss of an important win or even a best in show.

The standard of handling could be much improved in some breeds. There is no magic in handling and training a dog. It has all been accomplished by experience, observation and hard work and there are no short cuts. Handlers should develop a brisk, professional style, one which is most suitable for their age, figure and breed, and which gets the most out of their dog without showing off and detracting from the merits of the dog.

Clever handlers know what to do and when to do it with the minimum of fuss. They also know how to keep their dog cool, by standing so that their shadow shades the dog on exceptionally hot days. They know the judge's fetishes. As an example, some judges of Maltese have been known to make a song and dance as to whether the top-knots were plaited in two braids or one braid, or left loose with one bow, two bows or none and have judged the dogs accordingly, penalizing whichever they disliked. They should have been judging the dogs and not their individual preference of hair styles. Nevertheless it does happen.

FACE THE SAME DIRECTION

Judges prefer that all exhibits should face in the same direction as that in which the dogs moved round the ring, that is, in an anti-clockwise direction. If all the exhibits are set up facing the same way, it makes judging very much easier for the judge when he compares the dogs in the line-up. Some breeds are exceptions to this custom, such as the Bulldog, where exhibits are faced inwards towards the centre of the ring. Pekingese are placed on a table together, whilst Yorkshire Terriers are placed on their individual boxes in the ring, all facing in the normal direction.

THE LINE UP

The exhibitors should stand in line one behind the other, keeping well to the side of the ring. They should also try to remain equidistant from each other, so that each dog and handler can have their required 'pecking distance'. Handlers should not, however, stand directly at the end of the ring where they would be in the way of individual dogs being gaited.

From the moment that a dog enters the ring, he is liable to be summed up by the judge, and so it is important to keep the dog alert. He should not be permitted to sniff another exhibit nor to touch one, nor upset a rival in any way. As soon as the dogs are assembled, the judge will take his place in the centre of the ring and will stand back to scrutinize all the exhibits whilst they are standing. It must be remembered that no two judges will adopt identical methods and procedures. It is important, therefore, that the handlers should watch the judge carefully, so that when their turn comes, they will know exactly what they are expected to do.

The judge will probably ask all the handlers to move their dogs round the ring one behind the other making several circuits. This warms the dogs up, and they realize that judging has started.

THE JUDGE GOES OVER THE INDIVIDUAL DOGS

After the handlers and dogs have completed one or two laps of the ring the judge will call a halt. If the breed is to be examined on the table, the handler nearest the judging table will be asked to place his dog on it. The procedure for the judge going over the dog is identical, whether it is on the table or on the ground.

The judge will allow time for the handler to stack the dog. Most judges will stand back and scrutinize the dog as a whole from a short distance, first from the front and then from the side. When he goes over the dog in detail, he will start with the front. He will probably look first at the head, the ear placement and leathers, the depth of stop, the colour, size and shape of the eyes, and, in some breeds, the pigmentation of the rims of the eyes, and also the nose. The mouth will be examined by lifting up the lips, and the set of the teeth and the formation of the jaw will all be noticed. It is better if the handler opens the dog's mouth, because infections are less liable to be spread.

The length of neck will be noted and the judge will probably feel the shoulder placement, rib cage, depth of chest, whether the six vertebrae of the back are straight and parallel to the ground, the length and strength of loin, the angle of the croup, the depth of the flank, the set of tail and any tail idiosyncrasies. Then the judge is likely to feel the strength of the muscles of the hind-quarters and note the turn of stifle and the angulation and the let-down of the hock and whether the hind pasterns are vertical. The length of leg and bone structure and the shape of the feet and pads are often important. The judge may wish to lift a foreleg and observe how well the leg returns to position. In this manoeuvre the hardness of the pads and the length of nails are also noted. The condition, colour, and texture of the coat are all taken into consideration. The judge will be looking for soundness, quality and most important of all, the judge will be assessing type and temperament. Other qualities looked for by the judge will be balance, style, condition, harmony and beauty. The judge will pay special attention to characteristic breed points. For example, a judge going over a Yorkshire Terrier will examine the coat by using a brush, which will be provided by each dog's handler. He will lift the coat up carefully so as to observe the tan marking. This should be darker at the roots than in the middle and lighter at the tips. If the coat has been dyed it will all be of one colour. The dark steel blue from occiput to tail must not be mingled with fawn, bronze or dark hairs.

The fashion at the moment in the breed at the championship shows is for the handler to use a silver-backed brush. The judge, however, is not interested in such details; he is only examining the coat. He also examines idiosyncrasies and breed characteristics such as wrinkles, padding, dewlap, trace, colour of nails, lozenge, length of tail, size of ears, and length of breeches and petticoats, etc. Handlers know at once if the judge really knows the finer points of the dog he is going over.

MOVING THE DOG

As soon as the judge has examined the dog thoroughly, including whether or not he is 'entire' in the case of a male, he will next wish to see the dog move. If necessary, take him down from the table gently, allow him to shake and even to sneeze before starting to move him. Whether the dog has been examined on the ground or on the table, collect him up with a word of command and proceed to gait him in the direction that the judge has indicated. This is probably the most important moment that the exhibitor has paid for. The handler must emphatically therefore make the most of this opportunity, which is the longest time that the judge will watch his dog individually.

The judge will ask the handler to move his dog so that his action can be assessed from the rear and from the front and possibly also from the side. There are nine ways in which a judge may ask a handler to move his dog. Method three and four are most usually adopted by the majority of judges.

METHODS OF MOVING A DOG IN THE RING

1. Straight up and down the centre of the ring.
2. Straight up and down the side of the ring.
3. Diagonally across the ring and back.
4. In a triangle, starting up the side of the ring across to the left hand corner and back to the starting point.
5. In a triangle starting from the middle of the side nearest the judge, across to the right-hand far corner, along the top to the opposite corner and back to the starting point.
6. Up the centre of the ring turning left to the end, about turn, and straight back to the right-hand top corner of the ring, thus describing a letter 'T', back to the centre of the 'T', sharp left and back down the centre of the ring to the judge.
7. Up the right side of the ring to the corner, left turn to the far corner, about turn to the end and return down the side of the ring to the judge.
8. Straight across the ring and back to the line of dogs.
9. A complete circle of the ring.

In methods 2, 3, 4 and 7 the judge will be standing in the bottom right-hand corner of the ring, in methods 1, 5 and 6 he will be standing in the centre of one end of the ring, whilst in methods 8 and 9 the judge will be standing in the centre of the ring.

The judge chooses and adopts the method according to his own preference, the breed he is judging and the size of the ring. The number of dogs in a class may also be a deciding factor. Where the classes are large and time is at a premium, I personally prefer to stand in the centre at

Nine methods for gaiting

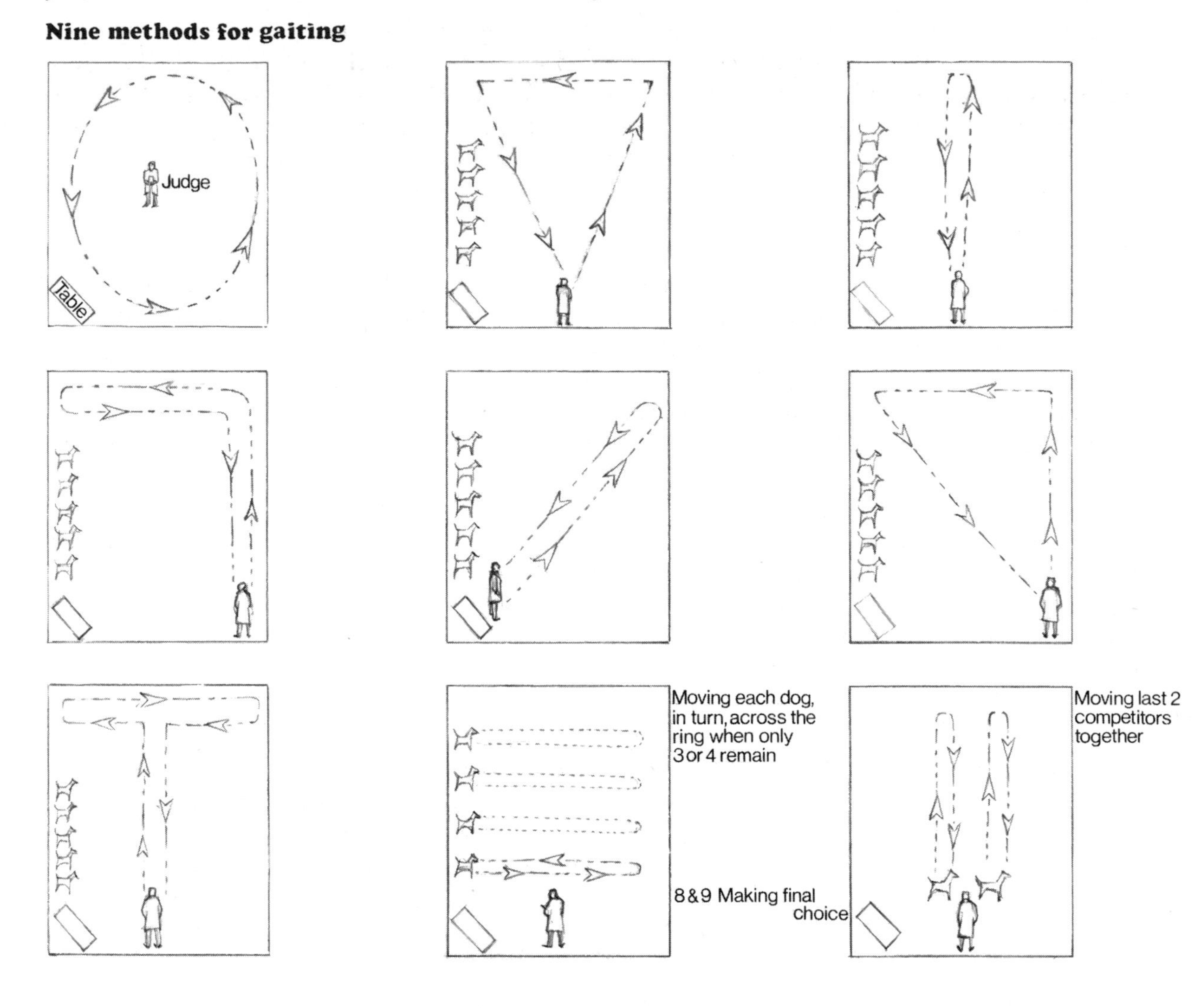

the bottom of the ring and to ask the handler first to move his dog straight up and down the centre of the ring, then diagonally across the ring to the right-hand top corner, along the top of the ring and back to me, thus forming a triangle. In this method the movement of the dog can be observed from three aspects.

The judge will expect that, whenever the dog is moved, he should be kept on the side of the handler nearest the judge, for obvious reasons. This is simple with the procedures for the straight-up-and-down or triangular method. For the 'T' method, however, it is a little more complicated. Since the dog will have to be changed from the handler's left-hand side at least twice, in order to keep him at all times in full view of the judge. The handler should move the dog at the correct gait, in a straight line up the centre of the ring and away from the judge, with the dog on his left-hand side. At the end of the ring the handler must turn sharp left and continue to the end of the ring. The handler should then turn so that the dog is on his right-hand side and should continue moving to the end of the ring. The handler once again turns, bringing the dog to his left-hand side, until he reaches the centre of the 'T', where he will turn at right angles again and proceed down the centre of the ring in a straight line towards the judge with the dog still on his left-hand side.

The handler should always start off walking with the foot nearest the dog and, when he reaches a point about a yard from the judge, the dog should be halted and his attention attracted, so that the dog is being shown alert and in full show stance. Luckily, method 'T' is not often used, because it is the most complicated way of moving a dog and does not, in my opinion show the exhibit to its best advantage. There are too many stops and turns in the 'T' method. When this method is used it is essential, moreover, that the ring should be sufficiently large.

Another method, which is often adopted when the ring is wide enough, is for the judge to go over each dog individually, when they are all lined up on one side of the ring. After going over the dog in the usual way and viewing him from the far side, the judge asks the handler to move his dog straight across the ring and back again. The judge then moves down the line of dogs, making each in turn move across the ring and back to his original position.

SEEN DOGS

As soon as the judge has finished examining the first exhibit the handler will be directed by a steward or by the judge to stand in the corner of the ring furthest away from the table, starting the line of the 'seen' dogs. The other handlers automatically join this line as soon as the judge has examined their dogs and must stand in the identical positions between the same exhibitors as previously, standing on the left of the leader.

If a class is large, then the wise handler will allow his dog to relax, since the judge will be fully occupied going over the other dogs. Toy breeds may be picked up and held in the arms. This is often the time when exhibitors gossip with one another. The serious handler will not indulge in this practice, because he should be fully alert watching the judge and also observing the movement and other show points of his fellow competitors. The handler must also be on the alert for the moment when to put his dog on the ground again, and from then on he should watch the judge as well as his dog.

JUDGES' PLACINGS

As soon as the judge has finished his individual examinations, the handlers must place their dogs in full show pose, according to the breed: whether, for instance, they are 'stacked' as for American Cocker Spaniels, 'stretched' for Setters, 'strung up' for Terriers, or left in a natural stance for many of the other breeds. The judge will look at each dog closely and will probably move the dogs he likes most to the top of the line in the order in which he likes them. If there is a previous class, he will line up the new dogs below them. Occasionally, judges prefer to place them above the previous class or he may line them up in front of them.

Many judges will then judge these two classes together, make the final line up with the exhibits still at the side of the ring, and they may then ask the exhibitors to move their dogs round the ring one final time before they make their ultimate decision. The handlers will be stopped, when the first one reaches a position near the table. The judge will then decide his placings one by one, and he will 'pull out' at least five and probably seven dogs so that they stand in the centre of the ring.

The dog placed first should always be on the left of the line-up as seen by the judge. Very often the judge may alter his placings by requesting a handler to move up or down this final line. In cases where there are several outstanding exhibits the judge may ask that two or more dogs be moved together, or, in the case of small breeds, he may ask the handlers to lift them up so that heads may be compared. Finally, the judge makes his placing in order of merit. It occasionally occurs in large classes of mixed sexes that a judge may decide to split the sexes for the convenience of judging. If this is done, a judge must select the same number of each sex as there are prizes and awards offered for the class. He must then judge all these dogs and bitches against each other for the final placings. The placed dogs, if judged first, must wait in the ring until the bitches have been placed, so that both may then be judged together for the final awards.

PROCEDURE FOR PEKINGESE

Pekingese are judged differently from the other breeds. A variety judge may ask the handlers to walk round the ring in the normal manner, but the specialist judge generally asks the handler to bring his dog out from the line of dogs. The handler should pick up his dog and carry it to the judge, who will then probably ask him to move the dog up and down the ring. The handler should put his dog on the ground, if necessary adjust his coat or tail with a brush, and then proceed slowly and carefully up and down the ring in a straight line with the dog on his left-hand side. As soon as the handler reaches the judge, he should pick up the dog and present him to the judge. The judge may just look at his head, but others prefer to take the dog from the handler and then will hand him back. The judge next directs the handler to place his dog on the table. When all the dogs have been seen and are on the table, the judge will examine them in turn. The handlers must make the most of their dogs by lifting up their manes with a brush and touching up their feathering. The judge will probably select five or six dogs from the table. The handlers of these will then place them in line on the ground on a slack lead and attract their attention. The judge may ask the handlers of these dogs to move again or he may just indicate his first dog, whose handler will automatically place his exhibit in the first place at the end of the table. The others will follow in order of merit. When all the remaining dogs are again on the table, and the handlers have refurbished them, making the head as flat and wide as possible, the judge will tap the table with his finger in front of one dog and then another, indicating them to change places to a higher or lower position. The other handlers have to move up or down the table in order to make room for the change of positions. The judge may make one or two more taps on the table until he has made his final decisions in order of merit. The handlers will probably finally be asked by the judge to place their dogs on the ground in the centre of the ring in the same order as they were chosen on the table.

AWARDS

It is not until the judging book is marked up by the judge and the handlers are actually holding the prize cards in their hands, that they can be absolutely certain of the judge's final decisions. Some judges have the irritating habit of juggling their placings and playing to the crowd. This is seldom good judging. As soon as the judge has decided on his order, the steward announces the placed dogs in a loud voice by calling out their ring numbers in order of merit. The judge enters up the numbers as they are announced in his judging book. At the same time the steward hands out the prize cards which often have a monetary prize in an envelope attached to each. If there should be rosettes, these will be presented at the same time. The judge will require the first, second, third and perhaps the fourth handlers to remain in their positions, until he has written up the critique of each dog in the judging book.

The first prize winner in the open classes should be congratulated by the runner-up before they move off; and the reserve best of opposite sex winner must always shake hands with the best of breed winner.

THE NEXT CLASS

Should the dog be entered in a subsequent class, whether he has been placed or not, the handler will be expected to move over to the furthest corner of the ring, as directed by the steward. The 'seen' line of dogs must stand in the order of their placings in the previous class. Here the handler may relax with his dog, until the judge has completed judging the dogs in the new class and has placed them too in order of merit. As soon as the judge is going over the last dogs of the new class, the handlers of the dogs which have already been seen must 'collect' up their dogs and stand them in full show pose. The judge will now bring the two sets of dogs together and will start comparing them whilst they are still lined up at the edge of the ring. He may place them in order and then see them all gait together. The judge will probably select seven or eight dogs before he makes his final placings. In the meantime, if the class is large, the judge may wish to excuse the other handlers and their dogs.

The steward generally tells the exhibitors with a charming smile that they may leave the ring, as they will all be disappointed not to have been awarded a card. A friendly smile can work wonders. The handlers should leave the ring with dignity and without showing any signs of disappointment. The judge will then proceed to select his final winners.

It should go without saying that no handler, however disappointed he may be regarding his placing, should ever show his ill feeling and bad manners by tearing up his card in the ring or, worse still, handing back the card to the judge. The Kennel Club could easily stop such offenders by suspending them for a period of three months. It is perfectly permissible for an exhibitor whose dog was placed below the two top dogs, to ask the judge what he thought of his dog, after the breed judging is finished. Winning dogs will have a report in the dog papers, and their owners should wait to see the judge's opinion in print.

ORDER OF PROCEDURE FOR TOP AWARDS

The judging in the open classes is identical to that in all the preceding classes. The winner of open dog or open bitch is placed in the centre of the ring, and the runner-up must remain at the side of the ring, unless he has been beaten in a previous class. The judge then, in fact, has the option as to whether all unbeaten dogs come forward or not; but most judges feel, quite rightly, that it is only fair that all unbeaten dogs should be given the kudos of parading in the ring with the winner, even if the judge has already himself decided on the winner.

UNBEATEN DOGS

Provided the judge wishes to see all the unbeaten dogs, the steward then calls for 'All unbeaten dogs in the ring please'. The handlers of all these dogs should be standing near the ring entrance with their dogs groomed and ready. The same will apply to the bitch classes and they must make certain that they are wearing the correct ring number for the dog they are handling. Occasionally, a handler may have several dogs unbeaten so that they will have to find other handlers to gait their dogs round the ring. If the dogs are not used to the adopted handler, the real one may take over each dog for the judge to go over and they will also gait the dog themselves, the assistants each time exchanging dogs. Afterwards, the dog will be handed back to the original assistant. If the dog is finally selected by the judge for best dog or bitch, the real handler will handle the dog from then on.

The best puppy, as long as he was not beaten in a subsequent class, will be brought forward together with any unbeaten dogs. The judge will ask the handlers to gait their dogs round the ring. He may possibly require them to move up and down the ring together, or two at a time, and he may even wish to refresh his memory as to the dog's bite or any other breed idiosyncrasies. The winner of these dogs is 'pulled out' into the centre of the ring and is awarded the challenge certificate (CC). The previous runner up to this winner will then be brought into the ring, and the judge will decide which dog is his reserve best of sex (sometimes erroneously called the reserve CC). These two winning dogs will normally parade round the ring, or only the winner will be asked to do so.

The dog classes are invariably judged before the bitch classes and the procedure is identical for both.

SPECIAL PRIZES

Clubs at large shows often offer special prizes, either donated by club members or individuals. These prizes may be spoons, trophies or even cash prizes or extra rosettes. Many exhibitors enjoy collecting perhaps a set of winning spoons. It is worth a novice perusing a catalogue just to see if there are any special prizes being presented at that particular show. It is not necessary to have won a first prize, because the first prize winner may not be a member of the club and so would not be eligible for the prize. If this is the case the judge will be told and the entry will be made in the judging book. Sometimes novices are unaware that they were entitled to a prize and it simply disappears. This is particularly sad, when the novice would be absolutely thrilled to have won a prize, whereas in later years the thrill has gone out of winning and the prize may be considered just as one more cup to clean!

BEST OF BREED

Finally, the judge must award the best of breed, and the best dog and the best bitch parade round the ring. The judge then proclaims the winner. The best of breed winner is entitled to go forward to the group judging, under another judge if this is to take place, or best in show, provided that the dog has not been beaten in a variety class. If a dog has been entered in a variety class, then he must be exhibited in such a class even though there is a high risk of his being beaten. The chances are that the group judging will be by another judge. The winner of the group then goes forward for the judging of best in show, and the runner-up must be prepared to stand by in the best in show ring.

BEST IN SHOW

The eligible winners of each group will stand in the ring with the runners-up standing behind them. There may be two judges for best in show, with a judge appointed as referee in case the two judges should not agree. The judges will go over the dogs in the normal manner. The dogs will parade round the ring, and the judges will make their selection for the dog which is to be best in show, and the dog will be brought forward to stand in the centre of the ring. The runner-up to the best in show winner is brought forward in line with the group winners, and the judges then select the reserve best in show. The best in show dog will parade round one circuit of the ring, which is called the 'lap of honour', and occasionally the dog may be adorned afterwards with a sash of honour. This is followed by the formal presentation of the best in show trophies.

CONGRATULATING THE WINNERS

It is extremely unsportsmanlike and very bad form, regardless of an exhibitor's personal feelings on a judge's placings, not to congratulate the winners. In all classes, those placed second and third should congratulate the winner whilst they are still in the ring. It is not done generally to shake the hand of the winner's handler. Only the handler of the reserve best of show does so. For the top awards in breed classes, all those in the final line up should also congratulate the winner and, if possible, the second and third placings too. All breed exhibitors should make an effort some-time during the show to congratulate the winners of the challenge certificates and best of breed winner.

RINGSIDE APPLAUSE

It is very easy for people at the ringside to pre-judge the dogs in loud voices, and to criticize a judge's placings; but it should be remembered that what the spectators see is by no means what the judge sees and feels when examining a dog at close quarters. The spectators, for instance, cannot see whether the dog has a good mouth or not, nor what goes on under a thick and heavy coat.

The spectators should be sporting enough to give applause to the winning dog, even if they do not agree with the judge's decision. It is exceedingly bad form to show disapproval of a judge's placings by refraining from clapping, by clapping the second and third placings and omitting the first, by making loud exclamations, or by any other method of showing disapproval, from slow handclapping to complete silence.

It is astonishing how catching an act like slow clapping catches on with the spectators, the majority of them not even knowing why they are doing so, but following the others like a lot of silly sheep. It is better to sway the sheep with vigorous and generous handclaps, than to be mean and unkind. After all, dog showing is meant to be a sport and everyone should enjoy themselves.

OBSERVE THE WINNING DOGS

However disappointed a handler may be in not winning a class or in not even being placed, he should never move off 'in a huff' with unseeing eyes. It is better by far to study the dogs which beat his exhibit, and to look at other breeders' dogs with dispassionate eyes, and to try to see why the judge preferred the other dogs. An intelligent handler or breeder can learn a great deal by observing other breeders' stock. Do not look for their faults but look quite calmly for their outstanding points. Gradually, the novice will eventually get 'an eye' for a good dog, and this is when a first-class stud dog can be chosen to bring in the points required to improve a line. Some owners are kennel blind, and really cannot bring themselves to see the faults in their own stock. A few are the reverse, and are so hyper-critical that they only see their own dog's faults and forget all they have put into the breed to obtain their outstanding features. The more a breeder or handler studies a breed and the more breeds he handles, studies and judges, the more knowledgeable he will become.

WHEN BREED JUDGING IS FINISHED

Many judges are doing a hard day's work for nothing or perhaps only for a very small remuneration. It is therefore much appreciated by judges if their work and skill is appreciated by the exhibitors. Most judges are only too pleased if the winners do spare a moment or two and go up to the judge quietly and perhaps thank him for their enjoyable day, and they might like to add that they were thrilled that the judge liked their dog so much. If the exhibitor is a novice and the win is her very first, the judge receives some satisfaction that perhaps he has launched yet another new exhibitor on his way.

If an exhibitor wishes to speak to the judge about his dog, then it is imperative that he should wait patiently until the judge has finished writing his notes and thanked his stewards. The judge may sit in the chair by the table resting his weary legs. This is the time that an exhibitor might ask one of the stewards to ask the judge if he could spare a few moments. Most judges are perfectly happy to comply, provided that the handler genuinely wants to learn and does not set about asking ridiculous questions. The exhibitor should think out carefully what he wants to ask the judge and then do so quietly, concisely and simply. He must, however, be satisfied with the judge's answers. The judge will not permit the conversation to deteriorate into an argument or a discussion. The exhibitor should never tell the judge that such-and-such a judge had given his dog high awards previously. He will only get a curt obvious answer to such a stupid remark. Nevertheless, it is confusing for the novice when a champion dog will win best of breed under an all-round judge and one week later the same dog under a specialist judge, in perfect condition, will be placed bottom in the open class of twenty dogs, most of whom he beat the previous week. This is known as breed 'politics' judging, and has to be accepted as part of the dog game.

The same kind of thing occurs in show reports, when one judge will remark, 'lovely head, moved soundly' the next says 'would prefer a finer head, movement will improve with age, elbows need tightening'. It is a matter of opinion on the day and some judges have quite frightening opinions!

FOLLOWING A JUDGE FROM SHOW TO SHOW

Many novices, after having won well under a particular judge at a show, erroneously feel that they should follow the judge from show to show wherever he is judging. Surprisingly, this is not considered a wise thing to do. The novice will often find to his astonishment that the next time he is under that judge, with the same dog, he may not even be placed at all. The dog will have other dogs to compete against whom he has never met previously. Some judges resent exhibitors following them around with the same dog hoping for more wins. What the novice should do is to enter another dog under the judge. If there is a promising puppy take that one under the judge. There is nothing a judge likes better than launching a promising puppy on his show career.

A puppy put up at a show under a well-known judge will often get away to a flying start, as other judges are often influenced by the opinion of a first-class judge.

A novice must not be taken in by judges who tout for entries saying how much they like a particular dog and indicating 'if you show under me. . . .' The chances are that such a judge, when the time comes, will not even place the dog at all.

A judge, who has perhaps done an exhibitor well, will always appreciate that exhibitor for giving him a courtesy entry with a nice dog, but not one with which he hopes to win top awards. Nice brood bitches are useful for these entries. They may not be good enough to become champions, perhaps, because of their size, but they may well produce better offspring than the champions. Breeders see the type and may well consider buying in a puppy when he has some These bitches are also useful to enter under a novice judge or a variety judge who is perhaps judging the breed for the first time. Obviously, well-known breeders would not be too happy with such judges practising on their champions. On the other hand, there is no need for the exhibitor to insult the judge by entering a really poor specimen. Some exhibitors will give a courtesy entry of several dogs, but not actually go to the show.

Judges always appreciate support from exhibitors. Everyone cannot win all the time every time, but with a good dog and perseverance his day will come.

It is a curious fact that once a dog or a team of dogs from a kennel start to win in the show ring they will go on winning and winning, although the same dogs may have been exhibited for a year with no spectacular wins at all. When a kennel has a run of luck then the dogs should be exhibited under as many different judges as possible.

There is much controversy about the ethics of taking a recently made-up champion to every possible show in order for the exhibitor to be able to boast that the dog has won the record number of challenge certificates in the breed. This may be a marvellous accomplishment; but on the other hand, if there is an excellent dog also doing the same circuit of shows, and he is always just pipped by the champion—particularly if the dog perhaps needs only one more certificate to 'make him up'—I feel that a sporting exhibitor should stand down and not show his dog until the other one is made up too. Many greedy people mutter about 'cheap champions'. It certainly does not mean necessarily that an inferior dog is becoming a champion.

Sometimes a dog may do a tremendous amount of winning and beat a rival dog more often than not over a period. Then suddenly comes a chance bit of luck. The other dog gets put up at an important show by a world-renowned judge and it seems that from that moment on all the other judges follow suit and the rival will never beat him again. This of course is all the luck of the dog game.

QUICK GUIDE TO SHOWING

Do give the dog a suppository before leaving home.
Do arrive at the show in good time.
Do exercise the dog before benching.
Do keep an eye on the dog all day, and see that he is comfortable.
Do keep the dog's bench chain short.
Do hang the bench card correctly.
Do find the show ring and check the time of judging.
Do exercise the dog before entering the ring.
Do ensure that the dog and handler are immaculately turned out.
Do take as little as possible into the ring.
Do get to the ringside in good time.
Do remember to wear the correct ring number for the dog you are showing.
Do know your ring number and the age of the exhibit.
Do stand in line at the edge of the ring.
Do ascertain that the slip lead is tight enough and under the angle of the jaw.
Do keep the surplus lead well concealed in the hand, or round the fingers.

Do not cut the corners when gaiting the dog.
Do keep the dog between you and the judge at all times.
Do set up the dog at the end of the table.
Do keep an eye on the judge all the time.
Do keep the dog alert and attentive at the appropriate times.
Do hold the bait at the correct height for the individual dog.
Do allow the dog to relax when the judge is occupied.
Do 'collect' the dog up in good time.
Do get the sparkle in your dog, don't let him look like a puppet on a string.
Do what the judge asks.
Do be 'on the ball', and concentrate.
Do be a good looser and a gracious winner.
Do congratulate the winners.
Do remember that the reserve best of sex handler shakes hands with the winner.
Do accept congratulations graciously.
Do always take a winning dog into the group and best in show rings.

DO ENJOY THE SHOW

Do not arrive late in the ring, and, if you do, apologize to the judge quietly.
Do not come in with a flurry after the judging is nearly finished.
Do not allow the end of the lead to trail on the ground, or table.
Do not mask another dog.
Do not 'crowd' the judge.
Do not step on another dog.
Do not allow your dog to touch another dog.
Do not allow a long end of the lead to swing about in the air when gaiting a dog.
Do not allow your dog out on a long lead.
Do not show off your dog at the expense of another exhibit.
Do not call a famous dog by name within earshot of the judge.
Do not speak to the judge unless spoken to.
Do not go into the ring armed with brushes and squeaky toys. Some judges may penalize these.
Do not carry previous prize cards ostentatiously in the ring.
Do not wear rosettes in the ring except for the best in show judging.
Do not move to a place higher than the judge has ordered.
Do not move into the centre of the ring when the judge has called another exhibitor.
Do not look too triumphant nor too dejected in the ring.
Do not tear up a prize card in pique, nor hand a card back to the judge or steward.
Do not make loud disparaging remarks about the judging.
Do not boast.
Do not take previous trophies up to the secretary's table whilst the judge is sitting at the table waiting to judge, announcing at the same time that your dog has won the cup twice before and if he wins it this time it will be yours for keeps!
Do not ever slap a dog in the ring: it is generally unnecessary and gives a most undesirable impression.
Do remember that the judge cannot choose the handler, but the exhibitors can always choose the judges.
Do not follow a judge you have just won under from show to show with the same dog.

CHAPTER X

Advertising, Show Photographs and Dinners

ADVERTISING

Anyone who takes up dog breeding and showing seriously will soon realize how important it is to win well at the shows. It is also important to follow up all wins by advertising. Keen followers of the dog game devour the weekly dog papers, reading them assiduously from cover to cover. Until the award of challenge certificates and champions has been published by the Kennel Club Gazette, advertisements relating to these awards should add the words, 'Subject to Kennel Club Approval'.

Winning dogs will appear in print in the judge's critiques and, if this is followed up by a good show-posed photograph, the impact of winning will be so much the greater. Obviously, the more a kennel's dogs win, and the more often a prefix appears in print, the better known a kennel becomes. Eventually, the kennel may be so well known that its prefix becomes synonymous with its breed or breeds. When this illustrious stage is reached, the kennel can keep going profitably for quite a period without advertising at all.

Regular advertising is, of course, expensive, but, provided that the stock is outstanding, it is the best possible way of ensuring the sale of all puppies, whether at home or abroad, and of becoming well known in the dog world. Advertisements which head the breed note columns always pay dividends, provided, of course, that there is sufficient stock to warrant the expense. Full page coverage in the two Christmas Annuals is also an excellent investment, although half a page or a third of a page is also useful. Advertising in the Kennel Gazette under the breed headings is almost essential, if a kennel is to become well known.

The choice of a prefix is extremely important. The best prefixes are short and easy to pronounce. It is sometimes a good idea to relate the prefix title to the breed, but this is only good provided that the breeder does not go into another breed at a later date.

A campaign of advertising should be planned in detail at the beginning of each year. Decide which photographs and blocks are to be used. Full page coverage in one annual and the advertisement above the breed notes would cost at the present time about £125. Another twenty-five pounds should be allotted to special advertisements for interim wins. Photographs should be taken in good time, because there will be a rush at the last moment before closing time for advertisements. Two or three breeders may care to club together for one visit by a photographer. Breed handbooks and catalogues are other ways of advertising. Regular advertising in the Cruft's issue of *The Field* and *Country Life* are also well worth doing. Sometimes these advertisements may not pay off for some time. I once sold a dog from such an advertisement two years afterwards. The buyer saw the advertisement at the hairdresser's. Advertisements in local papers and certain magazines may also pay dividends, depending on the time of year. Experience will prove that certain days are decidedly better than others for advertisements.

PHOTOGRAPHERS

The best dog photographs are generally taken by the top animal photographers. These photographic specialists are well worth the extra expense involved. Not only will they be able to take a better photograph of a particular dog, because they have special animal experience, but these people also have a great deal of patience. There is another great advantage in going to a well-known photographer, and that is because they themselves are well known. The press will often ask them for photographs of a particular breed, and, if your dog happens to be in their files, then the chances are that that dog will get into the press. Even if the dog is not named in the article, it is surprising how readers can find out who bred the dog, and from such photographs come more sales.

PHOTOGRAPHS

It is quite a good idea if several breeders club together and book a photographer to take photographs of their dogs at one session. This saves a tremendous amount of time for the photographer and becomes much cheaper for the individual breeders. They can assist each other in posing their dogs and in keeping them alert. Another way of saving money on photographs is to arrange for a particular photographer to take special photographs at one of the outdoor shows. Sometimes photographers advertise that they will be taking photographs for the Christmas Annuals of *Dog World* and *Our Dogs.* So many breeders leave the important photography of their dogs to the very last moment. They are then bitterly disappointed when the photographers cannot deliver the photographs in time so that the advertiser may receive the five per cent discount, which the dog papers generously allow if the advertisement copy is in by a certain early date.

Before embarking on the expense of dog photographs, it is well worth while studying good photographs of the breed involved. It is a great help to the photographer if the breeder knows what they want, and can pose their dog in the correct stance. It really requires a second person to attract the dog's attention and to make certain that he is standing correctly, and has not moved a leg out of place. Although animal photographers may know a great deal about a number of breeds, they may be more interested in the correct photographic technique rather than in the correct angulation of the legs or set of the tail, which could be very important in the breed concerned. Another point to remember is that, the better the camera, the less leeway there is for mistakes in accurate focusing. It is therefore, essential that the dog should be made to stand in a certain place and in the correct stance for each pose, so that all four legs are seen in the photograph. The second assistant can be a tremendous help to the photographer if he knows how to position the correct stance for the breed and how to attract the dog's attention, so that the show points that are required to be portrayed are shown to the best advantage. Many a beautiful photograph has been ruined by untidy lead ends spoiling the outline of the dog. The handler and assistant must remember that what the photographer sees through his lens, is not what the handler is seeing standing perhaps two or three feet to the side of the dog, nor what the assistant sees. So many photographs of dogs may be spoilt by the handler holding the bait or squeaky toy too high or at the wrong angle. The dog is then not portrayed in a natural stance with his head in the normal balanced position. There are a number of ways of attracting a dog; either with food, squeaky toys, or any sudden and interesting noise, or by a third person playing antics in front of the dog. A dog quickly becomes bored and most noises and antics will only attract him the first time. For head studies and certain positions the assistant should hold something beneath the camera to attract the dog's attention, but great care must be taken not to obstruct the lens with an arm or a hand. The attention of a greedy dog can easily be attracted by food, but some times this can backfire, and instead of getting a large, soft-eyed, doey expression, the photograph comes out with a pop-eyed 'greedy cheese' expression.

Breeds that require large, round eyes (for example Chihuahuas), are invariably better portrayed by flash photography. Frequently these breeds have eyes which are ultra-sensitive to light and instead of being wide open, the dogs appear in the photograph to have little, slit, almond-shaped eyes. Breeds that require small eyes are probably better not photographed by flash lights.

There are hints for some breeds which are useful to know, particularly the breeds which will have their mouth open at the crucial moment and pant with their tongues hanging out. If a fraction of a second before the photograph is taken, the handler or assistant can use a freshly cut lemon and just draw it over the tongue, the dog will automatically shut his mouth. Perhaps then, the perfect photograph can be taken.

It is horrifying how many superb photographs are spoilt by the handler forgetting to conceal the lead in the hand, allowing the lead to trail on the ground, or using too thick and cumbersome a lead and collar. Sometimes leads look as if they are coming out of the dog's mouth or ear, or even appear like an extra leg or tail. A good idea, if a lead is necessary, is to make a lead out of a length of fishing line with a clip fastener on one end and a loop on the other. If a slip lead is required, then the collar part of an ordinary slip lead could be used, attached to a length of fishing line. In this way the lead is almost invisible in the photograph, or could easily be obliterated by clever 'touching up'.

Thought must be given to a good background, and it is also important that the handler's or assistant's shadow should not be in the photograph. Many an excellent photograph is spoilt by the handler's fat legs being seen behind the dog. It is also necessary to keep each photographic session short, no longer than five or ten minutes at a time. A break for a cup of tea will prevent not only the photographer and handler becoming tired, but will also prevent the dog from becoming bored and despondent. It so often happens that after a whole day's photography, it is the last photograph that is the best, or the first. It is not unknown, even with the best of photographers, for a whole session to be wasted owing to a technical camera fault. When this occurs have pity on the photographer.

Photographing dogs is extremely tiring for photographer, handlers, assistants and dogs. The photographers know what they are doing and so do most dogs. It is so often the handlers who have not given the photographic session sufficient thought, and it is frequently their fault if the photographs are not what they had anticipated.

Many dog owners see their dogs through rose-tinted spectacles and literally will not believe that their dogs have any major faults. Obviously such faults appearing in photographs are not well received.

OCCASIONAL ADVERTISEMENTS

It is not worth while for a small kennel to advertise extensively, because it is time-consuming to have to answer endless enquiries when there is no stock for sale. The dog papers have advertisement space under various breeds. It is an excellent idea to advertise regularly in these columns. It is reasonably cheap and keeps a kennel prefix before the eyes of the dog fraternity. The advertisements can be placed in each paper on alternate weeks, or once a month, or just when there is stock for sale.

As soon as a kennel is well known, it becomes only necessary to advertise occasionally, making the most of past wins. One can live off the reputation of a challenge certificate at Cruft's for quite a few years!

Each kennel should try to work out the number of puppies that they expect to sell in any one year, and, if this is then totalled up, it would probably be found that about one tenth of the proceeds of the puppy sales should be spent on advertising.

PRE-SHOW DINNERS

I have never attended these events, but breeders who go to them, and the judges who also attend them, find them a great attraction and no doubt they can be great fun and most amusing. It can sometimes be awkward when a judge finds himself sitting next to a breeder who will be showing her breed under him, the following day. Not that this should make any difference to a good judge, however, but should the breeder win the challenge certificate under the judge then tongues begin 'to wag'. Such gatherings are an important contribution to the dog game because there are many extremely interesting people in dogs. The tremendous competition between breeders, striving for top honours, can bring out the worst traits in human nature. In some breeds the competitive spirit is so strong that only the hard and ruthless breeders can get to the top and remain there. Inevitably, people's opinions of successful dog people may be biased from what is seen of their characters in the show ring. If, however, these same people can be met at an interesting social function, it is quite surprising how tremendously interesting and charming some of these same people can be.

There are many social functions organized by energetic breed club committees for garden parties, tea and chatter parties, not to mention the annual club dinner parties. All these functions serve a very useful purpose in creating harmony amongst the members.

CHAPTER XI

Judging and Stewarding Regulations

JUDGES' TEACH-INS AND EXAMINATIONS

The Kennel Club do not require a judge to pass any form of examination or test, either practical or oral. Some countries, however, have extremely stiff requirements before a person is permitted to judge, and these include a written paper, a year's judging with an experienced judge, and a final judge's examination. Whether this produces better judging or not is a moot point, because undoubtedly the top British judges can be held second to none throughout the world without any formal training.

The modern trend in dog judging is slowly moving towards the idea of some formal education in the art of judging. There are quite a number of breed clubs and societies who are organizing what is known in the dog world as 'teach-ins' and 'judge-ins'. There is no doubt that these are an excellent idea, because they enable breeders to enlarge their knowledge and to assimilate the many idiosyncrasies in other breeds of which they would otherwise be completely unaware. A series of lectures, including one on dog kinetics, would also open the eyes of many people. To date, no breed club has actually set an examination paper for would-be judges, and possibly a written examination could be unfair, since there are many good judges to be found amongst comparatively uneducated people. If some form of examination were found necessary, it would probably be better to have 'viva' examinations and practical examinations of actually judging dogs in a ring, with the examinee having to give his reasons for selecting particular dogs. He should also be marked for his order of work, and how he filled up his judging book and treated his stewards, and for his general ring etiquette.

KENNEL CLUB JUDGING REGULATIONS

The Kennel Club are only concerned with the choice of judges for their championship shows, and these judges must have been passed by the Kennel Club before they are permitted to judge. The judges selected by the show committee for open, limited and sanction shows are not necessarily required to have any previous experience. The club secretaries are only interested in that any particular judge should draw a large entry.

The show executive must provide each judge with a special judging book. This book must contain detachable slips for the ring award board, and also one for the secretary's office. This is the slip which is eventually sent to the Kennel Club for official recognition. The book with the judge's original awards is kept by the judge for ever. The show executive must arrange that all the exhibit numbers of the dogs are entered in each class before judging commences. The steward informs the judge of any absentees and the judge is expected to fill in the numbers of those dogs in the judging book. If a breed is to be judged in any other ring than that which is catalogued, a notice of the change must be prominently posted in the original ring. Judges must judge the classes in each breed in the exact order in which they are entered in the judging book.

Should a judge, for any reason, be unable to fulfil his engagement to judge, he may be required by the Kennel Club committee to give his full reasons for not fulfilling his engagement. Should the reason be unsatisfactory to the Kennel Club committee, then a fine may be imposed which must be paid within the stipulated time laid down by the Kennel Club Committee. Should the judge default in this respect then he will be dealt with by the Kennel Club Committee under Kennel Club rule 17.

OFFICIATING JUDGES

No more than three judges may be appointed to judge for any prize or special award. Whenever two judges are appointed, the show committee must appoint a referee, and the name of the referee must be published in the schedule. A judge's award shall be final except in cases of fraud or misrepresentation, or where a genuine mistake has been made by the judge. No alteration of awards is permitted by the Kennel Club Committee after forty-two clear days since the date of the show, without special permission from the Kennel Club. A judge is empowered to withhold any awards for lack of merit, or if any exhibit has been improperly attracted after the handler has been warned by the judge. All judging slips must be marked accordingly. If a judge withholds a third prize for lack of merit, then the reserve award must also be withheld, but a judge may not withhold any prizes in sweepstake classes.

NUMBER OF DOGS TO BE PLACED

The judge must place his four (or more) best dogs in order, in the centre of the ring before marking awards in the judging book. The number of dogs placed depends on the number of prize cards. Any alterations made in the judging book must be initialled by the judge and endorsed on the slips, letter, or other documents, which must also include the time and date of any alteration. At the conclusion of judging a breed class, the judge must declare which exhibit is the best of breed. No judge is permitted to make a public commentary on the exhibits which he is judging or has judged at a show. No judge is permitted to award equal awards. The judge must sign all challenge certificates awarded, and the stewards and show committee are responsible for ensuring that the judge does sign them. The Kennel Club states that 'the dog must be in the show at the time the award is made'.

AWARDING CHALLENGE CERTIFICATES

A specialist judge is required to have had five years' experience of judging in specialist capacity. He may then be up-graded by the breed club to become a championship show judge, provided that his name is put forward to the Kennel Club Show Committee. The Kennel Club will send the prospective championship show judge a detailed form. This must be filled in clearly and must give all the details which the Kennel Club require. These will include all judging appointments over the previous five years at open shows, their respective dates, and the number of entries received. In due course, all being well, the Kennel Club will pass the judge, who is then entitled to award challenge certificates at any of the Kennel Club championship shows in the specified breed.

The judge's name must not be announced if he is awarding challenge certificates, until the name of the prospective judge has been submitted to the Kennel Club Committee and his name approved.

A judge should withhold a challenge certificate, should the winning exhibit not be considered by the judge to be worthy of this top award. In the event of the judge named in the schedule being unable to fulfil his engagement, a notice to this effect must be sent to the canine press, and a post-card must be sent to each exhibitor who has made an entry in all breeds affected. The name of another judge must then be submitted to the Kennel Club Committee for their approval. In an emergency, however, the show committee may substitute another judge, but he must be one who has already awarded challenge certificates to the breed previously.

FREQUENCY OF JUDGING APPOINTMENTS

A judge may not award more than one set of challenge certificates within a period of six months to the same sex of the same breed or variety. How often a judge accepts judging appointments depends entirely on each individual show committee's principles. Championship shows, such as

WELKS, often ask the judge not to judge the breed at open shows within a year or six months of the date of their particular show. If a judge accepts too many invitations to judge, exhibitors who have had their dogs unplaced are not likely to go under him again, and in this case the judge's entry is likely to be much smaller than if he judges less frequently. If, however, a judge has to accept more judging appointments, it is only fair that the shows should be at a good distance apart. Entries would not be affected, if a judge accepted an appointment to judge at open shows in a particular breed in, say, London, Birmingham and Edinburgh.

OTHER RULES FOR JUDGES

A judge may not exhibit for competition or handle in the ring any of his dogs on the same day that he is judging at a particular show. A judge may therefore enter his dogs at a two- or three-day show. This rule does not apply if a judge's appointment is changed in an emergency. An exhibitor may not enter a puppy that has been bred by the judge, or a dog that has been handled by the judge or boarded by or given any attention by the judge within a period of twelve months. In such a case the exhibitor would be penalized and not the judge.

UNWRITTEN LAWS

There are certain unwritten laws that exhibitors should comply with regarding judges. It is not a good idea to travel to a show with a judge, or to be seen carrying on a long conversation with a judge before exhibiting under him. To an honest judge and exhibitor the fact of talking to each other should make no difference whatsoever. Nevertheless, these actions could easily be misconstrued, just as it would be stupid to offer a judge a drink before judging; and perhaps even inviting the judge to a party a week or so before exhibiting under him. Making any other unnecessary contact with the judge, is bad form. All judges can see through those last-minute telephone calls, invitations to dinner, and the proverbial case of whisky or the television set which arrives on the eve of a show! There are other perhaps more subtle but equally underhand ways of endeavouring to curry a judge's favour, such as using a number of his stud dogs, buying in puppies from him or getting him judging appointments.

Another unwritten law regarding judges, particularly those awarding challenge certificates, is that on no account should they look at a catalogue before judging. This would be taking an unfair advantage of exhibitors by looking up and seeing what well-known dogs were being exhibited in each class. It is not, however, an unknown fact that some judges do resort to acquiring a catalogue, and then locking themselves in the lavatory where they make their decisions for each class. These would depend on whether they are friends of the committee, or whether they wish to become popular judges and allocate their quota of wins to each well-known kennel.

Strangely enough, judges who resort to this method of allotting awards are often the most popular. This is because exhibitors realize that these judges are not favouring just the mighty few, and that any exhibitor who regularly exhibits under the judge will get his quota of good placings, perhaps first or seconds in lower classes, provided that his dogs are good specimens.

SMOKING IN THE RING

No judge should demean himself by smoking either a cigarette or a pipe while on duty. It is extremely bad form, and it may also be dangerous. If the judge is going over a breed on the table, ash could inadvertently be dropped into a dog's eye, and a promising show career might be gone for ever.

DRINKING IN THE RING

A judge should never drink anything alcoholic in the ring whilst on duty, and he should not drink any form of alcohol until after judging is completed. It is horrible for exhibitors to have a judge's alcoholic breath near them, but it must be much worse for the dog with his ultra sensitive olfactory senses. There should, however, be nothing against a judge drinking a glass of water, lemonade, or Coca Cola, or even a cup of tea during the interval between classes of a long judging session.

JUDGING WHEN NOT FIT

No judge should contemplate accepting a judging appointment when not feeling well, and unless he is feeling absolutely fit and in tip-top condition. If he is not in perfect health he will obviously not be able to give of his best. Judging large and important classes is an arduous and tiring job, and one which requires a great deal of concentration. Any judge who has recently undergone a major operation or had a serious illness, should postpone all judging appointments until he is fit again. It may be a courageous man in the face of pain and adversity to try to carry on judging, but it is exceedingly hard on the exhibitors when the judge is feeling so ill that he can hardly see the dogs, let alone judge them. Exhibitors have probably travelled hundreds of miles to the show and spent large sums of money on entry fees and so it is only right that the judge should be capable of carrying out his duties efficiently.

BREED CLASSES AND REPORTS

The judge will know well in advance which breeds or varieties he will be judging. The shows are advertised in the dog papers, and very often the breeds are classified and the names of the judges also included, as well as the group judges and the best in show judge and referee. Soon after this the judge will receive a request from one or both of the dog papers to write a critique for them. This will state whether the paper concerned requires a show report on the first three placings in each class, or only on the first two. One of the papers also likes the number of entries in each class to be inserted. The critique appears in the dog papers the following week, provided that the judge gets his report in to the post at the week-end.

JUDGING APPOINTMENTS ABROAD

It is always an honour to be invited to judge abroad. The Kennel Club like to be informed of any foreign invitations to judge. The country concerned will accept judges in breeds in which they have awarded challenge certificates in Britain. A judge is permitted to accept any judging appointment he likes. It is not the responsibility of the Kennel Club, if foreign countries permit a judge to judge other breeds at small shows, even if the judge has not awarded challenge certificates. What is important, however, is that, whenever a judge accepts an appointment abroad, he should be absolutely certain that he really has sufficient knowledge to be a first-class judge. It should go without saying that judges should behave themselves when away from home, and they should remember that, all the time that they are away, they are unofficial ambassadors of their country. The inefficiency of their judging will be remembered for very many decades, especially any of the terrible boobs that all judges are liable to make at some time during their judging careers. The many correct decisions are invariably forgotten.

OVERSEAS JUDGES FOR CHAMPIONSHIP SHOWS

It is essential when judging breeds abroad that the judge should be fully aware of differences in breeds and breed standards and also of the particular method of judging procedures. Most countries require that a foreign judge should have been approved to judge his breeds by his own Kennel Club. It is normal practice for the would-be judge to have to fill in a form stating his qualification to judge any particular breed, where he has judged and the dates and also the size of his entries. The judge may also be required to fill in how many dogs of the breed to be judged he has owned, and he is expected to familiarize himself with the standards for the breed, and the regulations for judging of the country concerned. The experience required by American and British judges is similar. The system of approval, however, is different. The American Kennel Club will not approve persons who are licensed or professional handlers or who are occupationally ineligible under their rules. These qualifications, however, are not necessarily disqualifications for judging in the United Kingdom. In most countries, once the judge has been passed to judge a particular breed at championship show level, he is not normally required to fill in another form on another occasion. These regulations are a safeguard for the exhibitors so that they know that before a judge is accepted from another country he has at least had sufficient experience of the breed. Some judges have never had the opportunity of judging the large entries and enormous classes that are seen at the Kennel Club championship shows. A class of forty or fifty dogs is quite a different proposition compared with a judge's home experience of perhaps only three or four dogs in a class.

REGULATIONS REGARDING FOREIGN JUDGES

'When a foreign judge, other than one from the USA, is nominated to award Challenge Certificates in a particular breed at a Championship Show:

A letter is sent to his national Kennel Club asking:

(a) Whether the person nominated has been approved for that breed in their country.

(b) Whether the person nominated has in fact judged that particular breed in their country.

A letter is also sent to the person nominated asking:

(a) For details of the shows in his country at which he has judged the particular breed he has been invited to judge in Britain.

(b) For an indication of the number of entries he has drawn at such shows.

(c) How many dogs of the breed to be judged he has owned or exhibited.

(d) Any other information which he thinks will assist our Committee.

The procedure for American judges differs slightly.

A letter is sent to the American Kennel Club asking:

(a) Whether the person nominated has been approved for that breed by the AKC.

(b) Whether the person nominated has in fact judged that particular breed in the USA.

A letter is also sent to the person nominated asking:

(a) For details of the shows in the USA at which he had judged the particular breed he has been invited to judge in Britain.

(b) For an indication of the number of entries he has drawn at such shows.

All foreign judges will be expected to familiarize themselves with the British standard for the breed, and the regulations for judging at British shows.'

It is an expensive luxury for a show committee to pay the fare, fee, and hotel bill for several days for an unknown judge, unless there is some guarantee that he is an expert in his field and is therefore likely to draw a good entry. After all, this is what the show committee are hoping for. The exhibitors are also expecting expert, unbiased judging."

TETANUS PREVENTION

It is a sensible precaution for anyone who has much to do with dogs, and particularly judges with many judging appointments, to avail themselves of a series of injections against tetanus. There must be few judges indeed who have never been bitten by a dog.

A patient has one injection of tetanus vaccine. This should be followed by a second injection six to twelve weeks after the first injection. Six months to one year later a reinforcing injection is required. An injection is only required thereafter every five years, for permanent protection against tetanus. It is important that the tetanus prevention card should be carried and kept in a wallet or handbag at all times in case of accident or injury.

INVITATIONS FOR JUDGING APPOINTMENTS

The Kennel Club are not interested in the least which judges judge the various breeds at open, limited, sanction or exemption shows. Invitations are issued by show club committees to people whom someone on the committee feels would draw a good entry. These people probably all belong to one or more of the breed clubs. It is not actually necessary for a judge even to be on a breed club judging list, although people who are on the lists are more likely to be invited to judge, because secretaries of breed clubs are often asked to suggest judges for particular shows.

Invitations to judge are sometimes worded in such a way that the judge is not sure whether it is a definite invitation or not. A letter may be worded 'Are you free to judge such and such a breed on a particular date? Please state your fee.' The judge may hear no more as the committee may have decided to have a judge who will judge their breed for nothing. All-rounders in this country try and play safe and answer such a letter by confirming that they will judge.

JUDGING FEES

Most judges other than the professional judges do not normally demand a judging fee at open, limited and sanction shows, but they expect their expenses and meals to be covered. Fees are nearly always paid to judges at championship shows. Unfortunately, there is no set rate of payment and show secretaries generally write to a proposed judge and ask what fee he requires. This is often rather embarrassing and it very much depends on how hard a judge has to work and how big an entry he draws, and also on how many breeds he has been asked to judge.

Some judges, trying to curry favour with show secretaries, merely ask for a pound or two, whilst others will ask for their expenses and others will demand £5, £10, £15, or sometimes even more. Some judges judge for nothing in order to be asked to judge again. This is very hard on the professional all-rounders, who must earn their living by judging and save for a pension. Some clubs are extremely well off and often pay their all-rounder judges a pittance. Other clubs are struggling to survive and may even be a little more generous. Some of the largest shows expect the judge to judge for the honour only.

In the United States the judges are well paid. In Italy the judges must be given their out-of-pocket expenses and a night's lodging, but there is no judging fee. The fees vary from country to country.

All this seems a very haphazard arrangement and many championship shows only pay the judges if asked. Perhaps it might be a good idea if judges were paid a percentage of the profits above a certain number of entries. A judge who has an entry of 350 dogs with 200 dogs to go over has to work and concentrate exceedingly hard. This tiring day also includes perhaps a long journey by car, train or plane, and the following day which is generally a Sunday must be taken up with writing a good report on the first three dogs in each class.

Some form of sliding scale should be worked out, based on the experience of the judge and the total number of entries he draws.

Even at Cruft's, the largest show in the world, most of the judges are expected to judge solely for the honour of being invited to judge there; whilst others who are getting no larger entries, and perhaps judging the groups, may be paid as much as £50.

It is important and courteous that all judging invitations should be answered promptly, confirming one way or the other the judging appointment. It is essential to state the fee and any travelling expenses required. It might be as well to ask for confirmation, but this depends on the wording of the original letter.

The judging appointment with the name of the show, the address where the show is to be held, and the name and address of the secretary of the show, should be entered in a diary immediately. All correspondence relating to the show should be filed and kept in an accessible place.

BREED CLUB JUDGING LISTS

All breed clubs have judging lists and most have graded judging lists: an 'A' list and a 'B' list. These consist of all the names of judges who have been proposed and voted for at an Annual General Meeting. The 'A' list is the list for championship show judges, and the 'B' list is for those who may judge at open shows, limited shows and sanction shows. The lists are revised annually and the 'A' list is sent to the Kennel Club. Some clubs even have a 'C' list for shows below Open Shows. Other clubs have a challenge certificate list and then an 'A' and 'B' list.

The Kennel Club will permit judges to judge a numerically strong new breed at a championship show without the usual five-year experience. Normally this period has to elapse before a judge may award the Kennel Club Challenge Certificates. The number of challenge certificates offered by the Kennel Club is proportional to the number of the breed registrations in the preceding three years. A minimum of 150 dogs is essential. The Kennel Club are only interested in the judges who are to award their challenge certificates. There are 6000 judges recognized by the Kennel Club to award challenge certificates. Not all of them continue to judge and some may only be invited to judge once. The Kennel Club approve 3000 judges each year and there are about 100 judges at Cruft's.

CHANGES IN BREED CLUB JUDGING LISTS

Many people, including the all-rounders, feel that it should be very much more difficult to get on to a breed club judging list, but that, having once been accepted and placed on a list, it should be much more difficult to get judges removed from the list, unless of course there is some proved iniquity. The present system gives too much power to the club committees or strong charactered chairmen, who can lever judges off and on to their lists with impunity. A judge who is strong-minded enough to leave all the committee who have invited him to judge their breed championship show out of the winning cards is hardly likely to find himself invited to judge again. Judges with less character know which side their bread is buttered and the temptation to play ball is often too great. The lever that people have got today regarding who is to judge and who is not to judge is something that the Kennel Club should become more fully aware of. Having become aware of the situation, the Kennel Club Committee should take action to prevent abuse. Some clubs are perfectly aware of the advantages that committee members may be thought to have by some of the exhibitors, and some clubs actually mention in their catalogues 'EXHIBITORS PLEASE NOTE. MEMBERS OF THE COMMITTEE DO NOT EXHIBIT THEIR DOGS AT THIS SHOW.'

There are many club committees that choose their judges with the utmost fairness. Unfortunately, there are others where judging appointments are exchanged for wins in the show ring. A great deal of this could be eliminated, if the Kennel Club chose all judges on a rota system, and according to their ability and size of entries. This would avoid some of the scheming that goes on behind the scenes.

JUDGES' CLOTHING AND EQUIPMENT

It is undoubtedly most important that a judge, regardless of sex, should be suitably and neatly dressed for the occasion. After all, the judge will be in the centre of the ring, amongst most beautifully prepared and immaculately turned-out dogs. Although the exhibitors may often be dressed in the most unsuitable clothes, and many of them may unfortunately look unkempt and untidy, it is extremely important that it should be possible to pick out the officiating judge at a glance from his immaculate and alert appearance. Slovenly clothes often indicate a slovenly state of mind.

Male judges are expected to wear well pressed and tidy country suits and polished shoes, and the majority of male judges seem to favour wearing a hat, particularly at the outdoor shows when it is sunny. Many judges like to wear a buttonhole as well as their judge's badge and it is an excellent idea if a judge remembers to put several extra biros in a pocket. In case of wet weather, a judge should take a mackintosh and a spare pair of shoes or boots. He should also have some spare cash with which to stand his stewards a drink.

LADY JUDGES' CLOTHING AND EQUIPMENT

Lady judges should give considerable thought to their show-judging attire. It is most important that they should look neat and comfortable. There is a lot of bending and stretching to be done when going over a dog.

Shoes are extremely important. They must be comfortable, and should have reasonably flat heels. Nothing looks so unsuitable as a judge mincing up and down the ring in four-inch stiletto heels, or high platform shoes. In hot climates and when the judge has a full day's judging it is a good idea to take a second pair of shoes to wear in the afternoon.

The judge should certainly have her hair done the day before the show, unless she intends to wear a wig. Many judges nowadays do not normally wear hats when judging. There are, however, still some shows where hats are nearly always worn. There are certain considerations when choosing a hat to be worn when judging. First it should be attractive and it must be comfortable and well secured. It should also be of a size not to frighten a dog. Hats with long pheasant feathers in the rim or crown, moreover, would be most unsuitable when judging gun dogs. Brightly coloured, feathered creations are not particularly suitable either, nor are large jangling bracelets, beads and knuckle duster rings. Judging is a serious business and therefore there is no need for a judge to look as if she is just starting off for Ascot, nor, on the other hand, as if she is about to clean out a kennel.

DARK GLASSES

There are no rules or regulations laid down by the Kennel Club regarding a judge wearing tinted glasses. In some countries these are prohibited, because it is felt that many sun glasses distort colours, and some dogs might be alarmed at particularly large spectacles. However, if tinted glasses are worn by a judge, they should be removed at least once during an examination of a dog, where colour is important in a breed. Bifocals are particularly useful for older judges who require spectacles.

STEWARDING

STEWARDS

There are always at least one or two stewards in the judging ring. At the big championship shows there are often three. The stewards' job is a very important one, and on them depends the smooth running of the show. The stewards should take away from the judge all responsibility for everything which occurs in the ring other than actual judging. Stewarding is always done as a voluntary service. While on duty, the steward wears a badge in the form of a rosette with 'Steward' printed in the centre.

RESPONSIBILITIES

The senior steward is responsible for everything in the ring. He must check that there is a proper place for posting of awards, and that the prize cards for each class are complete. He must see that the judging table is in the correct position, and that it is not slippery for the dogs to stand on. If the surface is not suitable, then the table must be covered with something to prevent the dogs from slipping about. The steward must check that there are two chairs, a bucket of sawdust, a bowl of water, soap and a towel, and a dust pan and brush under the judging table for clearing away any accident made in the ring by the dogs. The blackboard must be clean, and there must be a duster and chalk for chalking up the number of the class being judged, followed by the numbers of the first four in it.

PRELIMINARY

The steward should arrive in good time at the show. He should report immediately at the secretary's office, where he will be told which ring he is to steward in. He will be given the number cards of all the entries in his ring for all the classes, a catalogue and the Kennel Club instructions leaflet. He must check that he has the correct numbers. The secretary will also hand over the prize cards, which are of different colours, the rosettes and the trophies. At the same time the steward will also be given his luncheon voucher. The steward will ask the judge how he would like the dogs lined up for the new and old classes, and also which way the award winning dogs are to stand in the centre of the ring.

EACH CLASS

When the judge is ready to start judging, it is the responsibility of one of the stewards to go round the benches, to announce the commencement of judging, and to go to the benches of any missing exhibits. It is, nevertheless, entirely the responsibility of the handlers to bring their dogs into the ring at the correct time. When the stewards are back in the ring, the handlers go to them to receive the numbers of their exhibits. If the stewards are wise, they will check the dog and the ring number in the catalogue before handing out the ring card. After they are sure that all the handlers are present, the senior steward informs the judge of any absentees and the judge marks these up in the judging book as ABS. One of the stewards will see that the handlers line up round the ring ready for the judge. The senior steward informs the judge that all are present.

The stewards then make themselves scarce in the corner of the ring where the table is placed. They must not converse with the judge unless requested by him to perform a specific duty. They must be constantly on the look-out for any irregularities that may occur during judging. A dog is not permitted to be attracted by anyone outside the ring. It is the duty of the stewards to see that this rule is observed. Their services may also be required should the ring become soiled.

The stewards must ensure that no other dogs are permitted in the ring except those being judged and that only the stewards and the judge other than the handlers may enter the ring without the authority of the show executive.

AT THE END OF EACH CLASS

When the judge has placed the dogs in the order of his preference, the senior steward hands the judge his judging book and ball-point pen and then proceeds to call out the numbers of the winning dogs in a loud voice, to enable the judge to enter the numbers in the judging book, and also so that spectators at the ringside can hear. He also presents the handlers with their award-winning cards. The steward will ask the handlers of the first four winning dogs to remain in their places so that the judge can write his report. If one of the handlers moves off the steward must retrieve him!

The judge will fill in his judging book and initial the three slips. The senior steward is responsible for seeing that the slips are initialed by the judge. He sends two slips by a runner to the secretary's office, or takes them there himself, and he pins the third on the notice board. The numbers of the winners must then be chalked up clearly and boldly for all to see.

The previous handlers who are in the next class must be placed in the order of their wins. If these exhibits have not previously met they should stand in order of seniority of classes in which they took part. They should stand in line from the furthest corner from the judge's table, and should be requested to keep those places until the judging of the new dogs is finished. The

PREPARATION FOR THE RING

Above: Last minute trimming of a Lakehead Terrier behind the scenes.

Right: Final preparations to an Old English Sheepdog. At his stage the chalk has already been brushed out of the coat.

Below: Preparing and chalking Old English Sheepdogs on the allotted tables.

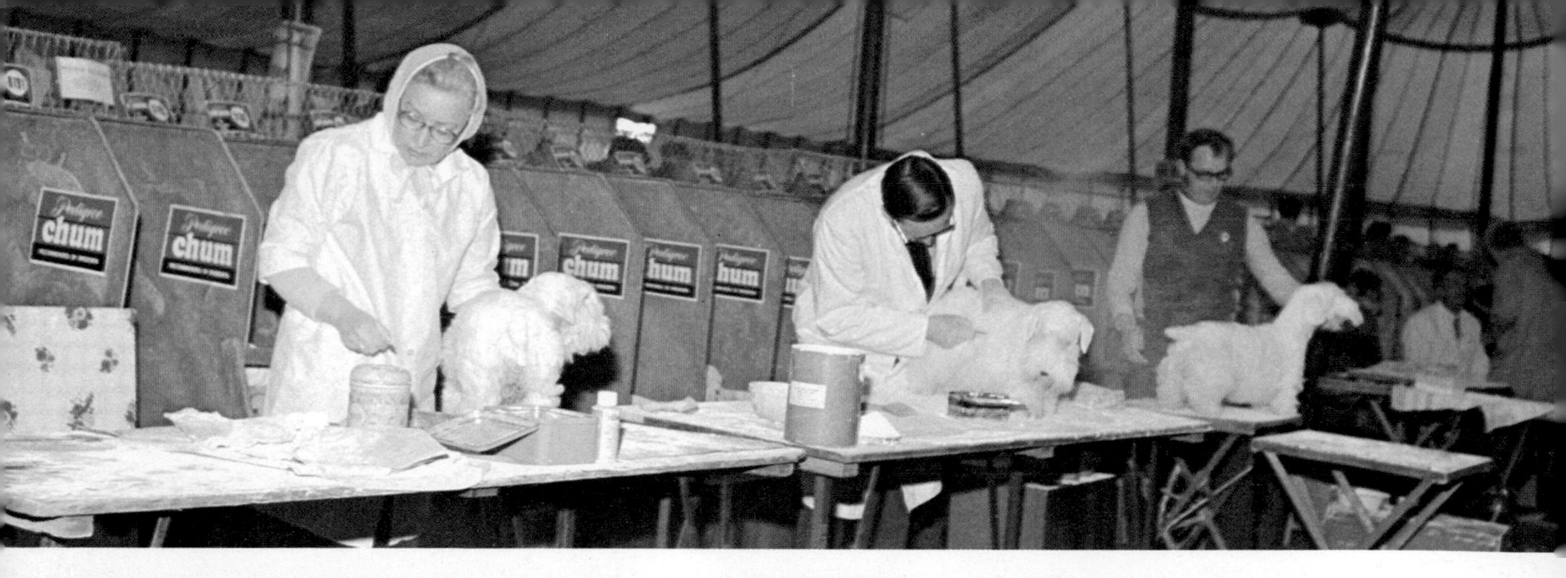

Top: Sealyham Terriers being chalked and brushed on the special tables provided. Handlers wear white overalls and hair is often protected with a scarf from flying chalk.

Above left: A Maltese having talcum powder brushed out of his coat on his grooming table. Chalk is used to whiten stained feet. A hand protects the eyes from both the brush and the powder.

Above right: A child handler at a country open show. The indoor rings are in the riding school in the background.

Right: A Skye Terrier having his parting made quite straight with a wet comb. A damp sponge is used to keep the hair lying flat on either side of the parting. The handler is studying her catalogue.

Above: The judge with her Cavalier King Charles Spaniel 'Best of Breed' and 'Best Opposite Sex', at Bath Championship Show.

Right: The judge watches the dog's gait coming towards him. He notes the elbows and the plane of the fore legs to each other, and also the position of the head. The handler is moving the dog at a fast trot, so that the diagonal feet are on the ground simultaneously.

Left: The senior steward fixing a judge's marked-up slip on the board in the ring.

Below left: A judge standing back to write up his notes on a Bloodhound at Bath Championship Show.

Below right: A Variety Class at an open outdoor show.

steward is responsible for seeing that the new dogs are placed separately. They generally stand diagonally opposite the old dogs, starting the new line near the judging table. The old class are then judged against the new.

The only time during judging that a steward should speak to a judge is to remind him before marking the judging book to place the first four dogs in order of merit if he has not already done so.

FINAL DUTIES

Whilst each class is being judged, one steward should warn the handlers in the next class that they must be ready in a certain time. Their ring numbers can be distributed to them at the same time. This standard of organization is a great help to both handlers and judge, because the time lag of handing out ring numbers in the ring is eliminated. In this way, classes can be judged very much more quickly. In large classes this may make all the difference as to whether handlers can get their dogs to the variety classes in time.

Stewards are responsible for ensuring that judges sign challenge certificates and awards for best of sex and reserve best of sex. The stewards must also see that the judge enters these winners in the judging book. Stewards very often fill in the numbers of the placed dogs on the two last slips after the judge has filled in the first slip. Before the next class starts the judge must be reminded to initial the slips, before they are sent to the secretary's office at the end of each class.

JUDGING BOOK SLIPS

All three slips are initialed by the judge, one is put up on the ring notice board and the other two are returned to the secretary, generally by a runner. One of the slips is put up in the secretary's office, and the other is sent to the Kennel Club for checking the winners in case of contravention of the regulations.

STEWARDS' SERVICE

The stewards may often be asked to steward for several breeds on the same day in the same ring. For this free service to the canine world, the stewards are given lunch and a drink. It is much appreciated if the stewards receive a letter of thanks from the judges for whom they have stewarded, but unfortunately, owing to the pressure of writing reports and the long journey home, many judges do not have time to comply with this courtesy and stewards often have to be content with verbal appreciation at the time.

CHAPTER XII

Judges and Judging Ability

JUDGES

There are two types of judge; the specialist judge who knows only one or two breeds, and the all-rounder who started life as a specialist judge, but who has graduated to being capable of judging all breeds. No judge probably can know all breeds perfectly, and this is why many specialist breeders do not like some all-rounders. The variety judge, usually has a good eye for a dog, and will judge the dog on soundness and the over-all appearance. The specialist judge often judges on a breed's finer points. Such a judge may look for black pigmentation, tracing, flat furry tail, tan markings, etc., and in so doing he may miss the overall quality of the dog. Both types of judge are, however, equally important for the good of breeds as a whole. Breed clubs should try to insist that almost half the judges in any one year should be outstanding all-rounders. The top dogs in any breed are those which are capable of winning equally under the specialist judge and the all-rounder. It is interesting to note that in Britain there are more specialist judges, whilst in the USA there are more all-rounder judges.

THE SPECIALIST JUDGE

The specialist judge compares each dog in the class feature by feature and point by point with the breed's standard, and then he compares each dog one with another. The specialist judge is looking for type, and the finer breed idiosyncrasies play a more important role. For example, he will often overlook a body fault, but he will seldom make allowances for a bad head.

THE ALL-ROUNDER JUDGE

The all-rounder or variety judge, on the other hand, judges the dog as a whole entity: soundness, balance and quality have a higher priority than individual breed characteristics. In a breed class, as soon as the all-rounder judge has summed up the individual dog, he then compares each dog of the same breed one with another. However, when the all-rounder judge is judging a variety class with perhaps forty or fifty dogs in the class, or a group class, there is no one standard for the judge to follow. The judge, therefore, judges each dog separately by its own standard and judges the dog as a whole entity. Is the dog a good specimen for its breed? The dog's individual breed features are less important than the overall quality of the dog. Each dog is therefore judged against its standard and not against a different breed in the class.

It is essential for the variety judge to keep up with the change of standards which occur from time to time. In the USA it is essential for the all-rounder judge to memorize the breed disqualifications. If he does not do so, he may well land himself in serious trouble. There are no breed standard disqualifications in Britain, only 'faults'.

THE CAREER JUDGE

A judge who wishes to make a career in judging may start in a number of ways. Most judges start as breeders of one breed. They then become well known within their breed and are first invited to judge at small shows, then at open shows. After about five years when they have been on their own club's judging list and bred a number of good dogs they are invited to judge at a championship show. The Kennel Club ask for information on all the judge's previous show experience both in judging, winning and breeding, before passing him as a championship show judge. Quite a number of kennel staff become excellent judges, obtaining their experience through their employer's dogs.

As soon as a person becomes efficient at judging his own breed he may progress to judging one or two other breeds at small shows and from then he may be invited to judge variety classes. These classes are an excellent way for a judge to obtain experience, and there is always a knowledgeable all-rounder who will give a novice judge very sound advice.

The variety judge next progresses to judging several breeds in one group and then concentrates on the rest of the breeds within that group. The serious judge may then progress to several breeds in another group and so on until after many years experience the judge becomes an accepted championship show variety judge.

To become a championship show all-rounder the Kennel Club require a judge to have been passed to award two but preferably three sets of challenge certificates in different breeds. By this time too the judge should have judged all breeds at open shows.

Many championship show judges who start by awarding one set of challenge certificates, find that they enjoy judging and are perhaps naturally good at it. They will soon accept any judging appointments at open shows which come their way. They may feel that it is a good idea to specialize within one group at open shows. If a judge has a good eye and wishes to learn, he can start by watching the judging at championship shows where he should see the best dogs and the best judges at work. It is then an excellent idea if he asks the judge, when the judging is finished, to give him a lesson with actual dogs. It is surprising how quickly you can learn even in one lesson by actually handling a dog and going over one, particularly if an outstanding specimen is produced and placed against an inferior one. A judge, who is already conversant in one breed at championship-show standard, will not take long to adjust to another breed and to having to memorize certain breed idiosyncrasies.

HOW THE ALL-ROUND JUDGE STARTS

Quite a number of prospective variety judges may buy in two or three outstanding dogs in different breeds and will have several litters and exhibit the dogs, so that they really know from first hand the construction, temperament and breed idiosyncrasies in respect of coat, colour, movement and soundness within a breed. Other prospective judges may be lucky enough to find an expert who will allow them to come into the ring with him as student judge and watch him going over the exhibits. The expert may even allow the novice judge actually to handle or go over a particularly bad or good dog after the judging, at the same time explaining the various merits or otherwise of the dogs. Kennel Club permission and also permission from the show committee must be obtained as no one other than the handlers, stewards and judge are permitted in the ring. Another method whereby a judge may gain experience is by being invited to judge variety classes at open, sanction and limited shows. At the smaller shows a would-be all-round judge can probably get a good idea of the different breeds likely to be exhibited at a particular show in any given area, because breeds are often regional.

By going to several shows in the same area and by talking to the show secretaries, the judge can probably get a good idea as to which breeds he is most likely to meet, and can therefore go home and 'swat up' the breed idiosyncrasies he is likely to encounter. In actual fact, variety judging is not nearly so difficult as it may appear. Judging unlike dogs each against its own standard has its compensations and there are nearly always sufficient outstanding dogs to make the final line-up reasonably easy. Each dog must be regarded as a whole and the nearest to the standard of its breed. Obviously, judges who are not sure of themselves will probably select the dogs from the breeds which they know really well and which they also like the best. Variety judging has no one standard to be guided by, so that individual breed points are of less importance than the overall picture of the dog.

STEWARD EXPERIENCE

There is still one more method whereby experience can be gained, and that is by an intelligent steward, who not only must be efficient at his stewardship, but at the same time can be observant of a judge's handling, technique and placings; and most judges are willing to impart their knowledge to a novice, whether he be a breeder, exhibitor, steward or a would-be judge.

WATCHING A GOOD JUDGE AT WORK

A novice can learn a great deal by watching a knowledgeable judge at work in the ring. Most successful, popular judges have worked out their own judging philosophy and their individual interpretations of the breed standards of the breeds in which they have become expert. Tremendous pleasure can be derived by watching a first-class judge working in a ring on a sunny day going over beautiful dogs all handled and presented immaculately by expert experienced handlers. Probably the first thing that a novice will notice is the calm, collected, self-assured manner in which the judge conducts himself. His personality permiates the ring, the handlers are on the alert, and the ring side has ceased its chatter. Everything has been organized before the commencement of judging right down to the last and most microscopic detail: the judge's own turnout; his organization of the stewards; the manner in which he intends to judge; where the dogs are to be lined up; the position of the table, its surface and the area over which the dogs are to be moved; the number of award cards; the checking of the judging book; and right down to the working of the ball-point pen.

The general routine and method of judging are adhered to throughout the day, so that exhibitors, stewards, handlers and the ringside onlookers, know exactly the order of work. The judge handles each dog, going over him with an eagle eye, which misses nothing, and in a gentle, authoritative manner. A judge who knows his breed and is deriving pleasure handling each exhibit displays such knowledge that it soon becomes apparent to the ringside followers exactly what he is looking for and what he dislikes. The knowledgeable spectators can follow the judging and understand why the judge is selecting certain dogs and discarding others. It soon becomes apparent that the ringside follow the judging with such concentration that many of the experts will know which dogs are likely to win the top honours or at least be in the cards.

These are the judges that the aspiring novice judge should spend hours watching, and he should make notes on their skills and procedures. Besides watching the judges, it is tremendously interesting watching the eyes of a dog while he is being gone over by the judge, and the knowing, experienced expression he will give the judge when the latter has to open the dog's mouth to see if it is correct. The dog looks at the judge in a supercilious way, as if he is saying: 'What nonsense all this is!'

The criteria of bad judging is when knowledgeable breeders cannot follow the judging, when there is no similarity in procedure, and when remarks are passed to the effect that the judge must be judging the other end of the lead. One of the worst and rudest forms of behaviour is for a supercilious judge to be abrupt and off-hand with the exhibitors and handlers dismissing them with curt or offensive remarks or laughing at novice handlers behind their backs as they move a dog. All this can be seen all too clearly from the ringside and is not admired. The judge who fails to bother to watch some of the dogs move round the ring or who takes his eyes off a dog being individually gaited for him, while he looks at the spectators or talks to a steward, is guilty of the depth of rudeness.

TRAITS OF A GOOD JUDGE

A good judge must be dedicated and confident. He also must be able to cope with every situation that arises in the ring. He requires presence, charm, tact, patience and above all integrity. He must be able to give confidence to the novice and to the dog lacking in ring experience, he must be kind and gentle, he must judge objectively, and it should go without saying that he must at all times be scrupulously fair. A good judge requires to be capable and strong-minded, and he often needs to be quick-witted too. He must be observant, have a retentive memory, and must be able to make rapid decisions when necessary. He must be decisive, calm and knowledgeable and authoritative. This paragon of all virtues must be courteous at all times with the exhibitors who have honoured him by giving him an entry for his efficient, unbiased, knowledgeable opinion on the day.

A good judge will never play to the gallery or cut corners when judging. He must be honest with any remarks he makes about a dog, false hopes must not be built up, nor should he pass criticism of a dog unless it is constructive. A judge must also be firm and know how to deal with a difficult, rude handler or breeder.

JUDGE TO THE STANDARD

Regardless of the breed they are judging, all judges must judge only to the breed standard. Each dog must be judged as a whole, balanced dog, and for type, temperament and soundness, in that order. A dog must be judged on merit and overall quality. Judging must always be positive judging and never negative. The virtues are assessed against the dog's faults. There is no such thing as a perfect dog any more than there is a perfect judge.

An outstanding dog with one fault is always preferable to a mediocre dog which excells in no particular feature. It is most important that a judge should suppress his foibles and likes and dislikes and should interpret the standard without bias.

A good judge must not only know what he is looking for: but he must also know how to look for it. Balanced judging is most important. In any breed, type must always be considered first. This consists of the breed characteristics and the breed features. A dog's temperament is incredibly important and so is soundness.

A sound dog must be able to stand and move correctly for its breed and be free from all disabilities. Beauty, symmetry, style and balance all go towards the makings of a superb show dog. Balance can be described as the proportions of each feature in turn one with another and as a whole. Personality, character, intelligence, alertness, pride of bearing and showmanship all go towards the sparkle and aura which makes one particular dog stand out from all the others. Condition comes into this too, with the perfect health of the dog, his general fitness, sparkling eye and glistening coat all going to make up the qualities a judge is looking for.

JUDGING ON THE DAY

Judging is judging the dog on the day and not on what the dog may be in a year's time, nor what it was five years ago. Judging at all times must be positive judging not on virtues only, nor on faults only, but on the whole dog as the type laid down in the standard and as a functionally sound dog too.

ABILITY AND INTEGRITY

Besides a judge having complete confidence in his opinion, he must also possess ability. It should go without saying that a judge must have integrity, or he should not be judging. He must also have sufficient character never to resent criticism. All judges are criticized and no judge can possibly please every exhibitor. His duty, however, is to judge the dogs, not to please the exhibitors. A good judge should never be taken in by showy, flashy dogs nor should they copy the placings of some other judge. Nor, for that matter, should a judge put a dog down because some other judge has placed it. A rival's dog must be judged with absolute integrity. No successful exhibitor is without a rival, and rivalry often leads to jealousy. It is this jealousy that unfortunately so often mars the dog game.

POPULARITY

A judge should remember that he is probably only popular before he starts judging, and that at the end of the show his friends for a time may well be limited to the winners. Luckily exhibitors' memories are short and most of them will try their luck again, probably with another dog under the same judge at another show. Exhibitors will always accept the judge's awards, if they realize that he is judging without bias and with complete integrity and is judging the dogs and nothing else. Judges are only human. They are by no means infallible and they can make mistakes just as anyone else can. Close decisions can be extremely difficult. Judges do not have to judge, any more than exhibitors have to exhibit. It is only the dogs that have no choice in the matter. However, it is quite surprising how much the dogs really do enjoy their outings to the shows, and how sad and despondent they are when they are left at home.

JUDGES AND THEIR RESPONSIBILITY TO THE BREEDS

All judges, before they accept judging appointments with too much alacrity, should realize the tremendous responsibility that they have towards the breeds which they accept to judge. Serious faults creep into a breed simply because the faults, instead of being penalized by judges, are ignored. In fact, almost by a wave of a hand type can be altered, so that judges can make or mar a breed. It might even be said that it is really the judges who are ultimately responsible for the many serious faults which are seen in far too many pedigree dogs today. The modern show dog has been developed by artificial selection over a very short period. The selection has often not been made with due consideration for the happiness or well being of the dog.

If judges were really sincere and absolutely adamant regarding soundness, then we should not see so many unsound dogs in the ring today. Breeders and exhibitors would not breed or show dogs which judges refused to place. How quickly roach-back little Chihuahuas disappeared from the ring when judges refused to place them. Not so, however, with Yorkshire Terriers, where roached backs are seen all too frequently and priority is given to colour and flowing coat.

SOME BREED STANDARDS

It is undoubtedly true, and many veterinary surgeons will agree, that some breed standards should be altered for the good of the dogs. For example the brachysaphilic breeds (Pugs, Bulldogs) would breathe better with longer muzzles, etc. Some breed standards are far too long-winded, so that they are seldom read and even less frequently understood or memorized. Some standards are not only vague and quite ambiguous, but they are also far from explicit, either for judges to interpret or for breeders to breed by. There are even a few standards which contain blatant contradictions.

In many standards there is the constant misuse of words which is really most confusing. The outstanding example is the hock. The hock is a joint, and it is a comparatively small area, with the point of hock at the top. Many standards state: 'hocks well let down, parallel when in motion'. To confuse the issue, there are many judges who actually think that the hock is the area from the point of hock to the heel pad. This is the hind pastern and it is this, with the hock, that 'should be perpendicular to the ground and that should move on parallel planes'. Such dogs, of course, lack kinetic balance and it would be better if the standard stated 'hind pasterns almost vertical when standing, with an inclination towards a centre line depending on speed'. Centre of hips to pad, and shoulder pad, must be in a straight line, when viewed from the front or the rear. The words 'plane', 'perpendicular', 'parallel', and 'vertical', should be used correctly. There are other words describing teeth, whose meaning is not clear. 'Scissor', 'level' and 'even' all have different meanings, but they are often used indiscriminately, although all three are required for a perfect scissor bite.

Standards should be positive and shortened considerably. The Kennel Club should lay down a general description of soundness, conformation, mouths and kinetic balance applying to all normal breeds. Breed idiosyncrasies, particularly head properties, should be comprehensive and concise. Rule-of-thumb measurements between forelegs, withers, hip bones, etc., should be given, but faults of unsoundness, being obvious, should be eliminated.

Standards were sometimes drawn up in the past by committee members, who were keen to launch a new breed but who obviously had no knowledge of anatomy or movement, and they were sometimes even incapable of writing good English. These people often described the dogs that they had at the time rather than the dogs that they should have had. In other words, they made the standard fit the dog instead of the other way round. If the committee could not make up their minds whether the dog should have an undercoat or not, they merely left such an important point out of the standard altogether. It is not, therefore, surprising that standards become misinterpreted.

If standards and judges were perfect, we should not see so many Pekingese with certain hereditary faults; Boston Terriers with such endless whelping problems and numerous breeds with straight and double jointed hocks, not to mention hip-displasia and many other problems which could be avoided to a certain extent with more sensible standards.

PHOTOGRAPHS AND WHERE TO STUDY THE BREEDS

It should really go without saying that judges must be conversant with the breed standards and understand the finer breed characteristics. Standards should be re-read before judging a breed as standards do become altered from time to time. Photographs of well-known dogs should be studied and compared and all judges should make an effort to read everything they can about a breed. They should talk to the knowledgeable breeders whenever possible in the various breeds and they should try and visit some of the top kennels from time to time but by appointment only. Most breeders are only too delighted to show off their stock and will point out the breed virtues and faults.

Never listen to the derogatory remarks some breeders are apt to make about their rivals' kennels. Not many people will bother to run down a bad dog and a bad kennel! It is generally only the good dogs and good kennels which create jealousy in others. It is a wise precaution to check first, before you believe anything in the dog world. Many normally charming people can be incredibly vicious about their rivals' dogs. There are too many scandal-mongers and ungenerous people in the dog game and it is these people who spoil the fun and enjoyment for others, and probably gain little satisfaction for themselves in the process.

TRAINING TO OBSERVE AND MEMORIZE

Judging is an art, some people are naturally good at it, others are not. A person who is knowledgeable of a breed does not by any means necessarily make a good judge. It is really a matter of the powers of observation. Seeing is quite different from looking. A good judge like an artist can judge inanimate objects too. He must train his memory to record what he sees and he must be able to catalogue the details. In other words he should be able to stare at a dog until he can shut his eyes and still visualize what he has seen. He should then try and jot down on paper what he thinks he has visualized and then take another good, hard, long look at the dog and see how far he was right. Then try the exercise with another dog or even another breed.

This exercise of memorizing and cataloguing all that the judge sees is particularly good regarding movement. Watch a superb Alsatian (German Shepherd Dog) move, and remember the beautiful extended trot, the position of the head and tail and so on. Watch and observe and memorize exactly how a Fox Terrier skims the ground; the hackney gait of the Miniature Pinscher; the Shih Tzu gait, the Pyrenean, the Pekingese, etc. How does the Dachshund manipulate his hindlegs in relation to his forelegs?

Many of the breed idiosyncrasies have been bred into the dogs' ancestors for useful purposes. The Bulldog, for example, has a curious receding nose, so that in the days of bull baiting the combination of the protruding jaw allowed the dog to breathe when it was fastened on to the bull's nose. The story also goes that the curious tail is due to the Bulldog's desire to keep it out of the bull's way; that its loose skin is to enable him to get out from beneath a bull's feet.

Spaniel - correct and incorrect heads

Ideal head

Too fine-temporal bone too pronounced

Skull too thick and rounded

Too wide at eye level: snipey muzzle

'Common' looking head; ears set too high; skull lacks modelling; short ear leathers

ASSESSING BREED CHARACTERISTICS

HEADS IN GENERAL

The head is probably a dog's most outstanding feature. A breed after all is first recognized by its head. The head indicates the breed function and the proportions and shape are designed or should be designed for maximum efficiency for the breed. There are the streamlined heads for speed, which are long and narrow and tight-lipped. There are the medium length heads which are moderately wide, found in the gun dogs and working breeds like the Pointers and Alsatians. There are the shorter-faced breeds which require a strong bite, such as the Boxer, and this type of head goes with a strong but not too short a neck. In fact length of head and neck nearly always correspond. Stayers with endurance require medium length of neck and head. Ground breeds require equal length of head and neck or possibly slightly longer heads. Terrier heads are rectangular when viewed from the side. Samoyeds are equilateral triangles as seen from on top or from the side. Some heads are described as 'double-brick', 'egg-' or as 'wedge-shaped', some have flat skulls, others are domed. Then there are all the variations in the stop from deep to almost none. Some breeds require massive heads, others must be long and fine. All breeds which are required to carry objects or game in their mouths must obviously have strong jaws. In such breeds any form of snipiness should be considered a major fault. The biting breeds, where strong bite is essential, must have good supporting bone below the eyes in order to give maximum strength for support to the molars. Any falling away below the eyes will indicate weak bite, and in such breeds this should be considered a major fault. Obviously, a muzzle which is snipey and narrow below the eyes will only be capable of holding short-rooted molar teeth, unless of course the teeth are set at an angle in the bone. Obviously too, teeth set at a slant will not have the power of straight set teeth nor will they have the all-important maximum bone support between the molars and a well filled-in muzzle.

The scenting breeds require large nostrils and long necks as do the trailers. The Toy breeds do not necessarily have to have functional heads in the same way as the working and sporting breeds. Their characteristics are more for beauty, so we find the flat head of the Pekingese, the apple-domed head of the Chihuahua, the triangular head of the Pomeranian, the cushioned face of the Japanese. In Toy breeds facial expression and beautiful eyes are essential for their functional use as pets for pleasure. Their expression must show their character of the quiet disdain of the oriental breeds, the perky aliveness of the Chihuahua and Pomeranian, the glamour of the Maltese, or the stolidness of the Pug.

VARIATIONS IN HEAD CONFORMATION

The great variation in head conformation in different breeds is not surprising, but what is perhaps surprising is that there can be so many variations within a breed, of which only one is considered as being correct for the standard.

Collie heads, correct and various faults

Ideal head

Too much stop and blunt square muzzle

Rounded skull, high over and between the eyes, lacking chin

Roman nosed

Two-angled head, skull and muzzle not parallel

Prick ears

Ears set and carried too low

'Borzoi-type' head, curving effect in relation of skull to muzzle; foreface too long in relation to skull

It is quite a useful exercise to trace a head study in profile of a perfect dog in any breed and then trace all the variations that may be found within that breed. The Collie head is perhaps the classic example of head variations. The skull may be too coarse or the head too cheeky, the eyes may be set too far apart or too close or just right, they may be too prominent, too deep, too large or too small. They may not be the desired shape, and there are also all the variations in colour.

The skull and muzzle can curve from occiput to nose, the fore face may be too long in relation to the skull. There may be an unwanted prominence above the stop, which spoils the correct line and the expression. The profile may be so straight that there is almost no stop. The stop may slope too much so that it is too long. There may be too deep a stop. The muzzle may be too long or too short. The muzzle may dip or dish or drop away at the nose. There may be an overshot bite making a weak chin or a slack jaw, perhaps caused by lack of teeth. The mouth may be undershot, so giving a heavy fore face with the wrong expression. Ears may be set too high or too low, with all the other ear faults. The boney structure beneath the eyes may not be strong enough or may be too heavy. The nose may vary in size. These are just some of the structural differences.

With some breeds optical illusions are created by the markings on the head. The shape or lack of lozenge, the coat, or even the way a dog has been clipped or stripped, can alter the finished appearance. It is the observation of the small details that make a good and knowledgeable specialist judge.

Any number of differences of construction may be found throughout the dog. The judge must realize all this and then with confidence he can commence to examine each dog thoroughly, allotting its relative importance to each breed characteristic, without bias for any particular feature.

FUNCTIONS OF A DOG

When going over any breed of dog, the judge must remember the prime function of the dog. If this is borne in mind the judge is less likely to make grave errors when judging. In variety judging the judge must make a mental picture of the requirements of that breed as he approaches the dog. The judge will find that he will then automatically switch his memory to the salient features required so that he will be able to go over the Miniature Pinscher equally easily as the Briard.

WHAT DOES A JUDGE SEE?

A judge looks down upon the dog so that the top-line is probably the greatest area seen. This area from withers to tail is varied in shape according to the breed: Terriers, Great Danes, Boston Terriers, Whippets, etc., each has its own breed top-line conformation. Some breeds are narrow at the withers and wide at the hindquarters; others require their greatest width the other way round being wide at the withers and narrow at the hindquarters and in addition are waisted.

Judge's first impressions

Good, happy show trot (diagonal gait) Sway back Shy sluggish showman

Other breeds, on the other hand, may have little variation of shape between the withers and tail and are almost equal in width all along the top line, having little or no waist. Try putting the body of a dog into an imaginary square or oblong box and visualize the shapes and spaces. Another useful exercise is to divide a breed like the Cocker Spaniel into squares and to see how each part fits.

Many breeds have roughly the same proportions. It is quite interesting to try to divide a well proportioned dog into the number of head measurements, if for no other reason than that it makes you not only look, but see what you are looking at. Many head proportions are half and half, that is nose to stop (i.e. muzzle), and stop to occiput (i.e. skull), are approximately equal. Two and a half head measurements would equal the top line, that is, withers to base of tail, and the same measurement of two and a half heads would be the height from withers to ground. A German Short Haired Pointer is a good example of this. A Great Dane's proportions would be half and half for the head, with three heads for height and length. A Samoyed head is roughly an equilateral triangle, either from on top or from the side, and its proportions are one and a quarter skull to one of muzzle. Some heads are described as 'double-brick', that is, head and muzzle on parallel planes. Other heads may be wedged or domed.

Ear shapes and leathers are tremendously varied, as are the set and use of the ears in individual breeds. Terriers have ear leathers which hang forward so as to protect the inner ear from dust and dirt when they are digging out earth. Prick-eared breeds are the breeds which work with their ears and have especially alert hearing. Breeds with large noses and wide nostrils work with their noses and generally have pendant ears.

Ear measurements can be judged by whether they meet at the end of the nose. The length of some must reach the base of the nose, whilst others extend to about an inch from the base. Some ears can be measured from the inner or outer corner of the eye, depending on the breed.

Noses are all constructed in the same way, yet look at the innumerable varieties found in the breeds. Tails are also different by breeds: the Saluki's turns over at the end just like a bunch of feathers; the Alsatian's sabre tail resembles a fox's brush; the Labrador's an otter's; the Setter's tail starts with short fringes near the root, and these gradually become longer until the middle where they are very long, and then taper to the tip. The whole is called the flag. The Pomeranian has his tail lying flat and flowing towards his head. The Chihuahua has the curious, flat, furry tail, shaped rather like a musquash. There is the Bulldog's fascinatingly knotted affair turning round on its tracks, and then suddenly reverting to its original direction. Tail measurements are interesting. Some are twice the length of head less the nose. Tails are seldom too long, though many are required to reach the hock. The tails of Italian Greyhounds are sometimes measured by drawing the tail round between the hindlegs and wrapping it round the upper thigh to see if it reaches the rear. Borzoi tails are drawn round a hindleg to see if they will reach the top of the hip bone. The hands of a clock may be used as a gauge for the set of a dog's tail. Ten minutes past twelve would be correct for the breeds requiring the tail to be at an angle of 60°.

Dewlaps have a definite effective pattern which is most interesting when the head is raised, the dewlap appears in the outline of the neck, but when the head is down the loose skin falls heavily beneath the angle of the lower jaw and, if the dog or hound is wearing a collar, the dewlap folds over the collar. This will be noticed in Bloodhounds and other similar breeds.

Feet are equally varied: Pekingese turn their feet out, Foxhounds turn theirs in, and Salukis have tufts of hair between their toes which are inclined to web. King Charles Spaniels (English Toy Spaniels) are extremely prone to web toes and also odd numbers of toes. A trainee judge can have endless interest in looking, memorising and cataloguing his own findings.

OPTICAL ILLUSIONS

Judges must beware of optical illusions. An optical illusion is given by the close proximity of one feature to another. It is possible that a dog's head, for instance, may look too narrow or too large when in fact the head is correct, but the illusion may only be because the dog's neck is perhaps too short or too thick. Possibly the dog may look as if his top-line is too long. The judge

Optical illusions: same size head on different bodies

'Smaller' appearance of head

Same size head, seemingly larger because on a smaller dog

must make certain whether the body is really too long, or whether it looks too long because the legs are too short? Perhaps the dog gives the appearance of being short coupled, or is this only an erroneous impression because the legs are too long?

A class of dogs may all be 'too low to ground' for the breed standard, but the one dog who is the correct height might give the impression that there was too much daylight beneath him, and vice versa. A well-balanced dog will often look surprisingly small. Occasionally, one finds a dog which seems point by point to be perfect, and yet the whole effect is wrong. Individual features may possibly be out of proportion to each other.

Some judges may well laugh at the idea of dividing a dog into head proportions, but the same judges are often caught out on optical illusions. Rough head measurement compared to other parts of the anatomy may sometimes prove surprisingly useful in resolving optical illusions, providing a ready explanation of why individually excellent parts of a dog do not make up a perfect whole.

Such measurements are not in the breed standards, and judges may say that they would always know when a dog was right. Do not press the point. It is not always easy to tell at first glance where a fault lies. Therefore a rule of thumb may be a most useful guide for a novice.

A DOG'S MOVEMENT

It may well be worth reminding a judge of some of the facts of movement in the majority of breeds. The exceptions are the low-slung broad-chested dogs or where standards specifically demand that 'both fore and hindlegs should be carried straight forward in travelling'. Terriers and American Cocker Spaniels are amongst these breeds. But this is neither a good nor efficient movement and dogs moving in this manner cannot be stayers. The excessive inclination of the shoulder blade towards the spine is one reason for such action. All other breeds must be judged on normal kinetic balance, and this is no more a frightening word than perspective.

For centuries there has been gross misconception on the movement of animals because all leg actions were frequently too fast for the human eye to follow correctly. It is only since the advent of the camera, and in particular of films of animals in slow motion, that it is now fully understood exactly how animals move. This particularly applies to horses and dogs. Artists in past centuries drew what they thought they saw, as may be seen from old paintings and prints of horses and dogs out hunting. There are, unfortunately, still far too many important people in dogs today who still believe that the correct movement for a dog moving from a stand still, regardless of speed, is that the legs 'should be carried straight forwards when travelling', and on parallel planes to each other, just as when the dog was standing. Some people are in fact so unreceptive of the conception of kinetic balance that they actually refer to it as mumbo jumbo clouded with scientific words, and they would still rather retain their erroneous delusions on movement. We are in the twentieth century and any doubting Thomas's could resolve their doubts by watching a slow motion film. People can see a dog stand and they can also see the first movements at a slow walk and some people are absolutely determined that thereafter the set of the dog's legs will not and should not change in any way whatever the speed. This has been so strongly felt that even in these days, when new standards are being made for a well established breed, as for example the American Cocker Spaniel, the standard specifically demands that '. . . hocks strong, well let down and parallel when in *motion and at rest*'. Yet the same standard requires a dog '*capable of speed combined* with *endurance*'. A dog moving with his legs on parallel planes at speed could not possibly have endurance because he would lack kinetic balance. The hocks are only joints; what the standard is looking for, is that the hind pasterns should be on parallel planes. It is easy to watch a wire-haired Fox Terrier move and to see that the forelegs really are moving in a parallel plane to each other and this complies with the standard. But it is neither efficient nor correct for kinetic balance. A normally proportioned dog's legs must incline in towards a central longitudinal line the faster he moves in order to maintain perfect kinetic balance, obtaining the maximum performance with the minimum of effort in order to achieve staying power, just as a Fox does when moving at speed. Many a Fox Terrier has been put down by a judge because they had moved with correct kinetic balance instead of the legs travelling straight forward as is required in the standard. One hears judges saying 'they should move their legs straight forward but oh dear how few of them do!' The dogs know better!

The misconception about movement probably grew in the first instance by misinterpretation of some of the breed standards and this has not been helped by the numerous drawings of the so called 'Correct Movement' of a dog which appear in authoritative books all over the world. It is high-time this erroneous belief were erased once and for all. See page 128.

Many standards state that the forelegs 'when viewed from any direction', or 'viewed from the front and from the side', 'must be straight', and mention 'legs perfectly straight both fore and aft', etc. The straightness in these standards refers to bone, that is the forearm, and pastern, and from hocks to pads as seen from the front and the rear. This is perfectly simple: the dog must

Static balance

1. Vertical or near vertical set to shoulder blade; does not have to bring feet in to get static balance.
2. Slight or decided slope of blade; feet must be set inside vertical of shoulder point.
3. Decided slope to blade and curved forearm sets pasterns much closer together than elbows.
4. Wide base of support, no bowing inward of leg. [Pad would have to come to A for balance of blade, and to B for complete static balance.] Extra leverage on serratus and pectoral muscles.

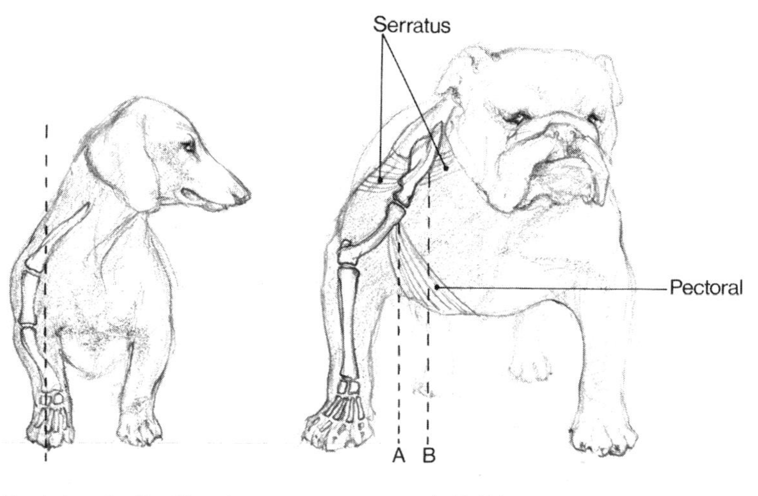

1. Alsatian
2. Pointer and many other breeds
3. Dachshunds, Scotties etc.
4. Bulldog

Pelvic Angulation

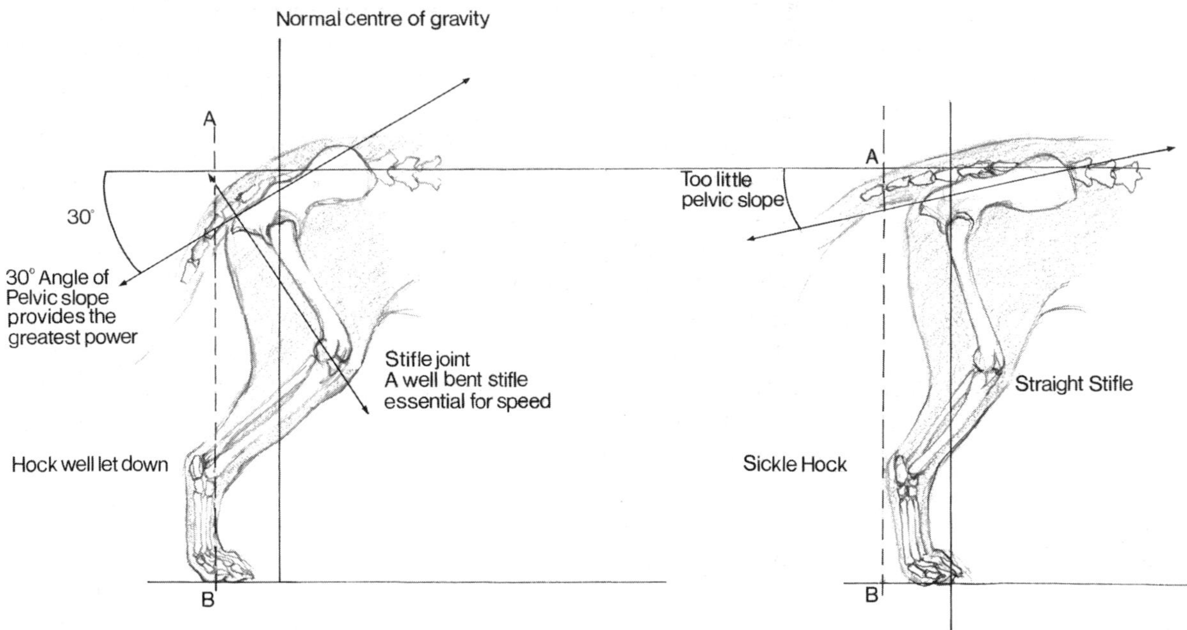

Correct hind angulation of Pelvis, Stifle and Hock: The dog is standing well up on hocks. Note line AB.

Incorrect hind angulation of pelvis, straight stifle and sickle hock.

have straight legs, but there is absolutely no mention that the legs must be perpendicular to the ground, nor that the right and left forelegs or hindlegs should move in parallel planes. This is erroneous interpretation of a standard. It is important for the judge to try to understand what efficiency and performance in movement is all about. What is required is maximum performance with minimum of effort at all speeds.

STATIC BALANCE

Looking at the dog from the front the inclination on which the shoulder blade lies on the rib cage will affect the position of the foreleg to attain static balance when the dog is standing. The

Stance - rear

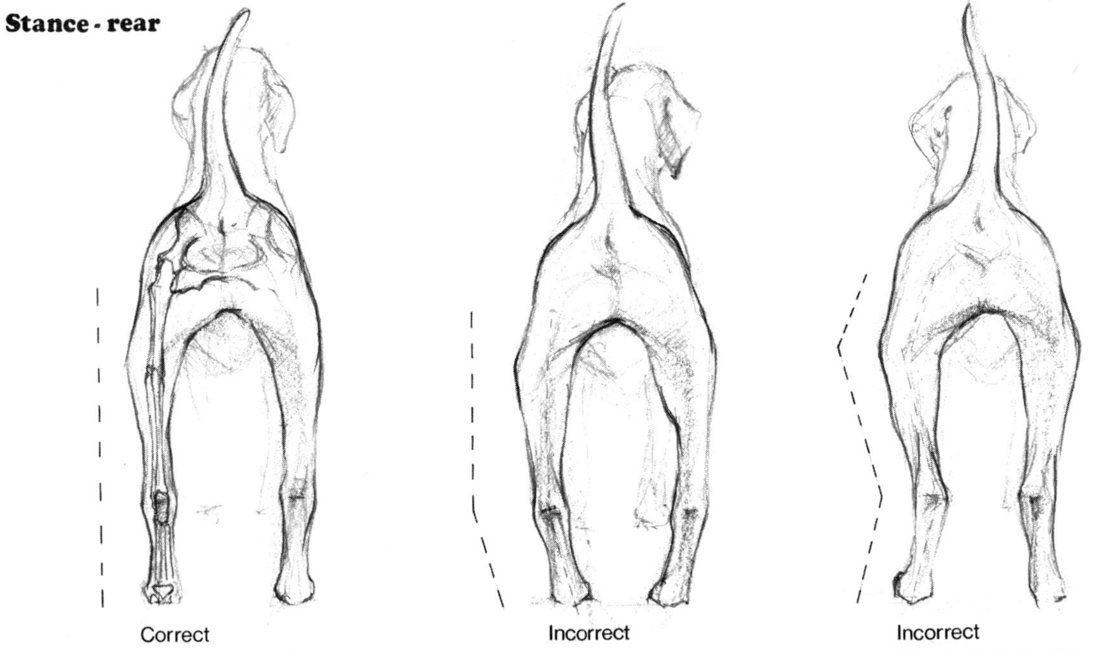

Correct
Straight line from centre of hip to pad.

Incorrect
Hocks turned out, not a common fault. Straight line from centre of hip to pad broken at hock.

Incorrect
'Cow-hocked'. Straight line broken twice, great weakness.

static centre of gravity of each shoulder blade is roughly the centre and in order to have static balance the dog must place his heel or the inner edge of the heel vertically under the centre of the shoulder blade. In a great many breeds, such as the Alsatian (German Shepherd Dog) the inclination of the shoulder towards the spine is very slight, whilst the variations of the inclination of the shoulder blade in some breeds become more and more extreme, until we find the Dachshund and, most extreme of all, the Bulldog. To obtain static balance the Dachshund generally has a curved forearm so that the pasterns are closer together, but the heel will still be in a vertical line with the centre of the shoulder blade, see diagram on page 125. Such breeds cannot move fast or work for long periods at speed. These breeds because of their faulty man-inspired anatomy will move with both fore and hindlegs travelling straight forward as demanded in their standards. The terriers move in this way too, owing to the narrowness of their withers, but none of these dogs can possibly have the staying power of a single tracking dog. However, since the standard demands that the legs must travel straight forward it is important that they do in fact travel straight forward. When viewed from the front or the rear the sequence of joints and the alignment of bones from shoulder to pad, or hip to pad, must remain in a straight line. A major fault is when the pad is lifted up and the leg is swung round in an arc only to bring the foot down straight ahead. This is wasted energy and obviously lacks efficiency for the greatest performance with the minimum of effort at any speed.

WIDE-SLUNG BREEDS AND LOW-SET DOGS

It is impossible for such dogs to single-track at any speed, but they should incline their legs inwards to the extent of their ability. Nevertheless, the sequence of joints must remain straight and there should be no deviation in this as the legs travel forward. Bow-legged dogs, or legs which are expected to turn out, obviously cannot move with the joints and bones in a straight line because they are not so initially, but they should move with the legs as straight as possible for the breed and with their greatest capacity for economy of movement. All the other breeds should single-track when moving at speed and should never be penalized by judges for legs which incline in towards a centre longitudinal line, provided the whole sequence of joints and bones remain in one straight line when viewed from the front or the rear. Needless to say, the legs should never cross, brush or interfere with each other in any way. The foreleg is always moved a split second in front of the on-coming hind foot and if the timing is right and the foot correctly flexed there will be no contact between the rear and front legs.

Kinetic balance, front and rear

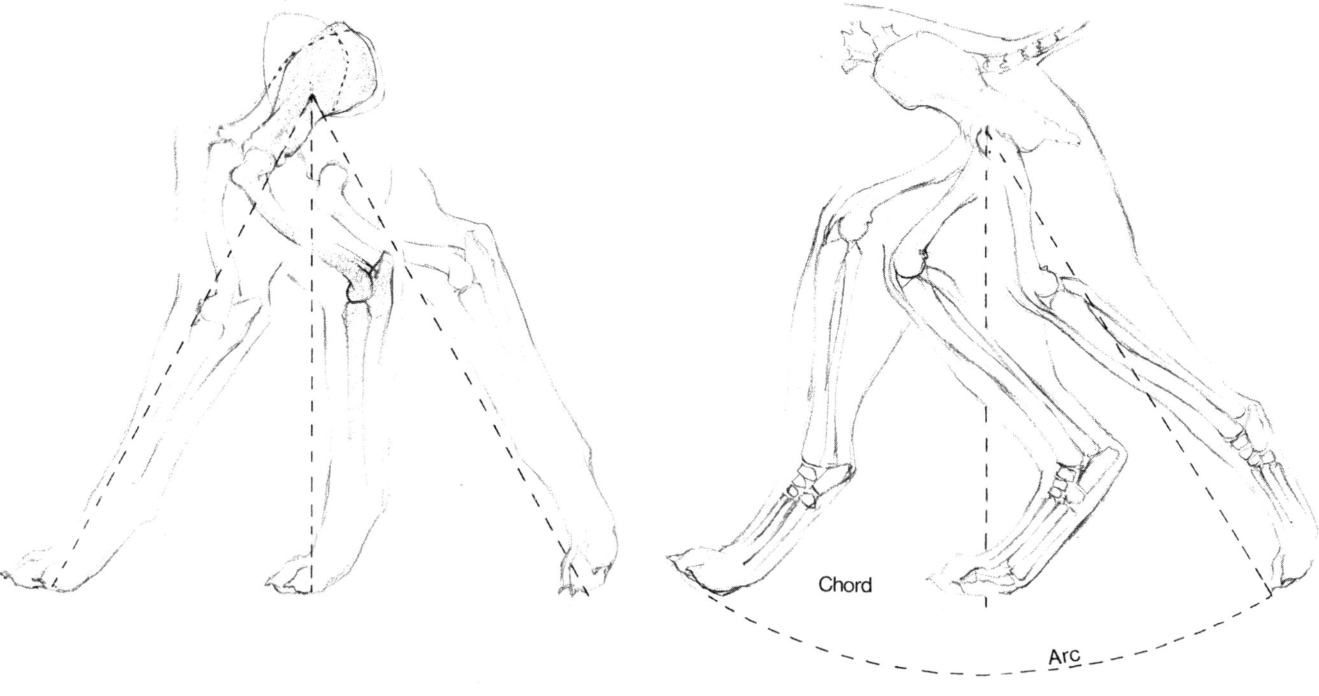

Standing and at three speeds – correct front movement (for hind movement see page 152)

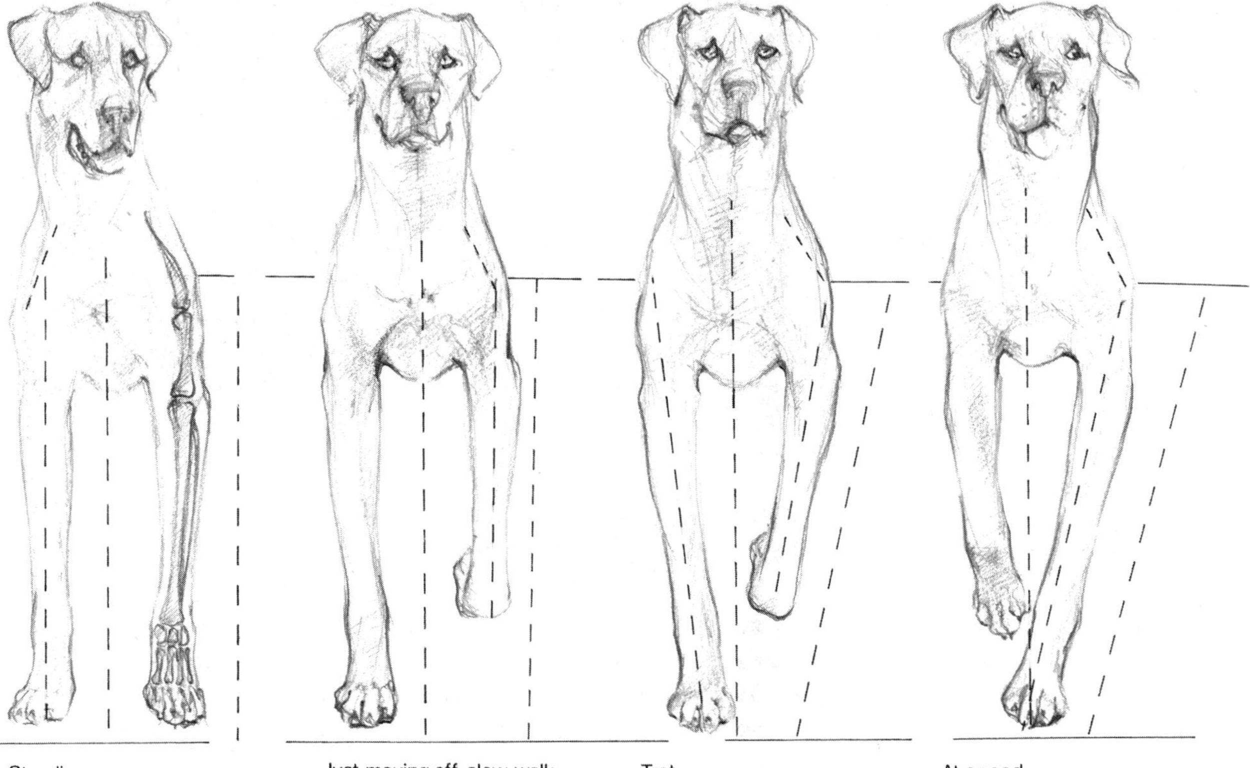

Standing
Static balance. Centre of shoulder blade to pad in one straight line. Paws turned slightly out.

Just moving off, slow walk
Weight on right leg. Straight line still almost vertical. Paws have straightened out.

Trot
Straight line from shoulder to pad, but now inclines inward.

At speed
Legs still in straight line, inclining further in; foot will not touch the weight-bearing leg as it is flexed and will step over it.

KINETIC BALANCE

Kinetic balance deals with forces in motion. When a dog commences to move, he will move from the position of his static balance and as his speed increases, in order to procure maximum efficiency in movement, the legs, when seen from the front or the rear, must incline inwards towards a longitudinal central line in order to maintain kinetic balance. The faster the dog moves, the more his legs will incline inwards until the speed is reached where he will single-track in order to maintain his balance. It is absolutely imperative that it be understood that the alignment of the bones from the centre of the shoulder blade, when viewed from the front, to the centre of the foot must be in one straight line, **but it is not a vertical line**. The same applies to the hindleg when seen from behind. The bone alignment from the hip joint to the foot must also be in a straight line but not a vertical line, except when the dog is standing.

EXPERIMENT OF HUMAN KINETIC BALANCE

As a simple experiment: stand with your legs slightly apart so that each foot is directly underneath its respective hip joint. Now try to walk forward keeping the legs at the same distance apart with the feet facing directly forward. This is how some people expect the dog to move forward. You will notice immediately that it is an unnatural movement, besides being an awkward and ungainly way of walking. There is no efficiency or economy of movement. You will notice as you move forward that the body has to sway from side to side in order to maintain its balance. It is certainly not a natural nor an attractive way of walking. It is even more ungainly when running.

Next try walking normally then fast and finally break into a run. You will notice immediately that at the fast speed you will be single-tracking too and your legs will be inclining inwards from your hips and will no longer be on a perpendicular plane to the ground, as when you first started to move. Your legs and feet, unless you are flat-footed, will still be in a straight line from hip to foot just as is required in a dog moving, or any other animal for that matter.

If, however, you have a weakness at your ankles and your feet turn inwards or outwards, then the straight alignment of your joints from hip to foot will be broken and you will be moving unsoundly. This is the equivalent of the dog moving close. If you happen to be knock-kneed (and most women are), and turn your feet out, then you have a similar double fault like a cow or a dog that is 'out at elbow' and has weak, turned-out pasterns. The required straight line from your hip to foot will be broken in two places, at the knees and at the ankle. In the cow-hocked dog the desired straight line, as seen from the rear is also broken twice, once at the stifle, throwing the hocks together, and again at the hocks, throwing the feet outwards.

At the slower speeds the inclination of the dog's legs inwards is much less in comparison than with the fast speeds. But whatever the speed, the importance is the straight alignment of the bones and joints from shoulder to pad and from hip to pad in order to procure maximum performance with the minimum of effort.

Pad mark pattern from static to speed, showing convergence and single-tracking —Foreshortened

SINGLE-TRACKING

There are unfortunately still too many people who do not perceive the difference between single-tracking and moving close. It is the difference between a sound dog and an unsound one. When a dog is moving fast and single-tracks at speed, his legs seen from the front are inclined inwards and the bone and joint alignment from the centre of the shoulder blade to the centre of the pad must be in one straight line. The forward-moving leg will not touch nor brush the weight-bearing leg as it passes it, because it is flexed and thus passes above the weight-bearing foot.

If the forward-moving leg brushes or interferes with the weight-bearing leg, then there is a constructional fault, and the alignment of bone and joints will not be in a straight line. If the alignment is correct and straight, then there will be a fault in timing or a constructional body fault.

MOVING CLOSE

The difference between moving close and single-tracking is that, when viewed from the front or the rear, the column of bones is not in a straight line: it is generally broken by the pasterns which either turn in or out. From the rear it may be the hocks which break the straight line of the bone assembly and this will be seen with cow-hocked dogs. This fault is a great weakness, because the line is broken twice between the hip and the pad (see diagram on page 152).

POUNDING AND PADDING

Pounding and padding are both caused by the same faults, an upright shoulder blade, which is frequently combined with too strong a rear action. Pounding is when the dog takes no action to compensate for the fault. Padding is the evasive action of a hackney gait which the dog employs, in order to lessen the excessive shock to the whole of the front of the dog through the pad.

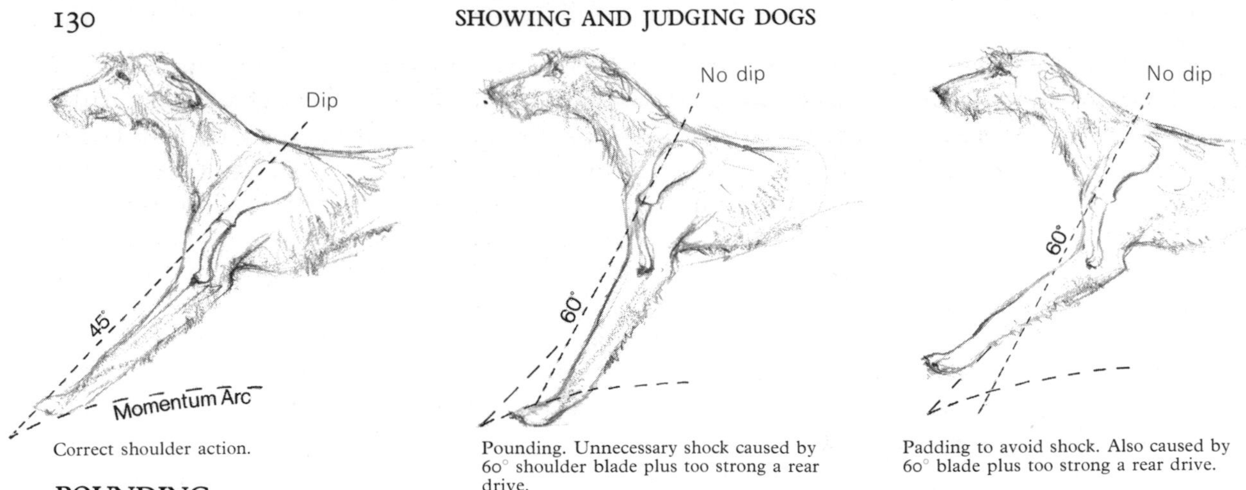

Correct shoulder action.

Pounding. Unnecessary shock caused by 60° shoulder blade plus too strong a rear drive.

Padding to avoid shock. Also caused by 60° blade plus too strong a rear drive.

POUNDING

The correct position for the pad to hit the ground in the fore limb is when the shoulder blade is set at an angle of 45°. The maximum reach of the momentum arc is reached when the leg is fully extended at any speed. For this it is also necessary for the hindquarters to be correct.

Pounding is the term used when the pad hits the ground just short of the momentum arc and therefore suffers unnecessary shock. The fault is due to the incorrect angulation of the shoulder blade lying at 60° instead of the more efficient 45°. This, combined with too strong a hind action, creates unnecessary shock through the pad to the whole of the front part of the dog's body. The dog does not try to compensate for the problem. The dog that pounds will obviously tire quickly and have no staying power.

PADDING OR HACKNEY GAIT

Padding is not to be confused with paddling when the dog moves with the forelegs wide apart. The term padding is used when the dog picks his forelegs up higher than is normally necessary during the forward stride, creating a hackney gait.

The fault lies in the faulty angulation of the shoulder blade lying at 60° instead of the more efficient 45°. This, combined with too strong a hind action, creates unnecessary shock through the pad to the whole of the front conformation. The dog compensates for the faults by the evasive action of a hackney gait which lessens the shock to the foreleg and the front assembly by using the muscles of the fore arm, thus causing the elbow to bend. The leg and pad are lifted higher and the pad is then dropped into the same position of the shortened momentum arc just as when the dog was pounding. The shock is less with this action, but the dog does not cover so much ground and unnecessary muscular energy is used, in order to bring the pad down in just the same place. A hackney gait may look attractive in some breeds but it is not a proficient performance nor an effortless one, and the dog will soon tire and have little staying power or endurance.

COMPENSATION FOR POUNDING

A dog with a 60° angle of the shoulder blade and too strong a rear action may learn to compensate for these faults in two ways in the ring. (There is a third way at the gallop.) The dog will use a padding, hackney gait in order to relieve the pounding action or he may change from using an almost full stride to short gaiting. A dog can learn to short-gait, even if he has a good turn of stifle with plenty of angulation.

When a dog short-gaits a judge should know why he is short-gaiting.

COMBINATION OF FORELEGS AND HINDLEGS IN LOCOMOTION

The forelegs endeavour to maintain the normal centre of gravity, but when the dog gaits, the drive from the hindleg action prevents this. The two assemblies are from then on in constant conflict and movement is in progress. The hind legs are not made to carry weight and there is much more stability at the withers. The heel pad is the first to strike the ground, when the hindleg has reached its maximum arc moving forward, and this pad takes the initial shock. As the leg commences to drive backwards, the toes come into play. As soon as the leg reaches the vertical position, power and push come into force, until the toes reach the furthest point of the arc, and the hindleg then starts to move forward again. Sometimes the leg is unable to fulfil the complete arc owing to a sickle hock or to the set of the croup. This will be found in dogs where the croup is either too steep or too flat. A 30° slope of the croup is considered as the most efficient.

Correct and incorrect hocks and dewclaws

Correct: Hocks and hind pasterns inclined very slightly forward

Hind dewclaw

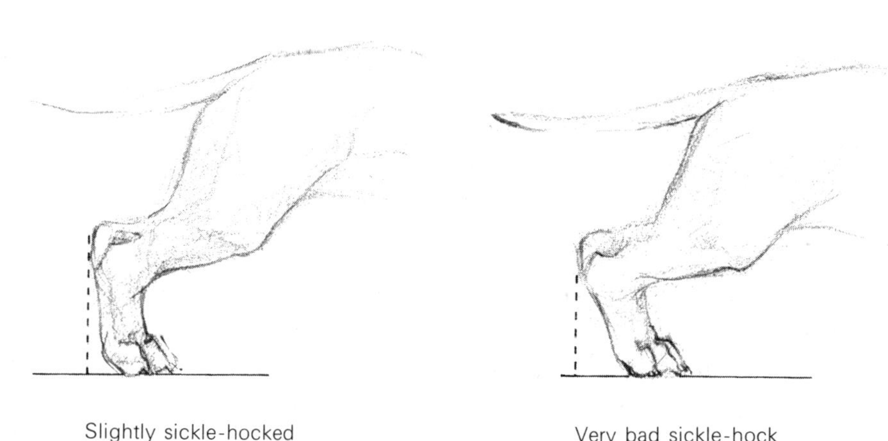

Slightly sickle-hocked

Very bad sickle-hock

SICKLE HOCKS

Sickle hocks are bad faults. The dog stands with a perpetual bend backwards, from the point of hock to the heel pad, so that the hind pastern leans back. This is frequently accompanied by acutely bent stifles. It is a fault frequently seen in Alsatians (German Shepherd Dogs). When a normal dog is 'standing well up on hocks', an imaginary line should go from the tip of the pelvis through the top bend of the pastern down through the centre of the hind pad to the ground. A good hind pastern from point of hock to ground should be inclined very slightly forward, although most standards require the hind pastern to be perpendicular from point of hock to the ground. The sickle hock causes the hind pastern to bend back considerably. However, provided that the Achilles tendon is sufficiently strong, and that it can straighten at the faster speeds, the fault is not so serious.

The two most important features to be correct in a dog are the shoulder, and the hock and hind pastern. If these two parts of the anatomy are correct there will be little fault to be found in movement, especially if there is a dip above the withers.

Incorrect movement

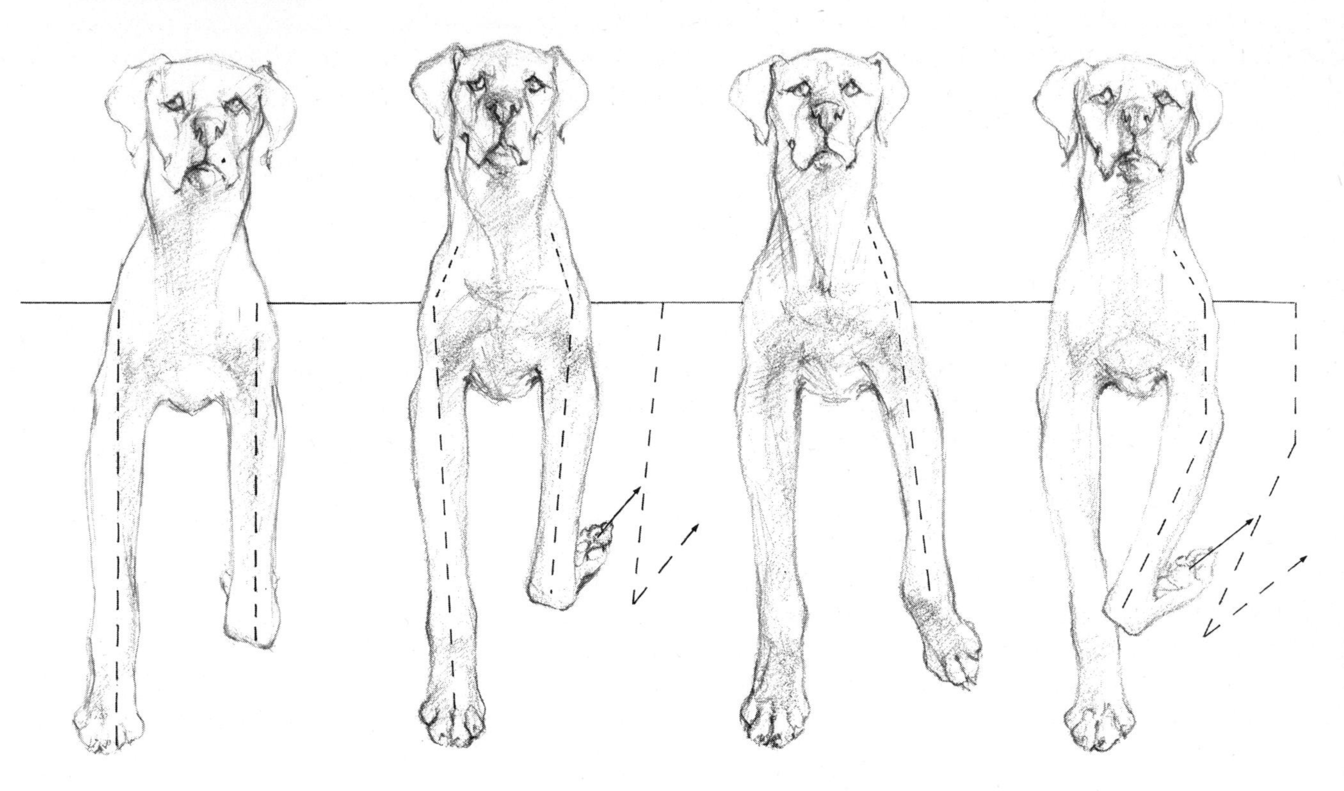

Parallel
Caused by lack of good angulation, kinetic balance, and tight shoulders.

Winging -
Bone alignment is broken at the pasterns.

Paddling

Weaving -
Bone alignment is broken at the elbows and pasterns.

Correct movement

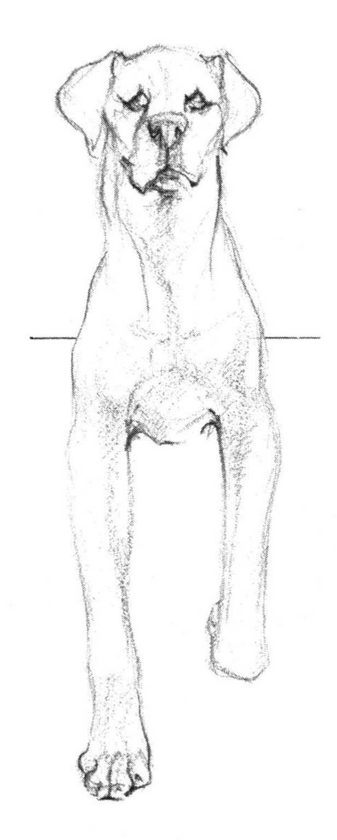

Correct

CHAPTER XIII

Judging Procedures

ARRIVAL AT THE SHOW

It is important that a judge should arrive at the show venue in plenty of time, and in a calm and composed state of mind. He should therefore aim at arriving at least an hour before judging is due to start, in order to have time to park his car and to find his way about the show ground. The judge must first make his way to the show secretary's office, to report his arrival. The judge will there be given his judge's badge and a luncheon and tea voucher. The judging book and a button hole may also be handed to him at the same time.

Once the judge has reported his arrival at the show, there is no objection if the judge wishes to wander round the show ground looking at all the stalls. It is perfectly in order for a judge to talk to friends, provided that they are unconnected with the breed which he is about to judge. It would, however, be unwise to indulge in conversation with anyone who is likely to be an exhibitor. There is, of course, no harm at all in saying 'Good morning' to friends and acquaintances. It is utterly stupid for friends of the judge to feel that they ought to cut him and to walk past him as if he did not exist. It is quite likely, however, that the judge may see some of the future exhibits trotting past him before judging, in which case it would certainly be better to look the other way. There are always too many people on the look out for something to criticize and quite harmless encounters are likely to be misconstrued.

Many judges, perhaps wisely, prefer to arrive at a show just in time to go straight into the ring. They also like to leave the show immediately judging is completed, so that they avoid any post mortems.

INSPECTION OF THE RING

The show secretary will have informed the judge of the expected time that he should be judging his breed or breeds, and he will also have been informed in which ring or rings he will be working. The judge must get to the ring at least ten minutes before he is due to judge. It is well worth while for a judge to inspect the ring or rings before he starts to judge. He may find that the grass is too long, or the ring too small for his breed; there may be irregularities, bumps or depressions in the ring, in which case the judge can decide to have the dogs gaited across the best area for assessing their movement. The judge may notice that some of the grass rings have been beautifully rolled and mown, whilst others resemble a ploughed field. Should the judge be judging a toy breed, he might consider asking the show secretary if he could judge his breed in a more suitable ring. Sometimes, at indoor shows, a judge may be asked to work in a ring which in his opinion is far too small. This is another case when a judge could ask a show secretary in the politest possible manner whether he could work in a better ring. There is no harm in asking for more suitable ring conditions, particularly when a ring really is unsuitable for a breed.

When matting is used, the judge should inspect it and make certain that there are no holes or tears and that the matting is laid flat. The table should also be inspected, to make certain that it is steady and non-slippery. If it is not, then something must be done to rectify the fault.

PROCEDURE BEFORE JUDGING

The judge should have time to become acquainted with his stewards and to sum them up, deciding how efficient they are likely to be. He may care to ask them to write their names and addresses at the back of the judging book for future reference. A wise judge will discuss his own particular judging technique with his stewards. This would include where the new dogs for each class are to stand, and that the winning dogs must be lined up going always in order of merit from left to right. A judge might care to remind stewards of the rule against dogs being attracted from outside the ring, and request them to inform him should they notice such an occurrence.

ORGANIZING THE ALLOTTED TIME

It is well worth while a judge asking the show secretary how many dogs he has had entered under him, if this has not been previously announced in the dog papers. Most judges are asked to make certain that they have finished judging by a specified time, either for the ring to be used by another judge, or in order to make certain that the group judging is finished on time, so that the best-in-show judging may commence promptly at 4 o'clock.

A judge can work comfortably with twenty to twenty-five dogs an hour. The Kennel Club recommend twenty dogs to the hour. The American Kennel Club allow 175 dogs to the day.

The judge should allow an hour's break for lunch, particularly when there is a large entry. If time is extremely short, the judge might consider taking his own box-lunch and reducing time to half an hour. It is important, however, to have a break, for, if a judge works for too long a period concentrating on the dogs, he may find that after four or five hours he is becoming over-tired. It is at this stage, when the most important judging is taking place, that the judge may possibly make a serious mistake: reversing an order, or even actually forgetting a good dog.

THE JUDGING BOOK

The judge is usually given the judging book on reporting to the secretary of the show. Otherwise the judge's book, prize cards and rosettes will be placed on the table by the senior steward. The judge's book will already have been marked up. At the top of each page is the class, and the bench number of each dog is entered down the first side column. The dogs which have already been seen have their bench numbers written either in red or in brackets. This indicates to the judge and the stewards that the dogs have been seen in a previous class.

ASSESSING THE TIME TO BE ALLOTTED TO THE BREED

It is an excellent idea at this stage, particularly if classes are large and time is short, for the judge to count the number of dogs he will have to go over in the time he has been allotted to judge the breed. Allowances must be made for change of classes, the distribution of ring numbers, and the award cards. The number of dogs should be divided into the time in minutes, and the expected time of starting each new class and finishing each class should be entered at the top of the page of judge's notes. In general, judges work to judging twenty dogs to the hour, so that the time that each class is expected to start should be written on the appropriate page. This should give sufficient time for the judge to go over each dog thoroughly and to watch his movement. If the judge has only small classes and the ring is not required immediately he has finished, the judge may decide to spend another minute on each dog. What must be avoided at all costs is for a judge to look hurried and not to spend sufficient time going over the individual dogs. Nor must the judge resort to slow tedious decisions. This is boring for everyone including the dogs and seldom produces good and efficient judging.

One more important point to be remembered is that the judge must judge the classes in the exact order in which they appear in the judging book.

THE ARRANGEMENT OF A JUDGING BOOK

The judge's book consists usually of a permanent reference column and three detachable slips (two if it is not a championship show). The four columns are each headed with the class number, the breed and variety, and sometimes the number of the class. There is also a line allocated for the number of prizes. After these headings the first section of each page is divided into three. On the left is the column for the bench numbers of each dog, one of the remaining columns is headed 'Judge's Notes' and the other 'Awards', where the judge enters 1, 2, 3, R (reserve), VHC (very highly commended) and HC (highly commended) against the number of the winning dogs. It must be realized that the judge does not know the name of the award-winning dogs. He has only the ring numbers to identify them, until he is afterwards presented with his catalogue by the secretary of the show, in order that he may obtain the names of dogs and exhibitors. Below the numbers the judge must enter any absentees in all the columns. There is one page allotted to each breed class and there is a final page where the winners of the challenge certificates are to be entered. Below these are the reserve best of sex dog, the reserve best of sex bitch, and finally a space for the best of breed.

SHOW REPORT

The judge's notes column should be divided by the judge, allowing roughly ten lines for the first award, ten lines for the second award, and seven lines for the third award. If for any reason this does not provide sufficient space, extend the dividing lines across on to the opposite page and continue the critique in these spaces. Some judges prefer to write the notes on the opposite page. If a judge intends to do this, he should, before judging commences, write the name of the class on the top of each opposite page, just in case two pages may be turned over by mistake. If this method is used, it is better to write the notes for the first class on the inside of the front cover, so that thereafter the judge's notes are facing the appropriate class.

Another method which is not often used but which some judges prefer is to divide up the inside of the back cover of the judging book into six or seven columns. The first column is marked 'Class'. Beneath this heading is written all the dog classes followed by all the bitch classes. The classes may be divided by lines drawn across the page. A space should be left between the dog classes and the bitch classes. The page is now divided into squares. As each class is finished, the number of the winning dog is entered in square one, the second in square two, and so on. In this way, the dogs from each class can be checked, so that an order is never reversed in subsequent classes.

EXAMPLES OF JUDGING BY THE SQUARE METHOD

CLASS	1st	2nd	3rd	4th	5th
Puppy Dog	1882	1889	1868	1888	1874
Novice Dog	1882	1889	1891	1868	1883
Graduate Dog	1878	1884	1889	1891	1873
Post Graduate Dog	1878	1873	1857	1880	1856
Limit Dog	1881	1885	1873	1857	1856
Open Dog	1881	1858	1885	1864	1869
Puppy Bitch					
Novice Bitch					
Graduate Bitch					
Post Graduate Bitch					
Limit Bitch					
Open Bitch					

ENGLISH JUDGING PAGE

BREED Chihuahuas (S/C)			Slip for Secretary's Office	Slip for Gen. Award Board	Slip for Ring Award Board
OPEN DOG			BREED	BREED	BREED
			Chihuahuas (S/C)	Chihuahuas (S/C)	Chihuahuas (S/C)
No. of Prizes 5					
Class No. 428			Class No. 428	Class No. 428	Class No. 428
Bench Number	Judge's Notes	Awards	Awards	Awards	Awards
3198		FIRST			
3199					
3221					
3223		SECOND			
3225					
3233					
3239		THIRD			
3245					
3247					
3255		RESERVE			
3261					
3266					
3278		VHC			
3279					
3280					
3283					
3286		ABSENTEES			
(3124)					
(3147)					
(3149)					
(3153)					
(3164)					
(3172)					
(3187)					

THE NERVOUS EXHIBITOR

The judge must remember that, if the handler is a novice and is also the owner of the dog, then he is very often kennel-blind. He is probably even convinced that his pet is the most beautiful dog in the world and is quite without faults! Patience is required for this type of exhibitor. Judges will encounter all too often in some breeds the hard and seasoned exhibitor, one who is not adverse to trying to pull a fast one should the opportunity arise. The judge must be on the alert and know exactly how to deal with any malpractices. At the other extreme, judges will encounter the nervous novice who is in such a trembling panic that his nervous state is being conveyed to perhaps an outstandingly good dog. A patient judge will try to be a little lenient and make encouraging remarks, such as telling the handler how nicely the dog moved, or when the handler cannot open the dog's mouth or stand him correctly, the judge could give a little friendly assistance and encourage the novice. This does not mean that the dog has to be placed, but it will help such an exhibitor and his good dog for a future occasion.

MIXED CLASSES

In over-large mixed classes judges may prefer to judge the class by sex. He may ask the steward to place all the dogs together and all the bitches together in line. If the classes are too large for the ring the judge may ask for the class to be divided in half, in which case it is probably better to divide the class by sex. If this practice is adopted, then the judge must select from each sex not less than the number of awards for the class and these dogs and bitches must then be judged together for the final placings. It is easier for the judge to have all the dogs together in a class, particularly since unilaterally and bilaterally cryptorchid dogs are now permitted to be exhibited in England and the disability is only counted against the dog as another fault. In some countries, quite rightly in my opinion, dogs which are not entire are not permitted to be exhibited, but what is more important such dogs should never be used at stud under any circumstances.

ENTRY OF DOGS IN INCORRECT CLASSES

This must be dealt with by the show secretary before the judging of a class has started. The dog can be withdrawn from the wrong class and transferred to an equivalent class of the correct breed, colour, sex, weight or height; otherwise it must be entered in the open class.

VARIETY CLASSES

In large variety classes it is probably a good idea to divide the classes into breeds and sexes. The smaller breeds should be kept at the end of the line, in order to avoid the risk of the larger breeds running into the smaller ones and causing congestion. In large classes the judge can place the dogs in order of merit as he works. This saves time re-organizing the final placings. The top five dogs in the line may have very little between them, in which case the judge would only have to concentrate perhaps on the top five dogs, after having seen them move for the final lap round the ring. It is quite in order for the judge to excuse the rest of the class down to the number of prize cards to be awarded. But every dog must be examined by the judge and seen at least once on a loose lead and from both sides. Many exhibitors prefer to stay in the ring rather than to be excused, busy handlers on the other hand prefer to leave the ring, so the judge must use his discretion.

WEIGHING AND MEASURING

There are certain breeds and varieties which are required to be measured or weighed for certain restricted classes. In the case of a dispute the decision of the judge is final.

MEASURING

The show executive must provide properly constructed measuring sticks or, for Poodles, fixed-bridge-type metal measures of 15 inches and 11 inches respectively and any other maximum height for the definition of any particular class for Poodles. All Poodles in restricted classes must be measured by the judge on a hard level surface before a class prize or reserve at a show may be awarded. A measure must also be provided for any breed at a show should the judge require one.

WEIGHING

Properly constructed and accurate weighing machines must be provided for every class where there is a weight restriction. Each dog must be weighed by the judge or his deputy before judging commences. Each Miniature Dachshund must be re-weighed by the judge before a class prize or a reserve may be awarded.

Miniature Bull Terriers and American Cocker Spaniels are amongst a number of breeds where measuring sticks are frequently required, owing to the diversity of size within the breed.

JUDGING THE FIRST CLASS

The judge should sit at the judge's table while the exhibitors and handlers are entering the ring. As soon as all the handlers have received their ring numbers and are assembled round the ring, the steward will inform the judge if there are any absentees and the judge must mark the numbers 'ABS' in the judging book. The stewards then take their place discreetly at the side of the ring or at the judging table.

Once the judge has taken up his place in the centre of the ring he is entirely on his own. However good and experienced the stewards may be, it is the judge who is entirely responsible for all that goes on in the ring. No two judges adopt identical methods or procedures of judging, but, whatever method the judge starts with, he should continue the same method for the entire breed. Most judges first watch the dogs gait round the ring, then examine them and watch them gait individually, and finally watch the class gait again.

The judge must remember that each exhibitor has paid him the compliment of entering a dog under him for his opinion on that day and at that particular show. The exhibitors have probably travelled great distances to reach the show. The exhibitors are probably all hard-working and many of them are busy housewives who have had to organize their homes, their kennels, their children, and their dogs before setting out. It is imperative that the judge should realize that on top of all this each exhibitor has had to spend a great deal of money on travelling, show entries, food and probably many other incidental expenses. It is, therefore, only fair that the judge should give each dog his full attention and allotted time when going over him, and also while watching him gait, regardless of whether he is a good, bad or indifferent specimen. The exhibitors have each paid their entry fee and are therefore entitled to have their dogs looked at properly. Most judges are able at the first summing up of the class to spot their top five specimens, but this does not mean that the other exhibits should not get his full attention. Rapid judging is unfair.

TALKING IN THE RING

It is a Kennel Club regulation that handlers must not speak to the judge in the ring unless spoken to, and this rule should be adhered to. However, on the other hand, the exhibitors have come to the show to enjoy themselves. Provided that the handlers know their place, so that judging can be made more fun and not too serious, it is perfectly legitimate for a judge to pass an amusing remark or two to ease the tension. Nevertheless, it is wiser to keep talking to a minimum.

FIRST IMPRESSIONS

The judge will take his place in the centre of the ring. He should look only at the dogs and not at the handlers nor at the people sitting at the ring side. He should first look at all the dogs from a distance, and he should consider each dog as a whole dog. The judge's glance should rest on each exhibit and should not pass over a bad specimen. He should endeavour to see each dog from all sides at least once during the class. Outstanding dogs will catch the judge's eye immediately, but perhaps on further examination a flashy specimen may not come up to his original expectation.

MOVING THE DOGS ROUND THE RING

Dogs should first be gaited round the ring in an anticlockwise direction. The movement enables them to become warmed up and get the feel of showmanship. It very much depends on the number of dogs in a class, the size of the ring, and on how short a time the judge has been given, as to whether the dogs are moved round the ring two or three times. Whatever the judge does, he must remain standing and facing the same direction in order to enable him to assess the side gait as each dog moves past him. He should, in fact, face the longest length of the ring. It is an unforgivable sin to allow a particular dog to catch his eye, and to follow it round the ring, the judge turning as the dog moves. In so doing the judge would allow certain other dogs to make one or two circuits of the ring without ever coming under his glance. Obviously, one or two outstanding dogs will catch the judge's eye and these may then be looked at on the second or third lap. Many variety judges judge the dogs while they are moving round the ring. It is invariably the judge's last impression of a dog's movement and always that of the spectators.

WHERE THE DOGS ARE TO STAND TO BE GONE OVER

Some breeds, including Spaniels and the Toy breeds, are gone over by the judge when they are standing on the table. Large breeds are examined on the ground. Yorkshire Terriers have individual boxes in the ring, but are examined on the table, while Pekingese are often all judged on one table together. Bulldogs are all set up facing the centre of the ring, whilst it is customary for some breeds to have their leads removed. All dogs, however, must wear a slip lead or collar and lead in the ring. Occasionally, a handler may ask a judge if he may show his dog without a lead, but this is generally not permitted.

GOING OVER THE INDIVIDUAL DOG

As soon as the dogs have completed one, two or three laps, the judge must order one handler to stop just before he reaches the table. The others will automatically stop and draw up at an equal distance apart, so that there is sufficient room for each dog. If the breed is one which is judged standing on the ground, the judge goes over the first one in the line, and then makes him move up and down or across the ring, or in a triangle. If, however, the breed is one which is judged upon a table, the judge should request the handler to place the dog there. In each case he must allow sufficient time for the handler to set up his dog in a show stance, or to stack it according to the breed. Whether the dog is on the ground or on the table, the judge should stand back and view the dog from a distance, observing it as a complete entity first from the side and then from the front. He must note type, balance, soundness, condition and showmanship. He should then approach the dog from the front, slowly, carefully and with confidence.

The judge should first extend the back of his hand towards the dog's nose, talking to him quietly and allowing sufficient time for the dog to appraise him. During this time the judge will assess temperament and experience. The judge must always avoid coming up suddenly from the dog's rear. There are some judges who prefer to look at a dog's front and throat first, but it is probably better to commence with the head. A good head is most important but not all-important. A judge must remember never to stare the dog in the eye. His glance should go along the dog as a whole. If the class is a mixed class, the judge must ask the handler whether the exhibit is a dog or a bitch, because, if it is a male the judge must remember in due course to ascertain if the dog is 'entire' or not. While the dog is on the table (or on the ground) conversation should be kept to a minimum, but a small quip which is light-hearted and to the point may relax a tense exhibitor.

AGE

Some judges like to ask the age of a dog, not perhaps because it has much importance to the judging assessment, but because it breaks the ice and paves the way for a more relaxed contact with the handler. Occasionally, age might be considered. When two dogs are of nearly equal standard the quality and quantity of the furnishings might have to be taken into account; or age may affect puppies in breeds where there is a size or weight limit, particularly in Poodles 'pushing the measure', or in an outstanding youngster still rather shelly and leggy.

If the breed is one which is judged on the table, the handler should always set up his dog at the end of the table and keep well out of the judge's way. As the judge advances towards the dog, having already looked at the head from the side, on top and in front, he should start by taking the dog's head in both hands, holding it behind the ears. Thereafter he should never lose actual contact with the dog until he has finished going over him in detail and has asked the handler to gait the dog for him.

ASSESSING BREED CHARACTERISTICS

EARS

The judge should proceed to go over the dog basically with the finger tips, using what might be described as a flowing, caressing movement. In no circumstances should a dog be poked or

Ears

Ear types

Erect - Alsatian
Prick - Scottish Terrier
Envelope - Pug
Semi-erect - Collie
Feathered - Papillon
Flaring - Chihuahua
Pendulous - Basset Hound
Rose-Whippet
Button - tips over eyes - Fox Terrier
Bat - French Bulldog
Lobular Cocker Spaniel
Pendant medium length Dachshund
High-set, rounded tip Mastiff
Lobular and clipped
American Cocker Spaniel
Filbert shape, hanging flat, tassle at end
Bedlington
Heart-shaped Pekingese

prodded. First, the set of the ears should be observed, noting their size, shape, length, placement and the thickness or fineness of the leathers. In some breeds the leathers are expected to meet when drawn forward at the tip of the nose. Some judges may show up their ignorance by performing this act with a Basset Hound only to find that the ear leathers exceed the point of expectation by a great margin. There are many breed idiosyncrasies regarding whether the ears are prick, drop, rose, pendant, button, tulip, bat, not to mention the varied angles at which the tips should lie or fall. In some breeds there are even certain ear carriages which may be disqualifications in the USA.

HEAD

The proportions of the head, the expression and typical breed characteristics must be noted. By placing the fingers behind the ears a judge can note the shape and breadth of the dome of the skull and the depth or slope of the stop. Eyes are particularly important, especially colour, expression and also placement. They may be deeply set or prominent, large, small or medium in size, and shapes vary from globular, oblique, triangular, almond or oval. Colour can be extremely important, ranging between black, dark brown, ruby red, light brown, hazel and yellow. In some breeds light eyes are looked on with great disfavour, although colour makes no difference to a dog's eyesight; and yellow eyes constitute a disqualification in some breeds in the USA. The width between the eyes is important and in some breeds the amount of white seen, or the size of the haw, must be taken into account. Black pigmentation to the eye-rims is essential in certain breeds.

The muzzle comes next under the scrutiny of the judge, and he must consider the width, depth and length of the muzzle in relation to the rest of the head. The fill-in and correct chiseling below the eyes, and in some breeds the depth of lip, is important. A judge may pull the upper lips down, in order to see if the two edges will meet beneath the chin. On the other hand some breeds require tight lips, whilst others must have well cushioned muzzles.

Wrinkles or lack of them are important points in some breeds and symmetrical markings on the head are important characteristics in other breeds. The diamond or thumb mark on the forehead, black moles on the cheek, a 'holy spot' or lozenge on the forehead and pencil-marking on the toes, are other breed idiosyncrasies. It will be seen how important it is for a judge to be conversant with the numerous small details in any breed that he takes on to judge. The size and colour of the nose varies enormously from breed to breed as does the shape and size of the nostrils and the line of the jaw. The separation of colour on the head is most important in some breeds.

MOUTH

The correct mouth is more important in working breeds than in some of the others. Many toy breeds lose teeth at an early age. One or two teeth missing may not necessarily be penalized, provided that the others are in good condition and of the correct bite required in the breed. Discoloured or pitted teeth which are caused by distemper should never really be penalized. As someone once said, 'they are the scars of victory' and surprisingly, though ugly, are often stronger than normal teeth. On the other hand if the texture of the tooth is poor then it is possible that the skeletal bones may be of poor quality too.

Many judges allow the handler to open the dog's mouth so that the teeth may be seen, or the teeth counted, and in some breeds that the colour of the tongue and membranes may be noted. This is a good idea in many ways as there is less likelihood of passing on an infection, but many judges prefer to open the mouth themselves. It is often quicker and easier, particularly if the handler is a novice. The judge must know what mouth is correct for the breed, whether the teeth are even, well set, clean, in good condition and also whether the dog has its full complement. In certain breeds it is necessary for the judge to count the teeth. This may be done by lifting the lip. In Germany, for example, teeth are considered tremendously important, far more so than many other more serious faults. For some reason it is believed that a dog with one premolar miss-

Mouths and bites

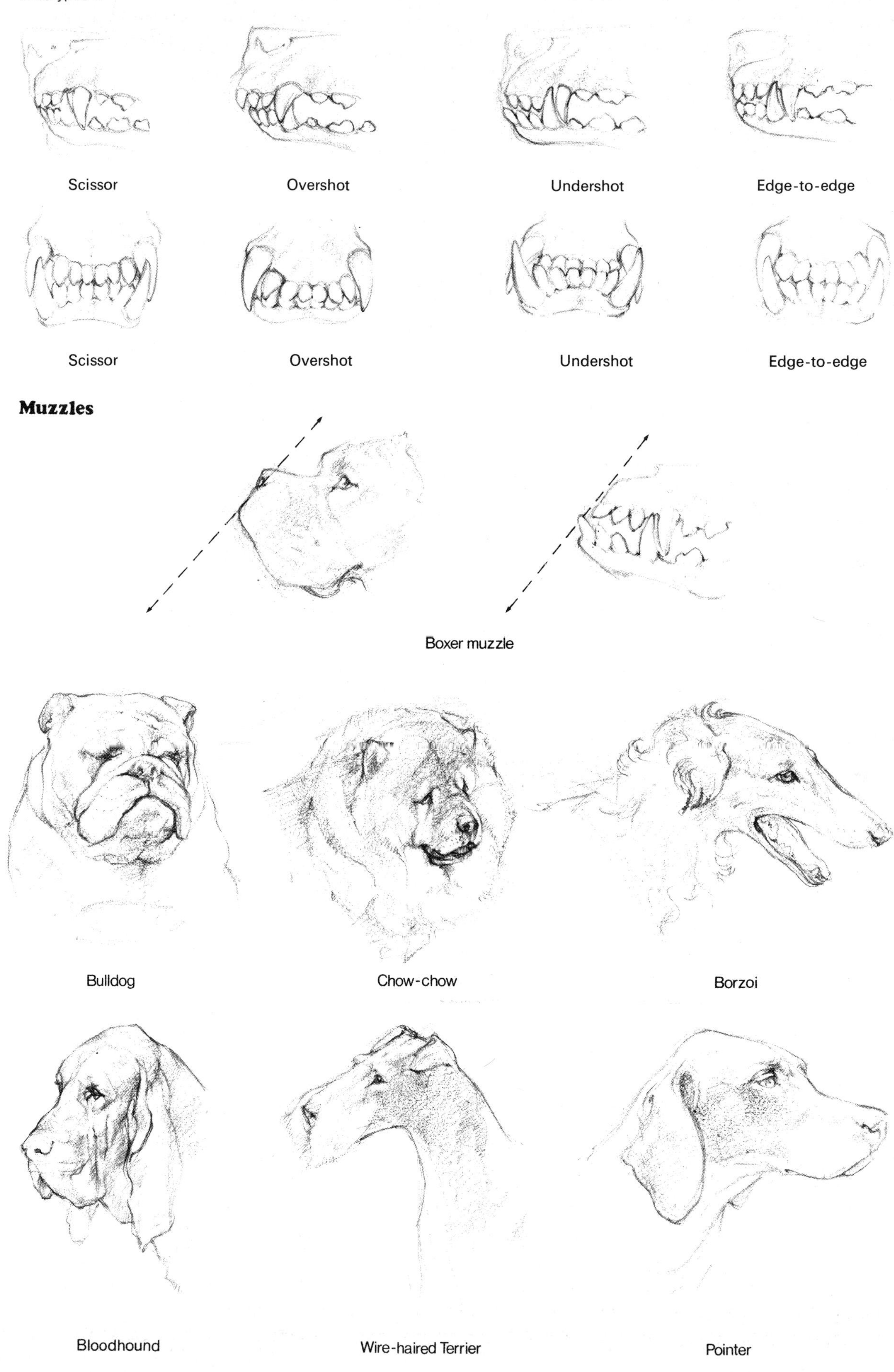

Bite, types of

Scissor | Overshot | Undershot | Edge-to-edge

Scissor | Overshot | Undershot | Edge-to-edge

Muzzles

Boxer muzzle

Bulldog | Chow-chow | Borzoi

Bloodhound | Wire-haired Terrier | Pointer

ing indicates a degenerate specimen, and, however good a dog may be in all other respects, it will automatically be discarded and will be unable to become a champion. Hairless breeds generally lack their premolar teeth altogether. Teeth should usually be strong, even, level and scissor.

NECK

The judge, having finished going over the head and assessed the proportions of each feature one to another, and realizing that heads and necks are related in length, must now examine the throat and neck and note whether it is long and refined enough, well arched, well muscled and sufficiently well set into the shoulders according to the breed standard; whether a dewlap is desirable or the throat is clean and dry. In some breeds it may entail pulling the ears forward over the nose so that the length of neck may be seen and any throatiness revealed. A useful method of gauging the length of neck is to measure the distance with the thumb and little finger from the tip of the sternum to the angle of the jaw. There must be a dip above the withers.

THE FRONT

The judge while still standing in front of the dog must look for static balance. This is not the same in all breeds, for example the Bulldog. The centre of gravity of the shoulder blade should be in a vertical line with the inner heel of the foot. The inward slope of the shoulder blade varies from being very slight in the Alsatian (German Shepherd Dog), to a much steeper slope in breeds like the Scottish Terrier or Dachshund, where the pasterns are set much closer together than the elbows in order to maintain static balance. The vertical line in these breeds will be further away from the upper arm. The judge must next look at the depth and breadth of the brisket and in heavily coated breeds the width should be felt with the palm of the hand uppermost. The shoulders can be assessed from the front, whether they are correct or perhaps over-loaded. Running his eye further down the dog he comes to the elbows. There are many dogs who suffer from dysplasia of the elbows. A clever, experienced handler may be able to stand his exhibit in such a way that this may pass unnoticed. The judge next examines the bone and muscle conformation of the forelegs and notices whether they are fine and straight, thick or bowed. In some breeds the bone should be round, in others, like the Borzoi, the bone is triangular with the greatest width behind. 'Bone' is the term used for the girth and substance of a dog's forelegs.

FORE PASTERNS

The judge must look carefully at the strength, length and shape and let down of the fore pasterns. They should be firm and there should be no variation in the width if the pasterns are strong. The bend sometimes comes from above the joint, or it may come from below, but it is generally agreed that some slope is necessary as it prevents knuckling over, absorbs shock and it provides lift to the centre of gravity. When knuckling-over occurs, due to the leg being too straight, the whole leg quivers so that there should always be some give at the pasterns. Too much slope is a weakness. On the other hand Alsatians (German Shepherd Dogs) require a pronounced slope owing to their particular construction.

FOREFEET AND HINDFEET

All four feet are particularly important in the large breeds as they are the weight carriers. The heel pads are generally larger on the forefeet than on the hindfeet. The reason for this is that the fore pad takes the greatest concussion whilst it is the toes on the hindfeet which help the heel pad when the greatest force is required. The judge must note the shape and size and tightness of the toes, whether the feet are cat-shaped (these being the stronger) or hare-shaped with the second digital bone at 45° or 60° respectively to the ground, and that the metacarpals are parallel to the ground; whether the toes are splayed or compact, webbed as required in some

Right: A poodle being measured by the judge.

Below right: The handler has set the dog up correctly at the end of the table. The judge has finished going over the dog's head and is now examining its hind quarters, whilst the handler keeps out of the judge's way by moving round to the front of the dog.

Bottom right: The judge is examining a Yorkshire Terrier. Normally the dog should be set up facing the end of the table, possibly the wind was blowing in the wrong direction for the coat.

Below: Some breeds have weight qualifications.

Left: A correctly stacked Airedale Terrier, showing his points to perfection.

Below left: The handler has set this Japanese up correctly at the end of the table. Instead of dropping the lead, which has allowed the dog to relax and sag she should have maintained control over it by keeping the lead well up under the angle of the jaw bone. Note how the judge is feeling the stifle in the crook of her fingers.

Below right: A well set-up West Highland White Champion. The handler is on one knee, the lead in the right hand and the left hand supporting the tail.

Right: A beautifully trained Beagle in a natural show stance.

Below left: The internationally renowned judge, Mr. Stanley Dangerfield, going over a beautifully presented Scottish Terrier.

Below right: A Staffordshire Bull Terrier facing forward as he would be presented in the ring.

The judge goes over a Pyrenean Mountain Dog at the Three Counties Championship Show.

A superb Standard Poodle winning 'Best in Show' at Windsor with the 'Reserve Best in Show', an outstanding keeshound.

Any adjustment to the fore leg is done by the handler grasping the dog's elbow and directing the foot to the desired position.

breeds and whether there are the correct number of toes. Pencilling on the toes and thumb marks are features to be looked for. In some breeds the colour of the pads is important and also the texture of the pads. There are also differences in the shapes and lengths of nail. In some breeds the colour of the nails must be black. Pekingese are required to have their forefeet turning outwards. There are some breed standards which state that the dog must have dew claws on the forelegs, whilst other standards require hind dew claws as with the Great Pyrenean Mountain Dog. King Charles Spaniels frequently have webbed toes as well as odd numbers of toes.

Up until now the dog has probably been standing motionless in the stance into which the handler has manoeuvred him or set him up. The judge may now, if he wishes, ask the handler to move the dog forward several paces. This will show up any faults if the dog is left to stand a moment or two. The judge may prefer to lift the dog up allowing his forelegs to drop naturally to the ground, or table, this will equally well show up any faults. Some judges prefer to place one hand on the withers and gently sway the dog from side to side, watching the front and elbows while so doing. Another method is to lift a foreleg and watch how it falls back into position. It is most important that the dog's head should be facing straight forward; otherwise, if it is slightly to one side, the dog will be off balance and the leg cannot return to the correct position. With this manoeuvre the judge can feel the hardness of the pads and the length of the nails as the pads touch his withdrawing hand when returning to the table. In some breeds the condition of the pads is most important. Some American Cocker Spaniels suffer from soft pads, and some may not have had their nails clipped sufficiently under the long, carefully trimmed feet. There must be some black on the back of a Gordon Setter's hindlegs; and so on.

The judge now moves to the side of the dog and, without losing actual contact, continues his examination. He may like to check the length of neck by hand and may ask the handler to draw the ears forward in breeds of the spaniel variety, or do so himself.

Measurements

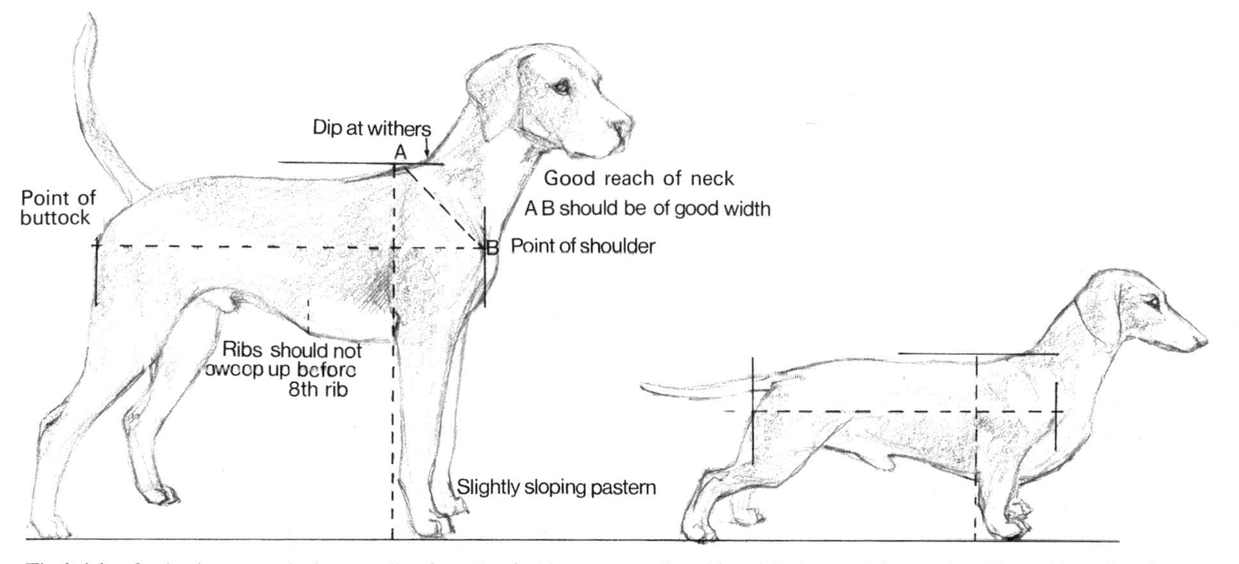

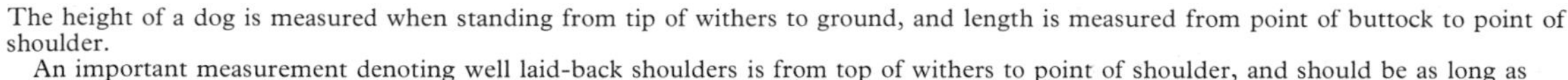

The height of a dog is measured when standing from tip of withers to ground, and length is measured from point of buttock to point of shoulder.

An important measurement denoting well laid-back shoulders is from top of withers to point of shoulder, and should be as long as possible. If shoulders are well laid back there will be a dip in front of the shoulder blade at the withers, and this goes with a good reach of neck, and slightly sloping pasterns.

Ribs should not sweep up before the eighth rib to allow for plenty of heart and lung room. To move well the body should be slightly longer than the height.

BODY

Next comes the examination of the shoulders from the side. In most breeds well laid-back shoulders are essential. To gauge a well laid-back shoulder it is important that the dog should be standing with his forelegs well under him. Many dogs have straight or upright shoulders and this generally goes with a short neck. Mr McDowell Lyon in his well-known book, *The Dog in*

Judging Terms

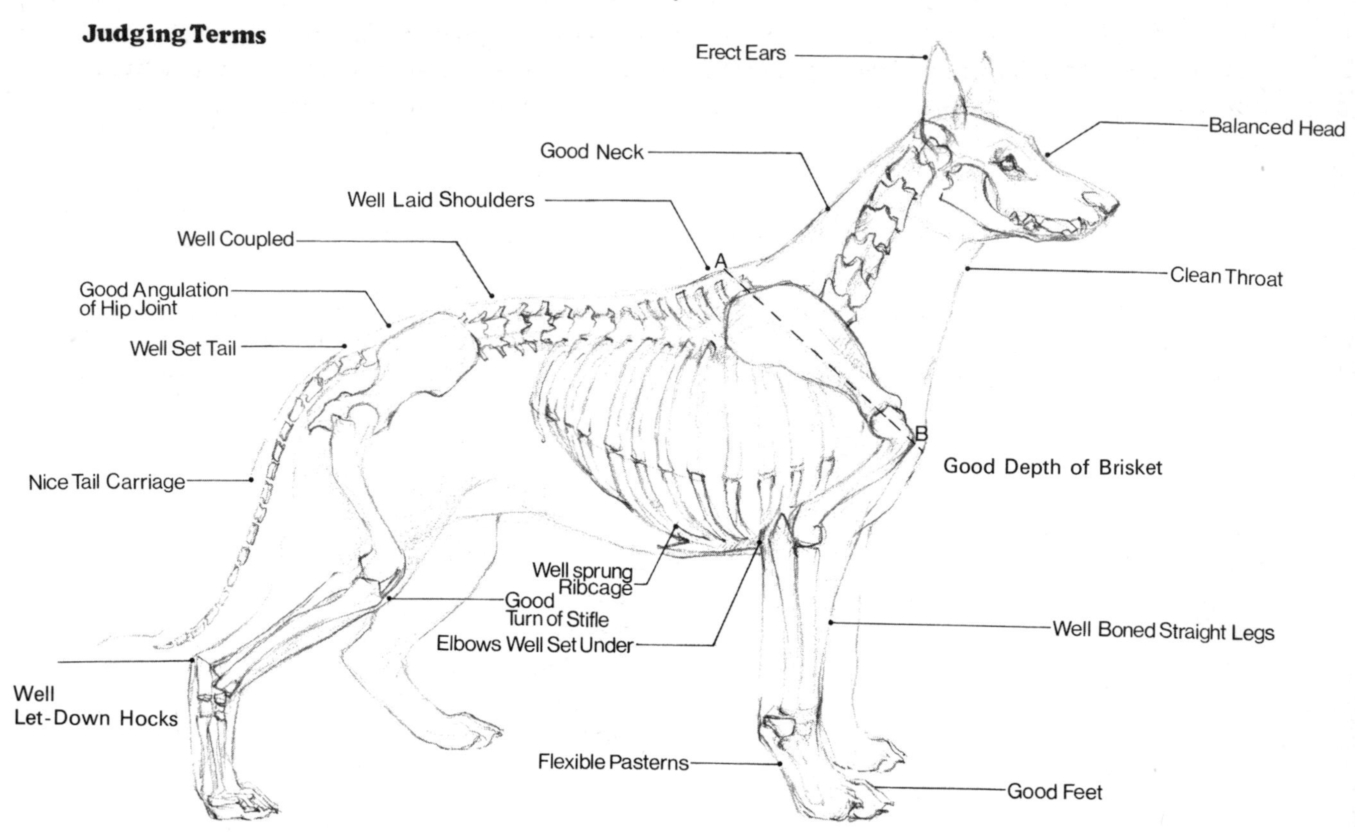

Action, states, that a 45° shoulder blade is twenty-five per cent more efficient than one of 60°. Many show dogs, however, have blades of 70°, which leads to even less efficiency.

The width between the withers (the top of the shoulder blades) varies considerably in different breeds. In some they are separated by a hand's breadth. In others it is essential that the withers should be close together and set high. Strength and stability are at the withers, not at the croup and loin. There should be a definite dip between the withers and the neck.

If the handler is a novice, it may be necessary for the judge to ask him to stand by the dog's head while he is going over the side and rear of the dog, and vice versa. Next comes the examination of the top-line, this is the largest expanse of the dog seen by the judge. The length of the top-line generally corresponds to the length of head. The judge must note if the top-line is broad and level and whether the back and loins are strong and straight or if the latter are slightly convex and whether they feel strong and firm and well muscled. Perhaps the withers are slightly higher than they should be. Look well at the croup as this gives the true angle of the pelvis and is controlled by the muscles: does it fall away sufficiently or too much? Is the body well coupled. Some breeds are inclined to roach. Notice the muscles on the shoulders and loins: are they overloaded, or correct for the breed? Regard the depth of the chest at the ninth rib for sufficient heart and lung room. Is the width correct with well sprung ribs or is the dog slab-sided? In the majority of breeds the chest cage reaches the elbows, which are half the height of the dog from the ground. The exceptions are the short-legged breeds where the bottom of the chest reaches the pasterns. Continuing along the top-line, the judge must note the strength of the loins and the tuck-up which should not sweep up before the ninth rib. Some breeds require a hand's length in the flank. If the dog is overbuilt, so that the hindquarters are higher than the withers, a constructional fault may be found to be at the stifles or the fore-pasterns. In some breeds, where stifles are weak, it may be worth pressing down on the hindquarters. The dog automatically resists, but the judge can watch what happens at the stifle joint. Pressure on the hindquarters does not show strength, the strength is at the withers and loins. Conversely, the fault may be caused by dysplasia of the elbows, which in dog parlance is known as 'out at elbow'. In some breeds clever trimming may hide a conformation fault by leaving more coat in a desired area and/or removing extra coat from another area. Too low a tail set can be successfully camouflaged in this way. Hindquarters in trimmed or heavily coated breeds can be most deceptive too, but an observant and knowledgeable judge will never be taken in by what lies under a coated dog.

TAIL

It has been said that a dog is no better than his tail and the many varied tail shapes and positions have often been caused by mutations. When referring to the root of the tail, judges actually mean the four coccygeal vertebrae of the tail. The fourth is the first one that comes into view, the previous three being the last of the sacreal vertebrae. Anything wrong with the tail vertebrae will invariably create problems with other bones near this area. This is the reason why

Tails

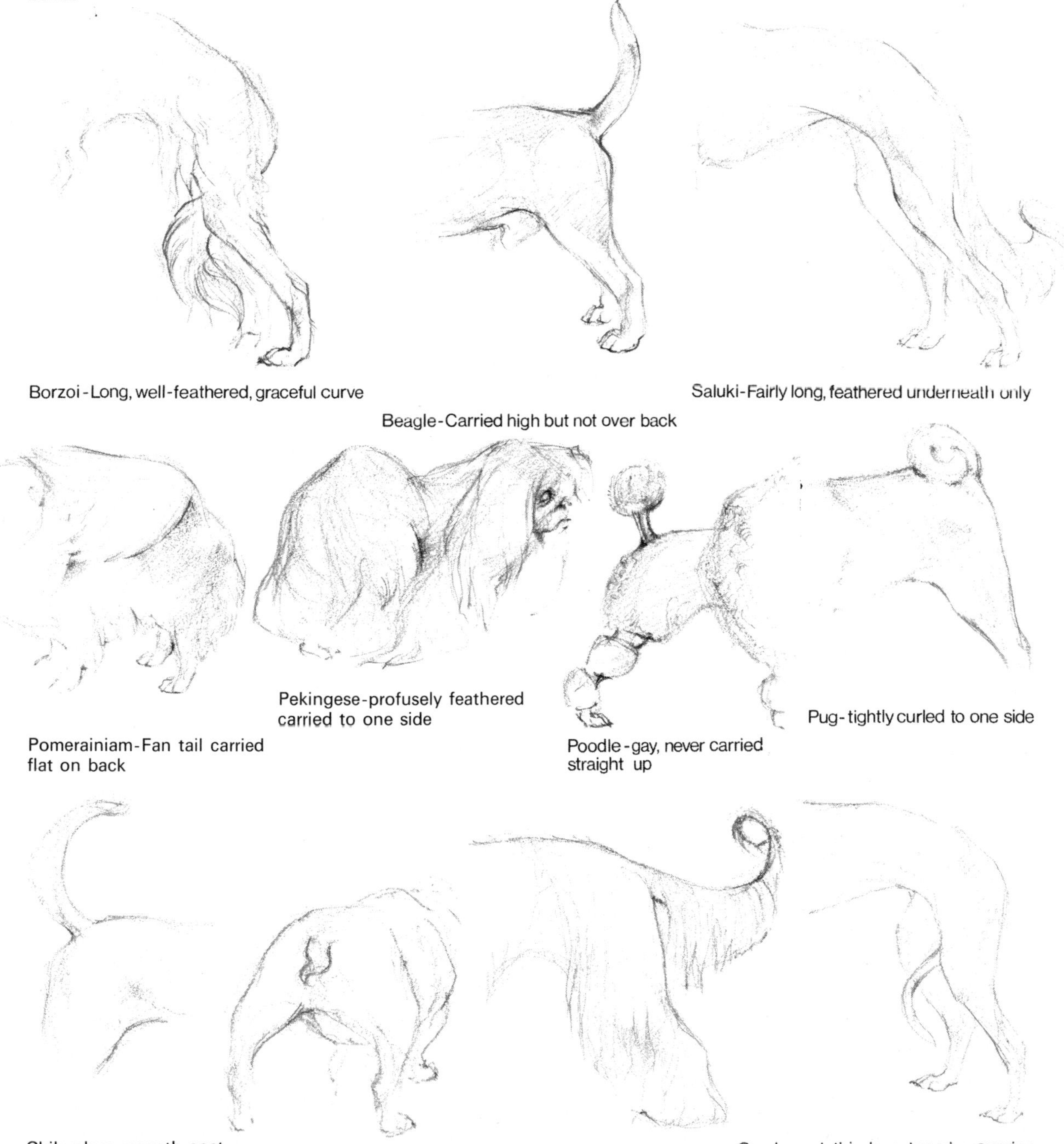

Borzoi - Long, well-feathered, graceful curve

Beagle - Carried high but not over back

Saluki - Fairly long, feathered underneath only

Pomerainiam - Fan tail carried flat on back

Pekingese - profusely feathered carried to one side

Poodle - gay, never carried straight up

Pug - tightly curled to one side

Chihuahua smooth coat - flat and furry, wider in centre

Bulldog - screwed or straight carried low

Afghan - carried high with ring at end, never bushy

Greyhound - thin, long, tapering curving up at end

Tails

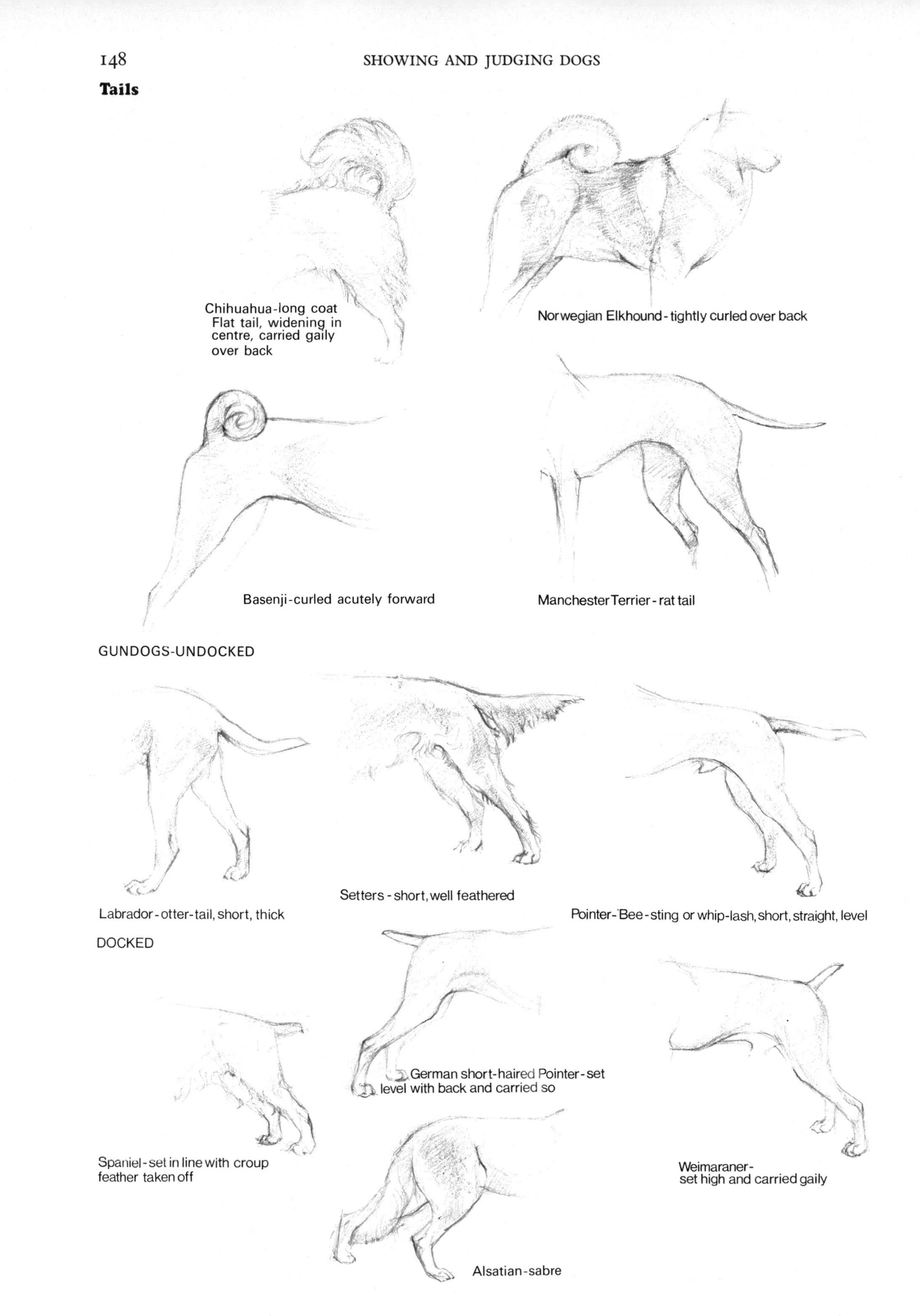
Chihuahua-long coat
Flat tail, widening in centre, carried gaily over back
Norwegian Elkhound - tightly curled over back
Basenji-curled acutely forward
Manchester Terrier - rat tail
GUNDOGS-UNDOCKED
Labrador - otter-tail, short, thick
Setters - short, well feathered
Pointer-'Bee-sting or whip-lash, short, straight, level
DOCKED
Spaniel - set in line with croup feather taken off
German short-haired Pointer - set level with back and carried so
Weimaraner-
set high and carried gaily
Alsatian-sabre

some breeds had their tails docked, so that they should all be uniform in the ring. Welsh Corgis (Pembroke), Dobermanns and Smooth Fox Terriers are some of these breeds. There are natural bobtails as well as some puppies in a litter having normal tails. The judge, however, must judge to the breed standard, however much he despises the docking of tails. He must first consider the tail set and the alignment. Some standards do not actually mention the docking of tails, and undocked tails are not mentioned as disqualifications. Occasionally, an outstanding dog will be exhibited with a tail that has either been docked too short or left too long. Some judges will penalize this but after all it is a man-made fault and should not influence the judges' decision.

On the other hand, some breeds are required to have long tails and breeders often have individual methods for gauging the correct length.

TESTICLES

If the dog is a male it is important to check that he is entire, but this must be done carefully and gently. In some countries dogs are examined by the veterinary surgeon before entry to the show and, if the dog is found not to be entire, he will automatically be disqualified from competing. In Britain the rule has been changed and the lack of one or even both testicles is treated merely as any other fault and the dog judged accordingly.

HINDQUARTERS AND LEGS

The judge must look at the hindquarters carefully and note the length and strength of the bones of the hindlegs, whether there is a good turn of stifle as required in some breeds, whether the hocks are well let down if speed is required, and if the thighs are strong and powerful. There are tremendous variations in the stifle joint. Some breeds are expected to have straight stifles and, unfortunately, there are very many breeds which suffer from weak or slipping stifle joints, and these are by no means all found in the toy breeds. The joint can be felt in the crook of the fingers for any suspected weakness. Many dogs can move most beautifully with stifle joints far from correct, but what few of them can do is to stand for long without the joint going straight. This in turn will cause the over-flection of the lower pastern joint. One joint cannot go out of alignment without affecting one or more of the nearest joints, which automatically have to compensate. Stifle joints which completely slip in and out are quite obvious, because the dog will hop and skip a few steps or even move for a few yards on three legs, until the joint slips back into its correct position. Judges will hear from the handlers many excuses for this movement: the usual ones are the length of the grass, or the slippery floor. Sadly, there are some breeds where it is comparatively rare to find a class of dogs without weak stifle joints. Cow-hocks are another weakness. The greater the fault, the more inefficient will be the movement. Pasterns which are below the hocks should be firm, and of one thickness, all the way down. The hock to pad assembly is extremely important. Well let-down hocks are indicative of endurance, higher hocks for speed. A bent sickle hock is a serious fault. This is when the line of the hind pastern, from the hock to the heel, lies back instead of upright or very slightly forward. A dog standing well up on hocks is in the ideal position for examining the angle of the pelvis and the thigh.

HINDFEET

The judge must look carefully at the hindfeet. These with the forefeet are the weight carriers. The hind pads are smaller than the fore pads, and he must note whether they are 'cat' or 'hare', whether the toes are well arched, slightly arched or slack or spread out. The hind toes are even more important than the front ones. The second digital toe should be at 45° to the ground. Some breeds require webbed toes, whilst others do not, and have them. Sometimes there are an odd number of toes. Nails must be examined carefully to see if they are the correct length and whether they touch the ground. Black nails are required in some breeds. Occasionally, nails are uncared for and they may be so long that they curl, and prevent the dog from moving correctly. Certain breeds must have exceptionally large feet with well-arched toes. A Borzoi should be able to have a tennis ball placed inside the arch. Cat feet are always stronger than hare feet and are not so liable to injury. The judge must not forget to notice the pencil marks required in some breeds. These are the dark lines down each toe required in the Miniature Pinscher.

DEWCLAWS

These are generally removed, but they are required on forelegs or hindlegs or both in some standards, notably Briards and Pyrenean Mountain Dogs.

SKIN AND COAT

Skin texture and quality are a great indication as to a dog's general health and fitness and are naturally important in the hairless breeds.

Coat is considerably more important in some breeds than in others, particularly in the long-coated breeds, such as Afghans, Maltese, Yorkshire Terriers, Shih Tzus and the Spitz breeds. It is not necessarily only the length and quantity, but also the quality and texture that are important. In many breeds a good undercoat is also necessary. Where breeds are judged on a points system, the judge will know how important coat is in relation to the other features in the standard. Only some breeds in the USA are judged on points, and none in England.

COLOUR

Colour or colours are rated extremely highly in some breeds. In the Yorkshire Terrier, for instance, it is extremely important that particular colours should appear only in certain areas, and also that the colour at the roots should be darker than at the tips, and that the tan should be bright and clear. Pugs require contrast between the main colour, trace and the mask. The tan in Dobermanns and American Cockers must be bright. Papillons require symmetrical markings and Dalmatians should have some spots on the tail and the ears. White patches in some breeds are a fault, as are certain colours. In the United States they may even be a disqualification. Buff American Cockers are expected to have the coat of one solid colour, but this is seldom possible as the hair is always lighter at the tips, though this does not show up so much on the silver-buffs.

FEATHERING AND FURNISHINGS

Furnishings are obviously more important in some breeds than in others. The fringes in Collies are called trousers in dogs, petticoats for bitches. The amount of ruff, fringes and tail feathering must conform with the standard; but it must be remembered that many dogs do not obtain their full coat until they are three years old, bitches often become out of coat after whelping, and many breeds have seasonal coats. Furnishings are important, but the judge must know what goes on beneath them. Coats which are too long and impede the dog's movement are generally penalized.

There are a number of breeds which are permitted to be trimmed and clipped. In some of these the standard states that excessive coats should be penalized. This clearly is a matter of interpretation. A heavily-coated dog may have been severely trimmed, whilst a less heavily-coated dog, which has been less severely trimmed, may be put down by a judge for having an excessive coat.

It should be remembered—as any breeder who has bred long- or heavily-coated dogs will know—that it is extremely difficult to preserve a long and flowing coat. Such a coat requires hours of work and great care with brushes and combs. These dogs require to be carefully exercised in selected countryside, where brambles and ferns will not destroy the coat. Take a heavily-coated American Cocker Spaniel out shooting in thick covert, and in a week he will probably have destroyed most of his flowing coat.

REVEALING THE JUDGE'S OPINION

A judge should always go over a dog as if he had never seen it before, however well he knows it. Many judges go over a dog without making any comment at all. Other judges perhaps toss an odd comment here and there, whilst some prefer to speak their thoughts out loud, giving the handler an opinion at that moment (provided that the opinion on the dog is not too derogatory). This method is nearly always well received by the novices, since it is from this that they learn about their exhibit. Seasoned exhibitors doubtless already know only too well the merits and faults of their dog, although a surprising number are quite kennel blind.

The exhibitors have come under the judge for his opinion of the dog on the day, and it saves time to comment immediately, because otherwise it may not be possible to remember the dog if asked about it later. Obviously, a judge is not judging on faults, and when he is thinking aloud he must minimize the faults and enlarge on the good qualities. Even rivals like to hear good remarks about their dogs. This method may occasionally attract back-chat, but, if so, the judge must assert himself immediately. It is often wiser to mention a fault verbally than to write it in your report, though I am not in favour of omitting faults from reports altogether.

APPRAISING THE DOG BEFORE GAITING

When the judge has gone over the dog carefully, appraising every feature and characteristic one with another, he should stand back and once again look at the dog as a whole for type, soundness, balance, harmony and beauty. A well balanced dog, for instance, may often appear surprisingly small. During the examination of the dog the judge will also obtain a good idea of the dog's natural temperament, but the most important factor is that the dog should be of the correct type for the breed. A clever, experienced handler knows how to make the most of his dog. The real test, however, will come when the judge sees the dog gait for him. Plaiting and weaving cannot be concealed and cow-hocks become very apparent. Head carriage, a level top line and tail set and the dog's aura and expression are given free rein for the judge to observe. Occasionally, a dog may be so tense on a table or standing on a slippery floor, that he will appear out at elbow or even cow-hocked, when in reality he is perfectly sound. These are occasions when an expert judge who knows his job is not fooled, just as he also knows what lies under a full and flowing coat.

GAITING

The next procedure is for the judge to ask the handler to gait his dog and in so doing it is important that the judge should indicate to the handler exactly how he wishes to see the dog being moved. This may be straight up and down or across the ring, in a triangle, or both, or any other method the judge prefers, such as diagonally across the ring obtaining the maximum length for gaiting, or in a 'T', or each dog starting from where he is standing and moving across the ring. The judge should not hustle the handler and should allow sufficient time for the handler to replace the lead in breeds where it is normal procedure for the lead to be removed. If the dog is on the table, the judge must allow the handler plenty of time to put his dog on the ground. The dog usually likes to sneeze or shake himself before starting to gait.

WHAT THE JUDGE MUST LOOK FOR IN THE GAIT

A normally proportioned dog moving with full efficiency from a stand-still starts off at a walk with one forefoot followed by the opposite hindfoot, then the other forefoot and its opposite

Movement–rear (for front movement see pages 128 and 132)

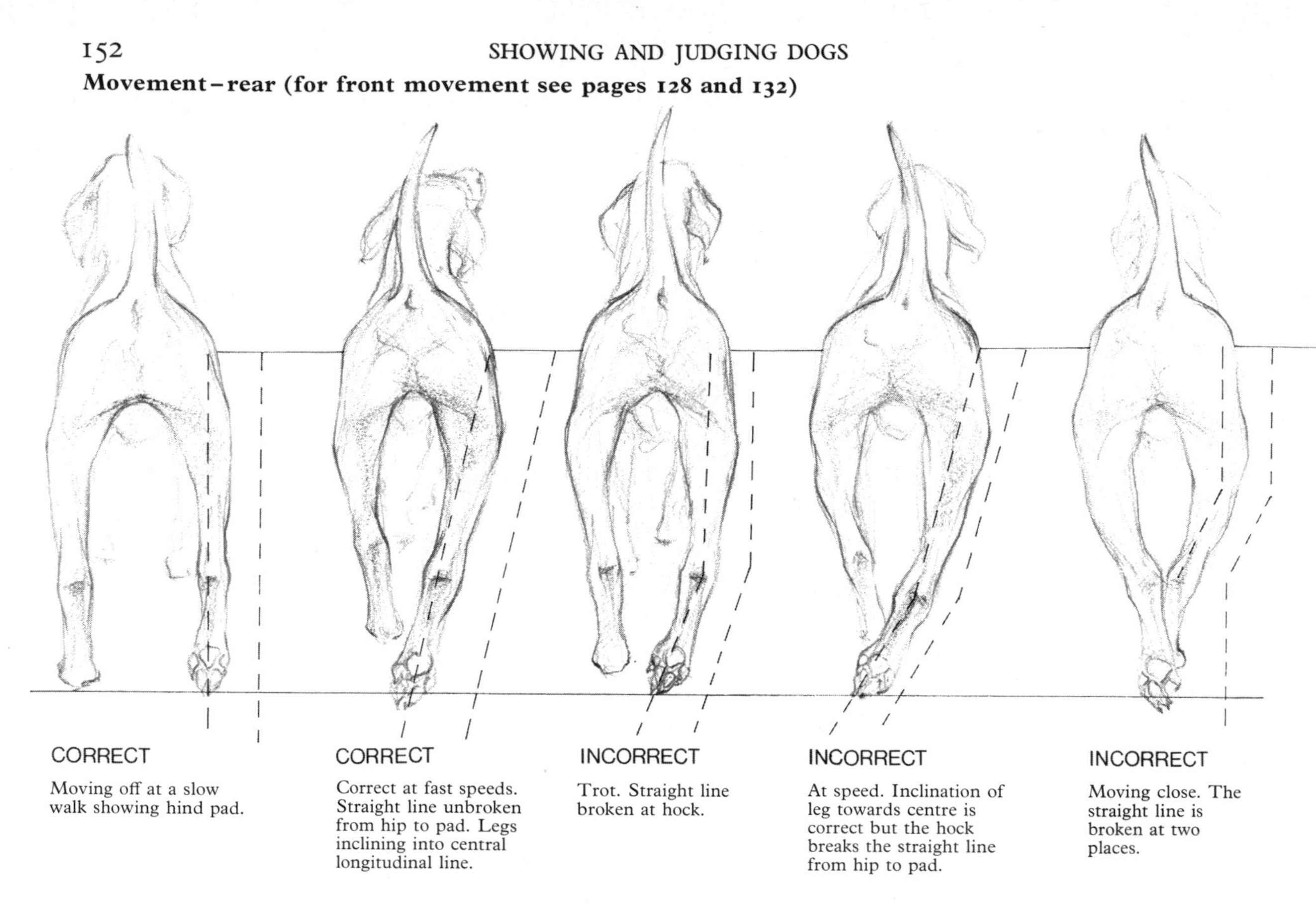

CORRECT
Moving off at a slow walk showing hind pad.

CORRECT
Correct at fast speeds. Straight line unbroken from hip to pad. Legs inclining into central longitudinal line.

INCORRECT
Trot. Straight line broken at hock.

INCORRECT
At speed. Inclination of leg towards centre is correct but the hock breaks the straight line from hip to pad.

INCORRECT
Moving close. The straight line is broken at two places.

hindfoot. This slow action with three legs on the ground together gives the impression that the legs are moved in the same lines and plane as those of the standing position. But as the speed increases to a trot, in order to enable the dog to keep his balance, he changes to a diagonal gait with only two legs on the ground at the same time, moving first with his right foreleg and left hindleg, and then changing to the opposite diagonals. The faster the dog moves at a flying trot, the closer the pads are placed to a longitudinal centre line, in order to maintain his balance. What a judge must look for, when the dog is moving towards him, is not that the forelegs are advancing absolutely in the same plane and parallel to each other, for this should not be so except when stated in a breed standard. They should angle in very slightly, depending on the speed. The important factor in movement, is that *from the shoulder to foot all the joints and bones should be in one straight line.* Equally, when the dog is moving away from the judge, *the sequence of bones and joints should also be in one straight line from the hip to the foot.* In other words if the dog is 'out at elbow' *or* is cowhocked, the alignment of bones and joints will not be in a straight line.

Except in the first paces at a very slow walk, the legs will not be in the same plane either. When the dog's movement is viewed from the side, it will be seen that the forefeet are moved slightly ahead of the hindfeet, so that they do not quite touch each other, and this enables the dog to move in a straight line.

Any lack of harmony will automatically show up in the gait. A long back produces a short stride and vice versa. When a long stride is expected and the stride is short, the judge must find where the fault lies. If it is accompanied with a hackney action the shoulder blade will be too upright at 60° instead of 45°. Low-placed hocks go with a great length of stride, and a good turn of stifle also produces a great length of stride. High-placed hocks and straight stifles obviously produce a short stride and invariably a stilted action. Breeds with a wide rib cage and short legs will not place their pads close to a centre line, even when moving at speed.

How many people, I wonder, are incapable of analysing movement, but receive a photographic impression of correct gait. Yet they would probably be incapable of saying exactly why one dog moved better than another.

Many breed standards mention that hocks should never turn in nor out. There are very few

Trot and Flying Trot

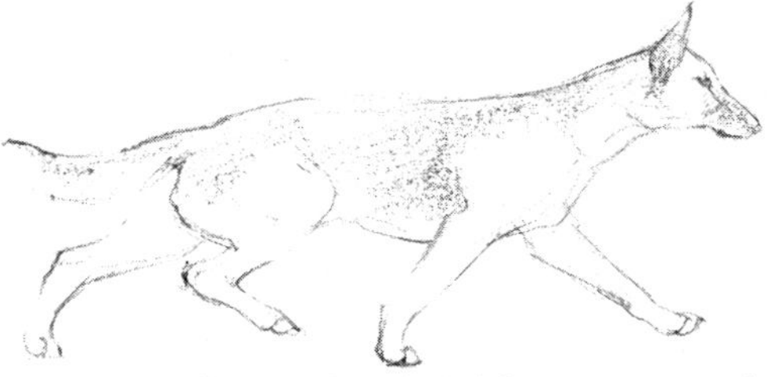

1 Left fore leading, with the left hind diagonal on ground

2 Suspension in a flying trot (provided back is long enough)

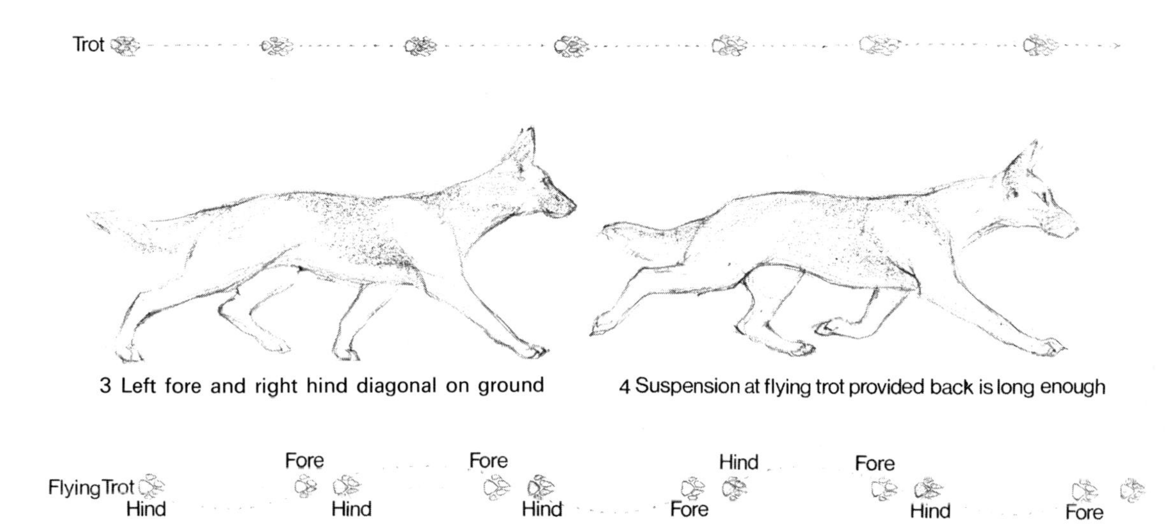

3 Left fore and right hind diagonal on ground

4 Suspension at flying trot provided back is long enough

Correct and incorrect movement, side view

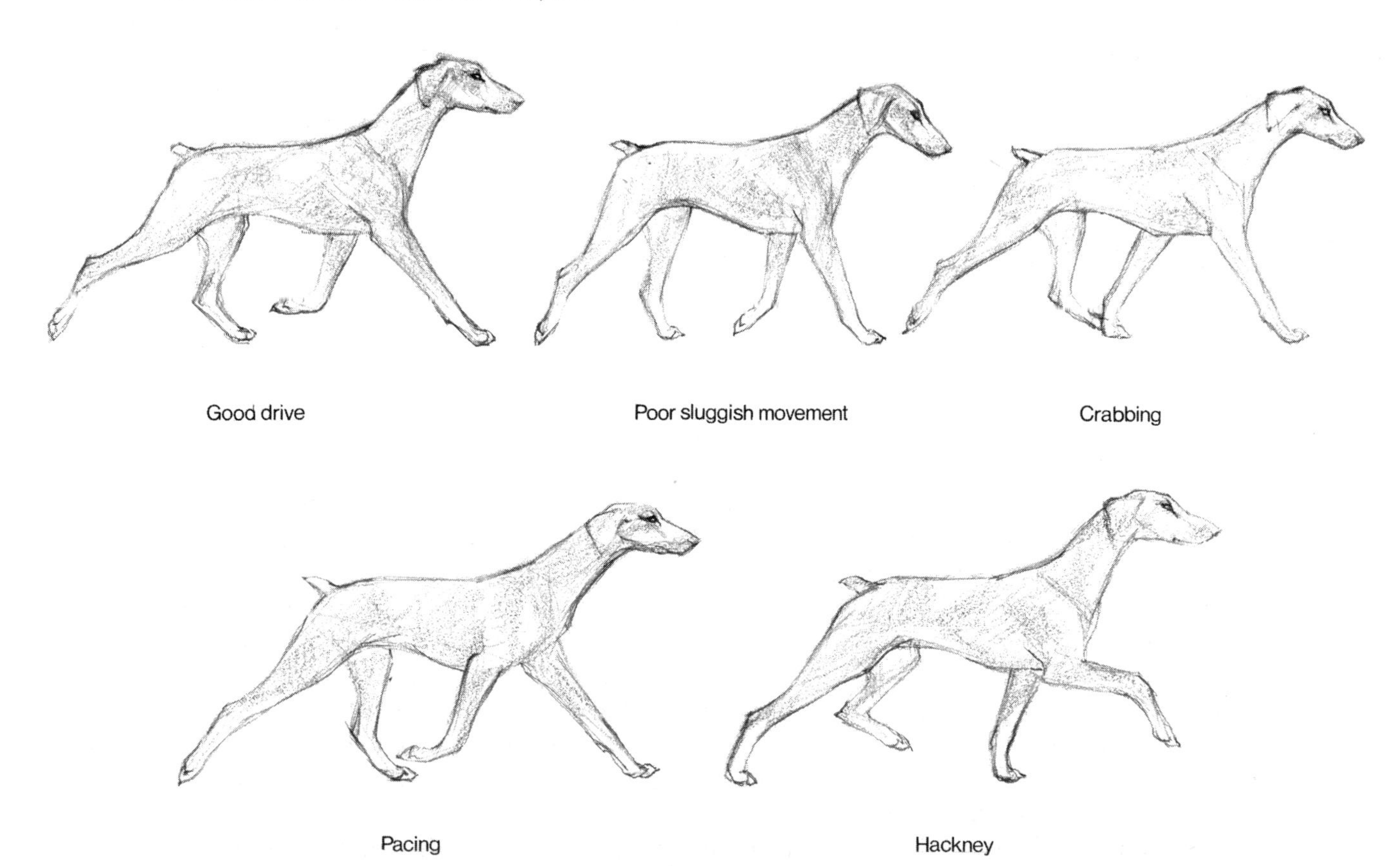

Good drive

Poor sluggish movement

Crabbing

Pacing

Hackney

The Walk

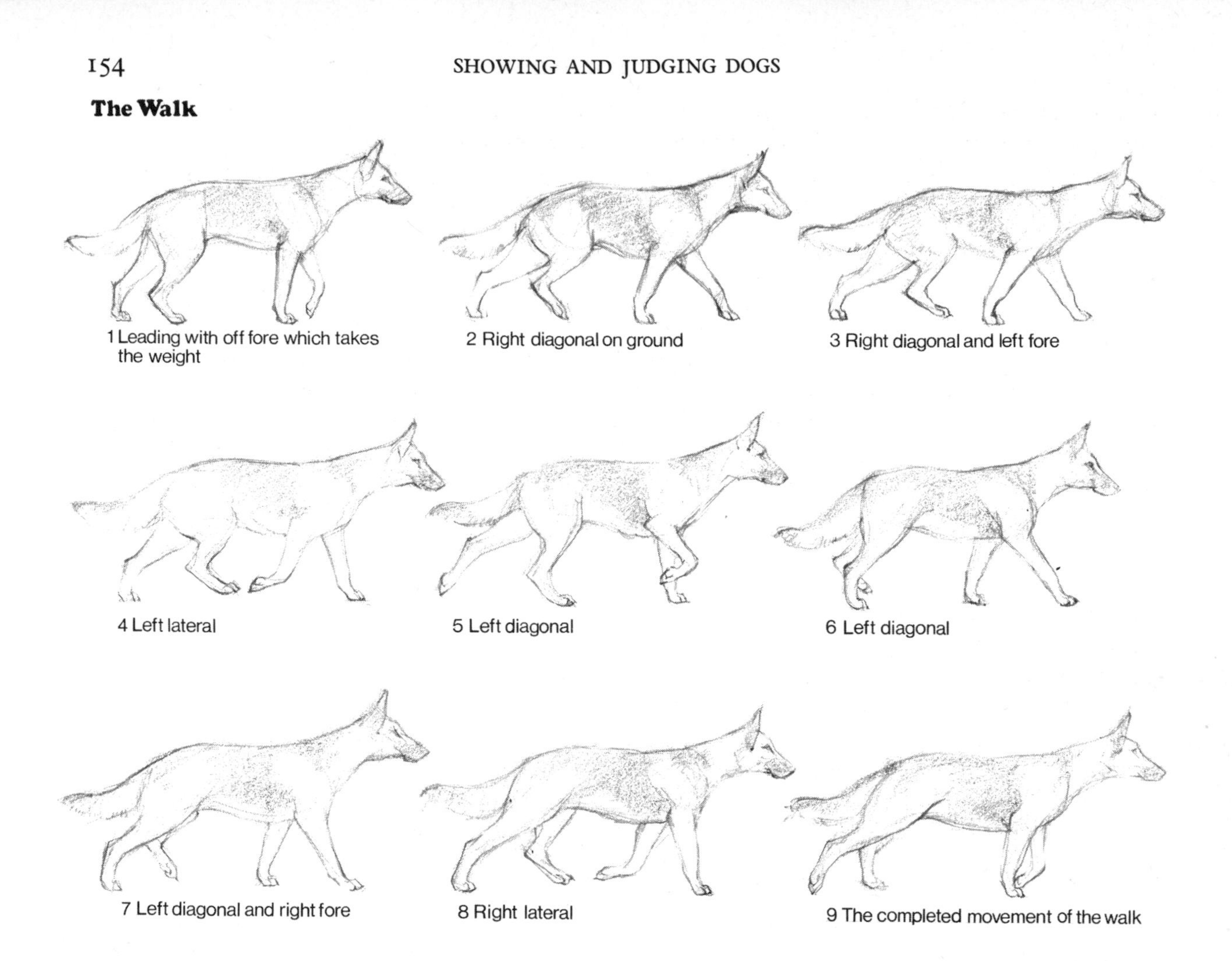

1 Leading with off fore which takes the weight
2 Right diagonal on ground
3 Right diagonal and left fore
4 Left lateral
5 Left diagonal
6 Left diagonal
7 Left diagonal and right fore
8 Right lateral
9 The completed movement of the walk

hocks which in fact turn out. Long bodies often go with upright shoulders and straight stifles, and in a great many breeds this leads to a short croup too. Every part of the body correlates with another. Many handlers prefer to move their dog at a fast trot and in some breeds to the point before they would break gait. Should a dog break gait, the judge should give him another chance. Trotting shows up more faults than any other gait. The judge usually prefers to watch a dog move at a moderate speed, in which case the handler may be asked to gait his dog more slowly.

ASSESSING THE GAIT

While the dog is being gaited, the judge must keep his eyes fixed on the dog, summing up his movement while going away, noticing whether his gait is sound, strong, fast, free, true and level, as well as being balanced and vigorous. While watching his action and drive, he must notice if the dog is cow-hocked and whether the pads can be seen. If the dog is being moved in a triangle, the judge will be able to see when he is moving across the far end of the ring whether the back is level, roached or dipped, or if the dog is padding or pounding. The judge must also note the position of the head, ears and tail. When the dog is coming towards him, he should notice whether the joints and bones of the forelegs from the shoulder to the pad are in one straight line, or if the dog perhaps toes in or out, or plaits or weaves. The more slowly the dog is moved, the less his legs will angle towards a longitudinal centre line. The judge will be able to see if the dog is pacing and whether the handler rectifies this tired gait. The judge may ask the handler to move the dog a second time, in case he wishes to verify a particular point. A dog must be seen at least once on a loose lead. The handler should then bring his dog to a standstill just in front of the judge, so that his dog stands facing to the right. In this way the dog will have been seen at least once from all sides. Many judges at this moment like to attract the dog's attention perhaps by throwing a bunch of keys or a match box, so that they can observe how well the dog uses his ears, and whether he has the correct expression and alertness for the breed.

The judge then dismisses the handler with a courteous 'Thank You'. If the handler is the first and is unsure where to go to stand, the judge should indicate this by pointing.

MONOSYLLABIC, CURT JUDGES

There are, unfortunately, a few judges who feel so self important that they prefer to give all their directions by hand signals only, or sometimes by curt, monosyllable words. This method of approach somewhat naturally is not popular with handlers and is considered high-handed and rude. Nevertheless, exhibitors would rather show under a good judge, even if he is high-handed and rude, than under a more charming one who is not so good. But such behaviour is quite unnecessary.

THE NEXT EXHIBIT

Before the judge has finished with the previous exhibit, the next handler will have already set up his dog either on the table or on the ground. Before advancing towards the dog, the judge should perhaps glance diagonally across the ring to ensure that the previous handler is standing where the new line of 'seen' exhibits is to be formed. This is particularly important if the dogs are being placed in order of merit.

The judge now follows the identical procedure with the next dog and all the subsequent exhibits.

PLACING THE EXHIBITS IN ORDER OF MERIT

Many a judge finds it a good idea and also a time-saving method, if he places each dog in the order that he likes them immediately after he has gone over them and watched their gait. When this method of judging is adopted, it is extremely important that the judge should make certain that the handler has indeed moved to the place that the judge has indicated. An artful handler may well try to place himself in a higher position, particularly if his neighbour is a young novice, who may be too over-awed to protest. A judge with a large number of dogs to go over might possibly not notice what had occurred.

JUDGING THE LINE UP

Whether the dogs have been placed in order of merit or not, the judge must, after examining the last dog, return to the centre of the ring and look at the whole class. The dogs will be set up and standing correctly for the breed. Some novice exhibitors may not all stand their dogs facing the same way, but a handler is perfectly entitled to stand his dog in the direction that he himself prefers. Some dogs may be too heavily marked on one side, and the handler may then consider that his dog will be shown to best advantage if he is set up so that the judge sees his better side. But it is naturally much simpler for the judge if all the dogs face the same way. Bulldogs and certain other breeds are set up facing the centre of the ring. The judge may walk behind the assembled dogs, so that he may see them from every direction.

If the judge has not already lined the dogs up in order of merit, or even if he has, he may possibly decide to alter a placing. As soon as the dogs are placed in order of merit, the judge will request the handlers to move their dogs once or twice more round the ring. If there are any dogs from a previous class, they should have been lined up and be standing in order of merit with the leader in the corner of the ring diagonally opposite the judging table. The new class of dogs, also in order of merit, is then joined up to the end of the line of the previous class. It is important for the judge to remember exactly which dog represents the top of the new ones. He must then assess the two sets of dogs together, bearing in mind type, soundness and presentation, and remembering that the new class is senior to the previous one. If the class is very large, the judge may at this stage, if he wishes, excuse the handlers and dogs below the first five or six of the new class. This makes more room in the ring, but not all exhibitors like being dismissed, and so the judge must use his discretion. The judge may decide to move some dogs up the line, or he may prefer to move dogs down the line, depending from which class they originated. It is important, however, not to juggle the placings, because this is a time when a judge may inadvertently reverse an order. Having placed the dogs in order of merit, they should be gaited round the ring once more as a class in order to compare them. The judge may find that the standard is extremely high or vice versa. He may wish to ask the handlers of a toy breed to hold up their dogs so that he can refresh his memory and compare the dogs' eyes, heads, ear placement or mouths. Soundness may be something the judge is looking for particularly, and he may wish to see the first three or four dogs move away from him, all moving together and all returning together. This is an excellent method of comparing the top three dogs in the class, and it is probably best if the judge has the dogs moved down and up the length of the ring, though this, of course, much depends on the size of the ring. As soon as the dogs return to their previous line up, the judge may alter the placings and once again, if necessary, watch the dogs gait. The judge may then call out the first dog, to stand in the centre of the ring, and then the second and the third and down to the number that are to receive prize cards.

BRINGING THE WINNING DOGS INTO THE CENTRE OF THE RING

The judge will know, before judging commences, how many dogs he must select from each class. The judge must 'pull out' not less than four dogs into the centre of the ring, and he must place them in order starting from left to right. Some judges like to go on changing the order in the centre of the ring, probably to keep up the suspense and perhaps even playing to the gallery. Occasionally, however, there may be so little to chose between the top three dogs that at the last moment the judge feels that one of them just has the edge on the others on temperament, or perhaps one of the exhibits has just become bored with the proceedings and let up at the last moment.

MALPRACTICES

Judges and stewards should be on the alert against cunning malpractices. For instance, a judge may ask a handler from the main line of dogs to go and stand in third place in the centre of the ring. Occasionally, if the handler is crafty, he may go and place himself first or second, hoping that the judge may forget, whilst he is deciding which other dogs to bring out into the centre of the ring. The other handlers may not have heard the judge's specific instructions, and there are always the cunning handlers who feel that all is fair in love and war. A novice may not like to stand up to an old hand and say that the judge told him to stand in second place. Luckily, this sort of behaviour does not happen frequently, but when it does it must be stamped on severely. Some top breeders dislike being placed third in the open dog class. They would rather the impression were given in the show report that they had not been present!

AWARD-WINNING DOGS

As soon as the judge has selected his award-winning dogs and they are lined up in order of merit in the centre of the ring, standing from left to right, he informs his steward that these are his final placings. The senior steward then hands the judge his judging book and ball-point pen and proceeds to call out the numbers of the prize winners, handing out at the same time the cards and rosettes. The handlers remain in line, while the judge makes notes on the winning dogs, having already written their numbers in each column, including the slips, as the steward called them out. A short report must be written on each of the first three dogs, and this must include the colour and sex, important features, movement and faults. It is essential that a judge be sure of his facts before they go into print. Not all countries require judges to write a report on the winning dogs.

DICTAPHONES

Many judges these days prefer to use a dictaphone for their reports. This is an excellent idea provided that it is checked and rechecked during each report to ensure that it is working correctly and that it has been switched on. Otherwise, the avid readers of the dog papers will find no report on their favourite breed! Some high-powered judges are lucky enough to have a wife, daughter or secretary, who will taken down the report in shorthand and type it out after each class. This is a great saver of time and mental effort. If a judge has had to go over more than two hundred dogs in a day, it may be difficult to recall each winner, even when writing a report the following day, unless the report in the judging book is written up clearly. Outstanding dogs are easily remembered but some may escape the memory.

SIGNING THE SLIPS

The judge next returns to the judge's table and initials all the slips. There are three of these if it is a championship show. Sometimes stewards will fill in the numbers on the slips for the judge, but the judge must make certain that he checks these. Efficient stewards will often offer to copy in the winning numbers on the last two tear out slips after each class. Where there are large classes this is a tremendous help. The judge must remember, however, that it is his responsibility to see that the numbers written on the slips have been copied correctly, and he should not initial the slips until he has verified this. Personally, I feel it is better for a judge to fill in the slips himself. In some countries only the judge may make entries in the judging book.

The senior ring steward is responsible for seeing that each slip is taken to the allotted place either by a steward or a runner. One slip is pinned on the ring award board, and two are sent to the secretary's office. One of the latter is placed on the general award board. If it is a championship show, the final slips are sent to the Kennel Club, where the awards are checked. Should the Kennel Club find any mistakes, such as a judge reversing an order—which is viewed with a very jaundiced eye by the Kennel Club Committee—the championship show judge who made such an error must satisfy the Kennel Club Committee as to why such a decision was taken. If the reason is not satisfactory, the judge will not be permitted to award challenge certificates again for some time.

The Kennel Club also check that the award-winning dogs were entered in correct classes, and, in the event of a dog being disqualified, it is published in the Kennel Gazette for all to see. Furthermore, the Kennel Club Committee imposes fines of £2, which must be paid within a specified time, and all prize cards and money must be returned to the show secretary.

THE INTERVAL BETWEEN CLASSES

Whilst the class of new dogs is forming, the judge should sit at the judge's table. He should never speak to an exhibitor, particularly about the placement of a dog in a previous class. This may only be discussed, if the judge so wishes, at the end of the breed judging, or variety or group judging, but certainly not before. The judge may have time to add to his notes, use his dictaphone, or dictate his notes to his secretary. As soon as all the dogs are present in the ring, the senior steward informs the judge of any absentees, which he must mark up in the judging book before taking his place in the centre of the ring. The whole procedure then starts again.

JUDGING SUBSEQUENT CLASSES

All the 'seen' dogs are lined up diagonally opposite the side of the ring where the new class is standing. As soon as the judge has gone over each exhibit the handler joins the line of the newly seen dogs. Most judges like to have a small gap left where one class joins the other. Each new class is senior to the preceding one. It is essential that the judge should first make certain that the 'seen' dogs are standing in order of merit, as well as the new class, in order that the two may be joined together. From a comparison of the two classes the judge proceeds to make his new order, which should go down to the requisite number of prize cards, although there are some judges who like to place the entire class in the order of merit as they work. This depends very much on the size of the class. If the class is large the judge may, if he wishes, dismiss the class beyond the number of prize cards. At this stage the remaining dogs should be moved together round the ring or in any other procedure that the judge favours. The dogs must then be called forward in order of merit into the centre of the ring, the winning dogs being lined up from the judge's left to right.

JUDGING BEST DOG

Open dog is the senior class. The procedure is identical. The winner, however, is left in the ring, with only the runner up left standing at the side. The judge may, if he wishes, request that all unbeaten dogs should be brought into the ring, and the stewards will consult their catalogue to make certain that all the unbeaten dogs are brought forward. The judge may have already decided that the winner of the open dog is his best dog, but it is only fair to allow all the other dogs to compete, so that they may have the honour and glory of parading with the ultimate dog winner. It is not, however, an automatic right for unbeaten dogs to be brought into the ring. It is left entirely to the judge's discretion. The unbeaten dogs and the winner of the open dog class should be moved round the ring, and the winner of these is the best dog, and is awarded the challenge certificate if it is a championship show. The second in the open-dog class now competes with the others for reserve best of sex. The cards and prizes should be given out, as soon as the judge has made his decision.

JUDGING THE BITCHES

After the dogs have been judged, then the bitch classes are started and the procedure is identical to that for the dogs, except for checking that they are entire.

JUDGING THE BEST OF BREED

The winning dog and the winning bitch are brought into the ring together. The judge should spend some time looking at these two. Then the judge should ask the two handlers to move their dogs round the ring at the same time. If the dogs are both so outstanding that there is little to choose between them, the judge may ask that the two dogs should be moved up and down the centre of the ring together, and his ultimate decision may depend on the finer breed points. The handlers by this time will be rather tense and the ringside spectators, who usually judge only by faults, will, of course, be trying to do the judge's judging for him. The right decision must be made without drawing out the judging too long. The judge must not play to the gallery. The judge shakes hands with the best-of-breed winner, and presents the rosettes and trophies with a few charming words of congratulations. The best opposite sex handler should shake hands with the best-of-breed handler and congratulate him with a complimentary word about his dog. It is a kind gesture on the part of the judge if he can pass a nice remark to the runner up. It helps his natural disappointment, especially if there was a close finish. The winning dog should do a lap of honour round the ring on his own with his handler, amidst suitable applause.

SIGNING CERTIFICATES

As soon as the judging is finished, the judge should return to the table and sign the necessary certificates, which the senior steward will have prepared for him.

TALKING TO THE EXHIBITORS

After finishing his judging, the judge would do well to remember that he probably has only two friends, the owners of the challenge certificate winners, and perhaps the winners of the other classes. Some exhibitors take their defeats well, others, unfortunately, can be most unsporting, and some become quite hot under the collar. Handlers may even come up to the judge and demand to know why the judge put their beautiful dog down, when so many well-known judges have put the dog up previously. Whatever happens the judge must remain absolutely calm, charming, admire the losing dog, and quite politely inform the disappointed exhibitor that, although his dog is extremely good, the other dog just had the edge on him on this particular day. Feelings are often high immediately after judging, so that it is probably better for the judge to beat a hasty retreat at this time and to avoid all unnecessary post mortems. It is not a good idea for him to go round the benches, chatting with the exhibitors and being particularly charming to the losers. The judge's task of appraising the exhibits should only take place in the ring.

There are always, however, a number of novices who genuinely want to learn from the judge and who may accost him at the end of the day to ask him to enlarge on his opinion.

Occasionally, a cantankerous exhibitor wants to know why a judge did not put their beloved Sammy up. He is so engrossed in his own disappointment, that he completely fails to realize that the judge may have gone over two hundred dogs that day. Brilliant as the judge may be, he is highly likely to have no recollection as to why he did what and when, without seeing all the rest of the class again, and in particular the dog in question. It may be better for the judge perhaps to pretend that he remembers the dog, and simply imply that he did like Sammy, but he just liked the other dogs a little bit better, and perhaps the exhibitor would like to show Sammy under him again another time.

However, if Sammy was a terrible specimen, the judge may get away by saying, 'I loved your dog, but he is *not* a good Fox Terrier' (or whatever the breed was). Exhibitors should not ask the judge what he thought of their dog, unless they really want to hear the truth. The truth may be unpalatable.

It is extremely boring for the judge to hear from an exhibitor, after he has put his dog down, that such and such famous judges have previously put the dog up. If all judges placed the dogs in the identical order, there would be little point in having classes of more than three dogs, and even the constant winners would find life boring and somewhat monotonous. Judging, after all, is only an opinion on a day.

REPORTING TO THE SHOW SECRETARY

As soon as the judge has accomplished his mission he must report to the show secretary's office. Here he will be given a catalogue, from which to write his report for the dog papers, and he will also be given his judging fee.

THE STEWARDS

It is always a kind gesture on the part of the judge to invite the stewards to have a drink with him. Sometimes this is difficult to arrange, particularly if the judge is first in the ring, because very often judges leave the show as soon as their appointment is over, whilst the stewards will continue stewarding all day. It is always appreciated if a judge can find time to write and thank each steward for his efficient co-operation in the ring.

VARIETY JUDGING

This is not as difficult as might be supposed, particularly if the classes are large. Few judges know all breeds equally well. Amongst the dogs in a variety class, the judge must look at each dog and decide if it is a good specimen for that breed. Would the dog stand out in a specialist class, or is he only a mediocre dog? Each dog is judged against its breed standard and not against another dog. The judge goes down the line of dogs, picking out the outstanding specimens. The finer breed points are less important than the whole dog's general appearance. The judge then lines these dogs up together, and there are nearly always sufficient dogs in the line-up which really stand out above the others in quality and temperament and in their primary breed functions.

GROUP JUDGING

After specializing in a breed, many judges promote themselves by becoming knowledgeable in a group. It may be the gun-dog group, the toy group or one of the other groups. Here again, each dog must be judged on how good a specimen he is of his breed. The dogs are selected accordingly, and once again there is generally just one which stands out for temperament, quality and perhaps the necessary added sparkle and style. Each dog has already won best of (his) breed and should be an outstanding specimen.

BEST IN SHOW JUDGING

The best in show judge is not necessarily technically an all-rounder judge. He is unlikely to have judged every single breed at open shows. However, a best in show judge must be someone with expert knowledge of a large number of breeds. He must be a person of outstanding honesty and complete integrity, and he must also be someone of considerable status in the dog world. The method of judging is exactly the same as for variety judging or group judging. The best in show judge must, however, whittle the dogs down to the final four, which are then brought out into the centre of the ring. Once again, there is usually one dog which stands out above all the others. By the time a dog has reached the best in show ring, he has already of course found favour with at least two if not three different judges, and one of these may well have been a specialist judge. So there is no reason why top exhibits should not all be outstanding specimens. This unfortunately is not always the case as occasionally breed politics rears its ugly head.

However, whatever the best in show judge does, he knows that at least two other judges will agree with his final placings, even if none of the others agree with his personal opinion on the day.

Complications sometimes arise when there are two judges judging best in show, and they refuse to agree on a particular dog. Perhaps one judge wants the Dalmatian and the other the Griffon Bruxellois. There are then two courses open. Either the two judges pull out a third dog which they both agree on, or, where there is a deadlock, a referee may be brought on to the scene. The referee's choice is, of course, final.

THE SHOW REPORT

Some judges use a dictaphone on the judge's table to make their critique, and this is excellent provided that the machine is working well. It is, however, not an unknown occurrence for the tape not to work, so that the judge finds that he has dictated his entire report on to nothing, and has no written notes from which to write his report. As a result, the disappointed exhibitors see no show reports in the dog papers. Other judges, who are lucky enough to have a wife and/or a secretary, can dictate excellent notes directly after each class. This is probably the best method of all, because, once the breed judging is over, he has also finished his critique.

It is surprising what a long time it can take to write up good reports on each dog, particularly if the notes have been skimped. The ring number of each winning dog must be looked up in the catalogue. The name of the exhibitor must be entered first, and then the full name of the dog, followed by its sex, if the classes were mixed. Exhibitors, and most of the dog people who cannot get to shows, read their dog papers avidly, and many of them read all the show reports from cover to cover. It is important, therefore, that the judge should try to write his report for the benefit of the people who were not at the show.

Right: German Short-haired Pointer.

Below: Mrs. Cecil-Wright presenting the cup to Champion Bournehouse Star Shine, with 54 challenge certificates. Reserve is the consistent winner Yorkshire Terrier Champion Blairsville Royal Seal. Judge Mr. Joe Braddon. What a wonderful sporting smile from the runner up!

Above left: Air Commodore Cecil-Wright presenting the cup to Champion Hawkhill Connaught, top winning Springer Spaniel.

Left: A good method of examining a mouth.

Below left: Good Companions.

Below: Show stance of a Doberman. A much shorter lead would have been better.

Opinions vary as to whether judges have the right to mention faults. Some judges avoid the difficulty by saying something to the effect that the dog would have been placed higher, except for one small fault. Readers are then kept guessing what the fault might be. It is probably better to be more explicit about the fault; but, whatever the judge puts down on paper, he must be accurate. The virtues of a dog should be emphasized and the faults minimised. A judge under contract to one paper normally only writes a report for that paper, and an outsider is then asked by the other dog paper to write a report for them. This always seems to be a strange and unsatisfactory arrangement. How can someone write a report about a dog which the judge has put up, when perhaps the person dislikes the dog intensely, did not agree at all with the judge's placings, and in any case may never have gone over it?

A JUDGING REPORT

Some judges are able to write excellent reports whilst others do not have this facility. There are numerous dog clichés which are used by judges to avoid writing what they really mean. I once made quite an amusing collection of these descriptions, for example: 'Could easily change places with the winner', 'Was not going too well on the day', 'Pressed the winner hard', 'Was not covering the ground on the day', 'Just scored on ears', 'Action not quite so good as winner', 'Not moving so steadily', 'Would like to take this one home.' Sometimes, one even reads such deplorable expressions as 'went like a bomb' or 'went like a train'. 'Not my type' is another expression used too frequently in reports. There is only one type: the standard!

It is quite a good idea to begin a show report with a summing up of the breed on the day. It is also an opportunity to thank the stewards. Unfortunately, sometimes space is short and the editor cuts out the preliminaries.

THE JUDGE'S OWN RECORD BOOK

Very many judges keep their own record book, giving details of each show, the date, the entry, and the number of classes and breeds judged. The exact critique as published is kept in the book, with the remarks about all the exhibits. This makes a good reference when judging a large show some years later. Some judges even add notes in between shows such as regarding how a particular dog is doing in the ring, particularly if the judge has launched a promising puppy on his show career. It is always gratifying to follow his show record to the top, when the dog becomes a champion. All judges like to give a dog its first challenge certificate and then follow its career, watching how long it takes before the dog is made up.

Some judges prefer to keep their notes on dogs under breeds, and in some ways this is simpler, especially for all-rounders, who perhaps are judging at dog shows regularly every week. I know several breed specialists who write a critique on every single dog in each class. this is a most useful record for breeding purposes, particularly for going out to stud.

THANKING A JUDGE

Occasionally a novice may make the mistake of going to a judge and thanking him for placing his dog or for giving him the challenge certificate. Sometimes thrilled exhibitors may even advertise their thanks to a particular judge or judges in the dog papers. A judge should not really be thanked, as he was not actually or directly doing the exhibitor a favour: he was really only doing his job. Most judges, however, appreciate the winners thanking them for an enjoyable day. There is no need to snub the thrilled novice and the judge can perhaps say how much he enjoyed going over such a beautiful dog and that the dog should be most useful to improve the breed.

USEFUL HINTS FOR JUDGES

Do read the breed standards frequently.
Never look at a catalogue before judging.
Go into the ring in plenty of time. Once in the ring never leave it except for lunch.
Decide on an allotted time for each dog.
Check where to write the reports in the judging book.
Arrange the judging procedure with the stewards and keep to the schedule.
Judge objectively and without fear or favour.
Give all instructions slowly and clearly.
Look only at the dogs and judge with confidence.
Make certain you understand kinetic balance.
Do not judge on faults or over-emphasize breed idiosyncrasies.
When the dogs move round the ring, stand in the centre and watch each dog as it passes you without following any one dog round. Otherwise you will miss some of them in the circuit.
Work from head to tail, gently and methodically, and with a minimum of prodding.
Concentrate all the time. Avoid tediously slow judging and hasty decisions.
Never risk being bitten by a dog.
Be on the alert for malpractices. Send an offending handler to the end of the line.
Keep to the same procedure all the time, and get the most out of each dog and handler.
Never underestimate a handler's intelligence or knowledge of a breed.
Do not be taken in by a flashy dog, a coated dog or a clever handler.
Make certain that each dog is seen once from all sides, and once on a loose lead.
Judge the dog on the day, not on what it has been or may be in the future.
Judge as if you have never seen the dog before.
Always feel free to alter your previous placings at other shows.
Never place a dog because a well-known judge has placed him previously.
Be deaf to ringside pressures, where clapping or conversations are aimed at the judge.
Be deaf to ringside applause every time a judge approaches a particular dog.
Be deaf to the handler who murmurs 'He only needs one more ticket.'
Always allow a professional handler to take over a client's dog in the ring after judging has started.
In extra large classes the dogs may be placed in order of merit immediately after examination and gaiting. This saves time.
In normal classes gait all dogs, examine, gait and gait all the dogs again.
Write up the judging book notes clearly or in personal shorthand. Do not forget to note the dog's colour and sex in mixed classes.
If using a dictaphone, check after each class that it is working.
Initial all slips immediately after each class.
Always judge in the order marked in the judging book.
After awarding best of breed and challenge certificates, check that all slips have been torn out of the judging book and sent to the correct destinations.
Offer your stewards a drink or a cup of tea.
Collect catalogue and judging fee from the secretary.
Never go round the benches after judging. All appraisal of dogs must be done in the ring.
Know how to deal with difficult and unsporting handlers.
Beware of an exhibitor pretending to ask an opinion, but who in fact is challenging the judge's decision.
Write a clear report, making certain that all facts are correct.
Post the report on time for the dog papers.
Do not resent criticism and always admit a mistake. Never apologise for your decisions.
Remember the importance of type, temperament, soundness and presentation in that order of priority.

Do not encourage future entries by praising unworthy dogs.
Judges in the USA must memorise all disqualifications.

A FEW GENERAL HINTS ON JUDGING

Judge the breeds on their individual uses. Gun dogs must be capable for shooting with; working breeds for their particular work; toy breeds for beauty and companionship, etc.

Breeds where strong teeth are demanded must never be snipey. There must always be a good fill-in under the eyes to ensure sufficient bony support for the molar teeth.

When viewed from the front or the rear the sequence of joints and bones from shoulder to pad and from hip to pad must always be in one straight line when the dog is gaiting, unless otherwise stated in the standard.

Legs inclining inwards towards a longitudinal central line are correct and should never be penalized, unless the sequence of joints and bones is *not* in a straight line when viewed from the front or the rear, or where the standard so demands.

Distemper teeth should not be penalized unless the teeth are in bad condition.

Never make a fetish over clipping, trimming or the number of bows or plaits a dog has been exhibited with.

Never be over-biased on breed points, thereby over-looking a major fault.

Never be deceived by a superb coat, make sure what lies beneath it.

Never be deceived by clever trimming, where a low set tail may be camouflaged.

If you suspect a mangy dog, do not take the exhibitor's excuses, and be sure to wash your hands before touching the next exhibit.

Always be on the alert for dyed dogs.

Learn the importance of colours in the breeds.

Know which dogs must be measured and when.

Always send for a measure when in doubt of a dog's size.

Learn the colour of eyes required in the breeds.

Know the importance of a slightly sloping fore pastern to avoid knuckling over.

Understand a good turn of stifle.

Know about well let-down hocks.

Learn to gauge a well laid-back shoulder. Withers to point of shoulder should be long.

Know all about straight stifles and slipping stifles.

Tails are important. They are seldom too long. Many must reach the hock or other designated length.

The six vertebrae of the (true) back must be parallel to the ground and straight.

Remember the back is not the same as the top-line.

Hocks are joints. It is the hind pasterns which must be in parallel planes to each other when the dog stands. Nature intends those to slope slightly forward, but some judges prefer them to be perpendicular.

Head measurements vary from nose to stop and from stop to occiput.

Remember the different proportions from stop to nose and from stop to occiput.

Stops are described as deep in numerous breeds, but remember which breeds require flat skulls, triangular heads, two-brick heads, domed heads, or wedge-shaped heads.

Remember how to gauge the length of ears. Some must reach the tip of the nose, others about an inch from the nose. Some reach the inside corner of the eye, others the outer corner.

Neck measurements can generally be made with the thumb and little finger stretched from the point of the jaw to the point of the sternum. There should be a dip between neck and withers.

Remember dogs are measured from the tip of the sternum to the point of the buttocks and from withers to ground.

'Bone' refers to the bones of the forearm. Good round bone is frequently required.

Good depth of brisket can be measured in the medium-sized, coated breeds by placing a hand on the dog's top-line from the withers down and the other hand beneath the rib cage. This will also show the spring of ribs. Muscular development in the hindquarters may be felt in the palms of both hands.

Some of the medium-sized breeds require the length of a hand at the flank.

There are various ways of measuring the desired width between the withers. In some breeds only a finger width is required; others require the width of one hand.

There are various widths required between the two hip bones, and these are again measured by finger widths.

The correct slope for the pastern is a vertical line passing through the slope from the centre of the shoulder blade to the pad.

A vertical line should pass from tip of pelvis below the tail and through to the centre pad of the hind foot when a dog stands well up on hocks.

The long third digital bones of the feet should be parallel to the ground. In the cat foot the second digital bone is 45° and in the hare foot it should be 60° to the ground.

Breeds which carry heavy objects must have strong maxillary bones.

The strength of the loin is important: through this area passes the drive from the hindlegs, the shock from the forelegs and the power to jump.

Do not press the rump down to feel strength: it is not there, and pressing down would merely show a good reflex action, or stifle problems.

Where good heart room is required, remember the sweep up towards the tuck-up should not start before the ninth rib.

A well sprung, longish floating rib will indicate how good the rest of the rib cage is likely to be.

Where low dogs are required, remember this is measured from the withers down, not from below the brisket to the ground.

Beware of optical illusions.

Remember to look at membranes, wrinkles, face padding, traces, pencilling, colour of nails, pads and toes, in breeds where they are important; also moles, lozenges and thumb marks.

Pekingese never have their mouths looked at. It is unnecessary to draw the ears of a Basset forward to see the length: they are always long enough. Bulldogs are always placed facing the centre of the ring.

Pekingese are all finally judged on a table together. Look for wry mouths and stiff backs.

As you become more experienced with breeds, keep a note book and enter up the important points to look for.

Find a photograph of the best specimen in the breed and paste it in the notebook for reference.

If you have a specimen photograph of a better dog or head study, paste it over the one illustrated in this book and keep it for reference in case one day you are invited to judge the breed. You can then memorize a good dog and recognize it when you see one.

Teeth generally should be strong, even, level and scissor. Remember to count teeth in breeds where this is important.

BREEDS WHERE KINETIC BALANCE IS DENIED.

(where standards state that legs should move straight forward)

KC	Daschshunds, Longhaired
KC	Dalmatians
KC	Dobermanns
AKC	Doberman Pinschers
KC	Fox Terriers
AKC	Gordon Setters
AKC	Great Danes
AKC	Irish Terriers
AKC	Italian Greyhounds
AKC	Kerry Blues
AKC	Maltese
AKC	Miniature Schnauzers
AKC	Norwich Terriers
AKC	Standard Poodles
KC	Retrievers, Labrador
AKC	Retrievers, Labrador
AKC	Skye Terriers
KC	American Cocker Spaniels
AKC	Spaniels, Cocker
KC	Spaniels, English Springer
AKC	Spaniels, English Springer
KC	West Highland White Terriers
KC	Belgian Shepherd Dogs
KC	Soft-Coated Wheaten Terriers

CHAPTER XIV

Anatomy Soundness and Joint Abnormalities

SIMPLE BASIC ANATOMY

A little insight into the anatomy of a dog can be most helpful to the breeder, exhibitor and judge. Far from being a dry subject it is in fact a most interesting one. A first-class breeder and judge should therefore try to understand the elementary anatomy and conformation of a dog. Faults creep into a breed, at first they are tolerated, then they become accepted until finally they are required! Serious faults should be easily recognized as each in turn effects another part of the anatomical conformation. In other words correct skeletal bone structure and placement are essential for soundness. Keen observation, particularly of movement, is imperative and also the ability to recognize sound movement. It is perhaps even more important to recognize why any particular movement is unsound.

Certain forms of unsoundness are not very noticeable when the dog is moving, and unsoundness may, for example, be detected by the characteristic way in which a dog with severe hip dysplasia stands. Similarly, a dog with weak stifles will from time to time stand with straight hocks and stifles, other dogs when standing may knuckle-over at the pastern joint. A straight stifle may alter the normally level top-line and give a tilted one. For example, over-angulation in one joint will automatically have to be compensated for in one or more of the joints nearest to the fault. Unsoundness is more often revealed when the dog gaits.

Although there is a tremendous difference in size amongst the 850 breeds which exist throughout the world, they all have the same number of bones, joints and muscles, and all are similarly constructed. Man, however, has over the centuries adapted the dog for his many requirements to such an extent that there are now more deviations in skeletal types in the dog than in any other species on earth. This, when you come to think of it, is quite an accomplishment. These deviations, however, have not always been to the advantage of the dog. But now is the time for breeders and judges to endeavour to put past mistakes right. This really means that over-exaggerated show points required in some breeds should be modified. The barbaric custom of ear cropping has already been stopped in many countries, and I hope that, as we all become more civilized, tail docking will no longer be tolerated either. It is interesting that undocked tails are only mentioned as a disqualification in a few breed standards.

PERMUTATIONS IN BREED CONSTRUCTION

There seems to be no end to the permutations that breeders have thought up for the construction of their show dogs. Sizes vary from Great Danes, weighing some two hundred pounds, to tiny Chihuahuas weighing only two or three pounds and some even less. Dogs have been developed, too, into the most curious shapes, not to mention vast deviations in weight and natural balance. Long necks are required with short backs, long backs with short necks, long backs may be expected to go with short legs. There are breeds which have large heads and small bodies and others with long snipy heads and narrow bodies. Heads, muzzles, ears, eyes, tails, all come into the permutations. Length of muzzle or lack of it may bring in added complications regarding alignment of the teeth which may be required in a particular breed standard. The shorter the muzzle, the more likelihood there is of an undershot mouth. The wrinkle that appears on the head, muzzle and dewlap is caused by the skin not having been reduced at the same rate as the bone structure. The numerous shapes and sizes of ear, nose and tail, the different shapes and length of the limbs, not to mention the variations of the shape of the foot, add to the list of almost unending permutations. It is fascinating that man has even contrived to breed dogs which have cat feet on the forelegs and hare feet on the hindlegs.

COMPARISON OF HUMAN AND CANINE LIMBS

It is interesting to compare the limbs of the dog with those of man. However, a novice is likely to find it a little complicated and somewhat confusing at first trying to visualize the comparative anatomy; particularly when it will be found that some of the joints in the dog may be referred to by several names. A typical example is that of the fore limb, where the bend at the top of the pastern is sometimes called the manus, knee, wrist or pastern joint, and on the hindleg, the joint is called the stifle, knee or patella. It is simpler to compare the joint at the top of the pastern on the fore limb to man's wrist and the pastern is the equivalent to man's hand and the dog's toes as man's fingers. The dewclaws are equivalent to man's big toe and thumb. The dog's heel is equivalent to the padded area just below man's fingers. Thus, on the forelegs the dog walks on his finger tips and on the hindlegs on his toes. The hocks downwards are equivalent to man's ankle and heel. When dog people mention the pasterns they are generally referring to the fore pasterns, but there are hind pasterns too, although they are frequently but erroneously, referred to as hocks.

THE SKELETON

The skeleton is the framework of the body which protects all the organs. The skull covers the brain and delicate organs of hearing and scenting. The rib cage covers the lungs, heart, liver, stomach, spleen, pancreas and the kidneys. The skeleton is held together by the muscles, and the skin covers the whole body. The bones of the skeleton vary. Some of the bones are solid, and some are hollow and are filled with marrow. The marrow is where the red blood cells are formed. Some bones are flat, such as the ribs, the skull bones and the shoulder blades. The breast bone (sternum) is not actually a bone but is made up of a tough springy cartilage.

Parts of a Dog

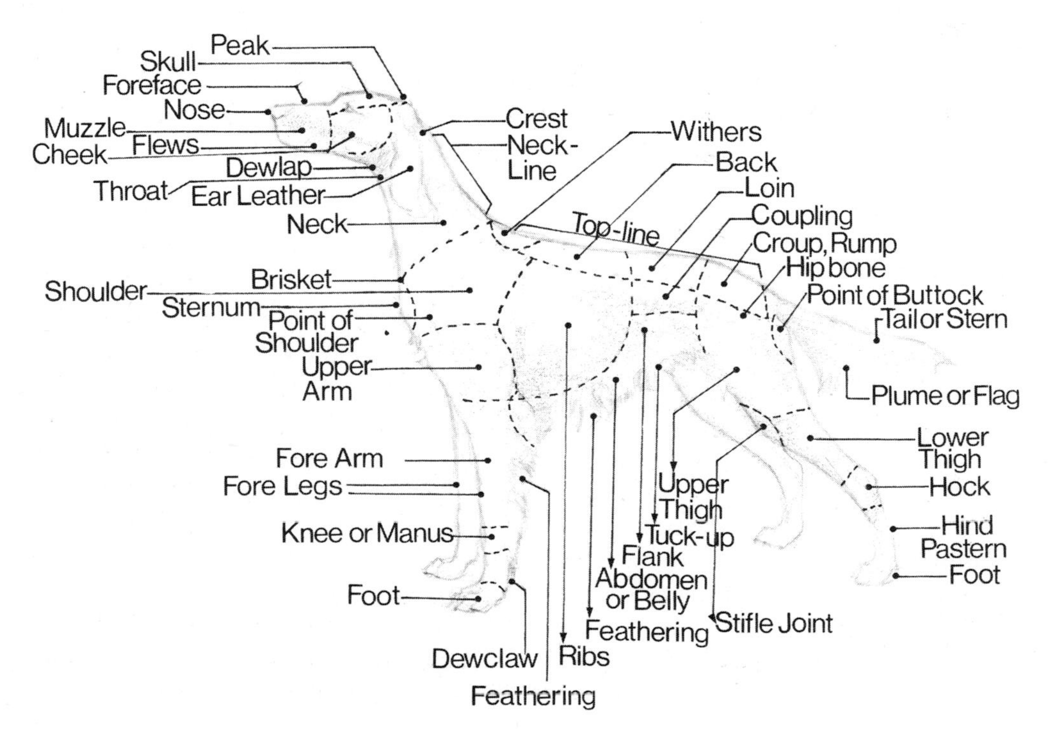

Skeletal Structure

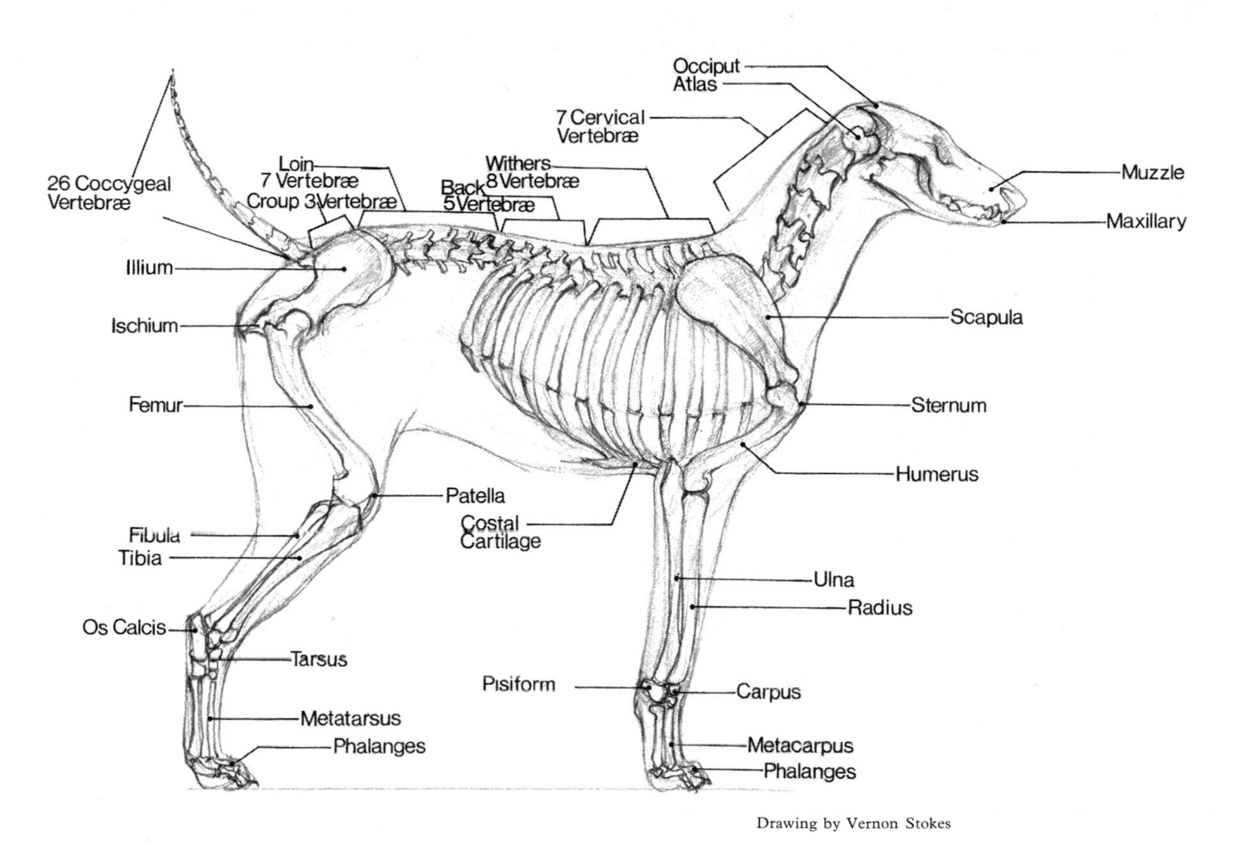

Drawing by Vernon Stokes

Muscular Structure

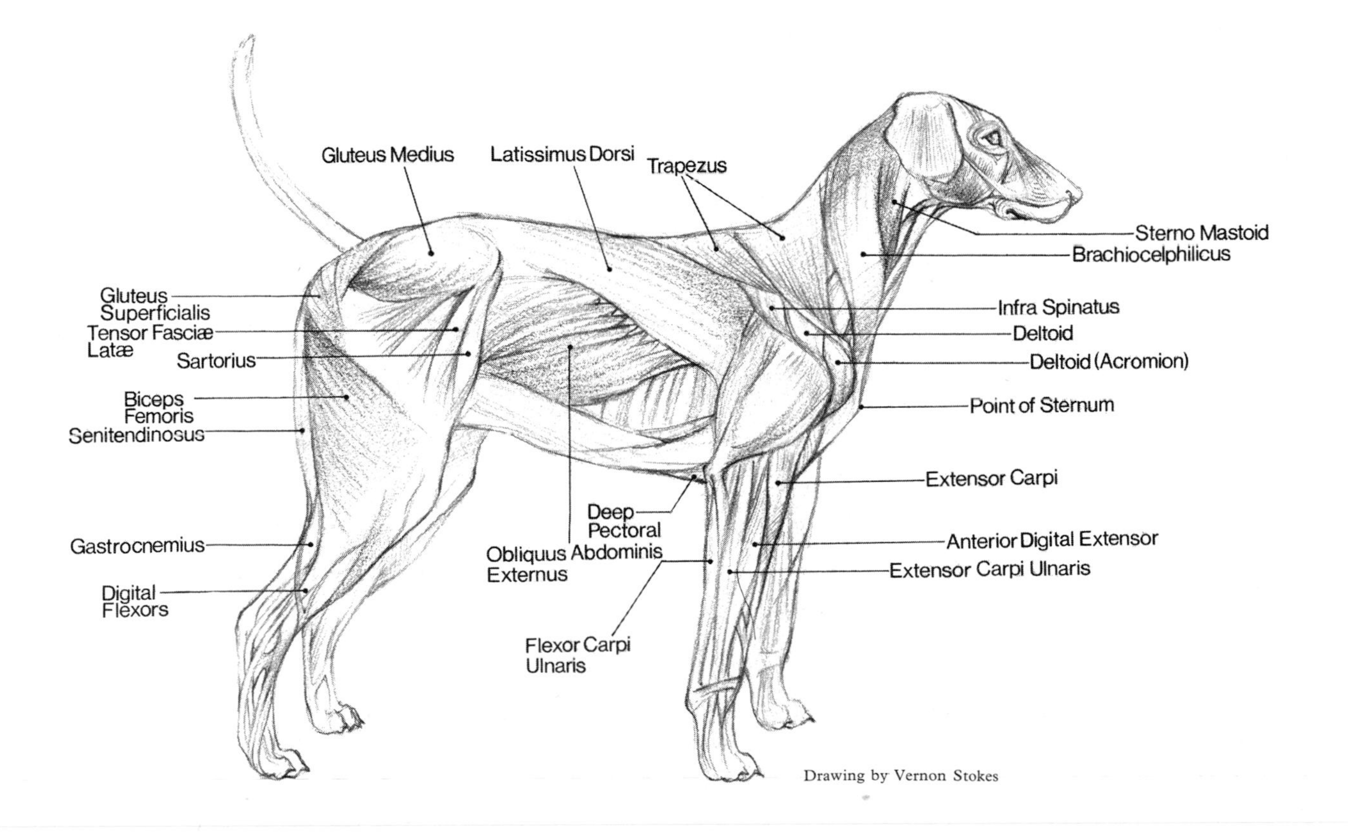

Drawing by Vernon Stokes

JOINTS

A joint is the structure where two bones come together. The joint is strengthened by muscles and ligaments. There are three kinds of joint: the ball and socket joint such as the hip joint, a hinge joint such as the knee or stifle joint and there are the vertebrae in the spine which are joined together by cartilage. A dog's spine is extremely flexible. The many other joints in the skeleton are variations of these three. The dog's limbs and joints are adapted for moving forward and there is little sideways movement in comparison with man's capability.

HEAD

The structure of the head and the varying proportions depend on the breed and its uses. The head is extremely important in the show dog and it is interesting how much heads can vary between breeds. Breeds where a strong bite is important must have a good fill-in beneath the eyes in order to give sufficient support for the molar teeth. Dogs which are required to carry heavy objects must have extra strong maxillary bone and must on no account ever be snipy.

The prominence at the top of the skull is called the occipital peak and is frequently mentioned in standards. The skull is attached to the neck by a ball and socket joint.

NECK

The neck has seven cervical vertebrae. All the muscles which are required to draw the leg forward depend on their attachment in the neck. The other important neck muscles are the ones which the dog uses to shake his prey which he uses in conjunction by keeping his legs firm as he shakes his head from side to side.

Trotting Alsatian showing skeletal structure

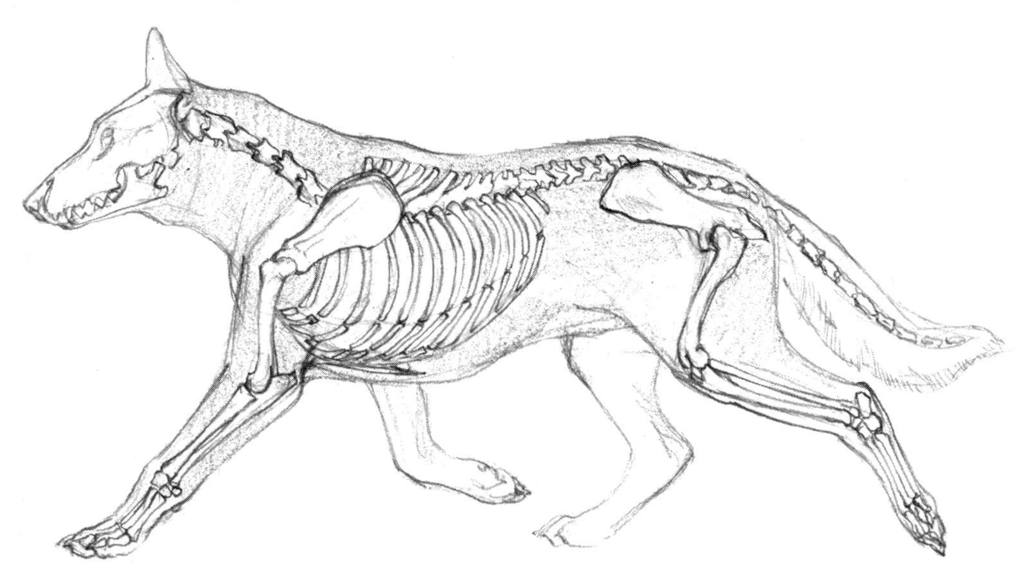

A dog with well laid-back shoulders, correct hind angulation, a good reach of neck, and slightly bent pasterns, moves with a long, effortless, free-swinging stride and correct foot timing. The feet are kept close to the ground to avoid unnecessary exertion. Good angulation also produces a greater expanse of muscle and stronger muscle attachments. The dog with such attributes has good substance, correct balance and covers the ground with the minimum of effort.

To move well, a dog must also be slightly longer in body than height at withers. Strong second thigh muscles enable the hindleg to straighten correctly, giving the maximum propulsion from the rear.

A dog with good width from the top of the withers to the point of shoulder will have well laid-back shoulders. A judge can see this without touching a dog. There should be a dip just in front of the shoulder blade at the withers and slightly sloping pasterns.

Over-reaching is caused by a shorter body than height. It occurs in growing puppies.

TOP LINE

This is the area referred to in show jargon which goes from the top of the withers to the base of the tail. It is frequently erroneously referred to as the back. Many standards require a level back. 'Stem to stern' is another expression used. Some standards divide the top-line in half, calling the first part the back, and the second, the loin. Such standards may demand back level and slightly arched loins. Large withers will have correspondingly large spines, but in either case the back line or top-line cannot be level.

Toplines

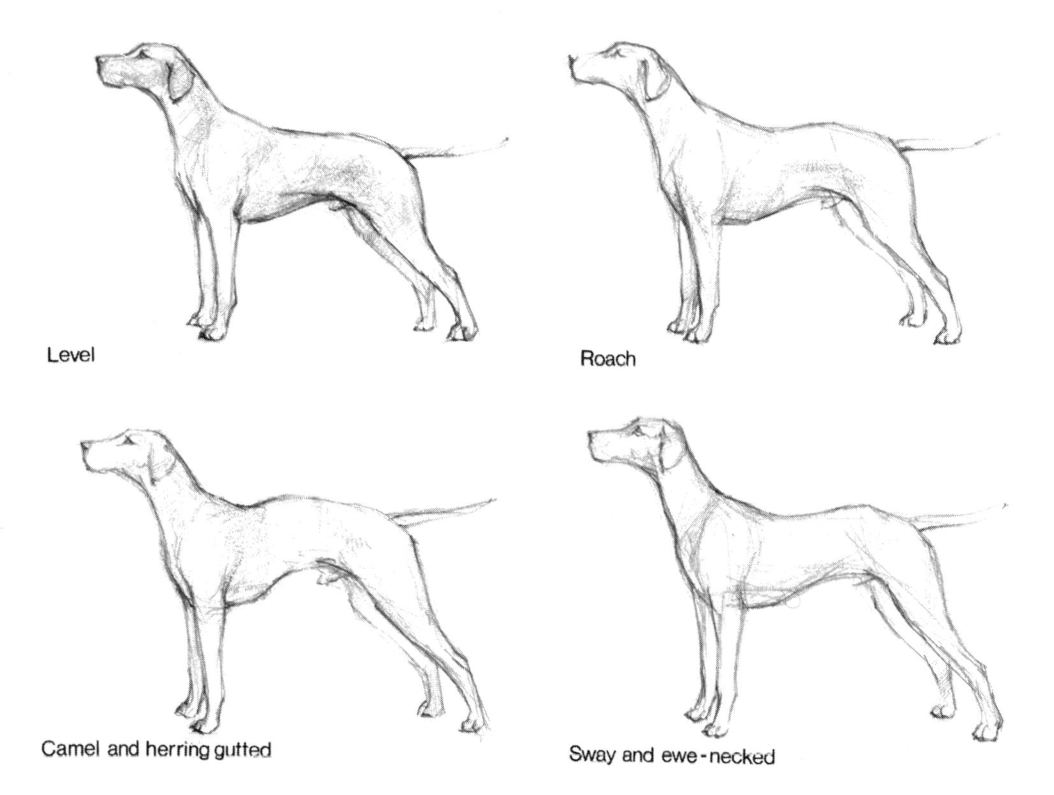

NOMENCLATURE OF THE SPINAL COLUMN

It is really most confusing when there is no one definite description for the various parts of the spinal column. If the nomenclature could be divided into neck, withers, back, loin and croup with the corresponding seven, eight, five, seven and three vertebrae for each, it would certainly help to lessen the confusion amongst breeders, judges and those who compile breed standards. The area between the neck and the start of the part of the tail that is first seen could be described as the top-line and nothing else.

THE SPINAL COLUMN

The spinal column goes from the head to the tip of the tail. The top-line goes from withers to tail. There are seven cervical vertebrae in the neck, eight at the withers which are highly important in shoulder action and five of the back. It is these five vertebrae which must be parallel to the ground. There are seven vertebrae in the arched loin and three fused ones forming the croup. The tail will have from three to twenty-six coccygeal vertebrae. The spines of the vertebrae for each group incline in different directions. The vertebrae of the neck are large and somewhat round, but at the withers the spines are long and slope back, the next section are the five much shorter spines of the back which are almost upright, these vertebrae carrying the floating rib and the other ribs which are connected to each other but not the ribs connected to the sternum.

LOIN

Between the rib section and the croup are the seven vertebrae of the loin. These bones are longer and wider than the others and the spines are much shorter and incline in the opposite direction to those on the withers and slope forward. They are extremely important for the rearing muscles. The loins have no support at all from any other bones and they act as the keystone bridge between the front assembly from the ribs forward and the rear assembly of bones that is the pelvis, legs and tail. A slight arch here is essential for structural strength, but there is no necessity for it to be too arched. A sag in this area is a much greater fault than a roach, as a sag becomes soft and will become worse with age. An arched loin must never be confused with a roach or sway back.

COUPLING

The distance between the front assembly and the rear assembly, which is the section of the loins, is called the coupling. There are often optical illusions here; particularly when a dog has good shoulders and acutely-angled hindquarters he will give the appearance of being short coupled. A deep body will do the same. Conversely a shallow body gives the impression of long coupling.

CROUP

To continue down the spinal column, after the vertebrae of the loin come those of the croup. There are three fused bones here, the spines of which slant further forward than those of the loin. To the croup is attached the pelvis, and the inclination of the croup will be the same as that of the pelvis. It is, however, actually controlled by muscles. If the muscles of the loin are pinched the croup will flatten. A natural flat croup indicates weak rearing muscles.

UNDULATIONS OF THE SPINAL COLUMN

Owing to the different angles of the spines of the vertebrae from the withers to the tail, it will be seen that the top-line could never be absolutely level. Obviously, since the spinal processes are in four distinct areas and in each area they incline in different directions, where they do meet there has to be a slight dip or rise. There is often a slight dip downwards at the withers and in the show world this is often considered a fault. Structurally, however, it is not a fault: it merely indicates that the spines are long. But where this dipped section meets the five vertebrae of the back, the top-line must change direction and this part of the back must be parallel to the ground. The forward slanting spines of the loins must now meet the more or less upright ones of the back and where they meet there must be another slight undulation, just as there will be where the croup starts. The whole spinal column will not and should not be absolutely straight. Just as the spinal column is not absolutely straight in the human. Yet we erroneously talk about straight backs in both humans and in dogs!

TAIL

The tail is all part of the spinal column and has from three to twenty-six coccygeal vertebrae, which become progressively smaller in size. The muscles of the tail affect the inclination of the pelvis and croup. Two main muscles work the tail, one on the top the other underneath. If the tail muscles are not working correctly, it will frequently be found that they are not working any better along the spine either. Another factor regarding the tail is that a mutation in this area often reflects itself in the vertebrae of the croup and in the pelvis, thus frequently causing whelping problems.

Any mutation in a vertebra of a tail will affect each consecutive one in a milder degree and therefore no mutations of a tail should start before the first two that can be seen. There are three coccygeal vertebrae of the tail before the first one comes into view. The tail acts as a rudder. It helps with balance and indicates every emotional feeling a dog has. For these reasons, it should never be docked.

FORE LIMB

The dog's fore limb is similar to man's arm, except that man's arm is free from the shoulder joint. The dog's foreleg looks as if the leg only starts below the elbow, but this is not so. The humerus or upper arm just as with man, joins the scapula or shoulder blade in a ball and socket joint, but instead of being free as in man, the upper arm is kept close to the dog's body by muscle, ligaments and skin. The length of this upper arm varies enormously in different breeds. The Fox Terrier has a very short upper arm, whereas the Dachshund has a very long one with short radius and ulna bones. These are the two bones between the elbows and the pasterns. The Fox Terrier radius and ulna on the other hand are long in comparison. Below these two bones are a group of bones forming a joint.

PASTERN JOINT

The pastern joint connects the forearm with the pastern, and it consists of a group of seven bones. This pastern joint is similar to man's wrist. It is at this joint that the slight bend or slope is given to the pastern. It is a little confusing because the pastern joint on the fore limb is sometimes called the manus, knee, or wrist.

Pasterns

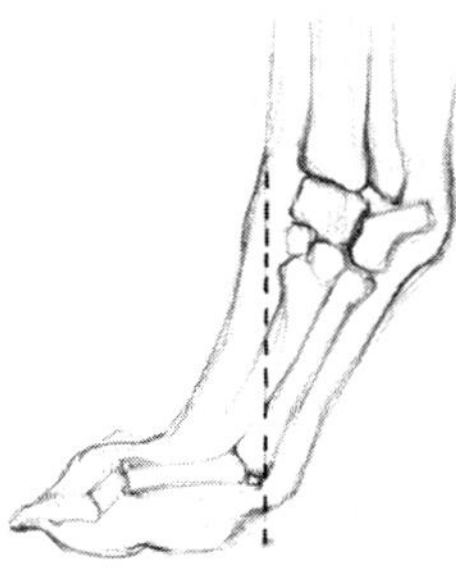

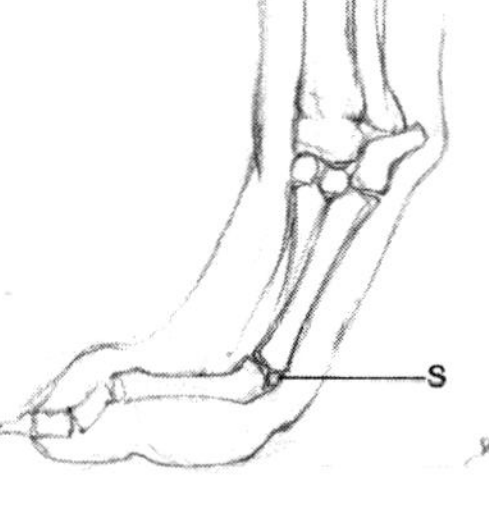

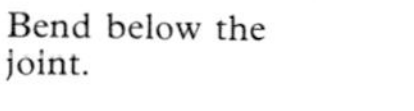

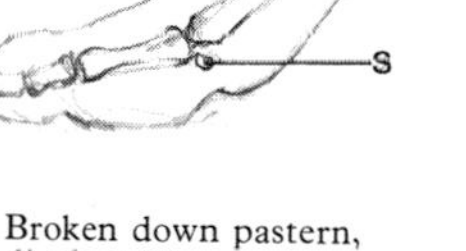

Well-bent pastern. Bend above the joint

Bend below the joint.

Broken down pastern, displaced bones including sesamoid(s).

Straight pastern.

Knuckled-over.

FORE PASTERN

The area between the pastern joint and the joint of the foot is called the pastern. It consists of five long metacarpal bones of which only four are used. The fifth ends in the dewclaw, which is equivalent to a man's thumb. The long bones of the hand correspond to the pastern in the dog and man's fingers correspond to the dog's toes on the foreleg. The toes have three phalanges in each toe.

The front bones of the pastern bear the dog's weight but do not provide for any leverage. The pastern joint at the top has a slight upward flexion as well as a hind flexion. It is important that the width of the pastern should be the same all the way down. The muscles of the pasterns are not particularly strong as they mainly swing the pad forward. It is these same muscles which prevent knuckling over. The back muscles are attached to the small bone called the pisiform, and other muscles help to keep the leg straight.

A great deal is heard about the pasterns at dog shows. How much slope should there be, where should it come and why is it there? The slope of the pastern must always be sufficient, so that the heel pad comes directly under the centre of gravity, in other words, in a vertical line from the centre of the shoulder blade to the pad. The slope is generally preferred to be at the top at the pastern joint where it articulates with the fore arm. The slope may, however, come at the bottom just above the foot. This in turn will make the pastern more upright, as is required in some breeds. The almost straight pastern has some advantages owing to there being more strength in a straight column of bones and the leg will therefore bear more weight, and at the same time there will be less strain on the muscles. On the other hand, if the pastern is too straight the leg will knuckle over at the group of bones at the pastern joint and the whole leg will then start to quiver, owing to the extra strain put on the muscles. The correct amount of flexion will prevent knuckling over and muscle strain. It will also absorb the shock of concussion through the pad. The correct slope will provide a better lift to the centre of gravity by permitting the lower bones to take part. The dog's heel pad is equivalent to the padded area just below man's fingers. So that a dog on his fore limbs walks on his fingers.

Breeds that are endowed with large shoulder blades and long upper arms require a greater slope to the pasterns than other breeds, the Alsatian or German Shepherd Dog being one breed renowned for sloping pasterns. The correct slope may be gauged by a vertical line going through the centre of the shoulder blade and the heel pad.

THE BROKEN DOWN PASTERN

This is a physical weakness, which is sometimes inherited. The foot becomes flat and the strain of the weight, instead of being carried by the straight bone assembly of the legs, is put on the muscles and the ligaments instead. The pisiform bone becomes displaced owing to the pull by the muscles and the little sesamoid bone at the bottom of the pastern also gets pulled out of position.

Feet

Cat foot-most breeds

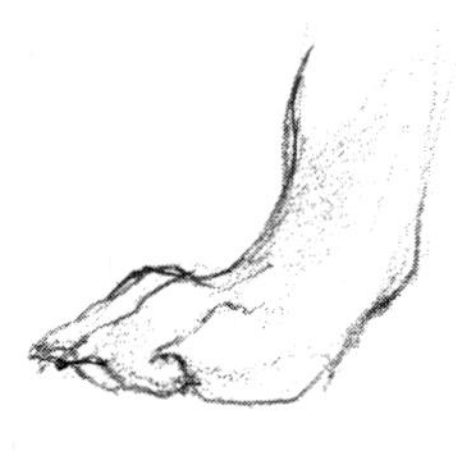

Hare foot- Papillons, Borzoi Japanese Spaniel etc.

Pekinese, flat turned (front view)

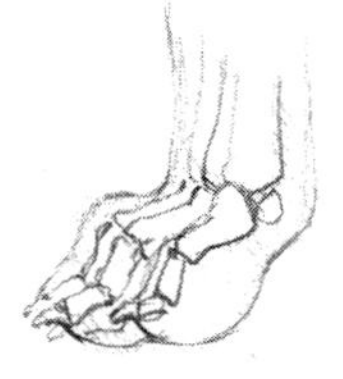

Cat foot

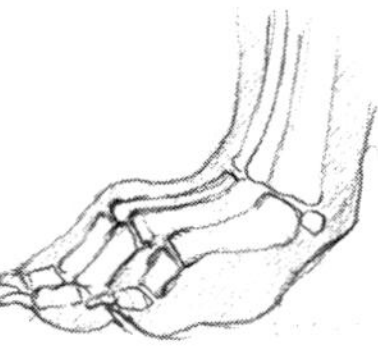

Hare foot

Splay foot

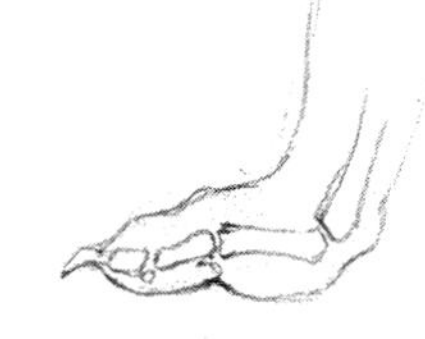

Paper foot

THE FORE FOOT AND HIND FOOT

Below the pasterns are a group of bones called the phalanges. These make up the four toes, each toe having three bones corresponding to man's fingers or on the hindleg to man's toes.

The main difference between a hare foot and a cat foot is the length of the third digital bone. These third digital bones, whether on a cat foot or a hare foot, should be parallel to the ground, but the second digital bone in the cat foot should lie at 45°. The hare foot is more likely to sustain injury than a cat foot.

The cat foot denotes endurance whilst the hare foot is for speed. A broken down cat foot should never be confused with a hare foot. The strength of the foot depends on the muscles and ligaments and tendons. The type of ground that a dog is exercised over and the amount of exercise a dog has have a considerable effect on the shape of the foot. A dog exercised over rough ground or kept on a pebble run will develop the muscles of his feet, so that they become thicker and stronger, and so that the toes are drawn up tightly to enable the dog to travel over the rough ground in comfort. If the ground is soft and even, the dog will not require to use the muscles of his feet like he does when negotiating hard rough ground, and consequently his feet will become slack and his toes will spread out, and his feet are likely then to become hare-shaped as opposed to cat-shaped. In general, bad feet tend to become worse. A man walking on soft sand or on a pebbly beach will use the muscles of his toes in much the same way as the dog.

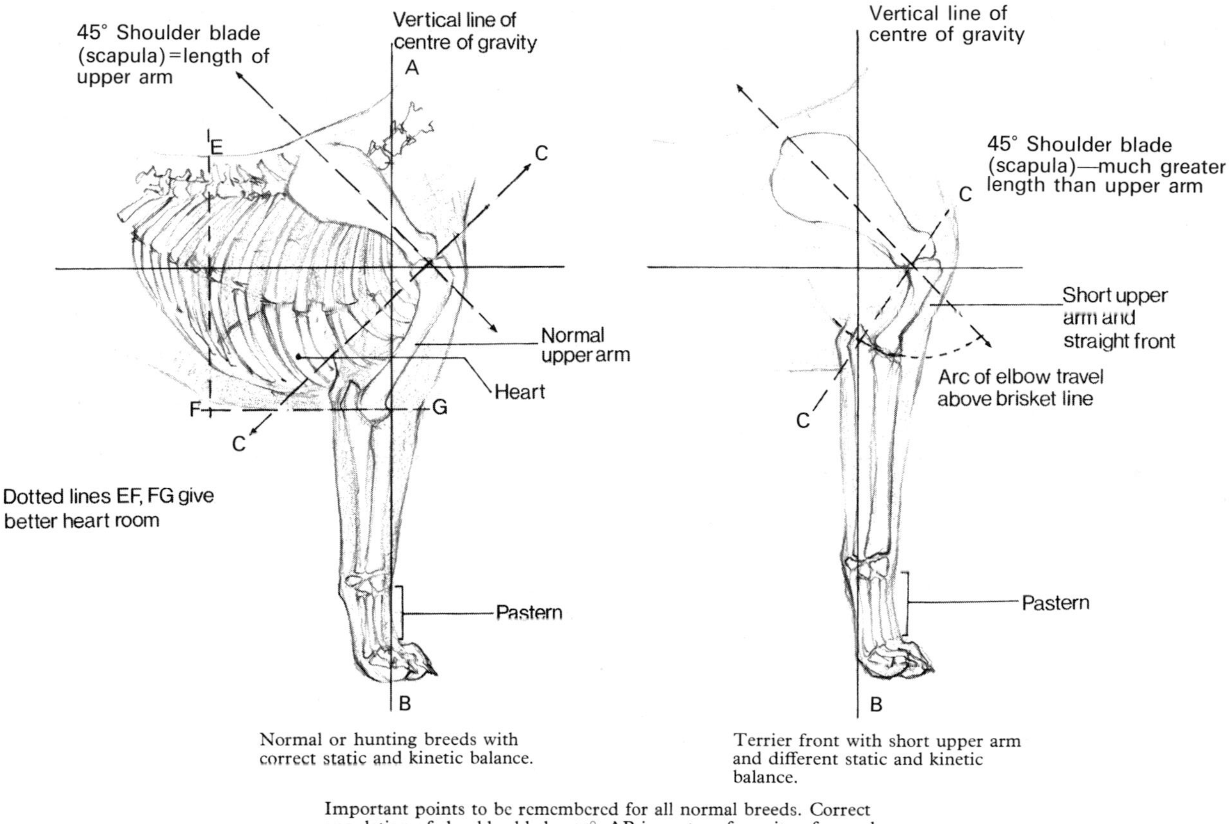

Normal or hunting breeds with correct static and kinetic balance.

Terrier front with short upper arm and different static and kinetic balance.

Important points to be remembered for all normal breeds. Correct angulation of shoulder blade: 45°. AB is centre of gravity of scapular and/or a vertical line with the heel pad for static balance. C. Ribs angled back at 45°. Last rib well sprung out from spinal column. D. Heart situated between third and eighth ribs. EF. Extremely important that there is good depth at the ninth ribs for heart and lung room, including length of sternum FG. Note: a dog has no collar bone.

SHOULDERS

The shoulder blades are extremely important. The shoulder blades or scapulae have to support weight. They absorb concussion from the gait, and they also propel on the turns. Another important function is to help with lateral displacement. The shoulder blade also aids the level of centre of gravity. Shoulders are particularly important for the working breeds. Perhaps the two most important parts of a dog are correct shoulders and hocks. If these are right then what goes on in between is likely to be correct too.

The angle at which a shoulder blade is set is most important. Correct shoulders are described in dog parlance as 'well laid back'. Some people perhaps do not understand exactly what angles are referred to and how they are measured or the importance of the way the dog is standing when the angle is measured. Every serious judge should study Mr Dowell Lyon's well-known book on 'The Dog in Action'. He states that a 45° shoulder blade is twenty-five per cent more efficient than a 60° or 70° shoulder blade. The latter are all too common in some breeds. It is helpful for the novice to study the illustrations of the various angles of shoulder blades and their placement on the different breeds, and then to relate the illustrations to actual dogs.

The shoulder blade in most breeds should slope back 45°, taking the dog's foreleg when well under him as the vertical line. At the same time the shoulder blade should be sloped inwards, hugging the rib cage. In some breeds the inclination is greater than in others and affects leg movement.

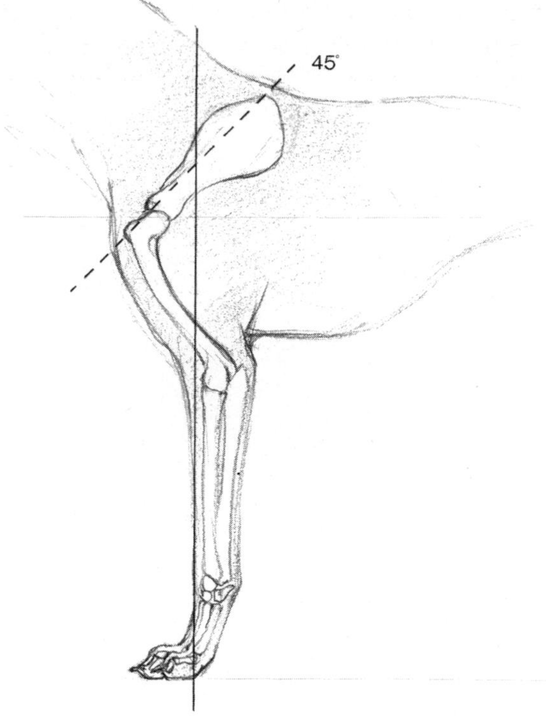

Dachshund front

Whole structure reduced in bone length and set high on the body. Elbow action arc is above brisket line. This front can be and often is in kinetic and static balance.

Racing front

Extremely long upper arm, often dropping the elbow below the brisket line. Pasterns sloping and longer in comparison with hocks than in other types. Feet set high on heel pad; long third digital bone and upright second digital bone.

The length of the humerus, which is the bone reaching from the shoulder to the elbow, determines the placement of the elbow on the chest wall. Many dogs which are loose at the elbow are tight at the shoulder joint and the forelegs tend to be thrown sideways in a circular movement. If the dog is tight at the elbow joint the whole leg inclines outwards, causing the dog to paddle.

Ribs

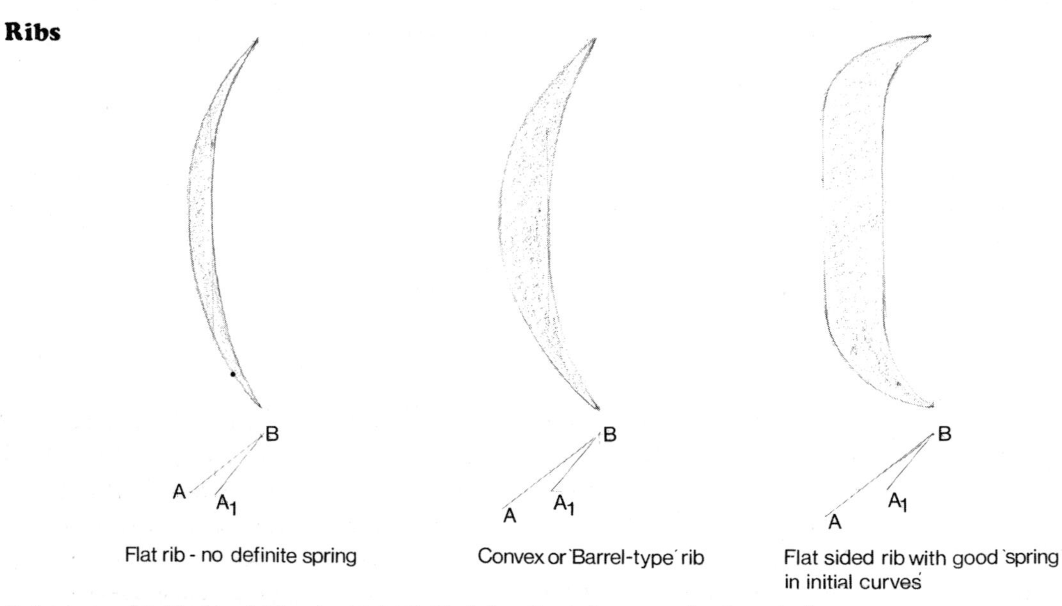

Flat rib - no definite spring

Convex or 'Barrel-type' rib

Flat sided rib with good 'spring in initial curves'

Each type angulated backward 45° and rotated 30°. Shaded portion indicates capacity change in thorax.

THE RIB CAGE

The depth of the chest is always greater than the width of the ribs. The cavity within the chest is pear-shaped and contains the lungs and the heart. The heart rests on the sternum bone

Static rear stance

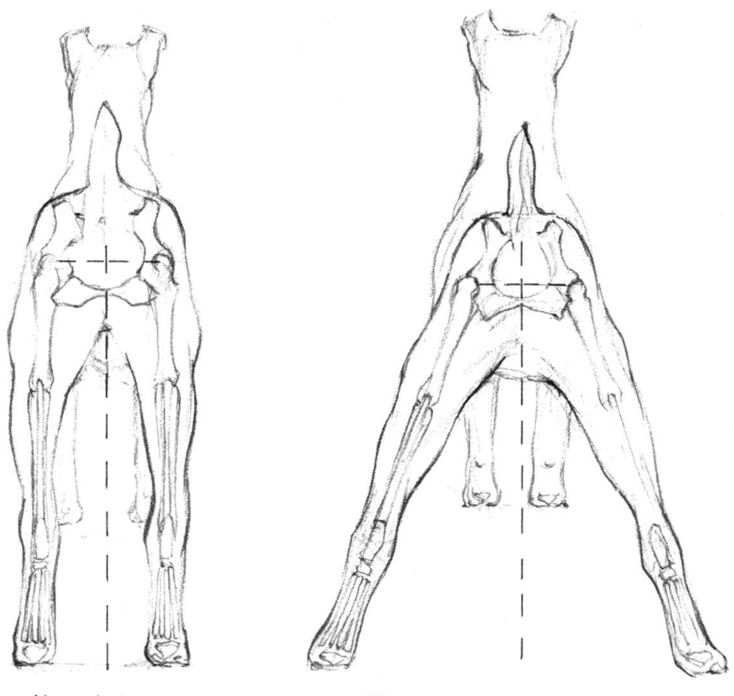

between the third and eighth ribs. A long diaphragm is important in all breeds, it is much more important than a wide rib cage. The muscle runs obliquely from loins to sternum. The depth should reach the ninth rib before turning up for the tuck up. The last three ribs are important. If they are well sprung out from the spinal column and are of a good size for the breed and angle back correctly at 45°, then the remainder of the ribs will be correct. It is not important whether the mid section of the rib is barrelled or flat, this depends on the breed standard. It is, however, important that the first four or five ribs should be less curved than the others, and they should also be flat-sided, so that there should be sufficient freedom for shoulder action.

HIND LIMB

The femur joins the sacrum or pelvis in a ball-and-socket joint forming the hip. This is where hip dysplasia occurs. The joint at the lower end of the femur corresponds to the knee in man and is called the stifle. There is often a great deal of trouble in this joint in some breeds. The femur is sometimes referred to as the upper thigh and the two bones below the stifle as the lower thigh.

HOCKS

The hock is a joint only, and must never be confused with the hind pastern. The bottom of the lower thigh consists of the tibia and fibula which articulate with the top of the hock. The hock joint consists of seven tarsal bones and corresponds to man's ankle. The point of hock is the equivalent of man's heel. It is the most important and longest bone, and is called the os calcis, which ends in the point of hock. Attached to it is the leverage muscle to the fibula.

Well let down hocks improve the leverage action and are required for endurance. High placed hocks are desirable for speed. There is, unfortunately, some confusion in dog parlance regarding hocks.

Although standards often ask for upright hocks or hocks perpendicular to the ground, what they intend should be applied to hind pasterns too. In fact, a more efficient hindleg is one where the hock and hind pastern slope very slightly forward.

SICKLE HOCKS

This is the description given when the hock inclines backwards. It is a most serious fault and is generally accompanied by acutely bent stifles. Long bones sometimes prevent the pads from reaching a point vertically under the centre of gravity. This problem is found in a great many Alsatians (German Shepherd Dogs) owing to the turn of stifle required in the breed. Provided that at high speed the hock can straighten sufficiently, so that the pad and stifle are in a straight line, then such a sickle hock can be forgiven.

GOOD MOVEMENT IN THE SHOW RING

All breeds are expected to move in the ring either at a slow or a fast trot. They are also expected to move with the head held high. This looks smart. Since show rings should be level and hard, the movement of the dog under these circumstances is all that concerns the judge and handler at this time. Many handlers prefer to move the dog at a fast trot, although the judge gets a better idea of movement when the gait is at a moderate speed. The trot gives more faults away to the judge than any other gait.

PERFECT MOVEMENT

Perfect movement varies with the conformation of breeds, and depends on correct skeletal and muscular conformation and complete co-ordination with both static and kinetic balance. This includes well laid-back shoulders, strong pasterns, hips, stifles, hocks and well-formed pads. The breeds which move best in the ring are those where the height of the withers from the ground is the same as the length of the body. Such dogs may be described as well proportioned. Those breeds with well laid-back shoulders and strong stifles gait with their forelegs and hindlegs working together in perfect harmony. At the trot there is a two-point support and only two feet touch the ground at the same moment. These are the diagonal feet. When a dog is well proportioned his fore foot and hind foot almost meet. In contrast to the movement of the dog, the wolf places each hind foot into the exact imprint of the fore foot. The well-proportioned dog is propelled along with equal propulsion by the fore limbs and the hind limbs. The gait should appear to be smooth and effortless.

All breeds walk, trot and pace and use three types of gallop. The *stride* is the distance covered from the imprint of one pad to the next imprint made by the same pad.

Suspension is the term used when the dog is in the process of being propelled by sheer momentum, when all four legs are off the ground at the same moment. *Time* is the number of leg changes which take place in order to support the body. *Walking* is a four-time gait with a wholly or partially three-point support. *Trotting* is a two-time gait with a two-point support. The *canter* is a three-time gait. There are in fact three types of walking and this is dependent upon the stride. *Sequence* is the term used to describe the complete action of all four legs. The dog always leads with one foreleg. This leg takes the weight and supports the body for one-third of the whole sequence. It is always a split second ahead of the hindleg.

When a dog commences to move forward from a standing position in static balance, where the legs have been parallel to each other and perpendicular to the ground, the parallel-plane relationship of the legs will be maintained for an extremely short time. As the dog gains speed, the whole length of the leg gradually tends to incline inwards until the gait is a fast trot, when the pads will be seen to be noticeably nearer a line directly under the longitudinal centre of the body. They reach this line at the fast speeds.

MISCONCEPTIONS OF MOVEMENT

There are still many knowledgeable dog people who have never realized that, the faster the dog moves, the nearer the dog will place his paws to a longitudinal centre line. Breeds must be judged to their standards. Some state categorically that the legs should move straight forward. Dalmations move in this way, whereas Collies do not. What is important, however, is that at whatever speed the dog is moving, whether at a slow trot or a flying trot, the entire leg when seen from the front or the rear should move in one straight line from mid-shoulder or the hip to the pad, without elbows, hocks or pads deviating from this straight line. This line, of course, is not in a plane perpendicular to the ground.

There are, however, a few breeds of dog whose proportions are such that the above movement would not hold true. Such dogs would not be stayers: they lack efficiency of movement having little kinetic balance. The inclination of the legs may be so slight in some breeds that this would only be seen in slow motion. Obviously, the longer a dog's legs the more easily can the inclination inwards be detected. If the joints and bones do not remain in line, then the dog either paddles, weaves or plaits. When the judge sees the dog moving away from him, the hind action should be strong and forceful with a good drive from the hocks propelling the dog forward. As with the fore limbs the hindlegs will gradually incline inwards with increasing speed. Thus, the joints and bones from the hip to the pad, as with the fore limbs, must be in a straight plane but not a vertical one. As the dog moves, the judge should be able to see the pads of the feet. When the dog is moving happily and freely and with alacrity, he will use his tail to maintain perfect balance and will carry it in the correct position for the breed.

THE SLOW WALK

The slow walk is not a speed normally seen in the show ring. It is described as a four-time movement. All legs move one after the other, with four different combinations of weight support. The dog always leads with one fore foot, and this takes the most weight, in fact one-third of the body weight. As the dog moves forward, one foreleg advances and reaches the ground on a plane below the dog's head, whilst the opposite hind limb moves forward to a line immediately below the dog's navel. At a given moment there will be three feet on the ground at the same time, and as the foreleg advances and comes in contact with the ground the dog's weight is changed from one foot to the other to prevent him from becoming top heavy and falling forward. All four legs move in a plane almost perpendicular to the ground. The tracks of a slow walk are on almost parallel planes with each other and are fairly wide apart. The slower the walk the further apart the tracks will be, and the more nearly perpendicular will the plane of the limbs be to the ground. A young puppy walking will have its legs much further apart, to enable him to balance; just as an elderly human or an invalid will walk with legs further apart, to help maintain his balance. The sequence of the walk is: left fore, right hind, right fore, left hind, the heel pad striking the ground first. The walk is the least tiring gait of all.

THE TROT AND THE FLYING TROT

The trot is the normal gait seen in the show ring. It is a two-time movement and is the simplest of all. Moreover, it shows up faults more than any other gait. It is a free swinging movement from shoulders and hips; the elbows, stifles, hocks, pasterns and pads all play their part and co-ordinate perfectly with each other. Whereas the weight in the walk has been taken by the opposite limbs, it is now taken by the diagonal pairs of legs, one diagonal after another, with the left fore and right hind moving together and vice versa. The passing foot will not touch the supporting leg, if it is sufficiently flexed, because it will pass above the lowest point of the supporting foot, and will not touch or brush. The same applies to the hindleg. Large breeds some times brush and move close, because the leg moves forward like a pendulum instead of being flexed.

For a split second in the flying trot while the legs change position, all four feet are off the ground at the same moment, so that there is a period of suspension. The passing foot will not touch the supporting leg, since it will be flexed backwards.

Each foot should only be lifted just high enough to clear the ground as the limb swings forward, thus giving the maximum muscular proficiency with the minimum of effort for the speed.

Few judges or exhibitors realize that, the faster the dog is made to trot, the nearer his tracks will be to a central line. It is well worth while trying out an experiment on a dog which the handler considers to have perfect movement. It will come as quite a surprise. A good way to set about the experiment is to walk a dog on a wet sandy beach or in snow, or to powder the hind pads with talcum powder and perhaps to crush up some red chalk and put the coloured chalk on the fore paws. Cooking oil on the fore pads will work equally well for the experiment. Start the dog in a standing position and make him walk slowly in a straight line across a floor and increase his speed after a few steps. It is extremely difficult to make a dog walk slowly as his natural gait is a slow or fast trot. It will be found that the tracks are perfectly regular and it will be easy to distinguish which were made by the fore limbs and which by the hind limbs. The distance between each hind limb and each fore limb, when moving slowly, will be considerable, but the moment the pace is accelerated to a fast speed the tracks of both fore pads will be found to be almost touching each other, as will the tracks of the two hind pads. The dog's body moving with perfect freedom may give the judge an optical illusion that at a trot the limbs are moving on the same plane with each other.

When the dog is seen by the judge from the side the gait will show the length of stride and the force of the propulsion. The five vertebrae of the back will remain parallel to the ground and the movement of diagonally opposite limbs will synchronize and be simultaneous.

When moving towards the judge a well balanced dog will have his head held correctly, supported by the strong muscles of the neck. The dog will move forward in a straight line along the ground and will not deviate from an imaginary vertical line. At a slow speed the forelegs should travel almost on the same plane with each other. There should be a slight upward flexion of the leading fore foot and the other fore foot should flex directly towards the rear. In other words the column of bones from the shoulder to the foot should always be in one straight line, but this line is not a vertical line except when the dog is standing. To sum up, in the perfect movement of a normally proportioned dog, that is to say, one with the height of withers being equal to the length of body, the gait should be sound, strong, quick, free, true and level.

The drawings on page 179 showing the correct movement of a dog are probably much easier for the novice to follow than any worded description, and it is probably useful for the novice to study drawings of poor movement and faulty rear and hind action.

BREEDS WITH OTHER PROPORTIONS

The gait of other breeds will obviously be as varied as their individual proportions, for example, Bulldogs will not be able to move with the ease and grace of a Whippet. Dachshunds, with their very long, low-to-ground bodies and short legs, and with their fore and hindlegs so far apart have compensated for their curious out-of-proportion anatomy by having a curved fore arm and by moving their hindlegs at a greater speed than their forelegs. Pekingese also have a curious gait caused by the combination of leg movement, rather resembling that of the Dachshund but made somewhat stiffer owing to a more rigid spine. This may not be so noticeable owing to the profuse coat. Pomeranians with their short backs and slightly longer legs skim over the ground in the daintiest of fashion. The Wire Fox Terrier gait is specifically mentioned in the standard and it is also typical for that breed. They skim over the ground but they lack staying power and kinetic balance, especially when they are strung up by their handlers, as they frequently are, and they then almost appear to be airborne. The large, heavy breeds often fail in hind movement. Pyrenean Mountain Dogs are built so heavily that hips, stifles and hocks are seldom as strong as they should be, and they too lack kinetic balance.

It is a strange fact that, although a dog may seemingly have perfect conformation when examined on the table or on the ground, it will often be found that a dog with a perfect front will paddle, weave or plait, and the same dog with apparently perfect hocks when in a show pose and cleverly set up by the handler will move with cow-hocks. Few breeds, however, turn their

Pace, side view, and Crabbing

Pacing, side view

Crabbing

Fore- and hindlegs operating on same training; the dog therefore has to sidestep to avoid the weight-bearing leg touching the over-reaching leg.

Correct movement. Front foot a split second out of the way of hind foot.

Trot and Pace

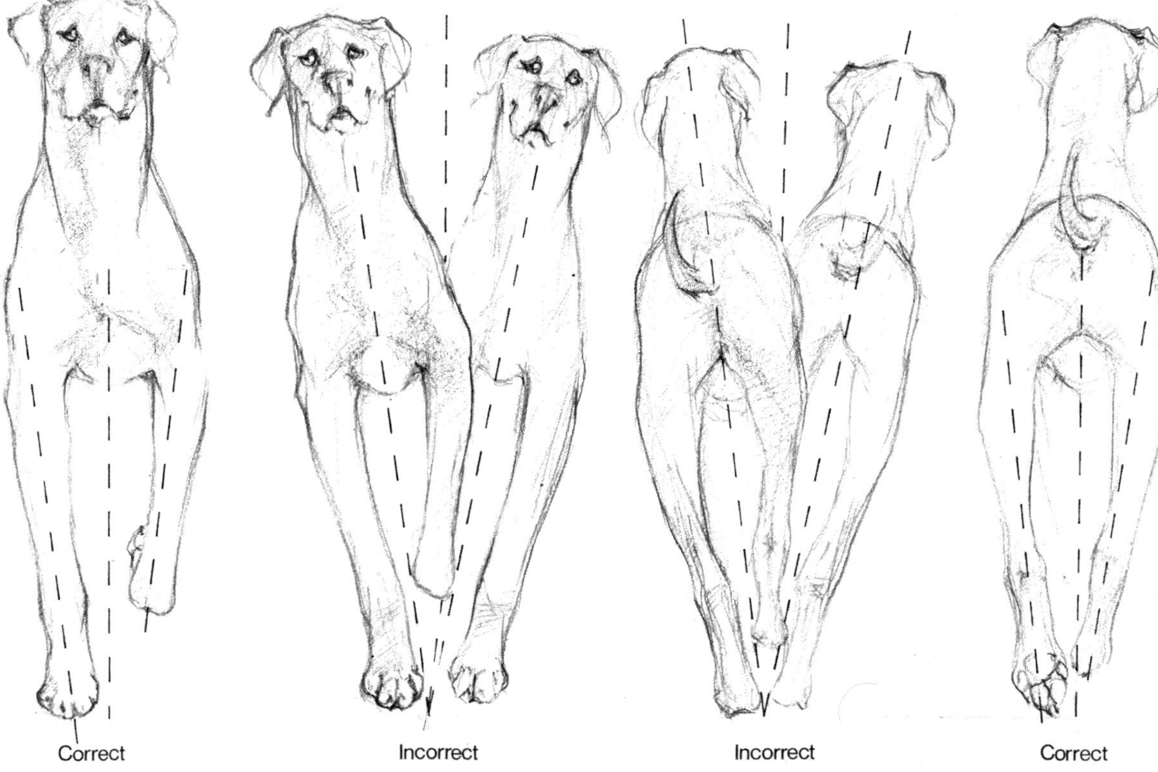

Correct

Trotting. Correct movement, head up, pads converging on or near centre line. Using normal diagonal gait with a two point support.

Incorrect

Pacing. Dogs roll from side to side using a lateral gait; both right legs moved at the same time; also with a two point support.

Incorrect

Pacing from the rear.

Correct

Trotting from rear. Correct movement. Head up; pads converging on or near centre line; normal diagonal gait; two point support.

hocks out. Some dogs will move soundly in an outdoor ring and unsoundly in an indoor one, or vice versa.

Tail carriage, ear carriage and coat all play an important part in the overall picture of a first-class show dog. Many faults can be hidden by a full and flowing coat, but this never deceives a judge who knows his dog.

DEVIATIONS IN PERFECT MOVEMENT

Since there are so many skeletal deviations and variations in show dogs, not to mention the many different weight distributions that are to be seen between the breeds, it stands to reason that there are bound to be similar variations in correct movement for any given breed. The nearer that movement can conform to the norm within a breed the better.

PACING

This is a movement which is sometimes called ambling. It is a two-time lateral gait. Instead of the diagonal legs co-ordinating together, the foreleg and the hindleg advance together on the same side. This gives the dog a curious, rolling side-to-side movement, which is particularly noticeable when the dog is moving in a straight line towards the judge. Instead of the dog moving without deviating from an imaginary vertical plane, the head and whole body will be seen to swing from side to side of such a vertical plane. Pacing is very much frowned on by judges, and the handler has to correct the faulty movement. Some breeds are more prone to pace than others, e.g. Alsatians, Dalmations, Pugs and Great Danes. Young puppies frequently pace before they learn to trot. Ambling is a restful gait adopted particularly by old, tired, out-of-condition dogs. Over-weight dogs are also inclined to pace. It is certainly not a gait for the show ring.

JOINT ABNORMALITIES

HIP DYSPLASIA

This is the name given to an abnormal development of the bones which form the hip joint. It is interesting that the severity of the condition is not always related to the unsoundness of the dog's gait. It will be noticed, however, that affected dogs show a distinct reluctance to jump. There is usually a decided lack of propulsive power and an excessive sideways movement of the pelvis and hips at each step, or there may be some exaggeration of the rise and fall of each step. Afflicted dogs tend to tire easily and prefer to sit rather than to stand.

CAUSES OF HIP DYSPLASIA

There are many theories regarding the cause of hip dysplasia and, from what one reads and hears, it seems as if not too much is known about the cause. Some authorities claim that it is hereditary and polygenetic. Others claim that it is not congenital, but that it occurs during the later growth of the puppy, and that it may occur as late as its second year. It is surprising to find, along with many other defects, that hip dysplasia has been known in man for several thousand years. It is found in many animals, including horses, cattle and even in cats. It was first noticed in dogs in 1935. A great many breeds are affected, but it does seem to occur more frequently in the large, heavy puppies.

The hip joint is a ball and socket joint, which simply means that the top of the thigh bone, or head of the femur, which should be round, fits into the deep socket of the pelvis, formed by the junction of the three pelvic bones. The bones normally fit each other perfectly, forming a stable ball-and-socket joint. But with hip dysplasia, instead of the femoral head being round, it loses its shape and becomes narrower, and the depth and shape of the socket are imperfect.

The bone no longer fits the socket snugly, and the socket in turn loses its shape and becomes too shallow. The strong ligaments which normally keep the ball-and-socket joint together do not work sufficiently well under the strain, and the malformed bone of the femur head moves about in the flattened socket. In severe cases there is complete dislocation of the hip, which causes a great deal of pain, and the dog is completely crippled. There are, of course, varying degrees of hip dysplasia, and in many cases it cannot be detected, except by X-ray, before the dog is a year old; but to be absolutely certain the dog should be at least two-years old. Dogs afflicted not too severely learn to compensate by developing and using particular muscles, and many dogs suffer no pain at all; but most dogs with even slight dysplasia tend to develop arthritis in old age.

One of the worst afflicted breeds at the present time is the Alsatian (German Shepherd Dog). It is worth watching the hind movement of Alsatians, since the dislocation of the hips is clearly visible in many of them.

OVER-ANGULATION OF THE HIND LIMB

The normal dog has correct angulation of the joints in the hind limbs. Fashion unfortunately has decreed in some breeds a decided over-angulation of the joints. Over the years, in order to achieve this, certain changes have had to take place in the length of the main bones. The tibia has increased in length and the distance between the hock and the ground has become shorter. In the normal dog, the leg from the hock joint to the ground is inclined very slightly forward, whereas in most show breeds it is considered correct for the leg from the hock to the ground to be perpendicular. A serious fault is a sickle hock, which angles backwards. The diagram of the hind limbs demonstrates what is known in show report terminology as a good turn of stifle. The angle at the rear of the stifle joint has been bred to become very much smaller than that found in the normal dog; the tibia, or lower thigh bone has become longer; and the leg from the hock to the ground has been made perpendicular. These skeletal changes of excessive angulation may possibly be a contributary cause of the pressure that now falls on the hip joint, where so much trouble is found.

Perhaps for a period judges might refrain from putting up dogs with over-angulated hind limbs and not enthuse on beautiful turn of stifle, and slowly the breeds affected might return to the shape that nature intended.

STIFLE DYSPLASIA

Stifle dysplasia, patella luxation, or slipping stifles as it is often referred to amongst dog people, is unfortunately far too common in a great many breeds. A slipped stifle is the dislocation of the patella, which is the equivalent of the dislocation of the knee cap in man. There are varying degrees of the abnormality. It seldom shows before the age of six months and may not show in the case of some bitches until after she has whelped her second litter. Dogs may develop partial dislocation in their old age. Obviously, the younger a dog is when partial or complete dislocation occurs, the worse it is for the dog, particularly when it occurs at about four to six months of age and develops until about ten to twelve months of age. The patella is a small bone which lies in a shallow groove at the lower end of the thigh bones. Normally, when the dog bends his knee the little bone moves along the shallow groove and is kept in place by the small ridges on either side of it, with the assistance of the ligaments. If the groove happens to be too shallow or the ridges too low, the knee cap slips out of the groove. The dog then 'carries' the affected leg and will run on three legs. It is more common for the patella to slip inwards from the mid-line.

There are at least six causes of styfle dysplasia. These are varied, and the majority are probably hereditary. Partial dislocation is what is most often observed in the ring in some breeds. The patella bone slides in and out of the trochlea depression on the femur with each step that the dog takes. When the dog is trotting, he may move astonishingly soundly. It is only when he is expected to stand that the slipping stifle may become obvious, since the joint becomes quite straight and, in order to compensate for this, the nearby joints are also affected. If the handler moves the dog slightly, the patella will return to the normal correct position. The more often that the patella slips out of the groove, the more strain is put on the surrounding ligaments and muscles. These become stretched and the general weakness at the joint increases.

If the dislocation becomes complete the patella over-rides the groove and the joint may lock. This is extremely painful, and if it occurs frequently an operation may be necessary. When the patella is locked, it slides over the outer edge of the trochlea groove, which acts rather like a pulley. The judge can feel the joint if it is grasped gently in the crooked fingers of the hand. The leg will often go straight and the joint above the foot becomes over-flexed. There is the tell-tale click, which can be heard quite distinctly in small breeds when the dog is picked up. Sometimes, a dog will perhaps be moving in the ring quite perfectly, when suddenly he will give a little skip and hop along on three legs. The moment the patella returns to its correct position in the groove the dog continues to move soundly.

Judges may have gone over a dog thoroughly, seen him move correctly and with alacrity and, just as the dog is about to be awarded a first prize, he may stand for just a fleeting second with his hindleg in such a position that the judge knows that he has a slipping stifle. In breeds where the fault is rife, it is never fair for a judge to put a dog in a lower place because he has seen the dog previously and already knows his weakness. If the judge does not actually see the stifle go out at that show on that day, he has every right to put the dog up, provided he is the better dog. The judge may decide to play safe and put another dog up whose stifles looked stronger, but he may in fact be just as weak in stifle as the first dog. It is up to handlers to show their dog without allowing the fault to betray him.

Extremely active small breeds seem particularly prone to patella luxation.

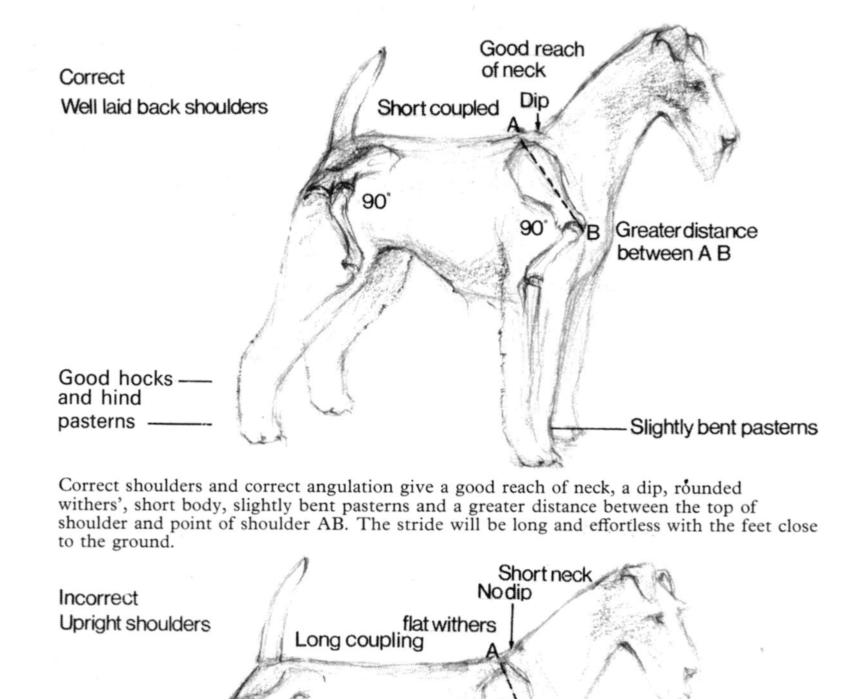

Correct shoulders and correct angulation give a good reach of neck, a dip, rounded withers', short body, slightly bent pasterns and a greater distance between the top of shoulder and point of shoulder AB. The stride will be long and effortless with the feet close to the ground.

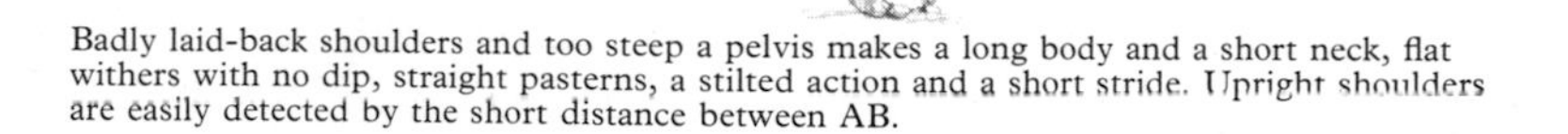

Badly laid-back shoulders and too steep a pelvis makes a long body and a short neck, flat withers with no dip, straight pasterns, a stilted action and a short stride. Upright shoulders are easily detected by the short distance between AB.

Conclusion

THE OBJECT OF SHOWS IS THE ADVANCEMENT OF PURE BRED DOGS
THE OBJECT OF THE KENNEL CLUB IS THE
PROMOTION AND IMPROVEMENT
OF DOGS

It is interesting that it matters very little whether it is easy to make up champions or difficult, whether the standards are good or bad, whether the judges are efficient or inefficient, whether the breeders have the good of the breed at heart or not. The crux of the matter is that, overall, pedigree dogs are improving. Breeders are more knowledgeable and judges on the whole put up the best dogs. Top breeders use the best studs and the veterinary profession cope with the breeders' mistakes. The exhibitors and handlers enjoy themselves; the suppliers of dog food and equipment make money; and the pedigree show dog trots along endeavouring to please master, judge and the public.

This state of affairs, however, will only continue provided that there is much less greed and far greater integrity and sportsmanship amongst the dog fraternity, whether they be breeders, handlers, judges or dealers. There should be more responsible supervision in all canine affairs by Kennel Clubs because the writing is already on the wall.

Dog shows must revert to the days when there was more integrity and they provided good sport and a happy day's outing that could be enjoyed by all.

A Glossary of Canine Terms

Abdomen The portion of the body that lies between the chest and the pelvis.
Achilles tendon The tendon and muscle that extends along the lower thigh, between the femur and the hock joint.
Action A dog's movement.
Affix A kennel name attached to the registered name of a dog. It may be placed before (prefix) or after (suffix) the dog's name.
AKC American Kennel Club.
Albinism Hereditary deficiency of colour pigment.
Almond eyes Narrow eyes, shaped like the almond nut.
Angulation Refers to the inclination of bones to each other. Front angulation at the hock, shoulder and upper arm. Rear angulation at stifles and hock in relation to the ground.
Anus Opening at end of rectum.
Apple-domed Rounded or domed skull.
Apron The long hair on the throat and front, which forms a frill.
ASCOB Any solid colour other than black. Pertains to American Cocker Spaniels.
Back The five vertebrae between the withers and the loin. Not to be confused with the top-line, or with length of body.
Back line The top-line from neck to base of tail, including withers, back, loin and croup.
Balanced Well proportioned, referring to the whole.
Barrel ribs Rounded ribs.
Bat ear An ear which is erect with a wide base and rounded tips.
Bay The sound a hound makes when on a trail.
Beard Bushy whiskers.
Beefy Over-heaviness of hindquarters.
Bell-ears Ears in the shape of a bell.
Belton A finely mottled colour-combination in the coat, seen in English Setters.
Benched show A dog show where there are benches to which dogs must be leashed, and cages for the Toy breeds.
Bilateral cryptorchid A dog with two undescended testicles.
BIS Best in Show.
Bird dog A breed of dog used for shooting birds. Pointers or Setters.
Bitch A female dog.
Bitchy Male with a bitch's characteristics.
Bite Refers to the set of the teeth when the mouth is closed.
Blade Shoulder.
Blaze A white mark running up the face between the eyes.
Blocky Head with rather square formation.
Bloom Glossiness of coat, denoting good condition.
Blue merle A grey-blue colour flecked with black, associated with a recessive gene.
Blue print Preconception of finished article.
Board The care of a dog for a fee.
BOB Best of Breed, a dog which is unbeaten in its breed at a particular show.
Bob-tail A dog born with a stump of a tail. Another name for the Old English Sheepdog.

Body, length of Tip of brisket to point of sacrum.
'Bone' The conformation and girth of a dog's forelegs.
Bossy When the muscles of the shoulder and upper arm are too thick and heavy.
Bow-legged Bandy legged, of fore or hindlegs.
Br. Breeder. The owner of a dog's dam at the time of whelping.
Brace Two dogs of a kind exhibited together.
Bracelets Long hair left on legs of Poodle after clipping.
Breaches Feathers on hindlegs.
Breeching The tan markings on the inside and back of thighs, e.g. Manchester Terrier.
Bridge of nose Bones between nostrils and stop.
Brindle A mixture of black hairs with light hairs, which are often in even stripes.
Brisket The lower part of the body below the chest and between the forelegs, and includes the breastbone.
Broken colour The main colour of a dog's coat broken up by another colour.
Broken-up face Deep stop, wrinkle, receding nose, undershot jaw.
Brood bitch A bitch which is kept for breeding.
Brush A tail like a fox, with thick bushy hair.
Bull neck Heavy, over-developed neck.
Burr The visible irregular inside formation of the ear.
Butterfly nose Mottled nose of two colours.
Buttocks Fleshy part of hindquarters.
Button ear The tip of the ear leather folding forward as in the Fox Terrier.
By Refers to the offspring of a stud dog.
CACIB Le Cértificat d'Aptitude Au Championnat International de Beauté. The European equivalent to a challenge certificate.
Camel back Roach back, the opposite of sway back.
Candle-flame ears The shape of the English Toy Terrier.
Canine Referring to an animal group including dogs, foxes, wolves, jackals, coyotes, etc.
Canines The two upper and two lower long, sharp, pointed teeth.
Carp back An arched back.
Carpals The small bones forming the pastern joint.
Cartilage Firm elastic tissue.
Castrate To remove the testicles in the male dog by surgery.
Cat foot A short round foot with the third digits short.
CC Challenge certificate. It is awarded by the Kennel Club and signed by the judge. It is given to the best dog and the best bitch in a breed at a championship show.
Ch. Champion. In Britain, the holder of three or more challenge certificates, awarded by three or more different judges. In the USA, the holder of 15 points won under three or more judges, and must include two wins of three or more points.
Chamois ear Ear that is soft and thin.
Character Disposition of a dog, or its essential breed characteristics.
Cheek Side of face below the eye.
Cheeky Heavy and pronounced cheek development, as in the Bulldog.
Chest The part of the body between the brisket and the belly, excluding the front part of the body, and enclosed by the ribs.
China eye A light blue eye.
Chiselled A well-defined moulding beneath the eyes or muzzle.
Choke collar A chain collar.
Chops The heavy pendulous lips which hang down below the lower jaw.
Chorea A nervous jerking of the muscles, generally affecting the legs.
Clip Trim with clippers for Poodles, American Cocker Spaniels, etc.
Clipping When hindfeet strike the forefeet when the dog gaits. To avoid this the dog 'crabs' or moves with his body at an angle to the line of progress.

Cloddy Low, thick-set build.
Close-coupled Short in loins.
Coat The hair covering a dog.
Cobby Short in length, stocky, compactly made, well ribbed up and muscled.
Collar A marking around a dog's neck. A chain or leather band as an ornament or means of restraint.
Common Coarse, not typey.
Companion dog Obedience title.
Condition Denoting health.
Conformation Structure of the dog.
Corky Compact, nimble body, and spirited in character.
Corny feet Horny pads.
Couple A brace of hounds.
Coupling The part of the body joining the forehand with the hindquarters; loin; the flank. Not to be confused with length of body.
Couplings A ring between the collar and lead on a brace of dogs.
Coursing Hunting hare with Greyhounds or Whippets.
Cow-hocked The hocks turned inwards, with hindlegs like those of a cow. This is a serious fault in most breeds. The hocks are out of a straight line from hip to pad.
Crank tail A short tail which curves down and away from the body, caused by mutation.
Crest The upper part of the neck.
Cropping The cutting off of a portion of a dog's ear in order to make it stand up on it own
Crabbing Moving like a crab. The hind feet step past the fore feet without clipping them. (illegal in the United Kingdom).
Cross-bred The offspring of dogs of two different pure breeds.
Croup The part of the spinal column between the loin and the tail. It consists of three fused vertebrae, usually set at an angle of 30°.
Crown The top part of the head.
Cry The baying of hounds on a trail.
Cryptorchid A dog with undescended testicles. Both sides undescended is 'bilateral cryptorchid', one side is 'unilateral cryptorchid'.
Cull To destroy puppies below breed standard, or weak puppies.
Culotte Long, thick hair on the thighs.
Cushion The pad of muscle over the foreface.
Dam The female parent of puppies.
Dappled A mottled colour.
Daylight The distance from the brisket to the ground between the four legs.
Dentition The number, arrangement and type of teeth in a dog's mouth.
Dewclaws The extra rudimentary claws, found on the inside of the lower portion of a dog's forelegs and sometimes on the hindlegs. The latter are required on Briards and Pyrenean Mountain Dogs (Great Pyrenees).
Dewlap Loose skin under the throat.
Dimples The depressions on either side of the breast bone.
Dish-face The description given when the tip of the nose is above the level of the stop as in Pointers.
Disqualification Ineligible for winning.
Distemper teeth Discoloured pitted teeth caused by a high temperature during distemper. Only the portion of the tooth above the gum line is affected.
Docked The cut or shortened dog's tail.
Dog A male dog.
Dome The rounded part of the skull.
Double coat Consisting of an undercoat of soft woolly hair, and an outer coat of coarse hair.
Down-faced Having a muzzle which is tilted downward from stop to muzzle.

Down in pastern Weak or faulty pastern with excessive slope.
Drop ears Soft, floppy ears hanging close to the head.
Dry neck A tight-skinned, steep neck.
Dual champion A dog who has won championships in show and field trials.
Dudley nose Flesh or liver-coloured nose.
Ear Organ for hearing; term often used for leather.
Ear fringes Long hair on edges of ears.
Earrings Hair on ears left unclipped.
Elbow Joint between upper arm and forearm.
Elbow, out at A dog whose elbows are not close to the body.
Endurance Staying power.
Erect pasterns With little angle at the knee joint.
Euthanasia An induced, gentle and easy death.
Even bite Incisor teeth meeting without overlap. Incorrect in most breeds.
Ewe neck A thin sheep-like neck, concave at the top.
Eye teeth The upper canines.
Ex. Refers to a puppy out of a bitch.
Expression An aspect of the face.
Face Front of head.
Faking A common but dishonest practice performed on a dog to make it appear better than it is.
Fall Long hair falling over the eyes.
Fallow Pale yellow colour.
False ribs Ribs which are not connected with sternum or cartilages of other ribs, also called 'floating ribs'.
Faults Inconsistencies with standard.
Fawn Cream colour.
FCI Féderation Cynologique Internationale.
Feathering The long-fringed hair on the ears, under the tail, and behind the legs.
Feet Tocs, nails and pads.
Felted A matted coat.
Femur Bone between hip and stifle joint.
Fiddle face An elongated, pinched-in foreface.
Fiddle front Crooked, bandy, front legs: out at elbows, pasterns close together and turned out feet. Forearm usually curved.
Fill-in Boney structure below the eyes.
Flag The long, fine, silky hair under the tail. In Setters this is the correct word for the tail.
Flank The fleshy part of the side between the ribs and the hip.
Flare Blaze which grows wider towards the top.
Flat bone Bones of the leg elliptical.
Flat croup Having insufficient downward slope, probably of less than 30°.
Flat-sided Lacking in roundness of the ribs, particularly from the fifth rib backwards.
Flecked Lightly speckled in spots of another colour.
Flesh nose Light nose, pink or tan.
Flews Pendulous inner corners of the upper lips.
Fly ears Semi-erect ears in breeds that have long pendulous ears.
Forearm The part of the foreleg between the elbow and the pastern.
Forc facc The part of the head from the ears to the nose.
Foreleg A front leg.
Fore pastern The group of bones below the pastern joint and the foot.
Fore quarters A misnomer frequently given to the forehand of a dog.
Foster-mother A bitch which nurses young other than its own.
Fraenum of lip The fold of mucous membrane which attaches lip to gum.

Frill The long hair on the front of the neck and fore chest.

Fringes The general feathering on the ears, ruff, legs and tail.

Frog face An excessive undershot jaw.

Front All that can be seen from the front other than the head. It includes the brisket, forelegs and shoulders.

Full eye Eye which is round and slightly protruding.

Furnished A term applied to dogs which have reached full growth of coat.

Furrow A groove running down the centre of the skull.

Gait The manner in which a dog moves.

Gay tail One that is carried up, 'when it should not be'.

Gaze hound A sight hound, who uses the eyes more than the nose when hunting game.

Geld See 'Castrate'.

Giving tongue Baying when on a trail.

Good doer A dog that eats well and thrives without trouble.

Goose rump A sharply sloping rump.

Grizzle Grey or steel colour.

Groom To brush and comb the coat.

Gun-dog A dog specially bred and trained for shooting.

Guns Those with the shooting party at a drive of game (not the beaters).

Gun-shy Frightened by gun fire.

Hackles Hair on the neck and back which is involuntarily raised when the dog is frightened.

Hackney gait A high stepping gait, padding to avoid pounding, generally a fault from a 60° shoulder blade combined with too strong a rear action.

Ham Well developed hindleg muscles.

Handler A person handling the dog in the ring at a dog show, field trial or obedience tests.

Hard mouth Biting hard on retrieved game.

Hare feet Long and narrow feet, with well separated toes. The third digital bone being longer than the others.

Harlequin A combination of colours, usually in patches on a white ground.

Harness A leather strap round shoulders and chest.

Haunches The rear part of the thighs on which a dog sits.

Haw A third eyelid.

Head From occiput to nose.

Heat The period during which the bitch is said to be in season (called the 'oestrum').

Heel! A command to a dog to walk close to its handler.

Heel free! A command for a dog to heel without a lead.

Height The measurement from the top of the withers to the ground.

Hind pasterns The group of bones between the hock joint and the foot.

Hocks The joints between the pasterns and the upper part of the hindlegs. These are equivalent to the ankle joint in man and the dog's true heel.

Hound colours White, tan, black.

Huckle-bone The top of the hip joints, only seen in thin dogs.

Inbreeding The mating of close relations.

Incisors The upper and lower front teeth between the canines.

In season During the oestrum.

Inter breeding The breeding between varieties of the same breed.

Int. Ch. International Champion. A dog which has become a champion in more than one country. An unofficial title.

Isabella A light bay colour seen in Dobermanns.

Jewel eyes Phosphorescent eyes, ruby red, emerald, or amethyst in colour.

Judge A person appointed to estimate the merits of the dogs at a show.

KC Kennel Club.

Kinetic Balance Balance when in motion.

Kink tail A short bent tail.
Kissing spots The tan markings on the cheek often found in Toy breeds.
Knee Manus, wrist or pastern joint.
Knuckle over Weak pastern joint. Double jointed.
Landseer A white and black Newfoundland.
Layback An undershot jaw with a receding nose.
Leather The skin and muscles of the ear flap.
Leggy Too high on the leg.
Level back Often misused for a level top line.
Level bite When the upper and lower front teeth meet.
Level gait Even movement.
Light eyes Yellow eyes.
Line breeding The mating of related dogs.
Lippy Thick hanging lips.
Litter The puppies born to a bitch at one whelping.
Liver A red-brown colour.
LK Ladies Kennel Association.
Loaded shoulders Thick, heavy muscular shoulders.
Locomotion Movement.
Loins The part of the body between the last rib and the croup.
Long-coupled Long loins between the two assemblies.
Low centre of gravity Short in leg.
Lumber Superfluous flesh, bone and bunchy muscles.
Lurcher A cross-bred hound usually a Greyhound with a Retriever or Collie.
Maiden An unmated bitch. In showing, it is a dog or a bitch which has not won a first prize of £1 or more.
Mane A profusion of long hair on throat and neck.
Mask A dark muzzle.
Mastitis Inflammation of the breasts.
Match A competition arranged more or less privately.
Mate To breed a dog and bitch.
Matron A proved brood bitch.
Measurement The height from withers to ground.
Merle A blue grey colour, flecked, with black, associated with a recessive gene.
Molera An American mis-spelling of the Spanish word 'mollera', used in Chihuahuas for an open fontanel. It is an abnormal ossification of the skull.
Mongrel A dog of mixed breed or type, a hybrid.
Monorchid A unilateral cryptorchid. A dog with only one testicle descended in the scrotum.
Muzzle The part of the head between the stop and the tip of the nose.
NAF 'Name Applied For'.
NFC 'Not for Competition'.
Nose An organ of smell.
Occiput The prominent bone at the peak of the skull.
Oestrum The period of ovulation. The season or heat.
Off colour Not well.
Other end of the lead Refers to the handler or owner of a dog in the show ring.
Ottertail A tail which is extra thick at the root and tapers gradually to a point.
Out at elbow Having the elbow joints turned away from the body.
Out-crossing The mating of unrelated dogs of the same breed.
Overbuilt A dog whose hindquarters are higher than the fore hand.
Overshot The front teeth of the upper jaw projecting over those of the lower jaw.
Pad The cushion sole of the foot.

Padding A dog with a 60° shoulder blade lifting his foreleg unnecessarily high to avoid pounding. A hackney gait.

Paddling Moving with the fore feet wide apart.

Paper foot Flat thin pads.

Parti-colour Term used for a coat of two colours, such as black and white, red and white or blue roan.

Pastern The part of the leg below the knee or hock and above the foot.

Peak A prominent occiput.

Pedigree A genealogical tree. In dogs, a record of four generations or more.

Pencilling Thin black lines on the tips of the toes, as in the Manchester Terrier.

Pepper and salt Even mixture of black and grey hair, as on a Schnauzer.

Pied Two colours of unequal proportions, generally unequal in shape.

Pigeon breast A prominent breast bone.

Plume A long fringe of hair growing from the tail.

Point The rigid stance a dog adopts naturally, indicating the presence of game.

Pom pom The hair left on the end of a Poodle's tail.

Pounding A dog with 60° shoulder blades. The pad hits ground too early, causing unnecessary shock.

Prefix A kennel name, which identifies the dogs belonging to one owner or owners.

Prick ear Erect, pointed ears.

Puppy A young dog up to the age of six months by law. At shows, however, it is a dog between the age of six months and a year.

Pure-bred A dog whose sire, dam and forebears belong to the same breed.

Put down To put a dog to sleep. In the USA, to prepare a dog for the show ring. When a judge 'put's down' a dog, it means that he did not give it a prize.

Quality Refinement.

Racy Slight in build and long in the legs, such as a Greyhound or Whippet.

Ram's nose A slightly convex muzzle.

Rat tail A thin round tail, rather long with short, thin hair.

Red A rich, brown colour.

Register To record with the Kennel Club a dog's particulars.

Reserve Fourth place in a class: or runner-up, e.g. reserve best in show.

Ribbed up A dog is said to be 'well ribbed up' when the ribs are neither too long nor too wide apart, making the animal appear compact.

Ring tail A tail curled over in a circle.

Roach back A back arched convexly along the spine, especially towards the hindquarters. It is an ugly hereditary fault in most breeds.

Roan White hair mixed equally with red or blue hair.

Root of the tail Where the tail joins the back.

Rose ear A backward folding ear showing the inner ear as in the Bulldog.

Rudder The tail.

Ruff The thick long hair around the neck.

Running on The keeping of a puppy, hoping that it will turn out well.

Russian Wolfhound Borzoi.

Sable Black hair incorporated in another coloured coat.

Saddle A solid area of colour extending over the shoulder and back.

Scissor bite A bite where the lower incisors touch the inside of the upper incisors. Correct for most breeds.

Screw tail A short, twisted tail.

Scrotum The sack containing the two testicles.

Season Another term of oestrum or heat in the bitch.

Second mouth A dog's mouth when the second or permanent teeth have replaced the first or milk teeth.

Second thigh The bones between the stifle and the hock.
Self-coloured A single colour with or without shadings.
Self-marked A whole- or solid-coloured dog with white or cream brisket, feet and tip of tail.
Semi-prick ears Straight, erect ears with the tips bent forward, as in the Collie.
Septum The division between the nostrils.
Service A mating.
Set-on Where the root of the tail is set on the hindquarters.
Shelley A weedy, narrow body, lacking in correct amount of bone.
Sickle hocks Hocks sloping backwards, a serious fault in all breeds.
Sickle tail One that curves upwards above the level of the back.
Sight hound A hound which hunts by eyesight in preference to scent.
Sire The male parent.
Skully A coarse skull.
Sloping shoulder A shoulder blade laid back.
Smoothcoat A dog with short close hair.
Smudge The dark thumb marking on the head of a puppy.
Snipy A long, narrow muzzle.
Soft-mouthed A dog which can retrieve game without damaging it.
Sound Moving and standing correctly on all four legs with static and kinetic balance and free from disease and defects. Of good quality throughout.
Spay To remove womb and ovaries to prevent a bitch from having puppies.
Spectacles Marking around the eyes.
Splashed A solid colour with irregular patches of another colour.
Splay foot A foot with the toes spread out.
Spring of rib The extent to which the ribs are well rounded.
Squirrel tail A tail curving over the back like a squirrel.
Stance Manner of standing.
Standard A description of the ideal dog of a breed, as a pattern for judges and breeders.
Stand-off coat A harsh coat which stands up as in the Spitz breeds.
Staring coat A coat which stands up when a dog is out of condition.
Static balance Balance when standing.
Stern Tail.
Stifle The joint in a dog's hindlegs between the upper and lower thigh. It is equivalent to the knee in man and is often weak in some breeds.
Stilted The uneven movement of a straight-hocked dog.
Stool Faeces.
Stop The depression at the junction of the nose and skull.
Straight-hocked Lacking in angulation of the hock joint.
Straight-shoulders Lacking in angulation, so that the shoulder blades are straight instead of lying well back.
Strain A family which are all related, and throw offspring good to type.
Stud Book A book issued by the Kennel Club once a year, relating to championship-show top wins.
Stud dog A male dog used for breeding purposes.
Substance Refers to strength of bone.
Suffix A breeder's kennel name attached to a dog's name to identify it as belonging to a certain kennel.
TAF 'Transfer applied for.'
Throaty Too much loose skin under the throat.
Thumb marks Round black marks on the pasterns.
Ticked The small dark flecks of colour on a white-coloured dog.
Tie The locking together of a dog and bitch during a mating, caused by the bulb of the dog's penis swelling inside the bitch.

Timber Generally refers to the bones of the legs.

Toe in The feet turning in.

Tongue The sound that hounds make when trailing.

Top-knot The long hair on the top of the head, usually tied together with an elastic band or ribbon.

Trace A dark line running down the centre of the back as in a Pug.

Transfer Change of ownership registered at the Kennel Club.

Tricolour A coat of three different colours, usually black, tan and white, blue, roan and tan, or liver, white and tan; the tan being at the eyebrows, cheeks, under tail and sometimes on feet.

Trim To groom a dog by clipping, plucking or cutting its coat.

Tucked up A dog not looking well.

Tulip ears Ears which are carried forward, slightly open but erect.

Type The quality of conforming to the breed standard.

Undercoat Soft woolly hair beneath the longer outer hair. It is often a different colour from the latter.

Undershot The lower incisor teeth projecting beyond the upper teeth.

Unilateral cryptorchid A dog with only one testicle descended in the scrotum.

Unsound Unable to move and stand correctly on all four legs, or suffering from a disease or defect, and not of good quality throughout.

Upper arm The humerus bone in the forelegs.

Uterus The womb.

Vagina The female genital passage.

Varminity A bright alert expression particularly in Terriers.

Vent The rectum and the area of lighter markings round the anus.

Vulva The external portion of the vagina.

Wall-eyed Eyes which are white and blue.

Wean To induce a puppy when old enough to feed otherwise than from the dam.

Weedy Lacking in substance.

WELKS West of England Ladies' Kennel Society.

Well sprung Well rounded ribs.

Wheaten Refers to a cream fawn colour as a Wheaten Terrier.

Wheel back A roach back.

Whelping Giving birth to puppies.

Whelps This term is not often used. It refers to the unborn puppy and to the puppy up till the time when it is weaned.

Whip tail A stiff straight tail as in the Pointer when pointing.

Whiskers The long hairs on the muzzle and the jaws.

Wire-haired A dense harsh coat.

Withers The eight vertebrae between the neck and the back between the shoulder blades.

Wolf sable The black, brown and grey hair distributed evenly over the coat, giving a wolf-coloured appearance.

Wrinkles The loose folds of skin on the head, particularly abundant in Bloodhounds.

Wry mouth The lower jaw set to one side. It is a very bad hereditary fault.

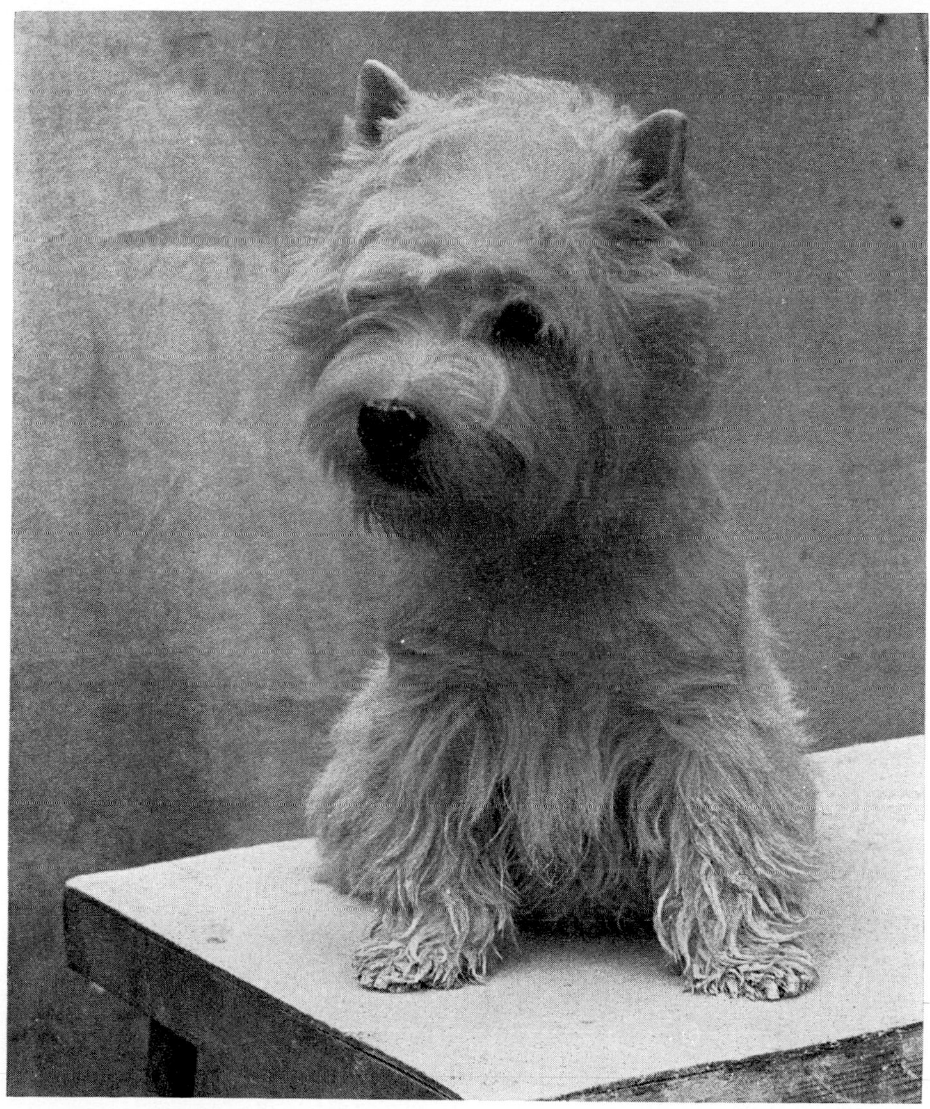

Above: A ringcraft class of gundogs. Leads would have been better hidden under the bent knees; they look unprofessional lying on the ground.

Left: A West Highland White Terrier with well-chalked feet which must be brushed out before entering the show ring.

Below: An excellent mackintosh to protect a long-coated breed on a wet day.

Left: Training a young boxer to stand.

Below: Ringcraft classes and matches are excellent training grounds for judges, handlers and dogs.

AMERICAN KENNEL CLUB INC.
51 MADISON AVENUE
NEW YORK, NEW YORK 10010

DOGS REGISTERED JANUARY 1, 1973 TO DECEMBER 31, 1973

Breed	Placings	1973	Placings	1972
Poodles	1	193,400	1	218,899
German Shepherd Dogs	2	90,907	2	101,399
Irish Setters	3	54,211	5	43,707
Beagles	4	54,125	3	57,050
Dachshunds	5	51,000	4	55,149
Miniature Schnauzers	6	41,745	6	43,280
St. Bernards	7	35,397	7	35,559
Doberman Pinschers	8	34,169	10	27,767
Labrador Retrievers	9	33,575	8	32,251
Cocker Spaniels	10	31,158	11	27,355
Collies	11	28,573	9	28,459
Pekingese	12	24,926	12	26,062
Chihuahuas	13	22,253	13	23,969
Shetland Sheepdogs	14	21,845	14	19,673
Great Danes	15	19,314	16	18,339
Brittany Spaniels	16	18,503	19	16,644
Yorkshire Terriers	17	18,073	17	16,879
Basset Hounds	18	17,843	15	18,989
Golden Retrievers	19	17,635	20	15,476
Pomeranians	20	16,708	18	16,723
Siberian Huskies	21	16,127	22	13,676
Lhasa Apsos	22	15,071	25	12,236
German Short-Haired Pointers	23	14,814	21	14,733
Old English Sheepdogs	24	14,751	23	13,321
English Springer Spaniels	25	12,421	27	11,364
Boxers	26	12,319	26	12,002
Boston Terriers	27	11,589	24	12,388
Afghan Hounds	28	10,549	30	9,023
Samoyeds	29	9,912	31	8,866
Scottish Terriers	30	9,502	28	10,011
Norwegian Elkhounds	31	8,826	34	8,398
Dalmatians	32	8,549	32	8,623
Pugs	33	8,420	29	9,257
Alaskan Malamutes	34	7,969	40	6,502
Cairn Terriers	35	7,497	35	7,753
Shih Tzu	36	7,473	41	5,704
Fox Terriers	37	7,273	33	8,559
Weimaraners	38	7,208	36	7,246
Airedale Terriers	39	6,687	37	6,974
Bulldogs	40	6,559	38	6,608
West Highland White Terriers	41	6,433	39	6,577
Maltese	42	5,416	42	5,101
Keeshonden	43	4,671	43	4,010
Silky Terriers	44	3,307	44	3,345
Chow Chows	45	3,163	46	2,789
Basenjis	46	2,400	45	2,894
Welsh Corgis (Pembroke)	47	2,290	47	2,256
Vizslas	48	2,233	48	2,206
Chesapeake Bay Retrievers	49	2,214	49	1,964
Newfoundlands	50	2,010	50	1,945
Akitas	51	1,859	89	255
Borzois	52	1,703	53	1,447
English Setters	53	1,603	51	1,518
Bichons Frises	54	1,578	77	430
Great Pyrenees	55	1,489	52	1,478
Schipperkes	56	1,366	54	1,411
Irish Wolfhounds	57	1,309	57	1,251
Bloodhounds	58	1,252	58	1,231
Australian Terriers	59	1,191	56	1,284
Welsh Terriers	60	1,167	55	1,312
Miniature Pinschers	61	1,079	59	1,159
Gordon Setters	62	1,071	61	1,028
Whippets	63	1,036	63	990
Kerry Blue Terriers	64	914	60	1,042
German Wire-Haired Pointers	65	888	65	700
Standard Schnauzers	66	851	62	1,011
Rottweilers	67	840	72	563
English Cocker Spaniels	68	768	68	657
Pulik	69	753	64	869
Rhodesian Ridgebacks	70	740	66	698
Italian Greyhounds	71	673	69	604
Soft-Coated Wheaten Terriers	72	652	—	—
Bullmastiffs	73	629	74	558
Bull Terriers	74	627	70	574
Salukis	75	607	76	495
Manchester Terriers	76	600	67	673
Bouviers des Flandres	77	585	75	511
Pointers	78	544	71	566
Mastiffs	79	516	81	394
Bedlington Terriers	80	515	73	560
Giant Schnauzers	81	449	85	327
Belgian Sheepdogs	82	422	78	416
American Staffordshire Terriers	83	411	82	389
Papillons	84	410	80	397
Tibetan Terriers	85	399	—	—
Welsh Corgis (Cardigan)	86	386	83	372
Irish Terriers	87	371	79	406
Belgian Tervuren	88	357	84	358
Japanese Spaniels	89	329	86	322
American Water Spaniels	90	307	87	316
Norwich Terriers	91	290	90	251
Skye Terriers	92	270	88	307
Dandie Dinmont Terriers	93	263	91	249
Scalyham Terriers	94	233	97	169
Brussels Griffons	95	222	92	247
Bernese Mountain Dogs	96	214	95	185
Wirehaired Pointing Griffons	97	207	94	188
Greyhounds	98	200	98	161
Black & Tan Coonhounds	99	198	93	221
Briards	100	165	100	147
French Bulldogs	101	155	99	154
Lakeland Terriers	102	135	96	171
Komondorok	103	121	103	103
Kuvaszok	104	120	101	127
Irish Water Spaniels	105	101	104	102
Scottish Deerhounds	106	97	102	108
Flat-Coated Retrievers	107	90	107	66
Border Terriers	108	74	108	58
Affenpinschers	109	73	109	55
Foxhounds (American)	110	72	105	78
Otter Hounds	111	55	110	41
Welsh Springer Spaniels	112	52	113	30
Curly-Coated Retrievers	113	40	112	31
English Toy Spaniels	114	38	106	75
Clumber Spaniels	115	31	111	37
Harriers	116	20	114	13
Foxhounds (English)	117	18	115	12
Sussex Spaniels	118	14	116	11
Field Spaniels	119	12	118	3
Belgian Malinois	120	11	116	11
		1,099,850		1,101,943

DOGS REGISTERED BY GROUPS

	1973	1972
Sporting Breeds	199,700	178,199
Hound Breeds	152,050	158,249
Working Breeds	305,350	297,449
Terrier Breeds	86,850	90,599
Toy Breeds	109,400	109,899
Non-Sporting Breeds	246,500	267,548
	1,099,850	1,101,943

LITTERS REGISTERED BY GROUPS

	1973	1972
Sporting Breeds	50,000	45,350
Hound Breeds	59,150	63,050
Working Breeds	90,099	87,750
Terrier Breeds	34,350	36,300
Toy Breeds	64,400	65,400
Non-Sporting Breeds	122,750	132,850
	420,749	430,700

Rules Applying to Registration and Dog Shows

Amended to April 1, 1971

By kind permission of
THE AMERICAN KENNEL CLUB
Incorporated
51 MADISON AVENUE
New York, N.Y. 10010

The *italicized* portions are not rules but are either regulations or explanations.

FOREWORD

The American Kennel Club was formed principally for the protection and advancement of pure-bred dogs.

The State of New York by Special Act of its legislature incorporated The American Kennel Club and granted it a charter in Section 2 of which the objects of the corporation are described to be 'to adopt and enforce uniform rules regulating and governing dog shows and field trials, to regulate the conduct of persons interested in exhibiting, running, breeding, registering, purchasing and selling dogs, to detect, prevent, and punish frauds in connection therewith, to protect the interests of its members, to maintain and publish an official stud book and an official kennel gazette, and generally to do everything to advance the study, breeding, exhibiting, running and maintenance of the purity of thoroughbred dogs.'

Section 2 of this charter further states that 'for these purposes it,' The American Kennel Club, 'shall have power to adopt a constitution, by-laws, rules and regulations, and enforce the same by fines and penalties, which it shall have the right to collect and enforce by suit, or by suspension or expulsion from membership, or by a suspension or denial of any or all of the privileges of said corporation.'

Forms for the registration of pure-bred dogs may be obtained by writing to or calling in person at the offices of The American Kennel Club.

The holding of dog shows at which pure-bred dogs may be exhibited and be given an opportunity to compete for prizes and thereby enable their breeders and owners to demonstrate the progress made in breeding for type and quality, and the holding of obedience trials and field trials at which pure-bred dogs may be run in competition for prizes and thereby enable their breeders and owners to demonstrate the progress made in breeding for practical use, stamina and obedience have been found to be the best methods by which the progress which has been made in breeding can be shown.

The American Kennel Club has adopted certain By-Laws, Rules and Regulations designed to carry out these objects. This book contains such of these by-laws, rules and regulations as affect the registration of pure-bred dogs; or the club or association which wishes to hold a dog show or obedience trial; or the person who wishes to exhibit, compete or take part therein; or the person who by unsportsmanlike conduct or wrong-doing is believed to be injuring the welfare of the sport of breeding and showing pure-bred dogs.

The American Kennel Club
Incorporated

Rules and Regulations
and
Extracts from By-Laws

CHAPTER 1
GENERAL EXPLANATIONS

SECTION 1. The word 'dog' wherever used in these Rules and Regulations includes both sexes.

SECTION 2. The words 'United States of America' wherever used in these Rules and Regulations shall be construed to include all territories and possessions of the United States of America and all vessels sailing under the American Flag.

CHAPTER 2
REGISTRABLE BREEDS BY GROUPS

The following breeds divided by groups shall be all the breeds now recognized by The American Kennel Club as being distinct breeds of pure-bred dogs eligible for registration in the Stud Book of The American Kennel Club.

GROUP 1
SPORTING DOGS

GRIFFONS (WIREHAIRED POINTING)
POINTERS
POINTERS (GERMAN SHORTHAIRED)
POINTERS (GERMAN WIREHAIRED)
RETRIEVERS (CHESAPEAKE BAY)
RETRIEVERS (CURLY-COATED)
RETRIEVERS (FLAT-COATED)
RETRIEVERS (GOLDEN)
RETRIEVERS (LABRADOR)
SETTERS (ENGLISH)
SETTERS (GORDON)
SETTERS (IRISH)
SPANIELS (AMERICAN WATER)
SPANIELS (BRITTANY)
SPANIELS (BRITTANY)
SPANIELS (CLUMBER)
SPANIELS (COCKER)
SPANIELS (ENGLISH COCKER)
SPANIELS (ENGLISH SPRINGER)
SPANIELS (FIELD)
SPANIELS (IRISH WATER)
SPANIELS (SUSSEX)
SPANIELS (WELSH SPRINGER)
VIZSLAS
WEIMARANERS
WIREHAIRED POINTING GRIFFON

GROUP 2—HOUNDS

AFGHAN HOUNDS
BASENJIS
BASSET HOUNDS
BLACK AND TAN COONHOUNDS
BLOODHOUNDS
BORZOIS
DACHSHUNDS
FOXHOUNDS (AMERICAN)
FOXHOUNDS (ENGLISH)
GREYHOUNDS
HARRIERS
IRISH WOLFHOUNDS
NORWEGIAN ELKHOUNDS
OTTER HOUNDS
RHODESIAN RIDGEBACKS
SALUKIS
SCOTTISH DEERHOUNDS
WHIPPETS

GROUP 3—WORKING DOGS

ALASKAN MALAMUTES
BELGIAN MALINOIS
BELGIAN SHEEPDOGS
BELGIAN TERVUREN
BERNESE MOUNTAIN DOGS
BOUVIERS DES FLANDERS
BOXERS
BRIARDS
BULLMASTIFFS
COLLIES
DOBERMAN PINSCHERS
GERMAN SHEPHERD DOGS
GIANT SCHNAUZERS
GREAT DANES
GREAT PYRENEES
KOMONDOROK
KUVASZOK
MASTIFFS
NEWFOUNDLANDS
OLD ENGLISH SHEEPDOGS
PULIK
ROTTWEILERS
ST. BERNARDS
SAMOYEDS
SHETLAND SHEEPDOGS
SIBERIAN HUSKIES
STANDARD SCHLAUZERS
WELSH CORGIS (CARDIGAN)
WELSH CORGIS (PEMBROKE)

GROUP 4—TERRIERS

AIREDALE TERRIERS
AMERICAN STAFFORDSHIRE TERRIERS
AUSTRALIAN TERRIERS
BEDLINGTON TERRIERS
BORDER TERRIERS
BULL TERRIERS
CAIRN TERRIERS
DANDIE DINMONT TERRIERS
FOX TERRIERS
IRISH TERRIERS
KERRY BLUE TERRIERS
LAKELAND TERRIERS
MANCHESTER TERRIERS
MINIATURE SCHNAUZERS
NORWICH TERRIERS
SCOTTISH TERRIERS
SEALYHAM TERRIERS
SKYE TERRIERS
SOFT-COATED WHEATEN TERRIERS
WELSH TERRIERS
WEST HIGHLAND WHITE TERRIERS

GROUP 5—TOYS

AFFENPINSCHERS
BRUSSELS GRIFFONS
CHIHUAHUAS
ENGLISH TOY SPANIELS
ITALIAN GREYHOUNDS
JAPANESE SPANIELS
MALTESE
MINIATURE PINSCHERS
PAPILLONS
PEKINGESE
POMERANIANS
PUGS
SHIH TZU
SILKY TERRIERS
YORKSHIRE TERRIERS

GROUP 6—NON-SPORTING DOGS

BICHONS FRISES
BOSTON TERRIERS
BULLDOGS
CHOW CHOWS
DALMATIANS
FRENCH BULLDOGS
KEESHONDEN
LHASA APSOS
POODLES
SCHIPPERKES
TIBETAN TERRIERS

The Board of Directors of The American Kennel Club may add other breeds to the foregoing list whenever in its opinion sufficient evidence is presented to said Board to justify its belief that such other breeds have been in existence as distinct breeds for such length of time as to justify being designated pure breeds. The Board of Directors also may remove any breed from the foregoing list or may transfer any breed from one group to another group whenever in its opinion sufficient evidence is presented to the Board to justify such removal or transfer.

CHAPTER 3

REGISTRATION

SECTION 1. The breeder of a dog is the person who owned the dam of that dog when the dam was bred; except that if the dam was leased at the time of breeding, the breeder is the lessee.

SECTION 2. An American-bred dog is a dog whelped in the United States of America by reason of a mating which took place in the United States of America.

SECTION 3. Any person in good standing with The American Kennel Club may apply for the registration of any pure-bred dog or litter of pure-bred dogs owned by him, by supplying The American Kennel Club with such information and complying with such conditions as it shall require.

SECTION 4. No individual dog from a litter whelped in the United States of America of which both parents are registered with The American Kennel Club shall be eligible for registration unless the litter has first been registered by the person who owned the dam at time of whelping; except that if the dam was leased at time of whelping, the litter may be registered only by the lessee.

SECTION 5. No dog or litter out of a dam under eight (8) months or over twelve (12) years of age at time of mating, or by a sire under seven (7) months or over twelve (12) years of age at time of mating, will be registered unless the application for registration shall be accompanied by an affidavit or evidence which shall prove the fact to the satisfaction of The American Kennel Club.

SECTION 6. No litter of pure-bred dogs and/or no single pure-bred dog which shall be determined by The American Kennel Club to be acceptable in all other respects for registration, shall be barred from registration because of the failure, by the legal owner of all or part of said litter, or said single dog to obtain some one or more of the signatures needed to complete the applicant's chain of title to the litter or dog sought to be registered, unless that person who, when requested, refuses so to sign the application form shall furnish a reason therefore satisfactory to The American Kennel Club, such as the fact that at the time of service an agreement in writing was made between the owner or lessee of the sire and the owner or lessee of the dam to the effect that no application for registration should be made and/or that the produce of such union should not be registered. In all cases where such an agreement in writing has been made, any person disposing of any of the produce of such union must secure from the new owner a statement in writing that he receives such produce upon the understanding that it shall not be registered. For the purpose of registering or refusing to register pure-bred dogs The American Kennel Club will recognize only such conditional sale or conditional stud agreements affecting the registration of pure-bred dogs as are in writing and are shown to have been brought to the attention of the applicant for registration. The American Kennel Club cannot recognize alleged conditional sale, conditional stud or other agreements not in writing which affect the registration of pure-bred dogs, until after the existence, construction and/or effect of the same shall have been determined by an action at law.

The owner or owners of a stud dog pure-bred and eligible for registration who in print or otherwise asserts or assert it to be pure-bred and eligible for registration and on the strength of such assertion secures or permits its use at stud, must pay the cost of its registration. The owner or owners of a brood bitch pure-bred and eligible for registration who in print or otherwise asserts or assert it to be pure-bred and eligible for registration and on the strength of such assertion leases it or sells its produce or secures the use of a stud by promising a puppy or puppies as payment of the stud fee in lieu of cash, must pay the cost of its registration.

That person or those persons refusing without cause to sign the application form or forms necessary for the registration of a litter of pure-bred dogs or of a single pure-bred dog and that person or those persons refusing without cause to pay the necessary fees due from him, her or them to be paid in order to complete the chain of title to a pure-bred litter or a pure-bred single dog sought to be registered, when requested by The American Kennel Club, may be suspended from the privileges of The American Kennel Club or fined as the Board of Directors of The American Kennel Club may elect.

The registration of a single pure-bred dog out of a litter eligible for registration may be secured by its legal owner as a one-dog litter registration and the balance of the litter may be refused registration where the breeder or the owner or lessee of the dam at the date of whelping wrongfully has refused to register the litter and that person or those persons so wrongfully refusing shall be suspended from the privileges of The American Kennel Club or fined as the Board of Directors of The American Kennel Club may elect.

SECTION 7. No change in the name of a dog registered with The American Kennel Club will be allowed to be made.

SECTION 8. Any person in good standing with The American Kennel Club may apply for transfer of ownership to him of any registered dog acquired by him by supplying The American Kennel Club with such information and complying with such conditions as it shall require.

SECTION 9. The American Kennel Club will not protect any person against the use by any other person of a kennel name in the registration of dogs with The American Kennel Club or in the entry of registered dogs in shows held under The American Kennel Club rules, unless the kennel name has been registered with The American Kennel Club.

SECTION 10. On and after October 1, 1948, application for the use of a kennel name as a prefix in the registering and showing of dogs shall be made to The American Kennel Club on a form which will be supplied by said Club upon request, and said application must be accompanied by a fee, the amount of which shall be determined by the Board of Directors of The American Kennel Club. The Board will then consider such application and if it approves of the name selected will grant the right to the use of such name only as a prefix for a period of five (5) years.

SECTION 11. The recorded owner shall have first consideration of the grant to use said kennel name for additional consecutive five (5) year terms upon receipt of the application for renewal accompanied by the renewal fee, the amount of which shall be determined by the Board of Directors, when received before the date of expiration of the original grant but the grant for any five (5) year renewal term will be made only at the expiration of the previous term.

In the event of the death of a recorded owner of a registered kennel name, his executors, administrators or legal heirs, upon submission of proper proof of their status, may use the name as a prefix during the remainder of the five (5) year term of use and the legal heir of the deceased recorded owner, or the executors or administrators acting in his behalf, shall have first consideration of the grant to the use of said name for additional terms, as provided heretofore in this section.

SECTION 12. If the recorded owner of a registered kennel name granted after October 1, 1948, desires to transfer ownership of or an interest in said kennel name to a new owner, application to transfer such name for the unexpired term must be made to The American Kennel Club on a form which will be supplied by said Club upon request. The application must be submitted for the approval of the Board of Directors of The American Kennel Club and accompanied by a fee, the amount of which shall be determined by the Board of Directors of The American Kennel Club.

Any kennel name granted by The American Kennel Club prior to October 1, 1948 may be transferred by its present owner or owners to another only by consent and on certain conditions and payment of fee as determined by the Board of Directors of The American Kennel Club.

SECTION 13. In the case of any registered kennel name which is recorded as jointly owned by two or more persons, application to transfer the interest of one co-owner to another co-owner, may be made to The American Kennel Club on a form which will be supplied by said Club upon request. The application must be submitted for the approval of the Board of Directors of The American Kennel Club but no fee will be charged for such a transfer.

SECTION 14. The protection of all kennel names registered between March 1, 1934 and October 1, 1948 shall depend upon their continuous use by registered owners. Neglect by the recorded owner of a registered kennel name to use such name in the registration of dogs for a continuous period of six years or more shall be considered such an abandonment of the name as to justify The American Kennel Club in refusing to protect its use unless the owner or owners thereof prior to the expiration of such six-year period shall notify The American Kennel Club of his, her or their desire to retain the same.

CHAPTER 3-A

IDENTIFICATION AND RECORDS

SECTION 1. The word 'person' as used in this chapter includes any individual, partnership, firm, corporation, association or organization of any kind.

The word 'dog' as used in this chapter includes a dog or puppy of any age and either sex.

SECTION 2. Each person who breeds, keeps, transfers ownership or possession of, or deals in dogs which are registered or to be registered with The American Kennel Club, whether he acts as principal or agent or sells on consignment, must make in connection therewith and preserve for five years adequate and accurate records. The Board of Directors shall by regulation designate the specific information which must be included in such records.

SECTION 3. Each person who breeds, keeps, transfers ownership or possession of, or deals in dogs that are registered or to be registered with The American Kennel Club, whether he acts as principal or agent or sells on consignment, must follow such practice as, consistent with the number of dogs involved, will preclude any possibility of error in identification of any individual dog or doubt as to the parentage of any particular dog or litter.

SECTION 4. The American Kennel Club or its duly authorized representative shall have the right to inspect the records required to be kept and the practices required to be followed by these rules and by any regulations adopted under them, and to examine any dog registered or to be registered with The American Kennel Club.

SECTION 5. Each person who transfers ownership or possession of a dog that is registered or to be registered with The American Kennel Club must describe the dog in the records of The American Kennel Club in writing to the person acquiring the dog at the time of transfer, either on a bill of sale or otherwise. The Board of Directors shall by regulation designate the descriptive information required.

SECTION 6. The American Kennel Club may refuse to register any dog or litter or to record the transfer of any dog, for the sole reason that the application is not supported by the records required by these rules and the regulations adopted under them.

SECTION 7. Any person who is required to keep records and who fails to do so or who fails or refuses when requested to make such records available for inspection by The American Kennel Club or its duly authorized representatives, may be suspended from all privileges of The American Kennel Club by the Board of Directors.

Any person who fails to follow such practices as will preclude any possibility of error in identification of an individual dog or doubt as to the parentage of a particular dog or litter, or who fails or refuses to permit the American Kennel Club or its duly authorized representatives to examine such practices, or to examine a dog that is registered or to be registered with The American Kennel Club, may be suspended from all privileges of The American Kennel Club by the Board of Directors.

CHAPTER 4

DOG SHOWS DEFINED

SECTION 1. A member show is a show at which championship points may be awarded, given by a club or association which is a member of The American Kennel Club.

SECTION 2. A licensed show is a show at which championship points may be awarded, given by a club or association which is not a member of The American Kennel Club but which has been specially licensed by The American Kennel Club to give the specific show designated in the license.

SECTION 3. A member or licensed all-breed club may apply to The American Kennel Club for approval to hold a show at which championship points may be awarded with entries restricted to puppies that are eligible for entry in the regular puppy class and dogs that have been placed first, second or third in a regular class at a show at which championship points were awarded, provided the club submitting such an application has held at least one show annually for at least ten years immediately prior to the year in which application for a show so restricted is made, and further provided that there shall not have been less than 900 dogs entered in its show (or in one of its shows if the club holds more than one show a year) in the year preceding the year in which application is made for its first show with entries so restricted.

When an application for this type of restricted entry show has been approved by The American Kennel Club the only dogs eligible for entry shall be puppies that are eligible for entry in the regular puppy class and those dogs that have been placed first, second or third in a regular class at a show at which championship points were awarded held not less than sixty days prior to the first day of the show at which entries will be so restricted.

However, a club making application to hold a show restricted to entries of dogs as specified above may further restrict entries by excluding all puppies or all puppies six months and under nine months and/or by excluding dogs that have placed third or dogs that have placed second and third, provided the extent of these further restrictions are specified on the application.

Any club whose application has been approved to hold a show with restricted entries as described in this section shall indicate the extent of the restrictions in its premium list.

SECTION 4. A member or licensed all-breed club may apply to The American Kennel Club for approval to hold a show at which championship points may be awarded with entries restricted to dogs that are champions on the records of The American Kennel Club and dogs that have been credited with one or more championship points, provided the club submitting such an application has held at least one show annually for at least 15 years immediately prior to the year in which application for a show so restricted is made, and further provided that there shall not have been less than 1200 dogs entered in its show (or in one of its shows if the club holds more than one show a year) in the year preceding the year in which application is made for its first show with entries so restricted.

When an application for this type of restricted entry show has been approved by the American Kennel Club, the only dogs eligible for entry shall be those dogs that have been recorded as champions and dogs that have been credited with one or more championship points as a result of competition at shows held not less than 60 days prior to the first day of the show at which entries will be so restricted.

However, a club making application to hold a show restricted to entries of dogs as specified above, may further restrict entries by excluding all puppies or all puppies six months and under nine months and/or by excluding dogs that have not been credited with at least one major championship point rating, provided the extent of these further restrictions are specified on the application.

Any club whose application has been approved to hold a show with restricted entries as described in this section shall indicate the extent of the restrictions in its premium list.

SECTION 5. A member or licensed show with a limited entry, at which championship points may be awarded may be given by a club or association in the event said club or association considers it necessary to LIMIT the TOTAL ENTRY at its show due to the limitations of space. The total number of entries to be accepted together with the reason therefore, must be indicated on the cover or title page of the PREMIUM LIST. A specified closing date, in accordance with Chapter 9, Section 9, must be indicated in the premium list together with a statement that entries will close on said date or when the limit has been reached, if prior thereto. No entries can be accepted, cancelled or substituted after the entry is closed. The specified closing date shall be used in determining whether a dog in eligible for the Novice Classes at the show.

SECTION 6. A specialty show is a show given by a club or association formed for the improvement of any one breed of pure-bred dogs, at which championship points may be awarded to said breed.

SECTION 7. An American-bred specialty show is a show for American-bred dogs only, given by a member club or association formed for the improvement of any one breed or pure-bred dogs at which championship points may be awarded to said breed.

SECTION 8. A sanctioned match is an informal meeting at which pure-bred dogs may compete but not for championship points, held by a club or association whether or not a member of The American Kennel Club by obtaining the sanction of The American Kennel Club.

CHAPTER 5

MAKING APPLICATION TO HOLD A DOG SHOW

SECTION 1. Each member club or association is entitled to hold one show and one field trial a year without payment of a fee to The American Kennel Club, but must pay a fee of fifteen ($15.00) dollars for each other show and/or field trial which it may hold during the same calendar year.

SECTION 2. Each member club or association which has held a show or shows in any one year shall have first right to claim the corresponding dates for its show or shows to be held in the next succeeding year.

SECTION 3. Each member club or association not a specialty club which shall hold a show at least once in every two consecutive calendar years shall have the sole show privilege in the city, town or district which has been assigned to it as its show territory.

SECTION 4. A member club or association must apply to The American Kennel Club on a regular official form, which will be supplied on request, over the signature of one of its officers, for permission to hold a show, stating in the application the day or days upon which, and the exact location where, it desires to hold such show, and sending a copy of any contract, or if verbal, a statement of the substance of the agreement made with the Superintendent or Show Secretary. This application will be referred to the Board of Directors of The American Kennel Club which will consider the same and notify the member club or association of its approval or disapproval of the dates and place selected.

SECTION 5. If a member club or association not a specialty club shall fail to hold a show at least once in every two consecutive calendar years, the Board of Directors of The American Kennel Club upon application may give a license to another club or association which need not be a member of The American Kennel Club to hold a show within the limits of the show territory of the member club or association which has so failed to hold its show.

SECTION 6. If a member club or association not a specialty club shall fail to hold a show within the next calendar year after a licensed show has been held within the show territory of said member club or association, the American Kennel Club will consider such failure sufficient reason to consider an application for membership in The American Kennel Club by any other club or association organized to hold shows within said territory which shall conform to the requirements and conditions of Article IV of the Constitution and By-Laws of The American Kennel Club although said member club or association so in default shall not consent thereto.

SECTION 7. Where there are two or more show-giving member clubs or associations not specialty clubs located in the same show territory, the jurisdiction of said clubs or associations shall be concurrent.

SECTION 8. The use of a club's name for show purposes cannot be transferred.

SECTION 9. If a non-member club or association wishes to hold a dog show, it must apply to The American Kennel Club on a regular official form, which will be supplied on request, over the signature of one of its officers, for permission to hold a show, stating in the application the day or days upon which, and the exact location where it desires to hold such show, and sending a copy of any contract, or if verbal, a statement of the substance of the agreement made with the Superintendent or Show Secretary. The American Kennel Club is to be supplied with such information with regard to Constitution, By-Laws, names of the officers and members, and the financial responsibility of the applying non-member club or association as The American Kennel Club may request. A non-member club shall pay a license fee for the privilege of holding such show under American Kennel Club rules, the amount of which fee shall be fixed and determined by the Board of Directors of The American Kennel Club. The application will be referred to the Board of Directors of The American Kennel Club, which will consider the same and notify the non-member club or association of its approval or disapproval of the dates and place selected. If the Board of Directors shall disapprove the application, the license fee will be returned to said non-member club or association.

SECTION 10. A member specialty club may hold a show confined to the breed which it sponsors and such show shall carry a championship rating according to the schedule of points of the breed for which the show is given.

SECTION 11. A member specialty club may hold a show confined to American-bred dogs only in which show winners classes may be included and championship points awarded, provided that the necessary regular classes are included in the classification.

SECTION 12. A non-member specialty club may be licensed to hold a show, if the consent in writing that it may be given first shall be obtained from the member specialty club formed for the improvement of the breed sought to be shown which first was admitted to be a member of The American Kennel Club, which member club is commonly known as the Parent Club.

If a Parent Club unreasonably shall withhold its consent in writing to the holding of such show, the non-member specialty club may appeal to the Board of Directors of The American

Kennel Club at any time after one month from the time when said consent was requested. A committee of said Board appointed by said Board or between sittings of said Board appointed by the President of The American Kennel Club, or, in his absence, by the Executive Vice-President of The American Kennel Club shall hear the parties who may present their respective contentions, either orally or in writing, and in its discretion may issue a license to the non-member specialty club to hold such show.

SECTION 13. Where a specialty club wishes to consider as its Specialty Show the breed classes at an all-breed show, written application must be made to The American Kennel Club and a fee of $15.00 sent with application. Consent of the parent member specialty club must be secured by the non-member specialty club and forwarded to The American Kennel Club.

SECTION 14. A specialty club that wishes to hold a futurity or sweepstake, either in conjunction with a show or as a separate event, must apply to The American Kennel Club on a form which will be supplied on request, for permission to hold the event, whether or not the futurity or sweepstake will be open to non-members.

SECTION 15. The Board of Directors of The American Kennel Club, may, in its direction grant permission to clubs to hold sanctioned matches, which sanctioned matches shall be governed by such rules and regulations as from time to time shall be determined by the Board of Directors.

SECTION 16. American Kennel Club sanction must be obtained by any club that holds American Kennel Club events, for any type of match for which it solicits or accepts entries from non-members.

SECTION 17. The Board of Directors of The American Kennel Club will not approve applications for shows where dates conflict, unless it be shown that the granting of such applications will not work to the detriment of either show.

SECTION 18. A show-giving club must not advertise or publish the date of any show which it proposes to hold until that date has been approved by The American Kennel Club.

SECTION 19. All clubs holding shows under American Kennel Club rules must have available at each show through their bench show committees, a copy of the latest edition of *The Complete Dog Book* and at least one copy of the rules of The American Kennel Club.

SECTION 20. Any club holding a show for charity if requested must submit to The American Kennel Club within ninety days of date of show, a complete financial statement and receipt from the organization for which the show was held.

SECTION 21. The duration of a dog show will not exceed two days, unless permission be granted by The American Kennel Club for a longer period.

CHAPTER 6

DOG SHOW CLASSIFICATIONS

SECTION 1. The following breeds and/or varieties of breeds, divided by groups, shall be all the breeds and/or varieties of breeds for which regular classes of The American Kennel Club may be provided at any show held under American Kennel Club rules. The Board of Directors may either add to, transfer from one group to another, or delete from said list of breeds and/or varieties of breeds, whenever in its opinion registrations of such breed and/or variety of breed in the Stud Book justify such action.

GROUP 1—SPORTING DOGS

POINTERS
POINTERS (GERMAN SHORTHAIRED)
POINTERS (GERMAN WIREHAIRED)
RETRIEVERS (CHESAPEAKE BAY)
RETRIEVERS (CURLY-COATED)
RETRIEVERS (FLAT-COATED)
RETRIEVERS (GOLDEN)
RETRIEVERS (LABRADOR)
SETTERS (ENGLISH)
SETTERS (GORDON)
SETTERS (IRISH)
SPANIELS (AMERICAN WATER)
SPANIELS (BRITTANY)
SPANIELS (CLUMBER)
SPANIELS (COCKER)
  Three varieties:
    Solid Color, Black.
    Solid Color Other Than Black including Black and Tan.
    Parti-color.
SPANIELS (ENGLISH COCKER)
SPANIELS (ENGLISH SPRINGER)
SPANIELS (FIELD)
SPANIELS (IRISH WATER)
SPANIELS (SUSSEX)
SPANIELS (WELSH SPRINGER)
VIZSLAS
WEIMARANERS
WIREHAIRED POINTING GRIFFONS

GROUP 2.—HOUNDS

AFGHAN HOUNDS
BASENJIS
BASSET HOUNDS
BEAGLES
  Two varieties:
    Not exceeding 13 inches in height.
    Over 13 inches but not exceeding 15 inches in height.
BLACK AND TAN COONHOUNDS
BLOODHOUNDS
BORZOIS
DACHSHUNDS
  Three varieties: Longhaired.
    Smooth.
    Wirehaired.
FOXHOUNDS (AMERICAN)
FOXHOUNDS (ENGLISH)
GREYHOUNDS
HARRIERS
IRISH WOLFHOUNDS
NORWEGIAN ELKHOUNDS
OTTER HOUNDS
RHODESIAN RIDGEBACKS
SALUKIS
SCOTTISH DEERHOUNDS
WHIPPETS

GROUP 3—WORKING DOGS

AKITAS
ALASKAN MALAMUTES
BELGIAN MALINOIS
BELGIAN SHEEPDOGS
BELGIAN TERVUREN
BERNESE MOUNTAIN DOGS
BOUVIERS DES FLANDRES
BOXERS
BRIARDS
BULLMASTIFFS
COLLIES
  Two varieties: Rough.
    Smooth.
DOBERMAN PINSCHERS
GERMAN SHEPHERD DOGS
GIANT SCHNAUZERS
GREAT DANES
GREAT PYRENEES
KOMONDOROK
KUVASZOK
MASTIFFS
NEWFOUNDLANDS
OLD ENGLISH SHEEPDOGS
PULIK
ROTTWEILERS
ST. BERNARDS
SAMOYEDS
SHETLAND SHEEPDOGS
SIBERIAN HUSKIES
STANDARD SCHNAUZERS
WELSH CORGIS (CARDIGAN)
WELSII CORGIS (PEMBROKE)

GROUP 4—TERRIERS

AIREDALE TERRIERS
AMERICAN STAFFORDSHIRE TERRIERS
AUSTRALIAN TERRIERS
BEDLINGTON TERRIERS
BORDER TERRIERS
BULL TERRIERS
  Two varieties: White.
  Colored.
CAIRN TERRIERS
DANDIE DINMONT TERRIERS
FOX TERRIERS
  Two varieties: Smooth.
  Wire.
IRISH TERRIERS
KERRY BLUE TERRIERS
LAKELAND TERRIERS
MANCHESTER TERRIERS
  Two varieties:
    Standard, over 12 pounds and not exceeding 22 pounds.
    Toy (in Toy Group)
MINIATURE SCHNAUZERS
NORWICH TERRIERS
SCOTTISH TERRIERS
SEALYHAM TERRIERS
SKYE TERRIERS
SOFT-COATED WHEATEN TERRIERS
WELSH TERRIERS
WEST HIGHLAND WHITE TERRIERS

GROUP 5—TOYS

AFFENPINSCHERS
BRUSSELS GRIFFONS
CHIHUAHUAS
  Two varieties: Smooth Coat.
  Long Coat.
ENGLISH TOY SPANIELS
  Two varieties:
    King Charles and Ruby.
    Blenheim and Prince Charles.
ITALIAN GREYHOUNDS
JAPANESE SPANIELS
MALTESE
MANCHESTER TERRIERS
  Two varieties:
    Toy, not exceeding 12 pounds
    Standard (in Terrier Group)
MINIATURE PINSCHERS
PAPILLONS
PEKINGESE
POMERANIANS
POODLES
  Three varieties:
    Toy, not exceeding 10 inches
    Miniature (in Non-Sporting Group)
    Standard (in Non-Sporting Group)
PUGS
SHIH TZU
SILKY TERRIERS
YORKSHIRE TERRIERS

GROUP 6—NON-SPORTING DOGS

BICHON FRISES
BOSTON TERRIERS
BULLDOGS
CHOW CHOWS
DALMATIANS
FRENCH BULLDOGS
KEESHONDEN
LHASA APSOS
POODLES
  Three varieties:
    Miniature, over 10 inches and not exceeding 15 inches
    Standard, over 15 inches
    Toy (in Toy Group)
SCHIPPERKES
TIBETAN TERRIERS

SECTION 2. No class shall be provided for any dog under six months of age except at sanctioned matches when approved by The American Kennel Club.

SECTION 3. The regular classes of The American Kennel Club shall be as follows:

Puppy
Novice
Bred-by-Exhibitor
American-bred
Open
Winners

These classes shall be divided by sex.

SECTION 4. The Puppy Class shall be for dogs that are six months of age and over, but under twelve months, that were whelped in the United States of America or Canada, and that are not champions. The age of a dog shall be calculated up to and inclusive of the first day of a show. For example, a dog whelped on January 1st is eligible to compete in a puppy class at a show the first day of which is July 1st of the same year and may continue to compete in puppy classes at shows up to and including a show the first day of which is the 31st day of December of the same year, but is not eligible to compete in a puppy class at a show the first day of which is January 1st of the following year.

SECTION 5. The Novice Class shall be for dogs six months of age and over, whelped in the United States of America or Canada, which have not, prior to the date of closing of entries, won three first prizes in the Novice Class, a first prize in Bred-by-Exhibitor, American-bred, or Open Classes, nor one or more points toward their championships.

SECTION 6. The Bred-By-Exhibitor Class shall be for dogs whelped in the United States of America, or, if individually registered in The American Kennel Club Stud Book, for dogs whelped in Canada, that are six months of age and over, that are not champions, and that are owned wholly or in part by the person or by the spouse of the person who was the breeder or one of the breeders of record.

Dogs entered in this class must be handled in the class by an owner or by a member of the immediate family of an owner.

For purposes of this section, the members of an immediate family are: husband, wife, father, mother, son, daughter, brother, sister.

SECTION 7. The American-bred Class shall be for all dogs (except champions) six months of age and over, whelped in the United States of America, by reason of a mating which took place in the United States of America.

SECTION 8. The Open Class shall be for any dog six months of age or over except in a member specialty club show held only for American-bred dogs, in which case the Open Class shall be only for American-bred dogs.

SECTION 9. The Winners Class shall be divided by sex and each division shall be open only to undefeated dogs of the same sex which have won first prizes in either the Puppy, Novice, Bred-by-Exhibitor, American-bred or Open Classes. There shall be no entry fee for competition in the Winners Class.

After the Winners prize has been awarded in one of the sex divisions, the second prize winning dog, if undefeated by the dog awarded Winners, shall compete with the other eligible dogs for Reserve Winners. No eligible dog may be withheld from competition.

Winners' Classes shall be allowed only at shows where American-bred and Open Classes shall be given.

A member specialty club holding a show for American-bred dogs only may include Winners' Classes, provided the necessary regular classes are included in the classification.

A member club holding a show with restricted entries may include Winners' classes, provided the necessary regular classes are included in the classification.

SECTION 10. No Winners' Class, or any class resembling it, shall be given at sanctioned matches.

SECTION 11. Bench show committees may provide such other classes of recognized breeds or recognized varieties of breeds as they may choose, provided they do not conflict with the conditions of the above mentioned classes and are judged before Best of Breed competition.

No class may be given in which more than one breed or recognized variety of breed may be entered, except as provided in these rules and regulations.

SECTION 12. A club that provides Winners classes shall also provide competition for Best of Breed or for Best of Variety in those breeds for which varieties are provided in this chapter.

The awards in this competition shall be Best of Breed or Best of Variety of Breed.

The following categories of dogs may be entered and shown in this competition.

Dogs that are Champions of Record.

Dogs which according to their owners' records have completed the requirements for a championship but whose championships are unconfirmed. The showing of dogs whose championships are unconfirmed is limited to a period of 90 days from the date of the show where a dog completed the requirements for a championship according to the owners' records.

In addition, the Winners Dog and Winners Bitch together with any undefeated dogs that have competed at the show only in additional non-regular classes shall compete for Best of Breed or Best of Variety of Breed.

If the Winners Dog or Winners Bitch is awarded Best of Breed or Best of Variety of Breed, it shall be automatically awarded Best of Winners; otherwise, the Winners Dog and Winners Bitch shall be judged together for the Best of Winners following the judging of Best of Breed or Best of Variety of Breed. The dog designated Best of Winners shall be entitled to the number of points based on the number of dogs or bitches competing in the regular classes, whichever is greater. In the event that Winners is awarded in only one sex, there shall be no Best of Winners award.

After Best of Breed or Best of Variety of Breed and Best of Winners have been awarded, the judge shall select Best of Opposite Sex to Best of Breed or Best of Variety of Breed. Eligible for this award are:

Dogs of the opposite sex to Best of Breed or Best of Variety of Breed that have been entered for Best of Breed competition.

The dog awarded Winners of the opposite sex to the Best of Breed or Best of Variety of Breed.

Any undefeated dogs of the opposite sex to Best of Breed or Best of Variety of Breed which have competed at the show only in additional non-regular classes.

SECTION 13. At specialty shows for breeds in which there are varieties as specified in Chapter 6, Section 1, and which are held apart from all-breed shows, Best of Breed shall be judged following the judging of Best of each variety and best of opposite sex to best of each variety. Best of Opposite Sex to Best of Breed shall also be judged. Dogs eligible for Best of Opposite Sex to Best of Breed competition will be found among the best of variety or the bests of opposite sex to bests of variety, according to the sex of the dog placed Best of Breed.

At an all-breed show (even if a specialty club shall designate classes as its specialty show), the judge of a breed in which there are show varieties shall make no placings beyond Best of Variety and Best of Opposite Sex to Best of Variety.

SECTION 14. A club or association holding a show may give six group classes not divided by sex, such groups to be arranged in same order and to comprise the same breeds and recognized varieties of breeds as hereinbefore set forth in Chapter 2 and Section 1 of Chapter 6. All dogs designated by their respective breed judges Best of Breed at the show at which these group classes shall be given shall be eligible to compete in the group classes to which they belong according to this grouping, and all dogs designated Best of Variety in those breeds with more than one recognized variety, shall be eligible to compete in the group classes to which they belong according to this grouping. All entries for these group classes shall be made after judging of the regular classes of The American Kennel Club has been finished and no entry fee shall be charged. In the event that the owner of a dog designated Best of Breed or Best of Variety shall not exhibit the dog in the group class to which it is eligible, no other dog of the same breed or variety of breed shall be allowed to compete.

SECTION 15. A club giving group classes must also give a Best in Show, the winner to be entitled 'Best Dog in Show'. No entry free shall be charged but the six group winners must compete.

SECTION 16. A club or association holding a show, if it gives brace classes in the several breeds and recognized varieties of breeds, may also give six brace group classes, not divided by sex; such groups to be arranged in the same order and to comprise the same breeds and recognized varieties of breeds as herein before set forth in Chapter 2 and Section 1 of Chapter 6. All braces of dogs designated by their respective breed judges as Best of Breed or Best of Variety as the case may be at shows at which these brace group classes shall be given, shall be eligible to compete in the brace group classes to which they belong according to this grouping. All entries for these brace group classes shall be made after the judging of the regular classes of The American Kennel Club has been finished and no entry fee shall be charged. In the event that the owner of a brace of dogs designated Best of Breed or Best of Variety shall not exhibit the brace of dogs in the group class to which it is eligible, no other brace of dogs of the same breed or variety of breed shall be allowed to compete.

SECTION 17. If a club or association holding a show shall give these six group classes, it must also give a 'Best Brace in Show' in which the six braces of dogs winning the first prizes in the six group classes must compete, but for which no entry fee shall be charged. The winner shall be entitled 'The Best Brace in Show'.

SECTION 18. A club or association holding a show, if it gives team classes in the several breeds and recognized varieties of breeds, may also give six team group classes not divided by sex, such groups to be arranged in the same order and to comprise the same breeds and recognized varieties of breeds as hereinbefore set forth in Chapter 2 and Section 1 of Chapter 6. All teams of dogs designated by their respective breed judges as Best of Breed or Best of Variety as the case may be at shows at which these team group classes shall be given, shall be eligible to compete in the team group classes to which they belong according to this grouping. All entries for these team group classes shall be made after the judging of the regular classes of The American Kennel Club has been finished and no entry fee shall be charged. In the event that the owner of a team of dogs designated Best of Breed or Best of Variety shall not exhibit the team of dogs in the group class to which it is eligible, no other team of dogs of the same breed or variety of breed shall be allowed to compete.

SECTION 19. If a club or association holding a show shall give these six group classes it must also give a 'Best Team in Show' in which the six teams of dogs winning the first prizes in the six group classes must compete, but for which no entry fee shall be charged. The winner shall be entitled 'The Best Team in Show'.

SECTION 20. A club or association holding a show may offer Junior Showmanship competition if it so chooses.

The classes and procedure shall conform to The American Kennel Club regulations governing Junior Showmanship as adopted by the Board of Directors.

SECTION 21. The Miscellaneous Class shall be for pure-bred dogs of such breeds as may be designated by the Board of Directors of The American Kennel Club. No dog shall be eligible for entry in the Miscellaneous Class unless the owner has been granted an Indefinite Listing Privilege, and unless the ILP number is given on the entry form. Application for an Indefinite Listing Privilege shall be made on a form provided by the AKC and when submitted must be accompanied by a fee set by the Board of Directors.

All Miscellaneous Breeds shall be shown together in a single class except that the class may be divided by sex if so specified in the premium list. There shall be no further competition for dogs entered in this class.

The ribbons for First, Second, Third and Fourth prizes in this class shall be Rose, Brown, Light Green, and Gray, respectively.

At present the Miscellaneous Class is open to the following breeds:

Akitas
Australian Cattle Dogs
Australian Kelpies
Bearded Collies
Bichons Frises
Border Collies
Cavalier King Charles Spaniels
Ibizan Hounds
Miniature Bull Terriers
Soft-Coated Wheaten Terriers
Spinoni Italiani
Tibetan Terriers

SECTION 22. A registered dog that is six months of age or over and of a breed for which a classification is offered in the premium list may be entered in a show for Exhibition Only at the regular entry fee provided the dog has been awarded first prize in one of the regular classes at a licensed or member show held prior to the closing of entries of the show in which the Exhibition Only entry is made, and provided further that the premium list has not specified that entries for Exhibition Only will not be accepted. The name and date of the show at which the dog was awarded the first prize must be stated on the entry form.

A dog entered for Exhibition Only shall not be shown in any class or competition at that show.

CHAPTER 7

APPROVAL OF JUDGES LISTS AND PREMIUM LIST PROOFS

SECTION 1. After a club or association has been granted permission by The American Kennel Club to hold a show, it must send for approval by and in time to reach The American Kennel Club at least TWELVE WEEKS before the closing date for entries of the show, a list of the names and addresses of the judges whom it has selected to judge its show, giving in each instance the particular breed or breeds of dogs and group classes, if any, which it is desired that each judge shall pass upon, and the name and address of the judge selected to pass upon Best in Show. No judge's name shall be submitted to pass upon any assignment unless the judge has agreed in writing to accept that assignment.

The show-giving club must not advertise or publish the name or names of any of the judges which it has selected until the complete list has been approved by The American Kennel Club.

SECTION 2. Each club or association which has been granted permission by The American Kennel Club to hold a dog show or obedience trial must submit in time to reach The American Kennel Club at least NINE WEEKS before its closing date for entries, two printer's proof copies of its proposed premium list. The Show Plans Department of The American Kennel Club will return, not later than seven weeks before the closing date for entries of the show or trial, one copy of the proof indicating thereon all necessary corrections, deletions and revisions. Attached to the returned proof will be a conditional authorization of The American Kennel Club to print and distribute the premium list. This authorization will list the conditions to be observed or carried out by the show or trial-giving club and its superintendent or show or trial secretary, before printing the premium list.

SECTION 3. Premium lists and entry forms must be printed and sent to prospective exhibitors at least FIVE WEEKS prior to the closing date for entries of the show if sent by other than first class mail and at least FOUR WEEKS if sent by first class mail. Four copies of the premium list must be sent to the American Kennel Club at the time of distribution accompanied with certification of mailing date signed by a U.S. Post Office employee.

SECTION 4. Premium lists and entry forms, in order to insure uniformity, must conform to The American Kennel Club official size of 6 × 9 inches and the entry form must conform in every respect with the official form, a sample of which may be had without charge by application to the Secretary of The American Kennel Club.

CHAPTER 8

RIBBONS, PRIZES AND TROPHIES

SECTION 1. All clubs or associations holding dog shows under the rules of The American Kennel Club, except sanctioned matches, shall use the following colors for their prize ribbons or rosettes, in the regular classes of The American Kennel Club and the regular group classes.

First prize—Blue.
Second prize—Red.
Third prize—Yellow.

Fourth prize—White.
Winners—Purple.
Reserve Winners—Purple and White.
Best of Winners—Blue and White.
Special prize—Dark Green.
Best of Breed and Best of Variety of Breed—Purple and Gold.
Best of Opposite Sex to Best of Breed and Best of Opposite Sex to Best of Variety of Breed—Red and White.

and shall use the following colors for their prize ribbons in all additional classes:

First prize—Rose.
Second prize—Brown.
Third prize—Light Green.
Fourth prize—Gray.

SECTION 2. The prize ribbon for Best Local Dog in Show shall be Blue and Gold, and the prize ribbons in local classes and local groups shall be:

First prize—Rose.
Second prize—Brown.
Third prize—Light Green.
Fourth prize—Gray.

SECTION 3. Each ribbon or rosette, except those used at sanctioned matches, shall be at least 2 inches wide, and approximately 8 inches long; and bear on its face a facsimile of the seal of The American Kennel Club, the name of the prize, and the name of the show-giving club with numerals of year, date of show, and name of city or town where show is given.

SECTION 4. If ribbons are given at sanctioned matches, they shall be of the following colors, but may be of any design or size:

First prize—Rose.
Second prize—Brown.
Third prize—Light Green.
Fourth prize—Gray.
Special prize—Green with pink edges.
Best of Breed—Orange.
Best of Match—Pink and Green.
Best of Opposite Sex to Best in Match—Lavender.

SECTION 5. If money prizes are offered in a premium list of a show, a fixed amount for each prize must be stated. All other prizes offered in a premium list of a show must be accurately described or their monetary value must be stated. Alcoholic beverages will not be acceptable as prizes.

SECTION 6. A show-giving club shall not accept the donation of a prize for a competition not provided for at its show.

SECTION 7. All prizes offered in a premium list of a show must be offered to be awarded in the regular procedure of judging, with the exception of those prizes provided for in Sections 9 and 13 of this Chapter.

SECTION 8. Prizes may be offered for outright award at a show for the following placings:

First, Second, Third, Fourth in the Puppy, Novice, Bred-by-Exhibitor, American-bred or Open Classes, or in any division of these designated in the Classification.
First, Second, Third, Fourth in any additional class which the show-giving club may offer in accord with the provisions of Chapter 6, Section 11, and in the Miscellaneous Class (at all-breed shows only).

Winners, Reserve Winners, Best of Winners, Best of Breed or Variety, Best of Opposite Sex to Best of Breed or Variety. At all-breed shows only; First, Second, Third, Fourth in a Group Class and for Best in Show, Best Brace in Show and Best Team in Show.

SECTION 9. At specialty shows held apart from all-breed shows, prizes, for outright award, may also be offered for:

Best in Puppy Classes, Best in Novice Classes, Best in Bred-by-Exhibitor Classes, Best in American-bred Classes, Best in Open Classes, Best in any additional classes which the show-giving club may offer in accord with the provisions of Chapter 6, Section 11, in which the sexes are divided.

(In breeds in which there are varieties, a prize may be offered for Best in any of the above classes within the variety.)

SECTION 10. At all-breed shows, prizes may be offered on a three-time win basis for the following awards, provided permanent possession goes to the owner winning the award three times not necessarily with the same dog, and further provided such prizes are offered by the show-giving club itself or through it for competition at its shows only:

Best in Show, Best in any one group class.

SECTION 11. At specialty shows, prizes may be offered on a three-time win basis for the following awards, provided permanent possession goes to the owner winning the award three times not necessarily with the same dog and further provided such prizes are offered by the specialty club itself or through it for competition at its specialty shows only:

Best of Breed or Best of Opposite Sex to Best of Breed (Where a specialty club considers the classes at an all-breed show as its specialty show, there can be no award for Best of Breed in those breeds in which there are varieties.) Best of Variety of Breed or Best of Opposite Sex to Best of Variety, Best of Winners, Winners Dog and Winners Bitch.

SECTION 12. Perpetual prizes and such three-time win prizes as have been in competition prior to September 9, 1952 and which would not be allowed under the terms of the sections in this Chapter will continue to be permitted to be offered under the terms of their original provisions until won outright or otherwise retired. Should premium list copy submitted to the AKC for approval contain such non-allowable prizes, a certification by the Club Secretary stating that the prizes have been in competition prior to September 9, 1952 must be included.

SECTION 13. Regular Specials are prizes offered by show-giving member or non-member specialty clubs for outright and automatic award at any show where the terms have been published in full in the premium list and catalog of the show. No prize may be offered for an award higher than Best of Breed or Best of Variety of Breed. It shall be the obligation of specialty clubs offering such regular specials to notify superintendents, show secretaries and show-giving clubs that said prizes may be offered provided the terms are set forth in full in the premium list and catalog of the show. The specialty club will be solely responsible for the distribution of such prizes within 60 days after the completion of a show when it has been determined that all the terms of the awards have been met. No show-giving club is obligated to accept an offering of regular specials.

CHAPTER 9

PREMIUM LISTS AND CLOSING OF ENTRIES

SECTION 1. The awards at a dog show, or the scores made at an obedience trial, will be officially recorded by The American Kennel Club only if the certification of the Secretary of The American Kennel Club is published on the first, second or third page of the premium list stating that permission has been granted by The American Kennel Club for the dog show or obedience trial to be held under American Kennel Club rules and regulations.

If the show shall be given by a club or association not a member of The American Kennel Club the words 'Licensed Show' must be plainly printed on the title page of the premium list.

SECTION 2. The premium list shall contain the following: A list of the officers of the show-giving club with the address of the secretary, a list of the members of the bench show committee (there must be at least five) together with the designation of 'Chairman' and the Chairman's address (and 'Obedience Trial Chairman' if an obedience trial is being held by a club in connection with its dog show), the names of the Veterinarians (or name of local Veterinary Association), the names and addresses of the judges, together with their assignments, and the name and address of the superintendent or show secretary who has been approved by The American Kennel Club. The premium list shall also specify whether the show is Benched or Unbenched, and shall give the exact location of the show, the date or dates on which it is to be held, and the times of opening and closing of the show.

SECTION 2A. An all-breed show-giving club may, at its option, use a condensed form of premium list which shall be identical with the content and format of a regular premium list, and comply with all the pertinent rules except that the listing of breed prizes and trophies offered is omitted as well as the listing of all prizes and trophies offered for an obedience trial if held by the show-giving club with its show. Such prizes and trophies as are offered for best in show and group placements are to be included in a condensed premium list as well as any schedule of class cash prizes that a club proposes to offer.

Two copies of the proposed list of breed and obedience prizes and trophies are to be submitted to AKC for approval at the same time that printers proof copies of the condensed premium list are submitted. The conditions of all prizes and trophies offered must conform to the provisions of Chapter 8 of these rules and Chapter 1, Section 32 of the Obedience Regulations. A club using a condensed form of premium list is obligated to prepare lists of the breed and obedience prizes and trophies for distribution to prospective entrants and exhibitors on request. Such lists can be printed, multilithed, multigraphed, mimeographed or typed (and photostated) on paper of any suitable size with both sides of the paper being used if the club wishes. In each condensed form of premium list there must be the notation, 'A list of breed and obedience prizes and trophies offered can be obtained by writing to (name and address of club secretary and/or superintendent and address).'

A club which chooses to use a condensed form of premium list may also prepare for printing a regular premium list for other than mail distribution. The regular premium list can then be used to fill requests for a listing of breed and obedience prizes and trophies offered and no separate list of breed and obedience prizes and trophies need be prepared.

However, if a regular premium list is used in addition to the condensed premium list, two copies of the printers proofs of the full premium list must be submitted to the AKC for approval with the notation that it is the club's intention to print a condensed premium list for mailing purposes.

An all-breed obedience trial-giving club may, at its option, use a condensed form of premium list which shall be identical with the content and format of a regular premium list, and comply with all the pertinent rules and regulations except that the listing of prizes and trophies offered is omitted. When a condensed form of premium list is used, the same procedure is to be followed with respect to the prize and trophy list as is required of show-giving clubs and as is set forth in this section.

SECTION 3. Except at specialty club shows, the general classification of recognized breeds divided into six groups and in the same order as set forth in Chapter 2, with the varieties of distinct breeds as described in Section 1 of Chapter 6 added thereto, in their proper groups and alphabetical position, shall be published in the premium list.

SECTION 4. If an all-breed club or association permits a specialty club to consider the classes at its show as their specialty show, the winner of Best of Breed or Best of Variety of Breed if no Best of Breed is awarded, may compete in the group classes of the all-breed show.

SECTION 5. If more than one judge has been approved to judge a specialty show held apart from an all-breed show, the premium list must designate the particular assignments of each judge as approved by The American Kennel Club, except when the specialty club has requested and received approval for the drawing of assignments at the show, in which case a statement to this effect shall appear in the premium list in place of designated assignments.

SECTION 6. A show-giving club shall assume the responsibility of collecting all recording fees for The American Kennel Club, which fact shall be stated in the premium list.

SECTION 7. Bench show committees may make such regulations or additional rules for the government of their shows as shall be considered necessary, provided such regulations or additional rules do not conflict with any rule of The American Kennel Club, and provided they do not discriminate between breeds or between dogs entered in show classes and those entered in obedience classes in the required hour of arrival and the hour of removal. If permission is granted to a club other than the show-giving club for the holding of an obedience trial in connection with a dog show, the obedience club so authorized, must comply with the show-giving club's rules adopted hereunder.

Such regulations or additional rules shall be printed in the premium list and violations thereof shall be considered the same as violations of the rules and regulations of The American Kennel Club.

SECTION 8. No prizes may be accepted or offered by a show-giving club unless they are published in the premium list of the show or in the separate list of prizes if the condensed form of premium list is used; nor may any be withdrawn or the conditions thereof changed after they have been published in the premium list or in the separate list of prizes.

If the donor of a prize that has been published in the premium list of a show or in the separate list of prizes shall fail to furnish the prize, the show-giving club shall promptly supply a prize of the same description and of no less value.

The show-giving club shall be responsible for all errors made in publishing offers of prizes and shall, in the event of error, award prizes of equal value; except that if an error has been made in the premium list or in the separate list of prizes in publishing the conditions of a specialty club's Regular Specials (as described in Chapter 8, Section 14) prizes shall be awarded according to the current terms of the specialty club's Regular Specials.

SECTION 9. Every premium list shall specify the date and time at which entries for a show shall close. The premium list shall also specify the name and address of the Superintendent or Show Secretary who is to receive the entries. For all shows other than specialty shows, the specified closing date and time must be no later than as outlined in the following schedule:

For a show which opens on Friday, Saturday, Sunday, or Monday, entries accepted not later than noon on the third Wednesday prior to the show.

For a show which opens on Tuesday, entries accepted not later than noon on the third Thursday prior to the show

For a show which opens on Wednesday, entries accepted not later than noon on the third Friday prior to the show.

For a show which opens on Thursday, entries accepted not later than noon on the third Saturday prior to the show.

Whenever the closing day noted above falls on a postal holiday, entries received in the first mail only on the following day may be accepted.

CHAPTER 10

JUDGES

SECTION 1. Any reputable person who is in good standing with The American Kennel Club may apply for leave to judge any breed or breeds of pure-bred dogs which in his or her opinion he or she is qualified by training and experience to pass upon, with the exception of persons connected with any publication in the capacity of solicitor for kennel advertisements, persons connected with dog food, dog remedy or kennel supply companies in the capacity of solicitor or salesman, persons employed in and about kennels, persons who buy, sell and in any way trade or traffic in dogs as a means of livelihood in whole or in part, whether or not they be known as dealers (excepting in this instance recognized private and professional handlers to a limited extent as will later appear) and professional show superintendents.

No Judge shall be granted a license to be an annual superintendent.

SECTION 2. The application for license to judge must be made on a form which will be supplied by The American Kennel Club upon request and when received by said club will be placed before the Board of Directors of The American Kennel Club who shall determine in each instance whether a license shall be issued.

SECTION 3. The American Kennel Club will not approve as judge for any given show the superintendent, show secretary, or show veterinarians, or club officials of said show acting in any one of these three capacities, and such persons cannot officiate or judge at such show under any circumstances.

SECTION 4. Only those persons whose names are on The American Kennel Club's list of eligible judges may, in the discretion of The American Kennel Club, be approved to judge at any member or licensed show, except that if it becomes necessary to replace an advertised judge after the opening of the show and no person on the eligible judges list is available to take his place, the Bench Show Committee may select as a substitute for the advertised judge a person whose name is not on the eligible judges list provided such person is not currently suspended from the privileges of The American Kennel Club, is not currently suspended as a judge and is not ineligible to judge under the provisions of Sections 1 and 3 of this Chapter.

SECTION 5. The American Kennel Club may in its discretion approve as a judge of any sanctioned match, futurity or sweepstake a person who is not currently suspended from the privileges of The American Kennel Club or whose judging privileges are not currently suspended.

SECTION 6. Bench show committees or superintendents shall, in every instance, notify appointed judges of the breeds and group classes upon which they are to pass, and such notification shall be given before the publication of the premium lists.

SECTION 7. Bench show committees or superintendents shall not add to or subtract from the number of breeds or variety groups which a selected judge has agreed to pass upon without first notifying said judge of and obtaining his consent to the contemplated change in his assigned breeds or variety groups, and the judge when so notified may refuse to judge any breeds or variety groups added to his original assignment.

SECTION 8. A bench show committee which shall be informed at any time prior to TEN DAYS before the opening day of its show that an advertised judge will not fulfill his or her engagement to judge shall substitute a judge in his or her place, which substitute judge must be approved by The American Kennel Club, and shall give notice of the name of the substitute judge to all those who have entered dogs in the classes allotted to be judged by the advertised judge. All those who have entered dogs to be shown under the advertised judge shall be permitted to withdraw their entries at any time prior to the opening day of the show and the entry fees paid for entering such dogs shall be refunded.

Since an entry can be made only under a breed judge, changes in Group or Best in Show assignments do not entitle an exhibitor to a refund.

SECTION 9. Should a Bench Show Committee be informed at any time within ten days before the opening of its show, or after its show has opened, that an advertised judge will not fulfill his or her engagement to judge, it shall substitute a qualified judge in his or her place, and shall obtain approval of the change from The American Kennel Club if time allows.

No notice need be sent to those exhibitors who have entered dogs under the advertised judge.

The Bench Show Committee will be responsible for having a notice posted in a prominent place within the show precincts as soon after the show opens as is practical informing exhibitors of the change in judges. An exhibitor who has entered a dog under an advertised judge who is being replaced may withdraw such entry and shall have the entry fee refunded, provided notice of such withdrawal is given to the Superintendent or Show Secretary prior to the start of the judging of the breed which is to be passed upon by a substitute judge.

SECTION 10. In case an advertised judge shall have judged part of the classes of a breed and then finds it impossible to finish, a substitute judge shall be selected by the bench show committee, and in that event the awards made by the regular judge shall stand, and his or her substitute shall judge only the remaining entries in the breed. No dogs entered under the regularly selected judge shall be withheld from competition.

SECTION 11. A substitute judge shall finish the judging of the breed class or group he or she is adjudicating upon if he or she has begun to judge before the advertised judge arrives at the show.

SECTION 12. Any club or association that holds a dog show must prepare, after the entries have closed and not before, a judging program showing that time scheduled for the judging of each breed and each variety for which entries have been accepted. If a substitute or additional page has been approved, Chapter 10, Section 8 or Chapter 10, Section 13 as appropriate will be quoted listing the changes. The judging program shall indicate the number of dogs entered and state the time for the start of group judging, if any. The program shall be based on the judging of about 25 dogs per hour by each judge. Each judge's breed and variety assignments shall be divided into periods of about one hour, except in those cases where the entry in a breed or variety exceeds 30. The total number of dogs assigned each judge will be indicated. One half to one hour must be allowed for rest or meals if a judge's assignment exceeds five hours. A copy of the program and identification slip for each dog entered shall be mailed to the owner and, if any, the professional handler no later than one week before the date of the event. Two copies of the program shall be mailed to the Show Plans Department at the time they are mailed to the exhibitors.

The judging program shall be printed in the catalog.

No judging shall occur at any show prior to the time specified in the judging program.

SECTION 13. The maximum number of dogs assigned in the breed judging to any judge, in one day, shall never exceed 175.

If a futurity or sweepstakes is offered in connection with a specialty show, which is held as part of an all-breed show, the above figure of 175 shall be reduced to 150 for the specialty show.

If a show-giving club so elects, it may place a limit of its own choosing lower than any of the limits provided for in the rule notifying The American Kennel Club of its intention at the time the judging panel is submitted for approval. This limit will then govern the need for additional judges if, when the entries for the show have closed, any judge on the panel has drawn more dogs than the limit set by the club.

When the entries have closed, if the entry under any judge exceeds the above limits, the Bench Show Committee must select some other judge or judges to whom sufficient breeds or varieties can be assigned to bring the total assignment of every judge within the limits. In the case of a specialty show, if the limits are exceeded, at least one additional judge shall be assigned to bring each judge's assignment within the limits. Approval must be obtained from The American Kennel Club for each such reassignment.

Notice must be sent to the owner of each dog affected by such a change in judges at least five days before the opening of the show, and the owner has the right to withdraw his entry and have his entry fee refunded provided notification of his withdrawal is received before the opening of the show by the Superintendent or Show Secretary named in the premium list to receive entries.

SECTION 14. A judge shall not exhibit his dogs or take any dog belonging to another person into the ring at any show at which he is officiating, nor shall he pass judgment in his official capacity upon any dog which he or any member of his immediate household or immediate family (as defined in Chapter 6, Section 6) has handled in the ring more than twice during the preceding twelve months.

SECTION 15. A judge's decision shall be final in all cases affecting the merits of the dogs. Full discretionary power is given to the judge to withhold any, or all, prizes for want of merit. After a class has once been judged in accordance with these rules and regulations, it shall not be rejudged. A class is considered judged when the judge has marked his book which must be done before the following class is examined. If any errors have been made by the judge in marking the awards as made, he may correct the same but must initial any such corrections.

Section 16. A judge may order any person or dog from the ring. For the purpose of facilitating the judging, judges are required to exclude from the rings in which they are judging all persons except the steward or stewards and the show attendants assigned to the ring and those actually engaged in exhibiting.

SECTION 17. A judge shall be supplied with a book called the judge's book in which he shall mark all awards and all absent dogs. The original judges' books at shows shall be in the custody of the judge, steward, superintendent, or superintendent's assistant. None other shall be allowed access to them. At the conclusion of the judging, the book must be signed by the judge and any changes which may have been made therein initialed by him.

SECTION 18. A judge's decision, as marked in the judge's book, cannot be changed by him after filing, but an error appearing in the judge's book may be corrected by The American Kennel Club after consultation with the judge.

SECTION 19. Only one judge shall officiate in each Group Class and only one judge shall select the Best in Show.

The Board of Directors suggests that whenever possible the Best in Show be determined by one who has not already judged any breed or group class of said show.

SECTION 20. If a judge disqualifies a dog at any show, he shall make a note in the judge's book giving his reasons for such disqualification. In computing the championship points for a breed, said dog shall not be considered as having been present at the show.

CHAPTER 11
HANDLERS

SECTION 1. Any person handling dogs for pay or acting as agent for another for pay at any show held under the rules of The American Kennel Club must hold a license from The American Kennel Club.

Any reputable person who is in good standing with The American Kennel Club may apply to said Club for license to act as a handler or as an agent, which application must be made on a form which will be supplied by said Club upon request. When the application is received by The American Kennel Club the Board of Directors shall determine whether a license shall be issued to the applicant.

SECTION 2. The fee for being granted a license to be a handler or an agent, or an assistant to a handler or an agent, shall be determined by the Board of Directors of The American Kennel Club from time to time in its discretion. Any such license may be granted for any such period of time that the Board of Directors deems appropriate in its discretion. All granted licenses shall expire December 31 of the year in which they are granted.

Effective January 1, 1954, no fee is required with applications for Handlers or Assistant Handlers licenses.

No handler's license will be granted to a person residing in the same household with a licensed judge.

CHAPTER 12

SELECTION OF SUPERINTENDENT, SHOW SECRETARY AND VETERINARIANS

When a club or association, which has been granted permission to hold a show, sends to The American Kennel Club its list of Judges to be approved, it must enclose with that list the names and addresses of its proposed Superintendent or Show Secretary, and Veterinarian or Veterinarians, all of whom must be approved by the Board of Directors of The American Kennel Club before the premium list of the show can be printed.

CHAPTER 13

SUPERINTENDENTS AND SHOW SECRETARIES

SECTION 1. The Superintendent of a Dog Show held under the rules of The American Kennel Club must hold a license from The American Kennel Club.

SECTION 2. Any qualified person may make application to The American Kennel Club for approval to act as Show Secretary of a dog show.

SECTION 3. Superintendents and Show Secretaries will be responsible along with bench show committees for making complete arrangements for attendance at a show with each one of the veterinarians selected to service a show. In the event that a recognized Veterinary Association is to furnish the veterinarians, the complete arrangements shall be made with the secretary of the Association.

SECTION 4. Superintendents and Show Secretaries shall have on hand at every show the various official American Kennel Club forms for the use of veterinarians.

SECTION 5. Superintendents and Show Secretaries shall be prepared, at any show, to furnish the forms to be used by any exhibitor or handler who seeks a health examination of a dog. Upon the filing of the completed form by an exhibitor or handler, it shall be the superintendent's and show secretary's duty to see that the owner or agent of the dog takes his dog to the 'Veterinarian Headquarters' for the examination.

SECTION 6. Superintendents and Show Secretaries will be responsible for providing at every show a suitable space which will serve as the headquarters of the show veterinarians. At an indoor show this space will be marked off in some adequate way and a sign 'Veterinarian Headquarters' must be prominently displayed. At an outdoor show, where canvas is available, the veterinarians' office shall be set up under its own individual tent. Where no tenting is used the Headquarters must be arranged so that the veterinarians are afforded protection from the weather.

SECTION 7. Superintendents and Show Secretaries are required, with their report of a show, to list the names of all veterinarians who served at a show and give the hours that each veterinarian was present.

SECTION 8. Superintendents and Show Secretaries shall have the sole authority to enforce the rules having to do with the benching of dogs.

SECTION 9. Superintendents and Show Secretaries shall have the sole authority to excuse a dog from being shown on the recommendation of the veterinarian under Chapter 15, Section 4 (*c*) and to release dogs from a show prior to the published time for the releasing of dogs, except in the event that a dog has been dismissed from a show by a veterinarian under Chapter 15, Section 4 (b).

SECTION 10. Bench show committees and superintendents of dog shows shall be held responsible for the enforcement of all rules and regulations relating to shows and must provide themselves with a copy of The American Kennel Club rules and regulations for reference.

SECTION 11. The Superintendent or Show Secretary will be held accountable for the maintenance of clean and orderly conditions throughout the precincts of the show during all hours when dogs are permitted to be present.

SECTION 12. Any reputable person who is in good standing with The American Kennel Club may apply to said Club for license to act as Superintendent of a Dog Show, which application must be made on a form which will be supplied by said Club upon request. When the application is received by The American Kennel Club its Board of Directors shall determine whether the applicant is reasonably qualified from training and experience to act as Superintendent of a Dog Show and whether a license shall be issued to said applicant.

The fee for being granted a yearly license to be a Superintendent and the fee for renewal of said license each year shall be determined by the Board of Directors of The American Kennel Club. The fee for being granted a license to superintend one show and/or one field trial only shall be determined in like manner.

No yearly license will be issued to any person until he or she has superintended at least three dog shows or field trials.

No annual superintendent shall be granted a license to be a judge.

CHAPTER 14

ADMISSION AND EXAMINATION OF DOGS ENTERED IN A SHOW

SECTION 1. The bench show committee of an all-breed club or a specialty club holding a dog show must elect whether all dogs are to be inspected in respect to their apparent health before being admitted to the show or whether dogs will be allowed to enter a show's premises without such inspection. If the bench show committee decides that all dogs are to be inspected, the designation 'Examined Show' shall be printed on the title page of the premium list and catalog.

SECTION 2. An 'Examined Show' is one at which each dog is subject to a health inspection by one of the show's verterinarians before being allowed to enter a show's premises.

SECTION 3. For an 'Examined Show' a club must employ a sufficient number of qualified veterinarians to insure the inspection and admission of dogs without undue delay, and shall arrange to have its full complement of veterinarians present during the hours of the show when dogs will be admitted. If dogs are to be admitted to a show's premises before the published opening hour, then the bench show committee of a club must arrange to have one or more of it veterinarians on duty during such time.

SECTION 4. For an 'Examined Show' a club or its superintendent shall provide a 'Veterinarian Enclosure' into which and through which every dog must pass before it is admitted to a show's premises. The 'Enclosure' is to be set up between an entrance to a show's building or grounds and the premises of a show and shall be of sufficient size to meet the needs of the veterinarians and allow for the orderly and prompt passage of exhibitors and dogs. Clubs and superintendents will be responsible for providing safeguards against the possibility of a dog getting into a show's premises without first having passed through the 'Enclosure.'

There shall also be provided within the 'Enclosure' a quarantine area in which there will be benches for dogs that the show veterinarians may wish to hold for an examination.

SECTION 5. For an 'Examined Show' a club or its superintendent shall provide in the enclosure for the use of its veterinarians the following items:

Examination tables (with non-slip footing surface and large enough to hold the largest dogs);
Tables for the use of the Veterinarians;
Rubber gloves;
Disinfectant (either zepheran chloride or roccal);
Wash bowls and paper towels;

Waste disposal cans;
'Passed' rubber stamps and stamp pads;

Forms to be completed by Veterinarians for all dogs not passed.

In addition a club or its superintendent shall appoint persons to serve in the Enclosure whose duty it will be to provide such help for the veterinarians as they may require and to direct the orderly passage of exhibitors and dogs through the Enclosure.

SECTION 6. If the bench show committee of a club chooses to hold an 'Examined Show' the chairman shall complete a form that shall be supplied by The American Kennel Club which is to be attached to the club's application for a date. This form will include a representation that the club is prepared to provide an adequate number of veterinarians, that the layout of the club's proposed building or grounds is such that an adequate 'Veterinarians Enclosure' (and benches) can be set up as described in these rules and that the club and its superintendent will properly administer the admission of dogs to the show premises in accordance with these rules.

SECTION 7. When a club is holding an 'Examined Show' of more than one day's duration, all of the requirements set forth in this chapter shall be applicable to all dogs that have been temporarily removed from the show premises at the close of the first day and are required to be returned to the show premises on the second day.

CHAPTER 15

DUTIES AND RESPONSIBILITIES OF SHOW VETERINARIANS

SECTION 1. Any reputable person who is in good standing with The American Kennel Club and who has been duly qualified to practice his profession by law may act as veterinarian of a dog show.

SECTION 2. Every club that holds a licensed or member show shall employ one or more veterinarians who are qualified as described in Section 1, to serve in an official capacity. At least one of these veterinarians shall be in attendance during the entire progress of the show. The duties of the veterinarians shall be to give advisory opinions to Judges and to Bench Show Committees on the physical conditions of dogs, when requested by such officials as provided for in these rules; to examine the health of the dogs at the request of exhibitors and handlers; and to render first aid to dogs in cases of sickness or injury occurring at the show. Show veterinarians are not required to be familiar with the Dog Show Rules or breed standards affecting the disqualification or eligibility of dogs, and should not attempt to interpret the effect of their advisory opinions on the status of dogs under the rules or standards. They should not discuss with exhibitors or handlers the advisory opinions given to Judges and Bench Show Committees. Show veterinarians are not to be called on to treat dogs for physical conditions that existed before they were brought to the show. In addition, at an Examined Show it will be the duty of the veterinarian to pass or reject all dogs coming into the Veterinarians Enclosure.

SECTION 3. At an 'Examined Show,' it will also be the duty of the show veterinarians to make a visual inspection of every dog that comes into the 'Veterinarian Enclosure.' Dogs with outward symptoms of illness or disease are to be held within the Enclosure for examination to determine whether they are to be admitted. The identification cards of admitted dogs shall be stamped 'passed' by the examining veterinarian.

SECTION 4. Veterinarians serving a show will have complete authority to:

(a) Reject any dog at the entrance to a show's premises which he considers may endanger the health of any other dogs;

(b) Dismiss any dog that has been admitted to a show which he considers may endanger the health of other dogs;

(c) Recommend to the superintendent or show secretary the excusing of any dog from being shown or from the show premises provided he considers that the showing of the dog in the ring or its remaining within the show premises would impair the dog's health.

In all cases where a dog is rejected, dismissed or recommended for excusing from judging or the show premises, the veterinarian shall complete a form, which will be provided giving the basis for his decision, or opinion, and shall file the form with the superintendent or show secretary.

SECTION 5. Veterinarians may request exhibitors and handlers to open dogs' mouths, but when they consider it necessary may do so themselves, provided however that in the latter instance they wear rubber gloves and take proper sanitary precautions.

SECTION 6. Upon the presentation at the 'Veterinarians Headquarters' of a dog whose health has been questioned by an exhibitor or handler, it shall be the duty of one of the show veterinarians, as soon as practical, to make an examination of the dog. If he considers that the dog should be dismissed from the show, he will ask the superintendent or show secretary to see that the dog is removed.

SECTION 7. Veterinarians serving a show will be expected to make full use of the area provided for them as a headquarters. Where practical, at least one veterinarian should be in attendance at the headquarters during the entire time that a show is in progress. At an 'Examined Show' the 'Veterinarians Enclosure' is to be used as a headquarters until such time as the entrance to the enclosure has been closed and no more dogs are to be admitted to it.

CHAPTER 16

DOG SHOW ENTRIES
CONDITIONS OF DOGS AFFECTING ELIGIBILITY

SECTION 1. No dog shall be eligible to be entered in a licensed or member dog show, except for dogs entered in the Miscellaneous Class, unless it is either individually registered in the AKC Stud Book or part of an AKC registered litter, or otherwise, if whelped outside the United States of America and owned by a resident of the U.S.A. or Canada, unless it has been registered in its country of birth with a foreign registry organization whose pedigrees are acceptable for AKC registration.

An unregistered dog that is part of an AKC registered litter or an unregistered dog with an acceptable foreign registration that was whelped outside the U.S.A. and that is owned by a resident of the U.S.A. or Canada may, without special AKC approval, be entered in licensed or member dog shows that are held not later than 30 days after the date of the first licensed or member dog show in which the dog was entered, but only provided that the AKC litter registration number or the individual foreign registration number and the name of the country of birth, are shown on the entry form, and provided further that the same name, which in the case of an imported or Canadian owned dog must be the name on the foreign registration, is used for the dog each time.

No dog that has not been individually registered with The American Kennel Club when first entered in a licensed or member dog show shall be eligible to be entered in any licensed or member dog show that is held more than 30 days after the date of the first licensed or member dog show in which it was entered, unless the dog's individual AKC registration number is shown on the entry form, or unless the owner has received from The American Kennel Club an extension notice in writing authorizing further entries of the dog for a specified time with its AKC litter number or individual foreign registration number. No such extension will be granted unless the owner can clearly demonstrate, in a letter addressed to the Show Records Department of The American Kennel Club requesting such extension, that the delay in registration is due to circumstances for which he is not responsible.

Such extension notice will be void upon registration of the dog or upon expiration of the period for which the extension has been granted if that occurs earlier, but upon application further extensions may be granted.

If a dog is later individually registered with a name that is not identical to the name under which it has been entered in dog shows prior to individual registration, each entry form entering the dog in a licensed or member dog show after the owner has received the individual registration certificate must show the registered name followed by 'formerly shown as' and the name under which the dog was previously shown, until the dog has been awarded one of the four places in a regular class at a licensed or member show.

SECTION 2. At every show held under the rules of The American Kennel Club, a recording fee not to exceed 25 cents may be required for every dog entered. This recording fee is to help defray expenses involved in keeping show records, and applies to all dogs entered. If a dog is entered in more than one class at a show, the recording fee applies only to first entry. The Board of Directors shall determine, from time to time, whether a recording fee shall be required, and the amount of it.

Effective June 1, 1954 recording fees are not required.

SECTION 3. Every dog must be entered in the name of the person who actually owned the dog at the time entries closed. The right to exhibit a dog cannot be transferred. A registered dog which has been acquired by some person other than the owner as recorded with The American Kennel Club must be entered in the name of its new owner at any show for which entries close after the date upon which the dog was acquired, and application for transfer of ownership must be sent to The American Kennel Club by the new owner within seven days after the last day of the show. The new owner should state on the entry form that transfer application has been mailed to The American Kennel Club or will be mailed shortly. If there is any unavoidable delay in obtaining the completed application required to record the transfer, The American Kennel Club may grant a reasonable extension of time, provided the new owner notifies the show records department of The American Kennel Club by mail within seven days after the show, of the reason for the delay. If an entry is made by a duly authorized agent of the owner, the name of the actual owner must be shown on the entry form. If a dog is owned by an association, the name of the association and a list of its officers must be shown on the entry form.

SECTION 4. To be acceptable, an entry must be submitted with required entry fee, on an official American Kennel Club entry form, signed by the owner or his duly authorized agent, and must include all of the following information: Name of the club holding the show; date of the show; breed; variety, if any; sex; full description of the class or classes in which entered; full name of dog; individual registration number or AKC litter number or, for a dog entered in the Miscellaneous Class, ILP number; name and address of the actual owner or owners. For a dog whelped outside the U.S.A. that is not AKC registered, the entry form must show the individual foreign registration number and country of birth. In addition, an entry in the Puppy, Novice, Bred-by-Exhibitor, or American-bred class must include the place of birth; an entry in the Puppy Class must include the date of birth; and an entry in the Bred-by-Exhibitor class must include the name or names of the breeder or breeders.

No entry may be accepted unless it is received by the Superintendent or Show Secretary named in the premium list to receive entries prior to the closing date and hour as published in the premium list, or in the case of a limited entry prior to the time the limit is reached. All the requirements of the fore-going paragraph and all other specific requirements printed in the premium list must be met before an entry can be considered acceptable.

SECTION 5. No entry shall be made and no entry shall be accepted by a Superintendent or Show Secretary which specifies any condition as to its acceptance.

SECTION 6. No entry may be changed or cancelled unless notice of the change or cancellation is received in writing or by telegram by the Superintendent or Show Secretary named in the premium list to receive entries, prior to the published closing date and hour for entries, except that a correction may be made in the sex of a dog at a show prior to the judging. No dog wrongly entered in a class may otherwise be transferred to another class. Owners are responsible for errors in entry forms, regardless of who may make such errors.

SECTION 7. No entry shall be received from any person who is not in good standing with The American Kennel Club on the day of the closing of the entries. Before accepting entries, a list of persons not in good standing must be obtained by the Show Superintendent or Show Secretary from The American Kennel Club.

SECTION 8. No entry shall be made under a kennel name unless that name has been registered with The American Kennel Club. All entries made under a kennel name must be signed with the kennel name followed by the word 'registered.' An 'exhibitor' or 'entrant' is the individual or, if a partnership, all the members of the partnership exhibiting or entering in a dog show. In the case of such an entry by a partnership every member of the partnership shall be in good standing with the American Kennel Club before the entry will be accepted; and in case of any infraction of these rules, all the partners shall be held equally responsible.

SECTION 9. A dog which is blind, deaf, castrated, spayed, or which has been changed in appearance by artificial means except as specified in the standard for its breed, or a male which does not have two normal testicles normally located in the scrotum, may not compete at any show and will be disqualified. A dog will not be considered to have been changed by artificial means because of removal of dew claws or docking of tail if it is of a breed in which such removal or docking is a regularly approved practice which is not contrary to the standard.

When a judge finds evidence of any of these conditions in any dog he is judging he must, before proceeding with the judging, notify the Superintendent or Show Secretary and must call an official show veterinarian to examine the dog in the ring and to give the judge an advisory opinion in writing on the condition of the dog. Only after he has seen the veterinarian's opinion in writing shall the judge render his own decision and record it in the judge's book, marking the dog 'disqualified' and stating the reason if he determines that disqualification is required under this rule. The judge's decision is final and need not necessarily agree with the veterinarian's opinion. The written opinion of the veterinarian shall in all cases be forwarded to The American Kennel Club by the Superintendent or Show Secretary.

When a dog has been disqualified under this rule or under the standard for its breed, either by a judge or by decision of a Bench Show Committee, any awards at that show shall be cancelled by The American Kennel Club and the dog may not again be shown unless and until, following application by the owner to The American Kennel Club, the owner has received official notification from The American Kennel Club that the dog's show eligibility has been reinstated. The American Kennel Club will not entertain any application for reinstatement of a male which has been disqualified as not having two normal testicles normally located in the scrotum until the dog is twelve (12) months old.

SECTION 9-A. A dog that is lame at any show may not compete and shall not receive any award at that show. It shall be the judge's responsibility to determine whether a dog is lame. He shall not obtain the opinion of the show veterinarian. If in the judge's opinion a dog in the ring is lame, he shall withhold all awards from such dog and shall excuse it from the ring. A dog so excused shall not be counted as having competed. When a judge excuses a dog from the ring for lameness, he shall mark his book 'Excused—lame.'

SECTION 9-B. No dog shall be eligible to compete at any show and no dog shall receive any award at any show in the event the natural color or shade of natural color or the natural markings of the dog have been altered or changed by the use of any substance whether such substance may have been used for cleaning purposes or for any other reason. Such cleaning substances are to be removed before the dog enters the ring.

If in the judge's opinion any substance has been used to alter or change the natural color or shade of natural color or natural markings of a dog, then in such event the judge shall withhold any and all awards from such dog, and the judge shall make a note in the judge's book giving his reason for withholding such award. The handler or the owner, or both, of any dog or dogs from which any award has been withheld for violation of this section of the rules, or any judge who shall fail to perform his duties under this section shall be subject to disciplinary action.

SECTION 9-C. Any dog whose ears have been cropped or cut in any way shall be ineligible to compete at any show in any state where the laws prohibit the same except subject to the provisions of such laws.

SECTION 10. No dog shall be eligible to compete at any show, no dog shall be brought into the grounds or premises of any dog show, and any dog which may have been brought into the grounds or premises of a dog show shall immediately be removed, if it

(a) shows clinical symptoms of distemper, infectious hepatitis, leptospirosis or other communicable disease, or

(b) is known to have been in contact with distemper, infectious hepatitis, leptospirosis or other communicable disease within thirty days prior to the opening of the show, or

(c) has been kenneled within thirty days prior to the opening of the show on premises on which there existed distemper, infectious hepatitis, leptospirosis or other communicable disease.

SECTION 11. A club may engage dogs not entered in its show as a special attraction provided the written approval of The American Kennel Club is first obtained.

SECTION 12. No dog not regularly entered in a show, other than one engaged as a special attraction, shall be allowed within the show precincts, except when the club has stated in its premium list that space will be provided for dogs not entered in the show. The club must then provide an area, clearly identified by an appropriate sign. This area shall be exclusively for dogs which are either en route to or from other shows in which entered, or which are being delivered to new owners or custodians, or being returned to their owners. No dog may be placed in this area if it is entered in the show, nor unless it is registered or registrable and eligible to be shown under American Kennel Club rules and the standard for its breed.

An owner or agent who wishes to use this facility shall, upon entering the show, file with the Superintendent or Show Secretary a form giving the dog's registration data and the reason for its presence. The Superintendent or Show Secretary will then issue a tag identifying the dog. This tag is to be attached to the crate or container which the owner or agent must supply.

No one except owners or agents in charge of these dogs and show officials shall be admitted to the area, and there shall be no benching, nor any offering for sale, breeding, nor displaying of these dogs. Such dogs will not be permitted in any other part of the show precincts except for minimum periods when necessary for exercising, and then only when accompanied by the owners or their agents.

Dogs in this area shall be subject to all the rules relating to health and veterinarians. The Superintendent or Show Secretary shall be responsible for compliance with this rule.

SECTION 13. Any person acting in the capacity of Superintendent (or Show Secretary where there is no Superintendent), official veterinarian, or judge at a show, or any member of his immediate household or immediate family (as defined in Chapter 6, Section 6) shall not exhibit, act as agent or handler at the show, and dogs owned wholly or in part by him or by any member of his immediate household or immediate family shall be ineligible to be entered at that show.

SECTION 14. No entry shall be made at any show under a judge of any dog which said judge or any member of his immediate household or immediate family (as defined in Chapter 6, Section 6) has been known to have owned, handled in the ring more than twice, sold, held under lease or boarded within one year prior to the date of the show.

SECTION 15. Any show-giving club which accepts an entry fee other than that published in its premium list, or in any way discriminates between exhibitors or entrants, shall be disciplined. No show-giving club shall offer to any one owner or handler any special inducement, such as trophies, reduced entry fees, rebates, additional prize money, or any other concession, for entering more than one dog in the show.

SECTION 16. A Bench Show Committee may decline any entries or may remove any dog from its show for cause, but in each such instance shall file good and sufficient reasons for so doing with The American Kennel Club.

CHAPTER 17

THE CATALOG

SECTION 1. Every Bench Show Committee shall provide a printed catalog which shall contain all particulars required of exhibitors entering dogs as herinafter provided. It shall also contain the exact location of the show, the date or dates on which it is to be held, the times of opening and closing of the show, a list of all officers and members of the Bench Show Committee, names and complete addresses of all judges and of the Superintendent or Show Secretary, the names of the veterinarians or local veterinary association providing veterinary service at the show, and the names and addresses of all exhibitors.

SECTION 2. Every catalog must bear on its cover or title page: 'This show is held under American Kennel Club rules.'

SECTION 3. If the show shall be given by a club or association not a member of The American Kennel Club the words 'Licensed Show' must be plainly printed on the title page of the catalog.

SECTION 4. The catalog shall be in book form 6×9 inches in size. It shall contain the names and particulars of all dogs entered in the show, arranged as follows: catalog number; name of dog; AKC registration number, or litter number or 'ILP' number for an unregistered dog, or foreign registration number and country for an unregistered imported dog; date of birth; name of breeder; names of sire and dam; name of owner. The catalog shall either give the address of the owner immediately after the owner's name under the identifying information for each dog entered, or shall include a separate alphabetical list of exhibiting names and addresses. The entries shall be catalogued by groups, breeds, varieties, and regular classes, in the order given in Chapter 6. The information on dogs entered in any additional classes shall appear following the space provided for recording Winners Bitch and Reserve Winners Bitch followed by the particulars of those dogs entered for Best of Breed except that the entries in Brace, Team, Stud Dog, Brood Bitch, or any other classes in which the judge's decision is based on the merits of more than one dog shall appear following the list of dogs entered for Best of Breed and the space provided for Best of Breed, Best of Winners and Best of Opposite Sex awards. The particulars of those dogs entered for Exhibition Only shall appear following all other entries in the breed or variety.

Additional requirements for format and contents of the catalog may be prescribed by the Board of Directors.

SECTION 5. The schedule of points toward championship governing each breed in the show shall be published in the catalog.

SECTION 6. All prizes offered in the premium list of a show or in the separate list of prizes if the condensed form of premium list is used, shall be printed in the catalog, and no change shall be made in the descriptions or conditions of these prizes, nor shall any prize or trophy be added that was not offered in the premium list or in the separate list of prizes.

CHAPTER 18

BENCHING OF DOGS

SECTION 1. At a Benched Show to which admission is charged, every dog twelve months old and over that is entered and present must be on its bench throughout the advertised hours of the show's duration, except for the necessary periods when it is actually being prepared for showing at its crate, or is being shown, or is in the exercise ring, or is being taken to or from these places. The advertised hours of the show's duration shall be the hours from the scheduled start of judging to the time shown in the premium list for the closing of the show.

No such dog shall be in its crate during the advertised hours of the show's duration except by written permission of the Superintendent or Show Secretary, and except for a period of one hour before the time printed in the program for the judging of its breed or variety and, if it becomes eligible for its Group or for Best in Show, for a period of one hour before the time printed in the program for the judging of such competition.

SECTION 2. The provisions of Section 1 also apply to a dog under 12 months of age except that it need not be benched until after the judging of the breed classes for which it is entered or becomes eligible and it may be in its crate until the judging of those classes. At a two day show it is required to be present only on the day it is to be judged.

SECTION 3. Failure to comply with these rules may cause cancellation of the dog's winnings, and subject the owner, handler, and Superintendent or Show Secretary to a fine and suspension of license and privileges.

SECTION 4. No signs shall be displayed on a bench except the plaque or emblem of a show-giving specialty club to which the dog's owner belongs, and signs not over 11 × 14 inches offering dogs or puppies for sale, or giving the kennel name and address of the owner, or the dog's name and a list of awards won by it at that show, or the name of a show-giving specialty club of which the dog's owner is a member. No prizes or ribbons shall be displayed on the bench except those won by the dog at that show.

SECTION 5. At an Unbenched Show, a sign stating that the show is unbenched shall be prominently displayed wherever admission tickets are sold.

CHAPTER 19

MEASURING, WEIGHING AND COLOR DETERMINATIONS WHEN FACTORS OF DISQUALIFICATION IN BREED STANDARDS OR ELIGIBILITY UNDER THE CONDITIONS OF A CLASS OR DIVISION OF A CLASS. CANCELLATION OF AWARDS

SECTION 1. Every dog entered and present at a show must compete in all competitions in its breed or variety for which it is entered or becomes eligible, unless it has been excused, dismissed, disqualified or found to be ineligible, under the rules.

SECTION 2. Any club or association giving a dog show must provide arm cards and shall see that every person exhibiting a dog wears, when in the ring, an arm card containing thereon the catalog number of the dog being exhibited; but no badges, coats with kennel names thereon or ribbon prizes shall be worn or displayed, nor other visible means of identification used, by an individual when exhibiting a dog in the ring.

SECTION 3. In those breeds where certain heights are specified in the standard as disqualifications, or in any class the conditions of which include a height specification, the judge shall have the authority to make a determination as to whether any dog measures within the specified limits, provided such a determination has not been made previously during the competition at the show.

If, in the opinion of a competing exhibitor or handler then in the ring, the height of a dog under judgment appears not to be in accord with the breed standard or the conditions of the class, such exhibitor may, prior to the time the judge has marked his book, request that the judge make a determination as to whether the dog measures within the specified limits, and the judge shall comply with the request, provided such a determination has not been made previously during competition at the show.

In all cases, the judge shall use equipment that meets AKC requirements.

If the judge finds that the dog's height is in accord with the breed standard or the conditions of the class, he shall mark his judge's book 'Measured in.'

If the judge finds that the dog's height is not in accord with the breed standard, he shall disqualify the dog, marking his judge's book 'Measured out–disqualified.' A dog thus disqualified may not again be shown unless and until, following application by the owner to The American Kennel Club, the owner has received official notification from The American Kennel Club that the dog's show eligibility has been reinstated.

If the judge finds that the dog's height is not in accord with the conditions of the class, he shall declare the dog ineligible for the class, marking his judge's book 'Measured out–ineligible.' A dog thus declared ineligible for its class shall be considered to have been wrongly entered and cannot be transferred to any other class at the show. Such a dog may not be shown in that class at any subsequent show unless and until, following application by the owner to The American Kennel Club, the owner has received official notification from The American Kennel Club that the dog's show eligibility has been reinstated; however, without making such application to The American Kennel Club, the owner of such a dog may enter the dog in a class with different height specifications, provided he is satisfied that the dog measures within the height limits of that class.

SECTION 4. In those breeds where certain weights are specified in the standard as disqualifications, or in any class or division of a class the conditions of which include a weight specification, the judge shall have the authority to make a determination as to whether any dog weighs within the specified limits, provided such a determination has not been made previously during competition at the show.

If, in the opinion of a competing exhibitor or handler then in the ring, the weight of a dog under judgment appears to be not in accord with the breed standard or the conditions of the class or division in which it is competing, such exhibitor or handler may, prior to the time the judge has marked his book, request that the judge make a determination as to whether the dog weighs within the specified limits, and the judge shall comply with the request, provided such a determination has not been made previously during competition at the show.

In all cases, the judge shall use scales that meet AKC requirements.

If the judge finds that the dog's weight is in accord with the breed standard or the conditions of the class or division in which it is competing, he shall mark his judge's book 'Weighed in.'

If the judge finds that the dog's weight is not in accord with the breed standard he shall disqualify the dog, marking his judge's book 'Weighed out—disqualified.' A dog thus disqualified may not again be shown unless and until, following application to The American Kennel Club, the owner has received official notification from The American Kennel Club that the dog's show eligibility has been reinstated.

If the judge finds that the dog's weight is not in accord with the conditions of the class or division in which it is competing, he shall declare the dog ineligible for the class, marking his judge's book 'Weighed out—ineligible.' A dog thus declared ineligible for a class or division of a class shall be considered to have been wrongly entered and cannot be transferred to any other class or division at that show.

SECTION 5. Bench Show Committees shall be responsible for providing suitable equipment for determining eligibility with respect o height, and accurate scales at every show.

SECTION 6. In those breeds where certain colors or markings are specified in the standard as disqualifications, or in any class or division of a class where a certain color, or colors or combinations of colors are required by the conditions of the class or division thereof, it shall be the judge's responsibility to determine whether a dog is to be disqualified or declared to be ineligible for the class.

If, in the opinion of the judge, the dog's color or markings are such as to require disqualification, the judge shall disqualify the dog, making note of the fact in the judge's book.

If, in the opinion of the judge, the dog's color or markings do not meet the requirements of the class or division of a class in which the dog is competing, the judge shall declare the dog ineligible to compete in that class or division of class, making note of the fact in the judge's book.

If, in the opinion of any competing exhibitor or handler then in the ring, the color or markings or combination of colors of a dog under judgment are such as to disqualify under the standard or are such as not to meet the requirements of the class or division thereof, such exhibitor or handler may, prior to the time the judge has marked his book, request the judge to render an opinion of the dog's color(s) and markings. Before proceeding with the judging, the judge must write his opinion on an AKC form that will be supplied by the superintendent or show secretary for that purpose, and shall disqualify the dog if its color or markings are such as to require disqualification under the breed standard or shall declare the dog ineligible if the color or markings do not meet the requirements of the class or division thereof in which the dog is competing, in either case making note of the fact in the judge's book.

Any dog thus disqualified by the judge under the standard may not again be shown unless and until, following application by the owner to The American Kennel Club, the owner has received official notification from The American Kennel Club that the dog's show eligibility has been reinstated.

Any dog thus declared by the judge to be ineligible for a class or division thereof shall be considered to have been wrongly entered in the class and cannot be transferred to any other class or division at that show.

SECTION 7. If an ineligible dog has been entered in any licensed or member dog show, or if the name of the owner given on the entry form is not that of the person or persons who actually owned the dog at the time entries closed, or if shown in a class for which it has not been entered, or if its entry form is deemed invalid or unacceptable by The American Kennel Club under these rules, all resulting awards shall be cancelled by The American Kennel Club. In computing the championship points such ineligible dogs, whether or not they have received awards, shall be not counted as having competed.

SECTION 8. If the catalog and/or the judge's book of any show shall by error or mistake set forth any information contrary to the information which appears on the entry form of the dog for that show, the Bench Show Committee and/or the Superintendent of the show, upon request of the owner or handler of said dog prior to the judging, shall correct the entry in the judge's book and in the marked catalog to be sent to The American Kennel Club and said dog properly may compete in all classes and for all prizes for which its entry form discloses it was properly entered.

SECTION 9. If an award in any of the regular classes is cancelled, the dog judged next in order of merit shall be moved up and the award to the dog moved up shall be counted the same as if it had been the original award. If there is no dog of record to move up, the award shall be void.

SECTION 10. If the win of a dog shall be cancelled by The American Kennel Club the owner of the dog shall return all ribbons and prizes to the show-giving club within ten days of receipt of the notice of the cancellation from The American Kennel Club. The show-giving club shall in each instance of failure to comply with this rule notify The American Kennel Club of such failure and The American Kennel Club upon receipt of such notice forthwith shall suspend the exhibitor so in default from all privileges of The American Kennel Club and notify the exhibitor so in default that it has done so, and said suspension shall continue until The American Kennel Club is notified that restitution has been made.

CHAPTER 20

PROTESTS AGAINST DOGS

SECTION 1. Every exhibitor and handler shall have the right to request through the superintendent or show secretary the examination, by one of a show's veterinarians, of any dog within a show's premises which is considered to endanger the health of other dogs in a show. The request is to be in writing and on a form obtainable from a superintendent or show secretary, whose duty it will be to see that the subject dog is promptly taken to the 'Veterinarian Headquarters' by its owner or the owner's agent.

SECTION 2. A protest against a dog may be made by any exhibitor, entrant or any member of a member club of The American Kennel Club. It shall be in writing, and be lodged with the secretary of the show-giving club within seven (7) days of the last day of the show unless the same be made by The American Kennel Club, provided, however, that a protest calling for a decision as to the physical condition of a dog which can be determined only with the advice of a veterinarian or at the time of showing shall be made before the closing of the show.

No protest will be entertained unless accompanied by a deposit of five ($5.00) dollars, which will be returned if the protest is sustained. This does not apply to protests by The American Kennel Club, nor to a protest made in the ring previous to the rendering of his decision by the judge.

SECTION 3. If a protest shall be made during the holding of a show the bench show committee shall hold a meeting as soon as possible and give all parties concerned an opportunity to be heard and shall at once render its decision. If a protest shall be made subsequent to the show it shall be decided by the show-giving club within thirty (30) days of its receipt. Five days' notice of the date and place of hearing shall be given to all parties concerned. Written copies of all decisions on protests shall be forwarded immediately to The American Kennel Club.

SECTION 4. An appeal to The American Kennel Club from a decision of a bench show committee where a dog has been protested may be taken and shall be forwarded to The American Kennel Club within seven (7) days of the date on which the decision was rendered together with a deposit of ten ($10.00) dollars. If the decision be sustained the deposit shall be forfeited, but if reversed, the deposit shall be returned.

SECTION 5. Any person who is handling a competing dog in the ring in any breed competition may then verbally protest to the judge before the judge has marked any award in his book, alleging that a dog being shown in the competition has a condition which makes it ineligible to compete under Chapter 16, Section 9, or Chapter 16, Section 9-B, of these rules, or a condition requiring disqualification under the standard for the breed; except that a verbal protest alleging that the height or weight or natural color and markings of a dog requiring its disqualification under the breed standard or a determination of its ineligibility under the conditions of its class must be made under Chapter 19, Sections 3, 4 or 6.

When such a protest is made, the judge, before proceeding with the judging, must notify the superintendent or show secretary and must call an official show veterinarian to examine the dog in the ring and give the judge an advisory opinion, in writing, on the condition of the dog. Only after he has seen the veterinarian's opinion in writing shall the judge render his own decision and record it in the judge's book, marking the dog 'Disqualified' and stating the reason if he determines that disqualification is required under Chapter 16, Section 9, or under the breed standard.

If the judge, after seeing the veterinarian's written opinion, determines that the dog is ineligible to compete because of violation of Chapter 16, Section 9-B, he shall withhold any award to the dog and mark the judge's book 'Ineligible to compete award withheld,' stating the reason for his decision.

A dog determined by a judge to be ineligible to compete under Chapter 16, Section 9-B, unless such determination is based on the use of a substance only for cleaning purposes, may not again be shown until an official record has been made by The American Kennel Club of its true color or markings. If the color and markings of the dog as recorded are such as not to be a disqualification under the standard of its breed, the dog's show eligibility will be reinstated.

The written opinion of the veterinarian shall in all cases be forwarded to The American Kennel Club by the Superintendent or Show Secretary.

CHAPTER 21

CHAMPIONSHIPS

SECTION 1. Championship points will be recorded for Winners Dog and Winners Bitch, for each breed or variety listed in Chapter 6, Section 1, at licensed or member dog shows approved by The American Kennel Club, provided the certification of the Secretary as described in Chapter 9, Section 1, has been printed in the premium list for the show.

Championship points will be recorded according to the number of eligible dogs competing in the regular classes of each sex in each breed or variety, and according to the Schedule of Points established by the Board of Directors. In counting the number of eligible dogs in competition, a dog that is disqualified, or that is dismissed, excused or ordered from the ring by the Judge, or from which all awards are withheld, shall not be included.

SECTION 2. A dog which in its breed competition at a show shall have been placed Winners and which also shall have won its group class at the same show shall be awarded championship points figured at the highest point rating of any breed or recognized variety of height of any breed entered in the show and entitled to winners points in its group, or if it also shall have been designated Best in Show, shall be awarded championship points figured at the highest point rating of any breed or recognized variety or height of any breed entered and entitled to winners points in the show. The final points to be awarded under this section shall not be in addition to but inclusive of any points previously awarded the dog in its breed competition or under the provisions of this section.

SECTION 3. At shows in which the winners' classes of certain breeds are divided into recognized varieties of those breeds as specified in Section 1 of Chapter 6 of these Rules and Regulations, the procedure for computing championship points shall be the same as if each recognized variety were a separate breed.

SECTION 4. Any dog which shall have won fifteen points shall become a Champion of Record, if six or more of said points shall have been won at two shows with a rating of three or more championship points each and under two different judges, and some one or more of the balance of said points shall have been won under some other judge or judges than the two judges referred to above. A dog becomes a champion when it is so officially recorded by The American Kennel Club and when registered in the Stud Book shall be entitled to a championship certificate.

SECTION 5. Any dog which has been awarded the title of Champion of Record may be designated as a 'Dual Champion' after it also has been awarded the title of Field Champion, but no certificate will be awarded for a Dual Championship.

CHAPTER 22
SUBMISSION OF A SHOW'S RECORDS TO AKC

SECTION 1. A show-giving club shall pay or distribute all prizes offered at its show within thirty (30) days after The American Kennel Club has checked the awards of said show.

SECTION 2. After each licensed or member club dog show a catalog marked with all awards and absent dogs, certified to by the superintendent or show secretary of the show, together with all judges' books, all original entry forms and a report of the show must be sent to The American Kennel Club so as to reach its office within seven (7) days after the close of the show. Penalty for noncompliance, one ($1.00) dollar for each day's delay and such other penalties as may be imposed by the Board of Directors of The American Kennel Club. All recording fees shall be paid to The American Kennel Club within seven (7) days after the close of the show.

CHAPTER 23
STEWARDS

The following policy has been adopted by the Board of Directors regarding stewarding at dog shows:

Clubs should appoint a chief steward well in advance of the date of their show whose duty it will be to invite a sufficient number of experienced persons to act as stewards in the judging rings on the day of the show. No person should be asked to serve as a steward whose judging or handling privileges are suspended or whose superintending privileges have been revoked. The chief steward should, as soon as practicable, confirm in writing, to each person who accepts an invitation to steward, the date and location of the show, the time at which they are to report for duty, and their particular ring assignment.

In preparing the schedule of ring assignments, the chief steward and other club officials should keep in mind that no person should serve as a steward with a judge under whom he has an entry, or under whom, in the course of the day's judging, such entry may become eligible to compete. If it becomes necessary during the show to reshuffle stewarding assignments, care should be taken to see that a person is not assigned to serve as steward with a judge if there is any possibility that the judge, later in the the show, will be passing upon an entry of the steward.

Persons should be selected who are familiar with judging procedure, breed classifications and rules. It should be borne in mind that a good steward makes the work of judging easier by relieving the judge of necessary detail; by assembling classes promptly, he will be able to keep the judging program on schedule and eliminate to a large extent delays between classes.

The chief steward should use his discretion in the assigning of more than one steward to a ring, but it is advisable that two stewards be asked to serve in those rings where judges have heavy assignments.

Stewards will notify the judge when all the dogs are in the ring for each class and call his attention to known absentees. Under no circumstances should a steward make any notation in the judge's book or erase or strike out any notation made by the judge.

Stewards will be responsible for returning to the chief steward or superintendent upon the completion of the judging all prize money, trophies and ribbons not awarded.

Stewards should have in mind that they have been selected to help the judge and not to advise him. They should carefully refrain from discussing or seeming to discuss the dogs or the exhibitors with the judge and should not, under any circumstances, show or give the appearance of showing the catalog to a judge. Stewards should not take or seem to take any part in judging. When they are not actively engaged in their duties, they should place themselves in such part of the rings as will not interfere with the view of those watching the judging, and should not permit persons to crowd about the ring entrance and interfere with access to the ring.

The foregoing policy should be observed by clubs holding member and licensed obedience trials, in addition to the applicable obedience regulations and the practices established for persons stewarding in obedience rings.

EXTRACTS FROM BY-LAWS

CHAPTER 24

DISCIPLINE

Article XII of the Constitution and By-Laws of The American Kennel Club provides:

SECTION 1. Any club or association or persons or persons interested in pure-bred dogs may prefer charges against any·other club or association, or person or persons, for conduct alleged to have been prejudicial to the best interests of pure-bred dogs, dog shows, obedience trials or field trials, or prejudicial to the best interests of The American Kennel Club, which charges shall be made in writing in duplicate setting forth in detail the nature thereof, shall be signed and sworn to by an officer of the club or association or by the person or persons making the same before some person qualified to administer oaths and shall be sent to The American Kennel Club together with a deposit of ten ($10,00) dollars, which sum shall become the property of The American Kennel Club if said charges shall not be sustained, or shall be returned if said charges are sustained, or if The American Kennel Club shall refuse to entertain jurisdiction thereof.

SECTION 2. The bench show, obedience trial or field trial committee of a club or association shall have the right to suspend any person from the privileges of The American Kennel Club for conduct prejudicial to the best interest of pure-bred dogs, dog shows, obedience trials, field trials or The American Kennel Club, alleged to have occurred in connection with or during the progress of its show, obedience trial or field trial, after the alleged offender has been given an opportunity to be heard.

Notice in writing must be sent promptly by registered mail by the bench show, obedience trial or field trial committee to the person suspended and a duplicate notice giving the name and address of the person suspended and full details as to the reasons for the suspension must be forwarded to The American Kennel Club within seven days.

An appeal may be taken from a decision of a bench show, obedience trial or field trial committee. Notice in writing claiming such appeal together with a deposit of five ($5.00) dollars must be sent to The American Kennel Club within thirty days after the date of suspension. The Board of Directors may itself hear said appeal or may refer it to a committee of the Board, or to a Trial Board to be heard. The deposit shall become the property of The American Kennel Club if the decision is confirmed, or shall be returned to the appellant if the decision is not confirmed.

SECTION 3. Upon receipt of duly preferred charges the Board of Directors of The American Kennel Club at its election either may itself consider the same or send the same to a Trial Board for hearing.

In either case a notice which shall state that said charges have been filed and shall set forth a copy of the same shall be sent to the club or association, or person or persons against which or whom said charges have been preferred, which club or association, or person or persons herein shall be known as and called the defendant. The club or association or person or persons which or who shall have preferred said charges herein shall be known as and called the complainant.

Said notice also shall set forth a time and place at which the defendant may attend and present any defense or answer which the defendant may wish to make.

If the complainant shall fail or refuse to appear and prosecute said charges or if the defendant shall fail or refuse to appear and present a defense at the time and place designated for the hearing of said charges, without giving a reasonable excuse for such failure or refusal, the Board of Directors or the Trial Board to which said charges have been referred may suspend whichever party shall be so in default from the privileges of The American Kennel Club for a period of six months or until such time as the party so in default shall be prepared to appear ready and willing to prosecute or defend said charges, as the case may be.

SECTION 4. The Board of Directors shall have the power to investigate any matters which may be brought to its attention in connection with the objects for which this Club was founded, or it may appoint a committee or Trial Board to investigate, in which event the same procedure shall be followed and the same rules shall apply as in a trial before a Trial Board.

If after such investigation the Board of Directors believes that sufficient evidence exists to warrant the filing of charges, it may file or direct the filing of such charges. The Board of Directors acting in accordance with the provisions of this Article may prefer charges for conduct prejudicial to the best interests of The American Kennel Club against persons who shall bring to its attention any matter which upon investigation shall be found to have been reported to it from malicious or untruthful motives or to have been based upon suspicion without foundation of fact or knowledge.

SECTION 5. The Board of Directors of The American Kennel Club shall have power to prefer charges against any association or other club, or person or persons, for conduct alleged to be prejudicial to pure-bred dogs, dog shows, obedience trials or field trials or to the best interests of The American Kennel Club, and pending the final determination of any such charges, may withhold the privileges of The American Kennel Club from any such other person or body against whom charges are pending.

SECTION 6. The Board of Directors shall have the power to suspend from the privileges of The American Kennel Club any member or delegate pending final action by the delegates in accordance with the provisions of this section, for conduct alleged to have been prejudicial to the best interest of The American Kennel Club or for violation of its constitution, by-laws or rules.

The Board of Directors shall then file charges and promptly set a date for a hearing and send to such suspended member or delegate by registered mail at least ten days prior to the date so fixed, notice of the time when and the place where the suspended member or delegate may be heard in its or his defense. Said notice shall also set forth a copy of the charges.

The Board of Directors may itself hear the evidence of the suspended member or delegate and any witnesses or may refer the charges to a committee of the Board or to a Trial Board to take the testimony and to report its findings or recommendations to the Board of Directors.

The Board of Directors, after hearing or reviewing the evidence, shall report its findings to The American Kennel Club at the next regular meeting of the Club, whereupon the delegates shall take action upon said findings and by a majority vote of the delegates present may reinstate, continue the suspension for a stated time or expel such member or delegate from The American Kennel Club.

SECTION 7. The American Kennel Club shall have the power by a two-thirds vote of the Delegates present and voting at any regular meeting to suspend from the privileges of The American Kennel Club any member or delegate for conduct alleged to have been prejudicial to the best interests of The American Kennel Club or for violation of its constitution, by-laws or rules.

The order of suspension thus made shall then be referred to the Board of Directors for hearing and report under the procedure as set forth in Paragraphs 2, 3 and 4 of Section 6 of this article.

SECTION 8. The Board of Directors of The American Kennel Club shall have power to hear as an original matter any charges preferred and to review and finally determine any appeal which may be made to the Board of Directors from the decision of a Trial Board or Bench Show, Obedience Trial or Field Trial Committee, and in each instance in which it shall find the charges to have been sustained, it shall impose such penalty as said Board of Directors may decide to be just and proper.

SECTION 9. The Board of Directors of The American Kennel Club and any Trial Board of The American Kennel Club with the permission of the Board of Directors of The American Kennel Club first obtained in writing, may in the discretion of said Board of Directors, and if necessary at the Club's expense, summon witnesses or a member of any Trial Board, Bench Show Committee, Obedience Trial Committee or Field Trial Committee to attend any and all hearings held under the provisions of Articles XII and XIII of the Constitution and By-Laws of The American Kennel Club. Said Board of Directors may suspend from the privileges of The American Kennel Club for a period of six months or until such time as he or she shall appear and be prepared and willing to testify any person so summoned who without reasonable excuse shall fail to appear and testify.

SECTION 10. The Board of Directors of The American Kennel Club shall, at the next meeting of the Board after an appeal is made from the decision of a Trial Board or Bench Show, Obedience Trial or Field Trial Committee, name a date for the hearing of such appeal and shall cause notice of the time when and place where said hearing is to be held to be sent to all parties in interest by registered mail at least fourteen (14) days prior to the date named.

SECTION 11. Penalties may range from a reprimand or fine to suspension for life from all privileges of The American Kennel Club.

SECTION 12. The Treasurer of The American Kennel Club shall enforce all monetary penalties.

SECTION 13. The suspension or disqualification of a person shall date from the day of the perpetration of the act or from any date subsequent thereto which shall be fixed after hearing by a Trial Board or by the Board of Directors of The American Kennel Club and shall apply to all dogs owned or subsequently acquired by the person so suspended or disqualified.

SECTION 14. All privileges of The American Kennel Club shall be withheld from any person suspended or disqualified.

SECTION 15. Any club, association or organization which shall hold a dog show, obedience trial, field trial or dog exhibition of any kind not in accordance with the rules of The American Kennel Club which apply to such show, obedience trial, field trial or exhibition may be disciplined even to the extent of being deprived of all privileges of The American Kennel Club for a stated period of time or indefinitely, and if such club, association or organization shall be a member of the American Kennel Club, it may be expelled from membership therein.

SECTION 16. No Club or association licensed by The American Kennel Club to give a show, obedience trial, hold a field trial or give a dog exhibition of any kind shall employ in any capacity, accept the donation of a prize or money from, or permit to be within the walls or boundaries of its building or grounds, if a dog show or obedience trial, or its grounds, if a field trial, save only as a spectator, any person known to be under suspension or disqualification from the privileges of The American Kennel Club or any employee or member of a corporation which shall be under suspension or disqualification from the privileges of The American Kennel Club. And any contract for floor space at a show, or contract for advertising space in a catalog, premium list or other printed matter, in connection with the giving of said show, shall bear upon it the following condition: 'This space is sold with the understanding that should the privileges of The American Kennel Club be withdrawn from the purchaser of this space prior to the carrying out of this contract, this contract is thereby automatically cancelled, and any money paid by the purchaser for such space shall be refunded.'

SECTION 17. No member club or association under suspension shall be represented by its delegate and no delegate under suspension shall act for a member or in any official capacity for The American Kennel Club during the period of suspension.

SECTION 18. Any association, club, person or persons suspended or disqualified by The American Kennel Club or from whom the privileges of The American Kennel Club have been withheld, may apply for reinstatement or restoration of privileges upon paying a fee, the amount of which may be fixed and determined by the Board of Directors of The American Kennel Club. Until said fee has been paid the application shall not be acted upon.

SECTION 19. As much of Article XII of these By-Laws as the Board of Directors of The American Kennel Club shall indicate shall be printed in any book or pamphlet which The American Kennel Club shall cause to be published containing the Rules of said Club.

CHAPTER 25

TRIAL BOARDS

Article XIII of the Constitution and By-Laws of The American Kennel Club provides:

SECTION 1. Trial Boards shall be appointed from time to time by the Board of Directors of The American Kennel Club and shall consist of three members for each Board, one of whom, if practicable, should be an attorney-at-law, and no one of whom shall be a director of The American Kennel Club. In case one or more members of a Trial Board shall be unable to sit in any given case, the President, or in his absence, the Executive Vice-President of The American Kennel Club, may appoint a substitute or substitutes for such case. In case of the absence of one or more members of said Board, the remaining member or members may hear and determine a case if the parties being heard shall consent thereto.

SECTION 2. Trial Boards shall hear and decide by a majority vote matters submitted to them by the Board of Directors and shall have power to impose a fine not to exceed twenty-five ($25.00) dollars and/or withhold the privileges of the Club for a period of not more than six months, or may recommend to said Board of Directors the withholding of privileges for a longer period or may recommend disqualification or the imposition of fines exceeding twenty-five ($25.00) dollars.

If a Trial Board recommends the withholding of privileges or disqualification to the Board of

Directors, the privileges of the Club shall be automatically withheld until the Board of Directors has adopted or refused to adopt such recommendation.

SECTION 3. Trial Boards shall have power to disqualify any person or withhold from any person all the privileges of The American Kennel Club for a period of not more than six months or to recommend to said Board of Directors the penalty of disqualification or the withholding of privileges for a longer period for improper or disorderly conduct during a hearing or a trial.

SECTION 4. Trial Boards shall keep minutes of their sittings.

SECTION 5. The decisions of Trial Boards shall be in writing signed by all members attending, and have annexed thereto all exhibits and papers offered before them. Each decision, together with complete copies of the minutes and testimony taken, shall be filed with the Secretary of The American Kennel Club within ten days of the date of the rendering of the decision. It shall be the duty of the Secretary of The American Kennel Club, when received, at once to notify in writing all parties in interest of the decision of a Trial Board.

SECTION 6. An appeal may be taken to the Board of Directors from any decision of a Trial Board, whether it be a decision in which the Trial Board itself imposes a certain penalty and/or fine, or one in which the Trial Board recommends that the Board of Directors shall impose a certain penalty and/or fine. Notice in writing claiming such appeal together with a deposit of twenty-five ($25.00) dollars must be sent to The American Kennel Club within thirty days after the receipt of the notice of the decision or recommendation of the Trial Board. The Board of Directors may itself hear said appeal or may refer it to a committee of the Board to be heard. The deposit of twenty-five ($25.00) dollars shall become the property of The American Kennel Club if the decision or recommendation of the Trial Board shall be confirmed, or shall be returned to the appellant if it shall not be confirmed. If the aggrieved party shall fail to take such appeal to the Board of Directors, there shall be no further right of appeal of any kind.

SECTION 7. Article XIII of these By-Laws shall be printed in any book or pamphlet which The American Kennel Club shall cause to be published containing the Rules of said club.

KENNEL CLUB
FIRST TWENTY BREEDS IN REGISTRATION ORDER
FOR THE YEARS 1968–75

	1968
1. Alsatians	14,958
2. Retrievers (Labrador)	12,544
3. Yorkshire Terriers	8,842
4. Poodles (Toy)	8,150
5. Poodles (Min.)	6,536
6. Spaniels (Cocker)	5,944
7. Shetland Sheepdogs	5,715
8. Collies (Rough)	5,064
9. Welsh Corgis (Pembroke)	4,593
10. Boxers	4,374
11. Retrievers (Golden)	4,251
12. West Highland White Terriers	4,160
13. Pekingese	3,980
14. Cairn Terriers	3,862
15. Beagles	3,841
16. Dalmatians	3,218
17. Dachshunds Min. (Smooth-Hrd)	2,745
18. Cavalier King Charles Spaniels	2,638
19. Basset Hounds	2,510
20. Chihuahuas (Smooth Coat)	2,502

	1969
1. Alsatians	16,546
2. Retrievers (Labrador)	14,498
3. Yorkshire Terriers	10,212
4. Poodles (Toy)	7,671
5. Spaniels (Cocker)	6,465
6. Poodles (Min.)	5,986
7. Shetland Sheepdogs	5,872
8. Collies (Rough)	5,736
9. West Highland White Terriers	4,837
10. Retrievers (Golden)	4,751
11. Boxers	4,457
12. Welsh Corgis (Pembroke)	4,165
13. Cairn Terriers	4,001
14. Beagles	3,979
15. Pekingese	3,890
16. Dalmatians	2,916
17. Cavalier King Charles Spaniels	2,899
18. Dachshunds Min. (Smooth-Hrd)	2,774
19. Chihuahuas (Smooth Coat)	2,714
20. Basset Hounds	2,679
Irish Setters	2,679

	1970
1. Alsatians	16,834
2. Labrador Retrievers	14,827
3. Yorkshire Terriers	11,016
4. Toy Poodles	7,926
5. Cocker Spaniels	7,121
6. Rough Collies	6,086
7. Shetland Sheepdogs	5,970
8. Miniature Poodles	5,291
9. Golden Retrievers	5,189
10. West Highland White Terriers	4,933

	1970 Contd.
11. Pekingese	4,243
12. Boxers	4,230
13. Pembroke Welsh Corgis	3,897
14. Cairn Terriers	3,860
15. Beagles	3,445
16. Irish Setters	3,277
17. Cavalier King Charles Spaniels	3,192
18. English Springer Spaniels	2,894
19. Smooth-Haired Miniature Dachshunds	2,872
20. Afghan Hounds	2,853

	1971
1. Alsatians	13,857
2. Labrador Retrievers	11,967
3. Yorkshire Terriers	10,577
4. Cocker Spaniels	6,825
5. Toy Poodles	6,362
6. Rough Collies	5,750
7. Shetland Sheepdogs	5,160
8. Golden Retrievers	4,766
9. Miniature Poodles	4,497
10. West Highland White Terriers	4,097
11. Pekingese	3,853
12. Irish Setters	3,764
13. Boxers	3,727
14. Afghan Hounds	3,606
15. Cavalier King Charles Spaniels	3,562
16. Beagles	3,209
17. Cairn Terriers	3,163
18. Pembroke Welsh Corgis	2,979
19. Old English Sheepdogs	2,896
20. Basset Hounds	2,837

	1972
1. Alsatians	15,078
2. Labrador Retrievers	13,880
3. Yorkshire Terriers	12,832
4. Cocker Spaniels	8,255
5. Poodles (Toy)	6,941
6. Rough Collies	6,597
7. Golden Retrievers	5,760
8. Shetland Sheepdogs	5,705
9. Irish Setters	4,792
10. Poodles (Miniature)	4,692
11. Pekingese	4,611
12. West Highland White Terriers	4,510
13. Cavalier Kind Charles Spaniels	4,471
14. Afghan Hounds	4,397
15. Boxers	3,984
16. English Springer Spaniels	3,658
17. Cairn Terriers	3,493
18. Old English Sheepdogs	3,188
19. Pembroke Welsh Corgis	3,180
20. Basset Hounds	3,173

	1973	
1.	Alsatians	15,185
2.	Yorkshire Terriers	13,780
3.	Retrievers (Labrador)	13,505
4.	Spaniels (Cocker)	8,193
5.	Poodles (Toy)	6,616
6.	Collies (Rough)	6,211
7.	Retrievers (Golden)	5,913
8.	Irish Setters	5,438
9.	Shetland Sheepdogs	5,328
10.	Cavalier King Charles Spaniels	5,071
11.	Afghan Hounds	4,820
12.	West Highland White Terriers	4,472
13.	Pekingese	4,313
14.	Poodles (Miniature)	4,104
15.	Boxers	4,039
16.	Old English Sheepdogs	3,976
17.	Spaniels (English Springer)	3,781
18.	Cairn Terriers	3,336
19.	Welsh Corgis (Pembroke)	2,936
20.	Basset Hounds	2,875

	1974	
1.	Yorkshire Terriers	15,147
2.	Alsatians	14,936
3.	Retrievers (Labrador)	12,849
4.	Spaniels (Cocker)	8,254
5.	Collies (Rough)	6,535
6.	Retrievers (Golden)	6,107
7.	Poodles (Toy)	6,086
8.	Cavalier King Charles Spaniels	5,795
9.	Irish Setters	5,590
10.	Shetland Sheepdogs	5,331

	1974 contd.	
11.	Old English Sheepdogs	4,921
12.	Afghan Hounds	4,890
13.	West Highland White Terriers	4,630
14.	Pekingese	4,491
15.	Spaniels (English Springer)	4,333
16.	Boxers	4,162
17.	Poodles (Miniature)	3,980
18.	Cairn Terriers	3,358
19.	Beagles	2,686
20.	Welsh Corgis (Pembroke)	2,621

	1975	
1.	Yorkshire Terriers	14,640
2.	Alsatians	11,357
3.	Retrievers (Labrador)	10,939
4.	Spaniels (Cocker)	7,210
5.	Retrievers (Golden)	5,950
6.	Cavalier King Charles Spaniels	5,407
7.	Collies (Rough)	5,395
8.	Poodles (Toy)	5,174
9.	Irish Setters	4,898
10.	Old English Sheepdogs	4,640
11.	Spaniels (English Springer)	4,472
12.	Shetland Sheepdogs	4,282
13.	West Highland White Terriers	3,913
14.	Afghan Hounds	3,867
15.	Pekingese	3,733
16.	Boxers	3,527
17.	Poodles (Miniature)	2,941
18.	Cairn Terriers	2,864
19.	Dobermanns	2,265
20.	Dachshunds (Miniature Long Haired)	2,103

CRUFT'S BEST IN SHOW WINNERS

Until 1928, there was no award of Best in Show at Cruft's. Since that time, the following dogs have gained this award:

1928 Greyhound PRIMLEY SCEPTRE, H. Whitley.

1929 Scottish Terrier HEATHER NECESSITY, E. Chapman.

1930 Cocker Spaniel LUCKYSTAR OF WARE, H. S. Lloyd.

1931 Cocker Spaniel LUCKYSTAR OF WARE, H. S. Lloyd.

1932 Labrador Retriever BRAMSHAW BOB, Lorna Countess Howe.

1933 Labrador Retriever BRAMSHAW BOB, Lorna Countess Howe.

1934 Greyhound SOUTHBALL MOONSTONE, B. Hartland Worden.

1935 Pointer PENINE PRIMA DONNA, A. Eggleston.

1936 Chow Chow CH. CHOONAN HUNG KWONG, Mrs V. A. M. Mannooch.

1937 Labrador Retriever CH. CHEVERELLA BEN OF BANCHORY, Lorna Countess Howe.

1938 Cocker Spaniel EXQUISITE MODEL OF WARE, H. S. Lloyd.

1939 Cocker Spaniel EXQUISITE MODEL OF WARE, H. S. Lloyd.

1948 Cocker Spaniel TRACEY WITCH OF WARE, H. S. Lloyd.

1950 Cocker Spaniel TRACEY WITCH OF WARE, H. S. Lloyd.

1951 Welsh Terrier TWYNSTAR BYMA-FI, Capt and Mrs I. M. Thomas.

1952 Bulldog CH. NOWAYS CHUCKLES, J. T. Barnard.

1953 Great Dane CH. ELCH ELDER OF OURBOROUGH, W. G. Siggers.

1954 (Cancelled).

1955 Poodle CH. TAIGANE AGGRI OF NASHEND, Mrs A. Proctor.

1956 Greyhound TREETOPS GOLDEN FALCON, Mrs W. de Casembroot and Miss H. Greenish.

1957 Keeshond CH. VOLRIJK OF VORDEN, Mrs I. M. Tucker.

1958 Pointer CH. CHIMING BELLS, Mrs W. Parkinson.

1959 Welsh Terrier CH. SANDSTORM SARACEN, Mes Leach and Thomas.

1960 Irish Wolfhound SULHAMSTEAD MERMAN, Mrs Nagle and Miss Clark.

1961 Airedale Terrier CH. RIVERINA TWEEDSBAIRN, Miss P. McCaughey and Mrs D. Schuth.

1962 Wire Fox Terrier CH. CRACKWYN COCKSPUR, H. L. Gill.
1963 Lakeland Terrier ROGERHOLM RECRUIT, W. Rogers.
1964 English Setter SH. CH. SILBURY SOAMES OF MADAVALE, Mrs A. Williams.
1965 Alsatian (G.S.D.) CH. FENTON OF KENTWOOD, Miss S. H. Godden.
1966 Toy Poodle OAKINGTON PUCKSHILL AMBER SUNBLUSH, Mrs C. E. Perry.
*1967 Lakeland Terrier CH. STINGRAY OF DERRYABAH, Mr and Mrs W. Postlethwaite.
1968 Dalmatian CH. FANHILL FAUNE, Mrs E. J. Woodyatt.
1969 Alsatian (G.S.D.) CH. HENDRAWEN'S NIBELUNG OF CHARAVIGNE, Mr and Mrs E. J. White.
1970 Pyrenean Mountain Dog BERGERIE KNUR, Mr and Mrs F. S. Prince.
1971 Alsatian (G.S.D.) CH. RAMACON SWASHBUCKLER, Prince Ahmed Husain.
1972 Bull Terrier CH. ABRASEAS AUDACITY, Miss V. Drummond-Wick.
1973 Cavalier King Charles Spaniel ALANSUEHE AQUARIUS, Messrs A. Hall and J.Evans.
1974 St. Bernard CH. BURTONSWOOD BOSSYBOOTS, Miss Hinde.
1975 Wire Fox Terrier CH. BROOKWIRE BRANDY OF LAYVEN, Messrs Benelli and Dondina.
1976 West Highland White Terrier CH. DIANTHUS BUTTON, Mrs K. Newstead.

* The only dog to win Cruft's and Westminster, the latter the following year.

WESTMINSTER BEST IN SHOW WINNERS

1936 Sealyham Terrier, CH. ST. MARGARET MAGNIFICENT OF CLAIREDALE, Clairedale Kennels.
1937 Fox Terrier (Wire) CH. FLORNELL SPICY PIECE OF HALLESTON, Halleston Kennels.
1938 English Setter CH. DARO OF MARIDOR, Maridor Kennels.
1939 Doberman Pinscher CH. FERRY V. RAUHFELSEN OF GIRALDA, Giralda Farms.
1940 Cocker Spaniel CH. MY OWN BRUCIE, H. E. Mellenthin.
1941 Cocker Spaniel CH. MY OWN BRUCIE, H. E. Mellenthin.
1942 West Highland White Terrier CH. WOLVEY PATTERN OF EDGERSTOUNE, Mrs. J. G. Winant.
1943 Miniature Poodle CH. PITTER PATTER OF PIPERSCROFT, Mrs. P. H. B. Frelinghuysen.
1944 Welsh Terrier CH. FLORNELL RARE-BIT OF TWIN PONDS, Mrs. Edward P. Alker.
1945 Scottish Terrier CH. SHIELING'S SIGNATURE, Mr. and Mrs. T. H. Snethen.
1946 Fox Terrier (Wire) CH. HETHERINGTON MODEL RHYTHM, Mr and Mrs T. H. Carruthers, III.
1947 Boxer CH. WARLORD OF MAZELAINE, Mr and Mrs Richard C. Kettles, Jr.
1948 Bedlington Terrier CH. ROCK RIDGE NIGHT ROCKET, Mr and Mrs William A. Rockefeller.
1949 Boxer CH. MAZELAINE ZAZARAC BRANDY, Mr and Mrs John Phelps Wagner.
1950 Scottish Terrier CH. WALSING WINNING TRICK OF EDGERSTOUNE, Mrs J. G. Winant.
1951 Boxer CH. BANG AWAY OF SIRRAH CREST, Dr and Mrs R. C. Harris.
1952 Doberman Pinscher CH. RANCHO DOBE'S STORM, Mr and Mrs Len Carey.
1953 Doberman Pinscher CH. RANCHO DOBE'S STORM, Mr and Mrs Len Carey.
1954 Cocker Spaniel CH. CARMOR'S RISE AND SHINE, Mrs Carl E. Morgan.
1955 Bulldog CH. KIPPAX FEARNOUGHT, John A. Saylor, M.D.
1956 Toy Poodle CH. WILBUR WHITE SWAN, Bertha Smith.
1957 Afghan Hound CH. SHIRKHAN OF GRANDEUR, Sunny Shay and Dorothy Chenade.
1958 Standard Poodle CH. PUTTENCOVE PROMISE, Puttencove Kennels.
1959 Miniature Poodle CH. FRONTCLAIR FESTOON, Dunwalke Kennels.
1960 Pekingese CH. CHIK T'SUN OF CAVERSHAM, Mr and Mrs C. C. Venable.
1961 Toy Poodle CH. CAPPOQUIN LITTLE SISTER, Miss Florence Michelson.
1962 West Highland White Terrier CH. ELFINBROOK SIMON, Wishing Well Kennels.
1963 English Springer Spaniel CH. WAKEFIELD'S BLACK KNIGHT, Mrs W. J. S. Borie.
1964 Whippet CH. COURTENAY FLEETFOOT OF PENNYWORTH, Pennyworth Kennels.
1965 Scottish Terrier CH. CARMICHAELS FANFARE, Mr and Mrs Charles C. Stalter.
1966 Fox Terrier (Wire) CH. ZELOY MOOREMAIDE'S MAGIC, Marion G. Bunker.
1967 Scottish Terrier CH. BARDENE BINGO, E. H. Stuart.
*1968 Lakeland Terrier CH. STINGRAY OF DERRYABAH, Mr and Mrs James A. Farrell, Jr.
1969 Skye Terrier CH. GLAMOOR GOOD NEWS, Walter F. Goodman and Mrs Adele F. Goodman.
1970 Boxer CH. ARRIBA'S PRIMA DONNA, Dr and Mrs P. J. Pagano and Dr Theodore S. Fickes.
1971 English Springer Spaniel CH. CHINOE'S ADAMANT JAMES, Milton E. Prickett.
1972 English Springer Spaniel CH. CHINOE'S ADAMANT JAMES, Milton E. Prickett.
1973 Standard Poodle CH. ACADIA COMMAND PERFORMANCE, Edward B. Jenner and Jo Ann Sering.
1974 German Short Pointer CH. GRETCHENOF COLUMBIA RIVER, Dr Richard Smith.

* Won Cruft's the previous year.

KENNEL CLUB CLASSIFICATION AND REGISTRATION OF BREEDS

SPORTING BREEDS

Hound Group
Afghan Hounds
Basenjis
Basset Hounds
Bassets Griffons Vendeen
Beagles
Bloodhounds
Borzois
Dachsbracke
Dachshunds (Long-Haired)
Dachshunds
(Miniature Long-Haired)
Dachshunds (Smooth-Haired)
Dachshunds
(Miniature Smooth-Haired)
Dachshunds (Wire-Haired)
Dachshunds
(Miniature Wire-Haired)
Deerhounds
Elkhounds
Finnish Spitz
Foxhounds
Greyhounds
Ibizan Hounds
Irish Wolfhounds
Otterhounds
Pharaoh Hounds
Portuguese Warren Hounds
Rhodesian Ridgebacks
Salukis
Sloughis
Swedish Foxhounds
Swiss Laufhunds (Jura)
Whippets

Gundog Group
English Setters
English Springer Spaniels
Field Spaniels
Flat Coated Retrievers
German Long haired Pointers
German Short haired Pointers
German Wire haired Pointers
Gordon Setters
Hungarian Vizslas
Irish Setters
Italian Spinones
Large Munsterlanders
Pointers
Pointing Wire-Haired Griffons
Retriever (Chesapeake Bay)
Retriever (Curly-Coated)
Retriever (Flat-Coated)
Retriever (Golden)
Retriever (Labrador)
Small Munsterlanders
Spaniel (American Cocker)
Spaniel (Clumber)
Spaniel (Cocker)
Spaniel (English Springer)
Spaniel (Field)
Spaniel (Irish Water)
Spaniel (Sussex)
Spaniel (Welsh Springer)
Sussex Spaniels
Weimaraners
Welsh Springer Spaniels

Terrier Group
Airedale Terriers
Australian Terriers
Bedlington Terriers
Border Terriers
Bull Terriers
Bull Terriers (Miniature)
Cairn Terriers
Dandie Dinmont Terriers
Glen of Imaal Terriers
Fox Terrier (Smooth)
Fox Terrier (Wire)
Irish Terriers
Soft-Coloured Wheaten Terriers
Staffordshire Bull Terriers
Kerry Blue Terriers
Lakeland Terriers
Manchester Terriers
Norfolk Terriers
Norwich Terriers
Scottish Terriers
Sealyham Terriers
Skye Terriers
Welsh Terriers
West Highland White Terriers

NON-SPORTING BREEDS

Utility Group
Boston Terriers
Bulldogs
Canaan Dogs
Chow Chows
Dalmatians
French Bulldogs
Giant Schnauzers
Iceland Dogs
Japanese Akitas
Keeshonds
Leonbergers
Lhasa Apsos
Mexican Hairless
Miniature Schnauzers
Poodles (Standard)
Poodles (Miniature)
Poodles (Toy)
Schipperkes
Schnauzers
Shih Tzus
Tibetan Spaniels
Tibetan Terriers

Working Group
Alaskan Malamutes
Alsatians (German Shepherd Dogs)
Anatolian (Karabash) Dogs
Australian Kelpies
Bearded Collies
Beaucerons
Belgian Shepherd Dogs
(Groendaels)
Belgian Shepherd Dogs
(Tervuerens)
Bernese Mountain Dogs
Bouviers Des Flandres
Boxers
Briards
Bullmastiffs
Collie (Rough)
Collie (Smooth)
Dobermanns
Great Danes
Hungarian Kuvasz
Hungarian Pulis
Huskies
Komondors
Maremma Italian Sheepdogs
Mastiffs
Newfoundlands
Norwegian Buhunds
Old English Sheepdogs
Polish Sheepdogs
Portuguese Water Dogs
Pyrenean Mountain Dogs
Rottweilers
St. Bernards
Samoyeds
Shetland Sheepdogs
Siberian Huskies
Tibetan Mastiffs
Welsh Corgi (Cardigan)
Welsh Corgi (Pembroke)

Toy Group
Affenpinschers
Bichons Frises
Cavalier King Charles Spaniels
Chihuahuas (Long Coat)
Chihuahuas (Smooth Coat)
Chinese Crested Dogs
English Toy Terriers
(Black and Tan)
Griffons Bruxellois
Italian Greyhounds
Japanese Chin
King Charles Spaniels
Lowchen
Maltese
Miniature Pinschers
Papillons
Pekingese
Pomeranians
Pugs
Silky Terriers
Yorkshire Terriers

KENNEL CLUB

List of Fees

on and after 1st April, 1976

For dogs born prior to 1st April 1976, applicable until 1st September 1976:	
Basic Registration by Breeder	£1.00
Basic Registration by any person other than Breeder	£2.00
Basic Registration (Breeder's declaration not signed)	£2.50
For dogs born on or after 1st April 1976:	
Litter Recording within four weeks of birth	£1.00
Basic Registration by Breeder	£1.00
Basic Registration by any person other than Breeder	£2.50
Registration in Active Register	£1.50
Registration in Obedience Record	£3.00
Registration Name Unchangeable (additional fee)	£2.00
Re-registration	£2.00
Transfer (in Basic or Active Register)	£2.00
Loan or use of bitch	£1.00
Change of name	£5.00
Pedigrees—3 generations	£5.00
,, 5 generations	£7.50
,, Export	£10.00
List of Wins (entered in Stud Book)	£0.50
Registration of Affix	£6.00
Affix Maintenance Fee (Annual)	£2.00
Holders of Affix may compound for 20 years on the payment of	£15.00
Assumed Name	£2.00
Registration of Title	£5.00
Maintenance of Title	£3.00
Formation of a Branch by a Registered Society	£3.00
Maintenance of Title of a Branch of a Registered Society	£3.00
Registration of Title of Dog Training Club	£5.00
Maintenance of Title of Dog Training Club	£3.00
For Shows held under Kennel Club Show Rules:	
Licence to hold a Championship Show	£5.00
Licence to hold an Open Show	£3.00
Licence to hold a Limited or Sanction Show	£2.00
The following Extra Fees are payable for Championship and Open Shows:	
For each 500 exhibits (or part)	£2.00
For permission to hold Matches under Kennel Club Regulations	£1.00
For permission to hold an Inter-Club Obedience Match	£1.00
For permission to hold an Exemption Show	£1.00
For permission to hold a Championship Obedience Show as a Separate Event or part of a Licence Show	£5.00
For permission to hold an Open Obedience Show as a Separate Event or part of a Licence Show	£3.00
For permission to hold a Limited or Sanction Obedience Show as a Separate Event or part of a Licence or Sanction Show	£2.00
For Working Trials held under Kennel Club Rules:	
Championship Working Trials	£5.00
Open Working Trials	£3.00
Members' Working Trials	£2.00
For Field Trials held under Kennel Club Rules:	
Two-day Meeting	£5.00
One-day Meeting	£3.00

VAT: All above fees are inclusive of Value Added Tax.

FIVE IMPORTANT
INHERITED ABNORMALITIES FOUND IN DOGS

Breed	Hip dysplasia	Patella luxation	Entropion	P.R.A.	Prolonged soft palate
Airedales			×		
Alsatians	×				
Beagles	×				
Bloodhounds			×		
Boston Terriers		×			
Boxers		×	×		×
Bulldogs	×	×	×		×
Bull Terriers			×		
Bull Terriers (Staffs)		×			
Cairn Terriers	×	×			
Chihuahuas	×	×	×		
Chow Chow			×		
Collies (Rough)				×	
Collies (Smooth)				×	
Dachshunds (Miniature)			×		
Dachshunds (Long haired)			×		
Dalmatians			×		
Fox Terriers (Wire)	×		×		
Griffon Bruxellois	×	×		×	
Irish Setters (Red)				×*	
Maltese		×			
Old English Sheep Dogs	×				
Papillons		×			
Pekingese	×	×	×		×
Pointers (German Short Haired)			×		
Pomeranians		×			
Poodles (Miniature)	×	×	×	×	×
Poodles (Toy)	×	×	×	×	
Poodles (Standard)		×		×	
Pugs	×	×			×
Retrievers (Golden)	×		×	×	
Retrievers (Labradors)	×	×	×	×	
Salukis			×		
Samoyeds	×				
Sealyhams				×	
Scotch Terriers		×			
Shetland Sheepdogs			×		
Spaniels (Cavalier)		×	×		
Spaniels (King Charles)		×			
Spaniels (Clumber)			×		
Spaniels (Cocker)			×	×	×
Spaniels (English Springer)			×	×	
St Bernards			×		
Welsh Corgis (Pembroke)	×	×	×		
Welsh Corgis (Cardigan)	×	×	×		
West Highland White	×	×			
Yorkshire Terriers	×	×	×		

* Formerly common, now controlled.

Breeds

KENNEL CLUB

COMPARATIVE TABLES OF REGISTRATIONS FOR THE YEARS 1966–72 INCLUSIVE

	1969	**1970**	**1971**	**1972**	1973	1974	1975
Hounds							
Afghan Hounds	2,194	2,853	3,606	4,397	4,820	4,890	**3,867**
Basenjis	215	238	258	220	220	202	**109**
Basset Hounds	2,679	2,642	2,837	3,173	2,875	2,379	**1,721**
Bassets Griffon Vendeen	—	—	—	5	7	10	**17**
Beagles	3,979	3,445	3,209	3,033	2,871	2,686	**1,895**
Bloodhounds	254	337	325	274	296	289	**196**
Borzois	271	293	206	393	333	371	**319**
Dachshunds (Long-Haired)	613	527	479	631	574	652	**499**
Dachshunds (Miniature Long-Haired)	1,837	1,938	2,051	2,599	2,469	2,433	**2,103**
Dachshunds (Smooth-Haired)	1,679	1,565	1,244	1,441	1,231	1,118	**836**
Dachshunds (Miniature Smooth-Haired)	2,774	2,872	2,428	2,802	2,478	2,098	**1,648**
Dachshunds (Wire-Haired)	287	235	227	313	315	318	**261**
Dachshunds (Miniature Wire-Haired)	516	513	545	579	765	744	**662**
Deerhounds	98	146	110	115	124	119	**117**
Elkhounds	405	343	304	349	274	284	**243**
Finnish Spitz	92	68	87	62	51	63	**78**
Foxhounds	—	—	—	—	—	—	—
Greyhounds	35	85	49	101	75	51	**72**
Ibizan Hounds	—	—	25	33	40	39	**60**
Irish Wolfhounds	303	258	431	511	654	695	**643**
Pharaoh Hounds	—	—	46	49	101	73	**42**
Portuguese Warren Hounds	—	—	—	2	—	—	—
Rhodesian Ridgebacks	230	253	207	314	260	217	**231**
Salukis	272	215	244	287	176	274	**249**
Sloughis (Algerian Greyhounds)	—	—	—	6	7	2	**19**
Swedish Foxhounds	—	—	—	6	—	4	—
Whippets	2,025	2,038	1,726	2,003	1,869	2,088	**1,615**
Gundogs							
American Cocker Spaniels	166	309	352	409	530	596	**488**
Chesapeake Bay Retrievers	—	—	4		—	1	**17**
Clumber Spaniels	96	107	53	109	94	98	**114**
Cocker Spaniels	6,465	7,121	6,825	8,255	8,193	8,254	**7,210**
Curly Coated Retrievers	93	63	108	71	100	38	**49**
English Setters	926	906	996	1,158	1,254	1,346	**1,217**
English Springer Spaniels	2,529	2,894	2,683	3,658	3781	4,333	**4,472**
Field Spaniels	19	30	31	24	43	34	**39**
Flat Coated Retrievers	241	237	293	306	427	421	**239**
German Shorthaired Pointers	353	421	434	491	564	568	**541**
Golden Retrievers	4,751	5,189	4,766	5,760	5,913	6,107	**5,950**
Gordon Setters	128	121	114	143	205	242	**255**
Hungarian Vizslas	—	—	71	78	99	86	**94**
Interbred Retrievers	17	27	—	—	—	—	—
Interbred Spaniels	2	18	—	—	—	—	—
Irish Setters	2,679	3,277	3,764	4,792	5,438	5,590	**4,898**
Irish Water Spaniels	35	31	56	62	117	94	**112**
Labrador Retrievers	14,498	14,827	11,967	13,880	13,505	12,849	**10,939**
Large Munsterlanders	—	—	9	38	27	65	**18**
Pointers	454	530	574	653	659	880	**641**
Sussex Spaniels	33	50	34	33	26	24	**36**
Weimaraners	187	211	213	330	456	327	**331**
Welsh Springer Spaniels	385	335	409	357	511	452	**466**
Terriers							
Airedale Terriers	943	1,038	971	1,112	1,052	1,077	**943**
Australian Terriers	121	142	84	117	85	112	**75**
Bedlington Terriers	273	282	273	326	311	267	**181**

	1969	1970	1971	1972	1973	1974	1975
Border Terriers	918	953	902	1,026	1,029	1,051	943
Bull Terriers	1,072	963	865	1,075	946	1,195	912
Cairn Terriers	4,001	3,860	3,163	3,493	3,336	3,358	2,864
Dandie Dinmont Terriers	217	182	208	195	203	224	188
Interbred Terriers	3	10	—	—	—	—	—
Irish Terriers	225	214	225	173	150	240	191
Kerry Blue Terriers	275	276	284	341	272	312	248
Lakeland Terriers	511	399	338	455	303	288	231
Manchester Terriers	46	81	57	49	83	61	58
Miniature Bull Terriers	43	62	96	54	53	63	52
Norfolk Terriers	291	294	233	269	216	250	247
Norwich Terriers	203	175	187	195	173	205	106
Scottish Terriers	1,505	1,614	1,273	1,554	1,356	1,302	1,176
Sealyham Terriers	522	442	407	333	304	292	211
Skye Terriers	144	198	187	196	240	237	147
Smooth Fox Terriers	600	545	548	613	519	510	400
Soft-Coated Wheaten Terriers	—	—	39	65	68	51	56
Staffordshire Bull Terriers	1,919	1,824	2,017	2,118	2,193	2,103	1,903
Welsh Terriers	304	308	224	310	296	291	191
West Highland White Terriers	4,837	4,933	4,097	4,510	4,472	4,630	3,913
Wire Fox Terriers	1,672	1,409	1,351	1,377	1,251	1,033	866
Utility							
Boston Terriers	402	329	361	356	250	325	204
Bulldogs	1,081	1,021	927	957	985	977	1059
Canaan Dogs	—	—	3	—	—	—	—
Chow Chows	1,033	1,088	1,332	1,488	1,518	1928	1447
Dalmatians	2,916	2,752	2,049	2,291	2,161	2044	1193
French Bulldogs	232	233	231	266	251	244	169
Giant Schnauzers	—	—	13	27	28	67	73
Iceland Dogs	—	—	—	7	—	—	—
Keeshonds	292	379	302	273	268	258	228
Lhasa Apsos	346	404	563	631	673	897	730
Miniature Schnauzers	524	503	625	664	658	544	595
Poodles (Miniature)	5,986	5,291	4,497	4,692	4,104	3,980	2,941
Poodles (Standard)	711	740	679	959	970	910	833
Poodles (Toy)	7,671	7,926	6,362	6,941	6,616	6,086	5,174
Schipperkes	125	119	112	128	91	88	98
Schnauzers	73	93	87	72	101	101	90
Shih Tzus	1,037	1,526	1,453	1,441	1,583	1,940	1,613
Tibetan Spaniels	305	445	511	582	616	669	559
Tibetan Terriers	136	116	114	166	215	297	226
Working							
Alaskan Malamutes	—	—	11	8	9	—	14
Alsatians (German Shepherd Dogs)	16,546	16,834	13,857	15,078	15,185	14,936	11,357
Anatolian Dogs	—	—	4	—	—	4	10
Bearded Collies	276	308	444	565	661	651	677
Belgian Shepherd Dogs (Groenendaels)	—	—	126	99	118	143	92
Belgian Shepherd Dogs (Tervueren)	—	—	—	6	15	17	24
Bernese Mountain Dogs	—	—	11	14	38	48	61
Boxers	4,457	4,230	3,727	3,984	4,039	4,162	3,527
Briards	—	—	59	65	106	156	200
Bullmastiffs	322	338	329	443	402	502	369
Cardigan Welsh Corgis	192	228	218	252	223	245	159
Dobermanns	1,553	1,645	1,566	1,594	1,891	2,029	2,265
Great Danes	2,140	2,174	1,999	2,310	2,500	2,330	1,953
Hungarian Kuvasz	—	—	1	—	—	2	8
Hungarian Pulis	—	—	21	34	45	34	36
Huskies	—	—	14	—	3	3	2
Komondors	—	—	—	1	7	1	5

	1969	1970	1971	1972	1973	1974	1975
Maremma Italian Sheepdogs	—	—	46	44	57	15	17
Mastiffs	171	84	154	152	226	203	206
Newfoundlands	117	138	159	207	220	227	238
Norwegian Buhunds	91	107	121	123	111	119	105
Old English Sheepdogs	1,806	2,343	2,896	3,188	3,976	4,921	4,640
Pembroke Welsh Corgis	4,165	3,897	2,979	3,180	2,936	2,621	1,922
Pyrenean Mountain Dogs	885	928	904	743	820	762	576
Rottweilers	163	164	249	263	306	332	401
Rough Collies	5,736	6,086	5,750	6,597	6,211	6,535	5,395
St Bernards	288	376	342	498	604	592	389
Samoyeds	666	697	727	834	814	1,002	854
Shetland Sheepdogs	5,872	5,970	5,160	5,705	5,328	5,331	4,282
Siberian Huskies	—	—	9	9	26	18	26
Smooth Collies	72	57	82	98	92	74	68
Toys							
Affenpinschers	—	—	—	1	—	—	1
Cavalier King Charles Spaniels	2,899	3,192	3,562	4,471	5,071	5,795	5,407
Chihuahuas (Long-Coat)	1,435	1,514	1,801	2,017	1,938	2,088	1,954
Chihuahuas (Smooth-Coat)	2,714	2,701	2,330	2,494	2,279	2,225	1,724
Chinese Crested	—	—	20	25	26	48	43
English Toy Terriers (Black and Tan)	87	79	58	73	38	48	64
Griffons Bruxellois	538	438	401	478	478	424	303
Interbred Toy Spaniels	1	—	—	—	—	—	—
Italian Greyhounds	111	167	105	125	124	134	95
Japanese Chin	175	194	179	237	222	221	172
King Charles Spaniels	145	185	114	193	171	168	135
Lowchen	—	—	28	13	82	88	84
Maltese	414	434	427	507	413	427	401
Miniature Pinschers	279	275	254	298	275	295	238
Papillons	751	764	781	962	832	963	697
Pekingese	3,890	4,243	3,853	4,611	4,313	4,491	3,733
Pomeranians	810	899	849	1,004	1,029	1,133	943
Pugs	1,263	1,226	1,076	1,068	892	1,012	709
Yorkshire Terriers	10,212	11,016	10,577	12,832	13,780	15,147	14,640
Total Non-Sporting Breeds	94,112	96,896	88,601	99,434	100,034	104,105	88,520
Total Sporting Breeds	75,460	77,772	72,444	84,264	83,748	83,675	71,754
Any other Breed or Variety	329	395	—		—	—	—
Crossbreeds	17	11	—	—	—	—	—
Development Register	—	—	20	24	2	—	—
Total Registrations	169,918	175,074	161,065	183,722	183,784	187,780	160,274

EXPORT PEDIGREES ISSUED DURING JANUARY–DECEMBER 1973

Breeds

Hounds

Breed	Number
Afghan Hounds	274
Basenjis	13
Basset Hounds	491
Beagles	135
Bloodhounds	40
Borzois	35
Dachshunds (Long Haired)	11
Dachshunds (Miniature Long Haired)	70
Dachshunds (Smooth Haired)	33
Dachshunds (Miniature Smooth Haired)	154
Dachshunds (Wire Haired)	6
Dachshund (Miniature Wire Haired)	26
Deerhounds	12
Elkhounds	8
Finnish Spitz	5
Greyhounds	24
Irish Wolfhounds	69
Pharaoh Hounds	24
Rhodesian Ridgebacks	23
Salukis	26
Whippets	57
Bassets Griffons Vendeen	4
Ibizan Hounds	2
	1,548

Terriers

Breed	Number
Airedale Terriers	128
Australian Terriers	7
Bedlington Terriers	25
Border Terriers	31
Bull Terriers	116
Bull Terriers (Miniature)	6
Cairn Terriers	225
Dandie Dinmont Terriers	27
Fox Terriers (Smooth)	82
Fox Terriers (Wire)	163
Irish Terriers	25
Kerry Blue Terriers	21
Lakeland Terriers	30
Manchester Terriers	5
Norfolk Terriers	10
Norwich Terriers	40
Scottish Terriers	210
Sealyham Terriers	27
Skye Terriers	34
Soft Coated Wheaten Terriers	4
Staffordshire Bull Terriers	30
Welsh Terriers	56
West Highland White Terriers	492
	1,794

Working

Breed	Number
Alsatians (German Shepherd Dogs)	321
Bearded Collies	55
Belgian Shepherd Dogs (Groenendaels)	13
Belgian Shepherd Dogs (Tervuerens)	1
Boxers	252
Briards	5
Bullmastiffs	50
Collies (Rough)	182
Collies (Smooth)	2
Dobermanns	122
Great Danes	172
Mastiffs	37
Newfoundlands	30
Old English Sheepdogs	469
Pyrenean Mountain Dogs	33
Rottweilers	18
St. Bernards	23
Samoyeds	49
Shetland Sheepdogs	178
Welsh Corgis (Cardigan)	19
Welsh Corgis (Pembroke)	137
Siberian Huskies	1
Bernese Mountain Dogs	2
Hungarian Pulis	11
Alaskan Malamutes	
	2,183

Gundogs

Breed	Number
English Setters	65
German Shorthaired Pointers	11
Gordon Setters	15
Hungarian Vizslas	11
Irish Setters	228
Pointers	60
Retrievers (Curly-Coated)	11
Retrievers (Flat-Coated)	65
Retrievers (Golden)	197
Retrievers (Labrador)	302
Spaniels (American Cocker)	46
Spaniels (Clumber)	12
Spaniels (Cocker)	618
Spaniels (English Springer)	99
Spaniels (Field)	6
Spaniels (Irish Water)	4
Spaniels (Sussex)	5
Spaniels (Welsh Springer)	18
Weimaraners	18
	1,791

Utility

Breed	Number
Boston Terriers	27
Bulldogs	266
Chow Chows	206
Dalmatians	90
French Bulldogs	43
Keeshonds	20
Lhasa Apsos	85
Miniature Schnauzers	52
Poodles (Standard)	47
Poodles (Miniature)	276
Poodles (Toy)	946
Schipperkes	12
Schnauzers	2
Shih Tzus	268
Tibetan Spaniels	43
Tibetan Terriers	8
Giant Schnauzers	5
	2,396

Toys

Breed	Number
Cavalier King Charles Spaniels	108
Chihuahuas (Long Coat)	84
Chihuahuas (Smooth Coat)	140
Chinese Crested Dogs	5
English Toy Terriers (Black and Tan)	1
Griffon Bruxellois	53
Italian Greyhounds	5
Japanese Chins	11
King Charles Spaniels	15
Lowchen	1
Maltese	73
Miniature Pinschers	28
Papillons	52
Pekingese	513
Pomeranians	121
Pugs	82
Yorkshire Terriers	2,395
	3,687

Countries

Country	Number
Afghanistan	0
Algeria	2
Angola	0
Argentina	24
Australia	281
Austria	86
Balearic Islands	1
Belgium	215
Bahamas	3
Bahrain	1
Bermuda	59
Brazil	57
Burma	1
China	2
Central African Republic	1
Canada	1,697
Canary Islands	4
Ceylon	1
Chile	0
Columbia	14
Costa Rica	1
Cyprus	0
Czechoslovakia	7
Dubai	1
Denmark	185
East Africa	1
Ethiopia	4
Ecuador	4
Falkland Islands	0
Finland	96
France	1,094
Germany (East)	1
Germany (Federal Republic)	1,660
Ghana	1
Gibraltar	10
Greece	28
Guyana	1
Guatemala	2
Hong Kong	37
Hungary	3
Indonesia	26
India	20
Iran	52
Iraq	0
Israel	29
Italy	2,398
Ivory Coast	1
Japan	30
Jordan	3
Kenya	26
Kuwait	0
Korea	5
Lebanon	67
Liberia	0
Libya	0
Luxembourg	3
Madeira	1
Malawi	0
Malaysia	88
Malta	9
Mexico	7
Monaco	3
Morocco	4
Mozambique	1
Mauritius	0
Netherlands	416
New Zealand	66
Nigeria	5
Norway	222
Pakistan	4
Peru	1
Philippines	1
Poland	10
Portugal	54
Puerto Rico	2
Republic of Panama	2
Rhodesia	35
Rumania	1
Seychelles	1
Senegal	0
Saudi Arabia	9
Sierra Leone	4
South Africa	152
Spain	643
Sweden	428
Switzerland	446
Taiwan	3
Tanzania	0
Thailand	16
Turkey	3
Uganda	0
U.S.S.R.	1
United Arab Republic	2
United States of America	2,333
Uruguay	1
Venezuela	38
Virgin Islands	0
West Indies	102
Windward Islands	1
Yugoslavia	24
Zambia	16
	13,399

Group	Number
Hound Group	1,548
Gundog Group	1,791
Terrier Group	1,794
Utility Group	2,396
Working Group	2,183
Toy Group	3,687
	13,399

METRIC CONVERSION TABLES

HEIGHT

Ins	Centimetres	Ins	Centimetres
1	2·54	19	48·26
2	5·08	20	50·80
3	7.62	21	53·34
4	10·16	22	55·88
5	12·70	23	58·42
6	15·24	24	60·96
7	17·78	25	63·50
8	20·32	26	66·04
9	22·86	27	68·58
10	25·40	28	71·12
11	27·94	29	73·66
12	30·48	30	76·20
13	33·02	31	78·74
14	35·56	32	81·28
15	38·10	33	83·82
16	40·64	34	86·36
17	43·18		
18	45·72		

WEIGHT

Lbs	Kilos	Lbs	Kilos
1	0·454	19	8·618
2	0·907	20	9·072
3	1·361	30	13·608
4	1·814	40	18·144
5	2·268	50	22·680
6	2·722	60	27·216
7	3·175	70	31·751
8	3·629	80	36·287
9	4·082	90	40·823
10	4·536	100	45·359
11	4·989	110	49·895
12	5·443	120	54·431
13	5·897	130	58·967
14	6·350	140	63·503
15	6·804	150	68·039
16	7·257	200	90·718
17	7·711		
18	8·165		

PART II

Alphabetical List of Breeds and their Kennel Club Standards

Note. A dog may be disqualified by the Committee of the Kennel Club from winning any award, whether an objection has been lodged or not, if proved, amongst other things, to have been: (i) Totally blind, (ii) defective in hearing, (iii) (a) if a dog, castrated or prevented from breeding as a result of a surgical operation, (b) if a bitch, spayed or prevented from breeding as a result of a surgical operation, except that this shall not apply to a bitch that has progeny registered at the Kennel Club.

AFFENPINSCHER

(AMERICAN KENNEL CLUB—GROUP V: TOYS)

General Appearance. Small, but rather sturdy in build and not delicate in any way. He carries himself with comical seriousness and he is generally quiet and a very devoted pal. He can get vehemently excited, however, when attacked and is fearless toward any aggressor.

Coat. A very important factor. It is short and dense in certain parts and shaggy and longer in others, but should be hard and wiry. It is longer and more loose and shaggy on the legs and around the eyes, nose and chin, giving the typical monkeylike appearance from whence comes his name. The best color is black, matching his eyes and fiery temperament. However, black with tan markings, red, grey and other mixtures are permissible. Very light colors and white markings are a fault.

Head. Should be round and not too heavy, with well-domed forehead.

Eyes. Should be round, of good size, black and very brilliant.

Ears. Rather small, set high, pointed and erect, usually clipped to a point.

Muzzle. Must be short and rather pointed with a black nose. The upper jaw is a trifle shorter than the lower jaw, while the teeth should close together; a slight undershot condition is not material. The teeth, however, should not show.

Neck. Short and straight.

Body. The back should be straight with its length about equal to the height at the shoulder. Chest should be reasonably deep and the body should show only a slight tuck-up at the loin.

Legs. Front legs should be straight as possible. Hind legs without much bend at the hocks and set well under the body.

Feet. Should be round, small and compact. Turned neither in nor out, with preferably black pads and nails.

Tail. Cut short, set and carried high.

Size. The smaller dog, if of characteristic type, is more valuable, and the shoulder height should not exceed $10\frac{1}{4}$ inches in any case.

Approved September 15, 1936

AFGHAN HOUND

(THE KENNEL CLUB—HOUND GROUP)

Characteristics. The Afghan Hound should be dignified and aloof with a certain keen fierceness. The Eastern or Oriental expression is typical of the breed. The Afghan looks at and through one.

General Appearance. The gait of the Afghan Hound should be smooth and springy with a style of high order. The whole appearance of the dog should give the impression of strength and dignity combining speed and power. The head must be held proudly.

Head and Skull. Skull long, not too narrow with prominent occiput. Foreface long with punishing jaws and slight stop. The skull well balanced and surmounted by a long 'top-knot'. Nose preferably black but liver is no fault in light coloured dogs.

Eyes. Should be dark for preference but golden colour is not debarred. Nearly triangular, slanting slightly upwards from the inner corner to the outer.

Ears. Set low and well back, carried close to the head. Covered with long silky hair.

Mouth. Level.

Neck. Long, strong with proud carriage of the head.

Forequarters. Shoulders long and sloping, well set back, well muscled and strong without being loaded. Forelegs straight and well boned, straight with shoulder, elbows held in.

Body. Back level, moderate length, well muscled, the back falling slightly away to the stern. Loin straight, broad and rather short. Hip-bones rather prominent and wide apart. A fair spring of ribs and good depth of chest.

Hindquarters. Powerful, well bent and well turned stifles. Great length between hip and hock with a comparatively short distance between hock and foot. The dew claws may be removed or remain at the discretion of the breeder.

Feet. Forefeet strong and very large both in length and breadth and covered with long thick hair, toes arched. Pasterns long and springy, especially in front and pads well let down on the ground. Hindfeet long, but not quite so broad as forefeet, covered with long thick hair.

Tail. Not too short. Set on low with ring at the end. Raised when in action. Sparsely feathered.

Coat. Long and very fine texture on ribs, fore and hind-quarters and flanks. From the shoulder backwards and along the saddle the hair should be short and close in mature dogs. Hair long from the forehead backward, with a distinct silky 'top knot'. On the foreface the hair is short as on the back. Ears and legs well coated. Pasterns can be bare. Coat must be allowed to develop naturally.

Colour. All colours are acceptable.

Weight and Size. Ideal height: Dogs 27 to 29 inches. Bitches 2 to 3 inches smaller.

Faults. Any appearance of coarseness. Skull too wide and foreface too short. Weak underjaw. Large round or full eyes. Neck should never be too short or thick. Back too long or too short.

AFGHAN HOUND

(AMERICAN KENNEL CLUB—GROUP II: HOUNDS)

General Appearance. The Afghan Hound is an aristocrat, his whole appearance one of dignity and aloofness with no trace of plainness or coarseness. He has a straight front, proudly carried head, eyes gazing into the distance as if in memory of ages past. The striking characteristics of the breed—exotic, or 'eastern,' expression, long silky topknot, peculiar coat pattern, very prominent hipbones, large feet, and the impression of a somewhat exaggerated bend in the stifle due to profuse trouserings—stand out clearly, giving the Afghan Hound the appearance of what he is, a king of dogs, that has held true to tradition throughout the ages.

Head. The head is of good length, showing much refinement, the skull evenly balanced with the foreface. There is a slight prominence of the nasal bone structure causing a slightly Roman appearance, the centre line running up over the foreface with little or no stop, falling away in front of the eyes so there is an absolutely clear outlook with no interference; the underjaw showing great strength, the jaws long and punishing; the mouth level, meaning that the teeth from the upper jaw and lower jaw match evenly, neither overshot nor undershot. This is a difficult mouth to breed. A scissors bite is even more punishing and can be more easily bred into a dog than a level mouth, and a dog having a scissors bite, where the lower teeth slip inside and rest against the teeth of the upper jaw, should not be penalized. The occipital bone is very prominent. The head is surmounted by a topknot of long silky hair.

Ears. The ears are long, set approximately on level with outer corners of the eyes, the leather of the ear reaching nearly to the end of the dog's nose, and covered with long silky hair.

Eyes. The eyes are almond-shaped (almost triangular), never full or bulgy, and are dark in colour.

Nose. Nose is of good size, black in colour.

Faults. Coarseness; snipiness; overshot or undershot; eyes round or bulgy or light in colour; exaggerated Roman nose; head not surmounted with topknot.

Neck. The neck is of good length, strong and arched, running in a curve to the shoulders which are long and sloping and well laid back.

Faults. Neck too short or too thick; a ewe neck; a goose neck; a neck lacking in substance.

Body. The back line appearing practically level from the shoulders to the loin. Strong and powerful loin and slightly arched, falling away toward the stern, with the hipbones very pronounced; well ribbed and tucked up in flanks. The height at the shoulders equals the distance from the chest to the buttocks; the brisket well let down, and of medium width.

Faults. Roach back, sway-back, goose rump, slack loin; lack of prominence of hipbones; too much width of brisket causing interference with elbows.

Tail. Tail set not too high on the body, having a ring, or a curve on the end; should never be curled over, or rest on the back, or be carried sideways; and should never be bushy.

Legs. Forelegs are straight and strong with great length between elbow and pastern; elbows well held in; forefeet large in both length and width; toes well arched; feet covered with long thick hair; fine in texture; pasterns long and straight; pads of feet unusually large and well down on the ground. Shoulders have plenty of angulation so that the legs are well set underneath the dog. Too much straightness of shoulder causes the dog to break down in the pasterns, and this is a serious fault. All four feet of the Afghan Hound are in line with the body, turning neither in nor out. The hind feet are broad and of good length; the toes arched, and covered with long thick hair; hindquarters powerful and well muscled with great length between hip and hock; hocks are well let down; good angulation of both stifle and hock; slightly bowed from hock to crotch.

Faults Front or back feet thrown outward or inward; pads of feet not thick enough; or feet too small; or any other evidence of weakness in feet; weak or broken down pasterns; too straight in stifle; too long in hock.

Coat. Hindquarters, flanks, ribs, forequarters, and legs well covered with thick, silky hair, very fine in texture; ears and all four feet well feathered; from in front of the shoulders, and also backwards from the shoulders along the saddle from the flanks and the ribs upwards, the hair is short and close, forming a smooth back in mature dogs—this is a traditional characteristic of the Afghan Hound. The Afghan Hound should be shown in its natural state; the coat is not clipped or trimmed; the head is surmounted (in the full sense of the word) with a topknot of long, silky hair—that is also an outstanding characteristic of the Afghan Hound. Showing of short hair on cuffs on either front or back legs is permissible.

Faults. Lack of shorthaired saddle in mature dogs.

Height. Dogs, 27 inches, plus or minus one inch; bitches, 25 inches, plus or minus one inch.

Weight. Dogs, about 60 pounds; bitches, about 50 pounds.

Color. All colors are permissible, but color or color combinations are pleasing; white markings, especially on the head, are undesirable.

Gait. When running free, the Afghan Hound moves at a gallop, showing great elasticity and spring in his smooth, powerful stride. When on a loose lead, the Afghan can trot at a fast pace; stepping along, he has the appearance of placing the hind feet directly in the foot prints of the front feet, both thrown straight ahead. Moving with head and tail high, the whole appearance of the Afghan Hound is one of great style and beauty.

Temperament. Aloof and dignified, yet gay.

Faults. Sharpness or shyness.

Approved September 14, 1948

AIREDALE TERRIER
(THE KENNEL CLUB—TERRIER GROUP)

Characteristics. Keen of expression, quick of movement, on the tip-toe of expectation at any movement. Character is denoted and shown by the expression of the eyes, and by the carriage of the ears and tail.

General Appearance. The various parts of the dog should be in proportion to each other giving a symmetrical appearance. In movement, the legs should be carried straight forward, the forelegs being perpendicular and parallel with the sides. The propulsive power is furnished by the hind legs, perfection of action being found in the Terrier possessing long thighs, and muscular second thighs well bent at the stifles, which admit of a strong forward thrust or snatch of the hocks. When approaching, the forelegs should form a continuation of the straight line of the front, the feet being the same distance apart as the elbows; when stationary it is often difficult to determine whether a dog is slightly out at shoulder, but directly he moves, the defect if it exists, becomes most apparent, the forefeet having a tendency to cross. When, on the contrary, the dog is tied at the shoulder, the tendency of the feet is to move wider apart. When the hocks are turned in (cow-hocks) the stifles and feet are turned outward, resulting in a serious loss of propulsive power. When the hocks are turned outward, the tendency of the hind feet is to cross.

Head and Skull. The skull should be long and flat, not too broad between the ears, and narrowing slightly to the eyes. It should be well balanced, with only little apparent difference in length between skull and foreface. The skull to be free from wrinkles, with stop hardly visible, and cheeks level and free from fullness. Foreface must be well filled up before the eyes, not dish-faced or falling away quickly below eyes, but on the other hand a little delicate chiselling should keep appearance from wedginess and plainness. Upper and lower jaws should be deep, powerful, strong and muscular, as strength of foreface is a great desideratum of the Airedale, but there must be no excess development of the jaws to give a rounded or bulging appearance to the cheeks, as 'cheekiness' is not desired. Lips to be tight. The nose should be black.

Eyes. Should be dark in colour, small, not prominent, full of terrier expression, keenness and intelligence.

Ears. Should be 'V' shaped with a side carriage, small, but not out of proportion to the size of the dog. The top line of the folded ear should be above the level of the skull. A pendulous ear, hanging dead by the side of the head like a hound's, is a fault.

Mouth. Teeth strong and level being capable of closing together like a vice.

Neck. Should be clean, muscular, of moderate length and thickness, gradually widening towards the shoulders, and free from throatiness.

Forequarters. Shoulders should be long, well laid back, and sloping obliquely into the back, shoulder blades flat. Forelegs should be perfectly straight, with plenty of bone. Elbows should be perpendicular to the body, working free of the sides.

Body. Back should be short, strong, straight and level, with no appearance of slackness. Loins muscular. Ribs well sprung. In a well ribbed-up or short-coupled dog there is little space between ribs and hips, when the dog is long in couplings some slackness will be shown here. Chest to be deep but not broad.

Hindquarters. Should be long and muscular with no droop. Thighs long and powerful with muscular second thigh, stifles well bent, not turned either in or out. Hocks well let down, parallel with each other when viewed from behind.

Feet. Should be small, round and compact, with a

good depth of pad, well cushioned, and the toes moderately arched, not turned either in or out.

Tail. Should be set on high and carried gaily, but not curled over the back. It should be of good strength and substance, and of fair length.

Coat. Should be hard, dense and wiry, and not too long as to appear ragged. It should also lie straight and close, covering the body and legs; the outer coat of hard, wiry, stiff hairs, the undercoat should be a shorter growth of softer hair. Some of the hardest coats are crinkling or just slightly waved; a curly coat is objectionable.

Colour. The head and ears, with the exception of dark markings on each side of the skull, should be tan, the ears being of a darker shade than the rest. The legs up to the thighs and elbows also should be tan. The body to be black or dark grizzle.

Weight and Size. Height about 23 to 24 inches for dogs, taken from top of shoulder, and bitches about 22 to 23 inches. Weight to be commensurate with height and type.

AIREDALE TERRIER

(AMERICAN KENNEL CLUB—GROUP IV: TERRIERS)

Head. Should be well balanced with little apparent difference between the length of skull and foreface.

Skull should be long and flat, not too broad between the ears and narrowing very slightly to the eyes. Scalp should be free from wrinkles, stop hardly visible and cheeks level and free from fullness.

Ears should be V-shaped with carriage rather to the side of the head, not pointing to the eyes, small but not out of proportion to the size of the dog. The topline of the folded ear should be above the level of the skull.

Foreface should be deep, powerful, strong and muscular. Should be well filled up before the eyes.

Eyes should be dark, small, not prominent, full of terrier expression, keenness and intelligence.

Lips should be tight.

Nose should be black and not too small.

Teeth should be strong and white, free from discoloration or defect. Bite either level or vise-like. A slightly overlapping or scissors bite is permissible without preference.

Neck. Should be of moderate length and thickness gradually widening towards the shoulders. Skin tight, not loose.

Shoulders and Chest. Shoulders long and sloping well into the back. Shoulder blades flat. From the front, chest deep but not broad. The depth of the chest should be approximately on a level with the elbows.

Body. Back should be short, strong and level. Ribs well sprung. Loins muscular and of good width. There should be but little space between the last rib and the hip joint.

Hindquarters. Should be strong and muscular with no droop.

Tail. The root of the tail should be set well up on the back. It should be carried gaily but not curled over the back. It should be of good strength and substance and of fair length.

Legs—Forelegs. Should be perfectly straight, with plenty of muscle and bone.

Elbows should be perpendicular to the body, working free of sides.

Thighs should be long and powerful with muscular second thigh, stifles well bent, not turned either in or out, hocks well let down parallel with each other when viewed from behind.

Feet should be small, round and compact with a good depth of pad, well cushioned; the toes moderately arched, not turned either in or out.

Coat. Should be hard, dense and wiry, lying straight and close, covering the dog well over the body and legs. Some of the hardest are crinkling or just slightly waved. At the base of the hard very stiff hair should be a shorter growth of softer hair termed the undercoat.

Color. The head and ears should be tan, the ears being of a darker shade than the rest. Dark markings on either side of the skull are permissible. The legs up to the thighs and elbows and the under-part of the body and chest are also tan and the tan frequently runs into the shoulder. The sides and upper parts of the body should be black or dark grizzle. A red mixture is often found in the black and is not to be considered objectionable. A small white blaze on the chest is a characteristic of certain strains of the breed.

Size. Dogs should measure approximately 23 inches in height at the shoulder; bitches, slightly less. Both sexes should be sturdy, well muscled and boned.

Movement. Movement or action is the crucial test of conformation. Movement should be free. As seen from the front the forelegs should swing perpendicular from the body free from the sides, the feet the same distance apart as the elbows. As seen from the rear the hind legs should be parallel with each other, neither too close nor too far apart, but so placed as to give a strong well-balanced stance and movement.The toes should not be turned either in or out. Yellow eyes, hound ears, white feet, soft coat, being much over or under the size limit, being undershot or overshot, having poor movement, are faults which should be severely penalized.

SCALE OF POINTS

Head	10
Neck, shoulders and chest	10
Body	10
Hindquarters and tail	10
Legs and feet	10
Coat	10
Color	5
Size	10
Movement	10
General characteristics and expression	15
Total	100

Approved July 14, 1959

ALASKAN MALAMUTES

(THE KENNEL CLUB—WORKING GROUP)

General Appearance and Characteristics. A powerful and substantially built dog with a deep chest and strong, compact body, not too short coupled, with a thick, coarse guard coat of sufficient length to protect a dense woolly under-coat, from 1 to 2 inches in depth when dog is in full coat. He stands well over his pads, and this stance gives the appearance of much activity, showing interest and curiosity. The head is broad, ears wedge-shaped and erect when alerted. The muzzle is bulky with only slight diminishing in width and depth from root to nose, not pointed or long, but not stubby. The Malamute moves with a proud carriage, head erect and eyes alert. Face markings are a distinguishing feature. These consist of either cap over head and rest of face solid colour, usually greyish-white, or face marked with the appearance of a mask. Combinations of cap and mask are not unusual. The tail is plumed and carried over the back, not like a fox brush or tightly curled, but more like a plume waving.

Malamutes are of various colours, but are usually wolfish grey or black and white. Their feet are of the 'snow shoe' type, tight and deep, with well-cushioned pads, giving a firm and compact appearance. Front legs are straight with big bone, hindlegs broad and powerful, moderately bent at stifles and without cow-hocks. The back is straight, gently sloping from shoulders to hips. The loin should not be so short or tight as to interfere with easy tireless movement. Endurance and intelligence are shown in body and expres-sion. The eyes have a 'wolflike' appearance by their position, but the expression is soft and indicates an affectionate disposition.

Temperament. The Alaskan Malamute is an affectionate, friendly dog, not a 'one-man' dog. He is a loyal, devoted companion, playful on invitation, but generally impressive by his dignity after maturity.

Head. The head should indicate a high degree of intelligence, and is broad and powerful as com-pared with other 'natural' breeds, but should be in proportion to the size of the dog so as not to make the dog appear clumsy or coarse.

Skull. The skull should be broad between the ears, gradually narrowing to the eyes, moderately rounded between the ears, flattening on top as it approaches the eyes, rounding off to cheeks, which should be moderately flat. There should be a slight furrow between the eyes; the top line of the skull and top line of the muzzle showing but little break downward from a straight line as they join.

Muzzle. The muzzle should be large and bulky in proportion to size of skull, diminishing but little in width or depth from junction with skull to nose; lips close fitting; nose black; upper and lower jaws broad with large teeth, front teeth meeting with a scissors grip but never overshot or undershot.

Eyes. Brown, almond shaped, moderately large for this shape of eye, set obliquely in skull. Dark eyes preferred.

Ears. The ears should be of medium size but small in proportion to the head. The upper halves of the ears are triangular in shape, slightly rounded at the tips, set wide apart on outside back edges of the skull with the lower part of the ear joining the skull on a line with the upper corner of the eye, giving the tips of the ears the appearance, erect, of standing off from the skull. When erect, the ears point slightly forward, but when the dog is at work the ears are sometimes folded against the skull. High set ears are a fault.

Neck. The neck should be strong and moderately arched.

Body. The body should be strong and compactly built but not short coupled, the chest strong and deep; the back straight and gently sloping to the hips. The loins should be well muscled and not so short as to interfere with easy rhythmic movement with powerful drive from the hindquarters. A long loin which weakens the back is also a fault. No excess weight.

Shoulders, Legs and Feet. Shoulders should be moderately sloping; forelegs heavily boned and muscled, straight to pasterns, which should be short and strong and almost vertical as viewed from the side. The feet should be large and compact, toes tight-fitting and well arched, pads thick and tough, toe nails short and strong. There should be a protective growth of hair between the toes. Hindlegs must be broad and powerfully muscled through thighs; stifles moderately bent, hock joints broad and strong, moderately bent and well let down. As viewed from behind, the hindlegs should not appear bowed in bone but stand and move truely in line with the movement of the front legs and not too close or too wide. The legs of the Malamute must indicate unusual strength and tremendous propelling power. Any indication of unsoundness in legs or feet, standing or moving, is to be considered a serious fault. Dewclaws on the hindlegs are undesirable and should be removed shortly after the pups are whelped.

Tail. The tail is moderately set and follows the line of the spine at the start. It is well-furred and carried over the back when the dog is not working, not tightly curled to rest on the back, or short-furred and carried like a fox brush, but of the appearance of a waving plume.

Coat. The Malamute should have a thick, coarse guard coat, not long and soft. The undercoat is dense, from 1 to 2 inches in depth, oily and woolly. The coarse guard coat stands out, and there is thick fur around the neck. The guard coat varies in length, as does the undercoat; however, in general, the coat is moderately short to medium along the sides of the body with the length of the coat increasing somewhat around the shoulders and neck, down the back and over the rump, as well as in the breeching and plume. Malamutes usually have shorter and less dense coats when shed out during the summer months.

Colour and Markings. The usual colours range from light gray through the intermediate shadings to black, always with white on underbodies, parts of legs, feet, and part of mask markings. Markings should be either caplike and/or mask-like on face. A white blaze on forehead and/or collar or spot on nape is attractive and acceptable, but broken colour extending over the body in spots or uneven splashings is undesirable. One should distinguish between mantled dogs and splash-coated dogs. The only solid colour allowable is the all-white.

Size. There is a natural range in size in the breed. The desirable freighting sizes are: **Males:** 25 inches at the shoulders—85 lbs. **Females:** 23 inches at the shoulders—75 lbs. However, size consideration should not outweigh that of type, proportion, and functional attributes, such as shoulders, chest, legs, feet, and movement. When dogs are judged equal in type, proportion, and functional attributes, the dog nearest the desirable freighting size is to be preferred.

Important: In judging Alaskan Malamutes their function as a sledge dog for heavy freighting must be given consideration above all else. The judge must bear in mind that this breed is designed primarily as the working sledge dog of the North for hauling heavy freight, and therefore he should be a heavy-boned, powerfully built, compact dog with sound legs, good feet, deep chest, powerful shoulders, steady, balanced, tireless gait, and the other physical equipment necessary for the efficient performance of his job. He isn't intended as a racing sled dog designed to compete in speed trials with the smaller Northern breeds. The Malamute as a sledge dog for heavy freighting is designed for strength and endurance and any characteristic of the individual specimen, including temperament, which interferes with the accomplishment of this purpose is to be considered the most serious of faults. Faults under this provision would be splayfootedness, any indication of unsoundness or weakness in legs, cowhocks, bad pasterns, straight shoulders, lack of angulation, stilted gait or any gait which isn't balanced, strong, and steady, ranginess, shallowness, ponderousness, lightness of bone, poor over-all proportion, and similar characteristics.

SCALE OF POINTS

General Appearance	20
Head	15
Body	20
Legs and Movement	20
Feet	10
Coat and Colour	10
Tail	5
Total	100

ALASKAN MALAMUTE

(AMERICAN KENNEL CLUB—GROUP III: WORKING DOGS)

General Appearance and Characteristics. The Alaskan Malamute is a powerful and substantially built dog with deep chest and strong, compact body, not too short coupled, with a thick, coarse guard coat of sufficient length to protect a dense, woolly undercoat, from 1 to 2 inches in depth when dog is in full coat. Stands well over pads, and this stance gives the appearance of much activity, showing interest and curiosity. The head is broad, ears wedge-shaped and erect when alerted. The muzzle is bulky with only slight diminishing in width and depth from root to nose, not pointed or long, but not stubby. The Malamute moves with a proud carriage, head erect and eyes alert. Face markings are a distinguishing feature. These consist of either cap over head and rest of face solid color, usually grayish white, or face marked with the appearance of a mask. Combinations of cap and mask are not unusual. The tail is plumed and carried over the back, not like a fox brush, or tightly curled, more like a plume waving.

Malamutes are of various colors, but are usually wolfish gray or black and white. Their feet are of the 'snowshoe' type, tight and deep, with well-cushioned pads, giving a firm and compact appearance. Front legs are straight with big bone. Hind legs are broad and powerful, moderately bent at stifles, and without cowhocks. The back is straight, gently sloping from shoulders to hips. The loin should not be so short or tight as to interfere with easy, tireless movement. Endurance and intelligence are shown in body and expression. The eyes have a 'wolf-like' appearance by their position, but the expression is soft and indicates an affectionate disposition.

Temperament. The Alaskan Malamute is an affectionate, friendly dog, not a 'one-man' dog. He is a loyal, devoted companion, playful on invitation, but generally impressive by his dignity after maturity.

Head. The head should indicate a high degree of intelligence, and is broad and powerful as compared with other 'natural' breeds, but should be in proportion to the size of the dog so as not to make the dog appear clumsy or coarse.

Skull. The skull should be broad between the ears, gradually narrowing to eyes, moderately rounded between ears, flattening on top as it approaches the eyes, rounding off to cheeks, which should be moderately flat. There should be a slight furrow between the eyes, the topline of skull and topline of the muzzle showing but little break downward from a straight line as they join.

Muzzle. The muzzle should be large and bulky in proportion to size of skull, diminishing but little in width and depth from junction with skull to nose; lips close fitting; nose black; upper and lower jaws broad with large teeth, front teeth meeting with a scissors grip but never overshot or undershot.

Eyes. Brown, almond shaped, moderately large for this shape of eye, set obliquely in skull. Dark eyes preferred.

Ears. The ears should be of medium size, but small in proportion to head. The upper halves of the ears are triangular in shape, slightly rounded at tips, set wide apart on outside back edges of the skull with the lower part of the ear joining the skull on a line with the upper corner of the eye, giving the tips of the ears the appearance, when erect, of standing off from the skull. When erect, the ears point slightly forward, but when the dog is at work the ears are sometimes folded against the skull. High-set ears are a fault.

Neck. The neck should be strong and moderately arched.

Body. The chest should be strong and deep; body should be strong and compactly built but not short coupled. The back should be straight and gently sloping to the hips. The loins should be well muscled and not so short as to interfere with easy, rhythmic movement with powerful drive from the hindquarters. A long loin which weakens the back is also a fault. No excess weight.

Shoulders, Legs and Feet. Shoulders should be moderately sloping; forelegs heavily boned and muscled, straight to pasterns, which should be short and strong and almost vertical as viewed from the side. The feet should be large and compact, toes, tight-fitting and well arched, pads thick and tough, toenails short and strong. There should be a protective growth of hair between toes. Hind legs must be broad and powerfully muscled through thighs; stifles moderately bent, hock joints broad and strong, moderately bent and well let down. As viewed from behind, the hind legs should not appear bowed in bone, but stand and move true in line with movement of the front legs, and not too close or too wide. The legs of the Malamute must indicate unusual strength and tremendous propelling power. Any indication of unsoundness in legs or feet, standing or moving, is to be considered a serious fault. Dewclaws on the hind legs are undesirable and should be removed shortly after pups are whelped.

Tail. Moderately set and following the line of the spine at the start, well furred and carried over the back when not working—not tightly curled to rest on back—or short furred and carried like a fox brush, a waving plume appearance instead.

Coat. The Malamute should have a thick, coarse guard coat, not long and soft. The undercoat is dense, from 1 to 2 inches in depth, oily and woolly. The coarse guard coat stands out, and there is a thick fur around the neck. The guard coat varies in length as does the undercoat, but in general the coat is moderately short to medium along the sides of the body with the length of the coat increasing somewhat around the shoulders and neck, down the back and over the rump, as well as in the breeching and plume. Malamutes usually have shorter and less dense coats when they shed out during the summer months.

Color and Markings. The usual colors range from light grey through the intermediate shadings to black, always with white on the underbody, parts of legs, feet and part of mask markings. The markings should be either cap-like and/or mask-like on the face. A white blaze on the forehead and/or the collar or spot on the nape is attractive and acceptable, but broken color extending over the body in spots or uneven splashings is undesirable. One should distinguish between mantled dogs and splash-coated dogs. The only solid color allowable is the all-white.

Size. There is a natural range in size in the breed. The desirable freighting sizes are: Males: 25 inches at the shoulders—85 pounds; Females: 23 inches at the shoulders—75 pounds.

However, size consideration should not outweigh that of type, proportion and functional attributes such as shoulders, chest, legs, feet and movement. When dogs are judged equal in type, proportion and functional attributes, the dog nearest the desirable freighting size is to be preferred.

Important: *In judging Alaskan Malamutes their function as a sledge dog for heavy freighting must be given consideration above all else.*

The judge must bear in mind that this breed is designed primarily as the working sledge dog of the North for hauling heavy freight, and therefore he should be a heavily-boned powerfully built, compact dog with sound legs, good feet, deep chest, powerful shoulders, steady, balanced, tireless gait, and other physical equipment necessary for the efficient performance of his job. He isn't intended as a racing sled dog designed to compete in speed trials with the smaller Northern breeds. The Malamute as a sledge dog for heavy freighting is designed for strength and endurance and any characteristic of the individual specimen, including temperament, which interferes with the accomplishment of this purpose is to be considered the most serious of faults. Faults under this provision would be splay-footedness, and indication of unsoundness or weakness in legs, cow-hocks, bad pasterns, straight shoulders, lack of angulation, stilted gaits or any gait which isn't balanced, strong and steady, ranginess, shallowness, ponderousness, lightness of bone, poor over-all proportion and similar characteristics.

SCALE OF POINTS

General Appearance	20
Head	15
Body	20
Legs and Movement	20
Feet	10
Coat and Color	10
Tail	5
Total	100

Approved April 12, 1960

ALSATIAN (GERMAN SHEPHERD DOG)

(THE KENNEL CLUB—WORKING GROUP)

Characteristics. The characteristic expression of the Alsatian gives the impression of perpetual vigilance, fidelity, liveliness and watchfulness, alert to every sight and sound, with nothing escaping attention; fearless, but with decided suspiciousness of strangers—as opposed to the immediate friendliness of some breeds. The Alsatian possesses highly developed senses, mentally and temperamentally. He should be strongly individualistic and possess a high standard of intelligence. Three of the most outstanding traits are incorruptibility, discernment and ability to reason.

General Appearance. The general appearance of the Alsatian is a well-proportioned dog showing great suppleness of limb, neither massive nor heavy, but at the same time free from any suggestion of weediness. It must not approach the greyhound type. The body is rather long, strongly boned, with plenty of muscle, obviously capable of endurance and speed and of quick and sudden movement. The gait should be supple, smooth and long-reaching, carrying the body along with the minimum of up-and-down movement, entirely free from stiltiness.

Head and Skull. The head is proportionate to the size of the body, long, lean and clean cut, broad at the back of the skull, but without coarseness, tapering to the nose with only a slight stop between the eyes. The skull is slightly domed and the top of the nose should be parallel to the forehead. The cheeks must not be full or in any way prominent and the whole head, when viewed from the top should be much in the form of a V, well filled in under the eyes. There should be plenty of substance in foreface, with a good depth from top to bottom. The muzzle is strong and long and, while tapering to the nose, it must not be carried to such an extreme as to give the appearance of being overshot. It must not show any weakness, or be snipy or lippy. The lips must be tight fitting and clean. The nose must be black.

Eyes. The eyes are almond-shaped as nearly as possible matching the surrounding coat but darker rather than lighter in shade and placed to look straight forward. They must not be in any way bulging or prominent, and must show a lively, alert and highly intelligent expression.

Ears. The ears should be of moderate size, but rather large than small, broad at the base and pointed at the tips, placed rather high on the skull and carried erect—all adding to the alert expression of the dog as a whole. (It should be noted, in case novice breeders may be misled, that in Alsatian puppies the ears often hang until the age of six months and sometimes longer, becoming erect with the replacement of the milk teeth.)

Mouth. The teeth should be sound and strong, gripping with a scissor-like action, the lower incisors just behind, but touching the upper.

Neck. The neck should be strong, fairly long with plenty of muscle, fitting gracefully into the body, joining the head without sharp angles and free from throatiness.

Forequarters. The shoulders should slope well back. The ideal being that a line drawn through the centre of the shoulderblade should form a right-angle with the humerus when the leg is perpendicular to the ground in stance. Upright shoulders are a major fault. They should show plenty of muscle, which is distinct from, and must not be confused with coarse or loaded bone, which is a fault. The shoulder-bone should be clean. The forelegs should be perfectly straight viewed from the front, but the pasterns should show a slight angle with the forearm when regarded from the side, too great an angle denotes weakness and while carrying plenty of bone, it should be of good quality. Anything approaching the massive bone of the Newfoundland, for example, being a decided fault.

Body. The body is muscular, the back is broadish and straight, strongly boned and well developed. The belly shows a waist without being tucked up. There should be a good depth of brisket or chest, the latter should not be too broad. The sides are flat compared to some breeds, and while the dog must not be barrel ribbed, it must not be so flat as to be actually slabsided. The Alsatian should be quick in movement and speedy but not like a Greyhound in body.

Hindquarters. The hindquarters should show breadth and strength, the loins being broad and strong, the rump rather long and sloping and the legs, when viewed from behind, must be quite straight, without any tendency to cow-hocks, or bow-hocks, which are both extremely serious faults. The stifles are well turned and the hocks strong and well let down. The ability to turn quickly is a necessary asset to the Alsatian, and this can only be if there is a good length of thigh-bone and leg, and by the bending of the hock.

Feet. The feet should be round, the toes strong, slightly arched and held close together. The pads should be firm, the nails short and strong. Dewclaws are neither a fault nor a virtue, but should be removed from the hind legs at 4 to 5 days old, as they are liable to spoil the gait.

Tail. When at rest the tail should hang in a slight curve, and reach at least as far as the hock. During movement and excitement it will be raised, but in no circumstances should the tail be carried past a vertical line drawn through the root.

Coat. The coat is smooth, but it is at the same time a double coat. The under-coat is woolly in texture, thick and close and to it the animal owes its characteristic resistance to cold. The outer-coat is also close, each hair straight, hard, and lying flat, so that it is rain-resisting. Under the body, to behind the legs, the coat is longer and forms near the thigh a mild form of breeching. On the head (including the inside of the ears), to the front of the legs and feet, the hair is short. Along the neck it is longer and thicker, and in winter approaches a form of ruff. A coat either too long or too short is a fault. As an average, the hairs on the back should be from 1 to 2 inches in length.

Colour. The colour of the Alsatian is in itself not important and has no effect on the character of the dog or on its fitness for work and should be a secondary consideration for that reason. All white or near white unless possessing black points are not desirable. The final colour of a young dog can only be ascertained when the outer coat has developed.

Weight and Size. The ideal height (measured to the highest point of the shoulder) is 22 to 24 inches for bitches and 24 to 26 inches for dogs. The proportion, of length to height, may vary between 10:9 and 10:8.5.

Faults. A long, narrow, Collie or Borzoi head. A pink or liver-coloured nose. Undershot or overshot mouth. Tail with curl or pronounced hook. The lack of heavy undercoat.

GERMAN SHEPHERD DOG

(AMERICAN KENNEL CLUB—GROUP III: WORKING DOGS)

General Appearance. The first impression of a good German Shepherd Dog is that of a strong, agile, well-muscled animal, alert and full of life. It is well balanced, with harmonious development of the forequarter and hindquarter. The dog is longer than tall, deep-bodied, and presents an outline of smooth curves rather than angles. It looks substantial and not spindly, giving the impression, both at rest and in motion, of muscular fitness and nimbleness without any look of clumsiness or soft living. The ideal dog is stamped with a look of quality and nobility—difficult to define, but unmistakable when present. Secondary sex characteristics are strongly marked, and every animal gives a definite impression of masculinity or femininity, according to its sex.

Character. The breed has a distinct personality marked by direct and fearless, but not hostile, expression, self-confidence and a certain aloofness that does not lend itself to immediate and indiscriminate friendships. The dog must be approachable, quietly standing its ground and showing confidence and willingness to meet overtures without itself making them. It is poised, but when the occasion demands, eager and alert; both fit and willing to serve in its capacity as companion, watchdog, blind leader, herding dog, or guardian, whichever the circumstances may demand. The dog must not be timid, shrinking behind its master or handler; it should not be nervous, looking about or upward with anxious expression or showing nervous reactions, such as tucking of tail, to strange sounds or sights. Lack of confidence under any surroundings is not typical of good character. Any of the above deficiencies in character which indicate shyness must be penalized as very serious faults. It must be possible for the judge to observe the teeth and to determine that both testicles are descended. Any dog that attempts to bite the judge must be disqualified. The ideal dog is a working animal with an incorruptible character combined with body and gait suitable for the arduous work that constitutes its primary purpose.

Head. The head is noble, cleanly chiseled, strong without coarseness, but above all not fine, and in proportion to the body. The head of the male is distinctly masculine, and that of the bitch distinctly feminine. The muzzle is long and strong with the lips firmly fitted, and its topline is parallel to the topline of the skull. Seen from the front, the forehead is only moderately arched, and the skull slopes into the long, wedge-shaped muzzle without abrupt stop. Jaws are strongly developed.

Ears. Ears are moderately pointed, in proportion to the skull, open toward the front, and carried erect when at attention, the ideal carriage being one in which the center lines of the ears, viewed from the front, are parallel to each other and perpendicular to the ground. A dog with cropped or hanging ears must be disqualified.

Eyes. Of medium size, almond shaped, set a little obliquely and not protruding. The color is as dark as possible. The expression keen, intelligent and composed.

Teeth. 42 in number—20 upper and 22 lower—are strongly developed and meet in a scissors bite in which part of the inner surface of the upper incisors meet and engage part of the outer surface of the lower incisors. An overshot jaw or a level bite is undesirable. An undershot jaw is a disqualifying fault. Complete dentition is to be preferred. Any missing teeth other than first premolars is a serious fault.

Neck. The neck is strong and muscular, clean-cut and relatively long, proportionate in size to the head and without loose folds of skin. When the dog is at attention or excited, the head is raised and the neck carried high; otherwise typical carriage of the head is forward rather than up and but little higher than the top of the shoulders, particularly in motion.

Forequarters. The shoulder blades are long and obliquely angled, laid on flat and not placed forward. The upper arm joins the shoulder blade at about a right angle. Both the upper arm and the shoulder blade are well muscled. The forelegs, viewed from all sides, are straight and the bone oval rather than round. The pasterns are strong and springy and angulated at approximately a 25-degree angle from the vertical.

Feet. The feet are short, compact, with toes well arched, pads thick and firm, nails short and dark. The dewclaws, if any, should be removed from the hind legs. Dewclaws on the forelegs may be removed, but are normally left on.

Proportion. The German Shepherd Dog is longer than tall, with the most desirable proportion as 10 to $8\frac{1}{2}$. The desired height for males at the top of the highest point of the shoulder blade is 24 to 26 inches; and for bitches, 22 to 24 inches. The length is measured from the point of the prosternum or breast bone to the rear edge of the pelvis, the ischial tuberosity.

Body. The whole structure of the body gives an impression of depth and solidity without bulkiness.

Chest. Commencing at the prosternum, it is well filled and carried well down between the legs. It is deep and capacious, never shallow, with ample room for lungs and heart, carried well forward, with the prosternum showing ahead of the shoulder in profile.

Ribs. Well sprung and long, neither barrel-shaped not too flat, and carried down to a sternum which reaches to the elbows. Correct ribbing allows the elbows to move back freely when the dog is at a trot. Too round causes interference and throws the elbows out; too flat or short causes pinched elbows. Ribbing is carried well back so that the loin is relatively short.

Abdomen. Firmly held and not paunchy. The bottom line is only moderately tucked up in the loin.

Topline—Withers. The withers are higher than and sloping into the level back.

Back. The back is straight, very strongly developed without sag or roach, and relatively short. The desirable long proportion is not derived from a long back, but from over-all length with relation to height, which is achieved by length of forequarter and length of withers and hindquarter, viewed from the side.

Loin. Viewed from the top, broad and strong. Undue length between the last rib and the thigh, when viewed from the side, is undesirable.

Croup. Long and gradually sloping.

Tail. Bushy, with the last vertebra extended at least to the hock joint. It is set smoothly into the croup and low rather than high. At rest, the tail hangs in a slight curve like a saber. A slight hook—sometimes carried to one side—is faulty only to the extent that it mars general appearance. When the dog is excited or in motion, the curve is accentuated and the tail raised, but it should never be curled forward beyond a vertical line. Tails too short, or with clumpy ends due to ankylosis, are serious faults. A dog with a docked tail must be disqualified.

Hindquarters. The whole assembly of the thigh, viewed from the side, is broad, with both upper and lower thigh well muscled, forming as nearly as possible a right angle. The upper thigh bone parallels the shoulder blade while the lower thigh bone parallels the upper arm. The metatarsus (the unit between the hock joint and the foot) is short, strong and tightly articulated.

Gait. A German Shepherd Dog is a trotting dog, and its structure has been developed to meet the requirements of its work.

General Impression. The gait is outreaching, elastic, seemingly without effort, smooth and rhythmic, covering the maximum amount of ground with the minimum number of steps. At a walk it covers a great deal of ground, with long stride of both hind legs and forelegs. At a trot the dog covers still more ground with even longer stride, and moves powerfully but easily, with co-ordination and balance so that the gait appears to be the steady motion of a well-lubricated machine. The feet travel close to the ground on both forward reach and backward push. In order to achieve ideal movement of this kind, there must be good muscular development and ligamentation. The hindquarters deliver, through the back, a powerful forward thrust which slightly lifts the whole animal and drives the body forward. Reaching far under, and passing the imprint left by the front foot, the hind foot takes hold of the ground; then hock, stifle and upper thigh come into play and sweep back, the stroke of the hind leg finishing with the foot still close to the ground in a smooth follow-through. The over-reach of the hindquarter usually necessitates one hind foot passing outside and the other hind foot passing inside the track of the forefeet, and such action is not faulty unless the locomotion is crabwise with the dog's body sideways out of the normal straight line.

Transmission. The typical smooth, flowing gait is maintained with great strength and firmness of back. The whole effort of the hindquarter is transmitted to the forequarter through the loin, back and withers. At full trot, the back must remain firm and level without sway, roll, whip or roach. Unlevel topline with withers lower than the hip is a fault. To compensate for the forward motion imparted by the hindquarters, the shoulder should open to its full extent. The forelegs should reach out close to the ground in a long stride in harmony with that of the hindquarters. The dog does not track on widely separated parallel lines, but brings the feet inward toward the middle line of the body when trotting in order to maintain balance. The feet track closely but do not strike or cross over. Viewed from the front, the front legs function from the shoulder joint to the pad in a straight line. Viewed from the rear, the hind legs function from the hip joint to the pad in a straight line. Faults of gait, whether from front, rear or side, are to be considered very serious faults.

Color. The German Shepherd Dog varies in color, and most colors are permissible. Strong rich colors are preferred. Nose black. Pale, washed-out colors and blues or livers are serious faults. A white dog or a dog with a nose that is not predominantly black, must be disqualified.

Coat. The ideal dog has a double coat of medium length. The outer coat should be as dense as possible, hair straight, harsh and lying close to the body. A slightly wavy outer coat, often of wiry texture, is permissible. The head, including the inner ear and foreface, and the legs and paws are covered with short hair, and the neck with longer and thicker hair. The rear of the forelegs and hind legs has somewhat longer hair extending to the pastern and hock, respectively. Faults in coat include soft, silky, too long outer coat, woolly, curly, and open coat.

DISQUALIFICATIONS

Cropped or hanging ears. Undershot jaw. Docked tail. White dogs. Dogs with noses not predominantly black. Any dog that attempts to bite the judge.

Approved April 9, 1968

AUSTRALIAN TERRIER

(THE KENNEL CLUB—TERRIER GROUP)

General Appearance. A rather low-set dog, compact and active.
Head and Skull. Head long, skull flat, full between the eyes; with a soft hair top-knot; long powerful jaw, nose black.
Eyes. Small, keen, dark colour.
Ears. Small, set high on skull, pricked, or dropped towards the front, free from long hair.
Mouth. Teeth level.
Neck. Neck inclined to be long in proportion to body, with a decided frill of hair.
Forequarters. Legs, perfectly straight, well set under the body, slight feather to the knee.
Body. Rather long in proportion to height; well ribbed up; back straight.
Hindquarters. Good strong thighs, hocks slightly bent.
Feet. Clean, small and well padded with no tendency to spread. Black toe nails.
Tail. Docked.
Coat. Straight hair from 2 to $2\frac{1}{2}$ inches long, of hard texture.
Colour. First, blue or silver grey body, tan colour on legs and face (the richer the tan the better). Top-knot blue or silver. Second, clear sandy or red with soft top-knot.
Weight and Size. Average weight about 10 or 11 lbs. Average height about 10 inches.
Faults. Flesh-coloured toe nails or nose; white on feet; white breast; curly or woolly coat; all black coat (puppies excepted). Overshot or undershot mouths.

AUSTRALIAN TERRIER

(AMERICAN KENNEL CLUB—GROUP IV: TERRIERS)

General Appearance. A small, sturdy, rough-coated terrier of spirited action and self-assured manner.
Head. Long, flat-skulled, and full between the eyes, with the stop moderate. The muzzle is no longer than the distance from the eyes to the occiput. Jaws long and powerful, teeth of good size meeting in a scissors bite, although a level bite is acceptable. Nose black.
Ears set high on the skull and well apart. They are small and pricked, the leather either pointed or slightly rounded and free from long hairs.
Eyes. Small, dark, and keen in expression; not prominent. Light-colored and protruding eyes are faulty.
Neck. Inclined to be long, and tapering into sloping shoulders; well furnished with hair which forms a protective ruff.
Body. Low-set and slightly longer from the withers to the root of the tail than from the withers to the ground.
Chest. Medium wide, and deep, with ribs well sprung but not round. Topline level.

Tail. Set on high and carried erect but not too gay; docked leaving two-fifths.
Legs and Feet. Forelegs straight and slightly feathered to the carpus or so-called knee; they are set well under the body with elbows close and pasterns strong. Hindquarters strong and well muscled but not heavy; legs moderately angulated at stifles and hocks, with hocks well let down. Bone medium in size. Feet are small, clean, and catlike, the toes arched and compact, nicely padded and free from long hair. Nails strong and black.
Coat. Outer coat harsh and straight, and about two and one half inches all over the body. Undercoat short and soft. The topknot, which covers only the top of the skull, is of finer texture and lighter color than the body coat.
Color. May be blue-black or silver-black, with rich tan markings on head and legs, sandy color or clear red. The blue-black is bluish at the roots and dark at the tips. In the silver-blacks each hair carries black and silver alternating with black at the tips. The tan is rich and deep, the richer the better. In the sandies, any suggestion of smuttiness is undesirable.
Gait. Straight and true; springy, indicating spirit and assurance.
Temperament. That of a hard-bitten terrier, with the aggressiveness of the natural ratter and hedge hunter, but as a companion, friendly, affectionate and biddable.
Size. Shoulder height, about 10 inches. Average weight 12 to 14 lbs.

Approved September 13, 1960

SILKY TERRIER

(THE KENNEL CLUB—TOY GROUP)

SILKY TERRIER

(AMERICAN KENNEL CLUB—GROUP V: TOYS)

The Silky Terrier is a lightly built, moderately low-set toy dog of pronounced terrier character and spirited action.
Head. The head is strong, wedge-shaped, and moderately long. The skull is a trifle longer than the muzzle, in proportion about three-fifths for the skull, two-fifths for the muzzle.
Skull. Flat, and not too wide between the ears.
Stop. Shallow.
Ears. Small, V-shaped and pricked. They are set high and carried erect without any tendency to flare obliquely off the skull.
Eyes. Small, dark in color, and piercingly keen in expression. Light eyes are a fault.
Teeth. Strong and well aligned, scissors bite. A bite markedly undershot or overshot is a serious fault.
Nose. The nose is black.
Neck and Shoulders. The neck fits gracefully into the sloping shoulders. It is medium long, fine and to some degree crested along its top line.
Body. Low-set, about one fifth longer than the dog's height at the withers. A too short body is a fault. The back line is straight, with a just perceptible rounding over the loins. Brisket medium wide, and deep enough to extend down to the elbows.
Tail. The tail is set high and carried erect or semi-erect but not over-gay. It is docked and well coated but devoid of plume.
Forequarters. Well laid back shoulders, together with good angulation at the upper arm, set the forelegs nicely under the body. Forelegs are strong, straight and rather fine-boned.
Hindquarters. Thighs well muscled and strong, but not so developed as to appear heavy. Legs moderately angulated at stifles and hocks, with the hocks low and equidistant from the hock joints to the ground.
Feet. Small, cat-like, round, compact. Pads are thick and springy while the nails are strong and dark colored. White or flesh colored nails are a fault. The feet point straight ahead, with no turning in or out. Dewclaws, if any, are removed.
Coat. Flat, in texture fine, glossy, silky; on matured specimens the desired length of coat from behind the ears to the set-on of the tail is from five to six inches. On the top of the head the hair is so profuse as to form a topknot, but long hair on face and ears is objectionable. Legs from knee and hock joints to feet should be free from long hair. The hair is parted on the head and down over the back to the root of the tail.
Color. Blue and tan. The blue may be silver blue, pigeon blue or slate blue, the tan deep and rich. The blue extends from the base of the skull to the tip of the tail, down the forelegs to the pasterns, and down the thighs to the hocks. On the tail the blue should be very dark. Tan appears on muzzle and cheeks, around the base of the ears, below the pasterns and hocks, and around the vent. there is a tan spot over each eye. The topknot should be silver or fawn.
Temperament. The keenly alert air of the terrier is characteristic, with shyness or excessive nervousness to be faulted. The manner is quick, friendly, responsive.
Movement. Should be free, light footed, lively, and straightforward. Hindquarters should have strong propelling power. Toeing in or out is to be faulted.
Size. Weight ranges from eight to ten pounds. Shoulder height from nine to ten inches. Pronounced diminutiveness (such as a height of less than 8 inches) is not desired; it accentuates the quality of toyishness as opposed to the breed's definite terrier character.

Approved April 14, 1959

BASENJI

(THE KENNEL CLUB—HOUND GROUP)

Characteristics. The Basenji does not bark but is not mute, its own special noise is a mixture of a chortle and a yodel. It is remarkable for its cleanliness in every way. The wrinkled forehead, tightly curled tail, and legs carried straight forward with a swift, long, tireless, swinging stride, are typical of the breed.

General Appearance. The Basenji should be a lightly built, finely-boned aristocratic looking animal, high on the leg compared with its length, always poised, alert and intelligent. The wrinkled head, with pricked ears, should be proudly carried on a well-arched neck. The deep brisket should run up into a definite waist and the tail be tightly curled, presenting a picture of a well-balanced dog of gazelle-like grace.

Head and Skull. The skull should be flat, well-chiselled and of medium width, tapering towards the nose, with only a slight stop. The distance from the top of the head to the stop is slightly more than from the stop to the tip of the nose. The side lines of the skull taper gradually towards the mouth, giving a clean-cheeked appearance. Fine and profuse wrinkles should appear on the forehead when the ears are pricked, side wrinkles are desirable but should not be exaggerated into dewlap. Wrinkles are more noticeable in puppies, but, because of lack of shadowing, are not as noticeable in tri-colours. A black nose is greatly desired.

Eyes. Dark, almond shaped, obliquely set, far-seeing and rather inscrutable in expression.

Ears. Small, pointed, erect and slightly hooded, of fine texture, set well forward on top of the head, the tip of the ear should be nearer the centre of the skull than the outside base.

Mouth. The mouth should be level, with scissors bite, the upper teeth slightly over-lapping and touching the lower teeth.

Neck. Strong and of good length, without thickness, well-crested and slightly full at the base of the throat with a graceful curve accentuating the crest. It should be well-set into laid back shoulders so as to give the head a 'lofty' carriage.

Forequarters. The shoulders must be well laid back, muscular but not loaded. The points of the scapulae should be fairly close at the withers. The elbows should be firmly tucked in against the brisket. When viewed from in front the elbows should be in line with the ribs and the legs should continue in a straight line to the ground giving a narrow front. The forelegs should be straight with fine bone and very long fore-arms. Pasterns should be of good length, straight but flexible.

Body. Balanced with short, level back. Ribs well sprung, deep and oval. The loin short-coupled and the deep brisket running up into a definite waist.

Hindquarters. Strong and muscular, with hocks well let down, turned neither in nor out, with long second thighs and moderately bent stifles.

Feet. Small, narrow and compact, with deep pads, well-arched toes and short nails.
Tail. The tail should be high set with the posterior curve of the buttock extending beyond the root of the tail giving a reachy appearance to the hindquarters. The tail curls tightly over the spine and lies closely to the thigh with a single or double curl.
Coat. Short, sleek and close, very fine. Skin very pliant.
Colour. Pure bright red, or pure black, or black and tan, all with white feet, chest and tail tips. White legs, white blaze and white collar optional.
Size and Weight. Ideal heights, Dogs 17 inches at shoulder; Bitches 16 inches, an inch either way should not penalize an otherwise well-balanced specimen. Ideal weights: Dogs 24 lbs, Bitches 21 lbs.
Faults. Coarse, domed or peaked skull. Muzzle too long or too broad. Cheekiness. Mouth over-shot or under-shot. Round or light eyes. Ears too low-set or too large. Wide chest, barrel ribs, shelly brisket. Short in the leg, out at elbows, toeing in. Heavy bone, cow hocks, low-set or straight tail, thin flat open feet. Long or heavy coat. Creams, sables, or any other colours than those defined in the Colour paragraphs above should be heavily penalised. Poor temperament.

BASENJI

(AMERICAN KENNEL CLUB—GROUP II: HOUNDS)

Characteristics. The Basenji should not bark, but it is not mute. The wrinkled forehead and the swift, tireless running gait (resembling a racehorse trotting full out) are typical of the breed.
General Appearance. The Basenji is a small, lightly built, short backed dog, giving the impression of being high on the leg compared to its length. The wrinkled head must be proudly carried, and the whole demeanor should be one of poise and alertness.
Head and Skull. The skull is flat, well chiseled and of medium width, tapering towards the eyes. The foreface should taper from eye to muzzle and should be shorter than the skull. Muzzle, neither coarse, nor snipy but with rounded cushions. Wrinkles should appear upon the fore-head, and be fine and profuse. Side wrinkles are desirable, but should never be exaggerated into dewlap.
Nose. Black greatly desired. A pinkish tinge should not penalize an otherwise first class specimen, but it should be discouraged in breeding.
Eyes. Dark hazel, almond shaped, obliquely set and far seeing.
Ears. Small, pointed and erect, of fine texture, set well forward on top of head.
Mouth. Teeth must be level with scissors bite.
Neck. Of good length, well crested and slightly full at base of throat. It should be well set into flat, laid back shoulders.
Forequarters. The chest should be deep and of medium width. The legs straight with clean fine bone, long forearm and well defined sinews. Pasterns should be of good length, straight and flexible.
Body. The body should be short and the back level. The ribs well sprung, with plenty of heart room, deep brisket, short coupled, and ending in a definite waist.
Hindquarters. Should be strong and muscular, with hocks well let down, turned neither in nor out, with long second thighs.
Feet. Small, narrow and compact, with well arched toes.
Tail. Should be set on top and curled tightly over to either side.
Coat. Short and silky. Skin very pliant.
Color. Chestnut red (the deeper the better) or pure black, or black and tan, all with white feet, chest and tail tip. White legs, white blaze and white collar optional.
Weight. Bitches 22 pounds approximately. Dogs 24 pounds approximately.
Size. Bitches 16 inches and dogs 17 inches from the ground to the top of the shoulder. Bitches 16 inches and dogs 17 inches from the front of the chest to the farthest point of the hindquarters.
Faults. Coarse skull or muzzle. Domed or peaked skull. Dewlap. Round eyes. Low set ears. Overshot or undershot mouths. Wide chest. Wide behind. Heavy bone. Creams, shaded or off colors, other than those defined above, should be heavily penalized.

Approved June 8, 1954

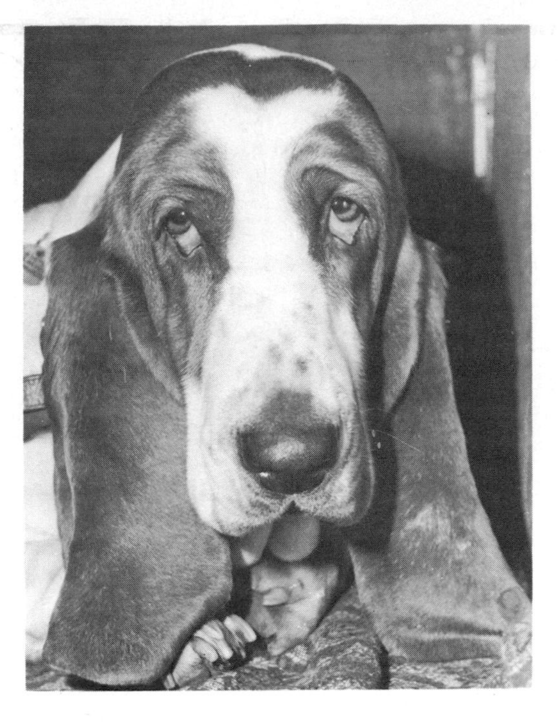

BASSET HOUND

(THE KENNEL CLUB—HOUND GROUP)

General Characteristics. A short-legged hound of considerable substance, well-balanced and full of quality. Action is most important. A smooth free action with forelegs reaching well forward and hind legs showing powerful thrust and the hound moving true both front and rear. Hocks and stifles must not be stiff in movement nor must any toes be dragged.

Head and Skull. Domes, with some stop and the occipital bone prominent; of medium width at the brow and tapering slightly to the muzzle; the general appearance of the foreface is lean but not snipy. The top of the muzzle nearly parallel with the line from stop to occiput and not much longer than the head from stop to occiput. There may be a moderate amount of wrinkle at the brows and beside the eyes and in any event the skin of the head should be so loose as to wrinkle noticeably when drawn forward or when the head is lowered. The flews of the upper lip overlap the lower substantially.

Nose. Entirely black, except in light-coloured hounds, when it may be brown or liver. Large with well opened nostrils and may protrude a little beyond the lips.

Eyes. Brown, but may shade to hazel in light-coloured hounds, neither prominent nor too deep set. The expression is calm and serious and the red of the lower lid appears, though not excessively.

Ears. Set on low but not excessively so and never above the line of the eye; very long, reaching at least to the end of a muzzle of correct length, narrow throughout their length and curling well inwards; very supple, fine and velvety in texture.

Mouth. The teeth level with a scissors bite although if they meet edge to edge it is not a fault.

Neck. Muscular and fairly long with pronounced dewlap but not exaggerated.

Forequarters. Shoulder-blades well laid back and shoulders not heavy. Forelegs short, powerful and with great bone, the elbows turned neither out nor in but fitting easily against the side. The knees at least slightly crooked inwards but not to so great an extent as to prevent free action or to result in legs touching each other when standing or in action. Knuckling-over is a bad fault. There may be wrinkles of skin between knee and foot.

Body. The breast bone slightly prominent but the chest not narrow or unduly deep; the ribs well-rounded and sprung and carried well back. The back rather broad, level, and with withers and quarters of approximately the same height, though the loins may arch slightly. The back from withers to the inset of the quarters not unduly long.

Hindquarters. Full of muscle and standing out well, giving an almost spherical effect when viewing the hound from the rear. Stifles well bent. The hocks as low to the ground as possible and slightly bent under the hound but not turned in or out. They should be placed just under the body when standing naturally. One or two wrinkles of skin may appear between hock and foot and at the rear of the joint a slight pouch resulting from the looseness of the skin.

Feet. Massive well knuckled-up and padded. The forefeet may point straight ahead or be turned slightly outwards but in every case the hound must stand perfectly true, the weight being borne equally by toes with pads together so that the feet would leave the imprint of a large hound and no unpadded areas in contact with the ground.

Tail. Well set-on, rather long, strong at the base and tapering with a moderate amount of coarse hair underneath. When the hound is moving the stern is carried well up and curves gently sabre-fashion over the back but is never curling or gay.

Coat. Smooth short and close without being too fine.

Colour. Generally black, white and tan or lemon and white, but any recognized hound colour is acceptable.

Height. Height 13 to 15 inches.

Faults. Any departure from the above Standard is a fault but the following should particularly be penalised:

(a) unsoundness of legs or feet.
(b) faulty mouth.
(c) lack of balance (i.e. undue exaggeration of any point).
(d) lack of typical Basset appearance and expression.

BASSET HOUND

(AMERICAN KENNEL CLUB—GROUP II: HOUNDS)

General Appearance. The Basset Hound possesses in marked degree those characteristics which equip it admirably to follow a trail over and through difficult terrain. It is a short-legged dog, heavier in bone, size considered, than any other breed of dog, and while its movement is deliberate, it is in no sense clumsy. In temperament it is mild, never sharp or timid. It is capable of great endurance in the field and is extreme in its devotion.

Head. The head is large and well proportioned. Its length from occiput to muzzle is greater than the width at the brow. In over-all appearance the head is of medium width.

Skull is well domed, showing a pronounced occipital protuberance. A broad flat skull is a fault. The length from nose to stop is approximately the length from stop to occiput. The sides are flat and free from cheek bumps. Viewed in profile the top lines of the muzzle and skull are straight and lie in parallel planes, with a moderately defined stop. The skin over the whole of the head is loose, falling in distinct wrinkles over the brow when the head is lowered. A dry head and tight skin are faults.

Muzzle is deep, heavy, and free from snipiness.

Nose is darkly pigmented, preferably black, with large wide-open nostrils. A deep liver-colored nose conforming to the coloring of the head is permissible but not desirable.

Teeth are large, sound, and regular, meeting in either a scissors or an even bite. A bite either overshot or undershot is a serious fault.

Lips are darkly pigmented and are pendulous, falling squarely in front and, toward the back, in loose hanging flews.

Dewlap is very pronounced.

Neck is powerful, of good length, and well arched.

Eyes are soft, sad, and slightly sunken, showing a prominent haw, and in color are brown, dark brown preferred. A somewhat lighter-colored eye conforming to the general coloring of the dog is acceptable but not desirable. Very light or protruding eyes are faults.

Ears are extremely long, low set, and when drawn forward, fold well over the end of the nose. They are velvety in texture, hanging in loose folds with the ends curling slightly inward. They are set far back on the head at the base of the skull and, in repose, appear to be set on the neck. A high set or flat ear is a serious fault.

Forequarters.

Chest is deep and full with prominent sternum showing clearly in front of the legs.

Shoulders and elbows are set close against the sides of the chest. The distance from the deepest point of the chest to the ground, while it must be adequate to allow free movement when working in the field, is not to be more than one-third the total height at the withers of an adult Basset. The shoulders are well laid back and powerful. Steepness in shoulder, fiddle fronts, and elbows that are out, are serious faults.

Forelegs are short, powerful, heavy in bone, with wrinkled skin. Knuckling over of the front legs is a disqualification.

The paw is massive, very heavy with tough heavy pads, well rounded and with both feet inclined equally a trifle outward, balancing the width of the shoulders. Feet down at the pastern are a serious fault.

Toes are neither pinched together nor splayed, with the weight of the forepart of the body borne evenly on each. The dewclaws may be removed.

Body. The rib structure is long, smooth, and extends well back. The ribs are well sprung, allowing adequate room for heart and lungs. Flat-sidedness and flanged ribs are faults. The topline is straight, level, and free from any tendency to sag or roach, which are faults.

Hindquarters. The hindquarters are very full and well rounded, and are approximately equal to the shoulders in width. They must not appear slack or light in relation to the over-all depth of the body. The dog stands firmly on its hind legs showing a well-let-down stifle with no tendency toward a crouching stance. Viewed from behind, the hind legs are parallel, with the hocks turning neither in nor out. Cowhocks or bowed legs are serious faults. The hind feet point straight ahead. Steep, poorly angulated hindquarters are a serious fault. The dewclaws, if any, may be removed.

Tail. The tail is not to be docked, and is set in continuation of the spine with but slight curvature, and carried gaily in hound fashion. The hair on the underside of the tail is coarse.

Size. The height should not exceed 14 inches. Height over 15 inches at the highest point of the shoulder blades is a disqualification.

Gait. The Basset Hound moves in a smooth, powerful, and effortless manner. Being a scenting dog with short legs, it holds its nose low to the ground. Its gait is absolutely true with perfect co-ordination between the front and hind legs, and it moves in a straight line with hind feet following in line with the front feet, the hocks well bent with no stiffness of action. The front legs do not paddle, weave, or overlap, and the elbows must lie close to the body. Going away, the hind legs are parallel.

Coat. The coat is hard, smooth, and short, with sufficient density to be of use in all weathers. The skin is loose and elastic. A distinctly long coat is a disqualification.

Color. Any recognized hound color is acceptable and the distribution of color and markings is of no importance.

DISQUALIFICATIONS

Height of more than 15 inches at the highest point of the shoulder blades. Knuckled over front legs. Distinctly long coat.

Approved January 14, 1964

BEAGLE

(THE KENNEL CLUB—HOUND GROUP)

Characteristics. A merry hound whose essential function is to hunt, primarily hare, by following a scent. Bold with great activity, stamina and determination. Alert, intelligent and of even temperament.

General Appearance. A sturdy and compactly-built hound, conveying the impression of quality without coarseness.

Head and Skull. Head fair length, powerful in the dog without being coarse, but finer in the bitch; free from frown and excessive wrinkle. Skull slightly domed, moderately wide, with indication of peak. Stop well defined and dividing length between occiput and tip of nose as equally as possible. Muzzle not snipy, lips reasonably well flewed. Nose broad and nostrils well expanded; preferably black, but less pigmentation permissible in the lighter coloured hounds.

Eyes. Dark brown or hazel, fairly large, not deep set or bulgy, set well apart and with a mild appealing expression.

Ears. Long with round tip, reaching nearly to end of nose when drawn out. Set on low, fine in texture and hanging gracefully close to cheek.

Mouth. Teeth strongly developed. Upper incisors just overlapping and touching outer surface of lower incisors to form scissor bite.

Neck. Sufficiently long to enable hound to come down easily to scent, slightly arched and showing a little dewlap.

Forequarters. Shoulders clean and sloping. Forelegs straight and upright, well under the hound, of good substance, strong, hard and round in bone. Not tapering off to feet. Pasterns short. Elbows firm, turning neither in nor out. Height to elbow about half the hound's height to withers.

Body. Topline straight and level. Chest well let down to below elbow. Ribs well sprung and extending well back. Short between the couplings. Loins powerful and supple, without excessive tuck-up.

Hindquarters. Very muscular about the thighs. Stifles well bent. Hocks firm, well let down and parallel to each other.

Feet. Tight and firm. Well knuckled up and strongly padded. Not hare-footed. Nails short.

Gait. Back level and no roll. Stride free, long-reaching and straight without high action. Hindlegs showing drive. Should not move close behind or paddle or plait in front.

Tail. Sturdy and of moderate length. Set on high and carried gaily but not curled over back or inclined forward from the root. Well covered with hair, especially on underside.

Coat. Short, dense and weatherproof.

Colour. Any recognized hound colour other than liver. Tip of stern white.

Weight and Size. It is desirable that height from ground to withers should neither exceed 16 inches nor fall below 13 inches.

Note. Male animals should have two apparently normal testicles fully descended into the scrotum.

BEAGLE

(AMERICAN KENNEL CLUB—GROUP II: HOUNDS)

Head. The skull should be fairly long, slightly domed at occiput, with cranium broad and full.

Ears. Ears set on moderately low, long, reaching when drawn out nearly, if not quite, to the end of the nose; fine in texture, fairly broad—with almost entire absence of erectile power—setting close to the head, with the forward edge slightly inturning to the cheek—rounded at tip.

Eyes. Eyes large, set well apart—soft and hound-like—expression gentle and pleading; of a brown or hazel color.

Muzzle. Muzzle of medium length—straight and square-cut—the stop moderately defined.

Jaws. Level. Lips free from flews; nostrils large and open.

Defects. A very flat skull, narrow across the top; excess of dome, eyes small, sharp and terrierlike, or prominent and protruding; muzzle long, snipy or cut away decidedly below the eyes, or very short. Roman-nosed, or upturned, giving a dish-face expression. Ears short, set on high or with a tendency to rise above the point of origin.

Body—Neck and Throat. Neck rising free and light from the shoulders strong in substance yet not loaded, of medium length. The throat clean and free from folds of skin; a slight wrinkle below the angle of the jaw, however, may be allowable.

Defects. A thick, short, cloddy neck carried on a line with the top of the shoulders. Throat showing dewlap and folds of skin to a degree termed 'throatiness.'

Shoulders and Chest. Shoulders sloping—clean, muscular, not heavy or loaded—conveying the idea of freedom of action with activity and strength. Chest deep and broad, but not broad enough to interfere with the free play of the shoulders.

Defects. Straight, upright shoulders. Chest disproportionately wide or with lack of depth.

Back, Loin and Ribs. Back short, muscular and strong. Loin broad and slightly arched, and the ribs well sprung, giving abundance of lung room.

Defects. Very long or swayed or roached back. Flat, narrow loin. Flat ribs.

Forelegs and feet—Forelegs. Straight, with plenty of bone in proportion to size of the hound. Pasterns short and straight.

Feet. Close, round and firm. Pad full and hard.

Defects. Out at elbows. Knees knuckled over forward, or bent backward. Forelegs crooked or Dachshund-like. Feet long, open or spreading.

Hips, Thighs, Hind Legs and Feet. Hips and thighs strong and well muscled, giving abundance of propelling power. Stifles strong and well let down. Hocks firm, symmetrical and moderately bent. Feet close and firm.

Defects. Cowhocks, or straight hocks. Lack of muscle and propelling power. Open feet.

Tail. Set moderately high; carried gaily, but not turned forward over the back; with slight curve; short as compared with size of the hound; with brush.

Defects. A long tail. Teapot curve or inclined forward from the root. Rat tail with absence of brush.

Coat. A close, hard, hound coat of medium length.

Defects. A short, thin coat, or of a soft quality.

Color. Any true hound color.

General Appearance. A miniature Foxhound, solid and big for his inches, with the wear-and-tear look of the hound that can last in the chase and follow his quarry to the death.

SCALE OF POINTS

Head			*Running Gear*		
Skull	5		Forelegs	10	
Ears	10		Hips, thighs and hind legs	10	
Eyes	5				
Muzzle	5	25	Feet	10	30
Body					
Neck	5		Coat	5	
Chest and shoulders	15		Stern	5	10
Back, loin and ribs	15	35	Total		100

Varieties. There shall be two varieties. Thirteen Inch—which shall be for hounds not exceeding 13 inches in height. Fifteen Inch—which shall be for hounds over 13 but not exceeding 15 inches in height.

DISQUALIFICATION

Any hound measuring more than 15 inches shall be disqualified.

PACKS OF BEAGLES

SCORE OF POINTS FOR JUDGING

Hounds—General levelness of pack	40%	
Individual merit of hounds	30%	
		70%
Manners		20%
Appointments		10%
Total		100%

Levelness of Pack. The first thing in a pack to be considered is that they present a unified appearance. The hounds must be as near to the same height, weight, conformation and color as possible.

Individual Merit of the Hounds. Is the individual bench-show quality of the hounds. A very level and sporty pack can be gotten together and not a single hound be a good Beagle. This is to be avoided.

Manners. The hounds must all work gaily and cheerfully, with flags up—obeying all commands cheerfully. They should be broken to heel up, kennel up, follow promptly and stand. Cringing, sulking, lying down to be avoided. Also, a pack must not work as though in terror of master and whips. In Beagle packs it is recommended that the whip be used as little as possible.

Appointments. Master and whips should be dressed alike, the master or huntsman to carry horn—the whips and master to carry light thong whips. One whip should carry extra couplings on shoulder strap.

RECOMMENDATIONS FOR SHOW LIVERY

Black velvet cap, white stock, green coat, white breeches or knickerbockers, green or black stockings, white spats, black or dark brown shoes. Vest and gloves optional. Ladies should turn out exactly the same except for a white skirt instead of white breeches.

Approved September 10, 1957

BEARDED COLLIE

(THE KENNEL CLUB—WORKING GROUP)

Characteristics. The Bearded Collie should be alert, lively and self confident, good temperament essential.

General Appearance. An active dog with long, lean body, and none of the stumpiness of the Bobtail and which though strongly made, shows plenty of daylight under the body and does not look too heavy. The face should have an enquiring expression. Movement should be free and active.

Head and Skull. Broad, flat skull with ears set high, fairly long foreface with moderate stop. Nose black except with brown or fawn coats, when brown is permitted.

Eyes. To tone with coat in colour, the eyes to be set rather widely apart, big and bright. Eyebrows arched and forward, but not long enough to obscure the eyes.

Ears. Medium size, drooping with longish hair, slight lift at the base denoting alertness.

Mouth. Teeth large and white, never undershot or overshot.

Neck. Must be fair length, muscular and slightly arched.

Forequarters. Legs straight with good bone, pasterns flexible without weakness, covered with shaggy hair all round.

Body. Fairly long, back level, with flat ribs and strong loins, ribcage both deep and long, shoulders flat, straight front essential.

Hindquarters. Legs muscular at thighs, with well bent stifles and hocks, free from exaggeration.

Feet. Oval in shape, soles well padded, toes arched and close together, well covered with hair including between the pads.

Tail. Set low, should be moderately long with abundant hair or brush, carried low when the dog is quiet, with an upward swirl at the tip, carried gaily when the dog is excited, but not over the back.

Coat. Must be double, the under one soft, furry and close the outer one harsh strong and flat, free from woolliness or any tendency to curl. Sparse hair on the ridge of the nose, slightly longer on the sides just covering the lips. Behind this falls the long beard. A moderate amount of hair under the chin, increasing in length to the chest.

Colour. Slate grey or reddish fawn, black, all shades of grey, brown and sandy, with or without white Collie markings.

Size. Ideal height at the shoulder: Dogs 21 to 22 inches. Bitches 20 to 21 inches.

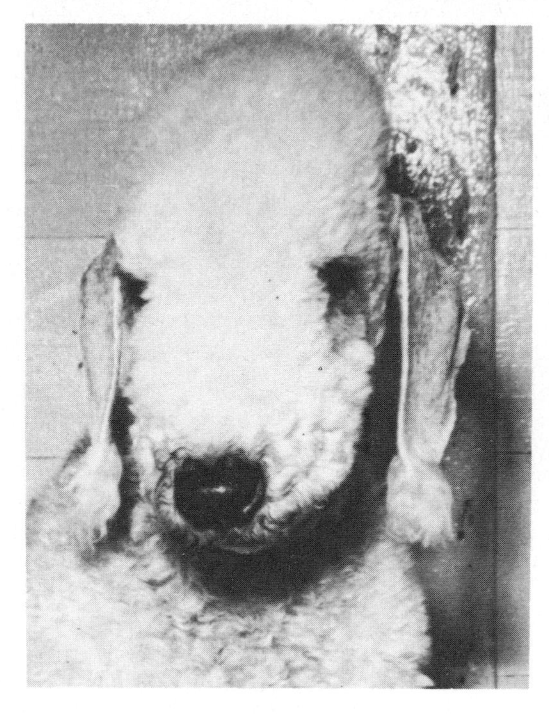

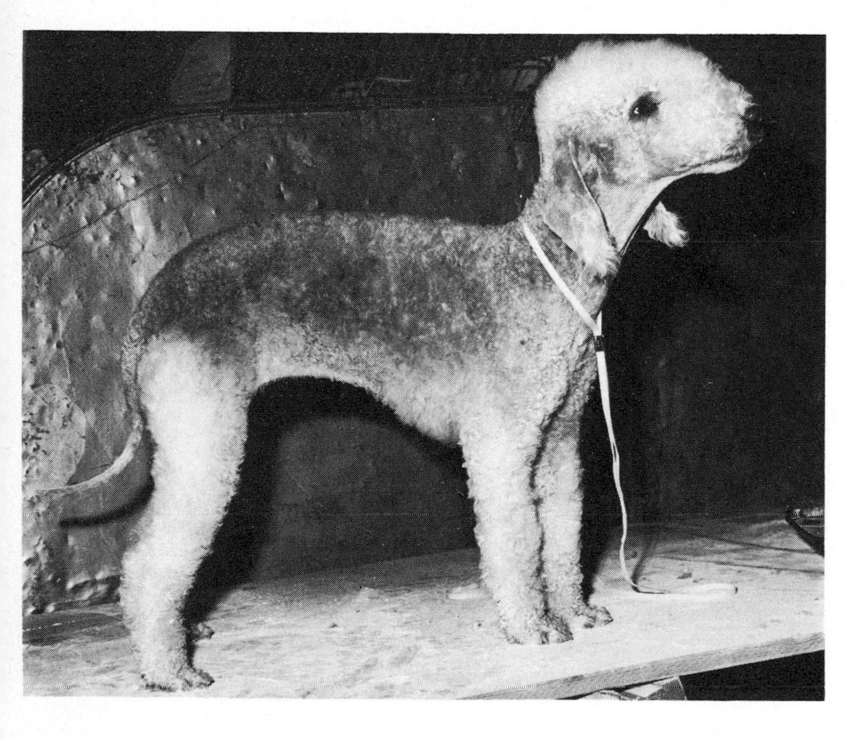

BEDLINGTON TERRIER

(THE KENNEL CLUB—TERRIER GROUP)

General Appearance. A graceful, lithe, muscular dog, with no sign of either weakness or coarseness. The whole head should be pear or wedge-shaped, and expression in repose mild and gentle, though not shy or nervous. When roused, the eyes should sparkle and the dog look full of temper and courage. Bedlingtons are capable of galloping at great speed and should have the appearance of being able to do so. This action is very distinctive. Rather mincing, light and springy in the slower paces, could have slight roll when in full stride. When galloping must use the whole body.

Head and Skull. Skull narrow, but deep and rounded; covered with profuse silky top-knot which should be nearly white. Jaw long and tapering. There must be no 'stop', the line from occiput to nose end being straight and unbroken. Well filled up beneath the eye. Close fitting lips, without flew. The nostrils must be large and well-defined. Blues and blue-and-tans must have black noses; livers and sandies must have brown noses.

Eyes. Small, bright and well sunk. The ideal eye has the appearance of being triangular. Blues should have a dark eye; blue-and-tans have lighter eyes with amber lights, and livers and sandies have a light hazel eye.

Ears. Moderate sized, filbert shaped, set on low, and hanging flat to the cheek. They should be covered with short fine hair with a fringe of whiteish silky hair at the tip.

Mouth. Teeth, level or pincer-jawed. The teeth should be large and strong.

Neck. Long tapering neck, deep at the base; there should be no tendency to throatiness. The neck should spring well up from the shoulders, and the head should be carried rather high.

Forequarters. The forelegs should be straight, but wider apart at the chest than at the feet. Pasterns long and slightly sloping without weakness. Shoulders flat and sloping.

Body. Muscular, yet markedly flexible; flat-ribbed and deep through the brisket; well ribbed up. The chest should be deep and fairly broad. The back should be roached and the loin markedly arched. Muscular galloping quarters which are also fine and graceful.

Hindquarters. Muscular and of moderate length. The hindlegs, by reason of the roach back and arched loin, have the appearance of being longer than the forelegs. The hocks should be strong and well let down.

Feet. Long hare feet with thick and well closed up pads.

Tail. Of moderate length, thick at the root, tapering to a point and gracefully curved. Should be set on low, and must never be carried over the back.

Coat. Very distinctive. Thick and linty, standing well out from the skin, but not wiry. There should be a distinct tendency to twist, particularly on the head and face.

Colour. Blue, blue and tan, liver, or sandy. Darker pigment to be encouraged.

Weight and Size. Height should be about sixteen inches at the shoulder. This allows of slight variation below in the case of a bitch and above in the case of a dog. Weight should be between eighteen and twenty-three pounds.

BEDLINGTON TERRIER

(AMERICAN KENNEL CLUB—GROUP IV: TERRIERS)

General Appearance. A graceful, lithe, well-balanced dog with no sign of coarseness, weakness or shelliness. In repose the expression is mild and gentle, not shy or nervous. Aroused, the dog is particularly alert and full of immense energy and courage. Noteworthy for endurance, Bedlingtons also gallop at great speed, as their body outline clearly shows.

Head. Narrow, but deep and rounded. Shorter in skull and longer in jaw. Covered with a profuse topknot which is lighter than the color of the body, highest at the crown, and tapering gradually to just back of the nose. There must be no stop and the unbroken line from crown to nose end reveals a slender head without cheekiness or snipiness. Lips are black in the blue and tans and brown in all other solid and bi-colors.

Eyes. Almond-shaped, small, bright and well sunk with no tendency to tear or water. Set is oblique and fairly high on the head. Blues have dark eyes; blues and tans, less dark with amber lights; sandies, sandies and tans, light hazel; liver, livers and tans, slightly darker. Eye rims are black in the blue and blue and tans, and brown in all other solid and bi-colors.

Ears. Triangular with rounded tips. Set on low and hanging flat to the cheek in front with a slight projection at the base. Points of greatest width approximately 3 inches. Ear tips reach the corners of the mouth. Thin and velvety in texture, covered with fine hair forming a small silky tassel at the tip.

Nose. Nostrils large and well defined. Blues and blues and tans have black noses. Livers, livers and tans, sandies, sandies and tans have brown noses.

Jaws. Long and tapering. Strong muzzle well filled up with bone beneath the eye. Close-fitting lips, no flews.

Teeth. Large, strong and white. Level or scissors bite. Lower canines clasp the outer surface of the upper gum just in front of the upper canines. Upper premolars and molars lie outside those of the lower jaw.

Neck and Shoulders. Long, tapering neck with no throatiness, deep at the base and rising well up from the shoulders which are flat and sloping with no excessive musculature. The head is carried high.

Body. Muscular and markedly flexible. Chest deep. Flat-ribbed and deep through the brisket, which reaches to the elbows. Back has a good natural arch over the loin, creating a definite tuck-up of the underline. Body slightly greater in length than height. Well-muscled quarters are also fine and graceful.

Legs and Feet. Lithe and muscular. The hindlegs are longer than the forelegs, which are straight and wider apart at the chest than at the feet. Slight bend to pasterns which are long and sloping without weakness. Stifles well angulated. Hocks strong and well let down, turning neither in nor out. Long hare feet with thick, well-closed-up, smooth pads. Dewclaws should be removed.

Coat. A very distinctive mixture of hard and soft hair standing well out from the skin. Crisp to the touch but not wiry, having a tendency to curl, especially on the head and face. When in show trim must not exceed 1 inch on body; hair on legs is slightly longer.

Tail. Set low, scimitar-shaped, thick at the root and tapering to a point which reaches the hock. Not carried over the back or tight to the underbody.

Color. Blue, sandy, liver, blue and tan, sandy and tan, liver and tan. In bi-colors the tan markings are found on the legs, chest, under the tail, inside the hindquarters and over each eye. The topknots of all adults should be lighter than the body color. Patches of darker hair from an injury are not objectionable, as these are only temporary. Darker body pigmentation of all colors is to be encouraged.

Height. The preferred Bedlington Terrier dog measures $16\frac{1}{2}$ inches at the withers, the bitch $15\frac{1}{2}$ inches. Under 16 inches or over $17\frac{1}{2}$ inches for dogs and under 15 inches or over $16\frac{1}{2}$ inches for bitches are serious faults. Only where comparative superiority of a specimen outside these ranges clearly justifies it, should greater latitude be taken.

Weight. To be proportionate to height within the range of 17 to 23 pounds.

Gait. Unique lightness of movement. Springy in the slower paces, not stilted or hackneyed. Must not cross, weave or paddle.

Approved September 12, 1967

BELGIAN MALINOIS

(THE KENNEL CLUB—WORKING GROUP)

BELGIAN MALINOIS

(AMERICAN KENNEL CLUB—GROUP III: WORKING DOGS)

General Appearance. The Belgian Malinois is a well-balanced, square dog, elegant in appearance, with an exceedingly proud carriage of the head and neck. The dog is strong, agile, well-muscled, alert and full of life. It stands squarely on all fours and viewed from the side, the topline, forelegs and hindlegs closely approximate a square. The whole conformation gives the impression of depth and solidity without bulkiness. The expression indicates alertness, attention and readiness for activity, and the gaze is intelligent and questioning. The male is usually somewhat more impressive and grand than its female counterpart, which has a distinctly feminine look.

Size and Substance. Males 24 to 26 inches in height, females 22 to 24 inches measured at the withers. The length, measured from point of breast bone to point of rump, should equal the height, but bitches may be slightly longer. Bone structure is moderately heavy in proportion to height so that the dog is well balanced throughout and neither spindly or leggy nor cumbersome and bulky.

Coat. Comparatively short, straight, with dense undercoat. Very short hair on the head, ears and lower legs. The hair is somewhat longer around the neck where it forms a collarette, and on the tail and the back of the thighs.

Color. Rich fawn to mahogany, with black overlay. Black mask and ears. The under parts of the body, tail, and breeches are lighter fawn, but washed-out fawn color on the body is a fault. The tips of the toes may be white and a small white spot on the chest is permitted.

Head. Clean-cut and strong, over-all size in proportion to the body.

Skull. Top flattened rather than rounded, the width approximately the same as the length but no wider.

Stop. Moderate.

Muzzle, Jaws, Lips. Muzzle moderately pointed, avoiding any tendency to snipiness, and approximately equal in length to that of the topskull. The jaws are strong and powerful. The lips tight and black, with no pink showing on the outside

Ears. Triangular in shape, stiff, erect and in proportion to the head in size. Base of the ear should not come below the center of the eye.

Eyes. Brown, preferably dark brown, medium size, slightly almond shaped, not protruding.

Nose. Black, without spots or discolored areas.

Teeth. A full complement of strong, white teeth,

evenly set and meeting in an even bite or a scissors bite, neither overshot nor undershot.

Torso—Neck. Round and rather outstretched, tapered from head to body, well muscled with tight skin.

Topline. The withers are slightly higher and slope into the back, which must be level, straight and firm from withers to hip joints. The loin section, viewed from above, is relatively short, broad and strong, but blending smoothly into the back. The croup is medium long, sloping gradually.

Tail. Strong at the base, bone to reach hock. At rest it is held low, the tip bent back level with the hock. In action it is raised with a curl, which is strongest toward the tip, without forming a hook.

Chest. Not broad, but deep. The lowest point reaches the elbow, forming a smooth ascendant curve to the abdomen, which is moderately developed, neither tucked-up nor paunchy.

Forequarters—Shoulders. Long and oblique, laid flat against the body, forming a sharp angle (approximately 90°) with the upper arm.

Legs. Straight, strong and paralleled to each other. Bone oval rather than round. Length and substance well proportioned to the size of the dog. Pastern: Medium length, strong and very slightly sloped. Dewclaws may be removed.

Feet. Round (cat footed), toes curved close together, well padded. Nails strong and black except that they may be white to match white toe tips.

Hindquarters—Thighs. Broad and heavily muscled. The upper and lower thigh bones approximately parallel the shoulder blade and upper arm respectively, forming a relatively sharp angle at stifle joint.

Legs. Length and substance well proportioned to the size of the dog. Bone oval rather than round. Legs are parallel to each other. The angle at the hock is relatively sharp, although the Belgian Malinois does not have extreme angulation. Metatarsus medium length, strong and slightly sloped. Dewclaws, if any, should be removed.

Feet. Slightly elongated, toes curved close together, well padded. Nails strong and black except that they may be white to match white toe tips.

Gait. Smooth, free and easy, seemingly never tiring, exhibiting facility of movement rather than a hard driving action. The dog tends to single track at a fast gait, the legs, both front and rear, converging toward the center line of gravity of the dog, while the backline remains firm and level, parallel to the line of motion with no crabbing. The Belgian Malinois shows a marked tendency to move in a circle rather than a straight line.

FAULTS

Any deviation from these specifications is a fault, the degree to which a dog is penalized depending on the extent to which the dog deviates from the standard and the extent to which the particular fault would actually affect the working ability of the dog.

DISQUALIFICATIONS

Ears hanging, as on a hound. Tail—cropped or stump. Males under 22½ or over 27½ inches in height. Females under 20½ or over 25½ inches in height.

Approved April 13, 1965

BELGIAN SHEPHERD DOG (GROENENDAELS)

(THE KENNEL CLUB—WORKING GROUP)

General Appearance. A medium-sized dog, well proportioned, intelligent, hardy, and bred to withstand adverse weather. It should be alert and attentive with a lively and enquiring mien.

Characteristics. With its fine proportions and proud carriage of the head, the Belgian Shepherd Dog should convey an impression of that graceful strength which has become the mark of selected representatives of a working breed. In addition to its inborn skill as a sheep-dog, it has a great potential as a guard dog.

Head and Skull. The head should be finely chiselled, long, but not excessively so, and gaunt. The skull and muzzle should be roughly equal in length, with at most a slight bias in favour of the muzzle, giving the impression of a balanced whole. The skull should be of medium width in proportion to the length of the head, flattened rather than rounded forehead and centre line not very pronounced; seen in profile it should be of medium length tapering gradually towards the nose. The nose should be black with well-flared nostrils. Moderate stop.

Eyes. Of medium size, neither protruding nor sunken, slightly almond-shaped, brownish coloured and preferably dark; black ringed eyelids. Direct, lively and inquiring look. Arches above the eyes not prominent, the muzzle finely chiselled under the eyes.

Ears. Distinctly triangular appearance, stiff and erect, set high, of proportionate length, with the external ear well rounded at the base.

Mouth. Wide. Lips thin-textured, very firm, strongly pigmented, not showing the red of the mucous membranes. Cheeks spare, quite flat but well-muscled. Strong, white, regular teeth firmly set in well-developed jaws. Scissor bite, i.e. the incisors of the upper jaw fitting closely over those of the lower jaw, extending slightly beyond them without losing contact with them. Edge to edge bite tolerated.

Neck. Very supple. The neck should be slightly elongated, well-muscled and without dewlap, broadening slightly towards the shoulders. The nape should be very slightly arched.

Forequarters. Strongly boned throughout with wiry and powerful muscle structure. The shoulder blades should be long and oblique, firmly attached, flat, forming an angle with the humerus, so as to enable the elbows to work easily. The forelegs should be long and well-muscled, and should move parallel. The bones joining the feet and pastern joint should be strong and short. Pastern joint clearly defined. Feet round, toes arched and very close together; soles thick and springy with large dark claws.

Body. The body should be powerful without being bulky. The length from the point of the shoulder to the point of the buttocks should be

approximately equal to the height at the withers in the case of the male; in the female it may be slightly greater. The chest should not be very broad but deep and low. Ribs should be well sprung. The upper line of the body (back and lumber region) should be straight, broad and powerfully muscled. The belly should be moderately developed neither drooping nor unduly cut-up, continuing the lower line of the chest in a graceful curve. The rump should be very slightly sloping, broad but not excessively so. Male animals should have two apparently normal testicles fully descended into the scrotum.

Hindquarters. The hindquarters should be well muscled and powerful but not bulky. Good, but not excessive, angulation, with hocks close to the ground. Viewed from behind the legs should be parallel. Dewclaws are not permitted. Feet slightly oval, toes arched and very close together; soles thick and springy with large dark claws.

Tail. The tail should be firmly set, strong at the base and of medium length. At rest the dog should carry it hanging down, with the tip slightly bent backwards at the level of the hock; on the move he should lift it, accentuating the curve towards the tip; however it should under no circumstances curl up or bend to one side.

Gait. The movement should be brisk and free, covering the maximum amount of ground, but not necessarily in a straight line.

Coat. The outer coat should be long, straight and abundant. It should not be silky or wiry, the texture should be of medium harshness. The undercoat should be extremely dense. The hair should be shorter on the head, outside of the ears and lower part of the legs. The opening of the ear should be protected by hair. The hair should be especially long and abundant, like a ruff around the neck, particularly in the male. There should be a fringe of long hair down the back of the forearm, long and abundant hair evident on the hindquarters and the tail. The male should be longer coated than the female.

Colour. Black. May be completely black or black with limited white as follows: Small to moderate patch or strip on chest, between pads of the feet and on the tips of the hind toes. Frosting (white or grey) on the muzzle.

Skin. Springy but quite taut over the whole body. All external mucous membranes highly pigmented.

Size. The ideal height for the male is $24\frac{1}{2}$ inches and for the female 23 inches.

Faults. Any departure from the foregoing points should be considered a fault and the seriousness of the fault should be in exact proportion to its degree.

BELGIAN SHEEPDOG

(AMERICAN KENNEL CLUB—GROUP III WORKING DOGS)

Personality. The Belgian Sheepdog should reflect the qualities of intelligence, courage, alertness, and devotion to master. To his inherent aptitude as guardian of flocks should be added protectiveness of the person and property of his master. He should be watchful, attentive, and always in motion when not under command. In his relationship with humans he should be observant and vigilant with strangers but not apprehensive. He should not show fear or shyness. He should not show viciousness by unwarranted or unprovoked attack. With those he knows well, he is most affectionate and friendly, zealous of their attention, and very possessive.

General Appearance. The first impression of the Belgian Sheepdog is that of a well-balanced, square dog, elegant in appearance, with an exceedingly proud carriage of the head and neck. He is a strong, agile, well-muscled animal, alert and full of life. His whole conformation gives the impression of depth and solidity without bulkiness. The male dog is usually somewhat more impressive and grand than his female counterpart. The bitch should have a distinctly feminine look.

Size and Substance. Males should be 24–26 inches in height and females 22–24 inches, measured at the withers. The length, measured from point of breast bone to point of rump, should equal the height. Bitches may be slightly longer. Bone structure should be moderately heavy in proportion to his height so that he is well balanced throughout and neither spindly or leggy nor cumbersome and bulky.

Stance. The Belgian Sheepdog should stand squarely on all fours. Side view: the topline, front legs, and back legs should closely approximate a square.

Expression. Indicates alertness, attention, readiness for activity. Gaze should be intelligent and questioning.

Coat. The guard hairs of the coat must be long, well-fitting, straight, and abundant. They should not be silky or wiry. The texture should be a medium harshness. The undercoat should be extremely dense, commensurate, however, with climatic conditions. The Belgian Sheepdog is particularly adaptable to extremes of temperature or climate. The hair is shorter on the head, outside of the ears, and lower part of the legs. The opening of the ear is protected by tufts of hair. Ornamentation: especially long and abundant hair, like a collarette, around the neck; fringe of long hair down the back of the forearm; especially long and abundant hair trimming the hindquarters, the breeches; long, heavy, and abundant hair on the tail.

Color. Black. May be completely black or may be black with white, limited as follows: Small to moderate patch or strip on forechest. Between pads of feet. On *tips* of hind toes. On chin and muzzle (frost—may be white or gray). On *tips* of front toes—allowable but a fault.

Head. Cleancut and strong, overall size should be in proportion to the body.

Skull. Top flattened rather than rounded. The width approximately the same, but not wider, than the length.

Stop. Moderate.

Muzzle, Jaws, Lips. Muzzle moderately pointed, avoiding any tendency to snipiness, and approximately equal in length to that of the topskull. The jaws should be strong and powerful. The lips should be tight and black, with no pink showing on the outside.

Ears. Triangular in shape, stiff, erect, and in proportion to the head in size. Base of the ear should not come below the center of the eye.

Eyes. Brown, preferably dark brown. Medium size, slightly almond shaped, not protruding.

Nose. Black, without spots or discolored areas.

Teeth. A full complement of strong, white teeth, evenly set. Should not be overshot or undershot. Should have either an even bite or a scissors bite.

Torso—Neck. Round and rather outstretched, tapered, well muscled, with tight skin.

Topline. The withers are slightly higher and slope into the back which must be level, straight, and firm from withers to hip joints. The loin section, viewed from above, is relatively short, broad and strong, but blending smoothly into the back. The croup is medium long, sloping gradually.

Tail. Strong at the base, bone to reach hock. At rest the dog holds it low, the tip bent back level with the hock. When in action he raises it and gives it a curl, which is strongest toward the tip, without forming a hook.

Chest. Not broad, but deep. The lowest point should read the elbow, forming a smooth ascendant curve to the abdomen.

Abdomen. Moderate development. Neither tuck-up nor paunchy.

Forequarters—Shoulder. Long and oblique, laid flat against the body, forming a sharp angle (approximately 90°) with the upper arm.

Legs. Straight, strong, and parallel to each other. Bone oval rather than round. Development (length and substance) should be well proportioned to the size of the dog. Pastern: medium length, strong, and very slightly sloped.

Feet. Round (cat footed), toes curved close together, well padded. Nails strong and black except that they may be white to match white toe tips.

Hindquarters—Thighs. Broad and heavily muscled. The upper and lower thigh bones approximately parallel the shoulder blade and upper arm respectively, forming a relatively sharp angle at stifle joint.

Legs. Length and substance well proportioned to the size of the dog. Bone oval rather than round. Legs are parallel to each other. The angle at the hock is relatively sharp, although the Belgian Sheepdog does not have extreme angulation. Metatarsus medium length, strong, and slightly sloped. Dewclaws, if any, should be removed.

Feet. Slightly elongated. Toes curved close together, well padded. Nails strong and black except that they may be white to match white toe tips.

Gait. Motion should be smooth, free and easy, seemingly never tiring, exhibiting facility of movement rather than a hard driving action. He tends to single-track on a fast gait; the legs, both front and rear, converging toward the center line of gravity of the dog. The backline should remain firm and level, parallel to the line of motion with no crabbing. He shows a marked tendency to move in a circle rather than a straight line.

Faults. Any deviation from these specifications is a fault. In determining whether a fault is minor, serious, or major, these two factors should be used as a guide: 1. The extent to which it deviates from the Standard. 2. The extent to which such deviation would actually affect the working ability of the dog.

DISQUALIFICATIONS

Visciousness. Color—any color other than black, except for white in specified areas. Ears—hanging (as on a hound). Tail—cropped or stump. Males under 22½ or over 27½ inches in height. Females under 20½ or over 25½ inches in height.

Approved June 9, 1959

BELGIAN TERVUREN

(THE KENNEL CLUB—WORKING GROUP)

BELGIAN TERVUREN

(AMERICAN KENNEL CLUB—GROUP III: WORKING DOGS)

Personality. The Belgian Tervuren should reflect the qualities of intelligence, courage, alertness and devotion to master. To his inherent aptitude as guardian of flocks should be added protectiveness of the person and property of his master. He should be watchful, attentive and usually in motion when not under command. In his relationship with humans he should be observant and vigilant with strangers but not apprehensive. He should not show fear or shyness. He should not show viciousness by unwarranted or unprovoked attack. With those he knows well, he is most affectionate and friendly, zealous for their attention and very possessive.

General Appearance. The first impression of the Belgian Tervuren is that of a well-balanced square dog, elegant in appearance, with proud carriage of the head and neck. He is a strong, agile, well-muscled animal, alert and full of life. His whole conformation gives the impression of depth and solidity without bulkiness. The male is usually somewhat more impressive and grand than the female. The female should have a distinctively feminine look. Because of frequent comparisons between the Belgian Tervuren and the German Shepherd Dog, it is to be noted that these two breeds differ considerably in size, substance and structure, the difference being especially noticeable in the formation of the topline and the hindquarters.

Size and Substance. Males 24–26 inches in height, and females 22–24 inches, measured at the withers. The length, measured from point of breastbone to point of rump, should equal the height. Bone structure medium in proportion to height so that he is well balanced throughout and neither spindly or leggy nor cumbersome and bulky

Stance. The Belgian Tervuren should stand squarely on all fours. Viewed from the side, the topline, ground level, front legs, and back legs should closely approximate a perfect square.

Expression. Intelligent and questioning, indicating alertness, attention and readiness for action.

Coat. The guard hairs of the coat must be long, well-fitting, straight and abundant. They should not be silky or wiry. The texture should be a medium harshness. The undercoat should be very dense commensurate, however, with climatic conditions. The Belgian Tervuren is particularly adaptable to extremes of temperature or climate. The hair is shorter on the head, outside the ears and on the lower part of the legs. The opening of the ear is protected by tufts of hair. Ornamentation: especially long and abundant hair, like a collarette, around the neck; fringe of long hair down the back of the forearm; especially long and abundant hair trimming the hindquarters—the breeches; long, heavy and abundant hair on the tail.

Color. Rich fawn to russet mahogany with black-overlay. The coat is characteristically double pigmented, wherein the tip of each fawn hair is blackened. On mature males, this blackening is especially pronounced on the shoulders, back and rib section. The chest color is a mixture of black and gray. The face has a black mask, and the ears are mostly black. The tail typically has a darker or black tip. The underparts of the body, tail and breeches are light beige. A small white patch is permitted on the chest, not to extend to the neck or breast. The tips of the toes may be white. White or gray hair (frost) on chin or muzzle is normal. Although some allowance is to be made for dogs under 18 months of age, when the true color is attained, washed-out color or color too black resembling the Belgian Sheepdog is undesirable.

Head. Well chiseled, dry, long without exaggeration. Skull and muzzle, measuring from the stop, should be of equal length. Over-all size should be in proportion to the body. Top of skull flattened rather than rounded, the width approximately the same but not wider than the length. Stop moderate. Muzzle moderately pointed, avoiding any tendency to snipiness. The jaws should be strong and powerful. The lips should be tight and black, with no pink showing on the outside. Ears are equilateral triangles in shape, well cupped, stiff, erect, not too large. Set high, the base of the ear should not come below the centre of the eye. Eyes brown, preferably dark brown, medium size, slightly almond shaped, not protruding. Light or yellow eyes are a fault. Nose black, without spots or discoloured areas. Nostrils well defined. There should be a full complement of strong white teeth evenly set. Either a scissors or even bite is acceptable. Should not be overshot or undershot. Teeth broken by accident should not be severely penalized, but worn teeth, especially incisors, are often indicative of the lack of proper bite, although some allowance should be made for age. Discoloured (distemper) teeth are not to be penalized.

Torso. Neck round, muscular, rather outstretched, slightly arched and tapered from head to body. Skin well fitting with no loose folds. Topline horizontal, straight and firm from withers to hip joints. The loin section, viewed from above, is relatively short, broad and strong, but blending smoothly into the back. The croup is medium long, sloping gradually. Tail strong at the base, the last vertebra to reach the hock. At rest the dog holds it low, the tip bent back level with the hock. When in action he raises it and gives it a curl, which is strongest toward the tip, without forming a hook. Tail should not be carried too high nor turned to one side. Chest not broad but deep, the lowest point should reach the elbow, forming a smooth ascendant curve to the abdomen. Abdomen moderately developed, neither tucked-up nor paunchy.

Forequarters. Legs straight, parallel, perpendicular to the ground. Shoulders long and oblique, laid flat against the body, forming a sharp angle (approximately 90°) with the upper arm. Top of the shoulder blades should be roughly a thumb's width apart. Arms should move in a direction exactly parallel to the axis of the body. Forearms long and well muscled. Bone flat rather than round. Pasterns short and strong, slightly sloped. Feet round (cat-footed), toes curved close together, well padded, strong nails. Nail colour can vary from black to transparent.

Hindquarters. Legs powerful without heaviness, moving in the same pattern as the limbs of the forequarters. Thighs broad and heavily muscled. Stifles clearly defined, with upper shank at right angles to the hip bones. Bone flat rather than round. Hocks moderately bent. Metatarsi short, perpendicular to the ground, parallel to each other when viewed from the rear. Dewclaws, if any, should be removed. Feet slightly elongated, toes curved close together, heavily padded, strong nails. Nail color may vary from black to transparent.

Gait. The gait is lively and graceful, covering the maximum of ground. Always in motion, seemingly never tiring, he shows facility of movement rather than a hard driving action. He tends to single-track at a fast gait, the legs both front and rear converging toward the centre line of gravity of the dog. The back line should remain firm and level, parallel to the line of motion with no crabbing. His natural tendency is to move in a circle rather than a straight line.

DISQUALIFICATIONS

Ears—hanging as on a hound. Tail—cropped or stump. Color—white markings anywhere except as specified. Teeth—pronounced undershot. Size—males under 22½ or over 24½ inches in height; females under 20½ or over 22½ inches in height.

Approved May 12, 1959

BERNESE MOUNTAIN DOG

(THE KENNEL CLUB—WORKING GROUP)

General Appearance. A well balanced dog, active and alert.

Height. Dogs 25 to 27½ inches; bitches 23 to 26 inches at the shoulder.

Body. Rather short than long in back, compact and well-ribbed up. Chest broad with good depth of brisket. Loins strong and muscular.

Head. Skull flat, defined stop and strong muzzle. Dewlaps very slightly developed, flews not too pendulous, jaw strong with good teeth, scissor bite. Eyes dark, haze-brown, full of fire. Ears V-shaped, set on high, not too pointed at tips, rather short. When in repose hanging close to head; when alert, brought slightly forward and raised at base.

Legs and Feet. Forelegs perfectly straight and muscular, thighs well developed and stifles well bent. Feet round and compact. Dewclaws should be removed.

Tail. Of a fair thickness and well covered with long hair but not to form a flag; moderate length. When in repose should be carried low, upward swirl permissible; when alert may be carried gaily but never curled over back.

Coat. Soft and silky, with a bright natural sheen long and slightly wavy but never curled.

Colour and Markings. Jet-black with russet brown or deep tan markings on all four legs, a brown spot over eyes, another just above forelegs and each side of white chest markings. Spots over the eyes must never be missing. White marks on tail end and white paws, pure white blaze up foreface. Between the white paws and the black thighs must always be brown. Allowed small white mark on back of neck size of a guinea. Brown on side of face between the white and the black.

Faults. Too massive in head, light or staring eyes, too heavy or long ears, too narrow or snipy muzzle, under or overshot mouth, pendulous dewlaps, too long or setter like body, splay or hare feet, tail curled or carried over back, cow-hocks and white legs. White boots, white collar, large white marks on back of neck.

BERNESE MOUNTAIN DOG

(AMERICAN KENNEL CLUB—GROUP III: WORKING DOGS)

General Appearance. A well-balanced dog, active and alert; a combination of sagacity, fidelity and utility.

Height. Dogs, 23 to 27½ inches; bitches, 21 to 26 inches at shoulder.

Head. Skull flat, defined stop and strong muzzle. Dewlaps very slightly developed, flews not too pendulous, jaw strong with good, strong teeth. Eyes dark, hazel-brown, full of fire. Ears V-shaped, set on high, not too pointed at tips and rather short. When in repose, hanging close to head; when alert, brought slightly forward and raised at base.

Body. Rather short than too long in back, compact and well ribbed up. Chest broad with good depth of brisket. Loins strong and muscular.

Legs and Feet. Forelegs perfectly straight and muscular, thighs well developed and stifles well bent. Feet round and compact. Dewclaws should be removed.

Tail. Of fair thickness and well covered with long hair, but not to form a flag; moderate length. When in repose, should be carried low, upward swirl permissible; when alert, may be carried gaily, but may never curl or be carried over back.

Coat. Soft and silky with bright, natural sheen; long and slightly wavy but may never curl.

Color and Markings. Jet-black with russet-brown or deep tan markings on all four legs, a spot just above forelegs, each side of white chest markings and spots over eyes, which may never be missing. The brown on the forelegs must always be between the black and white.

Preferable, but not a condition, are. White feet, tip of tail, pure white blaze up foreface, a few white hairs on back of neck, and white star-shaped markings on chest. When the latter markings are missing, it is not a disqualification.

Faults. Too massive in head, light or staring eyes, too heavy or long ears, too narrow or snipy muzzle, undershot or overshot mouth, pendulous dewlaps, too long or Setterlike body, spray or hare feet, tail curled or carried over back, cowhocks and white legs.

SCALE OF POINTS

General appearance	15	Tail	10
Size and height	5	Coat	10
Head	15	Colour and markings	15
Body	15	Total	100
Legs and feet	15		

Approved April 13, 1937

BICHONS FRISES

(AMERICAN KENNEL CLUB—GROUP IV: NON-SPORTING DOGS)

General Appearance. A sturdy, lively dog of stable temperament, with a stylish gait and an air of dignity and intelligence.

Color. Solid white, or white with cream, apricot, or grey on the ears and/or body.

Head. Proportionate to the size of the dog. Skull broad and somewhat round, but not coarse; covered with a topknot of hair.

Muzzle. Of medium length, not heavy or snipy. Slightly accentuated stop.

Ears. Dropped, covered with long flowing hair. The leather should reach approximately halfway the length of the muzzle.

Eyes. Black or dark brown, with black rims. Large, round, expressive, and alert.

Lips. Black, fine, never drooping.

Nose. Black, round, pronounced.

Bite. Scissors.

Neck. Rather long, and gracefully and proudly carried behind an erect head.

Shoulders. Well laid back. Elbows held close to the body.

Body. Slightly longer than tall. Well developed with good spring of ribs. The back inclines gradually from the withers to a slight rise over the loin. The loin is large and muscular. The brisket, well let down.

Tail. Covered with long flowing hair, carried gaily and curved to lie on the back.

Size. The height at the withers should not exceed 12 inches nor be under 8 inches.

Legs and Feet. Strong boned; forelegs appearing straight, with well-knit pasterns. Hindquarters well angulated. Feet, resembling cat's paws, are tight and round.

Coat. Profuse, silky and loosely curled. There is an undercoat.

Grooming. Scissored to show the eyes and give a full rounded appearance to the head and body. Feet should have hair trimmed to give a rounded appearance. When properly brushed, there is an overall 'powder puff' appearance. Puppies may be shown in short coat, but the minimum show coat for an adult is two inches.

Faults. Cowhocks, snipy muzzle, poor pigmentation, protruding eyes, yellow eyes, undershot or overshot bite.

Serious Faults. Corkscrew tail, black hair in the coat.

Approved November 14, 1972

BLACK AND TAN COONHOUND

(AMERICAN KENNEL CLUB—GROUP II: HOUNDS)

The Black and Tan Coonhound is first and fundamentally a working dog, capable of withstanding the rigors of winter, the heat of summer, and the difficult terrain over which he is called upon to work. Judges are asked by the club sponsoring the breed to place great emphasis upon these fact when evaluating the merits of the dog. The general impression should be that of power, agility, and alertness. His expression should be alert, friendly, eager, and aggressive. He should immediately impress one with his ability to cover the ground with powerful rhythmic strides.

Head. The head should be cleanly modeled, with medium stop occurring midway between occiput bone and nose. The head should measure from 9 to 10 inches in males and from 8 to 9 inches in females. Viewed from the profile the line of the skull is on a practically parallel plane to the foreface or muzzle. The skin should be devoid of folds or excess dewlap. The flews should be well developed with typical hound appearance. Nostrils well open and always black. Skull should tend toward oval outline. Eyes should be from hazel to dark brown in color, almost round and not deeply set. The ears should be low set and well back. They should hang in graceful folds giving the dog a majestic appearance. In length they should extend well beyond the tip of the nose. Teeth should fit evenly with slightly scissors bite.

Body—Neck, Shoulders, and Chest. The neck should be muscular, sloping, medium length, extending into powerfully constructed shoulders and deep chest. The dog should possess full, round, well-sprung ribs, avoiding flatsidedness.

Back and Tail. The back should be level, powerful and strong, with a visible slope from withers to rump. Tail should be strong, with base slightly below level of back line, carried free, and when in action at approximately right angle to back.

Legs and Feet. The forelegs should be straight, with elbows well let down, turning neither in nor out; pasterns strong and erect. Feet should be catlike with compact, well-arched toes and thick strong pads.

Hindquarters. Quarters should be well boned and muscled. From hip to hock well bent and not inclining either in or out. When standing on a level surface the hind feet should set back from under the body, and leg from pad to hock be at right angles to the ground when viewed both from profile and the rear. The stride of the Black and Tan Coonhound should be easy and graceful with plenty of reach in front and drive behind.

Coat and Color. The coat should be short but dense to withstand rough going. As the name implies, the color should be coal black, with rich tan markings above eyes, on sides of muzzle, chest, legs and breeching with black pencil markings on toes

Size. Measured at the shoulder: males, 25 to 27 inches; females, 23 to 25 inches. Height should be in proportion to general conformation so that dog appears neither leggy nor close to the ground. Dogs oversized should not be penalized when general soundness and proportion are in favor.

Judges should penalize the following defects: Undersize, elbows out at shoulder, lack of angulation in hindquarters, splay feet, sway- or roach back, flatsidedness, lack of depth in chest, yellow or light eyes, shyness and nervousness.

Faults. Dewclaws; white on chest or other parts of body is highly undesirable and if its exceeds 1½ inches in diameter should be disqualified.

DISQUALIFICATION

White on chest or other parts of the body if it exceeds 1½ inches in diameter.

Approved July 10, 1945

BLOODHOUND

(THE KENNEL CLUB—HOUND GROUP)

Characteristics. The Bloodhound possesses in a most marked degree, every point and characteristic of those dogs which hunt together by scent (Sagaces). He is very powerful and stands over more ground than is usual with hounds of other breeds. The skin is thin and extremely loose, this being especially noticeable about the head and neck, where it hangs in deep folds. In temperament he is affectionate, neither quarrelsome with companions nor with other dogs. His nature is somewhat reserved and sensitive.

General Appearance. The expression is noble and dignified and characterized by solemnity, wisdom and power. The gait is elastic, swinging and free; the stern being carried high scimitar fashion.

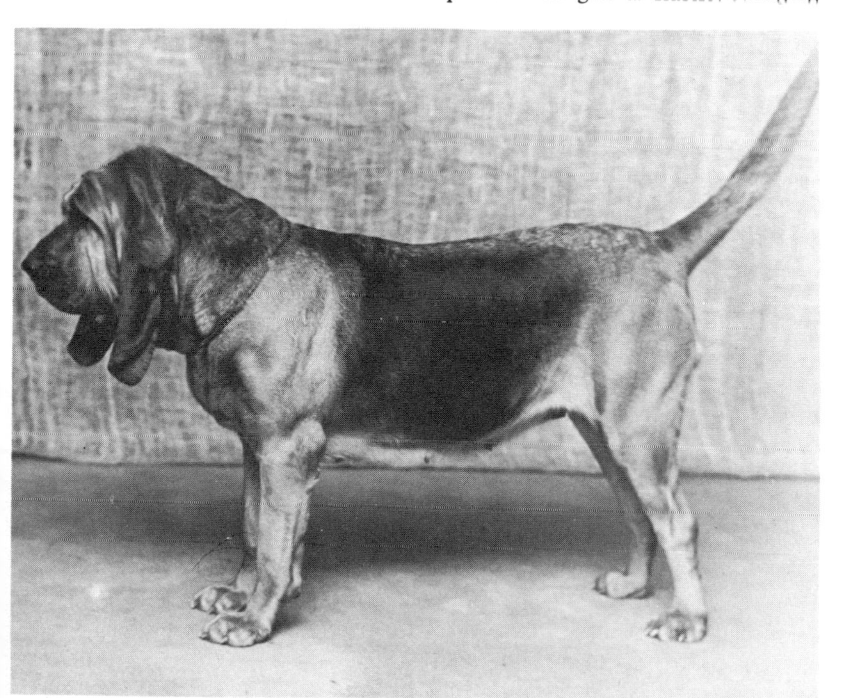

Head and Skull. The head is narrow in proportion to its length and long in proportion to the body, tapering but slightly from the temples to the muzzle, thus (when viewed from above and in front) having the appearance of being flattened at the sides and of being nearly equal in width throughout its entire length. In profile the upper outline of the skull is nearly in the same plane as that of the foreface. The length from the end of the nose to stop (midway between the eyes) should not be less than that from stop to back or occipital protuberance (peak). The entire length of head from the posterior part of the occipital protuberance to the end of the muzzle should be 12 inches or more in dogs and 11 inches or more in bitches. The skull is long and narrow, with the occipital peak very pronounced. The brows are not prominent although owing to the deep-set eyes they may have that appearance. The foreface is long, deep and of even width throughout, with square outline when seen in profile. The head is furnished with an amount of loose skin, which in nearly every position appears superabundant, but more particularly so when the head is carried low; the skin then falls into loose pendulous ridges and folds, especially over the forehead and sides of the face. The nostrils are large and open. In front the lips fall squarely making a right angle with the upper line of the foreface; whilst behind they form deep hanging flews, and, being continued into the pendant folds of loose skin about the neck, constitute the dewlap, which is very pronounced.

Mouth. A scissor bite with the inner faces of the upper incisors touching the outer faces of the lower incisors.

Eyes. The eyes are deeply sunk in the orbits, the lids assuming a lozenge or diamond shape, in consequence of the lower lids being dragged down and everted by the heavy flews. The eyes correspond with the general colour of the animal varying from deep hazel to yellow. The hazel colour is, however, to be preferred, although very seldom seen in liver and tan (red and tan) hounds. The eye should be free from any interference from the eyelashes.

Ears. The ears are thin and soft to the touch, extremely long, set on very low and fall in graceful folds, the lower parts curling inwards and backwards.

Neck. Should be long.

Forequarters. The shoulders muscular and well sloped backwards. The forelegs are straight, large and round in bone with elbows squarely set. The pasterns should be strong.

Hindquarters. The thighs and second thighs (gaskins) are very muscular, the hocks well bent and let down and squarely set.

Feet. Should be strong and well knuckled up.

Body. The ribs are well sprung and the chest well let down between the forelegs forming a deep keel.

The back and loins are strong, the latter deep and slightly arched.

Tail. The stern is long and thick tapering to a point, set on high with a moderate amount of hair underneath. It should be carried scimitar fashion, but not curled over the back or corkscrew at any time.

Colour. The colours are black and tan, liver and tan (red and tan) and red. The darker colours being sometimes interspersed with lighter or badger-coloured hair and sometimes flecked with white. A small amount of white is permissible on chest, feet and tip of stern.

Weight and Size. The mean average height of adult dogs is 26 inches and of bitches 24 inches. Dogs usually vary from 25 inches to 27 inches and bitches from 23 inches to 25 inches. The mean average weight of adult dogs in fair condition is 90 lbs and of adult bitches 80 lbs. Dogs attain the weight of 110 lbs and bitches 100 lbs. Hounds of the maximum height and weight are to be preferred providing always that quality, proportion and balance combine.

BLOODHOUND

(AMERICAN KENNEL CLUB—GROUP II: HOUNDS)

General Character. The Bloodhound possesses, in a most marked degree, every point and characteristic of those dogs which hunt together by scent (Sagaces). He is very powerful, and stands over more ground than is usual with hounds of other breeds. The skin is thin to the touch and extremely loose, this being more especially noticeable about the head and neck, where it hangs in deep folds.

Height. The mean average height of adult dogs is 26 inches, and of adult bitches 24 inches. Dogs usually vary from 25 inches to 27 inches, and bitches from 23 inches to 25 inches; but, in either case, the greater height is to be preferred, provided that character and quality are also combined.

Weight. The mean average weight of adult dogs, in fair condition, is 90 pounds, and of adult bitches 80. Dogs attain the weight of 110 pounds, bitches 100. The greater weights are to be preferred, provided (as in the case of height) that quality and proportion are also combined.

Expression. The expression is noble and dignified, and characterized by solemnity, wisdom, and power.

Temperament. In temperament he is extremely affectionate, neither quarrelsome with companions nor with other dogs. His nature is somewhat shy, and equally sensitive to kindness or correction by his master.

Head. The head is narrow in proportion to its length, and long in proportion to the body, tapering but slightly from the temples to the end of the muzzle, thus (when viewed from above and in front) having the appearance of being flattened at the sides and of being nearly equal in width throughout its entire length. In profile the upper outline of the skull is nearly in the same plane as that of the foreface. The length from end of nose to stop (midway between the eyes) should be not less than that from stop to back of occipital protuberance (peak). The entire length of head from the posterior part of the occipital protuberance to the end of the muzzle should be 12 inches, or more, in dogs, and 11 inches, or more, in bitches.

Skull. The skull is long and narrow, with the occipital peak very pronounced. The brows are not prominent, although, owing to the deep-set eyes, they may have that appearance.

Foreface. The foreface is long, deep, and of even width throughout, with aquare outline when seen in profile.

Eyes. The eyes are deeply sunk in the orbits, the lids assuming a lozenge or diamond shape, in consequence of the lower lids being dragged down and everted by the heavy flews. The eyes correspond with the general tone of colour of the animal, varying from deep hazel to yellow. The hazel colour is, however, to be preferred, although very seldom seen in red-and-tan hounds.

Ears. The ears are thin and soft to the touch, extremely long, set very low, and fall in graceful folds, the lower parts curling inwards and backwards.

Wrinkle. The head is furnished with an amount of loose skin, which in nearly every position appears superabundant, but more particularly so when the head is carried low; the skin then falls into loose, pendulous ridges and folds, especially over the forehead and sides of the face.

Nostrils. The nostrils are large and open.

Lips, Flews, and Dewlap. In front the lips fall squarely, making a right angle with the upper line of the foreface; whilst behind they form deep, hanging flews, and, being continued into the pendant folds of loose skin about the neck, constitute the dewlap, which is very pronounced. These characters are found, though in a less degree, in the bitch.

Neck, Shoulders, and Chest. The neck is long, the shoulders muscular and well sloped backwards; the ribs are well sprung; and the chest well let down between the forelegs, forming a deep keel.

Legs and Feet. The forelegs are straight and large in bone, with elbows squarely set; the feet strong and well knuckled up; the thighs and second thighs (gaskins) are very muscular; the hocks well bent and let down and squarely set.

Back and Loin. The back and loins are strong, the latter deep and slightly arched.

Stern. The stern is long and tapering, and set on rather high, with a moderate amount of hair underneath.

Gait. The gait is elastic, swinging and free, the stern being carried high, but not too much curled over the back.

Color. The colors are black and tan, red and tan, and tawny; the darker colours being sometimes interspersed with lighter or badger-coloured hair, and sometimes flecked with white. A small amount of white is permissible on chest, feet, and tip of stern.

BORDER TERRIER

(THE KENNEL CLUB—TERRIER GROUP)

Characteristics. The Border Terrier is essentially a working Terrier. It should be able to follow a horse and combine activity with gameness

Head and Skull. Head like that of an otter, moderately broad in skull, with a short strong muzzle; a black nose is preferable but a liver or flesh-coloured one is not a serious fault.

Eyes. Dark, with keen expression.

Ears. Small, V-shaped, of moderate thickness and dropping forward close to the cheek.

Mouth. Teeth should have a scissor-like grip, with the top teeth slightly in front of the lower, but level mouth is quite acceptable. An undershot or overshot mouth is a major fault and highly undesirable.

Neck. Of moderate length.

Forequarters. Forelegs straight and not too heavy in bone.

Body. Deep and narrow and fairly long; ribs carried well back, but not oversprung, as a terrier should be capable of being spanned by both hands behind the shoulder.

Hindquarters. Racy. Loin strong.

Feet. Small with thick pads.

Tail. Moderately short and fairly thick at the base, then tapering, set high and carried gaily but not curled over the back.

Coat. Harsh and dense with close undercoat. The skin must be thick.

Colour. Red, wheaten, grizzle and tan or blue and tan.

Weight and Size. Weight: Dogs, between 13–15½ lbs; Bitches, between 11½–14 lbs.

BORDER TERRIER

(AMERICAN KENNEL CLUB—GROUP IV: TERRIERS)

Since the Border Terrier is a working terrier of a size to go to ground and able, within reason, to follow a horse, his conformation should be such that he be ideally built to do his job. No deviations from this ideal conformation should be permitted, which would impair his usefulness in running his quarry to earth and in bolting it therefrom. For this work he must be alert, active and agile, and capable of squeezing through narrow apertures and rapidly traversing any kind of terrain. His head, 'like that of an otter,' is distinctive, and his temperament ideally exemplifies that of a terrier. By nature he is good-tempered, affectionate, obedient, and easily trained. In the field he is hard as nails, 'game as they come' and driving in attack. It should be the aim of Border Terrier breeders to avoid such over-emphasis of any point in the Standard as might lead to unbalanced exaggeration.

General Appearance. He is an active terrier of medium bone, strongly put together, suggesting endurance and agility, but rather narrow in shoulder, body and quarter. The body is covered with a somewhat broken though close-fitting and intensely wiry jacket. The characteristic 'otter' head with its keen eye, combined with a body poise which is 'at the alert,' gives a look of fearless and implacable determination characteristic of the breed. The proportions should be that the height at the withers is slightly greater than the distance from the withers to the tail, *i.e.* by possibly 1–1½ inches in a 14-pound dog.

Weight. Dogs, 13–15½ pounds, bitches, 11½–14 pounds, are appropriate weights for Border Terriers in hard-working condition.

Head. Similar to that of an otter. Moderately broad and flat in skull with plenty of width between the eyes and between the ears. A slight, moderately broad curve at the stop rather than a pronounced indentation. Cheeks slightly full.

Ears. Small V-shaped and of moderate thickness, dark preferred. Not set high on the head but somewhat on the side, and dropping forward close to the cheeks. They should not break above the level of the skull.

Eyes. Dark hazel and full of fire and intelligence. Moderate in size, neither prominent nor small and beady.

Muzzle. Short and 'well filled.' A dark muzzle is characteristic and desirable. A few short whiskers are natural to the breed.

Teeth. Strong, with a scissors bite, large in proportion to size of dog.

Nose. Black, and of a good size.

Neck. Clean, muscular and only long enough to give a well-balanced appearance. It should gradually widen into the shoulder.

Shoulders. Well laid back and of good length, the blades converging to the withers gradually from a brisket not excessively deep or narrow.

Forelegs. Straight and not too heavy in bone and placed slightly wider than in a Fox Terrier.

Feet. Small and compact. Toes should point forward and be moderately arched with thick pads.

Body. Deep, fairly narrow and of sufficient length to avoid any suggestion of lack of range and agility. Deep ribs carried well back and not oversprung in view of the desired depth and narrowness of the body. The body should be capable of being spanned by a man's hands behind the shoulders. Back strong but laterally supple, with no suspicion of a dip behind the shoulder. Loin strong and the underline fairly straight.

Tail. Moderately short, thick at the base, then tapering. Not set on too high. Carried gaily when at the alert, but not over the back. When at ease, a Border may drop his stern.

Hindquarters. Muscular and racy, with thighs long and nicely molded. Stifles well bent and hocks well let down.

Coat. A short and dense undercoat covered with a very wiry and somewhat broken top coat which should lie closely, but it must not show any tendency to curl or wave. With such a coat a Border should be able to be exhibited almost in his natural state, nothing more in the way of trimming being needed that a tidying-up of the head, neck and feet.

Hide. Very thick and loose fitting.

Movement. Straight and rhythmical before and behind, with good length of stride and flexing of stifle, and hock. The dog should respond to his handler with a gait which is free, agile and quick.

Color. Red, grizzle and tan, blue and tan, or wheaten. A small amount of white may be allowed on the chest but white on the feet should be penalized.

SCALE OF POINTS

Head, ears, neck and teeth	20	Back and loin	10
Legs and feet	15	Hindquarters	10
Coat and skin		Tail	5
Shoulders and chest	10	General appearance	10
Eyes and expression	10	Total	100

Approved March 14, 1950

BORZOI

(THE KENNEL CLUB—HOUND GROUP)

General Appearance. A very graceful, aristocratic and elegant dog possessing courage, muscular power, and great speed.

Head and Skull. Head, long and lean. Well filled in below the eyes. Measurement equal from the occiput to the inner corner of the eye and from the inner corner of the eye to tip of nose. Skull very slightly domed and narrow, stop not perceptible, inclining to Roman nose. Head fine so that the direction of the bones and principal veins can be clearly seen. Bitches heads should be finer than the dogs. Jaws long, deep and powerful; nose large and black, not pink or brown, nicely rounded, neither cornered nor sharp. Viewed from above the skull should look narrow, converging very gradually to tip of nose.

Eyes. Dark, intelligent, alert and keen. Almond shaped, set obliquely, placed well back but not too far apart. Eye rims dark. Eyes should not be light, round or staring.

Ears. Small and fine in quality; not too far apart. They should be active and responsive; when alert can be erect; when in repose nearly touching at the occiput

Mouth. Teeth even, neither pig-jawed not undershot.

Neck. Clean, slightly arched; reasonably long; powerful. Well set on, free from throatiness. Flat at the sides, not round

Forequarters. Shoulders clean, sloping well back, fine at withers, free from lumpiness. Forelegs, lean and straight. Seen from the front, narrow like blades; from the side, wide at shoulder narrowing down to foot; elbows neither turned in nor out, pasterns strong, flexible and springy.

Body. Chest, great depth of brisket, rather narrow. Ribs well sprung and flexible; neither flat sided nor barrel-shaped; very deep giving heart room and lung play, especially in the case of mature males. (It is from depth of chest rather than breadth that the Borzoi derives its heart room and lung play). Back, rising in a graceful arch from as near the shoulders as possible with a well balanced fallaway. The arch to be more marked in dogs than bitches. Rather bony, muscular and free from any cavity. Muscles, highly developed and well distributed.

Hindquarters. Loins, broad and very powerful, with plenty of muscular development. Quarters should be wider than shoulders, ensuring stability of stance. Thighs long, well developed with good second thigh. Hindlegs, long, muscular, stifles well bent, hocks broad, clean and well let down.

Feet. Front feet rather long, toes close together; well arched, never flat, neither turning in nor out. Hind feet hare-like, i.e., longer and less arched.

Tail. Long, rather low set. Well feathered, carried low, not gaily. In action may be used as rudder but not rising above level of back. From the level of the hocks may be sickle shaped but not ringed.

Coat. Long and silky (never woolly), or flat, or wavy, or rather curly. Short and smooth on head, ears and front legs; on the neck the frill profuse and rather curly; forelegs and chest well feathered; on hindquarters and tail, long and profuse feathering.

Weight and Size. Height at shoulder; Dogs from 29 inches upwards. Bitches from 27 inches upwards.

BORZOI

(AMERICAN KENNEL CLUB—GROUP II: HOUNDS)

General Appearance. The Borzoi was originally bred for the coursing of wild game on more or less open terrain, relying on sight rather than scent. To accomplish this purpose, the Borzoi needed particular structural qualities to chase, catch and hold his quarry. Special emphasis is placed on sound running gear, strong neck and jaws, courage and agility, combined with proper condition. The Borzoi should always possess unmistakeable elegance, with flowing lines, graceful in motion or repose. Males, masculine without coarseness; bitches, feminine and refined.

Head. Skull slightly domed, long and narrow, with scarcely any perceptible stop, inclined to be Roman-nosed. Jaws long, powerful and deep, somewhat finer in bitches but not snipy. Teeth strong and clean with either an even or a scissors bite. Missing teeth should be penalized. Nose large and black.

Ears. Small and fine in quality, lying back on the neck when in repose with the tips when thrown back almost touching behind occiput; raised when at attention.

Eyes. Set somewhat obliquely, dark in colour, intelligent but rather soft in expression; never round, full not staring, nor light in colour; eye rims dark; inner corner midway between tip of nose and occiput.

Neck. Clean, free from throatiness; slightly arched, very powerful and well set on.

Shoulders. Sloping, fine at the withers and free from coarseness or lumber.

Chest. Rather narrow, with great depth of brisket.

Ribs. Only slightly sprung, but very deep, giving room for heart and lung play.

Back. Rising a little at the loins in a graceful curve.

Loins. Extremely muscular, but rather tucked up, owing to the great depth of chest and comparative shortness of back and ribs.

Forelegs. Bones straight and somewhat flattened like blades, with the narrower edge forward. The elbows have free play and are turned neither in nor out. Pasterns strong.

Feet. Hare-shaped, with well-arched knuckles, toes close and well padded.

Hindquarters. Long, very muscular and powerful with well bent stifles; somewhat wider than the forequarters; strong first and second thighs; hocks clean and well let down; legs parallel when viewed from the rear.

Dewclaws. Dewclaws, if any, on the hindlegs are generally removed; dewclaws on the forelegs may be removed.

Tail. Long, set on and carried low in a graceful curve

Coat. Long, silky (not woolly), either flat, wavy or rather curly. On the head, ears and front of legs it should be short and smooth; on the neck the frill should be profuse and rather curly. Feather on hindquarters and tail, long and profuse, less so on chest and back of forelegs.

Color. Any color or combination of colors is acceptable.

Size. Mature males should be at least 28 inches at the withers and mature bitches at least 26 inches at the withers. Dogs and bitches below these respective limits should be severely penalized; dogs and bitches above the respective limits should not be penalized as long as extra size is not acquired at the expense of symmetry, speed, and staying quality. Range in weight for males from 75 to 105 pounds and for bitches from 15 to 20 pounds less.

Gait. Front legs must reach well out in front with pasterns strong and springy. Hackneyed motion with mincing gait is not desired nor is weaving and crossing. However, while the hind legs are wider apart than the front, the feet tend to move closer to the centre line when the dog moves at a fast trot. When viewed from the side there should be noticeable drive with a ground-covering stride from well-angulated stifles and hocks. The over-all appearance in motion should be that of effortless power, endurance, speed, agility, smoothness and grace.

Faults. The foregoing description is that of the ideal Borzoi. Any deviation from the above described dog must be penalized to the extent of the deviation, keeping in mind the importance of the contribution of the various features toward the basic original purpose of the breed.

Approved June 13, 1972

BOSTON TERRIER

(THE KENNEL CLUB—UTILITY GROUP)

Characteristics. A proportionate combination of "Colour" and "Ideal Markings" is a particularly distinctive feature of a representative specimen. A dog with a preponderance of white on body or without the proper proportion of brindle and white on head is at a disadvantage. The ideal "Boston Terrier Expression" as indicating "a high degree of intelligence" is also an important characteristic of the breed. "Colour and Markings" and "Expression" should be given particular consideration in determining the relative value of "General Appearance" to other points.

General Appearance. The general appearance of the Boston Terrier should be that of a lively, highly intelligent, smooth-coated, short-headed, compactly built, short-tailed, well balanced dog of medium size, of brindle colour and evenly marked with white. The head should indicate a high degree of intelligence and should be in proportion to the size of the dog; the body rather short and well knit; the limbs strong and neatly turned; tail short and no feature to be so prominent that the dog appears badly proportioned. The dog should convey an impression of determination, strength and activity, with style of a high order; carriage easy and graceful. The gait of the Boston Terrier is that of a sure-footed straight-gaited dog, forelegs and hindlegs moving straight ahead in time with perfect rhythm, each step indicating grace and power.

Head and Skull. Skull square, flat on top, free from wrinkles; cheeks flat; brow abrupt, stop well defined. Muzzle short, square, wide and deep, and in proportion to the skull; free from wrinkles; shorter in length than in width and depth, not exceeding in length approximately one-third of length of skull; width and depth carried out well to end; the muzzle from stop to end of nose on a line parallel to the top of the skull; nose black and wide with well-defined line between nostrils. The jaws broad and square. The chops of good depth but not pendulous, completely covering the teeth when mouth is closed.

Eyes. Wide apart, large and round, dark in colour, expression alert but kind and intelligent. The eyes should set square in the skull, and the outside corners should be on a line with the cheeks as viewed from the front.

Ears. Carried erect; small and thin; situated as near corner of skull as possible.

Mouth. Teeth short and regular, bite even, or sufficiently undershot to square muzzle.

Neck. Of fair length, slightly arched and carrying the head gracefully; neatly set into the shoulders.

Forequarters. Legs set moderately wide apart and on a line with the point of the shoulders straight in bone and well muscled; pasterns short and strong. Elbows standing neither in nor out.

Body. Deep with good width of chest; shoulders sloping, back short; ribs deep and well sprung, carried well back to loins; loins short and muscular; rump curving slightly to set-on of tail; flank very slightly cut up. The body should appear short but not chunky.

Hindquarters. Legs set true. bent at stifles, short from hocks to feet; hocks turning neither in nor out; thighs strong and well muscled.

Feet. Round, small and compact, and turned neither in nor out; toes well arched.

Tail. Set-on low; short, fine and tapering; straight or screw; devoid of fringes or coarse hair, and not carried above horizontal.

Coat. Short, smooth, bright and fine in texture.

Colour. Brindle with white markings; brindle must show throughout the body distinctly; black and white markings are permissible, but brindles with white markings are preferred. (Ideal colour shall be one in which the brindle colouring is evenly distributed throughout the body). Ideal markings: white muzzle, even white blaze over head, collar, breast, part or whole of forelegs, and hindlegs below hocks.

Weight and Size. Weight should not exceed 25 lbs., divided by classes as follows: Lightweight, under 15 lbs.; Middleweight, 15 and under 20 lbs.; Heavyweight, 20 and under 25 lbs.

Faults. Solid black, black and tan; liver or mouse colour; Dudley nose; docked tail. Skull 'domed' or inclined; furrowed by a medial line; skull too long for breadth, or vice versa; stop too shallow; brow and skull too slanting. Eyes small or sunken; too prominent; light colour or wall eye; showing too much white or haw. Muzzle wedge-shaped or lacking depth; down faced; too much cut out below the eyes; pinched or wide nostrils; butterfly nose; protruding teeth; weak lower jaw; showing 'turn-up'. Ears poorly carried or in size out of proportion to head. Neck: ewe-necked; throaty, short or thick. Body: flat sides; narrow chest; long or slack loins; roach back; sway back; too much cut-up in flank. Loose shoulders or elbows; hind legs too straight at stifles; hocks too prominent; long or weak pasterns; splay feet. A long or gaily carried tail; extremely gnarled or curled against body. (Note—The preferred tail should not exceed in length approximately half the distance from the set-on to hock). Colour and markings: all white; absense of white markings; preponderance of white on body; without the proper proportion of brindle and white on head; or any variations detracting from the general appearance. Coat: long or coarse; lacking lustre.

BOSTON TERRIER

(AMERICAN KENNEL CLUB—GROUP VI: NON SPORTING DOGS)

General Appearance. The general appearance of the Boston Terrier should be that of a lively, highly intelligent, smooth-coated, short-headed, compactly built, short-tailed, well-balanced dog of medium station, of brindle colour and evenly marked with white. The head should indicate a high degree of intelligence, and should be in proportion to the size of the dog; the body rather short and well knit, the limbs strong and neatly turned; tail short; and no feature be so prominent that the dog appears badly proportioned. The dog should convey an impression of determination, strength and activity, with style of a high order; carriage easy and graceful. A proportionate combination of 'color' and 'ideal markings' is a particularly distinctive feature of a representative specimen, and a dog with a preponderance of white on body, or without the proper proportion of brindle and white on head, should possess sufficient merit otherwise to counteract its deficiencies in these respects. The ideal 'Boston Terrier expression' as indicating 'a high degree of intelligence,' is also an important characteristic of the breed. 'Color and markings' and 'expression' should be given particular consideration in determining the relative value of 'general appearance' to other points.

Skull. Square, flat on top, free from wrinkles; cheeks flat; brow abrupt, stop well defined.

Eyes. Wide apart, large and round, dark in color, expression alert, but kind and intelligent. The eyes should set square in the skull, and the outside corners should be on a line with the cheeks as viewed from the front.

Muzzle. Short, square, wide and deep, and in proportion to skull; free from wrinkles; shorter in length than in width and depth, not exceeding in length approximately one third of length of skull; width and depth carried out well to end; the muzzle from stop to end of nose on a line parallel to the top of the skull; nose black and wide, with well defined line between nostrils. The jaws broad and square, with short regular teeth. Bite even or sufficiently undershot to square muzzle. The chops of good depth but not pendulous, completely covering the teeth when mouth is closed.

Ears. Carried erect, either cropped to conform to the shape of head, or natural bat, situated as near the corners of skull as possible.

Head Faults. Skull 'domed' or inclined; furrowed by a medial line; skull too long for breadth, or *vice versa*; stop too shallow; brow and skull too slanting. Eyes small or sunken; too prominent; light color or walleye; showing too much white or haw. Muzzle wedge-shaped or lacking depth; downfaced; too much cut out below the eyes; pinched or wide nostrils; butterfly nose; protruding teeth; weak lower jaw; showing turn-up, layback, or wrinkled. Ears poorly carried or in size out of proportion to head.

Neck. Of fair length, slightly arched and carrying the head gracefully; setting neatly into shoulders.

Neck Faults. Ewe-necked; throatiness; short and thick.

Body. Deep with good width of chest; shoulders sloping; back short; ribs deep and well sprung, carried well back to loins; loins short and muscular; rump curving slightly to set-on of tail; flank very slightly cut up. The body should appear short but not chunky.

Body Faults. Flat sides; narrow chest; long or slack loins; roach back; sway-back; too much cut up in flank.

Elbows. Standing neither in nor out.

Forelegs. Set moderately wide apart and on a line with the point of the shoulders; straight in bone and well muscled; pasterns short and strong.

Hind Legs. Set true; bent at stifles; short from hocks to feet; hocks turning neither in nor out; thighs strong and well muscled.

Feet. Round, small and compact and turned neither in nor out; toes well arched.

Leg and Feet Faults. Loose shoulders or elbows; hind legs too straight at stifles; hocks too prominent; long or weak pasterns; splay feet.

Gait. The gait of the Boston Terrier is that of a sure-footed, straight-gaited dog, forelegs and hind legs moving straight ahead in line with perfect rhythm, each step indicating grace with power.

Gait Faults. There shall be no rolling, paddling or weaving when gaited and any crossing movement, either front or rear, is a serious fault.

Tail. Set-on low; short, fine and tapering; straight; or screw; devoid of fringe or coarse hair, and not carried above horizontal.

Tail Faults. A long or gaily carried tail; extremely gnarled or curled against body. (Note—The preferred tail should not exceed in length approximately half the distance from set-on to hock.)

Ideal Color. Brindle with white markings. The brindle to be evenly distributed and distinct. Black with white markings permissible but brindle with white markings preferred.

Ideal Markings. White muzzle, even white blaze over head, collar, breast, part or whole of fore-legs, and hind legs below hocks.

Color and Markings Faults. All white; absence of white marking; preponderance of white on body; without the proper proportion of brindle and white on head; or any variations detracting from the general appearance.

Coat. Short, smooth, bright and fine in texture.

Coat Faults. Long or coarse; lacking luster.

Weight. Not exceeding 25 pounds, divided by classes as follows: lightweight, under 15 pounds; middleweight, 15 and under 20 pounds; heavy-weight, 20 and not exceeding 25 pounds.

SCALE OF POINTS

General appearance	10	Forelegs	5
Skull	10	Hind legs	5
Eyes	5	Gait	10
Muzzle	10	Feet	5
Ears	2	Tail	5
Neck	3	Color	4
Body	15	Ideal markings	5
Elbows	4	Coat	2
		Total	100

DISQUALIFICATIONS

Solid black; black and tan; liver or mouse colors. Dudley nose. Docked tail or any artificial means used to deceive the judge.

Approved April 9, 1957

BOUVIERS DES FLANDERS

(THE KENNEL CLUB—WORKING GROUP)

BOUVIERS DES FLANDRES

(AMERICAN KENNEL CLUB—GROUP III: WORKING DOGS)

The Bouvier des Flandres is a rough-coated dog of notably rugged appearance as befitting an erstwhile cattle driver and farmers' helper of Flandres, and later an ambulance dog and messenger in World War I. He is a compact-bodied, powerfully built dog of upstanding carriage and alert, intelligent expression.

Head. The head is medium long, with the skull slightly longer than the muzzle.

Skull. Almost flat on top, moderately wide between the ears, and sloping slightly toward the muzzle. The brow is noticeably arched over the eyes. The stop is shallow, and the under-eye fill-in good.

Ears. Rough-coated, set high on the head and cropped to a triangular contour. They stand erect and are carried straight up.

Eyes. Neither protruding nor sunken, the eyes are set a trifle obliquely in the skull and not too far apart. They are of medium size and very nearly oval. Preferred color, a dark nut-brown. Black eyes, although not considered faulty, are less desirable as contributing to a somber expression. Light-colored eyes, and staring or wild expression are faulty.

Muzzle. Wide, deep and well filled out, the width narrowing gradually toward the tip of the nose. Cheeks are clean or flat-sided, the jaws powerful, and the lips dry and tight-fitting. A narrow muzzle, suggestive of weakness, is faulty.

Teeth. Strong and white, with the canines set well apart, the teeth meet in a scissors bite.

Nose. Black and well developed, the nostrils wide open. Across the top the contour is a trifle rounded as opposed to flat. Brown, pink and spotted noses are faulty.

Neck and Shoulders. The neck is well rounded, slightly arched, and carried almost upright, its thickness gradually increasing as it fits gracefully into the shoulders. Clean and dry at the throat. The shoulders are long and sloping.

Body. The brisket is deep, extending down at least to the point of the elbows, and of moderate width.

Back. Short, strong and straight.

Loins. Short, taut, and slightly arched in topline, while the rump is broad and square rather than sloping. Ribs are deep and well sprung. As advantageous for breeding purposes, slightly greater length of loin is permissible in bitches.

Tail. Set high, carried up, and docked to about 4 inches.

Legs and Feet. The leg bones, although only moderate in girth, are made to appear heavy because of their covering with thick, rough hair.

Forelegs. Straight as viewed from the front or side, with elbows turned neither in nor out.

Hind Legs. Hindquarters are firm and well muscled, with large, powerful hams. Legs are strong and sturdy, with hocks well let down and wide apart. They are slightly angulated at stifle and hock joints. Viewed from the back, they are absolutely parallel.

Feet. Round, compact, with toes arched and close. The nails are black, the pads thick and tough.

Coat. Rough, tousled and unkempt in appearance, the coat is capable of withstanding the hardest work in the most inclement weather.

Topcoat. Harsh, rough and wiry, and so thick that when separated by the hand the skin is hardly visible.

Undercoat. Fine and soft in texture, and thicker in winter. On the skull the hair is shorter and almost smooth. On the brows it is longer, thus forming eyebrows. Longer growth on muzzle and underjaw form mustache and beard. On the legs it is thick and rough, on the feet rather short. Soft, silky or woolly topcoats are faulty.

Color. From fawn to black; pepper and salt, gray and brindle. A white star on the chest is allowed. Chocolate brown with white spots is faulty.

Height. Dogs from $23\frac{1}{2}$ to $27\frac{1}{2}$ inches; bitches, a minimum of $22\frac{3}{4}$ inches.

SCALE OF POINTS

Coat	20	Back, loin, brisket, belly	15
Head (eyes, ears, skull, foreface)	20	Feet and legs	10
Shoulders and style	10	Symmetry, size and character	15
Hindquarters (hams and legs)	10	Total	100

Approved April 14, 1959

BOXER

(THE KENNEL CLUB—WORKING GROUP)

Characteristics. The character of the Boxer is of the greatest importance and demands the most careful attention. He is renowned from olden times for his great love and faithfulness to his master and household, his alertness and fearless courage as a defender and protector. The Boxer is docile but distrustful of strangers. He is bright and friendly in play but brave and determined when roused. His intelligence and willing tractability, his modesty, and cleanliness make him a highly desirable family dog and cheerful companion. He is the soul of honesty and loyalty. He is never false or treacherous even in his old age.

General Appearance. The Boxer is a medium sized, sturdy, smooth-haired dog of short square figure and strong limb. The musculation is clean and powerfully developed, and should stand out plastically from under the skin. Movement of the Boxer should be alive with energy. His gait, although firm, is elastic. The stride free and roomy; carriage proud and noble. As a service and guard dog he must combine a considerable degree of elegance with the substance and power essential to his duties; those of an enduring escort dog whether with horse, bicycle or carriage and as a splendid jumper. Only a body whose individual limbs are built to withstand the most strenuous 'mechanical' effort and assembled as a complete and harmonious whole, can respond to such demands. Therefore to be at its highest efficiency, the Boxer must never be plump or heavy. Whilst equipped for great speed, it must not be racy. When judging the Boxer the first thing to be considered is general appearance, the relation of substance to elegance and the desired relationship to the individual parts of the body to each other. Consideration, too, must be given to colour. After these, the individual parts should be examined for their correct construction and their functions. Special attention should be devoted to the head.

Head and Skull. The head imparts to the Boxer a unique individual stamp peculiar to the breed. It must be in perfect proportion to his body; above all it must never been too light. The muzzle is the most distinctive feature. The greatest value is to be placed on its being of correct form and in absolute proportion to the skull. The beauty of the head depends upon the harmonious proportion between the muzzle and the skull. From whatever direction the head is viewed, whether from the front, from the top or from the side, the muzzle should always appear in correct relationship to the skull. That means that the head should never appear too small or too large. The length of the muzzle to the whole of the head should be as 1 is to 3. The head should not show deep wrinkles. Normally wrinkles will spring up on the top of the skull when the dog is alert. Folds are always indicated from the root of the nose running downwards on both sides of the muzzle. The dark mask is confined to the muzzle. It must be in distinct relief to the colour of the head so that the face will not have a 'sombre' expression. The muzzle must be powerfully developed in length, in breadth and in height. It must not be pointed or narrow; short or shallow. Its shape is influenced through the formation of both jaw-bones, the placement of teeth in the jaw-bones, and through the quality of the lips. The top of the skull should be slightly arched. It should not be so short that it is rotund, too flat, or too broad. The occiput should not be too pronounced. The forehead should form a distinct stop with the top line of the muzzle, which should not be forced back into the forehead like that of a Bulldog. Neither should it slope away (downfaced). The tip of the nose should lie somewhat higher than the root of the muzzle. The forehead should show a suggestion of furrow which, however, should never be too deep, especially between the eyes. Corresponding with the powerful set of teeth, the cheeks accordingly should be well developed without protruding from the head with 'too bulgy' an appearance. For preference they should taper into the muzzle in a slight, graceful curve. The nose should be broad and black, very slightly turned up. The nostrils should be broad with a naso-labial line between them. The two jaw-bones should not terminate in a normal perpendicular level in the front but the lower jaw should protrude beyond the upper jaw and bend slightly upwards. The Boxer is normally undershot. The upper jaw should be broad where attached to the skull, and maintain this breadth except for a very slight tapering to the front.

Eyes. The eyes should be dark brown; not too small or protruding; not deep set. They should disclose an expression of energy and intelligence, but should never appear gloomy, threatening or piercing. The eyes must have a dark rim.

Ears. Some American and Continental Boxers are cropped and are ineligible for competition under Kennel Club Regulations. The Boxer's natural ears are defined as: moderate in size (small rather than large), thin to the touch, set on wide apart at the highest points of the sides of the skull and lying flat and close to the cheek when in repose. When the dog is alert the ears should fall forward with a definite crease.

Mouth. The canine teeth should be as widely separated as possible. The incisors (6) should be all in one row, with no projection of the middle teeth. In the upper jaw they should be slightly concave. In the lower they should be in a straight line. Both jaws should be very wide in front; bite powerful and sound, the teeth set in the most normal possible arrangement. The lips complete the formation of the muzzle. The upper lip should be thick and padded and fill out the hollow space in front formed by the projection of the lower jaw and be supported by the fangs of the jaw. These fangs must stand as far apart as possible and be of good length so that the front surface of the muzzle becomes broad and almost square; to form an obtuse (rounded) angle with the top line of the muzzle. The lower edge of the upper lip should rest on the edge of the lower lip. The repandous (bent upward) part of the under-jaw with the lower lip (sometimes called the chin) must not rise above the front of the upper lip. On the other hand it should not disappear under it. It must, however, be plainly perceptible when viewed from the front as well as the side, without protruding and bending upward as in the English Bulldog. The teeth of the under-jaw should not be seen when the mouth is closed, neither should the tongue show when the mouth is closed.

Neck. The neck should be not too thick and short but of ample length, yet strong, round, muscular and clean-cut throughout. There should be a distinctly marked nape and an elegant arch down the back.

Forequarters. The chest should be deep and reach down to the elbows. The depth of the chest should be half the height of the dog at the withers. The ribs should be well arched but not barrel-shaped. They should extend far to the rear. The loins should be short, close and taught and slightly tucked up. The lower stomach line should blend into an elegant curve to the rear. The shoulders should be long and sloping, close lying but not excessively covered with muscle. The upper arm should be long and form a right-angle to the shoulder-blade. The forelegs when seen from the front should be straight, parallel to each other and have strong, firmly articulated (joined) bones. The elbows should not press too closely to the chest-wall or stand off too far from it. The underarm should be perpendicular, long and firmly muscled. The pastern joint of the foreleg should be clearly defined, but not distended. The pastern should be short, slightly slanting and almost perpendicular to the ground

Body. The body viewed in profile should be of square appearance. The length of the body from the front of the chest to the rear of the body should equal the height from the ground to the top of the shoulder, giving the Boxer a short-coupled, square profile. The torso rests on trunk-like straight legs with strong bones. The withers should be clearly defined. The whole back should be short, straight, broad, and very muscular

Hindquarters. The hindquarters should be strongly muscles. The musculation should be hard and stand out plastically through the skin. The thighs should not be narrow and flat but broad and curved. The breech musculation should also be strongly developed. The croup should be slightly sloped, flat arched and broad. The pelvis should be long and, in females especially, broad. The upper and lower thighs should be long. The hip and knee joints should have as much angle as possible. In a standing position the knee should reach so far forward that it would meet a vertical line drawn from the hip protuberance to the floor.

The hock angle should be about 140 degrees; the lower part of the foot at a slight slope of about 95 to 100 degrees from the hock joint to the floor; that is, not completely vertical. Seen from behind the hind legs should be straight. The hocks should be clean and not distended, supported by powerful rear pads.

Feet. The feet should be small with tightly-arched toes (cat feet) and hard soles. The rear toes should be just a little longer than the front toes, but similar in all other respects.

Tail. The tail attachment should be high. The tail should be docked and carried upwards and should be not more than 2 inches long.

Coat. The coat should be short and shiny, lying smooth and tight to the body.

Colour. The permissible colours are fawn, brindle and fawn in various shades from light yellow to dark deer red. The brindle variety should have black stripes on a golden-yellow or red-brown background. The stripes should be clearly defined and above all should not be grey or dirty. Stripes that do not cover the whole top of the body are not desirable. White markings are not undesirable, in fact, they are often very attractive in appearance. The black mask is essential but when white stretches over the muzzle, naturally that portion of the black mask disappears. It is not possible to get black toe-nails with white feet. It is desirable, however, to have an even distribution of head markings.

Weight and Size. Dogs: 22 to 24 inches at the withers. Bitches: 21 to 23 inches at the withers. heights above or below these figures not to be encouraged. Dogs around 23 inches should weigh about 66 lbs. and Bitches of about 22 inches should weigh about 62 lbs.

Faults. Visciousness; treachery; unreliability; lack of temperament; cowardice. Head: a head that is not typical. A plump, bulldoggy appearance. Light bone. Lack of proportion. Bad physical condition. Lack of nobility and expression. 'Sombre' face. Unserviceable bite whether due to disease or to faulty tooth placement Pinscher or Bulldog head. Showing the teeth or the tongue. A sloping top line of the muzzle. Too pointed or too light a bite (snipy). Eyes: visible conjunctiva (Haw). Light eyes. Ears: flying ears; rose ears; semi-erect or erect ears. Neck: dewlap. Front: too broad and low in front; loose shoulders; chest hanging between the shoulders; hare feet; turned legs and toes. Body: carp (roach) back; sway back; thin, lean back; long narrow, sharp-sunken in loins. Weak union with the croup, hollow flanks; hanging stomach. Hindquarters: a falling off or too arched or narrow croup. A low-set tail; higher in back than in front; steep, stiff or too little angulation of the hindquarters; light thighs; cow-hocks; bow-legs; hind dewclaws; soft hocks, narrow heel, tottering, waddling gait; hare's feet; hindquarters too far under or too far behind. Colour; Boxers with white or black ground colour, or entirely white or black or any other colour than fawn or brindle. (White markings are allowed but must not exceed one-third (1/3) of the ground colour.)

BOXER

(AMERICAN KENNEL CLUB—GROUP III: WORKING DOGS)

General Appearance. The Boxer is a medium-sized, sturdy dog, of square build, with short back, strong limbs, and short, tight-fitting coat. His musculation, well developed, should be clean, hard and appear smooth (not bulging) under taut skin. His movements should denote energy. The gait is firm yet elastic (springy), the stride free and ground-covering, the carriage proud and noble. Developed to serve the multiple purposes of guard, working and escort-dog, he must combine elegance with substance and ample power, not alone for beauty but to ensure the speed, dexterity and jumping ability essential to arduous hike, riding expedition, police or military duty. Only a body whose individual parts are built to withstand the most strenuous efforts, assembled as a complete and harmonious whole, can respond to these combined demands. Therefore, to be at his highest efficiency he must never be plump or heavy, and, while equipped for great speed, he must never be racy.

The head imparts to the Boxer a unique individual stamp, peculiar to him alone. It must be in perfect proportion to the body, never small in comparison to the over-all picture. The muzzle is his most distinctive feature, and great value is to be placed on its being of correct form and in absolute proper proportion to the skull.

In judging the Boxer, first consideration should be given to general appearance; next, over-all balance, including the desired proportions of the individual parts of the body to each other, as well as the relation of substance to elegance—to which an attractive color or arresting style may contribute. Special attention is to be devoted to the head, after which the dog's individual components are to be examined for their correct construction and function, and efficiency of gait evaluated.

General Faults. Head not typical, plump, bull-doggy appearance, light bone, lack of balance, bad condition, lack of noble bearing.

Head. The beauty of the head depends upon the harmonious proportion of the muzzle to the skull. The muzzle should always appear powerful, never small in its relationship to the skull. The head should be clean, not showing deep wrinkles. Folds will normally appear upon the forehead when the ears are erect, and they are always indicated from the lower edge of the stop running downward on both sides of the muzzle. The dark mask is confined to the muzzle and is in distinct contrast to the color of the head. Any extension of the mask to the skull, other than dark shading around the eyes, creates a somber, undesirable expression. When white replaces any of the black mask, the path of any upward extension should be between the eyes. The muzzle is powerfully developed in length, width and depth. It is not pointed, narrow, short or shallow. Its shape is influenced first through the formation of both jawbones, second through the placement of the teeth, and third through the texture of the lips.

The Boxer is normally undershot. Therefore, the lower jaw protrudes beyond the upper and curves slightly upward. The upper jaw is broad where attached to the skull and maintains this breadth except for a very slight tapering to the front. The incisor teeth of the lower jaw are in a straight line, the canines preferably up front in the same line to give the jaw the greatest possible width. The line of incisors in the upper jaw is slightly convex toward the front. The upper corner incisors should fit snugly back of the lower canine teeth on each side, reflecting the symmetry essential to the creation of a sound, non-slip bite.

The lips, which complete the formation of the muzzle, should meet evenly. The upper lip is thick and padded, filling out the frontal space created by the projection of the lower jaw. It rests on the edge of the lower lip and, laterally, is supported by the fangs (canines) of the lower jaw. Therefore, these fangs must stand far apart, and be of good length so that the front surface of the muzzle is broad and squarish and, when viewed from the side, forms an obtuse angle with the topline of the muzzle. Over-protrusion of the overlip or underlip is undesirable. The chin should be perceptible when viewed from the side as well as from the front without being over-repandous (rising above the bite line) as in the Bulldog. The Boxer must not show teeth or tongue when the mouth is closed. Excessive flews are not desirable.

The top of the skull is slightly arched, not rotund, flat, nor noticeably broad, and the occiput not too pronounced. The forehead forms a distinct stop with the topline of the muzzle, which must not be forced back into the forehead like that of a Bulldog. It should not slant down (down-faced), nor should it be dished, although the tip of the nose should lie somewhat higher than the root of the muzzle. The forehead shows just a slight furrow between the eyes. The cheeks, though covering powerful masseter muscles compatible with the strong set of teeth, should be relatively flat and not bulge, maintaining the clean lines of the skull. They taper into the muzzle in a slight, graceful curve. The ears are set at the highest points of the sides of the skull, cut rather long without too broad a shell, and are carried erect. The dark brown eyes, not too small, protruding or deep-set, are encircled by dark hair, and should impart an alert, intelligent expression. Their mood-mirroring quality combined with the mobile skin furrowing of the forehead gives the Boxer head its unique degree of expressiveness. The nose is broad and black, very slightly turned up; the nostrils broad, with the nasolabial line running between them down through the upper lip, which, however, must not be split.

Faults. Lack of nobility and expression, somber face, unserviceable bite. Pinscher or Bulldog head, sloping topline of muzzle, muzzle too light for skull, too pointed a bite (snipy). Teeth or tongue showing with mouth closed, driveling, split upper lip. Poor ear carriage, light ('Bird of Prey') eyes.

Neck. Round, of ample length, not too short; strong, muscular and clean throughout, without dewlap; distinctly marked nape with an elegant arch running down to the back. **Faults.** Dewlap.

Body. In profile, the build is of square proportions in that a horizontal line from the front of the forechest to the rear projection of the upper thigh should equal a vertical line dropped from the top of the withers to the ground.

Chest and Forequarters. The brisket is deep, reaching down to the elbows; the depth of the body at the lowest point of the brisket equals half the height of the dog at the withers. The ribs, extending far to the rear, are well arched but not barrel-shaped. Chest of fair width and forechest well defined, being easily visible from the side. The loins are short and muscular; the lower stomach line, lightly tucked up, blends into a graceful curve to the rear. The shoulders are long and sloping, close-lying and not excessively covered with muscle. The upper arm is long, closely approaching a right angle to the shoulder blade. The forelegs, viewed from the front, are straight, stand parallel to each other, and have strong, firmly joined bones. The elbows should not press too closely to the chest wall or stand off visibly from it. The forearm is straight, long and firmly muscled. The pastern joint is clearly defined but not distended. The pastern is strong and distinct, slightly slanting, but standing almost perpendicular to the ground. The dewclaws may be removed as a safety precaution. Feet should be compact, turning neither in nor out, with tightly arched toes (cat feet) and tough pads.

Faults. Chest too broad, too shallow or too deep in front, loose or overmuscled shoulders, chest hanging between shoulders, tied-in or bowed-out elbows, turned feet, hare feet, hollow flanks, hanging stomach.

Back. The withers should be clearly defined as the highest point of the back; the whole back short, straight and muscular with a firm topline. **Faults.** Roach back, sway back, thin lean back, long narrow loins, weak union with croup.

Hindquarters. Strongly muscled with angulation in balance with that of forequarters. The thighs broad and curved, the breech musculature hard and strongly developed. Croup slightly sloped, flat and broad. Tail attachment high rather than low. Tail clipped, carried upward. Pelvis long and, in females especially, broad. Upper and lower thigh long, leg well angulated with a clearly defined, well-let-down hock joint. In standing position, the leg below the hock joint (metatarsus) should be practically perpendicular to the ground, with a slight rearward slope permissible. Viewed from behind, the hind legs should be straight, with the hock joints leaning neither in nor out. The metatarsus should be short, clean and strong, supported by powerful rear pads. The rear toes just a little longer than the front toes, but similar in all other respects. Dewclaws if any, may be removed

Faults. Too rounded, too narrow, or falling off of croup; low-set tail; higher in back than in front; steep, stiff, or too slightly angulated hindquarters; light thighs; bowed or crooked legs; cow-hocks; overangulated hock joints (sickle hocks); long metatarsus (high hocks); hare feet; hindquarters too far under or too far behind.

Gait. Viewed from the side, proper front and rear angulation is manifested in a smoothly efficient, level-backed, ground-covering stride with powerful drive emanating from a freely operating rear. Although the front legs do not contribute impelling power, adequate 'reach' should be evident to prevent interference, overlap or 'side-winding' (crabbing). Viewed from the front, the shoulders should remain trim and the elbows not flare out. The legs are parallel until gaiting narrows the track in proportion to increasing speed, then the legs come in under the body but should never cross. The line from the shoulder down through the leg should remain straight, although not necessarily perpendicular to the ground. Viewed from the rear, a Boxer's breech should not roll. The hind feet should 'dig in' and track relatively true with the front. Again, as speed increases, the normally broad rear track will become narrower.

Faults. Stilted or inefficient gait, pounding, paddling or flailing out of front legs, rolling or waddling gait, tottering hock joints, crossing over or interference—front or rear, lack of smoothness.

Height. Adult males—$22\frac{1}{2}$ to 25 inches; females —21 to $23\frac{1}{2}$ inches at the withers. Males should not go under the minimum nor females over the maximum.

Coat. Short, shiny, lying smooth and tight to the body.

Color. The colors are fawn and brindle. Fawn in various shades from light tan to dark deer red or mahogany, the deeper colors preferred. The brindle variety should have clearly defined black stripes on fawn background. White markings on fawn or brindle dogs are not to be rejected and are often very attractive, but must be limited to one third of the ground color and are not desirable on the back of the torso proper. On the face, white may replace a part or all of the otherwise essential black mask. However, these white markings should be of such distribution as to enhance and not detract from true Boxer expression.

Character and Temperament. These are of paramount importance in the Boxer. Instinctively a 'hearing' guard dog, his bearing is alert, dignified and self-assured, even at rest. In the show ring, his behavior should exhibit constrained animation. With family and friends, his temperament is fundamentally playful, yet patient and stoical with children. Deliberate and wary with strangers, he will exhibit curiosity, but, most importantly, fearless courage and tenacity if threatened. However, he responds promptly to friendly overtures when honestly rendered. His intelligence, loyal affection and tractability to disipline make him a highly desirable companion.

Faults. Lack of dignity and alertness, shyness, cowardice, treachery and viciousness (belligerency toward other dogs should not be considered viciousness).

DISQUALIFICATIONS

Boxers with white or black ground color, or entirely white or black, or any color other than fawn or brindle. (White markings, when present, must not exceed one third of the ground color.)

Approved December 12, 1967

BRIARD

(BERGER DE BRIE)

(THE KENNEL CLUB—WORKING GROUP)

General Appearance. A dog of rugged appearance; supple; muscular and well proportioned, gay and lively.
Size. Dogs $24\frac{1}{2}$ to 27 inches. Bitches 23 to $25\frac{1}{2}$ inches.
Faults. Less than the minimum, except for those under 18 months of age.
Serious Faults. Adults below the minimum or more than 1 inch above the maximum.
Head. Strong, fairly long with well defined stop, placed exactly midway in the length of the head. The head must carry hair forming moustache, beard and eye-brows which slightly veil the eyes.
Faults. Short or overlong head; unbalanced head; carrying too much hair so detracting from the shape of the head; too little moustache or beard or eyebrows. Too pronounced or too little stop.
Serious Faults. Any of the above carried to excess.
Muzzle. Neither narrow nor pointed.
Faults. Nose too small, narrow or pointed, light coloured, or with flesh coloured spots.
Serious Faults. Chocolate coloured, light or flesh coloured nose.
Forehead. Slightly rounded.
Faults. Flat, too round, too wide, or shading the eyes.
Skull. Rectangular in shape.
Faults. Too long; too short or bumpy.
Teeth. Strong, white and well fitting.
Faults. Defective teeth.
Serious Faults. Incisors or pre-molars missing; seriously under or over-shot.
Eyes. Horizontal in shape, well opened and rather large; intelligent and gentle in expression.
Faults. Too small; almond shaped or light in colour.
Serious Faults. Eyes of different colour one from the other; wild in expression or very light.
Ears. Set on high. They should not lie too flat against the side of the head, and they should be fairly short. The length of an uncropped ear should be equal to, or slightly less than half the length of the head. Covered with long hair. In case of equality between two specimens the advantage should be given to the one whose ears are carried erect without being cropped.
Faults. Short hair on ears, ears too long or badly carried.
Serious Faults. Ears set on too low; or half folded.
Conformation.
Neck. Well muscled and arching well away from the shoulders.
Faults. Neck too long, thin or short.
Chest. Broad, deep and well let down.
Faults. Narrow; too deep; or not deep; flat ribbed or too rounded.
Back. Straight.

Faults. Dipped or roached back.
Serious Fault. Rump higher than withers.
Rump. Slightly sloping.
Faults. Straight rump or 'goose-rumped'.
Legs. Well muscled with heavy bone, well balanced stance.
Faults. Light bone; loose shoulders; thighs too wide apart; weak or straight pastern;
Serious Faults. Badly laid shoulder; short hair on legs.
Hocks. Not too low set, well angulated, the leg below the hock being not quite vertical.
Faults. Hock set low or high.
Serious Faults. Badly angulated hock.
Tail. Full length. Well covered in hair, with a slight upward curl at the tip. Carried low and neither twisted to one side nor the other. The bone of the tail should reach at least to the point of the hock.
Faults. Short, carried gaily or sideways, carrying short hair.
Serious Fault. Carried over the back.
Feet. Strong and round, (mid-way between a cat foot and a hare foot).
Faults. Long, flat or narrow feet; feet turning either in or out; insufficient hair.
Nails. Black.
Faults. Grey nails.
Serious Faults. White nails.
Pads. Thick and hard.
Faults. Flat, soft or spongey.
Toes. Close together.
Faults. Toes spread out, long or flat.
Coat. Long, slightly wavy, harsh (like the hair of a goat).
Faults. Soft, curly or short coat.
Serious Fault. Coat less than three inches long.
Colour. All solid colours are allowed except those mentioned below. The darker colours are preferred. Disallowed colours are: white, chestnut, bi-colour; white stripe on head, white hair on feet. Do not confuse bi-colour with the lighter shadings at the ends of the hairs. This lighter shading must, however, be of the same tone as the rest of the coat, i.e. light fawn on dark fawn, light grey on dark grey.
Fault. Slight white marking on chest.
Dewclaws. Double dewclaws on hindlegs. Even dogs of first rate quality cannot be awarded a prize if they do not have these double dewclaws.
Faults. Double dewclaws on front legs.

BRIARD

(AMERICAN KENNEL CLUB GROUP III: WORKING DOGS)

General Appearance. A strong and substantially built dog, fitted for field work, lithe, muscular, and well proportioned, alert and active.
Size. Height at shoulders: Dogs, 23 to 27 inches; bitches, 22 to $25\frac{1}{2}$ inches. Young dogs may be below the minimum.
Head. Large and rather long. Stop well marked and placed at equal distance from top of head and tip of nose. Forehead very slightly rounded. Line from stop to tip of nose straight. Teeth strong, white, and meeting exactly even. Muzzle neither narrow nor pointed. Nose rather square than rounded, always black. Hair heavy and long on top of head, the ears, and around the muzzle forming eyebrows standing out and not veiling the eyes too much. Eyes horizontal, well opened, dark in color and rather large; intelligent and gentle in expression.
Ears. Placed high, alert, may be cropped or left natural. If cropped the ears are carried erect; if uncut they should not be too large or carried too flat. There shall be no preference shown to either cropped or uncropped ears.
Conformation. Neck muscular and distinct from the shoulders. Chest broad and deep. Back straight. Rump slightly sloped. Legs muscular with heavy bones. Hock not too near the ground, making a well-marked angle, the leg below the hock being not quite vertical.
Tail. Uncut, well feathered, forming a crook at the end, carried low and twisted neither to right nor left. The length of the tail should equal the distance from the root of the tail to the point of the hock.
Feet. Strong, round, with toes close together and hard pads; nails black.
Coat. Long, slightly wavy, stiff and strong.
Color. All solid colors are allowed except white. Dark colors are preferable. Usual colors; black, and black with some white hairs, dark and light gray, tawny, and combinations of two of these colors, provided there are no marked spots and the transition from one to the other takes place gradually and symmetrically.
Dewclaws. Two dewclaws on each hind leg are required. A dog with only one cannot be given a prize.
Faults. Muzzle pointed. Eyes small, almond-shaped or light in color. Rump straight or too sloped. White spot on the breast (a large white spot is very bad). Tail too short or carried over the back. White nails.

DISQUALIFICATIONS

Size below the limit. Absence of dewclaws. Short hair on the head, face or feet. Tail lacking or cut. Nose light in color or spotted. Eyes spotted. Hair curled. White hair on feet. Spotted colors of the coat.

Approved March 12, 1963

BULL TERRIER

(THE KENNEL CLUB—TERRIER GROUP)

General Appearance. The Bull Terrier is the Gladiator of the canine race and must be strongly built, muscular, symmetrical and active, with a keen, determined and intelligent expression, full of fire and courageous but of even temperament and amenable to discipline. Irrespective of size, dogs should look masculine, and bitches feminine. The moving dog shall appear well-knit, smoothly covering the ground with free easy strides and with a typical jaunty air. Fore and hind legs should move parallel each to each when viewed from in front or behind, the forelegs reaching out well and the hindlegs moving smoothly at the hip and flexing well at the stifle and hock with great thrust.

Head. The head should be long, strong and deep, right to the end of the muzzle, but not coarse. Viewed from the front it should be egg-shaped and completely filled, its surface being free from hollows or indentations. The top of the skull should be almost flat from each to ear. The profile should curve gently downwards from the top of the skull to the tip of the nose, which should be black and bent downwards at the tip. The nostrils should be well developed. The underjaw should be strong.

Eyes. The eyes should appear narrow, obliquely placed and triangular, well sunken, as dark as possible and with a piercing glint. The distance from the tip of the nose to the eyes should be perceptibly greater than that from the eyes to the top of the skull.

Ears. The ears should be small, thin and placed close together. The dog should be able to hold them stiffly erect, when they should point straight upwards.

Mouth. The teeth should be sound, clean, strong, of good size and perfectly regular. The upper front teeth should fit in front of and closely against the lower front teeth. The lips should be clean and tight.

Neck. The neck should be very muscular, long, arched, tapering from the shoulders to the head, and free from loose skin.

Forequarters. The shoulders should be strong and muscular but without loading. The shoulder blades should be wide, flat and attached closely to the chest wall, and should have a very pronounced backward slope of the front edge from bottom to top. The forelegs should have the strongest type of round quality bone and the dog should stand solidly upon them; they should be moderately long and perfectly parallel. The elbows should be held straight and the strong pasterns upright.

Body. The body should be well rounded with marked spring of rib, and great depth from withers to brisket, so that the latter is nearer the ground than the belly. The back should be short and strong with the top line level behind the withers and arching or roaching slightly over the loin. The underline from brisket to belly should form a graceful upward curve. The chest should be broad viewed from in front.

Hindquarters. The hind legs should be in parallel viewed from behind. The thigh must be muscular and the second thigh well developed. The stifle joint should be well bent and the hock well angulated, with the bone to the foot short and strong.

Feet. The feet should be round and compact with well arched toes.

Tail. The tail should be short, set on low, it should be carried horizontally. Thick at the root it should taper to a fine point.

Coat. The coat should be short, flat, even and

harsh to the touch, with a fine gloss. The skin should fit the dog tightly.
Colour. For white, pure white coat, markings on the head are permissible. For coloured, colour (preferably brindle) to predominate. Skin pigmentation should not be penalized.
Weight and Size. There neither weight nor height limits but there should be the impression of the maximum of substance to the size of the dog.
Faults. Any departure from the foregoing points should be considered a fault and the seriousness of the fault should be in exact proportion to its degree.
N.B.—Under Kennel Club Show Regulations, deafness is a disqualification.

(MINIATURE)

The Standard of the Miniature Bull Terrier is the same as that of the Bull Terrier with the exception of the following:—
Weight and Size. Height should be not more than 14 inches, weight should be not more than 20 lbs.

BULL TERRIER

(AMERICAN KENNEL CLUB—GROUP IV: TERRIERS)

WHITE

The Bull Terrier must be strongly built, muscular, symmetrical and active, with a keen determined and intelligent expression, full of fire but of sweet disposition and amenable to discipline.
The Head should be long, strong and deep right to the end of the muzzle, but not coarse. Full face it should be oval in outline and be filled completely up giving the impression of fullness with a surface devoid of hollows or indentations, *i.e.*, egg shaped. In profile it should curve gently downwards from the top of the skull to the tip of the nose. The forehead should be flat across from ear to ear. The distance from the tip of the nose to the eyes should be perceptibly greater than that from the eyes to the top of the skull. The underjaw should be deep and well defined.
The Lips should be clean and tight.
The Teeth should meet in either a level or in a scissors bite. In the scissors bite the upper teeth should fit in front of and closely against the lower teeth, and they should be sound, strong and perfectly regular.
The Ears should be small, thin and placed close together. They should be capable of being held stiffly erect, when they should point upwards.
The Eyes should be well sunken and as dark as possible, with a piercing glint and they should be small, triangular and obliquely placed; set near together and high up on the dog's head. Blue eyes are a disqualification.
The Nose should be black, with well developed nostrils bent downwards at the tip.
The Neck should be very muscular, long, arched and clean, tapering from the shoulders to the head and it should be free from loose skin.
The Chest should be broad when viewed from in front, and there should be great depth from withers to brisket, so that the latter is nearer the ground than the belly.
The Body should be well rounded with marked spring of rib, the back should be short and strong. The back ribs deep. Slightly arched over the loin. The shoulders should be strong and muscular but without heaviness. The shoulder blades should be wide and flat and there should be a very pronounced backward slope from the bottom edge of the blade to the top edge. Behind the shoulders there should be no slackness or dip at the withers. The underline from the brisket to the belly should form a graceful upward curve.
The Legs should be big boned but not to the point of coarseness; the forelegs should be of moderate length, perfectly straight, and the dog must stand firmly upon them. The elbows must turn neither in nor out, and the pasterns should be strong and upright. The hind legs should be parallel viewed from behind. The thighs very muscular with hocks well let down. Hind pasterns short and upright. The stifle joint should be well bent with a well developed second thigh.
The Feet round and compact with well arched toes like a cat.
The Tail should be short, set on low, fine, and ideally should be carried horizontally. It should be thick where it joins the body, and should taper to a fine point.
The Coat should be short, flat, harsh to the touch and with a fine gloss. The dog's skin should fit tightly.
The Color is white though markings on the head are permissible. Any markings elsewhere on the coat are to be severely faulted. Skin pigmentation is not to be penalized.
Movement. The dog shall move smoothly, covering the ground with free, easy strides, fore and hind legs should move parallel each to each when viewed from in front or behind. The forelegs reaching out well and the hind legs moving smoothly at the hip and flexing well at the stifle and hock. The dog should move compactly and in one piece but with a typical jaunty air that suggests agility and power.
Faults. Any departure from the foregoing points shall be considered a fault, and the seriousness of the fault shall be in exact proportion to its degree, *i.e.* a very crooked front is a very bad fault; a rather crooked front is a rather bad fault; and a slight crooked front is a slight fault.

DISQUALIFICATION

Blue eyes.

COLORED

The Standard for the Colored Variety is the same as for the White except for the sub-head 'Color' which reads: *Color.* Any color other than white, or any color with white markings. Preferred color, brindle. A dog which is predominantly white shall be disqualified.

DISQUALIFICATIONS

Blue eyes. Any dog which is predominantly white.

Approved September 10, 1968

BULLDOG

(THE KENNEL CLUB—UTILITY GROUP)

General Appearance. In forming a judgement on any specimen of the breed, the general appearance, which is the first impression the dog makes as a whole on the eye of the judge, should be first considered. Secondly should be noticed its size, shape and make, or rather its proportions in the relation they bear to each other. No point should be so much in excess of the others as to destroy the general symmetry, or make the dog appear deformed, or interfere with its powers of motion, etc. Thirdly its style, carriage, gait, temper and its several points should be considered separately in detail, due allowance being made for the bitch, which is not so grand or as well developed as the dog.

The general appearance of the Bulldog is that of a smooth-coated, thick-set dog, rather low in stature, but broad, powerful, and compact. The head strikingly massive and large in proportion to the dog's size. The face extremely short. The muzzle very broad, blunt, and inclined upwards. The body short and well knit; the limbs stout and muscular. The hindquarters high and strong but rather lightly made in comparison with its heavily made foreparts. The dog should convey an impression of determination, strength, and activity, similar to that suggested by the appearance of a thick-set Ayrshire Bull.

From its formation the dog has a peculiar heavy and constrained gait, appearing to walk with short, quick steps on the tips of its toes, its hind-feet not being lifted high, but appearing to skim the ground, and running with the right shoulder rather advanced, similar to the manner of a horse in cantering.

Head and Skull. The skull should be very large—the larger the better—and in circumference should measure (round in front of the ears) at least the height of the dog at the shoulders. Viewed from the front it should appear very high from the corner of the lower jaw to the apex of the skull, and also very broad and square. The cheeks should be well rounded and extended sideways beyond the eyes. Viewed at the side, the head should appear very high, and very short from its back to the point of the nose. The forehead should be flat, neither prominent nor overhanging the face; the skin upon it and about the head very loose and well wrinkled. The projections of the frontal bones should be very prominent, broad, square, and high, causing a deep and wide indention between the eyes termed the 'stop'. From the 'stop' a furrow both broad and deep should extend up to the middle of the skull, being traceable to the apex. The face, measured from the front of the cheek-bone to the nose, should be as short as possible, and its skin should be deeply and closely wrinkled. The muzzle should be short, broad, turned upwards and very deep from the corner of the eye to the

corner of the mouth. The nose should be large, broad and black, and under no circumstances should it be liver coloured or brown; its top should be deeply set back almost between the eyes. The distance from the inner corner of the eye (or from the centre of the stop between the eyes) to the extreme tip of the nose should not exceed the length from the tip of the nose to the edge of the under lip. The nostrils should be large, wide, and black, with a well-defined vertical straight line between them. The flews, called the 'chop' should be thick, broad, pendant, and very deep, hanging completely over the lower jaw at the sides (not in front). They should join the under lip in front and quite cover the teeth. The jaws should be broad, massive and square, the lower jaw should project considerably in front of the upper and turn up. Viewed from the front, the various properties of the face must be equally balanced on either side of an imaginary line down the centre of the face.

Eyes. The eyes seen from the front, should be situated low down in the skull, as far from the ears as possible. The eyes and 'stop' should be in the same straight line, which should be at right angles to the furrow. They should be as wide apart as possible, provided their outer corners are within the outline of the cheeks. They should be quite round in shape, of moderate size, neither sunken nor prominent, and in colour should be very dark—almost, if not quite, black, showing no white when looking directly forward.

Ears. The ears should be set high on the head—i.e., the front inner edge of each ear should (as viewed from the front) join the outline of the skull at the top corner of such outline, so as to place them as wide apart, and as high and as far from the eyes as possible. In size they should be small and thin. The shape termed 'rose ear' is correct, and folds inwards at its back, the upper or front edge curving over outwards and backwards, showing part of the inside of the burr.

Mouth. The jaw should be broad and square and have the six small front teeth between the canines in an even row. The canine teeth or tusks wide apart. The teeth should not be seen when the mouth is closed. The teeth should be large and strong. When viewed from the front, the under-jaw should be centrally under the upper jaw to which it should also be parallel.

Neck. Should be moderate in length (rather short than long) very thick, deep and strong. It should be well arched at the back, with much loose, thick and wrinkled skin about the throat, forming a dewlap on each side, from the lower jaw to the chest.

Forequarters. The shoulders should be broad, sloping and deep, very powerful and muscular, and giving the appearance of having been 'tacked on' to the body. The brisket should be capacious, round and very deep from the top of the shoulders to the lowest part where it joins the chest, and be well let down between forelegs. It should be large in diameter and round behind the forelegs (not flat-sided, the ribs being well rounded). The forelegs should be very stout and strong, set wide apart, thick, muscular, and straight, with well-developed forearms, presenting a rather bowed outline, but the bones of the legs should be large and straight, not bandy or curved. They should be rather short in proportion to the hind-legs, but not so short as to make the back appear long, or detract from the dog's activity, and so cripple him. The elbows should be low, and stand well away from the ribs. The pasterns should be short, straight and strong.

Body. The chest should be very wide, laterally round, prominent, and deep, making the dog appear very broad and short-legged in front. The body should be well ribbed up behind, with the belly tucked up and not pendulous. The back should be short and strong, very broad at the shoulders, and comparatively narrow at the loins. There should be a slight fall to the back close behind the shoulders (its lowest part), whence the spine should rise to the loins (the top of which should be higher than the top of the shoulders), thence curving again more suddenly to the tail, forming an arch—a distinctive characteristic of the breed—termed 'roach back'.

Hindquarters. The legs should be large and muscular, and longer in proportion than the fore-legs, so as to elevate the loins. The hocks should be slightly bent and well let down, so as to be long and muscular from the loins to the point of the hock. The lower part of the leg should be short, straight and strong. The stifles should be round and turned slightly outwards away from the body. The hocks are thereby made to approach each other, and the hind feet to turn outwards.

Feet. The hind feet, like the fore feet, should be round and compact, with the toes well split up and the knuckles prominent. The fore feet should be straight and turn very slightly outward, of medium size and moderately round. The toes compact and thick, being well split up, making the knuckles prominent and high

Tail. The tail, termed the 'stern', should be set on low, jut out rather straight, then turn downwards. It should be round, smooth and devoid of fringe or coarse hair. It should be moderate in length—rather short than long—thick at the root, and tapering quickly to a fine point. It should have a downward carriage (not having a decided upward curve at the end), and the dog should not be able to raise it over its back.

Coat. Should be fine in texture, short, close and smooth (hard only from the shortness and closeness, not wiry).

Colour. The colour should be whole or smut (that is, a whole colour with a black mask or muzzle). The only colours (which should be brilliant and pure of their sort) are whole colours—viz., brindles, reds, with their varieties, fawns, fallows, etc., white and also pied (i.e., a combination of white with any other of the foregoing colours). Dudley, black and black with tan are extremely undesirable colours

Weight and Size. The most desirable weight for the Bulldog is 55 lbs. for a dog and 50 lbs. for a bitch.

BULLDOG

(AMERICAN KENNEL CLUB—GROUP VI: NON-SPORTING DOGS)

General Appearance, Attitude, Expression, etc. The perfect Bulldog must be of medium size and smooth coat; with heavy, thick-set, low-swung body, massive short-faced head, wide shoulders and sturdy limbs. The general appearance and attitude should suggest great stability, vigour and strength. The disposition should be equable and kind, resolute and courageous (not vicious and aggressive), and demeanor should be pacific and dignified. These attributes should be countenanced by the expression and behavior.

Gait. The style and carriage are peculiar, his gait being a loose-jointed, shuffling, sidewise motion, giving the characteristic 'roll.' The action must, however, be unrestrained, free and vigorous.

Proportion and Symmetry. The 'points' should be well distributed and bear good relation one to the other, no feature being in such prominence from either excess or lack of quality that the animal appears deformed or ill-proportioned.

Influence of Sex. In comparison of specimens of different sex, due allowance should be made in favour of the bitches, which do not bear the characteristics of the breed to the same degree of perfection and grandeur as do the dogs.

Size. The size for mature dogs is about 50 pounds; for mature bitches about 40 pounds.

Coat. The coat should be straight, short, flat, close, of fine texture, smooth and glossy. (No fringe, feather or curl.)

Color of Coat. The color of coat should be uniform, pure of its kind and brilliant. The various colors found in the breed are to be preferred in the following order: (1) red brindle, (2) all other brindles, (3) solid white, (4) solid red, fawn or fallow, (5) piebald, (6) inferior qualities of all the foregoing.

Note. A perfect piebald is preferable to a muddy brindle or defective solid colour. Solid black is very undesirable, but not so objectionable if occurring to a moderate degree in piebald patches. The brindles to be perfect should have a fine, even and equal distribution of the composite colors. In brindles and solid colors a small white patch on the chest is not considered detrimental. In piebalds the color patches should be well defined, of pure color and symmetrically distributed.

Skin. The skin should be soft and loose, especially at the head, neck and shoulders.

Wrinkles and Dewlap. The head and face should be covered with heavy wrinkles, and at the throat, from jaw to chest, there should be two loose pendulous folds, forming the dewlap.

Skull. The skull should be very large, and in circumference, in front of the ears, should measure at least the height of the dog at the shoulders. Viewed from the front, it should appear very high from the corner of the lower jaw to the apex of the skull, and also very broad and square. Viewed at the side, the head should appear very high, and very short from the point of the nose to occiput. The forehead should be flat (not rounded or domed), neither too prominent not overhanging the face.

Cheeks. The cheeks should be well rounded, protruding sideways and outward beyond the eyes.

Stop. The temples or frontal bones should be very well defined, broad, square and high, causing a hollow or groove between the eyes. This indentation, or stop, should be both broad and deep and extend up the middle of the forehead, dividing the head vertically, being traceable to the top of the skull.

Eyes and Eyelids. The eyes, seen from the front, should be situated low down in the skull, as far from the ears as possible, and their corners should be in a straight line at right angles with the stop. They should be quite in front of the head, as wide apart as possible, provided their outer corners are within the outline of the cheeks when viewed from the front. They should be quite round in form, of moderate size, neither sunken nor bulging, and in color should be very dark. The lids should cover the white of the eyeball, when the dog is looking directly forward, and the lid should show no 'haw'.

Ears. The ears should be set high in the head, the front inner edge of each ear joining the outline of the skull at the top back corner of skull, so as to place them as wide apart, and as high, and as far from the eyes as possible. In size they should be small and thin. The shape termed 'rose ear' is the most desirable. The rose ear folds inwards at its back lower edge, the upper front edge curving over, outwards and backwards, showing part of the inside of the burr. (The ears should not be carried erect or prick-eared or buttoned and should never be cropped.)

Face. The face, measured from the front of the cheekbone to the tip of the nose, should be extremely short, the muzzle being very short, broad, turned upwards and very deep from the corner of the eye to the corner of the mouth.

Nose. The nose should be large, broad and black, its tip being set back deeply between the eyes. The distance from bottom of stop, between the eyes, to the tip of nose should be as short as possible and not exceed the length from the tip of nose to the edge of under lip. The nostrils should be wide, large and black, with a well-defined line between them. Any nose other than black is objectionable and 'Dudley' or flesh-colored nose absolutely disqualified from competition.

Chops. The chops or 'flews' should be thick, broad, pendant and very deep, completely overhanging the lower jaw at each side. They join the under lip in front and almost or quite cover the teeth, which should be scarcely noticeable when the mouth is closed.

Jaws. The jaws should be massive, very broad, square and 'undershot,' the lower jaw projecting considerably in front of the upper jaw and turning up.

Teeth. The teeth should be large and strong, with the canine teeth or tusks wide apart, and the 6 small teeth in front, between the canines, in an even, level row.

Neck. The neck should be short, very thick, deep and strong and well arched at the back.

Shoulders. The shoulders should be muscular, very heavy, wide-spread and slanting outward, giving stability and great power.

Chest. The chest should be very broad, deep and full.

Brisket and Body. The brisket and body should be very capacious, with full sides, well-rounded ribs and very deep from the shoulders down to its lowest part, where it joins the chest. It should be well let down between the shoulders and forelegs, giving the dog a broad, low, short-legged appearance. The body should be well ribbed up behind with the belly tucked up and not rotund.

Back. The back should be short and strong, very broad at the shoulders and comparatively narrow at the loins. There should be a slight fall in the back, close behind the shoulders (its lowest part), whence the spine should rise to the loins (the top of which should be higher than the top of the shoulders), thence curving again more suddenly to the tail, forming an arch (a very distinctive feature of the breed), termed 'roach back' or, more correctly, 'wheelback.'

Forelegs. The forelegs should be short, very stout, straight and muscular, set wide apart, with well developed calves, presenting a bowed outline, but the bones of the legs should not be curved or bandy, nor the feet brought too close together.

Elbows. The elbows should be low and stand well out and loose from the body.

Hind Legs. The hind legs should be strong and muscular and longer than the forelegs, so as to elevate the loins above the shoulders. Hocks should be slightly bent and well let down, so as to give length and strength from loins to hock. The lower leg should be short, straight and strong, with the stifles turned slightly outward and away from the body. The hocks are thereby made to approach each other, and the hind feet to turn outward.

Feet. The feet should be moderate in size, compact and firmly set. Toes compact, well split up, with high knuckles and with short stubby nails. The front feet may be straight or slightly outturned, but the hind feet should be pointed well outward.

Tail. The tail may be either straight or 'screwed' (but never curved or curly), and in any case must be short, hung low, with decided downward carriage, thick root and fine tip. If straight, the tail should be cylindrical and of uniform taper. If 'screwed' the bends or kinks should be well defined, and they may be abrupt and even knotty, but no portion of the member should be elevated above the base or root.

SCALE OF POINTS

General Properties		
Proportion and symmetry	5	
Attitude	3	
Expression	2	
Gait	3	
Size	3	
Coat	2	
Color of coat	4	22
Head		
Skull	5	
Cheeks	2	
Stop	4	
Eyes and eyelids	3	
Ears	5	
Wrinkle	5	
Nose	6	
Chops	2	
Jaws	5	
Teeth	2	39
Body, Legs, etc.		
Neck	3	
Dewlap	2	
Shoulders	5	
Chest	3	
Ribs	3	
Brisket	2	
Belly	2	
Back	5	
Forelegs and elbows	4	
Hind legs	3	
Feet	3	
Tail	4	39
Total		100

DISQUALIFICATION

Dudley or flesh-colored nose.

BULLMASTIFF

(THE KENNEL CLUB—WORKING GROUP)

Characteristics. The temperament of the Bullmastiff combines high spirits, reliability, ability, endurance and alertness.

General Appearance. The Bullmastiff is a powerfully built, symmetrical dog, showing great strength, but not cumbersome.

Head and Skull. The skull should be large and square, viewed from every angle, with fair wrinkle when interested, but not when in repose. The circumference of the skull may equal the height of the dog measured at the top of the shoulder; it should be broad and deep with good cheeks. The muzzle short, the distance from the tip of the nose to the stop should be approximately one-third of the length from the tip of the nose to the centre of the occiput, broad under the eyes and nearly parallel in width to the end of the nose; blunt and cut off square, forming a right-angle with the upper line of the face, and at the same time proportionate with the skull. Underjaw broad to the end. Nose broad with widely spreading nostrils when viewed from the front; flat, not pointed or turned up in profile. Flews not pendulous, and not hanging below the level of the bottom of the lower jaw. Stop definite.

Eyes. Dark or hazel, and of medium size, set apart the width of the muzzle with furrow between. Light or yellow eyes a fault.

Ears. V-shaped, or folded back, set on wide and high, level with occiput, giving a square appearance to the skull, which is most important. They should be small and deeper in colour than the body, and the point of the ear should be level with the eye when alert. Rose ears to be penalised.

Mouth. Mouth to be level, slight undershot allowed, but not preferred. Canine teeth large and set wide apart, other teeth strong, even and well-placed Irregularity of teeth a fault.

Neck. Well-arched, moderate length, very muscular and almost equal to the skull in circumference.

Forequarters. Chest, wide and deep, well set down between forelegs, with deep brisket. Shoulders muscular sloping and powerful, not overloaded. Forelegs powerful and straight, well boned and set wide apart, presenting a straight front. Pasterns straight and strong.

Body. Back short and straight, giving a compact carriage, but not so short as to interfere with activity. Roach and sway backs a fault.

Hindquarters. Loins wide and muscular with fair depth of flank. Hindlegs strong and muscular, with well developed second thighs, denoting power and activity, but not cumbersome. Hocks moderately bent. Cow-hocks a fault.

Feet. Not large, with rounded toes, well-arched (cat feet), pads hard. Splay feet a fault.

Tail. Set high, strong at root and tapering, reaching to the hocks, carried straight or curved, but not hound fashion. Crank tails a fault.

Coat. Short and hard, giving weather protec-

tion, lying flat to the body. A tendency to long, silky or woolly coats to be penalised.
Colour. Any shade of brindle, fawn or red, but the colour to be pure and clear. A slight white marking on chest permissible but not desirable. Other white markings a fault. A dark muzzle is essential, toning off towards the eyes, with dark markings around the eyes, giving expression. Dark toenails desirable.
Weight and Size. Dogs should be 25 to 27 inches at shoulder, and 110 lbs to 130 lbs in weight. Bitches should be 24 to 26 inches at the shoulder and 90 lbs to 110 lbs in weight. It must be borne in mind that size must be proportionate with weight, and soundness and activity is most essential.

BULLMASTIFF

(AMERICAN KENNEL CLUB—GROUP III: WORKING DOGS)

Generao Appearance. That of a symmetrical animal, showing great strength; powerfully built but active. The dog is fearless yet docile, has endurance and alertness. The foundation breeding was 60% Mastiff and 40% Bulldog.
Head. Skull large, with a fair amount of wrinkle when alert; broad, with cheeks well developed. Forehead flat. Muzzle broad and deep; its length, in comparison with that of the entire head, approximately as 1 is to 3. Lack of foreface with nostrils set on top of muzzle is a reversion to the Bulldog and is very undesirable. Nose black with nostrils large and broad. Flews not too pendulous, stop moderate, and the mouth (bite) preferably level or slightly undershot. Canine teeth large and set wide apart. A dark muzzle is preferable.
Eyes. Dark and medium size.
Ears. V-shaped and carried close to the cheeks, set on wide and high, level with occiput and cheeks, giving a square appearance to the skull; darker in color than the body and medium in size.
Neck. Slightly arched, of moderate length, very muscular, and almost equal in circumference to the skull.
Body. Compact. Chest wide and deep, with ribs well sprung and well set down between the forelegs.
Forequarters. Shoulders muscular but not loaded, and slightly sloping. Forelegs straight, well boned and set well apart; elbows square. Pasterns straight, feet of medium size, with round toes well arched. Pads thick and tough, nails black.
Back. Short, giving the impression of a well balanced dog.
Loins. Wide, muscular and slightly arched, with fair depth of flank.
Hindquarters. Broad and muscular with well developed second thigh denoting power, but not cumbersome. Moderate angulation at hocks. Cow-hocks and splay feet are bad faults.
Tail. Set on high, strong at the root and tapering to the hocks. It may be straight or curved, but never carried hound fashion.
Coat. Short and dense, giving good weather protection.
Color. Red, fawn or brindle. Except for a very small white spot on the chest, white marking is considered a fault.
Size. Dogs, 25 to 27 inches at the shoulder, and 110 to 130 pounds weight. Bitches, 24 to 26 inches at the shoulder, and 100 to 120 pounds weight. Other things being equal, the heavier dog is favored.

Approved February 6, 1960

CAIRN TERRIER

(THE KENNEL CLUB—TERRIER GROUP)

Characteristics. This terrier should impress with his fearless and gay disposition.

General Appearance. Active, game, hardy, and 'shaggy' in appearance; strong, though compactly built. Should stand well forward on forepaws. Strong quarters, deep in ribs. Very free in movement. Coat hard enough to resist rain. Head small, but in proportion to body, a general foxy appearance is the chief characteristic of this working terrier.

Head and Skull. Skull broad in proportion; strong, but not too long or heavy jaw. A decided indentation between eyes; hair should be full on forehead. Muzzle powerful but not heavy. Very strong jaw, which should be neither undershot not overshot.

Eyes. Set wide apart; medium in size; dark hazel, rather sunk, with shaggy eyebrows.

Ears. Small, pointed, well carried and erect, but not too closely set.

Mouth. Large teeth. Jaw strong and level.

Neck. Well set on, but not short.

Forequarters. Sloping shoulder and a medium length of leg; good, but not too large, bone. Forelegs should not be out at elbow. Legs must be covered with hard hair.

Body. Compact, straight back; well sprung deep ribs; strong sinews. Back medium in length and well-coupled.

Hindquarters. Very strong.

Feet. Forefeet, larger than hind, may be slightly turned out. Pads should be thick and strong. Thin and ferrety feet are objectionable.

Tail. Short, well furnished with hair, but not feathery; carried gaily, but should not turn down towards back.

Coat. Very important. Must be double-coated, with profuse, hard, but not coarse, outer coat and undercoat which resembles fur, and is short, soft and close. Open coats are objectionable. Head should be well furnished.

Colour. Red, sandy, grey, brindled, or nearly black. Dark points such as ears and muzzle, very typical.

Weight and Size Ideal weight, 14 lbs.

Faults. Muzzle: undershot or overshot. Eyes; too prominent or too light. Ears; too large or at points; they must not be heavily coated with hair. Coat; silkiness or curliness objectionable; a slight wave permissible. Nose; flesh or light coloured, most objectionable. In order to keep this breed to the best old working type, any resemblance to a Scottish Terrier will be considered objectionable.

CAIRN TERRIER

(AMERICAN KENNEL CLUB—GROUP IV: TERRIERS)

General Appearance. That of an active, game, hardy, small working terrier of the short-legged class; very free in its movements, strongly but not heavily built, standing well forward on its forelegs, deep in the ribs, well coupled with strong hindquarters and presenting a well-proportioned build with a medium length of back, having a hard, weather-resisting coat; head shorter and wider than any other terrier and well furnished with hair giving a general foxy expression.

Skull. Broad in proportion to length with a decided stop and well furnished with hair on the top of the head, which may be somewhat softer than the body coat.

Muzzle. Strong but not too long or heavy. Teeth large—mouth neither overshot nor undershot. Nose black.

Eyes. Set wide apart, rather sunken, with shaggy eyebrows, medium in size, hazel or dark hazel in color, depending on body color, with a keen terrier expression.

Ears. Small, pointed, well carried erectly, set wide apart on the side of the head. Free from long hairs.

Tail. In proportion to head, well furnished with hair but not feathery. Carried gaily but must not curl over back. Set on at back level.

Body. Well muscled, strong, active body with well-sprung, deep ribs, coupled to strong hindquarters, with a level back of medium length, giving an impression of strength and activity without heaviness.

Shoulders, Legs and Feet. A sloping shoulder, medium length of leg, good but not too heavy bone; forelegs should not be out at elbows, and be perfectly straight, but forefeet may be slightly turned out. Forefeet larger than hind feet. Legs must be covered with hard hair. Pads should be thick and strong and dog should stand well up on its feet.

Coat. Hard and weather resistant. Must be double-coated with profuse harsh outer coat and short, soft, close furry undercoat.

Color. May be of any color except white. Dark ears, muzzle and tail tip are desirable.

Ideal Size. Involves the weight, the height at the withers and the length of body. Weight for bitches, 13 pounds, for dogs, 14 pounds. Height at the withers—bitches, $9\frac{1}{2}$ inches, dogs, 10 inches. Length of body from $14\frac{1}{4}$ to 15 inches from the front of the chest to back of hindquarters. The dog must be of balanced proportions and appear neither leggy nor too low to ground; and neither too short nor too long in body. Weight and measurements are for matured dogs at two years of age. Older dogs may weigh slightly in excess and growing dogs may be under these weights and measurements.

Condition. Dogs should be shown in good hard flesh, well muscled and neither too fat nor thin. Should be in full good coat with plenty of head furnishings, be clean, combed, brushed and tidied up on ears, tail, feet and general outline. Should move freely and easily on a loose lead, should not cringe on being handled, should stand up on their toes and show with marked terrier characteristics.

FAULTS

1. Skull. Too narrow in skull. **2. Muzzle.** Too long and heavy a foreface; mouth overshot or undershot. **3. Eyes.** Too large, prominent, yellow, and ringed are all objectionable. **4. Ears.** Too large, round at points, set too close together, set too high on the head; heavily covered with hair. **5. Legs and Feet.** Too light or too heavy bone. Crooked forelegs or out at elbow. Thin, ferrety feet; feet let down on the heel or too open and spread. Too high or too low on the leg. **6. Body.** Too short back and compact a body, hampering quickness of movement and turning ability. Too long, weedy and snaky a body, giving an impression of weakness. Tail set on too low. Back not level. **7. Coat.** Open coats, blousy coats, too short or dead coats, lack of sufficient undercoat, lack of head furnishings, lack of hard hair on the legs. Silkiness or curliness. A slight wave permissible **8. Nose.** Flesh or light-colored nose. **9. Color.** White on chest, feet or other parts of body.

Approved May 10, 1938

CAVALIER KING CHARLES SPANIEL

(THE KENNEL CLUB—TOY GROUP)

General Appearance. An active, graceful, well-balanced dog. Absolutely fearless and sporting in character and very gay and free in action.
Head and Skull. Head almost flat between the ears, without dome. Stop shallow; length from base of stop to tip about $1\frac{1}{2}$ inches. Nostrils should be well developed and the pigment black. Muzzle well tapered to the point. Lips well covering, but not hound-like.
Eyes. Large, dark and round, but not prominent. The eyes should be spaced well apart.
Ears. Long and set high, with plenty of feather.
Mouth. Level.
Neck. Should be well set on.
Forequarters. Shoulders not too straight. Legs; moderate bone, straight.
Body. Should be short-coupled with plenty of spring of rib. Back level. Chest moderate, leaving ample heart room.
Hindquarters. Legs; moderate bone, straight.
Feet. Compact, well cushioned and well feathered.
Tail. The docking of tails is optional. The length of the tail should be in balance with the body.
Coat. Long silky and free from curl. A slight wave is permissible. There should be plenty of feather.
Colour. The only recognized colours are: Black and Tan, Raven black with tan markings above the eyes, on cheeks, inside ears, on chest and legs and underside of tail. The tan should be bright.
Ruby: Whole coloured rich red.
Blenheim: Rich chestnut marking well broken up on a pearly white ground. The markings should be evenly divided on the head, leaving room between the ears for the much valued lozenge mark or spot (a unique characteristic of the breed). Tricolour: Black and white well spaced and broken up, with tan markings over the eyes, on cheeks, inside ears, inside legs, and on underside of tail. Any other colour or combination of colours is most undesirable.
Weight and Size. Weight: 10 to 18 lbs. A small well balanced dog well between these weights is desirable.
Faults. Light eyes. Undershot and crooked mouths and pig jaws. White marks on whole coloured specimens. Coarseness of type. Putty noses. Flesh marks. Nervousness.

CHIHUAHUA (SMOOTH COAT)

(THE KENNEL CLUB—TOY GROUP)

Characteristics. An alert and swift moving little dog with a saucy expression.
General Appearance. Small, dainty and compact with a brisk forceful action.
Head and Skull. A well rounded 'Apple Dome' skull with or without Molero, cheeks and jaws lean, nose moderately short, slightly pointed. Define stop.
Eyes. Full, round but not protruding, set well apart, dark or ruby. (Light eyes in light colours permissible).
Ears. Large, set on at an angle of about 45 degrees; this gives breadth between the ears.
Mouth. Level, scissor bite.
Neck. Slightly arched, of medium length.
Forequarters. Shoulders should be well up, lean, sloping into a slightly broadening support above straight forelegs that are set well under, giving free play at the elbows.
Body. Level back, slightly longer than the height at shoulder. Well sprung ribs with deep brisket.
Hindquarters. Muscular with hocks well apart, neither out nor in, well let down.
Feet. Small with toes well split up, but not spread, pads cushioned. Fine pasterns (neither 'Hare' nor 'Cat' foot). A dainty foot with nails moderately long.
Tail. Medium length carried up or over the back. Preferred furry, flattish in appearance, broadening slightly in the centre and tapering to a point.
Coat. Smooth, of soft texture, close and glossy.
Colour. Any colour or mixture of colours.
Weight. Up to six pounds, with two to four pounds preferable. If two dogs are equally good in type, the more diminutive preferred.
Faults. Cropped tail, brokendown ears.

CHIHUAHUA (LONG COAT)

The Standard of the Chihuahua (Long Coat) is the same as the Standard of the Chihuahua (Smooth Coat) with the exception of the following:
Coat. Long, of soft texture (never coarse or harsh to the touch) either flat or slightly wavy. No tight curly coat. There should be feathering on the feet and legs, pants on the hind legs, a large ruff on the neck is desired and preferred, the tail should be long and full as a plume.

CHIHUAHUAS

(AMERICAN KENNEL CLUB—GROUP V: TOYS)

Head. A well-rounded 'apple dome' skull, with or without molera. Cheeks and jaws lean. Nose moderately short, slightly pointed (self-colored, in blond types, or black). In moles, blues, and chocolates, they are self-colored. In blond types, pink nose permissible.
Ears. Large, held erect when alert, but flaring at the sides at about an angle of 45 degrees when in repose. This gives breadth between the ears. In Long Coats, ears fringed. (Heavily fringed ears may be tipped slightly, never down.)
Eyes. Full, but not protruding, balanced, set well apart—dark ruby, or luminous. (Light eyes in blond types permissible.)
Teeth. Level or scissors bite. Overshot or undershot bite or any distortion of the bite should be penalized as a serious fault.
Neck and Shoulders. Slightly arched, gracefully sloping into lean shoulders, may be smooth in the

very short types, or with ruff about neck preferred. In Long Coats, large ruff on neck desired and preferred. Shoulders lean, sloping into a slightly broadening support above straight forelegs that are set well under, giving a free play at the elbows. Shoulders should be well up, giving balance and soundness, sloping into a level back. (Never down or low.) This gives a chestiness and strength of forequarters, yet not of the 'Bulldog' chest; plenty of brisket.

Back and Body. Level back, slightly longer than height. Shorter backs desired in males. Ribs rounded (but not too much 'barrel-shaped').

Hindquarters. Muscular, with hocks well apart, neither out nor in, well let down, with firm sturdy action.

Tail. Moderately long, carried sickle either up or out, or in a loop over the back, with tip just touching the back. (Never tucked under.) Hair on tail in harmony with the coat of the body, preferred furry in Smooth Coats. In Long Coats, tail full and long (as a plume).

Feet. Small, with toes well split up but not spread, pads cushioned, with fine pasterns. (Neither the hare nor the cat-foot.) A dainty, small foot with nails moderately long.

Coat. In the Smooth, the coat should be soft texture, close and glossy. (Heavier coats with undercoats permissible.) Coat placed well over body with ruff on neck, and more scanty on head and ears. In Long Coats, the coat should be of a soft texture, either flat or slightly curly, with undercoat preferred. Ears fringed (heavily fringed ears may be tipped slightly, never down), feathering on feet and legs, and pants on hind legs. Large ruff on neck desired and preferred. Tail full and long (as a plume).

Color. Any color—solid, marked or splashed.

Weight. A well-balanced little dog not to exceed 6 pounds.

General Appearance. A graceful, alert, swift-moving little dog with saucy expression. Compact, and with terrierlike qualities.

SCALE OF POINTS

Head, including ears	20
Body, including tail	20
Coat	20
Legs	20
General Appearance and Action	20
Total	100

DISQUALIFICATIONS

Cropped tail, bobtail. Broken down or cropped ears. Any dog over 6 pounds in weight. In Long Coats, too thin coat that resembles bareness.

CHINESE CRESTED

(THE KENNEL CLUB—TOY GROUP)

Translation: Mrs NIZET de LEEMANS.

This sturdy toy breed of rare hairless dogs comes in numerous colours, or shades, and markings, and in either solid colour or all-over spotted. They are dainty, alert, intelligent, courageous, gentle, clean, odourless, and very affectionate. They are 'free whelpers', seldom requiring veterinary aid; they adjust to cold or warm climates, as their body temperature is about four degrees higher than that of humans. Neither noisy nor 'yappy', nevertheless they are excellent watch-dogs.

General Appearance. A small, active and graceful dog; medium to fine boned; smooth hairless body, with hair on feet, head and tail.

Head. Long skull, slightly rounded, slight stop; moderately long muzzle, cheeks lean.

Crest. Flat, high or long flowing; sparse crest acceptable; full crest preferred.

Ears. Large upstanding ears, with or without ear fringe.

Eyes. Medium size, round and set wide apart.

Teeth. Level or scissors bite. Canine teeth or tusks extended towards front. Pre-molars absent.

Neck. Long, graceful neck. Slightly arched, carried high. Sloping gracefully to shoulders.

Body. Should be medium to long. Level back. Rump slightly rounded. Chest deep and fairly broad. Belly moderately tucked up.

Tail. Up and over back or lopped, never curled. Plume on lower two-thirds of tail. Sparse plume acceptable. Full plume preferred.

Forelegs. Straight, medium to fine boned.

Hindlegs. Hocks well let down.

Feet. Hare foot. Nails moderately long. Hair should not come above first joint from floor.

Colour. Any colour, plain or spotted.

Skin. Smooth and soft. Warm to touch.

Weight. Varies considerably, maximum 12 lbs.

CHOW CHOW

(THE KENNEL CLUB—UTILITY GROUP)

Characteristics. A well-balanced dog, leonine in appearance, with proud dignified bearing; loyal yet aloof; unique in its stilted gait and bluish-black tongue.

General Appearance. An active, compact, short-coupled and well-balanced dog, well knit in frame, with tail carried well over the back.

Head and Skull. Skull flat and broad, with little stop, well filled out under the eyes. Muzzle moderate in length, broad from the eyes to the point (not pointed at the end like a fox). Nose black, large and wide in all cases (with the exception of cream and white in which case a light-coloured nose is permissible and in blues and fawns a self-coloured nose); but in all colours a black nose is preferable.

Eyes. Dark and small, preferably almond-shaped (in blue or fawn dog a light colour is permissible).

Ears. Small, thick, slightly rounded at the tip, carried stiffly erect but placed well forward over the eyes and wide apart, which gives the dog the peculiar characteristic expression of the breed, viz., a scowl.

Mouth. Teeth strong and level, giving scissor bite. Tongue bluish black. Flews and roof of mouth black. Gums preferably black.

Neck. Strong, full, set well on the shoulders and slightly arched.

Forequarters. Shoulders muscular and sloping. Forelegs perfectly straight, of moderate length and with good bone.

Body. Chest broad and deep. Back short, straight and strong. Loins powerful.

Hindquarters. Hindlegs muscular and hocks well let down and perfectly straight which are essential in order to produce the Chow's characteristic stilted gait.

Feet. Small, round and catlike, standing well on the toes.

Tail. Set high and carried well over the back.

Coat. Abundant, dense, straight and stand-off. Outer-coat rather coarse in texture and with a soft woolly undercoat. The Chow Chow is a profusely coated dog and balance should therefore be assessed when the coat is at its natural length.

Colour. Whole coloured black, red, blue, fawn, cream or white, frequently shaded but not in patches or parti-coloured (the underpart of tail and back of thighs frequently of a light colour).

Weight and Size. Minimum height for Chows to be 18 inches, but in every case balance should be the outstanding feature and height left to the discretion of the judges.

Faults. Drop ears, tongues splashed or patchy, tail not carried over the back, parti-coloured, off black noses except in the colours specified, viz., creams, whites, blues or fawns. Any artificial shortening of the coat which alters the natural outline or expression of the dog should be penalized. (The standard of the smooth variety is

identical with the above except that the coat is smooth.)

CHOW CHOW

(AMERICAN KENNEL CLUB—GROUP VI: NON-SPORTING DOGS)

General Appearance. A massive, cobby, powerful dog, active and alert, with strong, muscular development, and perfect balance. Body squares with height of leg at shoulder; head, broad and flat, with short, broad, and deep muzzle, accentuated by a ruff; the whole supported by straight, strong legs. Clothed in a shining, offstanding coat, the Chow is a masterpiece of beauty, dignity, and untouched naturalness.

Head. Large and massive in proportion to size of dog, with broad, flat skull; well filled under the eyes; moderate stop; and proudly carried.

Expression. Essentially dignified, lordly, scowling, discerning, sober, and snobbish—one of independence.

Muzzle. Short in comparison to length of skull; broad from eyes to end of nose, and of equal depth. The lips somewhat full and overhanging.

Teeth. Strong and level, with scissors bite; should neither be overshot, nor undershot.

Nose. Large, broad, and black in color.

Disqualification. Nose spotted or distinctly other color than black, except in blue Chows, which may have solid blue or slate noses.

Tongue. A blue-black. The tissues of the mouth should approximate black.

Disqualification. Tongue red, pink, or obviously spotted with red or pink.

Eyes. Dark, deep-set, of moderate size, and almond-shaped.

Ears. Small, slightly rounded at tip, stiffly carried. They should be placed wide apart, on top of the skull, and set with a slight, forward tilt.

Disqualification. Drop ear or ears. A drop ear is one which is not stiffly carried or stiffly erect, but which breaks over at any point from its base to its tip.

Body. Short, compact, with well-sprung ribs, and let down in the flank.

Neck. Strong, full, set well on the shoulders.

Shoulders. Muscular, slightly sloping.

Chest. Broad, deep, and muscular. A narrow chest is a serious fault.

Back. Short, straight, and strong.

Loins. Broad, deep, and powerful.

Tail. Set well up and carried closely to the back, following line of spine at start.

Forelegs. Perfectly straight, with heavy bone and upright pasterns.

Hind Legs. Straight-hocked, muscular, and heavy boned.

Feet. Compact, round, cat-like, with thick pads.

Gait. Completely individual. Short and stilted because of straight hocks.

Coat. Abundant, dense, straight, and off-standing; rather coarse in texture with a soft, woolly undercoat. It may be any clear color, solid throughout, with lighter shadings on ruff, tail, and breechings.

DISQUALIFICATIONS

Nose spotted or distinctly other color than black, except in blue Chows, which may have solid blue or slate noses. Tongue red, pink or obviously spotted with red or pink. Drop ear or ears.

Approved March 11, 1941

COLLIE (ROUGH)

(THE KENNEL CLUB—WORKING GROUP)

Characteristics. To enable the Collie to fulfil a natural bent for sheepdog work, its physical structure should be on the lines of strength and activity, free from cloddiness and without any trace of coarseness. Expression, one of the most important points in considering relative values, is obtained by the perfect balance and combination of skull and foreface; size, shape, colour and placement of eye, correct position and carriage of ears.

General Appearance. The Collie should instantly appeal as a dog of great beauty, standing with impassive dignity, with no part out of proportion to the whole.

Eyes. These are a very important feature and give a sweep expression to the dog. They should be of medium size, set somewhat obliquely, of almond shape and of dark brown colour, except in the case of blue merles when the eyes are frequently (one or both, or part of one of both), blue or blue flecked. Expression full of intelligence, with a quick, alert look when listening.

Head and Skull. The head properties are of great importance and must be considered in proportion to the size of the dog. When viewed from both front and profile the head bears a general resemblance to a well-blunted, clean wedge, being smooth in outline. The sides should taper gradually and smoothly from the ears to the end of the black nose, without prominent cheek bones or pinched muzzle. Viewed in profile the top of the skull and the top of the muzzle lie in two parallel, straight planes of equal length, divided by a slight, but perceptible 'stop' or break. A mid-point between the inside corners of the eyes, (which is the centre of a correctly placed 'stop') is the centre of balance in length of head. The end of the smooth, well-rounded muzzle is blunt, but not square. The underjaw is strong, clean cut and the depth of the skull from the brow to the underpart of the jaw, must never be excessive (deep through). Whatever the colour of the dog, the nose must be black.

Ears. These should be small and not too close together on top of the skull, nor too much to the side of the head. When in repose they should be carried thrown back, but when on the alert brought forward and carried semi-erect, that is, with approximately two-thirds of the ear standing erect, the top third tipping forward naturally, below the horizontal.

Mouth. The teeth should be of good size, with the lower incisors fitting closely behind the upper incisors; a very slight space not to be regarded as a serious fault.

Neck. The neck should be muscular, powerful, of fair length and well arched.

Forequarters. The shoulders should be sloped and well-angulated. The forelegs should be straight and muscular, neither in nor out at elbows, with a moderate amount of bone.

Body. The body should be a trifle long compared to the height, back firm with a slight rise over the loins; ribs well-sprung, chest deep and fairly broad behind the shoulders.

Hindquarters. The hind legs should be muscular at the thighs, clean and sinewy below, with well bent stifles. Hocks well let-down and powerful.

Feet. These should be oval in shape with soles well padded, toes arched and close together. The hind feet slightly less arched.

Gait. Movement is a distinct characteristic of this breed. A sound dog is never out at elbow, yet it moves with its front feet comparatively close together. Plaiting, crossing or rolling are highly undesirable. The hindlegs, from the hock joint to the ground, when viewed from the rear, should be parallel. The hindlegs should be powerful and full of drive. Viewed from the side the action is smooth. A reasonably long stride is desirable and this should be light and appear quite effortless.

Tail. The tail should be long with the bone reaching at least to the hock joint. To be carried low when the dog is quiet, but with a slight upward swirl at the tip. It may be carried gaily when the dog is excited, but not over the back.

Coat. The coat should fit the outline of the dog and be very dense. The outer coat straight and harsh to the touch, the undercoat soft, furry and very close; so close as to almost hide the skin. The mane and frill should be very abundant, the mask or face, smooth, also the ears at the tips, but they should carry more hair towards the base; the forelegs well feathered, the hindlegs above the hocks profusely so, but smooth below. Hair on the tail very profuse

Colour. The three recognized colours are sable and white, tricolour and blue merle.

Sable. Any shade from light gold to rich mahogany or shaded sable. Light straw or cream colour is highly undesirable.

Tricolour. Predominantly black with rich tan markings about the legs and head. A rusty tinge in the top coat is highly undesirable.

Blue Merle. Predominantly clear, silvery blue, splashed and marbled with black. Rich tan markings to be preferred, but their absence should not be counted as a fault. Large black markings, slate colour, or a rusty tinge either of the top or undercoat are highly undesirable.

White Markings. All the above may carry the typical white Collie markings to a greater or lesser degree. The following markings are favourable—White collar, full or part; white shirt, legs and feet; white tail tip. A blaze may be carried on muzzle or skull or both.

Weight and Size. Dogs 22 to 24 inches at shoulder, bitches 20 to 22 inches. Dogs 45 to 65 lbs, bitches 40 to 55 lbs.

Faults. Length of head apparently out of proportion to body; receding skull or unbalanced head to be strongly condemned. Weak, snipy muzzle; domed skull; high peaked occiput, prominent cheek bones; dish-faced or Roman-nosed; under-shot or over-shot mouth; missing teeth; round or light coloured and glassy or staring eyes are highly objectionable. Body flat sided, short or cobby; straight shoulder or stifle; out at elbow; crooked fore-arms; cow-hocks or straight hocks, large, open or hare feet; feet turned in or out; long, weak pasterns; tail short, kinked or twisted to one side or carried over the back; a soft, silky or wavy coat or insufficient undercoat; prick ears, low-set ears; nervousness.

COLLIE (SMOOTH)

(The Smooth Collie only differs from the Rough in its coat, which should be hard, dense and quite smooth.)

COLLIE

(AMERICAN KENNEL CLUB—GROUP III: WORKING DOGS)

ROUGH

General Character. The Collie is a lithe, strong, responsive, active dog, carrying no useless timber, standing naturally straight and firm. The deep, moderately wide chest shows strength, the sloping shoulders and well-bent hocks indicate speed and grace, and the face shows high intelligence. The Collie presents an impressive, proud picture of true balance, each part being in harmonious proportion to every other part and to the whole. Except for the technical description that is essential to this Standard and without which no Standard for the guidance of breeders and judges is adequate, it could be stated simply that no part of the Collie ever seems to be out of proportion to any other part. Timidity, frailness, sullenness, visciousness, lack of animation, cumbersome appearance and lack of over-all balance impair the general character.

Head. The head properties are of great importance. When considered in proportion to the size of the dog the head is inclined to lightness and never appears massive. A heavy-headed dog lacks the necessary bright, alert, full-of-sense look that contributes so greatly to expression. Both in front and profile view the head bears a general resemblance to a well-blunted lean wedge, being smooth and clean in outline and nicely balanced in proportion. On the sides it tapers gradually and smoothly from the ears to the end of the black nose, without being flared out in backskull ('cheeky') or pinched in muzzle ('snipy'). In profile view the top of the backskull and the top of the muzzle lie in two approximately parallel, straight planes of equal length, divided by a very slight but perceptible stop or break. A mid-point between the inside corners of the eyes (which is the center of a correctly placed stop) is the center of balance in length of head.

The end of the smooth, well-rounded muzzle is blunt but not square. The underjaw is strong,

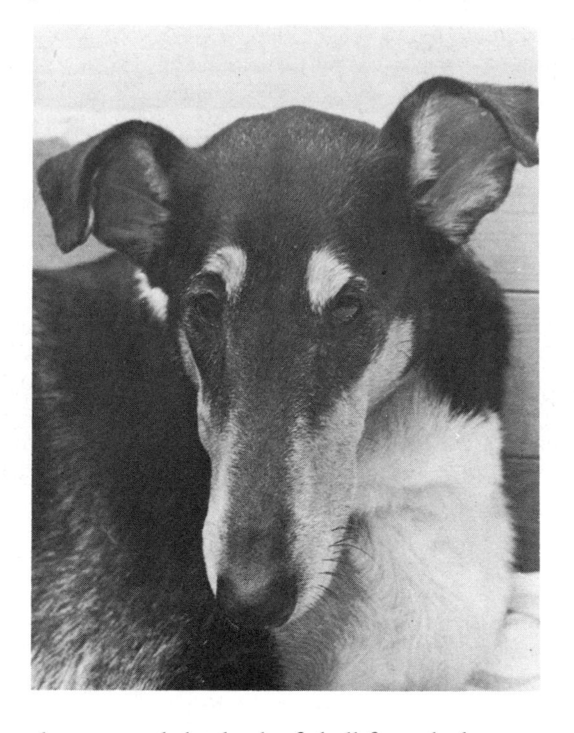

clean-cut and the depth of skull from the brow to the under part of the jaw is not excessive. The teeth are of good size, meeting in a scissors bite. *Overshot or undershat jaws are undesirable the latter being more severely penalized.* There is a very slight prominence of the eyebrows. The backskull is flat, without receding either laterally or backward and the occipital bone is not highly peaked. The proper width of backskull necessarily depends upon the combined length of skull and muzzle and the width of the back skull is less than its length. Thus the correct width varies with the individual and is dependent upon the extent to which it is supported by length of muzzle. Because of the importance of the head characteristics, *prominent head faults are very severely penalized.*

Eyes. Because of the combination of the flat skull, the arched eyebrows, the slight stop and the rounded muzzle, the foreface must be chiseled to form a receptacle for the eyes and they are necessarily placed obliquely to give them the required forward outlook. Except for the blue merles, they are required to be matched in color. They are almond-shaped, of medium size and never properly appear to be large or prominent. The color is dark and the eye does not show a yellow ring or a sufficiently prominent haw to affect the dog's expression. The eyes have a clear, bright appearance, expressing intelligent inquisitiveness, particularly when the ears are drawn up and the dog is on the alert. In blue merles, dark brown eyes are preferable, but either or both eyes may be merle or china in color without specific penalty. A large, round, full eye seriously detracts from the desired 'sweet' expression. *Eye faults are heavily penalized.*

Ears. The ears are in proportion to the size of the head and, if they are carried properly and unquestionably 'break' naturally, are seldom too small. Large ears usually cannot be lifted correctly off the head, and even if lifted, they will be out of proportion to the size of the head. When in repose the ears are folded lengthwise and thrown back into the frill. On the alert they are drawn well up on the backskull and are carried about three-quarters erect, with about one-fourth of the ear tipping or 'breaking' forward. *A dog with prick ears or low ears cannot show true expression and is penalized accordingly.*

Neck. The neck is firm, clean, muscular, sinewy and heavily frilled. It is fairly long, carried upright with a slight arch at the nape and imparts a proud, upstanding appearance showing off the frill.

Size. Dogs are from 24 to 26 inches at the shoulder and weigh from 60 to 74 pounds. Bitches are from 22 to 24 inches at the shoulder, weighing from 50 to 65 pounds. *An undersize or an oversize Collie is penalized according to the extent to which the dog appears to be undersize or oversize.*

Body. The body is firm, hard and muscular, a trifle long in proportion to the height. The ribs are well-rounded behind the well-sloped shoulders and the chest is deep, extending to the elbows. The back is strong and level, supported by powerful hips and thighs and the croup is sloped to give a well-rounded finish. The loin is powerful and slightly arched. *Noticeably fat dogs, or dogs in poor flesh, or with skin disease, or with no undercoat are out of condition and are moderately penalized accordingly.*

Legs. The forelegs are straight and muscular, with a fair amount of bone considering the size of the dog. A cumbersome appearance is undesirable. *Both narrow and wide placement are penalized.* The forearm is moderately fleshy and the pasterns are flexible but without weakness.

The hind legs are less fleshy, muscular at the thighs, very sinewy and the hocks and stifles are well bent. *A cowhocked dog or a dog with straight stifles is penalized.* The comparatively small feet are approximately oval in shape. The soles are well padded and tough, and the toes are well arched and close together. When the Collie is not in motion the legs and feet are judged by allowing the dog to come to a natural stop in a standing position so that both the forelegs and the hind legs are placed well apart, with the feet extending straight forward. Excessive 'posing' is undesirable.

Gait. The gait or movement is distinctly characteristic of the breed. A sound Collie is not out at the elbows but it does, nevertheless, move toward an observer with its front feet tracking comparatively close together at the ground. The front legs do not 'cross over,' nor does the Collie move with a pacing or rolling gait. Viewed from the front, one gains the impression that the dog is capable of changing its direction of travel almost instantaneously, as indeed it is. When viewed from the rear, the hind legs, from the hock joint to the ground, move in comparatively close-together, parallel, vertical planes. The hind legs are powerful and propelling. Viewed from the side, the gait is smooth not choppy. The reasonably long, 'reaching' stride is even, easy, light and seemingly effortless.

Tail. The tail is moderately long, the bone reaching to the hock joint or below. It is carried low when the dog is quiet, the end having an upward twist or 'swirl.' When gaited or when the dog is excited it is carried gaily but not over the back.

Coat. The well-fitting, proper-texture coat is the crowning glory of the rough variety of Collie. It is abundant except on the head and legs. The outer coat is straight and harsh to the touch. *A soft, open outer coat or a curly outer coat, regardless of quantity, is penalized.* The undercoat, however, is soft, furry and so close together that it is difficult to see the skin when the hair is parted. The coat is very abundant on the mane and frill. The face or mask is smooth. The forelegs are smooth and well feathered to the back of the pasterns. The hind legs are smooth below the hock joints. Any feathering below the hocks is removed for the show ring. The hair on the tail is very profuse and on the hips it is long and bushy. The texture, quantity and the extent to which the coat 'fits the dog' are important points.

Color. The four recognized colors are sable and white, tri-color, blue merle and white. There is no preference among them. The sable and white is predominantly sable (a fawn sable color of varying shades from light gold to dark mahogany) with white markings usually on the chest, neck, legs, feet and the tip of the tail. A blaze may appear on the foreface or backskull or both. The tri-color is predominantly black, carrying white markings as in a sable and white and has tan shadings on and about the head and legs. The blue merle is a mottled or 'marbled' color, predominantly blue-gray and black with white markings as in the sable and white and usually has tan shadings as in the tri-color. The white is predominantly white, preferably with sable or tri-color markings. Blue merle coloring is undesirable in whites.

Expression. Expression is one of the most important points in considering the relative value of Collies. *Expression,* like the term 'character' is difficult to define in words. It is not a fixed point as in color, weight or height and it is something the uninitiated can properly understand only by optical illustration. In general, however, it may be said to be the combined product of the shape and color of the eye and the position, size and carriage of the ears. An expression that shows sullenness or which is suggestive of any other breed is entirely foreign. The Collies cannot be judged properly until its expression has been carefully evaluated.

SMOOTH

The Smooth Variety of Collie is judged by the same Standard as the Rough Variety, except that the references to the quantity and the distribution of the coat are not applicable to the Smooth Variety, which has a hard, dense, smooth coat.

Approved March 10, 1959

DACHSHUND (Long-Haired)

(THE KENNEL CLUB—HOUND GROUP)

Characteristics. The long-haired Dachshund is an old, fixed sub-variety of the 'Teckel,' and its history extends back to the beginning of Teckel breeding. The breed is full of character, quick in attack and defence, faithful when properly brought up and very obedient. All the senses are well developed. It has the reputation of being extraordinarily intelligent and easy to train. Its build and temperament fit it to hunt quarry both above and below ground; its eagerness, keen sight and hearing and its sonorous bark make it especially suitable for tracking. In these respects it compares very favourably with any other variety.

The thick, soft hair protects it against thorns, enables it to endure both cold and heat and is rain-proof. It is especially suited to water work. In following a trail its highly developed sense of smell stands it in good stead. It is easily trained to retrieve. The long-haired Dachshund can therefore be used in many different ways by the sportsman.

General Appearance. Form, colour, size and character similar in all respects to those of the smooth Dachshund, except for the long, soft hair. The form is compact, short-legged and long, but sinewy and well muscled, with bold and defiant head carriage, and intelligent expression. In spite of the shortness of the legs the body should be neither too plump nor so slender as to have a weasel-like appearance. Height at shoulder should be half the length of the body measured from the breast bone to the set-on of the tail, and the girth of the chest double the height at the shoulder. The length from the tip of the nose to the eyes should be equal to the length from the eyes to the base of the skull. The tail should not touch the ground when at rest, neither should the ears (i.e., the leather) extend beyond the nose when pulled to the front.

Head and Skull. Long and conical when seen from above, and in profile, sharp and finely modelled. Skull neither too broad nor too narrow, only slightly arched, without prominent stop. Foreface long and narrow, finely modelled. Lips should be tightly drawn, well covering the lower jaw, neither too heavy nor too sharply cut away, the corners of the mouth slightly marked.

Eyes. Medium in size, oval, set obliquely, clear, expressive and dark in colour.

Ears. Broad and placed, relatively well back, high and well set on lying close to the cheeks, broad and long, nicely feathered and very mobile.

Mouth. Wide, extending back to behind the eyes, furnished with strong teeth which should fit into one another exactly, the inner side of the upper incisors closing on the outer side of the under ones.

Neck. Sufficiently long, muscular, showing no dewlap, slightly arched at the nape, running gracefully into the shoulders, carried well up and forward.

Forequarters. Muscular, with deep chest. Shoulders long and broad, set obliquely, lying firmly on well developed ribs. Muscles hard and plastic. Breast bone prominent, extending so far forward as to show depressions on both sides. Upper arm the same length as the shoulder blade, jointed at right angles to the shoulder, well boned and muscled, set on close to the ribs but moving freely as far as the shoulder blade. Lower arm comparatively short, inclined slightly inwards, solid and well muscled.

Body. Long and well muscled, the back showing oblique shoulders and short and strong pelvic region. Ribs very oval, deep between the forelegs and extending far back. Loin short, strong and

broad. The line of the back only slightly depressed over the shoulders and slightly arched over the loin, with the outline of the belly moderately tucked up.

Hindquarters. Rump round, full, broad, with muscles well modelled and plastic. Pelvis bone not too short, broad, strongly developed and set obliquely. Thigh bone strong, of good length and jointed to the pelvis at right angles. Second thigh short, set at right angles to the upper thigh, well muscled. Hocks set wide apart, strongly bent and, seen from behind, the legs should be straight.

Feet. Broad and large, straight or turned slightly outwards; the hind feet smaller and narrower than the fore. Toes close together and with a distinct arch to each toe. Nails strong. The dog must stand equally on all parts of the foot.

Tail. Set on fairly high, not too long, tapering and without too marked a curve. Not carried too high. Fully feathered.

Coat. Soft and straight or slightly waved, of shining colour. Longer under the neck, the underparts of the body and, particularly, on the ears, behind the legs, where it should develop into abundant feathering, and reach the greatest length on the tail, where it should form a flag. The feathering should extend to the outsides of the ears, where short hair is not desired. Too heavy a coat gives an appearance of undue plumpness and hides the outline. The coat should resemble that of an Irish Setter, giving the dog an appearance of elegance. Too much hair on the feet is ugly and useless.

Colour. Black and tan, dark brown with lighter shadings, dark red, light red, dappled, tiger-marked or brindle. In black and tan, red and dappled dogs the nose and nails should be black, in chocolate they are often brown.

Weight and Size. As a rule Long-Haired Dachshunds are classified as follows:—Middle weight up to 17 lbs for bitches and 18 lbs for dogs. Heavy weight over 17 lbs for bitches and over 18 lbs for dogs. The Middle-weights are best suited for badger and fox drawing and the Heavy-weights for tracking, hunting larger animals and for water work. The last named are also very useful for retrieving rabbits and water fowl.

DACHSHUND (Smooth-Haired)

(THE KENNEL CLUB—HOUND GROUP)

Characteristics. First and foremost a sporting dog, the Smooth Dachshund is remarkably versatile, being equally adaptable as a house pet; his smooth, close coat is impervious to rain and mud. His temperament and acute intelligence make him the ideal companion for town or country. In the field of sport he is unequalled, combining the scenting powers of a Foxhound with unflinching courage, and will go to ground to fox, otter or badger.

General Appearance. Long and low, but with compact and well-muscled body, not crippled, cloddy, or clumsy, with bold defiant carriage of head and intelligent expression.

Head and Skull. Long and appearing conical when seen from above, and, from a side view tapering to the point of the muzzle. Stop not pronounced, skull should be slightly arched in profile, appearing neither too broad nor too narrow. Jaw neither too square nor snipy but strong, the lips lightly stretched fairly covering the lower jaw.

Eyes. Medium in size, oval, and set obliquely. Dark in colour, except in the case of Chocolates, in which they may be lighter; in Dapples one or both wall eyes are permissible.

Ears. Broad, of moderate length, and well rounded (not narrow, pointed or folded), relatively well back, high and well set on, lying close to the cheek very mobile as in all intelligent dogs; when at attention the back of the ear directed forward and outward.

Mouth. Teeth must be strongly developed. The powerful canine teeth must fit closely. The correct bite is a scissors bite, any deviation being a fault.

Neck. Sufficiently long, muscular, clean, no dewlap, slightly arched in the nape, running in graceful lines into the shoulders, carried well up and forward.

Forequarters. Shoulder blades long, broad and set on sloping, lying firmly on fully-developed ribs, muscles hard and plastic. Chest very oval, with ample room for the heart and lungs, deep and with ribs well sprung out towards the loins, breast-bone very prominent. The front legs should, when viewed from one side, cover the lowest point of the breastline. Forelegs very short and in proportion to size strong in bone. Upper arm of equal length with, and at right angles to, the shoulder blade; elbows lying close to ribs, but moving freely up to shoulder blades. Lower arm short as compared with other animals, slightly inclined inwards (crook), seen in profile moderately straight; not bending foward or knuckling over (which indicates unsoundness).

Body. Long and muscular, the line of back slightly depressed at shoulders and slightly arched over the loin, which should be short and strong; outline of belly moderately tucked up. What is required is a general levelness of the back, the hindquarters (the rump) not being higher than the shoulders.

Hindquarters. Rump round, full, broad; muscles hard and plastic; hip bone or pelvic bone not too short, broad and strongly developed, set moderately sloping, thigh bones strong, of good length, and joined to pelvis at right-angles; lower thighs short in comparison with other animals; hocks well developed and seen from behind the legs should be straight (not cow-hocked). The dog should not appear higher at the quarters than at shoulders.

Feet. The front feet should be full, broad and close-knit, and straight or very slightly turned outwards, the hind feet smaller and narrower. The toes must be close together with a decided arch to each toe, with strong regularly placed nails and firm pads. The dog must stand true, i.e. equally on all parts of the foot.

Tail. Set on fairly high, strong and tapering, but not too long and not too curved or carried too high.

Coat. Short, dense and smooth, but strong. The hair on the underside of the tail coarse in texture; skin loose and supple, but fitting the dog closely all over, without much wrinkle.

Colour. Any colour other than white (except a white spot on breast). Nose and nails should be black. In red dogs a red nose is permissible but not desirable. In Chocolate and Dapples the nose may be brown or flesh-coloured. In Daples large spots of colour are undesirable, and the dog should be evenly dappled all over.

Weight and Size. Dogs should not exceed 25 lbs. Bitches should not exceed 23 lbs.

Faults. In general appearance weak or deformed, too high or too low to the ground; ears set on too high or too low, eyes too prominent; muzzle too short or pinched, either undershot or overshot; forelegs too crooked; hare or terrier feet, or flat spread toes (flat-footed); out at elbows; body too much dip behind the shoulders; loins weak or too arched; chest too flat or too short; hindquarters weak or cow-hocked, quarters higher than the shoulders.

DACHSHUND (Wire-Haired)

(THE KENNEL CLUB—HOUND GROUP)

Characteristics. The Dachshund should be clever, lively, courageous to the point of rashness, sagacious and obedient. He is especially suited for going to ground because of his low build, very strong forequarters and forelegs, long, strong jaw and the immense power of his bite and hold. His loose skin enables him to manoeuvre with ease for attack or defence. His deep, loud bay indicates his position to those working him. He is also well equipped for field work on account of his good nose and sound construction. He can force his way through cover so dense that it would stop even the smallest gundog. Because of his nose, voice, good sight and perseverence he makes a good tracking dog.

General Appearance. Low to ground, short legged, the body long but compact and well muscled. The head should be carried boldly and the expression be very intelligent. Despite his short legs, compared with the length of his body, he must not be awkward, cramped, crippled or lacking in substance.

Head and Skull. Looked at from above or from the side, the head should taper uniformly to the tip of the nose and be clean cut. The skull is only slightly arched, being neither too broad nor too narrow and slopes gradually, without marked stop, to a finely formed, slightly arched muzzle, the nasal bones and cartilage (Septum) being long and narrow. The ridges of the frontal bones are well developed giving prominence to the nerve bosses over the eyes. Jaw has extremely strong bones, is very long and opens very wide. It should not be too square nor yet snipy. The lips are lightly stretched, the corners just marked and the upper lip covers the lower jaw neatly.

Eyes. Oval, medium in size, set obliquely, lustrous and expressive. The colour should be dark except in the case of Chocolates, when they may be lighter, and of dapples, when one or both wall eyes are allowed.

Ears. Broad and rounded, the front edge touching the cheek. They are relatively well back and high and are well set on. The length is such that when the ears are pulled forward they reach a point approximately half-way between the eyes and the tip of the nose.

Mouth. The powerful canine teeth fit closely. The correct bite is a scissor bite, any deviation being a fault.

Neck. Sufficiently long, muscular, clean cut, not showing any dewlap, slightly arched in the nape, extending in a graceful line into the shoulders and carried erect.

Forequarters. The shoulder blades are long, broad and placed firmly and obliquely upon a very robust rib cage. The upper arm is the same length as the shoulder blade, set at right angles to it and, like the shoulder blade, is very strong and covered with hard but supple muscles. The upper arm lies close to the ribs but is able to move freely. The forearm is comparatively short, inclined slightly inwards to form the crook, when seen in profile is moderately straight and must not bend forward or knuckle over, a state which indicates unsoundness. A correctly placed front leg covers the lowest point of the breast bone.

Body. The breast bone is strong and prominent enough to show a dimple at each side. Looked at from the front the thorax should be very oval allowing ample room for the heart and lungs; seen from the side it should intersect the forearm just above the wrist. The top line, very slightly depressed at the shoulders and slightly arched over the loin, is parallel to the ground. The whole trunk should be long, well ribbed up and underneath should merge gradually into the line of a moderately tucked up belly. The rump is full, round and wide with strong and pliant muscles.

Hindquarters. The pelvis is strong, set obliquely and not too short. The upper thigh, set at right angles to the pelvis, is strong and of good length, the lower thigh is short, set at right angles to the upper thigh and is well muscled. The hocks are well developed. The legs when seen from behind, are set well apart, straight and parallel to one another.

Feet. The front feet are full, broad in front, straight or turned just a trifle outwards. The four toes forming the foot are compact, well arched and have tough pads. The fifth toe (dewclaw) is usually left on. The nails are strong and short. The dog must stand true and equally on all parts of the foot. The hind feet are smaller and narrower than the fore feet and placed straight. There should be no dewclaw. In all other respects the hind feet and toes are similar to the forefeet and toes.

Tail. Continues line of the spine; is but slightly curved, must not be carried too gaily or reach the ground when at rest.

Coat. With the exception of the jaw, eyebrows and ears, the whole body is covered with a completely even, short, harsh coat and an undercoat. There should be a beard on the chin. The eyebrows are bushy. The hair on the ears is almost smooth.

Colour. All colours are allowed but a white patch on the chest, though not a fault, is not desirable. Except in the case of Chocolates, when it may be brown or flesh-coloured, the nose should be black.

Weight and Size. It is recommended that dogs should weigh from 20 to 22 lbs and bitches from 18 to 20 lbs.

Faults. *Primary Faults.* An overshot or undershot jaw. Out at elbow. Knuckling over. Toes turned inwards. Splayed feet. Cow hocks. A bad coat. *Secondary Faults.* Very light eyes. A narrow chest. Breast bone insufficiently prominent. A dip behind the shoulders. A hollow back. A roach back. Rump higher than withers. Weak loins. Excessively drawn up flanks. Bad angulation of forequarters or hindquarters. Legs too long, too close in front, or behind. Toes turned too much outwards. Bowed hind legs. A sluggish, clumsy or waddling gait. Poor muscle. Too long a tail. *Minor Faults.*

Ears too high, too low, sticking out, folded or narrow. Too marked a stop. Head too wide, too narrow or too short. Too pointed or too weak a jaw. Short neck or swan neck. Dewlaps. Goggle eyes. Too short a tail.

DACHSHUND MINIATURE (Long-Haired)

(THE KENNEL CLUB—HOUND GROUP)

Characteristics. The Miniature Dachshund should be gay, alert, bold and highly intelligent. Despite its small size it should be strong, extremely active, hardy and game. Movement should be free and gay. Both fore and hind feet should move straight forward without plaiting or crossing in front and free from any tendency to throw out the hind feet sideways.

General Appearance. In conformation the Miniature Dachshund should be in all respects similar to the Dachshund of standard size. It should be compact, short-legged and long in body, well muscled and strong, with bold and intelligent expression. The body should be neither so plump as to give an impression of cobbiness, nor so slender as to impart a weasel-like appearance. Height at shoulder should be half the length of the body measured from the breast bone to the base of the tail, and the girth of the chest double the height at the shoulder. The length from the tip of the nose to the eyes should equal the length similar to the Dachshund of standard size. It should be compact, short-legged and long in body, well muscled and strong, with bold and intelligent expression. The body should be neither so plump as to give an impression of cobbiness, nor so slender as to impart a weasel-like appearance. Height at shoulder should be half the length of the body measured from the breast bone to the base of the tail, and the girth of the chest double the height at the shoulder. The length from the tip of the nose to the eyes should equal the length from eyes to base of skull.

Head and Skull. Long and conical when seen from above, sharp in profile and finely modelled. Skull neither too broad nor too narrow, only slightly arched and without prominent stop. Foreface long and narrow, finely modelled. The lips should be tightly drawn but well covering the lower jaw, neither heavy nor too sharply cut away. The corners of the mouth slightly marked.

Eyes. Of medium size, neither prominent nor too deeply set, oval in shape, placed obliquely. They should be clear and expressive and dark in colour except in Dapples and Chocolates, in which wall or light eyes are permissible.

Ears. Broad and placed relatively well back, high and well set on, lying close to the cheeks and very mobile. The leather of the ears when pulled to the front should not extend beyond the tip of the nose.

Mouth. Wide, extending back to behind the eyes. Teeth sound and strong, the inner side of the upper incisors closing on the outer side of the under ones.

Neck. Long and muscular, showing no dewlap, slightly arched at the nape, running cleanly into the shoulders, carried well up, giving the dog an alert, defiant appearance.

Forequarters. Muscular, with deep chest. Shoulder blades should be long and broad, set obliquely and lying firmly on well-developed ribs. The breast bone should be prominent, extending so far forward as to show depressions on both sides. Upper arm equal in length to the shoulder blade, which it should join at an angle of 90 degrees, well boned and muscled, set on close to the ribs but moving freely. Lower arm short, inclined slightly inwards, well boned and free from wrinkle.

Body. Long and well muscled with oblique

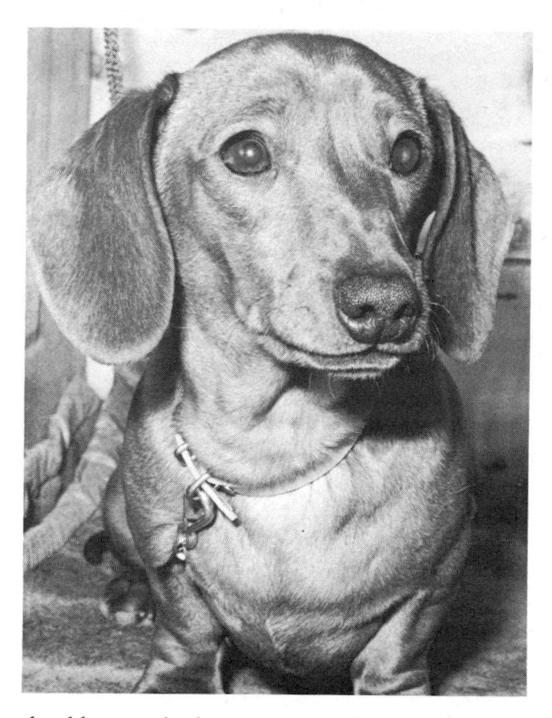

shoulders and short strong pelvic region. Ribs well-sprung and extending far back. Chest oval, well let down between the forelegs, with the deepest point of the keel level with the wrist-joints. The line of the back level or only slightly depressed over the shoulders and slightly arched over the loin, with the belly moderately tucked up.

Hindquarters. Rump full, round and broad. Pelvis bone not too short, broad, strong and set obliquely. Thigh bone strong, of good length and jointed to the pelvis at an angle of 90 degrees. Second thighs short, set at right angles to the upper thigh and well muscled. Hocks well let down, set wide apart, strongly bent. Seen from behind the legs should be straight, with no tendency for the hocks to turn inwards or outwards.

Feet. Broad and large in proportion to the size of the dog, straight or turned only slightly outwards. The hind feet smaller than the fore. Toes close together and with each toe well arched. Nails strong. The dog must stand equally on all parts of the foot.

Tail. Set on fairly high, not too long, tapering and without too marked a curve. It should not be carried too high and never curled over the back.

Coat. The coat should be soft and straight or only slightly waved. It is longest under the neck, on the under-parts of the body and behind the legs, where it should form abundant feathering and on the tail where it should form a flag. The outside of the ears should also be well feathered. The coat should be flat, resembling that of an Irish Setter, and should not obscure the outline. Too much hair on the feet is not desired.

Colour. Any colour. No white is permissible except for a small spot on the breast and even this is undesirable. The nose should be black except in Dapples and Chocolates in which it may be flesh coloured or brown. In all cases the coat colour should be bright and clearly defined. In black and tans the tan should be rich and sharp. Dapples should be free from large unbroken patches, the dappling being evenly distributed over the whole body.

Weight and Size. The ideal weight is 10 lbs and it is of the utmost importance that judges should not award a prize to any dog exceeding 11 lbs in weight. Other points being equal the smaller the better, but mere diminutiveness must never take precedence over general type and soundness. Any appearance of weediness or toyishness is to be avoided at all costs.

Faults. Round skull. Round or protruding eyes. Short ears. Shallow chest. Narrowness in front or behind. Short body. Long legs. Splayed feet. Cow hocks. Mouth under or overshot. Nervous or cringing demeanour.

DACHSHUND MINIATURE (Smooth-Haired)

(THE KENNEL CLUB—HOUND GROUP)

The Standard of the Dachshund Miniature (Smooth-Haired) is identical with the Standard of the Dachshund Miniature (Long-Haired) with the following exceptions:

Coat. In Smooths, short, dense and smooth, adequately covering all the parts of the body; coarsest on the under-side of the tail.

Weight and Size. The ideal weight is 10 lbs and it is of the utmost importance that judges should not award a prize to any dog exceeding 11 lbs in weight. Other points being equal the smaller the better, but mere diminutiveness must never take precedence over general type and soundness. Any appearance of weediness or toyishness is to be avoided at all costs.

Faults. Woolly or curly coat.

DACHSHUND MINIATURE (Wire-Haired)

(THE KENNEL CLUB—HOUND GROUP)

The Standard of the Dachshund Miniature (Wire-Haired) is identical with the Standard of the Dachshund Miniature (Long-Haired) with the following exceptions.

Coat. With the exception of the jaw, eyebrows and ears, the whole body is covered with a completely even, short, harsh coat and undercoat. There should be a beard on the chin. The eyebrows are bushy. The hair on the ears is almost smooth.

Weight and Size. The ideal weight is 10 lbs and it is of the utmost importance that judges should not award a prize to any dog exceeding 11 lbs in weight. Other points being equal the smaller the better, but mere diminutiveness must never take precedence over general type and soundness. Any appearance of weediness or toyishness is to be avoided at all costs.

DACHSHUND

(AMERICAN KENNEL CLUB—GROUP II: HOUNDS)

SUMMARY

General Appearance. Short-legged, long-bodied, low-to-ground; sturdy, well muscled, neither clumsy nor slim, with audacious carriage and intelligent expression; conformation pre-eminently fitted for following game into burrows.

Head. Long, uniformly tapered, clean-cut; teeth well fitted, with scissors bite; eyes medium oval; ears broad, long, rounded, set on high and well back; neck long, muscular.

Forequarters. Muscular, compact. Chest deep, long, full and oval; breastbone prominent. Broad, long shoulder, and oblique humerus forming right angle; heavy, set close; forearm short, inclined slightly in. Foreleg straight and vertical in profile, covering deepest point of chest. Feet broad, firm, compact, turned slightly out.

Hindquarters. Well-muscled and rounded. Pelvis, femur and tibia oblique, forming right angles; tarsus inclined forward. Hip should be level with shoulder, back strong, neither sagged nor more than very slightly arched. Tail strong, tapered, well-covered with hair, not carried gaily.

Varieties. Three coat types: *Smooth* or Short-haired, short and dense, shining, glossy. *Wire-haired*, like German Wirehaired Pointer, hard, with good undercoat. *Longhaired*, like Irish Setter.

Note—In each coat variety there are divisions of open classes restricted to Miniatures, under 9 pounds, minimum age 12 months.

Color. Solid red (tan) of various shades, and black with tan points, should have black noses and nails, and narrow black line edging lips and eyelids; chocolate with tan points permits brown nose. Eyes of all, lustrous, the darker the better.

Faults. Overshot or undershot, knuckling over, loose shoulders; high on legs, clumsy gait, long, splayed or twisted feet, sagged or roached back, high croup, small, narrow or short chest, faulty angulation of fore or hindquarters, weak loins, narrow hindquarters, bowed legs, cowhocks; weak or dish-faced muzzle, dewlaps, uneven or scanty coat.

GENERAL FEATURES

General Appearance. Low to ground, short-legged, long-bodied, but with compact figure and robust muscular development; with bold and confident carriage of the head and intelligent facial expression. In spite of his shortness of leg, in comparison with his length of trunk, he should appear neither crippled, awkward, cramped in his capacity for movement, nor slim and weasel-like.

Qualities. He should be clever, lively, and courageous to the point of rashness, persevering in his work both above and below ground; with all the senses well developed. His build and disposition qualify him especially for hunting game below ground. Added to this, his hunting spirit, good nose, loud tongue, and small size, render him especially suited for beating the bush. His figure and his fine nose give him an especial advantage over most other breeds of sporting dogs for trailing.

CONFORMATION OF BODY

Head. Viewed from above or from the side, it should taper uniformly to the tip of the nose, and should be clean-cut. The skull is only slightly arched, and should slope gradually without stop (the less stop the more typical) into the finely-formed slightly-arched muzzle (ram's nose). The bridge bones over the eyes should be strongly prominent. The nasal cartilage and tip of the nose are long and narrow; lips tightly stretched, well covering the lower jaw, but neither deep nor pointed; corner of the mouth not very marked. Nostrils well open. Jaws opening wide and hinged well back of the eyes, with strongly developed bones and teeth.

Teeth. Powerful canine teeth should fit closely together, and the outer side of the lower incisors should tightly touch the inner side of the upper. (Scissors bite.)

Eyes. Medium size, oval, situated at the sides, with a clean, energetic, though pleasant expression; not piercing. Color, lustrous dark reddish-brown to brownish-black for all coats and colors. Wall eyes in the case of dapple dogs are not a very bad fault, but are also not desirable.

Ears. Should be set near the top of the head, and not too far forward, long but not too long, beautifully rounded, not narrow, pointed, or folded. Their carriage should be animated, and the forward edge should just touch the cheek.

Neck. Fairly long, muscular, clean-cut, not showing any dewlap on the throat, slightly arched in the nape, extending in a graceful line into the shoulders, carried proudly but not stiffly.

Front. To endure the arduous exertion underground, the front must be correspondingly muscular, compact, deep, long and broad. Forequarters in detail: (*a*) Shoulder Blade: Long, broad, obliquely and firmly placed upon the fully developed thorax, furnished with hard and plastic muscles. (*b*) Upper Arm: Of the same length as the shoulder blade, and at right angles to the latter, strong of bone and hard of muscle, lying close to the ribs, capable of free movement. (*c*) Forearm: This is short in comparison to other breeds, slightly turned inwards; supplied with hard but plastic muscles on the front and outside, with tightly stretched tendons on the inside and at the back. (*d*) Joint between forearm and foot (wrists): These are closer together than the shoulder joints, so that the front does not appear absolutely straight. (*e*) Paws: Full, broad in front, and a trifle inclined outwards; compact, with well-arched toes and tough pads. (*f*) Toes: There are five of these, though only four are in use. Dewclaws may be removed. They should be close together, with a pronounced arch; provided on top with strong nails, and underneath with tough toe-pads.

Trunk. The whole trunk should in general be long and fully muscled. The back, with sloping shoulders, and short, rigid pelvis, should lie in the straightest possible line between the withers and the very slightly arched loins, these latter being short, rigid, and broad. (*a*) Chest: The breastbone should be strong, and so prominent in front that on either side a depression (dimple) appears. When viewed from the front, the thorax should appear oval, and should extend downward to the mid-point of the forearm. The enclosing structure of ribs should appear full and oval, and when viewed from above or from the side, full-volumed, so as to allow by its ample capacity, complete development of heart and lungs. Well ribbed up, and gradually merging into the line of the abdomen. If the length is correct, and also the anatomy of the shoulder and upper arm, the front leg when viewed in profile should cover the lowest point of the breast line. (*b*) Abdomen: Slightly drawn up.

Hindquarters. The hindquarters viewed from behind should be of completely equal width. (*a*) Croup: Long, round, full, robustly muscled, but plastic, only slightly sinking toward the tail. (*b*) Pelvic Bones: Not too short, rather strongly developed, and moderately sloping. (*c*) Thigh Bone: Robust and of good length, set at right angles to the pelvic bones. (*d*) Hind Legs: Robust and well-muscled, with well-rounded buttocks. (*e*) Knee Joint: Broad and strong. (*f*) Calf Bone: In comparison with other breeds, short; it should be perpendicular to the thigh bone, and firmly muscled. (*g*) The bones at the base of the foot (*tarsus*) should present a flat appearance, with a strongly prominent hock and a broad tendon of Achilles. (*h*) The central foot bones (*metatarsus*) should be long, movable towards the calf bone, slightly bent toward the front, but perpendicular (as viewed from behind). (*i*) Hind Paws: Four compactly closed and beautifully arched toes, as in the case of the front paws. The whole foot should be posed equally on the ball and not merely on the toes; nails short

Tail. Set in continuation of the spine, extending without very pronounced curvature, and should not be carried too gaily.

Note—Inasmuch as the Dachshund is a hunting dog, scars from honorable wounds shall not be considered a fault.

SPECIAL CHARACTERISTICS OF THE THREE COAT-VARIETIES

The Dachshund is bred with three varieties of coat: (1) Shorthaired (or *Smooth*); (2) Wirehaired; (3) Longhaired. All three varieties should conform to the characteristics already specified. The longhaired and shorthaired are old, well-fixed varieties, but into the wirehaired Dachshund, the blood of other breeds has been purposely introduced; nevertheless, in breeding him, the greatest stress must be placed upon conformity to the general Dachshund type. The following specifications are applicable separately to the three coat-varieties, respectively:

SHORTHAIRED (OR SMOOTH) DACHSHUND

(1) Hair: Short, thick, smooth and shining; no bald patches. Special faults are: Too fine or thin hair, leathery ears, bald patches, too coarse or too thick hair in general. Tail: Gradually tapered to a point, well but not too richly haired; long, sleek bristles on the underside are considered a patch of strong-growing hair, not a fault. A brush tail is a fault, as is also a partly or wholly hairless tail.

Color of hair, nose and nails. (*a*) *One-colored Dachshund*—This group includes red (often called tan), red-yellow, yellow, and brindle with or without a shading of interspersed black hairs. Nevertheless a clean color is preferable, and red is to be considered more desirable than red-yellow or yellow. Dogs strongly shaded with interspersed black hairs belong to this class, and not to the other color groups. A small white spot is admissible but not desirable. Nose and Nails—Black; brown is admissible, but not desirable.

(*b*) *Two-colored Dachshund*—'These comprise deep black, chocolate, gray (blue), and white; each with tan markings over the eyes, on the sides of the jaw and underlip, on the inner edge of the ear, front, breast, inside and behind the front legs, on the paws and around the anus, and from there to about one-third to one-half of the length of the tail on the under side. The most common two-colored Dachshund is usually called black-and-tan. A small white spot is admissible but not desirable. Absence, undue prominence or extreme lightness of tan markings is undesirable. Nose and nails—In the case of black dogs, black; for chocolate, brown (the darker the better); for gray (blue) or white dogs, gray or even flesh color, but the last named color is not desirable; in the case of white dogs, black nose and nails are to be preferred.'

(*c*) *Dappled Dachshund*—The color of the dappled Dachshund is a clear brownish or grayish color, or even a white ground, with dark irregular patches of dark-gray, brown, red-yellow or black (large areas of one color not desirable). It is desirable that neither the light nor the dark color should predominate. Nose and Nails—As for One- and Two-Colored Dachshund.

WIREHAIRED DACHSHUND

(2) The general appearance is the same as that of the shorthaired, but without being long in the legs, it is permissible for the body to be somewhat higher off the ground. Hair: With the exception of jaw, eyebrows, and ears, the whole body is covered with a perfectly uniform tight, short, thick, rough, hard coat, but with finer, shorter hairs (undercoat) everywhere distributed between the coarser hairs, resembling the coat of the German Wirehaired Pointer. There should be a beard on the chin. The eyebrows are bushy. On the ears the hair is shorter than on the body; almost smooth, but in any case conforming to the rest of the coat. The general arrangement of the hair should be such that the wirehaired Dachshund, when seen from a distance should resemble the smooth-haired. Any sort of soft hair in the coat is faulty, whether short or long, or wherever found on the body; the same is true of long, curly, or wavy hair, or hair that sticks out irregularly in all directions; a flag tail is also objectionable. Tail: Robust, as thickly haired as possible, gradually coming to a point, and without a tuft. Color of Hair, Nose and Nails: All colors are admissible. White patches on the chest, though allowable, are not desirable.

LONGHAIRED DACHSHUND

(3) The distinctive characteristic differentiating this coat from the shorthaired, or smooth-haired Dachshund is alone the rather long silky hair. Hair: The soft, sleek, glistening, often slightly wavy hair should be longer under the neck, on the underside of the body, and especially on the ears and behind the legs, becoming there a pronounced feather; the hair should attain its greatest length on the underside of the tail. The hair should fall beyond the lower edge of the ear. Short hair on the ear, so-called 'leather' ears, is not desirable. Too luxurious a coat causes the longhaired Dachshund to seem coarse, and masks the type. The coat should remind one of the Irish Setter, and should give the dog an elegant appearance. Too thick hair on the paws, so-called 'mops,' is inelegant, and renders the animal unfit for use. It is faulty for the dog to have equally long hair over all the body, if the coat is too curly, or too scrubby, or if a flag tail or overhanging hair on the ears are lacking; or if there is a very pronounced parting on the back, or a vigorous growth between the toes. Tail: Carried gracefully in prolongation of the spine; the hair attains here its greatest length and forms a veritable flag. Color of Hair, Nose and Nails: Exactly as for the smooth-haired Dachshund, except that the red-with-black (heavily sabled) color is permissible and is formally classed as red.

Note—Miniature Dachshunds are bred in all three coats. Within the limits imposed, symmetrical adherence to the general Dachshund conformation, combined with smallness, and mental and physical vitality, should be the outstanding characteristics of Miniature Dachshunds. They have not been given separate classification but are a division of the Open Class for 'under 10 pounds, and 12 months old or over.'

GENERAL FAULTS

Serious Faults: Overshot or undershot jaws, knuckling over, very loose shoulders.

'Secondary Faults—A weak, long-legged, or dragging figure, body hanging between the shoulders; sluggish, clumsy, or waddling gait; toes turned inwards or too obliquely outwards; splayed paws, sunken back, roach (or carp) back; croup higher than withers; short-ribbed or too-weak chest; excessively drawn-up flanks like those of a Greyhound; narrow, poorly-muscled hindquarters; weak loins; bad angulation in front or hindquarters; cow hocks; bowed legs; wall eyes, except for dapple dogs; a bad coat.'

'Minor Faults—Ears wrongly set, sticking out, narrow or folded; too marked a stop; too pointed or weak a jaw? pincer teeth; too wide or too short a head; goggle eyes, wall eyes in the case of dapple dogs; insufficiently dark eyes in the case of all other coat-colors; dewlaps; short neck; swan neck; too fine or too thin hair; absence of, or too profuse or too light tan markings in the case of two-colored dogs.'

Approved January 12, 1971

DALMATIAN

(THE KENNEL CLUB—UTILITY GROUP)

General Appearance. The Dalmatian should be a balanced, strong, muscular, active dog of good demeanour. Symmetrical in outline, free from coarseness and lumber, capable of great endurance with a fair amount of speed.

Head and Skull. The head should be of fair length, the skull flat, reasonably broad between the ears but refined, moderately well defined at the temples, i.e. exhibiting a moderate amount of stop; not in one straight line from nose to occiput bone. Entirely free from wrinkle. The muzzle should be long and powerful, never snipy, the lips clean, fitting the jaw moderately close. The nose in the black spotted variety should always be black, in the liver spotted variety always brown.

Eyes. The eyes, set moderately well apart should be of medium size, round, bright and sparkling, with an intelligent expression, their colour, depending on the marking of the dog; dark in the black spotted, amber in the liver spotted. The rim round the eyes should be complete; black in the black spotted and liver brown in the liver spotted.

Ears. The ears should be set on rather high, of moderate size, rather wide at the base, gradually tapering to a rounded point. Fine in texture, carried close to the head. The marking should be well broken up, preferably spotted.

Mouth. The teeth should meet. The upper slightly overlapping the lower (Scissor bite.)

Neck. The neck should be fairly long, nicely arched, light and tapering. Entirely free from throatiness.

Forequarters. The shoulders should be moderately oblique, clean and muscular. Elbows close to the body. The forelegs perfectly straight with strong round bone down to the feet, with a slight spring at the pastern joint.

Body. The chest should not be too wide but deep, spacious with plenty of lung and heart room. The ribs well sprung, well defined wither, powerful level back, loins strong, clean and muscular, and slightly arched.

Hindquarters. Rounded, muscles clean with well developed second thigh, good turn of stifle and hocks well defined.

Tail. In length reaching approximately to the hocks. Strong at the insertion gradually tapering towards the end, it should not be inserted too low or too high, be free from coarseness and carried with a slight upward curve, never curled. Preferably spotted.

Feet. Round, compact, with well arched toes (cat feet) and round tough elastic pads. Nails black or white in the black spotted variety, in the liver spotted—brown or white.

Gait. The Dalmatian should have great freedom of movement. A smooth, powerful rhythmic action with a long stride. Viewed from behind, the legs should move in parallel, the hindlegs tracking the fore. A short stride and paddling action is incorrect.

Coat. The coat should be short, hard and dense, sleek and glossy in appearance. The ground colour should be pure white. Black spotted dogs should have dense spots and liver spotted dogs liver-brown spots They should not run together but be round and well defined, the size of sixpence to a half crown, as well distributed as possible. Spots on the extremities should be smaller than those on the body.

Size. Overall balance of prime importance, but the ideal height to be aimed at is dogs 23 to 24 inches, bitches 22 to 23 inches.

Faults. Patches, black and liver spots on the same dog (tri colours). Lemon spots. Blue eyes. Bronzing and other faults of pigmentation.

DALMATIAN

(AMERICAN KENNEL CLUB—GROUP VI: NON-SPORTING DOGS)

The Dalmatian should represent a strong, muscular, and active dog; poised and alert; free of shyness; intelligent in expression; symmetrical in outline; and free from coarseness and lumber. He should be capable of great endurance, combined with a fair amount of speed.

Head. Should be of a fair length, the skull flat, proportionately broad between the ears, and moderately well defined at the temples, and not in one straight line from the nose to the occiput bone as required in a Bull Terrier. It should be entirely free from wrinkle.

Muzzle. Should be long and powerful—the lips clean. The mouth should have a scissors bite. Never undershot or overshot. It is permissible to trim whiskers.

Eyes. Should be set moderately well apart, and of medium size, round, bright, and sparkling, with an intelligent expression; their color greatly depending on the markings of the dog. In the black-spotted variety the eyes should be dark (black or brown or blue). In the liver-spotted variety they should be lighter than in the black-spotted variety (golden or light brown or blue). The rim around the eyes in the black-spotted variety should be black; in the liver-spotted variety, brown. Never flesh-colored in either. Lack of pigment a major fault.

Ears. Should be set rather high, of moderate size, rather wide at the base, and gradually tapering to a rounded point. They should be carried close to the head, be thin and fine in texture, and preferably spotted.

Nose. In the black-spotted variety should always be black; in the liver-spotted variety, always brown. A butterfly or flesh-colored nose is a major fault.

Neck and Shoulders. The neck should be fairly long, nicely arched, light and tapering, and entirely free from throatiness. The shoulders should be oblique, clean, and muscular, denoting speed.

Body, Back, Chest, and Loins. The chest should not be too wide, but very deep and capacious, ribs well sprung but never rounded like barrel hoops (which would indicate want of speed). Back powerful; loin strong, muscular and slightly arched.

Legs and Feet. Of great importance. The forelegs should be straight, strong, and heavy in bone; elbows close to the body; feet compact, well-arched toes, and tough, elastic pads. In the hind legs the muscles should be clean, though well defined; the hocks well let down. Dewclaws may be removed from legs.

Nails. In the black-spotted variety, black or white; or a nail may be both black and white. In the liver-spotted variety, brown or white; or a nail may be both brown and white.

Gait. Length of stride should be in proportion to the size of the dog, steady in rhythm of 1, 2, 3, 4 as in the cadence count in military drill. Front legs should not paddle, nor should there be a straddling appearance. Hind legs should neither cross nor weave; judges should be able to see each leg move with no interference of another leg. Drive and reach are most desirable. Cowhocks are a major fault.

Tail. Should ideally reach the hock joint, strong at the insertion, and tapering toward the end, free from coarseness. It should not be inserted too low down, but carried with a slight curve upwards, and never curled.

Coat. Should be short, hard, dense, and fine, sleek and glossy in appearance, but neither woolly nor silky.

Color and Markings. Are most important points. The ground color in both varieties should be pure white, very decided, and not intermixed. The color of the spots in the black-spotted variety should be dense black; in the liver-spotted variety they should be liver brown. The spots should not intermingle, but be as round and well defined as possible, the more distinct the better. In size they should be from that of a dime to a half-dollar. The spots on the face, head, ears, legs, and tail to be smaller than those on the body. Patches, tri-colors, and any color markings other than black or liver constitute a disqualification. A true patch is a solid, sharply defined mass of black or liver that is appreciably larger than any of the markings on the dog. Several spots that are so adjacent that they actually touch one another at their edges do not constitute a patch.

Size. The desirable height of dogs and bitches is between 19 and 23 inches at the withers, and any dog or bitch over 24 inches at the withers is to be disqualified.

MAJOR FAULTS

Butterfly or flesh-colored nose. Cowhocks. Flat feet. Lack of pigment in eye rims. Shyness. Trichiasis (abnormal position or direction of the eyelashes).

FAULTS

Ring or low-set tail. Undersize or oversize.

SCALE OF POINTS

Body, back, chest and loins	5
Coat	5
Color and markings	25
Ears	5
Gait	10
Head and eyes	10
Legs and feet	10
Neck and shoulders	10
Size, symmetry, etc.	10
Tail	5
Total	100

DISQUALIFICATIONS

Any color markings other than black or liver. Any size over 24 inches at the withers. Patches. Tri-colors. Undershot or overshot bite.

Approved December 11, 1962

DANDIE DINMONT TERRIER

(THE KENNEL CLUB—TERRIER GROUP)

Head and Skull. Head strongly made and large, not out of proportion to the dog's size, the muscles showing extraordinary development, more especially the maxillary. Skull broad between the ears, getting gradually less towards the eye, and measuring about the same from the inner corner of the eye to back of skull as it does from ear to ear. The forehead well domed. The head is covered with very soft silky hair, which should not be confined to a mere top-knot, and the lighter in colour and silkier it is the better. The cheeks, starting from the ears proportionately with the skull, have a gradual taper towards the muzzle, which is deep and strongly made, and measures about three inches in length, or in proportion to skull as three is to five. The muzzle is covered with hair of a little darker shade than top-knot, and of the same texture as the feather of the forelegs. The top of the muzzle is generally bare for about an inch from the back part of the nose, the bareness coming to a point towards the eye, and being about one inch broad at the nose. The nose black.

Eyes. Set wide apart, large, full, round but not protruding, bright, expressive of great determination, intelligence, and dignity, set low and prominent in front of the head, colour, a rich dark hazel.

Ears. Pendulous, set well back wide apart and low on the skull, hanging close to the cheek, with a very slight projection at the base, broad at the junction of the head and tapering almost to a point, the fore part of the ear coming almost straight down from its junction with the head to the tip. They shall harmonise in colour with the body colour. In the case of a pepper dog they are covered with a soft, straight, dark hair (in some cases almost black). In the case of a mustard dog, the hair should be mustard in colour, a shade darker than the body, but not black. All should have a thin feather of light hair starting about two inches from the tip, and of nearly the same colour and texture as the top-knot, which gives the ear the appearance of a distinct point. The animal is often one or two years old before the feather is shown. The cartilage and skin of the ear should not be thick, but very thin. Length of ear, from three to four inches.

Mouth. The inside of the mouth should be black or dark coloured. The teeth very strong, especially the canine, which are of extraordinary size for such a small dog. The canines fit well into each other, so as to give the greatest available holding and punishing power, and the teeth are level in front, the upper ones very slightly overlapping the under ones. Undershot or overshot mouths are equally objectionable.

Neck. Very muscular, well developed, and strong, showing great power of resistance, being well set into the shoulders.

Forequarters. The forelegs short, with immense muscular development and bone, set wide apart and chest coming well down between them. Bandy legs are objectionable. The hair on the forelegs of a pepper dog should be tan, varying according to the body colour from a rich tan to a pale fawn; of a mustard dog they are of a darker shade than its head, which is a creamy white. In both colours there is a nice feather about two inches long, rather lighter in colour than the hair on the fore part of the leg.

Body. Long, strong, and flexible; ribs well sprung and round, chest well developed and let well down between the forelegs; the back rather low at the shoulders having a slight downward curve and a corresponding arch over the loins, with a very slight gradual drop from top of loin to root of tail; both sides of backbone well supplied with muscle.

Hindquarters. The hind legs are a little longer than the fore ones, and are set rather wide apart, but not spread out in an unnatural manner; the thighs are well developed, and the hair of the same colour and texture as the fore ones, but having no feather or dew claws.

Feet. Flat feet are objectionable. The whole claws should be dark, but the claws of all vary in shade according to the colour of the dog's body. The feet of a pepper dog should be tan, varying according to the body colour from a rich tan to a pale fawn; of a mustard dog they are a darker shade than its head. Hind feet should be much smaller than the fore feet.

Tail. Rather short, say from eight to ten inches, and covered on the upper side with wiry hair of a darker colour than that of the body, the hair on the under side being lighter in colour, and not so wiry, with a nice feather about two inches long, getting shorter as it nears the tip; rather thick at the root, getting thicker for about four inches, then tapering off to a point. It should not be twisted or curled in any way, but should come up with a curve like a scimitar, the tip, when excited, being in a perpendicular line with the root of the tail. It should neither be set too high nor too low. When not excited it is carried gaily, and a little above the level of the body.

Coat. This is a very important point. The hair should be about two inches long; that from the skull to root of tail a mixture of hardish and soft hair, which gives a sort of crisp feel to the hand. The hard should not be wiry; the coat is what is termed pily or pencilled. The hair on the under part of the body is lighter in colour and softer than that on the top. The skin on the belly accords with the colour of the dog.

Colour. The colour is pepper or mustard. The pepper ranges from a dark bluish black to a light silvery grey, the intermediate shades being preferred, the body colour coming well down the shoulder and hips, gradually merging into the leg colour. The mustards vary from a reddish brown to a pale fawn, the head being a creamy white, the legs and feet of a shade darker than the head. The claws are dark as in other colours. (Nearly all Dandie Dinmont Terriers have some white on the chest, and some have white claws.) White feet are objectionable.

Weight and Size. The height should be from eight to eleven inches at the top of shoulder. Length from top of shoulder to root of tail should not be more than twice the dog's height, but, preferably, one or two inches less. The ideal weight as near eighteen pounds as possible. This weight is for dogs in good working order.

DANDIE DINMONT TERRIER

(AMERICAN KENNEL CLUB—GROUP IV: TERRIERS)

Head. Strongly made and large, not out of proportion to the dog's size, the muscles showing extraordinary development, more especially the maxillary.

Skull broad between the ears, getting gradually less towards the eyes, and measuring about the same from the inner corner of the eye to back of skull as it does from ear to ear. The forehead well domed. The head is *covered* with very soft silky hair, which should not be confined to a mere topknot, and the lighter in color and silkier it is the better.

The Cheeks, starting from the ears proportionately with the skull have a gradual taper towards the muzzle, which is deep and strongly made, and measures about three inches in length, or in proportion to skull as 3 is to 5.

The Muzzle is covered with hair of a little darker shade than the topknot, and of the same texture as the feather of the forelegs. The top of the muzzle is generally bare for about an inch from the back part of the nose, and bareness coming to a point towards the eye, and being about 1 inch broad at the nose. The nose and inside of mouth black or dark-coloured.

The Teeth very strong, especially the canines, which are of extraordinary size for a small dog. The canines mesh well with each other, so as to give the greatest available holding and punishing power. The incisors in each jaw are evenly spaced and six in number, with the upper incisors overlapping the lower incisors in a tight, scissors bite.

Eyes. Set wide apart, large, full, round, bright, expressive of great determination, intelligence and dignity; set low and prominent in front of the head; color, a rich dark hazel.

Ears. Pendulous, set well back, wide apart, and low on the skull, hanging close to the cheek, with a very slight projection at the base, broad at the junction of the head and tapering almost to a point, the forepart of the ear tapering very little—the tapering being mostly on the back part, the forepart of the ear coming almost straight down from its junction with the head to the tip. They should harmonize in color with the body color. In the case of a Pepper dog they are covered with a soft straight brownish hair (in some cases almost black). In the case of a Mustard dog the hair should be mustard in color, a shade darker than the body, but not black. All should have a thin feather of light hair starting about 2 inches from the tip, and of nearly the same color and texture as the topknot, which gives the ear the appearance of a *distinct point.* The animal is often 1 or 2 years old before the feather is shown. The cartilage and skin of the ear should not be thick, but rather thin. Length of ear from 3 to 4 inches.

Neck. Very muscular, well-developed and strong, showing great power of resistance, being well set into the shoulders.

Body. Long, strong and flexible; ribs well sprung and round, chest well developed and let well down between the forelegs; the back rather low at the shoulder, having a slight downward curve and a corresponding arch over the loins, with a very slight gradual drop from top of loins to root of tail; both sides of backbone well supplied with muscle.

Tail. Rather short, say from 8 inches to 10 inches, and covered on the upper side with wiry hair of darker color than that of the body, the hair on the under side being lighter in color and not so wiry, with nice feather about 2 inches long, getting shorter as it nears the tip; rather thick at the root, getting thicker for about 4 inches, then tapering off to a point. It should not be twisted or curled in any way, but should come up with a curve like a scimitar, the tip, when excited, being in a perpendicular line with the root of the tail. It should neither be set on too high nor too low. When not excited it is carried gaily, and a little above the level of the body.

Legs. The forelegs short, with immense muscular development and bone, set wide apart, the chest coming well down between them. The feet well formed *and not flat,* with very strong brown or dark-colored claws. Bandy legs and flat feet are objectionable. The hair on the forelegs and feet of a Pepper dog should be tan, varying according to the body color from a rich tan to a pale fawn; of a Mustard dog they are of a darker shade than its head, which is a creamy white. In both colors there is a nice feather, about 2 inches long, rather lighter in color than the hair on the forepart of the leg. The hind legs are a little longer than the forelegs, and are set rather wide apart but not spread out in an unnatural manner, while the feet are much smaller; the thighs are well developed, and the hair of the same color and texture as the forelegs, but having no feather or dewclaws; the whole claws should be dark; but the claws of all vary in shade according to the color of the dog's body.

Coat. This is a very important point; the hair should be about 2 inches long; that from skull to root of tail, a mixture of hardish and soft hair, which gives a sort of crisp feel to the hand. The hard should not be wiry; the coat is what is termed piley or penciled. The hair on the under part of the body is lighter in color and softer than on the top. The skin on the belly accords with the color of dog.

Color. The color is pepper or mustard. The pepper ranges from a dark bluish black to a light silvery gray, the intermediate shades being preferred, the body color coming well down the shoulder and hips, gradually merging into the leg color. The mustards vary from a reddish brown to a pale fawn, the head being a creamy white, the legs and feet of a shade darker that the head. The claws are dark as in other colors. (Nearly all Dandie Dinmont Terriers have some white on the chest, and some have also white claws.)

Size. The height should be from 8 to 11 inches at the top of shoulder. Length from top of shoulder to root of tail should not be more than twice the dog's height, but preferably 1 or 2 inches less.

Weight. The preferred weight from 18 to 24 pounds. These weights are for dogs in good working condition.

The relative value of the several points in the standard are apportioned as follows:

SCALE OF POINTS

Head	10	Legs and feet	10
Eyes	10	Coat	15
Ears	10	Color	5
Neck	5	Size and weight	5
Body	20	General appearance	5
Tail	5	Total	100

Approved June 10, 1969

DEERHOUND

(THE KENNEL CLUB—HOUND GROUP)

Head and Skull. The head should be broadest at the ears, tapering slightly to the eyes, with the muzzle tapering more decidedly to the nose. The muzzle should be pointed but the lips level. The head should be long, the skull rather flat than round, with a very slight rise over the eyes, but with nothing approaching a stop. The skull should be coated with moderately long hair, which is softer than the rest of the coat. The nose should be black (though in some blue-fawns the colour is blue) and slightly aquiline. In the lighter coloured dogs a black muzzle is preferred. There should be a good moustache or rather silky hair, and a fair beard.

Eyes. The eyes should be dark; generally they are dark-brown or hazel. A very light eye is not liked. The eye is moderately full, with a soft look in repose, but a keen, far-away look when the dog is roused. The rims of the eyelids should be black.

Ears. The ears should be set on high, and, in repose, folded back like the Greyhound's, though raised above the head in excitement without losing the fold, and even in some cases semi-erect. A prick ear is bad. A big thick ear hanging flat to the head, or heavily coated with long hair, is the worst of faults. The ear should be soft, glossy, and like a mouse's coat to the touch, and the smaller it is the better. It should have no long coat or long fringe, but there is often a silky silvery coat on the body of the ear and the tip. Whatever the general colour, the ears should be black or dark-coloured.

Mouth. Teeth level.

Neck. The neck should be long; that is, of the length that befits the Greyhound character of the dog. An over-long neck is not necessary or desirable, for the dog is not required to stoop to his work like a Greyhound, and it must be remembered that the mane, which every good specimen should have, detracts from the apparent length of neck. Moreover, a Deerhound requires a very strong neck to hold a stag. The nape of the neck should be very prominent where the head is set on, and the throat should be clean cut at the angle and prominent.

Forequarters. The shoulders should be well sloped, the blades well back and not too much width between them. Loaded and straight shoulders are very bad faults. The forelegs should be straight, broad and flat, a good broad forearm and elbow being desirable.

Body. The body and general formation is that of a Greyhound of larger size and bone. Chest deep rather than broad, but not too narrow and flat-sided. The loin well arched and drooping to the tail. A straight back is not desirable, this formation being unsuitable for going uphill, and very unsightly.

Hindquarters. Drooping, and as broad and powerful as possible, the hips being set wide apart.

The hindlegs should be well bent at the stifle, with great length from the hip to the hock, which should be broad and flat.

Feet. Should be close and compact, with well arranged toes. Nails strong.

Tail. Should be long, thick at the root, tapering, and reaching to within about $1\frac{1}{2}$ inches to the ground. When the dog is still, dropped perfectly straight down, or curved. When in motion it should be curved when excited, in no case to be lifted out of the line of the back. It should be well-covered with hair; on the inside, thick and wiry; on the underside longer, and towards the end a slight fringe is not objectionable. A curl or ring tail is very undesirable.

Coat. The hair on the body, neck and quarters should be harsh and wiry, and about three or four inches long; that on the head, breast and belly is much softer. There should be a slight hairy fringe on the inside of the fore- and hindlegs, but nothing approaching the 'feather' of a Collie. The Deerhound should be a shaggy dog, but not over-coated. A woolly coat is bad. Some good strains have a mixture of silky coat with the hard, which is preferable to a woolly coat; but the proper coat is a thick, close-lying, ragged coat, harsh or crisp to the touch.

Colour. Colour is much a matter of fancy. But there is no manner of doubt that the dark blue-grey is the most preferred because quality tends to follow this colour. Next comes the darker and lighter greys or brindles, the darkest being generally preferred. Yellow and sandy-red or red-fawn, especially with black points, i.e., ears and muzzles, are also in equal estimation, this being the colour of the oldest-known strains, the McNeil and Cheethill Menzies. White is condemned by all the old authorities, but a white chest and white toes, occurring as they do in a great many of the darkest-coloured dogs, are not so greatly objected to, but the less the better, as the Deerhound is a self-coloured dog. A white blaze on the head, or a white collar should be heavily penalised. In other cases, though passable, yet an attempt should be made to get rid of white markings. The less white the better, but a slight white tip to the stern occurs in the best strains.

Weight and Size. Should be from 85 to 105 lbs in dogs and from 65 to 80 lbs in bitches. Height of dogs should not be less than 30 inches and bitches 28 inches, at the shoulder, respectively.

Faults. Thick ear hanging flat to the head, or heavily coated with long hair. Curl or ring tail. Light eye. Straight back. Cow hocks, weak pasterns, straight stifles, splay feet, woolly coat, loaded and straight shoulders, white markings.

SCOTTISH DEERHOUND

(AMERICAN KENNEL CLUB—GROUP II: HOUNDS)

Head. Should be broadest at the ears, narrowing slightly to the eyes, with the muzzle tapering more decidedly to the nose. The muzzle should be pointed, but the teeth and lips level. The head should be long, the skull flat rather than round with a very slight rise over the eyes but nothing approaching a stop. The hair on the skull should be moderately long and softer than the rest of the coat. The nose should be black (in some blue fawns—blue) and slightly aquiline. In lighter colored dogs the black muzzle is preferable. There should be a good mustache of rather silky hair and a fair beard.

Ears. Should be set on high; in repose, folded back like a Greyhound's, though raised above the head in excitement without losing the fold, and even in some cases semierect. A prick ear is bad. Big thick ears hanging flat to the head or heavily coated with long hair are bad faults. The ears should be soft, glossy, like a mouse's coat to the touch and the smaller the better. There should be no long coat or long fringe, but there is sometimes a silky, silvery coat on the body of the ear and the tip. On all Deerhounds, irrespective of color of coat, the ears should be black or dark colored.

Neck and Shoulders. The neck should be long—of a length befitting the Greyhound character of the dog. Extreme length is neither necessary nor desirable. Deerhounds do not stoop to their work like Greyhounds. The mane, which every good specimen should have, sometimes detracts from the apparent length of the neck. The neck, however, must be strong as is necessary to hold a stag. The nape of the neck should be very prominent where the head is set on, and the throat clean cut at the angle and prominent. Shoulders should be well sloped; blades well back and not too much width between them. Loaded and straight shoulders are very bad faults.

Tail. Should be tolerably long, tapering and reaching to within $1\frac{1}{2}$ inches of the ground and about $1\frac{1}{2}$ inches below the hocks. Dropped perfectly down or curved when the Deerhound is still, when in motion or excited, curved, but in no instance lifted out of line of the back. It should be well covered with hair, on the inside, thick and wiry, underside longer and towards the end a slight fringe is not objectionable. A curl or ring tail is undesirable.

Eyes. Should be dark—generally dark brown, brown or hazel. A very light eye is not liked. The eye should be moderately full, with a soft look in repose, but a keen, far-away look when the Deerhound is roused. Rims of eyelids should be black.

Body. General information is that of a Greyhound of larger size and bone. Chest deep rather than broad but not too narrow or slab-sided. Good girth of chest is indicative of great lung-power. The loin well arched and drooping to the tail. A straight back is not desirable, this formation being unsuited for uphill work, and very unsightly.

Legs and Feet. Legs should be broad and flat, and good broad forearms and elbows are desirable. Forelegs must, of course, be as straight as possible. Feet close and compact, with well-arranged toes. The hindquarters drooping, and as broad and powerful as possible, the hips being set wide apart. A narrow rear denotes lack of power. The stifles should be well bent, with great length from hip to hock, which should be broad and flat. Cowhocks, weak pasterns, straight stifles and splay feet are very bad faults.

Coat. The hair on the body, neck and quarters should be harsh and wiry, about 3 or 4 inches long; that on the head, breast and belly much softer. There should be a slight fringe on the inside of the forelegs and hindlegs but nothing approaching the 'feather' of a Collie. A woolly coat is bad. Some good strains have a mixture of silky coat with the hard which is preferable to a woolly coat. The climate of the United States tends to produce the mixed coat. The ideal coat is a thick, close-lying ragged coat, harsh or crisp to the touch.

Color is a matter of fancy, but the dark blue-gray is most preferred. Next come the darker and lighter grays or brindles, the darkest being generally preferred. Yellow and sandy red or red fawn, especially with black ears and muzzles, are equally high in estimation. This was the color of the oldest known strains—the McNeil and Chesthill Menzies. White is condemned by all authorities, but a white chest and white toes, occurring as they do in many of the darkest-colored dogs, are not objected to, although the less the better, for the Deerhound is a self-colored dog. A white blaze on the head, or a white collar, should entirely disqualify. The less white the better but a slight white tip to the stern occurs in some of the best strains.

Height of Dogs. From 30 to 32 inches, or even more if there be symmetry without coarseness, which is rare.

Height of Bitches. From 28 inches upwards. There is no objection to a bitch being large, unless too coarse, as even at her greatest height she does not approach that of the dog, and therefore could not be too big for work as overbig dogs are.

Weight. From 85 to 110 pounds in dogs, and from 75 to 95 pounds in bitches.

POINTS OF THE DEERHOUND
ARRANGED IN ORDER OF IMPORTANCE

1. **Typical.** A Deerhound should resemble a rough-coated Greyhound of larger size and bone. 2. **Movements.** Easy, active and true. 3. As tall as possible consistent with quality. 4. **Head.** Long, level, well balanced, carried high. 5. **Body.** Long, very weak in brisket, well-sprung ribs and great breadth across hips. 6. **Forelegs.** Strong and quite straight, with elbows neither in nor out. 7. **Thighs.** Long and muscular, second thighs well muscled, stifles well bent. 8. **Loins.** Well arched, and belly well drawn up. 9. **Coat.** Rough and hard, with softer beard and brows. 10. **Feet.** Close, compact, with well-knuckled toes. 11. **Ears.** Small (dark) with Greyhoundlike carriage. 12. **Eyes.** Dark, moderately full. 13. **Neck.** Long, well arched, very strong with prominent nape. 14. **Shoulders.** Clean, set sloping. 15. **Chest.** Very deep but not too narrow. 16. **Tail.** Long and curved slightly, carried low. 17. **Teeth.** Strong and level. 18. **Nails.** Strong and curved.

DISQUALIFICATION

White blaze on the head, or a white collar.

Approved March, 1935

DOBERMANN

(THE KENNEL CLUB—WORKING GROUP)

Characteristics. The Dobermann is a dog of good medium size with a well-set body, muscular and elegant. He has a proud carriage and a bold, alert temperament. His form is compact and tough and owing to his build capable of great speed. His gait is light and elastic. His eyes show intelligence and firmness of character, and he is loyal and obedient. Shyness or viciousness must be heavily penalised.

Head and Skull. Has to be proportionate to the body. It must be long, well filled under the eyes and clean cut. Its form seen from above and from the side must resemble a blunt wedge. The upper part of the head should be as flat as possible and free from wrinkle. The top of the skull should be flat with a slight stop, and the muzzle line extend parallel to the top line of the skull. The cheeks must be flat and the lips tight. The nose should be solid black in black dogs, solid dark brown in brown dogs, and solid dark grey in blue dogs. Head out of balance in proportion to body, dish-faced, snipy or cheeky should be penalised.

Eyes. Should be almond-shaped, not round, moderately deep set, not prominent, with vigorous, energetic expression. Iris of uniform colour, ranging from medium to darkest brown in black dogs, the darker shade being the more desirable. In browns or blues the colour of the iris should blend with that of the markings, but not be of lighter hue than that of the markings. Light eyes in black dogs to be discouraged.

Ears. Should be small, neat and set high on the head. Erect or dropped, but erect preferred.

Mouth. Should be very well developed, solid and strong, with a scissor bite. The incisors of the lower jaw must touch the inner face of the incisors of the upper jaw. Overshot or undershot mouths, badly arranged or decayed teeth to be penalised.

Neck. Should be fairly long and lean, carried erect and with considerable nobility, slightly convex and proportionate to the whole shape of the dog. The region of the nape has to be muscular. Dewlap and loose skin are undesirable.

Forequarters. The shoulder blade and upper arm should meet at an angle of 90 degrees. Relative length of shoulder and upper arm should be as one, excess length of upper arm being much less undesirable than excess length of shoulder blade. The legs, seen from the front and side, are perfectly straight and parallel to each other from elbow to pastern, muscled and sinewy, with round bone proportionate to body structure. In a normal position and when gaiting, the elbow should lie close to the brisket.

Body. Should be square, height measured vertically from the ground to the highest point of the withers, equalling the length measured horizontally, from the forechest to rear projection of the upper thigh. The back should be short and firm with the topline sloping slightly from the withers to the croup, the female needing room to carry litters may be slightly longer to loin. The belly should be fairly well tucked up. Ribs should be deep and well-sprung, reaching to elbow. Long, weak or roach backs to be discouraged.

Hindquarters. Should be parallel to each other and wide enough apart to fit in with a properly built body. The hip bone should fall away from the spinal column at an angle of about 30 degrees. Croup well filled out. The hindquarters should be well developed and muscular, with long bent stifle and their hocks turning neither in nor out. While the dog is at rest, hock to heel should be perpendicular to the ground.

Feet. Fore feet should be well arched, compact and cat-like, turning neither in nor out. All dewclaws to be removed, Long, flat deviating paws and weak pasterns should be penalised. Hind feet should be well arched, compact and cat-like, turning neither in nor out.

Gait. Should be free, balanced and vigorous with good reach in the forequarters, and a driving power in the hindquarters. When trotting, there should be a strong rear action drive with rotary motion of hindquarters. Rear and front legs should be thrown neither in nor out. Back should remain strong and firm.

Tail. The tail should be docked at the first or second joint and should appear to be a continuation of the spine, without material drop.

Coat. Should be smooth-haired, short, hard, thick and close lying. Invisible grey undercoat on neck permissible.

Colour. Colours allowed are definite black, brown or blue with rust red markings. Markings must be sharply defined and appearing above each eye and on the muzzle, throat and forechest, and on all legs and feet, and below tail. White markings of any kind are highly undesirable.

Weight and Size. Ideal height at withers: Males 27 inches; Females $25\frac{1}{2}$ inches. Considerable deviation from this ideal to be discouraged.

Faults. Shyness or viciousness must be heavily penalized. Head out of balance in proportion to body, dish-faced, snipy or cheeky should be penalized. Light eyes in black dogs to be discouraged. Overshot or undershot mouths, badly arranged or decayed teeth to be penalized. Dewlap and loose skin are undesirable. Long, weak or roach backs to be discouraged. White markings of any kind are highly undesirable

DOBERMAN PINSCHERS

(AMERICAN KENNEL CLUB—GROUP III: WORKING DOGS)

General Conformation and Appearance. The appearance is that of a dog of medium size, with a body that is square; the height, measured vertically from the ground to the highest point of the withers, equalling the length measured horizontally from the forechest to the rear projection of the upper thigh. *Height* at the withers—*Dogs* 26 to 28 inches, ideal about $27\frac{1}{2}$ inches; *Bitches* 24 to 26 inches, ideal about $25\frac{1}{2}$ inches. Length of head, neck and legs in proportion to length and depth of body. Compactly built, muscular and powerful, for great endurance and speed. Elegant in appearance, of proud carriage, reflecting great nobility and temperament. Energetic, watchful, determined, alert, fearless, loyal and obedient.

The judge shall dismiss from the ring any shy or vicious Doberman.

Shyness. A dog shall be judged fundamentally shy if, refusing to stand for examination, it shrinks away from the judge; if it fears an approach from the rear; if it shies at sudden and unusual noises to a marked degree.

Viciousness. A dog that attacks or attempts to attack either the judge or its handler, is definitely vicious. An aggressive or belligerent attitude towards other dogs shall not be deemed viciousness.

Head. Long and dry, resembling a blunt wedge in both frontal and profile views. When seen from the front, the head widens gradually towards the base of the ears in a practically unbroken line. Top of skull flat, turning with slight stop to bridge of muzzle, with muzzle line extending parallel to top line of skull. Cheeks flat and muscular. Lips lying close to jaws. Jaws full and powerful, well filled under the eyes.

Eyes. Almond shaped, moderately deep set, with vigorous, energetic expression. Iris, of uniform color, ranging from medium to darkest brown in black dogs; in reds, blues, and fawns the color of the iris blends with that of the markings, the darkest shade being preferable in every case.

Teeth. Strongly developed and white. Lower incisors upright and touching inside of upper incisors—a true scissors bite. *42 correctly placed teeth,* 22 in the lower, 20 in the upper jaw. Distemper teeth shall not be penalized.

Disqualifying Faults. Overshot more than $\frac{3}{16}$ of an inch. Undershot more than $\frac{1}{8}$ of an inch. Four or more missing teeth

Ears. Normally cropped and carried erect. The upper attachment of the ear, when held erect, is on a level with the top of the skull.

Neck. Proudly carried, well muscled and dry. Well arched, with nape of neck widening gradually toward body. Length of neck proportioned to body and head.

Body. Back short, firm, of sufficient width, and muscular at the loins, extending in a straight line from withers to the *slightly* rounded croup.

Withers pronounced and forming the highest point of the body.

Brisket reaching deep to the elbow.

Chest broad with forechest well defined.

Ribs well sprung from the spine, but flattened in lower end to permit elbow clearance.

Belly well tucked up, extending in a curved line from the brisket.

Loins wide and muscled.

Hips broad and in proportion to body, breadth of hips being approximately equal to breadth of body at rib cage and shoulders.

Tail docked at approximately second joint, appears to be a continuation of the spine, and is carried only slightly above the horizontal when the dog is alert.

Forequarters—Shoulder Blade sloping forward and downward at a 45 degree angle to the ground meets the upper arm at an angle of 90 degrees. Length of shoulder blade and upper arm are equal. Height from elbow to withers approximately equals height from ground to elbow.

Legs, seen from front and side, perfectly straight and parallel to each other from elbow to pastern; muscled and sinewy, with heavy bone. In normal pose and when gaiting, the elbows lie close to the brisket.

Pasterns firm and almost perpendicular to the ground.

Feet well arched, compact, and catlike, turning neither in nor out. Dewclaws may be removed.

Hindquarters. The angulation of the hindquarters balances that of the forequarters.

Hip Bone falls away from spinal column at an angle of about 30 degrees, producing a slightly rounded, well-filled-out croup.

Upper Shanks, at right angles to the hip bones, are long, wide, and well muscled on both sides of thigh, with clearly defined stifles. Upper and lower shanks are of equal length. While the dog is at rest, hock to heel is perpendicular to the ground. Viewed from the rear, the legs are straight, parallel to each other, and wide enough apart to fit in with a properly built body.

Cat Feet, as on front legs, turning neither in nor out. Dewclaws, if any, are generally removed.

Gait. Free, balanced, and vigorous, with good reach in the forequarters and good driving power in the hindquarters. When trotting, there is strong rear-action drive. Each rear leg moves in line with the foreleg on the same side. Rear and front legs are thrown neither in nor out. Back remains strong and firm. When moving at a fast trot, a properly built dog will singletrack.

Coat, Color, Markings—Coat, smooth-haired, short, hard, thick and close lying, invisible gray undercoat on neck permissible.

Allowed Colors. Black, red, blue, and fawn (Isabella).

Markings. Rust, sharply defined, appearing above each eye and on muzzle, throat and forechest, on all legs and feet, and below tail.

Nose Solid black on black dogs, dark brown on red ones, dark gray on blue ones, dark tan on fawns. White patch on chest, not exceeding $\frac{1}{2}$ square inch, permissible.

Faults. *The foregoing description is that of the ideal Doberman Pinscher. Any deviation from the above described dog must be penalized to the extent of the deviation.*

DISQUALIFICATIONS

Overshot more than $\frac{3}{16}$ of an inch; undershot more than $\frac{1}{8}$ of an inch. Four or more missing teeth.

Approved October 14, 1969

ELKHOUND

(THE KENNEL CLUB—HOUND GROUP)

Characteristics. The Elkhound is a hardy sporting dog of Nordic type of a bold and virile nature, and has good scenting power. Its disposition should be friendly and intelligent, with great energy and independence of character, and without any sign of undue nervousness.

General Appearance. It has a compact and proportionately short body, a coat thick and bundant but not bristling, and prick ears; tail tightly curled over back.

Head and Skull. Broad between the ears; the forehead and back of the head are slightly arched with a clearly marked but not large stop. Muzzle moderately long, broader at the base and gradually tapering—whether seen from above or from the side—but not pointed; bridge of the nose straight, jaw strong with lips tightly closed.

Eyes. Not prominent, in colour brown and as dark as possible, giving a frank, fearless and friendly expression.

Ears. Set high, firm and upstanding, height slightly greater than their width at the base, pointed and very mobile.

Neck. Of medium length, firm, muscular and well set up.

Forequarters. Legs firm, straight and powerful with good bone; elbows closely set on

Body. Short in the couplings; back, wide and straight from neck to stern; chest, wide and deep with well-rounded ribs, loins, muscular; stomach, very little drawn up.

Hindquarters. Legs straight at the hock and when viewed from behind. There should be no dewclaws on the hindlegs

Feet. Compact, oval in shape and not turned outwards; toes, tightly closed; tòe nails, firm and strong.

Tail. Set high, tightly curled over the back but not carried on either side; hair, thick and close.

Coat. Thick, abundant, coarse and weather-resisting; short on the head and on the front of the legs; longest on the chest, neck, buttocks, behind the forelegs and on the underside of the tail. It is composed of a longish and coarse top coat, dark at the tips with a light-coloured, soft and woolly undercoat. About the neck and front of the chest the longer coat forms a sort of ruff which, with the pricked ears, the energetic eyes and the curled tail, gives the animal its unique and alert appearance.

Colour. Grey, of various shades with black tips to the long outer coat; lighter on the chest, stomach, legs, and the underside of the tail. Any distinctive variation from the grey colour is most undesirable and too dark or too light colourings should be avoided. Pronounced markings on legs and feet are also not desirable.

Weight and Size. For dogs, the height at the shoulder is about $20\frac{1}{2}$ inches, and for bitches, about $18\frac{1}{2}$ inches. Weight approximately 50 lbs and 43 lbs respectively.

NORWEGIAN ELKHOUNDS

(AMERICAN KENNEL CLUB—GROUP II: HOUNDS

General Description. The Norwegian Elkhound is a hardy gray hunting dog. In appearance, a typical northern dog of medium size and substance, square in profile, close coupled and balanced in proportions. The head is broad with prick ears, and the tail is tightly curled and carried over the back. The distinctive gray coat is dense and smooth-lying. In temperament, the Norwegian Elkhound is bold and energetic, an effective guardian yet normally friendly, with great dignity and independence of character. As a hunter, the Norwegian Elkhound has the courage, agility and stamina to hold moose and other big game at bay by barking and dodging attack, and the endurance to track for long hours in all weather over rough and varied terrain.

In the show ring, presentation in a natural, unaltered condition is essential.

Head. Broad, at the ears, wedge-shaped, strong, and dry (without loose skin). Viewed from the side, the forehead and back of the skull are only slightly arched; the stop not large, yet clearly defined. The bridge of the nose is straight, parallel to and about the same length as the skull. The muzzle is thickest at the base and, seen from above or from the side, tapers evenly without being pointed. Lips are tightly closed and teeth meet in a scissors bite.

Ears. Set high, firm and erect yet very mobile. Comparatively small; slightly taller than their width at the base with pointed (not rounded) tips. When the dog is alert, the orifices turn forward and the outer edges are vertical.

Eyes. Very dark brown, medium in size, oval, not protruding.

Neck. Of medium length, muscular, well set up with a slight arch and with no loose skin on the throat.

Body. Square in profile and close coupled. Distance from brisket to ground appears to be half the height at the withers. Distance from forechest to rump equals the height at the withers. Chest deep and moderately broad; brisket level with points of elbows; and ribs well sprung. Loin short and wide with very little tuck-up. The back is straight and strong from its high point at the withers to the root of the tail.

Forequarters. Shoulders sloping with elbows closely set on. Legs well under body and medium in length; substantial, but not course, in bone. Seen from the front, the legs appear straight and parallel. Single dewclaws are normally present.

Hindquarters. Moderate angulation at stifle and hock. Thighs are broad and well muscled. Seen from behind, legs are straight, strong and without dewclaws.

Feet. Paws comparatively small, slightly oval with tightly closed toes and thick pads. Pasterns are strong and only slightly bent. Feet turn neither in nor out.

Tail. Set high, tightly curled, and carried over the centerline of the back. It is thickly and closely haired, without brush, natural and untrimmed.

Coat. Thick, hard, weather-resisting and smooth-lying; made up of soft, dense, woolly undercoat and coarse, straight covering hairs. Short and even on head, ears and front of legs; longest on back of neck, buttocks and underside of tail. The coat is not altered by trimming, clipping or artificial treatment. Trimming of whiskers is optional.

Color. Gray, medium preferred, variations in shade determined by the length of black tips and quantity of guard hairs. Undercoat is clear light silver as are legs, stomach, buttocks, and underside of tail. The gray body color is darkest on the saddle, lighter on the chest, mane and distinctive harness mark (a band of longer guard hairs from shoulder to elbow). The muzzle, ears, and tail tip are black. The black of the muzzle shades to lighter gray over the forehead and skull. Yellow or brown shading, white patches, indistinct or irregular markings, 'sooty' coloring on the lower legs and light circles around the eyes are undesirable. Any overall color other than gray as described above, such as red, brown, solid black, white or other solid color, disqualifies.

Gait. Normal for an active dog constructed for agility and endurance. At a trot the stride is even and effortless; the back remains level. As the speed of the trot increases, front and rear legs converge equally in straight lines toward a center line beneath the body so that the pads appear to follow in the same tracks (single track). Front and rear quarters are well balanced in angulation and muscular development.

Size. The height at the withers for dogs is $20\frac{1}{2}$ inches; for bitches $19\frac{1}{2}$ inches. Weight for dogs about 55 pounds; for bitches about 48 pounds.

DISQUALIFICATIONS

Any overall color other than gray as described above, such as red, brown, solid black, white or other solid color.

Approved February 13, 1973

ENGLISH SETTER

(THE KENNEL CLUB—GUNDOG GROUP)

Characteristics. An intensely friendly and quiet-natured dog with a keen game sense.

General Appearance. Of medium height, clean in outline, elegant in appearance and movement.

Head and Skull. Head should be long and reasonably lean, with a well-defined stop. The skull oval from ear to ear, showing plenty of brain room, and with a well-defined occipital protuberance. The muzzle moderately deep and fairly square; from the stop to the point of the nose should equal the length of skull from occiput to eyes; the nostrils wide and the jaws of nearly equal length; flews not to be too pendulous; the colour of the nose should be black or liver, according to the colour of the coat.

Eyes. The eyes should be bright, mild and intelligent, and of a dark haze, colour, the darker the better.

Ears. The ears of moderate length, set on low, and hanging in neat folds close to the cheek; the tip should be velvety, the upper part clothed in fine silky hair.

Mouth. To be level.

Neck. Neck should be rather long, muscular and lean, slightly arched at the crest, and clean cut where it joins the head; towards the shoulder it should be larger and very muscular, not throaty or pendulous below the throat, but elegant in appearance.

Forequarters. The shoulders should be well set back or oblique, the chest should be deep in the brisket, and of good depth and width between the shoulder blades. The forearm big and very muscular, with rounded bone, and the elbow well let down. Pasterns short, muscular, round and straight.

Body. The body should be of moderate length, the back short and level with good round widely-sprung ribs and deep in the back ribs, i.e., well ribbed up.

Hindquarters. The loins should be wide, slightly arched, strong and muscular, with defined second thigh. Stifles well bent and rugged, thighs long from hip to hock.

Feet. The feet should be very close and compact and well protected by hair between the toes.

Tail. The tail should be set on almost in line with the back; medium length, nor curly or ropy, to be slightly curved or scimitar-shaped but with no tendency to turn upwards; the flag or feather hanging in long pendant flakes. The feather should not commence at the root, but slightly below, and increase in length to the middle, then gradually taper off towards the end; the hair long, bright, soft and silky, wavy, but not curly

Coat. The coat from the back of the head in a line with the ears ought to be slightly wavy, long and silky, which should be the case with the coat generally; the breeches and forelegs, nearly down to the feet, should be well feathered.

Colour. The colour may be either black and white, lemon and white, liver and white or tricolour—that is black, white and tan; those without heavy patches of colour on the body, but flecked all over, preferred.

Weight and Size. Should be: Dogs, 60 to 66 lbs, height $25\frac{1}{2}$ to 27 inches. Bitches, 56 to 62 lbs, height, 24 to $25\frac{1}{2}$ inches.

Faults. Coarse lumpy' shoulders; short foreface; tapering to nose; lack of 'stop'; light or obliquely set eyes; high ear placement; loose elbows from bad shoulder placement; flat ribs; too long loin; wide feet; weak pasterns; straight stifles; narrow quarters; gay 'flag'; lightness of bone; mouth undershot or overshot; lacking freedom of action.

SETTERS, ENGLISH

(AMERICAN KENNEL CLUB—GROUP I: SPORTING DOGS)

Head. Long and lean, with a well-defined stop. The skull oval from ear to ear, of medium width, giving brain room but with no suggestion of coarseness, with but little difference between the width at base of skull and at brows and with a moderately defined occipital protuberance. Brows should be at a sharp angle from the muzzle. Muzzle should be long and square, of width in harmony with the skull, without any fullness under the eyes and straight from eyes to tip of the nose. A dish face or Roman nose objectionable. The lips square and fairly pendant. Nose should be black or dark liver in color, except in white, lemon and white, orange and white, or liver and white dogs, when it may be of lighter color. Nostrils should be wide apart and large in the openings. Jaws should be of equal length. Overshot or undershot jaw objectionable. Ears should be carried close to the head, well back and set low, of moderate length, slightly rounded at the ends, and covered with silky hair. Eyes should be bright, mild, intelligent and dark brown in color.

Neck. The neck should be long and lean, arched at the crest, and not too throaty.

Shoulders. Shoulders should be formed to permit perfect freedom of action to the forelegs. Shoulder blades should be long, wide, sloping moderately well back and standing fairly close together at the top.

Chest. Chest between shoulder blades should be of good depth but not of excessive width.

Ribs. Ribs, back of the shoulders, should spring gradually to the middle of the body and then taper to the back ribs, which should be of good depth.

Back. Back should be strong at its junction with the loin and should be straight or sloping upward very slightly to the top of the shoulder, the whole forming a graceful outline of medium length, without sway or drop. Loins should be strong, moderate in length, slightly arched, but not to the extent of being roached or wheel-backed. Hipbones should be wide apart without too sudden drop to the root of the tail.

Forelegs. The arms should be flat and muscular, with bone fully developed and muscles hard and devoid of flabbiness; of good length from the point of the shoulder to the elbow, and set at such an angle as will bring the legs fairly under the dog. Elbows should have no tendency to turn either in or out. The pastern should be short, strong and nearly round with the slope from the pastern joint to the foot deviating very slightly forward from the perpendicular.

Hind Legs. The hind legs should have wide, muscular thighs with well developed lower thighs. Stifles should be well bent and strong. Hocks should be wide and flat. The hind pastern or metatarsus should be short, strong and nearly round.

Feet. Feet should be closely set and strong, pads well developed and tough, toes well arched and protected with short, thick hair.

Tail. Tail should be straight and taper to a fine point, with only sufficient length to reach the hocks, or less. The feather must be straight and silky, falling loosely in a fringe and tapering to the point when the tail is raised. There must be no bushiness. The tail should not curl sideways or above the level of the back.

Coat. Coat should be flat and of good length, without curl; not soft or woolly. The feather on the legs should be moderately thin and regular.

Height. Dogs about 25 inches; bitches about 24 inches.

Colors. Black, white and tan; black and white; blue belton; lemon and white; lemon belton; orange and white; orange belton; liver and white; liver belton; and solid white.

Markings. Dogs without heavy patches of color on the body, but flecked all over preferred.

Symmetry. The harmony of all parts to be considered. Symmetrical dogs will have level backs or be very slightly higher at the shoulders than at the hips. Balance, harmony of proportion, and an appearance of breeding and quality to be looked for, and coarseness avoided.

Movement and Carriage. An easy, free and graceful movement, suggesting rapidity and endurance. A lively tail and a high carriage of head. Stiltiness, clumsiness or a lumbering gait are objectionable.

SCALE OF POINTS

Head		
Skull	5	
Ears	5	
Eyes	5	
Muzzle	5	20
Body		
Neck	5	
Chest and shoulders	12	
Back, loin and ribs	10	27
Running Gear		
Forelegs	5	
Hips, thighs and hind legs	12	
Feet	6	23
Coat		
Length and texture	5	
Color and marking	3	8
Tail		
Length and carriage	5	5
General Appearance and Action		
Symmetry, style and movement	12	
Size	5	17
Total	100	100

Approved May 8, 1951

ENGLISH TOY TERRIER (BLACK AND TAN)

(THE KENNEL CLUB—TOY GROUP)

General Appearance. A well balanced, elegant and compact Toy with Terrier temperament and characteristics. It must be borne in mind that in the past the breed was required frequently to be able to acquit itself satisfactorily in the rat pit. Therefore present day specimens should be sleek and cleanly built giving an appearance of alertness combined with speed of movement but not of whippet type.

In realization of the fact that this is a Toy Dog with Terrier characteristics unduly nervous specimens cannot rank as wholly typical representatives of the breed. Judges, when officiating, should bear this in mind.

Head and Skull. The head should be long and narrow with a flat skull, wedge-shaped without emphasis of cheek muscles and well filled up under the eyes. The top and bottom jaws should be held tightly together within compressed lips. Upon close inspection of the foreface one finds indications of a slight 'stop'. The foreface then tapers gently to provide a wedge-shaped impression in profile similarly corresponding to that given when it is viewed direct. Although an illusion of being 'overshot' can result, any suggestion of a snipy appearance is undesirable. Nose—Black.

Eyes. These should be very dark to black without light shading from the iris. They should be small, almond shaped, obliquely set and sparkling.

Note: Light, large and round, protruding or disproportionately wide or narrow set eyes should be regarded as faults.

Ears. These should be of 'candle-flame' shape, slightly pointed at the tips, placed high upon the back of the skull and proportionately close together. A guide to the size can be obtained by bending the ear forward. It should not reach the eye. From nine months of age the ear carriage must be erect. The entire inside of the ear should face the front. The leather of the ear should be thin. A cat ear appearance is wrong.

Note. Large or 'flapping' ears should be regarded as faults.

Mouth. Teeth should be level and strong. The upper front teeth should close slightly over the lower front teeth, the latter to lean forward fractionally thus establishing the correct level bite.

Neck. The neck should be long, graceful and slightly arched. The shoulders should be well laid back not straight. The pattern of the neck line flowing into the shoulders, and sloping off elegantly. Throatiness is undesirable.

Forequarters. The chest narrow and deep. Legs falling straight from the shoulders, with the elbows close to the chest providing a straight front. Loose elbows and wide fronts are faults. Fine bone is eminently desirable. The ideal fore-movement is that akin to the 'extended trot', hackney action is not desirable; equally to be discouraged is a 'shuffling' gait.

Body. The body is compact, head and legs proportionate thus producing correct balance. The back very slightly curving from behind the shoulder to the loin falling again to the root of the tail. The chest should be narrow and deep with the ribs well sprung to a well cut up loin. The buttocks should be gently rounded.

Faults. A roached, dipped or dead flat back, hindquarters higher than the shoulders.

Hindquarters. A well-rounded loin leading to a good turn of stifle is required, hocks well let down, a 'tucked under' appearance is undesirable. Hind-action should be smooth and suggest ease and precision combined with drive. There should be a 'flowing quality' to give true soundness.

Feet. Dainty compact, split up between the toes, and well arched, with jet black nails; the two middle toes of the front feet rather longer than the others and the hind feet shaped like those of a cat. Hare feet are not desirable, and should be regarded as a fault.

Tail. The tail should be thick at the root, tapering to a point. Set low and not reaching below the hock. A 'gay' tail carriage is undesirable if displayed to excess.

Coat. The texture should be thick, close, smooth and of glossy appearance. A density of short hair is required.

Note: Sparse, weak coats should be regarded as faults.

Colour. Black and Tan. The black should be ebony and the tan can be likened to a new chestnut, deeply rich. These colours should not run, or blend into each other, but should meet abruptly, forming clear and well defined lines of colour division. Forelegs tanned to the knee in front. The tan then continuing inside and at the back of the foreleg to a point just below the elbow. A thin black line up each toe (Pencilling) and a clearly defined black mark 'thumb mark' on the centre of each pastern, and under the chin. The hindlegs should be well tanned in front and the inside, with a black 'bar' dividing the tan at the centre of the lower thigh. Each toe 'pencilled'. Heavy tan on the outside of the hindquarters, 'breeching', is a fault. On the head the muzzle is well tanned, nose black, the black continuing along the top of the muzzle, curving below the eyes to the base of the throat. A tan spot above each eye and a small tan spot on each cheek. The under jaw and throat are tanned, the lip line black. The hair inside the ears tanned (tan behind the ears a fault). Each side of the chest is slightly tanned. The vent and under root of the tail tanned. White hairs forming a patch anywhere are a serious fault.

Weight and Size. The ideal weight is between that of 6 to 8 lbs and a height of 10 to 12 inches at the shoulders is most desirable.

Judges are encouraged to use scales, as it is hoped this will help to establish uniformity.

MANCHESTER TERRIER (TOY)

(AMERICAN KENNEL CLUB—GROUP V: TOYS)

The Standard for the Manchester Terrier (Toy Variety) is the same as for the Manchester Terrier except as regards weight and ears.

Head. Long, narrow, tight-skinned, almost flat, with a slight indentation up the forehead; slightly wedge-shaped, tapering to the nose, with no visible cheek muscles, and well filled up under the eyes; tight-lipped jaws, level in mouth, and functionally level teeth, or the incisors of the upper jaw may make a close, slightly overlapping contact with the incisors of the lower jaw.

Eyes. Small, bright, sparkling and as near black as possible; set moderately close together; oblong in shape, slanting upwards on the outside; they should neither protrude nor sink in the skull.

Nose. Black.

Ears (Toy Variety). Of moderate size; set well up on the skull and rather close together; thin, moderately narrow at base; with pointed tips; naturally erect carriage. Wide, flaring, blunt-tipped or 'bell' ears are a serious fault; cropped or cut ears shall disqualify.

Ears (Standard Variety). Erect, or button, small and thin; smaller at the root and set as close together as possible at the top of the head. If cropped, to a point, long and carried erect.

Neck and Shoulders. The neck should be a moderate length, slim and graceful; gradually becoming larger as it approaches, and blend smoothly with the sloping shoulders; free from throatiness; slightly arched from the occiput.

Chest. Narrow between the legs; deep in the brisket.

Body. Moderately short, with robust loins; ribs well sprung out behind the shoulders; back slightly arched at the loin, and falling again to the tail to the same height as the shoulder.

Legs. Forelegs straight, of proportionate length, and well under body. Hind legs should not turn in or out as viewed from the rear; carried back; hocks well let down.

Feet. Compact, well arched, with jet black nails; the two middle toes in the front feet rather longer than the others; the hind feet shaped like those of a cat.

Tail. Moderately short, and set on where the arch of the back ends; thick where it joins the body, tapering to a point, not carried higher than the back.

Coat. Smooth, short, thick, dense, close and glossy; not soft.

Color. Jet black and rich mahogany tan, which should not run or blend into each other but abruptly forming clear, well-defined lines of color division. A small tan spot over each eye; a very small tan spot on each cheek; the lips of the upper and lower jaws should be tanned, extending under the throat, ending in the shape of the letter V; the inside of the ears partly tanned. Tan spots, called rosettes, on each side of the chest above the front legs, more pronounced in puppies than in adults. There should be a black 'thumb mark' patch on the front of each foreleg between the pastern and the knee. There should be a distinct black 'pencil mark' line running lengthwise on the top of each toe on all four feet. The remainder of the fore-legs to be tan to the knee. Tan on the hind legs should continue from the penciling on the feet up the inside of the legs to a little below the stifle joint; the outside of the hindlegs to be black. There should be tan under the tail, and on the vent, but only of such size as to be covered by the tail. White in any part of the coat is a serious fault, and shall disqualify whenever the white shall form a patch or stripe measuring as much as one-half inch in its longest dimension.

Weight (Toy Variety). Not exceeding 12 pounds. It is suggested that clubs consider dividing the American-bred and open classes by weight as follows: 7 pounds and under, over 7 pounds and not exceeding 12 pounds.

Weight (Standard Variety). Over 12 pounds and not exceeding 22 pounds. Dogs weighing over 22 pounds shall be disqualified. It is suggested that clubs consider dividing the American-bred and open classes by weight as follows: over 12 pounds and not exceeding 16 pounds, over 16 pounds and not exceeding 22 pounds.

DISQUALIFICATIONS

Color. White in any part of the coat, forming a patch or stripe measuring as much as $\frac{1}{2}$ inch in its longest dimension.

Weight (Standard Variety). Over 22 pounds.

Ears (Toy Variety). Cropped or cut ears.

Approved June 12, 1962

FINNISH SPITZ

(THE KENNEL CLUB—HOUND GROUP)

Characteristics. The Finnish Spitz characteristics are eagerness to hunt, courage and fidelity.
General Appearance. Body almost square. Bearing bold. The whole appearance, and particularly eyes, ears and tail, indicates liveliness.
Head and Skull. Medium sized and clean cut, forehead slightly arched, stop pronounced. Muzzle narrow and clean cut, seen from above and from the sides evenly tapering. Nose pitch black. Lips tightly closed and thin.
Eyes. Medium sized, lively, preferably dark.
Ears. Cocked, sharply pointed, fine in texture, exceedingly mobile.
Neck. Muscular, in males it looks rather short, due to the thick coat, in bitches medium long.
Forequarters. Strong and straight.
Body. Back, straight and strong. Chest, deep. Belly, slightly drawn up.
Hindquarters. Strong, hocks comparatively straight.
Feet. Preferably roundish.
Tail. Curves vigorously from its root in an arch, forward, downward and backward, then pressing down against the thigh, with its tip extending to the middle part of the thigh. Extended, the tail vertebrae usually reaches to the hock joint.
Coat. On head and legs, except their back sides, short and close-lying, on the body longish, semi-erect, on the neck and back stiffer. The outer coat on the shoulders, particularly in males, considerably longer and coarser. On the back of the thighs the hair is long and dense, also on the tail. Undercoat short, soft, dense, light in colour.
Colour. On the back reddish-brown or yellowish-red, preferably bright. The hairs on innersides of the ears, cheeks, under the muzzle, on the breast, abdomen, inside the legs, at the back of thighs, under the tail are of a lighter shade. White markings on feet and a narrow white stripe on the breast can be permitted, also some black hairs on the lips and sparse separate hairs with black points along the back.
Weight and Size. Height at withers and length of body in males $17\frac{1}{2}$ inches, 20 inches; in bitches $15\frac{1}{2}$ inches, 18 inches.
Faults. Fleshy head, coarse muzzle, ears pointing forward at a sharp angle or their tips pointing outwards or towards one another, ears curving backwards or with slack points or with long hairs inside. Yellow or wall-eyes, elbows turned inwards, too weak pastern, slack tail or too excessively curled tail, long, soft or too short, close wavy or curly coat, dirty colour particularly distinctly defined differences between the colours, disfiguring dewclaws.

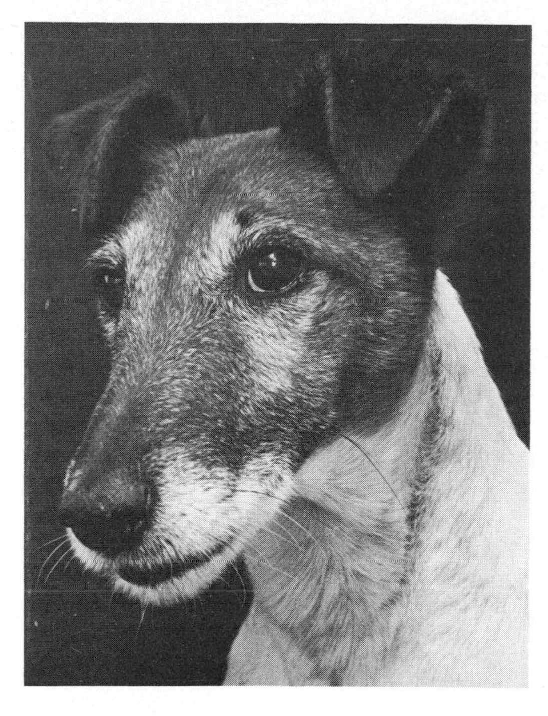

FOX TERRIER (SMOOTH)

(THE KENNEL CLUB—TERRIER GROUP)

General Appearance. The dog must present a general gay, lively, and active appearance; bone and strength in a small compass are essentials, but this must not be taken to mean that a Fox Terrier should be cloggy, or in any way coarse, speed and endurance must be looked to as well as power, and the symmetry of the Foxhound taken as a model. The Terrier, like the Hound, must on no account be leggy, nor must he be too short in the leg. He should stand like a cleverly made Hunter, covering a lot of ground, yet with a short back. He will then attain the highest degree of propelling power, together with the greatest length of stride that is compatible with the length of his body.

Head and Skull. The skull should be flat and moderately narrow, and gradually decreasing in width to the eyes. Not much 'stop' should be apparent, but there should be more dip in the profile between the forehead and the top jaw than is seen in the case of the Greyhound. The cheeks must not be full. The jaw, upper and under, should be strong and muscular, should be of fair punishing strength, but not so in any way to resemble the Greyhound. There should not be much falling away below the eyes. This part of the head should, however, be moderately chiselled out, so as not to go down in a straight line like a wedge. The nose, towards which the muzzle must gradually taper, should be black.

Eyes. Should be dark in colour, small and rather deep set, full of fire, life and intelligence; as nearly as possible circular in shape.

Ears. Should be V-shaped and small, of moderate thickness, and dropping forward close to the cheek, not hanging by the side of the head like a Foxhound's.

Mouth. The teeth should be nearly as possible level, i.e., the upper teeth on the outside of the lower teeth.

Neck. Should be clean and muscular, without throatiness, of fair length, and gradually widening to the shoulders.

Forequarters. The shoulders should be long and sloping, well laid back, fine at the points, and clearly cut at the withers.

Body. Chest deep and not too broad. Back should be short, straight and strong, with no appearance of slackness. Loin should be powerful and very slightly arched. The fore ribs should be moderately arched, the back ribs deep; and the dog should be well ribbed up.

Hindquarters. Should be strong and muscular, quite free from droop or crouch; the thighs long and powerful; hocks near the ground, the dog standing well up on them like a Foxhound, and not straight in stifle.

Feet. Should be round, compact and not large. The soles hard and tough. The toes moderately arched, and turned neither in nor out.

Tail. Should be set on rather high, and carried gaily, but not over the back nor curled. It should be of good strength.

Coat. Should be straight, flat, smooth, hard, dense and abundant. The belly and under side of the thighs should not be bare.

Colour. White should predominate; brindle, red or liver markings are objectionable. Otherwise this point is of little or no importance.

Weight and Size. Weight is not a certain criterion of a Terrier's fitness for his work—general shape, size and contour are the main points—and if a dog can gallop and stay, and follow his fox up a drain, it matters little what

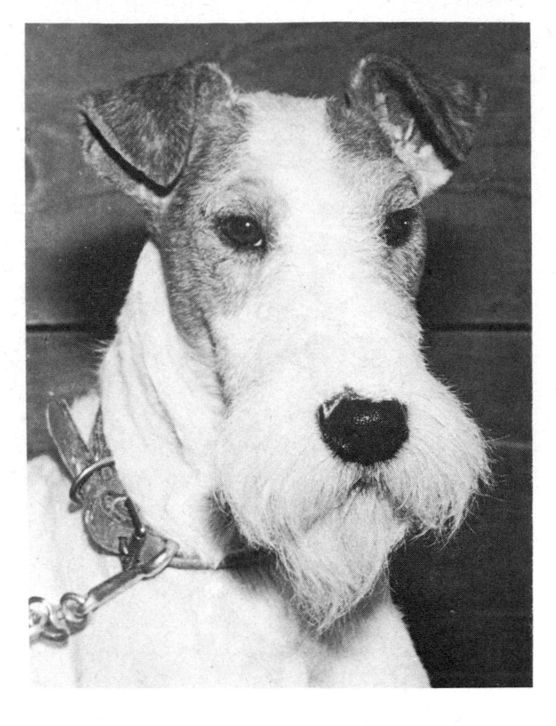

his weight is to a pound or so, though, roughly speaking, 15 to 17 lbs for a bitch and 16 to 18 lbs for a dog in Show condition are appropriate weights.

Faults. Nose, white, cherry, or spotted to a considerable extent with either of these colours. Ears, prick, tulip or rose. Mouth, much undershot or much overshot.

FOX TERRIER (WIRE)

(THE KENNEL CLUB—TERRIER GROUP)

Characteristics. The Terrier should be alert, quick of movement, keen of expression, on the tip-toe of expectation at the slightest provocation. Character is imparted by the expression of the eyes and by the carriage of ears and tail.

General Appearance. The dog should be balanced and this may be defined as the correct proportion of a certain point or points, when considered in relation to a certain other point or points. It is the keystone of the Terrier's anatomy. The chief points for consideration are the relative proportions of skull and foreface; head and back; height at withers; and length of body from shoulder-point to buttock—the ideal of proportion being reached when the last two measurements are the same. It should be added that, although the head measurements can be taken with absolute accuracy, the height at withers and length of back are approximate, and are inserted for the information of breeders and exhibitors rather than as a hard-and-fast rule. The movement of action is the crucial test of conformation. The Terrier's legs should be carried straight forward while travelling, the forelegs hanging perpendicular and swinging parallel to the sides, like the pendulum of a clock. The principal propulsive power is furnished by the hind legs, perfection of action being found in the Terrier possessing long thighs and muscular second-thighs well bent at the stifles, which admit of a strong forward thrust or 'snatch' of the hocks. When approaching, the forelegs should form a continuation of the straight of the front, the feet being the same distance apart as the elbows. When stationary it is often difficult to determine whether a dog is slightly out at shoulder but directly he moves the defect—if it exists—becomes more apparent, the fore feet having a tendency to cross, 'weave' or 'dish'. When, on the contrary, the dog is tied at the shoulder, the tendency of the feet is to move wider apart, with a sort of padding action. When the hocks are turned in—cow-hocks—the stifles and feet are turned outwards, resulting in a serious loss of propulsive power. When the hocks are turned outwards the tendency of the hind feet is to cross, resulting in an ungainly waddle.

Head and Skull. The top line of the skull should be almost flat, sloping slightly and gradually decreasing in width towards the eyes. In a well-balanced head there should be little apparent difference in length between skull and foreface. If, however, the foreface is noticeably shorter, it amounts to a fault, the head looking weak and 'unfinished'. On the other hand, when the eyes are set too high up in the skull, and too near the ears, it also amounts to a fault, the head being said to have a 'foreign appearance'. Although the foreface should gradually taper from eye to muzzle and should dip slightly at its juncture with the forehead, it should not 'dish' or fall away quickly below the eyes, where it should be full and well made up, but relieved from 'wedginess' by a little delicate chiselling. While well-developed jaw bones, armed with a set of strong white teeth, impart that appearance of strength to the fore-face which is desirable. An excessive bony or muscular development of the jaws is both unnecessary and unsightly, as it is partly responsible for the full and rounded contour of the cheeks to which the term 'cheeky' is applied. Nose should be black.

Eyes. Should be dark in colour, moderately small and not prominent, full of fire, life and intelligence; as nearly as possible, circular in shape and not too far apart. Anything approaching a yellow eye is most objectionable.

Ears. Should be small and V-shaped and of moderate thickness, the flaps neatly folded over and drooping forward close to the cheeks. The top line of the folded ear should be well above the level of the skull. A pendulous ear, hanging dead by the side of the head like a hound's is uncharacteristic of the Terrier, while an ear which is semi-erect is still more undesirable

Mouth. Both upper and lower jaws should be strong and muscular, the teeth as nearly as possible level and capable of closing together like a vice—the lower canines locking in front of the upper and the points of the upper incisors slightly overlapping the lower.

Neck. Should be clean, muscular, of fair length, free from throatiness and presenting a graceful curve when viewed from the side.

Forequarters. Shoulders when viewed from the front, should slope steeply downwards from their juncture, with the neck towards the points, which should be fine. When viewed from the side they should be long, well laid back, and should slope obliquely backwards from points to withers, which should always be clean cut. A shoulder well laid back gives the long fore-hand, which, in combination with a short back, is so desirable in Terrier or Hunter. Chest deep and not broad, a too narrow chest being almost as undesirable as a very broad one. Excessive depth of chest and brisket is an impediment to a Terrier when going to ground. Viewed from any direction the legs should be straight, the bone of the forelegs strong right down to the feet. The elbows should hang perpendicular to the body, working free of the sides, carried straight through in travelling.

Body. The back should be short and level, with no appearance of slackness—the loins muscular and very slightly arched. The brisket should be deep, the front ribs moderately arched, and the back ribs deep, and well sprung. The term 'slackness' is applied both to the portion of the back immediately behind the withers when it shows any tendency to dip, and also the flanks when there is too much space between the back-ribs and hip-bone. When there is little space between the ribs and hips, the dog is said to be 'short in couplings', 'short-coupled', or 'well-ribbed up'. A Terrier can scarcely be too short in back, provided he has sufficient length of neck and liberty of movement. The bitch may be slightly longer in couplings than the dog.

Hindquarters. Should be strong and muscular, quite free from droop or crouch; the thighs long and powerful; the stifles well curved and turned neither in nor out; the hock-joints well bent and near the ground; the hocks perfectly upright and parallel with each other when viewed from behind. The worst possible form of hindquarters consists of a short second-thigh and a straight stifle, a combination which causes the hindlegs to act as props rather than instruments of propulsion. The hindlegs should be carried straight through in travelling.

Feet. Should be round, compact, and not large—the pads tough and well cushioned, and the toes moderately arched and turned neither in nor out. A Terrier with good-shaped forelegs and feet will wear his nails down short by contact with the road surface, the weight of the body being evenly distributed between the toe-pads and the heels.

Tail. Should be set on rather high and carried gaily but not curled. It should be of good strength and substance and of fair length—a three-quarters dock is about right—since it affords the only safe grip when handling working Terriers. A very short tail is suitable neither for work nor show.

Coat. The principal difference between that of the Smooth and Wire variety is that, whereas the former is straight and flat, that of the latter appears to be broken—the hairs having a tendency to twist. The best coats are of a dense, wiry texture—like cocoa-nut matting—the hairs growing so closely and strongly together that when parted with the fingers the skin cannot be seen. At the base of these stiff hairs is a shorter growth of finer and softer hair—termed the undercoat. The coat on the sides is never quite so hard as that on the back and quarters. Some of the hardest coats are 'crinkly' or slightly waved, but a curly coat is very objectionable. The hair on the upper and lower jaws should be crisp and only sufficiently long to impart an appearance of strength to the foreface, thus effectually differentiating them from the Smooth variety. The hair on the forelegs should also be dense and crisp. The coat should average in length from $\frac{3}{4}$ to 1 inch on shoulders and neck, lengthening to $1\frac{1}{2}$ inches on withers, backs, ribs and quarters. These measurements are given rather as a guide to exhibitors than as an infallible rule, since the length of coat varies in different specimens and seasons. The judge must form his own opinion as to what constitutes a 'sufficient' coat.

Colour. White should predominate: brindle, red, liver, or slaty blue are objectionable. Otherwise, colour is of little or no importance.

Weight and Size. Bone and strength in a small compass are essential, but this must not be taken to mean that a Terrier should be 'cloddy', or in any way coarse—speed and endurance being requisite as well as power. The Terrier must on no account be leggy, nor must he be too short on the leg. He should stand like a cleverly-made, short-backed Hunter, covering a lot of ground. According to present-day requirements, a full-sized, well-balanced dog should not exceed $15\frac{1}{2}$ inches at the withers—the bitch being proportionately lower—nor should the length of back from withers to root of tail exceed 12 inches, while to maintain the relative proportions, the head—as before mentioned—should not exceed $7\frac{1}{4}$ inches or be less than 7 inches. A dog with these measurements should scale 18 lbs in show condition—a bitch weighing some 2 lbs less—with a margin of 1 lb either way.

Faults. Nose: white, cherry, or spotted to a considerable extent with either of these colours. Ears: prick, tulip, or rose. Mouth: much undershot or much overshot.

Note: Old scars or injuries, the result of work or accident, should not be allowed to prejudice a Terrier's chance in the show-ring, unless they interfere with its movement or with its utility for work or stud.

FOX TERRIER—SMOOTH

(AMERICAN KENNEL CLUB—GROUP IV: TERRIERS)

SMOOTH

The following shall be the standard of the Fox Terrier amplified in part in order that a more complete description of the Fox Terrier may be presented. The standard itself is set forth in ordinary type, the amplification in italics.

Head. The skull should be flat and moderately narrow, gradually decreasing in width to the eyes. Not much stop should be apparent, but there should be more dip in the profile between the forehead and the top jaw than is seen in the case of a Greyhound. The cheeks must not be full. The ears should be V-shaped and small, of moderate thickness, and drooping forward close to the cheek, not hanging by the side of the head like a Foxhound. *The topline of the folded ear should be well above the level of the skull.* The jaws, upper and lower, should be strong and muscular and of fair punishing strength, but not so as in any way to resemble the Greyhound or modern English Terrier. There should not be much falling away below the eyes. This part of the head should, however, be moderately chiseled out, so as not to go down in a straight slope like a wedge. The nose, toward which the muzzle must gradually taper, should be black. *It should be noticed that although the foreface should gradually taper from eye to muzzle and should tip slightly at its juncture with the forehead, it should not 'dish' or fall away quickly below the eyes, where it should be full and well made up, but relieved from 'wedginess' by a little delicate chiseling.* The eyes and the rims should be dark in color, *moderately* small and rather deep-set, full of fire, life and intelligence and as nearly as possible circular in shape. *Anything approaching a yellow eye is most objectionable.* The teeth should be as nearly as possible together, *i.e. the points* of the upper (*incisors*) teeth on the outside of or *slightly overlapping* the lower teeth. *There should be apparent little difference in length between the skull and foreface of a well-balanced head.*

Neck. Should be clean and muscular, without throatiness, of fair length, and gradually widening to the shoulders.

Shoulders. Should be long and sloping, well laid back, fine at the points, and clearly cut at the withers.

Chest. Deep and not broad.

Back. Should be short, straight (*i.e. level*), and strong, with no appearance of slackness. *Brisket should be deep, yet not exaggerated.*

Loin. Should be very powerful, *muscular* and very slightly arched. The foreribs should be moderately arched, the back ribs deep *and well sprung*, and the dog should be well ribbed up.

Hindquarters. Should be strong and muscular, quite free from droop or crouch; the thighs long and powerful; *stifles well curved and turned neither in nor out*; hocks *well bent* and near the ground *should be perfectly upright and parallel each with the other when viewed from behind*, the dog standing well up on them like a Foxhound, and not straight in the stifle. *The worst possible form of hindquarters consists of a short second thigh and a straight stifle.*

Stern. Should be set on rather high and carried gaily, but not over the back or curled. It should be of good strength, anything approaching a 'pipe-stopper' tail being especially objectionable.

Legs. The forelegs viewed from any direction must be straight with bone strong right down to the feet, showing little or no appearance of ankle in front, and being short and straight in pasterns. Both forelegs and hind legs should be carried straight forward in traveling, the stifles not turning outward. The elbows should hang perpendicularly to the body, working free of the sides.

Feet. Should be round, compact and not large; the soles hard and tough; the toes moderately arched and turned neither in nor out.

Coat. Should be smooth, flat, but hard, dense and abundant. The belly and under side of the thighs should not be bare.

Color. White should predominate; brindle, red, or liver markings are objectionable. Otherwise this point is of little or no importance.

Symmetry, Size and Character. The dog must present a generally gay, lively and active appearance; bone and strength in a small compass are essentials, but this must not be taken to mean that a Fox Terrier should be cloddy, or in any way coarse—speed and endurance must be looked to as well as power, and the symmetry of the Foxhound taken as a model. The terrier, like the hound, must on no account be leggy, nor must he be too short in the leg. He should stand like a cleverly made hunter, covering a lot of ground, yet with a short back, as before stated. He will then attain the highest degree of propelling power, together with the greatest length of stride that is compatible with the length of his body. Weight is not a certain criterion of a terrier's fitness for his work—general shape, size and contour are the main points; and if a dog can gallop and stay, and follow his fox up a drain, it matters little what his weight is to a pound or so; *According to present-day requirements, a full-sized, well-balanced dog should not exceed 15½ inches at the withers, the bitch being proportionately lower—nor should the length of back from withers to root of tail exceed 12 inches, while, to maintain the relative proportions, the head should not exceed 7¼ inches or be less than 7 inches. A dog with these measurements should scale 18 pounds in show condition—a bitch weighing some 2 pounds less—with a margin of 1 pound either way.*

Balance. *This may be defined as the correct proportions of a certain point, or points, when considered in relation to a certain other point or points. It is the keystone of the terrier's anatomy. The chief points for consideration are the relative proportions of skull and foreface; head and back; height at withers and length of body from shoulder-point to buttock—the ideal of proportion being reached when the last two measurements are the same. It should be added that, although the head measurements can be taken with absolute accuracy, the height at withers and length of back and coat are approximate, and are inserted for the information of breeders and exhibitors rather than as a hard and fast rule.*

Movement. *Movement, or action, is the crucial test of conformation. The terrier's legs should be carried straight forward while traveling, the forelegs hanging perpendicular and swinging parallel with the sides, like the pendulum of a clock. The principal propulsive power is furnished by the hind legs, perfection of action being found in the terrier possessing long thighs and muscular second thighs well bent at the stifles, which admit of a strong forward thrust or 'snatch' of the hocks. When approaching, the forelegs should form a continuation of the straight line of the front, the feet being the same distance apart at the elbows. When stationary, it is often difficult to determine whether a dog is slightly out at shoulder, but, directly he moves, the defect—if it exists—becomes more apparent, the forefeet having a tendency to cross, 'weave,' or 'dish'. When, on the contrary, the dog is tied at the shoulder, the tendency of the feet is to move wider apart, with a sort of paddling action. When the hocks are turned in—cowhock—the stifles and feet are turned outwards, resulting in a serious loss of propulsive power. When the hocks are turned outwards the tendency of the hind feet is to cross, resulting in an ungainly waddle.*

N.B. Old scars or injuries, the result of work or accident, should not be allowed to prejudice a terrier's chance in the show ring, unless they interfere with its movement or with its utility for work or stud

FOX TERRIER—WIRE

(AMERICAN KENNEL CLUB—GROUP V: TERRIERS, WIRE)

This variety of the breed should resemble the smooth sort in every respect except the coat, which should be broken. The harder and more wiry the texture of the coat is, the better. On no account should the dog look or feel woolly; and there should be no silky hair about the poll or elsewhere. The coat should not be too long, so as to give the dog a shaggy appearance, but, at the same time, it should show a marked and distinct difference all over from the smooth species.

SCALE OF POINTS

Head and ears	15	Legs and feet	15
Neck	5	Coat	15
Shoulders and chest	10	Symmetry, size and character	10
Back and loin	10	Total	100
Hindquarters	15		
Stern	5		

DISQUALIFICATIONS

Nose. White, cherry or spotted to a considerable extent with either of these colors. Ears. Prick, tulip or rose. Mouth. Much undershot, or much overshot.

FOXHOUND

(THE KENNEL CLUB—HOUND GROUP)

Head and Skull. Skull broad.
Neck. Long, but not thick. A short-necked hound is deficient in pace.
Forequarters. Shoulders should show quality and no lumber. A shoulder with an excessive amount of fleshy conformation will prevent the hound from running up or down hill at top pace. Legs full of bone right down to the feet, and not tapering off in any way.
Body. Girth should be deep with plenty of heart room. Back broad, and a hound should be well ribbed up; but there should be a fair space between the end of the ribs and the commencement of the hindquarters, otherwise the hound will be deficient in stride and therefore lack pace.
Hindquarters. Full, and of great muscular proportions. Hocks should be well let down, and the bone of the hindlegs (as in the forelegs) should continue all the way down to the foot, and not become light under the pastern.
Feet. The toes of the feet should be close together, and not open.
Tail. Should be well put on at the end of good quarters, and these quarters should in no way end abruptly and be of the type that hound-men term 'chopped off behind'. A curly stern, although unsightly, will not be detrimental to the hound's hunting qualities.

FOXHOUND, ENGLISH

(AMERICAN KENNEL CLUB—GROUP II: HOUNDS)

Head. Should be of full size, but by no means heavy. Brow pronounced, but not high or sharp. There should be a good length and breadth, sufficient to give in a dog hound a girth in front of the ears of fully 16 inches. The nose should be long ($4\frac{1}{2}$ inches) and wide, with open nostrils. Ears set on low and lying close to the cheeks. Most English hounds are 'rounded' which means that about $1\frac{1}{2}$ inches is taken off the end of the ear. The teeth must meet squarely, either a *pig-mouth* (overshot) or undershot being a disqualification.
Neck. Must be long and clean, without the slightest throatiness, not less than 10 inches from cranium to shoulder. It should taper nicely from shoulders to head, and the upper outline should be slightly convex.
Shoulders should be long and well clothed with muscle, without being heavy, especially at the points. They must be well sloped, and the true arm between the front and the elbow must be long and muscular, but free from fat or lumber.
Chest and Back Ribs. The chest should girth over 31 inches in a 24-inch hound, and the back ribs must be very deep.
Back and Loin. Must both be very muscular, running into each other without any contraction between them. The couples must be wide, even to

raggedness, and the topline of the back should be absolutely level, the *Stern* well set on and carried gaily but not in any case curved *over* the back like a squirrel's tail. The end should taper to a point and there should be a fringe of hair below.

Hindquarters or propellers are required to be very strong, and as endurance is of even greater consequence than speed, straight stifles are preferred to those much bent as in a Greyhound.

Elbows set quite straight, and neither turned in nor out are a *sine qua non.* They must be well let down by means of the long true arm above mentioned.

Legs and Feet. Every Master of Foxhounds insists on legs as straight as a post, and as strong; size of bone at the ankle being especially regarded as all important. The desire for straightness had a tendency to produce knuckling-over, which at one time was countenanced, but in recent years this defect has been eradicated by careful breeding and intelligent adjudication, and one sees very little of this trouble in the best modern Foxhounds. The bone cannot be too large, and the feet in all cases should be round and catlike, with well-developed knuckles and strong horn, which last is of the greatest importance.

Color and Coat. Not regarded as very important, so long as the former is a good 'hound color,' and the latter is short, dense, hard, and glossy. Hound colors are black, tan, and white, or any combination of these three, also the various 'pies' compounded of white and the color of the hare and badger, or yellow, or tan. The *Symmetry* of the Foxhound is of the greatest importance, and what is known as 'quality' is highly regarded by all good judges.

SCALE OF POINTS

Head	5	Elbows	5
Neck	10	Legs and feet	20
Shoulders	10	Color and coat	5
Chest and back ribs	10	Stern	5
Back and loin	15	Symmetry	5
Hindquarters	10	Total	100

DISQUALIFICATION

Pig-mouth (overshot) or undershot.

Approved 1935

FOXHOUND, AMERICAN

(AMERICAN KENNEL CLUB—GROUP II: HOUNDS)

Head. *Skull.* Should be fairly long, slightly domes at occiput, with cranium broad and full. **Ears.** Ears set on moderately low, long, reaching when drawn out nearly, if not quite, to the tip of the nose; fine in texture, fairly broad, with almost entire absence of erectile power—setting close to the head with the forward edge slightly inturning to the cheek—round at tip.
Eyes. Eyes large, set well apart—soft and hound-like—expression gentle and pleading; of a brown or hazel color.
Muzzle. Muzzle of fair length—straight and square-cut—the stop moderately defined.
Defects. A very flat skull, narrow across the top; excess of dome; eyes small, sharp and terrier-like, or prominent and protruding; muzzle long and snipy, cut away decidedly below the eyes, or very short. Roman-nosed, or upturned, giving a dish-face expression. Ears short, set on high, or with a tendency to rise above the point of origin.
Body. Neck and Throat. Neck rising free and light from the shoulders, strong in substance yet not loaded, of medium length. The throat clean and free from folds of skin, a slight wrinkle below the angle of the jaw, however, is allowable.
Defects. A thick, short, cloddy neck carried on a line with the top of the shoulders. Throat showing dewlap and folds of skin to a degree termed 'throatiness'.
Shoulders, Chest and Ribs. Shoulders sloping—clean, muscular, not heavy or loaded—conveying the idea of freedom of action with activity and strength. Chest should be deep for lung space, narrower in proportion to depth than the English hound—28 inches (*girth*) in a 23-inch hound being good. Well-sprung ribs—back ribs should extend well back—a three-inch flank allowing springiness.
Back and Loins. Back moderately long, muscular and strong. Loins broad and slightly arched.
Defects. Very long or swayed or roached back. Flat, narrow loins.
Forelegs and Feet. Forelegs. Straight, with fair amount of bone. Pasterns short and straight. **Feet.** Foxlike. Pad full and hard. Well-arched toes. Strong nails.
Defects. Straight, upright shoulders, chest disproportionately wide or with lack of depth. Flat ribs. Out at elbow. Knees knuckled over forward, or bent backward. Forelegs crooked. Feet long, open or spreading.
Hips, Thighs, Hind Legs and Feet. Hips and thighs, strong and muscled, giving abundance of propelling power. Stifles strong and well let down. Hocks firm, symmetrical and moderately bent. Feet close and firm.
Defects. Cowhocks, or straight hocks. Lack of muscle and propelling power. Open feet.
Tail. Set moderately high; carried gaily, but not turned forward over the back; with slight curve; with very slight brush.
Defects. A long tail. Teapot curve or inclined forward from the root. Rat tail, entire absence of brush.
Coat. A close, hard, hound coat of medium length.
Defects. A short thin coat, or of a soft quality.
Height. Dogs should not be under 22 or over 25 inches. Bitches should not be under 21 or over 24 inches measured across the back at the point of the withers, the hound standing in a natural position with his feet well under him.
Color. Any color.

SCALE OF POINTS

Head			*Running Gear*		
Skull	5		Forelegs	10	
Ears	5		Hips, thighs and hind legs	10	
Eyes	5		Feet	15	35
Muzzle	5	20	*Coat and Tail*		
Body			Caot	5	
Neck	5		Tail	5	10
Chest and shoulders	15		Total		100
Back, loins and ribs	15	35			

FRENCH BULLDOG

(THE KENNEL CLUB—UTILITY GROUP)

General Appearance. A French Bulldog should be sound, active and intelligent, of compact build, medium or small sized, with good bone, a short smooth coat, and the various points so evenly balanced that the dog does not look ill-proportioned.

Head and Skull. Head massive, square and broad. Skull nearly flat between the ears, with a domed forehead, the loose skin forming symmetrical wrinkles. Muzzle broad, deep and laid back with the muscles of the cheek well developed; nose and lips black. Stop well defined. Lower jaw should be deep square, broad, slightly undershot and well turned up. Nose extremely short, black and wide, with open nostrils and the line between well defined. Lips thick, the lower meeting the upper in the middle, completely hiding the teeth. The upper lip should cover the lower on each side with plenty of cushion, but not so exaggerated as to hang too much below the level of the lower jaw.

Eyes. Should be dark, of moderate size, round, neither sunken nor prominent, showing no white when looking straight, set wide apart and low down in the skull.

Ears. 'Bat ears' of medium size, wide at the base, rounded at the top, set high, carried upright and parallel, a sufficient width of skull preventing them being too close together; the skin soft and fine and the orifice, as seen from the front, showing entirely.

Mouth. Teeth sound and regular, but not visible when the mouth is closed. Tongue must not protrude.

Neck. Should be powerful, with loose skin at the throat, but not exaggerated. Well arched and thick, but not too short.

Forequarters. Legs set wide apart, straight bones, strong, muscular and short.

Body. Should be short, cobby, muscular and well rounded, with deep wide brisket, roach back, strong, wide at the shoulders and narrowing at the loins, good 'cup up' and well sprung.

Hindquarters. Legs strong, muscular and longer than the forelegs so as to raise the loins above the shoulders. Hocks well let down and with very fine movement.

Feet. Should be small, compact and placed in continuation of the line of the leg, with absolutely sound pastern. The hind rather long than the fore feet. Toes compact, knuckle high, nails short, thick and preferably black.

Tail. Very short, set low, thick at the root, and tapering quickly towards the tip, either straight or kinked, but never curling over the back. A good tail is placed so that it cannot be carried gaily.

Coat. Texture fine, smooth, lustrous, short and close.

Colour. The colours allowed are brindle, pied and fawn.

1 The brindle is a mixture of black and coloured hairs. This variety may contain white on condition that brindle predominates.
2 The pied is a dog in which the white predominates over the brindle. White dogs are classified with the pieds, but their eyelashes and eyerims should be black. In pieds the white should be clear with definite brindle patches and no ticking or black spots.
3 The fawn dog may contain brindle hairs but must have black eyerims and eyelashes.

Weight and Size. The ideal weight is 28 lbs for dogs and 24 lbs for bitches but soundness must not be sacrificed to smallness.

Faults. Nose other than black. Eyes of different colours. Ears not erect. Hare lip. Tail docked. Colour-Tan, Mouse Grey (blue).

FRENCH BULLDOG

(AMERICAN KENNEL CLUB—GROUP VI:
(NON-SPORTING DOGS)

General Appearance. The French Bulldog should have the appearance of an active, intelligent, muscular dog, of heavy bone, smooth coat, compactly built, and of medium or small structure.

Proportion and Symmetry. The points should be well distributed and bear good relation one to the other, no feature being in such prominence from either excess or lack of quality that the animal appears deformed or poorly proportioned.

Influence of Sex. In comparison of specimens of different sex, due allowance should be made in favor of the bitches, which do not bear the characteristics of the breed to the same marked degree as do the dogs

Weight. A lightweight class under 22 pounds; heavyweight class, 22 pounds, and not over 28 pounds.

Head. The head should be large and square. The top of the skull should be flat between the ears; the forehead should not be flat but slightly rounded. The stop should be well defined, causing a hollow or groove between the eyes. The muzzle should be broad, deep and well laid back; the muscles of the cheeks well developed. The nose should be extremely short; nostrils broad with well defined line between them. The nose and flews should be black, except in the case of the lighter-colored dogs, where a lighter color nose is acceptable. The flews should be thick and broad, hanging over the lower jaw at the sides, meeting the underlip in front and covering the teeth which should not be seen when the mouth is closed. The underjaw should be deep, square, broad, undershot and well turned up.

Eyes. The eyes should be wide apart, set low down in the skull, as far from the ears as possible, round in form, of moderate size, neither sunken nor bulging, and in color dark. Now haw and no white of the eye showing when looking forward.

Neck. The neck should be thick and well arched, with loose skin at throat.

Ears. The ears shall hereafter be known as the bat ear, broad at the base, elongated, with round top, set high on the head, but not too close together, and carried erect with the orifice to the front. The leather of the ear, fine and soft.

Body. The body should be short and well rounded. The chest, broad, deep and full, well ribbed with the belly tucked up. The back should be a roach back, with a slight fall close behind the shoulders. It should be strong and short, broad at the shoulders and narrowing at the loins.

Legs. The forelegs should be short, stout, straight and muscular, set wide apart. The hind leg should be strong and muscular, longer than the forelegs, so as to elevate the loins above the shoulders. Hocks well let down.

Feet. The feet should be moderate in size, compact and firmly set. Toes compact, well split up, with high knuckles and short, stubby nails; hind feet slightly longer than forefeet.

Tail. The tail should be either straight or screwed (but not curly), short, hung low, thick root and fine tip; carried low in repose.

Color, Skin and Coat. Acceptable colors are: All brindle, fawn, white, brindle and white, and any color except those which constitute disqualification. The skin should be soft and loose, especially at head and shoulders, forming wrinkles. Coat moderately fine, brilliant, short and smooth.

SCALE OF POINTS

General Properties		
Proportion and symmetry	5	
Expression	5	
Gait	4	
Color	4	
Coat	2	20
Head		
Skull	6	
Cheeks and chops	2	
Stop	5	
Ears	8	
Eyes	4	
Wrinkles	4	
Nose	3	
Jaws	6	
Teeth	2	40
Body, Legs, etc.		
Shoulders	5	
Back	5	
Neck	4	
Chest	3	
Ribs	4	
Brisket	3	
Belly	2	
Forelegs	4	
Hindlegs	3	
Feet	3	
Tail	4	40
Total		100

DISQUALIFICATIONS

Other than bat ears; black and white, black and tan, liver, mouse or solid black (black means black without any trace of brindle) eyes of different color; nose other than black except in the case of the lighter-colored dogs, where a lighter color nose is acceptable; hare lip; any mutilation; over 28 pounds in weight.

Approved February 11, 1947

GERMAN SHORTHAIRED POINTER

(THE KENNEL CLUB—GUNDOG GROUP)

Characteristics. The German Short-haired Pointer is a dual-purpose Pointer-Retriever and this accounts for his excellence in the field, which requires a very keen nose, perseverance in searching, and enterprise. His style attracts attention; he is equally good on land and in water, is biddable, an extremely keen worker, and very loyal.

General Appearance. A noble, steady dog showing powers, endurance and speed, giving the immediate impression of an alert and energetic (not nervous) dog whose movements are well co-ordinated. Neither unduly small nor conspicuously large, but of medium size, and like the hunter, 'With a short back stands over plenty of ground'. Grace of outline, clean cut head, sloping long shoulders, deep chest, short back and powerful hindquarters, good bone composition, adequate muscle, well carried tail and taut coat giving a thoroughbred appearance.

Head and Skull. Clean-cut, neither too light nor too heavy, but well proportioned to the body. The skull sufficiently broad and slightly rounded. The furrow between the eyes not so deep, and the occiput not so pronounced as in the English Pointer. The nasal bone rises gradually from nose to forehead (this is more pronounced in the male) and should never possess a definite stop as in the English Pointer, but when viewed from the side there is a well defined stop effect due to the position of the eye-brows. The lips fall away almost vertically from a somewhat protruding nose and continue in a slight curve to the corner of the mouth. Lips well developed but not over hung. Jaws powerful and sufficiently long to enable the dog to pick up and carry game. Dish-face and snipy muzzle are not desirable. Nose solid brown, wide nostrils well opened and soft.

Eyes. Medium size, soft and intelligent, not protruding nor too deep set. Varying in shades of brown to tone with coat. Light eye not desirable. Eyelids should close properly.

Ears. Broad and set high; neither too fleshy nor too thin with a short soft coat; hung close to the head, no pronounced fold, rounded at the tip and should reach almost to the corner of the mouth when brought forward.

Mouth. Teeth sound and strong. Molar teeth meeting exactly and the eyeteeth should fit close in a true scissor bite. Neither overshot nor undershot.

Neck. Moderately long, muscular and slightly arched, becoming larger towards the shoulders. Skin should not fit too loosely.

Forequarters. Shoulders sloping and very muscular with top of shoulder blades close; upper arm bones between shoulder and elbow long. Elbows well laid back, neither pointing outwards nor inwards. Forelegs straight and lean, sufficiently muscular and strong but not coarse-boned. Pasterns slightly sloping, almost straight but not quite.

Body. Chest must appear deep rather than wide but not out of proportion to the rest of the body; ribs deep and well sprung, never barrel-shaped nor flat as in the hound; back ribs reaching well down to tucked up loins. Chest measurement immediately behind the elbows smaller than that about a handsbreadth behind the elbows, so that the upper arm has freedom of movement. Firm, short back, not arched. The loin wide and slightly arched; the croup wide and sufficiently long, neither too heavy nor too sloping starting on a level with the back and sloping gradually towards the tail. Bones solid and strong not clumsy and porous.

Hindquarters. The hips broad and wide falling slightly towards the tail. Thighs strong and well muscled. Stifles well bent. Hocks square with the body and slightly bent, turning neither in nor out. Pasterns nearly upright.

Feet. Compact, close-knit, round to spoon-shaped, well padded, should turn neither in nor out. Toes well arched and heavily nailed.

Tail. Starts high and thick growing gradually thinner. Docked to medium length by two-fifths to half its length. When quiet tail should be carried down and when moving horizontally, never held high over the back or bent.

Coat. Skin should not fit loosely or fold. Coat short, flat and coarse to the touch, slightly longer under the tail.

Colour. Solid liver, liver and white spotted, liver and white spotted and ticked, liver and white ticked, black and white.

Weight and Size. Dogs 55 to 70 lbs, bitches 45 to 60 lbs. Size—dogs 23 to 25 inches and bitches 21 to 23 inches at the shoulder. Symmetry is most essential.

Faults. Bone structure too clumsy, sway-back, head too large, deep wrinkles in forehead, cone-shaped skull or occiput too prominent. Ears too long, pointed, fleshy or undue folds. Flesh coloured nose. Eyes too light, too round or too closely set together, eyelids not closing properly. Wrinkles in neck. Feet or elbows turned inwards or outwards. Soft, sunken or splayed toes; cow-hocks, straight hindlegs, or down on pasterns. Tail starting too low, undocked, too thick, curled up or too furry. Tri-coloured.

POINTER (GERMAN SHORT-HAIRED)

(AMERICAN KENNEL CLUB—GROUP I: SPORTING DOGS)

General Appearance. The over-all picture which is created in the observer's eye should be that of an aristocratic, well-balanced, symmetrical animal with conformation indicating power, endurance and agility and a look of intelligence and animation. The dog should be neither unduly small nor conspicuously large. It should rather give the impression of medium size, but be like the proper hunter, 'with a short back, but standing over plenty of ground'. Tall, leggy individuals seldom possess endurance or sound movement.

Dogs which are ponderous or unbalanced because of excess substance should be definitely rejected. The first impression should be that of a keenness which denotes full enthusiasm for work without indication of nervous or flighty character. Movement should be alertly co-ordinated without waste motion. Grace of outline, clean-cut head, sloping shoulders, deep breast, powerful back, strong quarters, good bone composition, adequate muscle, well-carried tail and taut coat, all of which should combine to produce a look of nobility and an indication of anatomical structure essential to correct gait which must indicate a heritage of purposefully conducted breeding.

Head. Clear cut, neither too light nor too heavy, in proper proportion to the body. Skull should be reasonably broad, arched on side and slightly round on top. Scissura (median line between the eyes at the forehead) not too deep, occipital bone not as conspicuous as in the case of the Pointer. The foreface should rise gradually from nose to forehead—not resembling the Roman nose. This is more strongly pronounced in the dog than in the bitch, as befitting his sex. The chops should fall away from the somewhat projecting nose. Lips should be full and deep, never flewy. The chops should not fall over too much, but form a proper fold in the angle. The heavy, in proper proportion to the body. Skull should be reasonably broad, arched on side and slightly round on top. Scissura (median line between the eyes at the forehead) not too deep, occipital bone not as conspicuous as in the case of the Pointer. The foreface should rise gradually from nose to forehead—not resembling the Roman nose. This is more strongly pronounced in the dog than in the bitch, as befitting his sex. The chops should fall away from the somewhat projecting nose. Lips should be full and deep, never flewy. The chops should not fall over too much, but form a proper fold in the angle. The jaw should be powerful and the muscles well developed. The line to the forehead should rise gradually and should never possess a definite stop as in the case of the Pointer, but rather a stop-effect when viewed from the side, due to the position of the eyebrows. The muzzle should be sufficiently long to enable the dog to seize properly and to facilitate his carrying game a long time. A pointed muzzle is not desirable. The entire head should never give the impression of tapering to a point. The depth should be in the right proportion to the length, both in the muzzle and in the skull proper.

Ears. Ears should be broad and set fairly high, lie flat and never hang away from the head. Placement should be above eye level. The ears, when laid in front without being pulled, should about meet the lip angle. In the case of heavier dogs, they should be correspondingly longer.

Eyes. The eyes should be of medium size, full of intelligence, and expressive, good-humored, and yet radiating energy, neither protruding nor sunk. The eyelids should close well. The best color is a dark shade of brown. Light yellow, china or wall (bird of prey) eyes are not desirable.

Nose. Brown, the larger the better; nostrils well opened and broad. Flesh-colored and spotted noses are not desirable.

Teeth. The teeth should be strong and healthy. The molars should intermesh properly. Incisors should fit close in a true scissors bite. Jaws should be neither overshot nor undershot.

Neck. Of adequate length to permit the jaws reaching game to be retrieved, sloping downwards on beautifully curving lines. The nape should be rather muscular, becoming gradually larger towards the shoulders. Moderate houndlike throatiness permitted.

Breast and Thorax. The breast in general should give the impression of depth rather than breadth; for all that, it should be in correct proportion to the other parts of the body with fair depth of chest. The ribs forming the thorax should be well-curved and not flat; they should not be absolutely round or barrel-shaped. Ribs that are entirely round prevent the necessary expansion of the chest when taking breath. The back ribs should reach well down. The circumference of the breast immediately behind the elbows should be smaller than that of the breast about a hand's-breadth behind elbows, so that the upper arm has room for movement.

Back and Loins. Back should be short, strong and straight with slight rise from root of tail to withers. Excessively long or hog-backed should be penalized. Loin strong, of moderate length and slightly arched. Tuck-up should be apparent.

Assembly of Back Members. The hips should be broad with hip sockets wide apart and fall slightly toward the tail in a graceful curve. Thighs strong and well muscled. Stifles well bent. Hock joints should be well angulated with strong, straight bone structure from hock to pad. Angulation of both stifle and hock joints should be such as to combine maximum combination of both drive and traction. Hocks should turn neither in nor out.

Assembly of Front Members. The shoulders should be sloping, movable, well covered with muscle. The shoulder blades should lie flat. The upper arm (also called the cross bar, i.e. the bones between the shoulder and elbow joints) should be as long as possible, standing away somewhat from the trunk so that the straight and closely muscled legs, when viewed from in front, should appear to be parallel. Elbows which stand away from the body or are pressed right into same indicate toes turning inwards or outwards, which should be regarded as faults. Pasterns should be strong, short and nearly vertical.

Feet. Should be compact, close-knit and round to spoon-shaped. The toes sufficiently arched and heavily nailed. The pad should be strong and hard.

Coat and Skin. The skin should look close and tight. The hair should be short and thick and feel tough and hard to the hand; it is somewhat longer on the underside of the tail and the back edge of the haunches. It is softer, thinner and shorter on the ears and the head.

Tail. Is set high and firm, and must be docked, leaving approximately two-fifths of length. The tail hangs down when the dog is quiet, is held horizontally when he is walking, never turned over the back or considerably bent but violently wagged when he is on the search.

Bones. Thin and fine bones are by no means desirable in a dog which should be able to work over any and every country and should possess strength. The main importance accordingly is laid not so much on the size as being in proper proportion to the body. Dogs with coarse bones are handicapped in agility of movement and speed.

Desirable Weight and Height. Dogs—55 to 70 pounds. Bitches—45 to 60 pounds. Dogs—23 to 25 inches. Bitches—21 to 23 inches at the shoulders.

Color. Solid liver, liver and white spotted, liver and white spotted and ticked, liver and white ticked, liver roan. Any colors other than liver and white (gray white) are not permitted.

Symmetry and field quality are most essential. A dog well balanced in all points is preferable to one with outstanding good qualities and defects. A smooth, lithe gait is most desirable.

Faults. Bone structure too clumsy or too light, head too large, too many wrinkles in forehead, dish-faced, snipy muzzle, ears too long, pointy or fleshy; flesh-colored nose, eyes too light, too round or too closely set together, excessive throatiness, cowhocks, feet or elbows turned inward or outward, down on pasterns, loose shoulders, sway-back, black coat or tri-colored, any colors except liver or some combination of liver and white.

Approved May 7, 1946

GIANT SCHNAUZER

(THE KENNEL CLUB—UTILITY GROUP)

General Appearance. The Schnauzer is a powerfully built, robust, sinewy, nearly square dog (length of body equal to height at shoulders). His temperament combines high spirits, reliability, strength, endurance and vigour. Expression keen and attitude alert. Correct conformation is of more importance than colour or other purely 'beauty' points.

Head and Skull. Head strong and elongated, gradually narrowing from the ears to the eyes and thence forward towards the tip of the nose. Upper part of the head (occiput to the base of the forehead) moderately broad between the ears—with flat, creaseless forehead and well muscled, but not too strongly developed cheeks. The powerful muzzle formed by the upper and lower jaws (base of forehead to the tip of nose) should end in a moderately blunt line, with bristly, stubby moustache and chin whiskers. Ridge of the nose straight and running almost parallel to the extension of the forehead. The nose is black and full. Lips tight and not overlapping. Medium stop to accentuate eye-brows.

Eyes. Medium sized, dark, oval, set forward, with arched bushy eye-brows.

Ears. Neat and 'V' shaped, set high and dropping forward to temple.

Mouth. Scissor teeth, slightly overlapping from the top; with strongly developed fangs; healthy and pure white.

Neck. Moderately long, nape strong and slightly arched, skin close to throat, neck set cleanly on shoulders.

Forequarters. Shoulders flat and sloping. Forelegs straight viewed from any position. Muscles smooth and lithe rather than prominent; bones strong, straight and carried well down to the feet, elbows set close to the body and pointing directly backward.

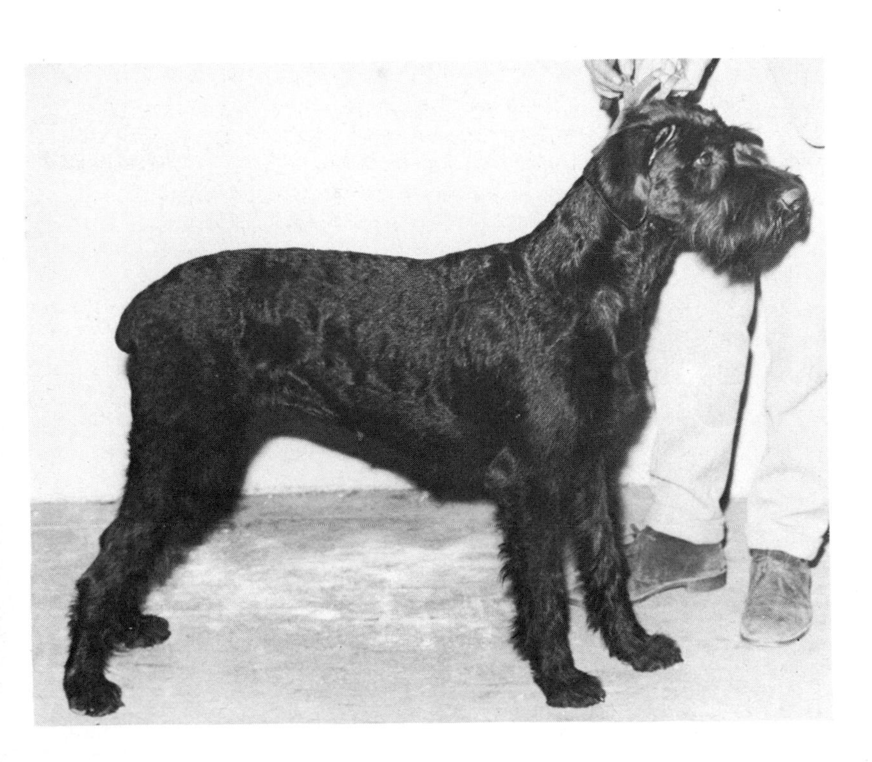

Body. Chest moderately broad, deep, with visible strong breast bone reaching down to at least the height of elbow and slightly rising backward to loins. Back strong and straight, slightly higher at the shoulder than at the hindquarters, with short well developed loins. Ribs well sprung. Length of body equal to height from top withers to ground.

Hindquarters. Thighs slanting and flat, but strongly muscled. Hindlegs (upper and lower thighs) at first vertical to the stifle, from stifle to hock in line with the extension of the upper neck line, from hock vertical to ground.

Feet. Short, round, extremely compact with close-arched toes (cat's paws) dark nails and hard soles. The feet also deep or thickly padded, pointing forward.

Tail. Set on and carried high, cut down to three joints.

Coat. Hard and wiry and just short enough for smartness, clean on neck, shoulder, ears and skull, plenty of good hard hair on front legs. Good undercoat is essential.

Colour. All pepper and salt colours in even proportions, or pure black.

Height. The ideal height for bitches shall be 60 cms (23½ inches) and for dogs 70 cms (27½ inches). Any variation or more than 3 cms (1 inch) in these heights should be penalised.

Faults. Too heavy or too light; too low or high on the leg. Head too heavy or round; creased forehead; sticking out or badly carried ears; light eye, with yellow or light grey rings; strongly protruding cheek-bones; flabby throat skin; undershot or overshot jaw. Muzzle too pointed or too small. Back too long, sunken or roached; barrel-shaped ribs; slanting crupper; elbows turned out; heels turned in, handpart overbuilt (too Steep). Toes spread open; paws long and flat (hare). Coat too short and sleek, or too long, soft or curled. All white, spotty, tigered or red colours. Small white breast spot or marking is not a fault. Among other serious faults are cow-hocks, sunken pasterns, or any weakness of joint, bone or muscular development.

Note. Male animals should have two apparently normal testicles fully descended into the scrotum.

GIANT SCHNAUZERS

(AMERICAN KENNEL CLUB—GROUP III: WORKING DOGS)

General Description. The Giant Schnauzer should resemble, as nearly as possible, in general appearance, a larger and more powerful version of the Standard Schnauzer, on the whole a bold and valiant figure of a dog. Robust, strongly built, nearly square in proportion of body length to height at withers, active, sturdy, and well-muscled. Temperament which combines spirit and alertness with intelligence and reliability. Composed, watchful, courageous, easily trained, deeply loyal to family, playful, amiable in repose, and a commanding figure when aroused. The sound, reliable temperament, rugged build, and dense weather-resistant wiry coat make for one of the most useful, powerful, and enduring working breeds.

Head. Strong, rectangular in appearance, and elongated; narrowing slightly from the ears to the eyes, and again from the eyes to the tip of the nose. The total length of the head is about one-half the length of the back (withers to set-on of tail). The head matches the sex and substance of the dog. The top line of the muzzle is parallel to the top line of the skull; there is a slight stop which is accentuated by the eyebrows.

Skull. (Occiput to Stop). Moderately broad between the ears; occiput not too prominent. Top of skull flat; skin unwrinkled.

Cheeks. Flat, but with well-developed chewing muscles; there is no 'cheekiness' to disturb the rectangular head appearance (with beard).

Muzzle. Strong and well-filled under the eyes; both parallel and equal in length to the topskull; ending in a moderately blunt wedge. The nose is large, black, and full. The lips are tight, and not overlapping, black in color.

Bite. A full complement of sound white teeth (6/6 incisors, 2/2 canines, 8/8 premolars, 4/6 molars) with a scissors bite. The upper and lower jaws are powerful and well-formed. *Disqualifying Faults:* Overshot or undershot.

Ears. When cropped, identical in shape and length with pointed tips. They are in balance with the head and are not exaggerated in length. They are set high on the skull and carried perpendicularly at the inner edges with as little bell as possible along the other edges. When uncropped, the ears are 'V'-shaped button ears of medium length and thickness, set high and carried rather high and close to the head.

Eyes. Medium size, dark brown, and deep-set. They are oval in appearance and keen in expression with lids fitting tightly. Vision is not impaired nor eyes hidden by too long eyebrows.

Neck. Strong and well-arched, of moderate length, blending cleanly into the shoulders, and with the skin fitting tightly at the throat; in harmony with the dog's weight and build.

Body. Compact, substantial, short-coupled, and strong, with great power and agility. The height at the highest point of the withers equals the body length from breastbone to point of rump. The loin section is well-developed, as short as possible for compact build.

Forequarters. The forequarters have flat, somewhat sloping shoulders and high withers. Forelegs are straight and vertical when viewed from all sides with strong pasterns and good bone. They are separated by a fairly deep brisket which precludes a pinched front. The elbows are set close to the body and point directly backwards.

Chest. Medium in width, ribs well-sprung but with no tendency toward a barrel chest; oval in cross-section; deep through the brisket. The breastbone is plainly discernible, with strong forechest; the brisket descends at least to the elbows, and ascends gradually toward the rear with the belly moderately drawn up. The ribs spread gradually from the first rib so as to allow space for the elbows to move close to the body.

Shoulders. The sloping shoulder blades (scapulae) are strongly-muscled yet flat. They are well laid back so that from the side the rounded upper ends are in a nearly vertical line above the elbows. They slope well forward to the point where they join the upper arm (humerus), forming as nearly as possible a right angle. Such an angulation permits the maximum forward extension of the forelegs without binding or effort. Both shoulder blades and upper arm are long, permitting depth of chest at the brisket.

GORDON SETTER

(THE KENNEL CLUB—GUNDOG GROUP)

General Appearance. A stylish dog, built on galloping lines, having a thoroughbred appearance consistent with its build which can be compared to a weight carrying hunter. Must have symmetrical conformation throughout, showing true balance. Strong, fairly short and level back. Shortish tail. Head fairly long, clearly lined and with intelligent expression, clear colours and long flat coat.

Head and Skull. Head deep rather than broad, but definitely broader than the muzzle, showing brain room. Skull slightly rounded and broadest between the ears. The head should have a clearly indicated stop and length from occiput to stop should be slightly longer than from stop to nose. Below and above the eyes should be lean and the cheeks as narrow as the leanness of the head allows. The muzzle should be fairly long with almost parallel lines and not pointed, as seen from above or from the side. The flews not pendulous but with clearly indicated lips. Nose big and broad, with open nostrils and black in colour. The muzzle should not be quite as deep as its length.

Eyes. Of fair size, not too deep nor too prominent but sufficiently under the brows to show keen and intelligent expression. Dark brown and bright.

Ears. Set low on the head and lying close to it, of medium size and thin.

Mouth. Must be even and not under nor overshot.

Neck. Long, lean and arched to the head and without any throatiness.

Forequarters. Shoulders should be long and slope well back; with wide flat bone and fairly close at withers; should not be loaded, i.e., too thick, which interferes with liberty of movement. Elbows well let down and showing well under the body, which gives freedom of action. Forelegs big, flat-boned and straight, with strong upright pasterns, well feathered.

Body. Of moderate length, deep in brisket, with ribs well sprung. Deep in back ribs, i.e. well-ribbed up. Loins wide and slightly arched. Chest not too broad.

Hindquarters. Hindlegs from hip to hock should be long, broad and muscular; hock to heel short and strong, stifles well bent; hocks straight, not inclined either in or out. Pelvis should tend to the horizontal, i.e. opposite of goose rump.

Feet. Oval, with close knit, well-arched toes, with plenty of hair between. Full toe pads and deep heel cushions.

Tail. Fairly short, straight or slightly scimitar shaped and should not reach below the hocks. Carried horizontal or below line of back. Thick at the root tapering to a fine point. The feather or flag which starts near the root should be long and straight, and growing shorter uniformly to the point.

Coat. On the head and front of legs and tips of

ears should be short and fine, but on all other parts of the body and legs it ought to be of moderate length, fairly flat and free as possible from curl or wave. The feather on the upper portion of the ears should be long and silky, on the back of the hind legs long and fine; a fair amount of hair on the belly forming a nice fringe which may extend on chest and throat. All feathering to be as flat and straight as possible.

Colour. Deep shining coal-black, with no sign of rustiness, with tan markings of a rich chestnut red, i.e., colour of a ripe horse-chestnut as taken from shell. Tan should be lustrous. Black pencilling allowed on toes and also black streak under jaw. *Tan Markings:* two clear spots over the eyes not over threequarters of an inch in diameter. On the sides of the muzzle, the tan should not reach above the base of nose, resembling a stripe around the end of the muzzle from one side to the other. On the throat. Two large, clear spots on the chest. On the inside of the hindlegs and inside the thighs showing down the front of the stifle and broadening out to the outside of the hindlegs from the hock to the toes. It must, however, not completely eliminate the black on the back of the hindlegs. On the forelegs, up to the elbows behind, and to the knees or a little above, in front. Around the vent. A white spot on chest is allowed but the smaller the better.

Weight and Size. As a guide to size, shoulder height for males 26 inches and weight about 65 lbs. Females, 24½ inches and weight about 56 lbs. In show condition.

Faults. General Impression: unintelligent appearance. The bloodhound type with heavy and big head and ears and clumsy body; the collie type with pointed muzzle and curved tail. The Head: pointed, snipy, down or upturned muzzle, too small or large mouth. The Eyes: too light in colour, too deep set or too prominent. The Ears: set too high, or unusually broad or heavy. The Neck: thick and short. Shoulders and Back: irregularly formed. The Chest: too broad. The Legs and Feet: crooked legs. Out-turned elbows. The toes scattered, flat footed. The Tail: too long, badly carried or hooked at the end. The Coat: curly, like wool, not shining. The Colour: yellow, or straw-coloured tan, or without clearly defined lines between the different colours. White feet. Too much white on the chest. In the black there should be no tan hairs.

SETTERS, GORDON

(AMERICAN KENNEL CLUB—GROUP I: SPORTING DOGS)

General Impression. The Gordon Setter is a good-sized, sturdily built, black and tan dog, well muscled, with plenty of bone and substance, but active, upstanding, and stylish, appearing capable of doing a full day's work in the field. He has a strong, rather short back, with well-sprung ribs and a short tail. The head is fairly heavy and finely chiseled. His bearing is intelligent, noble, and dignified, showing no signs of shyness or viciousness. Clear colors and straight or slightly waved coat are correct. He suggests strength and stamina rather than extreme speed. Symmetry and quality are most essential. A dog well-balanced in all points is preferable to one with outstanding good qualities and defects. A smooth, free movement, with high head carriage, is typical.

Size. Shoulder height for males, 24 to 27 inches. For females, 23 to 26 inches.

Weight. Males, 55 to 80 pounds; females, 45 to 70 pounds. Animals that appear to be over or under the prescribed weight limits are to be judged on the basis of conformation and condition. Extremely thin or fat dogs should be discouraged on the basis that under- or overweight hampers the true working ability of the Gordon Setter. The weight-to-height ratio makes him heavier than other setters.

Head. The head is deep, rather than broad, with plenty of brain room; a nicely rounded, good-sized skull, broadest between the ears. The head should have a clearly indicated stop. Below and above the eyes should be lean, and the cheek as narrow as the leanness of the head allows. The muzzle is fairly long and not pointed, either as seen from above or from the side. The flews should not be pendulous. The nose should be broad, with open nostrils and black in color. The muzzle is the same length as the skull from occiput to stop, and the top of the muzzle is parallel to the line of the skull extended. The lip line from the nose to the flews shows a sharp, well-defined, square contour.

Eyes. Of fair size, neither too deep-set, nor too bulging, dark brown, bright, and wise. The shape is oval rather than round. The lids should be tight.

Ears. Set low on the head approximately on line with the eye, fairly large and thin, well folded and carried close to the head.

Teeth. The teeth should be strong and white, and preferably should meet in front in a scissors bite, with the upper incisors slightly forward of the lower incisors. A level bite is not to be considered a fault. Pitted teeth from distemper or allied infections should not be penalized.

Neck. Long, lean, arched to the head, and without throatiness.

Shoulders. Should be fine at the points, and lying well back, giving a moderately sloping topline. The tops of the shoulder blades should be close together. When viewed from behind, the neck appears to fit into the shoulders in smooth, flat, lines that gradually widen from neck to shoulder.

Chest. Deep and not too broad in front; the ribs well sprung, leaving plenty of lung room. The chest should reach to the elbows. A pronounced forechest should be in evidence.

Body. The body should be short from shoulder

to hips, and the distance from the forechest to the back of the thigh should approximately equal the height from the ground to the withers. The loins should be short and broad and not arched. The croup is nearly flat, with only a slight slope to the tailhead.

Forequarters. The legs should be big-boned, straight, and not bowed, with elbows free and not turned in or out. The angle formed by the shoulder blade and upper arm bone should be approximately 90° when the dog is standing so that the foreleg is perpendicular to the ground. The pasterns should be straight.

Hindquarters. The hind legs from hip to hock should be long, flat, and muscular; from hock to heel, short and strong. The stifle and hock joints are well bent and not turned either in or out. When the dog is standing with the hock perpendicular to the ground the thigh bone should hang downward parallel to an imaginary line drawn upward from the hock.

Feet. The feet should be formed by close-knit, well-arched toes with plenty of hair between; with full toe pads and deep heel cushions. Feet should not be turned in or out. Feet should be catlike in shape.

Tail. Short and should not reach below the hocks, carried horizontal or nearly so; thick at the root and finishing in a fine point. The feather which starts near the root of the tail should be slightly waved or straight, having triangular appearance, growing shorter uniformly toward the end. The placement of the tail is important for correct carriage. If the croup is nearly flat, the tail must emerge nearly on the same plane as the croup to allow for horizontal carriage. When the angle of the tail bends too sharply at the first coccygeal bone, the tail will be carried too gaily or will droop. The tail placement should be judged in its relationship to the structure of the croup.

Temperament. The Gordon Setter should be alert, gay, interested, and aggressive. He should be fearless and willing, intelligent and capable. He should be loyal and affectionate, and strong-minded enough to stand the rigors of training.

Gait. The action of the Gordon Setter is a bold, strong, driving, free-swinging gait. The head is carried up and the tail 'flags' constantly while the dog is in motion. When viewed from the front the forefeet move up and down in straight lines so that the shoulder, elbow, and pastern joints are approximately in line with each other. When viewed from the rear, the hock, stifle, and hip joints are approximately in line. Thus the dog moves in a straight pattern forward without throwing the feet in or out. When viewed from the side the forefeet are seen to lift up and reach forward to compensate for the driving hindquarters. The hindquarters reach well forward and stretch far back, enabling the stride to be long and the drive powerful. The over-all appearance of the moving dog is one of smooth-flowing, well-balanced rhythm, in which the action is pleasing to the eye, effortless, economical and harmonious.

Coat. Should be soft and shining, straight or slightly waved, but not curly, with long hair on ears, under stomach and on chest, on back of the fore- and hind legs, and on the tail.

Color and Markings. Black with tan markings, either of rich chestnut or mahogany color. Black penciling is allowed on the toes. The borderline between black and tan colors should be clearly defined. There should not be any tan hairs mixed in the black. The tan markings should be located as follows (1) Two clear spots over the eyes and not over three quarters of an inch in diameter; (2) On the sides of the muzzle. The tan should not reach to the top of the muzzle, but resembles a stripe around the end of the muzzle from one side to the other; (3) On the throat; (4) Two large clear spots on the chest; (5) On the inside of the hind legs showing down the front of the stifle and broadening out to the outside of the hind legs from the hock to the toes. It must not completely eliminate the black on the back of the hind legs; (6) On the forelegs from the carpus, or a little above, downward to the toes; (7) Around the vent; (8) A white spot on the chest is allowed, but the smaller the better. Predominantly tan, red, or buff dogs which do not have the typical pattern of markings of a Gordon Setter are ineligible for showing and undesirable for breeding.

SCALE OF POINTS

While not a part of the official breed standard, may be helpful in placing proper emphasis upon qualities desired in the physical make-up of the breed.

Head and neck (incl. ears and eyes)	10	Coat	8
Body	15	Color and markings	5
Shoulders, forelegs, forefeet	10	Temperament	10
Hind legs and feet	10	Size, general appearance	15
Tail	5	Gait	12
		Total	100

DISQUALIFICATIONS

Predominantly tan, red, or buff dogs which do not have the typical pattern of markings of a Gordon Setter.

Approved November 13, 1962

GREAT DANE

(THE KENNEL CLUB—WORKING GROUP)

General Appearance. The Great Dane should be remarkable in size and very muscular, strongly though elegantly built; the head and neck should be carried high, and the tail in line with the back, or slightly upwards but not curled over the hindquarters. Elegance of outline and grace of form are most essential to a Dane; size is absolutely necessary, but there must be that alertness of expression and briskness of movement without which the Dane character is lost. He should have a look of dash and daring, of being ready to go anywhere and do anything. The action should be lithe, springy and free, the hocks move freely and the head be carried high except when galloping.

Head and Skull. The head, taken altogether, should give the idea of great length and strength of jaw. The muzzle or foreface is broad, and the skull proportionately narrow, so that the whole head, when viewed from above and in front, has the appearance of equal breadth throughout. The entire length of head varies with the height of the dog; 13 inches from the tip of the nose to the back of the occiput is a good measurement for a dog of 32 inches at the shoulder. The length from the end of the nose to the point between the eyes should be about equal, or preferably of greater length than from this point to the back of the occiput. The skull should be flat and have a slight indentation running up the centre, the occipital peak not prominent. There should be a decided rise or brow over the eyes but no abrupt stop between them; the face should be well chiselled, well filled in below the eyes with no appearance of being pinched; the foreface long, of equal depth throughout. The cheeks should show as little lumpiness as possible, compatible with strength. The underline of the head, viewed in profile, should run almost in a straight line from the corner of the jawbone, allowing for the fold of the lip, but with no loose skin to hang down. The bridge of the nose should be very wide, with a slight ridge where the cartilage joins the bone. (This is a characteristic of the breed.) The nostrils should be large, wide and open, giving a blunt look to the nose. A butterfly or flesh-colored nose is not objected to in Harlequins. The lips should hang squarely in front, forming a right-angle with the upper line of foreface.

Eyes. Fairly deep set, of medium size and preferably dark. Wall or odd eyes permissible in Harlequins.

Ears. Should be small, set high on the skull and carried slightly erect with the tips falling forward.

Mouth. The teeth should be level and not project one way or the other.

Neck. The neck should be long, well arched, and quite clean and free from loose skin, held well up, well set in the shoulders, and the junction of the head and neck well defined.

Forequarters. The shoulders should be muscular but not loaded, and well sloped back, with the elbows well under the body. The forelegs should be perfectly straight with big bone, which must be flat.

Body. The body should be very deep, with ribs well sprung and belly well drawn up. The back and loins should be strong, the latter slightly arched.

Hindquarters. The hindquarters and thighs should be extremely muscular giving the idea of great strength and galloping power. The second thigh is long and well developed, the stifle and hock well bent, the hocks set low, turning neither in nor out.

Feet. The feet should be catlike and should not turn in or out. The toes well arched and close, the nails strong and curved. Nails should be black but light nails are permissible in Harlequins.

Tail. The tail should be thick at the root, and taper towards the end, reaching to or just below the hocks. It should be carried in a straight line level with the back, when the dog is in action, slightly curved towards the end, but in no case should it curl or be carried over the back.

Coat. The hair is short and dense and sleek-looking, and in no case should it incline to roughness.

Colour. (*a*) Brindles must be striped, ground colour from the lightest yellow to the deepest orange, and the stripes must always be black. Eyes and nails preferably dark. (*b*) Fawns, the colour varies from lightest buff to deepest orange, darker shadings on the muzzle and the ears and around the eyes are by no means objectionable. Eyes and nails preferably dark. (*c*) Blues, the colour varies from light grey to deepest slate. (*d*) Blacks, black is black. (In all the above colours white is only admissible on the chest and feet, but it is not desirable even there. The nose is always black (except in blues). Eyes and nails preferably dark. (*e*) Harlequins, pure white underground with preferably black patches (blue patches permitted), having the appearance of being torn. In Harlequins, wall eyes, pink noses or butterfly noses are permissible but are not desirable.

Weight and Size. The minimum height of an adult dog over eighteen months must be 30 inches, that of a bitch, 28 inches. Weight, the minimum weight of an adult dog over eighteen months should be 120 lbs, that of a bitch, 100 lbs.

Faults. Cow-hocks. Out at elbows. Straight stifles. Undershot or overshot mouth. Round bone. Snipy muzzle. Straight shoulders. Shelly body. Ring tail.

GREAT DANE

(AMERICAN KENNEL CLUB—GROUP III: WORKING DOGS)

STANDARD OF POINTS

1. General Conformation		
(*a*) General appearance	10	
(*b*) Color and markings	8	
(*c*) Size	5	
(*d*) Condition of coat	4	
(*e*) Substance	3	30
2. Movement		
(*a*) Gait	10	
(*b*) Rear end (croup, legs, paws)	10	
(*c*) Front end (shoulders, legs, paws)	8	28
3. Head		
(*a*) Head conformation	12	
(*b*) Teeth	4	
(*c*) Eyes (nose and ears)	4	20
4. Torso		
(*a*) Neck	6	
(*b*) Loin and back	6	
(*c*) Chest	4	
(*d*) Ribs and brisket	4	20
5. Tail		2
Total		100

1. General Conformation 30 points

(a) General Appearance (10 points)—The Great Dane combines in its distinguished appearance dignity, strength and elegance with great size and a powerful, well-formed, smoothly muscled body. He is one of the giant breeds, but is unique in that his general conformation must be so well-balanced that he never appears clumsy and is always a unit—the Apollo of dogs. He must be spirited and courageous—never timid. He is friendly and dependable. This physical and mental combination is the characteristic which gives the Great Dane the majesty possessed by no other breed. It is particularly true of this breed that there is an impression of great masculinity in dogs as compared to an impression of femininity in bitches. The male should appear more massive throughout than the bitch, with larger frame and heavier bone. In the ratio between length and height, the Great Dane should appear as square as possible. In bitches, a somewhat longer body is permissible. Faults: Lack of unity; timidity; bitchy dogs; poor musculature; poor bone development; out of condition; rickets; doggy bitches.

(b) Color and Markings (8 points)—(*i*) Color: Brindle Danes. Base color ranging from light golden yellow to deep golden yellow always brindled with strong black cross stripes. The more intensive the base color and the more intensive the brindling, the more attractive will be the color. Small white marks at the chest and toes are not desirable. Faults: Brindle with too dark a base color; silver-blue and grayish-blue base color; dull (faded) brindling; white tail tip.

(*ii*) Fawn Danes. Golden yellow up to deep golden yellow color with a deep black mask. The golden deep-yellow color must always be given the preference. Small white spots at the chest and toes are not desirable. Faults: Yellowish-gray, bluish-yellow, grayish-blue, dirty yellow color (drab color), lack of black mask.

(*iii*) Blue Danes. The color must be a pure steel blue as far as possible without any tinge of yellow, black or mouse gray. Faults: Any deviation from a pure steel-blue coloration.

(*iv*) Black Danes. Glossy black. Faults: Yellow-black, brown-black or blue-black. White markings, such as stripes on the chest, speckled chest and markings on the paws are permitted but not desirable.

(*v*) Harlequin Danes. Base color: pure white with black torn patches irregularly and well-distributed over the entire body; pure white neck preferred. The black patches should never be large enough to give the appearance of a blanket nor so small as to give a stippled or dappled effect. (Eligible but less desirable are a few small gray spots, also pointings where instead of a pure white base with black spots there is a white base with single black hairs showing through which tend to give a salt and pepper or dirty effect.) Faults: White base color with a few large spots; bluish-gray pointed background.

(c) Size (5 points)—The male should not be less than 30 inches at the shoulders, but it is preferable that he be 32 inches or more, providing he is well proportioned to his height. The female should not be less than 28 inches at the shoulders, but it is preferable that she be 30 inches or more, providing she is well proportioned to her height.

(d) Condition of Coat (4 points)—The coat should be very short and thick, smooth and glossy. Faults: Excessively long hair (stand-off coat); dull hair (indicating malnutrition, worms and negligent care).

(e) Substance (3 points)—Substance is that sufficiency of bone and muscle which rounds out a balance with the frame. Faults: Lightweight whippety Danes; coarse, ungainly proportioned Danes; always there should be balance.

2. Movement 28 points

(a) Gait (10 points). Long, easy, springy stride with no tossing or rolling of body. The back line should move smoothly, parallel to the ground. The gait of the Great Dane should denote strength and power. The rear legs should have drive. The forelegs should track smoothly and straight. The Dane should track in two parallel straight lines. Faults: Short steps. The rear quarters should not pitch. The forelegs should not have a hackney gait (forced or choppy stride). When moving rapidly the Great Dane should not pace for the reason that it causes excessive side-to-side rolling of the body and thus reduces endurance.

(b) Rear End (Croup, Legs, Paws) (10 points)—The croup must be full, slightly drooping and must continue imperceptibly to the tail root. Hind legs, the first thighs (from hip joint to knee) are broad and muscular. The second thighs (from knee to hock joint) are strong and long. Seen from the side, the angulation of the first thigh with the body, of the second thigh with the first thigh, and the pastern root with the second thigh should be very moderate, neither too straight nor too exaggerated. Seen from the rear, the hock joints appear to be perfectly straight, turned neither towards the inside nor towards the outside. Faults: A croup which is too straight; a croup which slopes downward too steeply; and too narrow a croup. Hind legs: Soft, flabby, poorly muscled thighs; cowhocks which are the result of the hock joint turning inward and the hock and rear paws turning outward; barrel legs, the result of the hock joints being too far apart; steep rear. As seen from the side, a steep rear is the result of the angles of the rear legs forming almost a straight line; overangulation is the result of exaggerated angles between the first and second thighs and the hocks and is very conducive to weakness. The rear legs should never be too long in proportion to the front legs.

Paws, round and turned neither towards the inside nor towards the outside. Toes short, highly arched and well closed. Nails short, strong and as dark as possible. Faults: Spreading toes (splay foot); bent, long toes (rabbit paws); toes turned towards the outside or towards the inside. Furthermore, the fifth toe on the hind legs appearing at a higher position and with wolf's claw or spur; excessively long nails; light-colored nails.

(c) Front End (Shoulders, Legs, Paws) (8 points)—**Shoulders.** The shoulder blades must be strong and sloping and seen from the side, must form as nearly as possible a right angle in its articulation with the humerus (upper arm) to give a long stride. A line from the upper tip of the shoulder to the back of the elbow joint should be as nearly perpendicular as possible. Since all dogs lack a clavicle (collar bone) the ligaments and muscles holding the shoulder blade to the rib cage must be well developed, firm and secure to prevent loose shoulders. Faults: Steep shoulders, which occur if the shoulder blade does not slope sufficiently; overangulation; loose shoulders which occur if the Dane is flabby muscled, or if the elbow is turned toward the outside; loaded shoulders.

Forelegs. The upper arm should be strong and muscular. Seen from the side or front the strong lower arms run absolutely straight to the pastern joints. Seen from the front, the forelegs and the pastern roots should form perpendicular lines to the ground. Seen from the side, the pastern root should slope only very slightly forward. Faults: Elbows turned toward the inside or toward the outside, the former position caused mostly by too narrow or too shallow a chest, bringing the front legs too closely together and at the same time turning the entire lower part of the leg outward; the latter position causes the front legs to spread too far apart, with the pastern roots and paws usually turned inwards. Seen from the side, a considerable bend in the pastern toward the front indicates weakness and is in most cases connected with stretched and spread toes (splay foot); seen from the side a forward bow in the forearm (chair leg); an excessively knotty bulge in the front of the pastern joint.

Paws. Round and turned neither toward the inside nor toward the outside. Toes short, highly arched and well closed. Nails short, strong and as dark as possible. Faults: Spreading toes (splay foot), bent, long toes (rabbit paws); toes turned toward the outside or toward the inside; light-colored nails.

3. Head 20 points

(a) Head Conformation (12 points)—Long, narrow, distinguished, expressive, finely chiseled,

HUNGARIAN VIZSLA

(THE KENNEL CLUB—GUNDOG GROUP)

Characteristics. The Hungarian Vizsla should be lively and intelligent, obedient but sensitive, very affectionate and easily trained. It was bred for hunting for fur and feather on open ground or in thick cover, pointing and retrieving from both land and water.

General Appearance. A medium sized dog of distinguished appearance, robust but not too heavily boned.

Head and Skull. The head should be gaunt and noble. The skull should be moderately wide between the ears with a median line down the forehead and a moderate stop. The muzzle should be a little longer than the skull and although tapering should be well squared at the end. The nostrils should be well developed, broad and wide. The jaws strong and powerful. The lips should cover the jaws completely and should be neither loose nor pendulous. The nose should be brown.

Eyes. Neither deep nor prominent, of medium size, being a shade darker in colour than the coat. The shape of the eyes should be slightly oval and the eyelids should fit tightly. A yellow or black eye is objectionable.

Ears. The ears should be moderately low set, proportionately long with a thin skin and hang down close to the cheeks, should be rounded 'V' shaped, not fleshy.

Mouth. Sound white teeth meeting in a scissor bite, full dentition is desirable.

Forequarters. Shoulders should be well laid and muscular, elbows straight pointing neither in nor out, the forearm should be long.

Body. Back should be level, short, well muscled, withers high. The chest should be moderately broad and deep with prominent breast bone. The distance from the withers to the lowest part of the chest should be equal to the distance from the chest to the ground. The ribs should be well sprung and the belly should be tight with a slight tuck up beneath the loin. The croup should be well muscled.

Hindquarters. Should be straight when viewed from the rear, the thighs should be well developed with moderate angulation, the hocks well let down.

Feet. Rounded with toes short, arched and well closed. A cat like foot is desirable, hare foot is objectionable. Nails short, strong and a shade darker in colour than coat, dewclaws should be removed.

Gait. Graceful and elegant with a lively trot and ground covering gallop.

Tail. Should be of moderate thickness, rather low set, with one third docked off. Whilst moving should be held horizontally.

Coat. Should be short and straight, dense and coarse and feel greasy to the touch.

Colour. Russet gold. Small white marks on chest and feet, though acceptable, are not desirable.

Weight and Size. Optimum Weight $48\frac{1}{2}$ to 66 lbs. Height at Withers; dogs $22\frac{1}{2}$ to 25 inches, bitches 21 to $23\frac{1}{2}$ inches.

VIZSLA

(AMERICAN KENNEL CLUB—GROUP I: SPORTING DOGS)

General Appearance. That of a medium-sized hunting dog of quite distinguished appearance. Robust but rather lightly built, his short coat is an attractive rusty-gold, and his tail is docked. He is a dog of power and drive in the field, and a tractable and affectionate companion in the home.
Head. Lean but muscular. The skull is moderately wide between the ears, with a median line down the forehead. Stop moderate. The muzzle is a trifle longer than the skull and, although tapering, is well squared at its end. Jaws strong, with well-developed white teeth meeting in a scissors bite. The lips cover the jaws completely but they are neither loose nor pendulous. Nostrils slightly open, the nose brown. A black or slate-gray nose is objectionable.
Ears. Thin, silky, and proportionately long, with rounded-leather ends; set fairly low and hanging close to the cheeks.
Eyes. Medium in size and depth of setting, their surrounding tissue covering the whites, and the iris or color portion harmonizing with the shade of the coat. A yellow eye is objectionable.
Neck. Strong, smooth, and muscular; moderately long, arched, and devoid of dewlap. It broadens nicely into shoulders which are well laid back.
Body. Strong and well proportioned. The back is short, the withers high, and the topline slightly rounded over the loin to the set-on of the tail. Chest moderately broad and deep, and reaching down to the elbows. Ribs well sprung, and underline exhibiting a slight tuck-up beneath the loin.
Legs and Feet. Forelegs straight, strong, and muscular, with elbows close. The hindlegs have well-developed thighs, with moderate angulation at stifles and hocks. Too much angulation at the hocks is as faulty as too little. The hocks, which are well let down, are equidistant from each other from the hock joint to the ground. Cowhocks are faulty. Feet are cat-like, round and compact, with toes close. Nails are brown and short; pads thick and tough. Dewclaws, if any, to be removed. Hare feet are objectionable.
Tail. Set just below the level of the back, thicker at the root, and docked one third off.
Coat. Short, smooth, dense, and close-lying, without woolly undercoat.
Color. Solid. Rusty gold or rather dark sandy yellow in different shades, with darker shades preferred. Dark brown and pale yellow are undesirable. Small white spots on chest or feet are not faulted.
Temperament. That of the natural hunter endowed with a good nose and above-average ability to take training. Lively, gentle-mannered, and demonstratively affectionate. Fearless, and with well-developed protective instinct.
Gait. Far-reaching, light-footed, graceful, smooth.
Size. Males, 22 to 24 inches; females, 21 to 23 inches at the highest point of the shoulders. Any dog measuring over or under these limits shall be considered faulty, the seriousness of the fault depending on the extent of the deviation. Any dog that measures more than 2 inches over or under these limits shall be disqualified.

DISQUALIFICATION

Deviation in height of more than 2 inches from standard either way.

Approved December 10, 1963

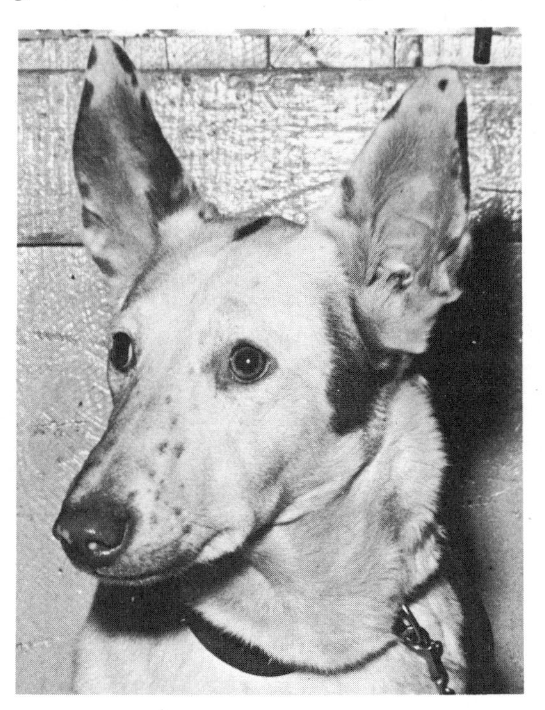

IBIZAN HOUND

(THE KENNEL CLUB—HOUND GROUP)

Characteristics. The skeleton is very strong; the gait is a hesitant trot; they are highly agile, very astute, intelligent and docile; they jump to a great height without a take-off run. They hunt more by scent and hearing that by sight and only bark when sighting or hearing the quarry. They all retrieve and point to the game; they break off the point easily and as a rule they whirl their tails during the point. They are good retrievers.

Head. Long and narrow, shaped like a sharp cone truncated near its base, extremely lean.

Skull. Long and flattened, prominent occipital bone, frontal depression (stop) lightly defined, forehead narrow.

Ears. Always pricked, turned forwards, horizontally sideways or backwards: upwards when the dog is alert, very mobile; the centre of their base placed at the level of the eyes, in shape that of an elongated rhomboid, truncated at one third of its longer diagonal, slender and short, without hair inside.

Eyes. Slanting and small, light amber in colour, resembling caramel, very intelligent but not very noble glance.

Nose. Slightly convex, its length from the eyes to the point of the muzzle is the same as from between the eyes to the occiput.

Muzzle. Prominent, protruding beyond the lower jaw: flesh coloured, harmonizing with the coat, open nostrils.

Jaws. Very strong and lean.

Lips. Delicate and puckered.

Teeth. Exactly opposed (level bite), white and well arranged.

Neck. Very lean, fairly long, muscular and slightly arched.

Withers. Loose.

Shoulders. Sloping.

Back. Straight.

Loins. Arched and of medium width.

Rump. Sloping.

Tail. Long, when passed between the legs should reach at least to the spine; in repose, hangs naturally; in action, at times shaped like a very stiff sickle and at times erect, but never curled at all.

Chest. Deep, narrow and long, breastbone forming a very sharp and prominent angle; rib-cage flattened.

Belly. Good waistline.

Hindquarters. Long thighs, strong and lean; hocks bent, broad and well let down.

Feet. Like a hare's; paws long and tight; well feathered between the toes; claws very strong and generally white, sometimes the colour of the coat; pads very firm.

Coat. Smooth, wire or long, but the last rough; rather shorter on the head and ears and longer on the back of the thighs and the underside of the tail.

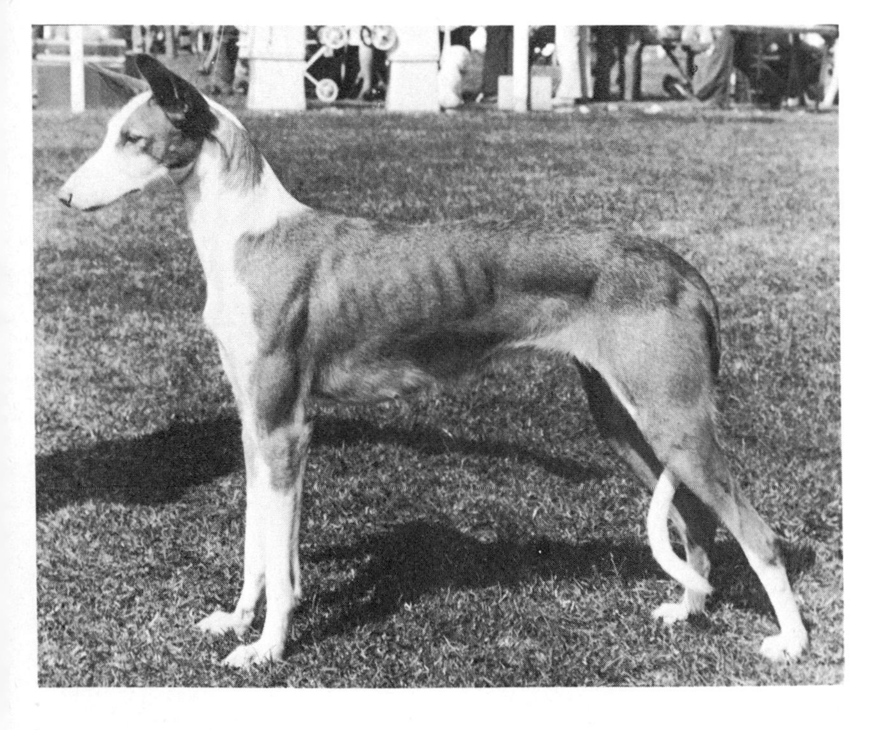

Colour. White and red, white and tawny; or all one colour, white, red or tawny; red is preferable to tawny and all other colours are barred.
Height. Dogs $23\frac{1}{2}$ to 26 inches. Bitches $22\frac{1}{2}$ to 25 inches.
Weight. Dogs, about $49\frac{1}{2}$ lbs, Bitches about 42 lbs.
Faults. Folded (button) ears, dark eyes, teeth which do not exactly meet top and bottom; breastbone poorly defined; forelegs spread, narrowing a lot towards the lower end of the forearms; forefeet turned out; broad loins; broad rump; broad, rounded thighs with large veins.

POINTS

General Appearance, stature and movement	25
Head	10
Eyes	4
Ears	6
Neck	5
Body	20
Limbs	20
Tail	4
Coat and Colour	6
Total	100

ICELAND DOG

(THE KENNEL CLUB—UTILITY GROUP)

General Appearance. A Spitz type of slightly under middle size, lightly built, with a game temperament.
Head. Light, rather broad between the ears.
Skull. Broad and domed.
Muzzle. Rather shorter than long; stop, marked but not sharp.
Nose. Black.
Lips. Short and tight.
Ears. Large at the base, triangular in shape, pointed and erect.
Eyes. Small and round; dark in colour with a lively expression.
Neck. Short, strong and slightly arched, carrying the head high.
Shoulders. Straight, not sloping.
Chest. Large and deep.
Belly. Drawn up.
Body. Strong and rather short but light.
Legs. Clean, straight and muscular; stifles not too bent.
Feet. Oval, pads well-developed.
Tail. Of moderate length, very bushy and carried curled over the back.
Coat. Hard, of medium length, longer round the neck, on the thighs and at the underside of the tail. The coat is flat on the body and is short on the head and the legs; forelegs, without feather.
Colour. White with fawn markings, golden, light fawn with black tips to long hairs, and occasionally all black.
Height. From 15 to 18 inches.
Weight. About 30 lbs.

IRISH SETTER (RED)

(THE KENNEL CLUB—GUNDOG GROUP)

General Appearance. Must be racy, full of quality, and kindly in expression

Head and Skull. The head should be long and lean, not narrow or snipy, and not coarse at the ears. The skull oval (from ear to ear), having plenty of brain room, and with well-defined occipital protuberance. Brows raised, showing stop. The muzzle moderately deep, and fairly square at end. From the stop to the point of the nose should be long, the nostrils wide, and the jaws of nearly equal length, flews not to be pendulous. The colour of the nose: dark mahogany, or dark walnut, or black.

Eyes. Should be dark hazel or dark brown and ought not to be too large.

Ears. The ears should be of moderate size, fine in texture, set on low, well back; and hanging in a neat fold close to the head.

Mouth. Not over or undershot.

Neck. Should be moderately long, very muscular, but not too thick, slightly arched, free from all tendency to throatiness.

Forequarters. The shoulders to be fine at the points, deep and sloping well back. The chest as deep as possible, rather narrow in front. The fore-legs should be straight and sinewy, having plenty of bone, with elbows free, well let down, not inclined either in or out.

Body. Should be proportionate, the ribs well sprung, leaving plenty of lung room. Loins muscular, slightly arched.

Hindquarters. Should be wide and powerful. The hindlegs from hip to hock should be long and muscular; from hock to heel short and strong. The stifle and hock joints well bent, and not inclined either in or out.

Feet. Should be small, very firm, toes strong, close together and arched.

Tail. Should be of moderate length, proportionate to the size of the body, set on rather low, strong at root, and tapering to a fine point; to be carried as nearly as possible on a level with or below the back.

Coat and Feathering. On the head, front of the legs, and tips of the ears, should be short and fine, but on all other parts of the body and legs it ought to be of moderate length, flat, and as free as possible from curl or wave. The feather on the upper portion of the ears should be long and silky; on the back of fore- and hindlegs should be long and fine; a fair amount of hair on the belly, forming a nice fringe, which may extend on chest and throat. Feet to be well feathered between the toes. Tail to have a nice fringe of moderately long hair, decreasing in length as it approaches the point. All feathering to be as straight and as flat as possible.

Colour. The colour should be rich chestnut, with no trace whatever of black; white on chest, throat or toes, or a small star on the forehead, or a narrow streak or blaze on the nose or face not to disqualify.

SETTER, IRISH

(AMERICAN KENNEL CLUB—GROUP I: SPORTING DOGS)

General Appearance. The Irish Setter is an active, aristocratic bird-dog, rich red in color, substantial yet elegant in build. Standing over two feet tall at the shoulder, the dog has a straight, fine, glossy coat, longer on ears, chest, tail, and back of legs. Afield he is a swift-moving hunter; at home, a sweet-natured, trainable companion. His is a rollicking personality.

Head. Long and lean, its length at least double the width between the ears. The brow is raised, showing a distinct stop midway between the tip of nose and the well-defined occiput (rear point of skull). Thus the nearly level line from occiput to brow is set a little above, and parallel to, the straight and equal line from eye to nose. The skull is oval when viewed from above or front; very slightly domed when viewed in profile. Beauty of head is emphasized by delicate chiseling along the muzzle, around and below the eyes, and along the cheeks. Muzzle moderately deep, nostrils wide, jaws of nearly equal length. Upper lips fairly square but not pendulous, the underline of the jaws being almost parallel with the top line of the muzzle. The teeth meet in a scissors bite in which the upper incisors fit closely over the lower, or they may meet evenly.

Nose. Black or chocolate.

Eyes. Somewhat almond-shaped, of medium size, placed rather well apart; neither deep-set nor bulging. Color, dark to medium brown. Expression soft yet alert.

Ears. Set well back and low, not above level of eye. Leather thin, hanging in a neat fold close to the head, and nearly long enough to reach the nose.

Neck. Moderately long, strong but not thick, and slightly arched; free from throatiness, and fitting smoothly into the shoulders.

Body. Sufficiently long to permit a straight and free stride. Shoulder blades long, wide, sloping well back, fairly close together at the top, and joined in front to long upper arms angled to bring the elbows slightly rearward along the brisket. Chest deep, reaching approximately to the elbows; rather narrow in front. Ribs well sprung. Loins of moderate length, muscular and slightly arched. Top line of body from withers to tail slopes slightly downward without sharp drop at the croup. Hindquarters should be wide and powerful with broad, well-developed thighs.

Legs and Feet. All legs sturdy, with plenty of bone, and strong, nearly straight pastern. Feet rather small, very firm, toes arched and close. Forelegs straight and sinewy, the elbows moving freely. Hind legs long and muscular from hip to hock, short and nearly perpendicular from hock to ground; well angulated at stifle and hock joints, which, like the elbows, incline neither in nor out.

Tail. Strong at root, tapering to fine point, about long enough to reach the hock. Carriage straight or curving slightly upward, nearly level with the back.

Coat. Short and fine on head, forelegs, and tips of ears; on all other parts, of moderate length and flat. Feathering long and silky on ears; on back of forelegs and thighs long and fine, with a pleasing fringe of hair on belly and brisket extending onto the chest. Feet well feathered between the toes. Fringe on tail moderately long and tapering. All coat and feathering as straight and free as possible from curl or wave.

Color. Mahogany or rich chestnut red, with no trace of black. A small amount of white on chest, throat, or toes, or a narrow centered streak on skull, is not to be penalized.

Size. There is no disqualification as to size. The make and fit of all parts and their over-all balance in the animal are rated more important. Twenty-seven inches at the withers and a show weight of about 70 pounds is considered ideal for a dog; the bitch 25 inches, 60 pounds. Variance beyond an inch up or down to be discouraged.

Gait. At the trot the gait is big, very lively, graceful, and efficient. The head is held high. The hindquarters drive smoothly and with great power. The forelegs reach well ahead as if to pull in the ground, without giving the appearance of a hackney gait. The dog runs as he stands: straight. Seen from the front or rear, the forelegs, as well as the hindlegs below the hock joint, move perpendicularly to the ground, with some tendency toward a single track as speed increases. But a crossing or weaving of the legs, front or back, is objectionable.

Balance. At his best the lines of the Irish Setter so satisfy in over-all balance that artists have termed him the most beautiful of all dogs. The correct specimen always exhibits balance whether standing or in motion. Each part of the dog flows and fits smoothly into its neighboring parts without calling attention to itself.

Approved June 14, 1960

IRISH TERRIER

(THE KENNEL CLUB—TERRIER GROUP)

Characteristics. Dogs that are very game are usually surly or snappish. The Irish Terrier as a breed is an exception, being remarkably good tempered, notably so with humans, it being admitted, however, that he is perhaps a little too ready to resent interference on the part of other dogs. There is a heedless, reckless pluck about the Irish Terrier which is characteristic, and coupled with the head-long dash, blind to all consequences, with which he rushes at his adversary, has earned for the breed the proud epithet of 'The Dare Devils.' When 'off duty' they are characterized by a quiet caress-inviting appearance, and when one sees them endearingly, timidly pushing their heads into their master's hands, it is difficult to realize that on occasions, at the 'set on', they can prove that they have the courage of a lion, and will fight unto the last breath in their bodies. They develop an extraordinary devotion for, and have been known to track their masters almost incredible distances.

General Appearance. The dog must present an active, lively, lithe and wiry appearance; with lots of substance, at the same time free of clumsiness, as speed and endurance, as well as power, are very essential. They must be neither 'cloddy' nor 'cobby', but should be framed on the 'lines of speeds', showing a graceful 'racing outline'.

Head and Skull. Head long; skull flat, and rather narrow between ears, getting slightly narrower towards the eye; free from wrinkles; stop hardly visible except in profile. The jaw must be strong and muscular, but not too full in the cheek, and of a good punishing length. The foreface should not 'dish' or fall away quickly between or below the eyes, where it should be well made up, being relieved of 'wedginess' by delicate chiselling. The hair should be crisp and only sufficiently long to impart an appearance of additional strength to the foreface. Lips should be well fitting and externally almost black in colour. The nose must be black.

Eyes. A dark colour, small, not prominent, and full of life, fire and intelligence. A light or yellow eye is a fault.

Ears. Small and V-shaped, of moderate thickness, set well on the head, and dropping forward closely to the cheek. The top of the folded ear should be well above the level of the skull. The ear must be free of fringe, and the hair thereon shorter and darker in colour than the body.

Mouth. The teeth should be even, strong and free from discoloration, the top teeth slightly overlapping the lower.

Neck. Should be of a fair length and gradually widening towards the shoulders, well carried, and free of throatiness. There is generally a slight frill at each side of the neck, running nearly to the corner of the ear.

Forequarters. The shoulders must be fine, long,

and sloping well into the back. The legs moderately long, well set from the shoulders, perfectly straight, with plenty of bone and muscle; the elbows working freely clear of the sides; pasterns short and straight, hardly noticeable. The forelegs should be moved straight forward when travelling. The hair on the legs should be dense and crisp.

Body. Chest deep and muscular, but neither full nor wide. Body moderately long; back should be strong and straight, with no appearance of slackness behind the shoulders; the loin muscular and slightly arched; ribs fairly sprung, rather deep than round, and well-ribbed back.

Hindquarters. Should be strong and muscular, the thighs powerful, hocks near the ground, stifles moderately bent. The hindlegs should be moved straight forward when travelling, the stifles not turned outwards. The hair on the legs should be dense and crisp.

Feet. Should be strong, tolerably round, and moderately small, toes arched, and neither turned out nor in; black toe nails most desirable. Pads must be sound and free from cracks or horny excrescences.

Tail. Generally docked to about three quarters; should be free of fringe or feather, but well covered with rough hair, set on pretty high, carried gaily, but not over the back or curled.

Coat. Hard and wiry, having a broken appearance, free of softness or silkiness, not so long as to hide the outline of the body, particularly in the hindquarters, straight and flat, no shagginess and free of lock or curl. At the base of these stiff hairs is a growth of finer and softer hair, usually termed the undercoat.

Colour. Should be 'whole-coloured', the most preferable colours being a bright red, red wheaten, or yellow red. White sometimes appears on chest and feet and is more objectionable on the latter than on the former, as a speck of white on chest is frequently to be seen in all self-coloured breeds.

Weight and Size. The most desirable weight in Show condition is, for a dog, 27 lbs, and for a bitch, 25 lbs. Height at shoulders, approximately 18 inches.

IRISH TERRIER

(AMERICAN KENNEL CLUB—GROUP IV: TERRIERS)

Head. Long, but in nice proportion to the rest of the body; the skull flat, rather narrow between the ears, and narrowing slightly toward the eyes; free from wrinkle, with the stop hardly noticeable except in profile. The jaws must be strong and muscular, but not too full in the cheek, and of good punishing length. The foreface must not fall away appreciably between or below the eyes; instead, the modeling should be delicate. An exaggerated foreface, or a noticeably short foreface, disturbs the proper balance of the head and is not desirable. The foreface and the skull from occiput to stop should be approximately equal in length. Excessive muscular development of the cheeks, or bony development of the temples, conditions which are described by the fancier as 'checky', or 'strong in head', or 'thick in skull' are objectionable. The 'bumpy' head, in which the skull presents two lumps of bony structure above the eyes, is to be faulted. The hair on the upper and lower jaws should be similar in quality and texture to that of the body, and of sufficient length to present an appearance of additional strength and finish to the foreface. Either the profuse, goat-like beard, or the absence of beard, is unsightly and undesirable.

Teeth. Should be strong and even, white and sound; and neither overshot nor undershot.

Lips. Should be close and well-fitting, almost black in color.

Nose. Must be black.

Eyes. Dark brown in color; small, not prominent; full of life, fire and intelligence, showing an intense expression. The light or yellow eye is most objectionable, and is a bad fault.

Ears. Small and V-shaped; of moderate thickness; set well on the head, and dropping forward closely toward the outside corner of the eye. The top of the folded ear should be well above the level of the skull. A 'dead' ear, hound-like in appearance, must be severely penalized. It is not characteristic of the Irish Terrier. The hair should be much shorter and somewhat darker in color than that on the body.

Neck. Should be of fair length and gradually widening toward the shoulders; well and proudly carried, and free from throatiness. Generally there is a slight frill in the hair at each side of the neck, extending almost to the corner of the ear.

Shoulders and Chest. Shoulders must be fine, long, and sloping well into the back. The chest should be deep and muscular, but neither full nor wide.

Body. The body should be moderately long. The short back is not characteristic of the Irish Terrier, and is extremely objectionable. The back must be strong and straight, and free from an appearance of slackness or 'dip' behind the shoulders. The loin should be strong and muscular, and slightly arched, the ribs fairly sprung, deep rather than round, reaching to the level of the elbow. The bitch may be slightly longer than the dog.

Hindquarters. Should be strong and muscular; thighs powerful; hocks near the ground; stifles moderately bent.

Stern. Should be docked, taking off about one quarter. It should be set on rather high, but not curled. It should be of good strength and substance; of fair length and well covered with harsh, rough hair.

Feet and Legs. The feet should be strong, tolerably round, and moderately small; toes arched and turned neither out nor in, with dark toenails.

The pads should be deep, and must be perfectly sound and free from corns. Cracks alone do not necessarily indicate unsound feet. In fact, all breeds have cracked pads occasionally, from various causes.

Legs moderately long, well set from the shoulders, perfectly straight, with plenty of bone and muscle; the elbows working clear of the sides; pasterns short, straight, and hardly noticeable. Both fore and hind legs should move straight forward when traveling; the stifles should not turn outwards. 'Cowhocks'—that is, the hocks turned in and the feet turned out—are intolerable. The legs should be free from feather and covered with hair of similar texture to that on the body to give proper finish to the dog.

Coat. Should be dense and wiry in texture, rich in quality, having a broken appearance, but still lying fairly close to the body, the hairs growing so closely and strongly together that when parted with the fingers the skin is hardly visible; free of softness or silkiness, and not so long as to alter the outline of the body, particularly in the hindquarters. On the sides of the body the coat is never as harsh as on the back and quarters, but it should be plentiful and of good texture. At the base of the stiff outer coat there should be a growth of finer and softer hair, lighter in color, termed the undercoat. Single coats, which are without any undercoat, and wavy coats are undesirable; the curly and the kinky coats are most objectionable.

Color. Should be whole-colored: bright red, golden red, red wheaten, or wheaten. A small patch of white on the chest, frequently encountered in all whole-colored breeds, is permissible but not desirable. White on any other part of the body is most objectionable. Puppies sometimes have black hair at birth, which should disappear before they are full grown.

Size. The most desirable weight in show condition is 27 lbs for the dog and 25 lbs for the bitch. The height at the shoulder should be approximately 18 inches. These figures serve as a guide to both breeder and judge. In the show ring, however, the informed judge readily identifies the oversized or undersized Irish Terrier by its conformation and general appearance. Weight is not the last word in judgement. It is of the greatest importance to select, insofar as possible, terriers of moderate and generally accepted size, possessing the other various characters.

General Appearance. The overall appearance of the Irish Terrier is important. In conformation he must be more than a sum of his parts. He must be all-of-a-piece, a balanced vital picture of symmetry, proportion and harmony. Furthermore, he must convey character. This terrier must be active, lithe and wiry in movement, with great animation; sturdy and strong in substance and bone structure, but at the same time free from clumsiness, for speed, power and endurance are most essential. The Irish Terrier must be neither 'cobby' or 'cloddy', but should be built on lines of speed with a graceful, racing outline.

Temperament. The temperament of the Irish Terrier reflects his early background: he was family pet, guard dog, and hunter. He is good tempered, spirited and game. It is of the utmost importance that the Irish Terrier show fire and animation. There is a heedless, reckless pluck about the Irish Terrier which is characteristic, and which, coupled with the headlong dash, blind to all consequences, with which he rushes at his adversary, has earned for the breed the proud epithet of 'Daredevil'. He is of good temper, most affectionate, and absolutely loyal to mankind. Tender and forebearing with those he loves, this rugged, stout-hearted terrier will guard his master, his mistress and children with utter contempt for danger or hurt. His life is one continuous and eager offering of loyal and faithful companionship and devotion. He is ever on guard, and stands between his home and all that threatens.

Approved December 10, 1968

IRISH WOLFHOUND

(THE KENNEL CLUB—HOUND GROUP)

General Appearance. The Irish Wolfhound should not be quite so heavy or massive as the Great Dane, but more so than the Deerhound, which in general type he should otherwise resemble. Of great size and commanding appearance, very muscular, strongly though gracefully built, movements easy and active; head and neck carried high; the tail carried with an upward sweep with a slight curve towards the extremity.
Head and Skull. Long, the frontal bones of the forehead very slightly raised and very little indentation between the eyes. Skull, not too broad. Muzzle, long and moderately pointed.
Eyes. Dark.
Ears. Small and Greyhound-like in carriage.
Neck. Rather long, very strong and muscular, well arched, without dewlap or loose skin about the throat.
Forequarters. Shoulders muscular, giving breadth of chest, set sloping. Elbows well under, turned neither inwards nor outwards. Leg and forearm muscular, and the whole leg strong and quite straight.
Body. Chest, very deep. Breast, wide. Back, rather long than short. Loins arched. Belly well drawn up.
Hindquarters. Muscular thighs and second thighs; long and strong as in the Greyhound, and hocks well let down and turning neither in nor out.
Feet. Moderately large and round, turned neither inwards nor outwards. Toes well arched and closed. Nails very strong and curved.
Tail. Long and slightly curved, of moderate thickness, and well covered with hair.
Coat. Rough and hardy on body, legs and head; especially wiry and long over eyes and under jaw.
Colour. The recognized colours are grey, brindle, red, black, pure white, fawn, or any colour that appears in the Deerhound.
Weight and Size. The minimum height and weight of dogs should be 31 inches and 120 lb; of bitches, 28 inches and 90lb. *Anything below this should be heavily penalized.* Great size, including height at shoulder and proportionate length of body, is the desideratum to be aimed at, and it is desired to firmly establish a breed that shall average from 32 to 34 inches in dogs, showing the requisite power, activity, courage and symmetry.
Faults. Too light or heavy a head, too highly arched frontal bone. Large ears. Ears hanging flat to the face. Short neck. Full dewlap. Too narrow or too broad a chest. Sunken, hollow or quite straight back. Bent forelegs. Overbent fetlocks. Twisted feet. Spreading toes. Too curly a tail. Weak hindquarters and a general want of muscle. Too short in body. Pink or liver-coloured eyelids. Lips and nose any colour other than black. Very light eyes.

IRISH WOLFHOUND

(AMERICAN KENNEL CLUB—GROUP II: HOUNDS)

General Appearance. Of great size and commanding appearance, the Irish Wolfhound is remarkable in combining power and swiftness with keen sight. The largest and tallest of the galloping hounds, in general type he is a rough-coated, Greyhoundlike breed; very muscular, strong though gracefully built; movements easy and active; head and neck carried high, the tail carried with an upward sweep with a slight curve towards the extremity. The minimum height and weight of dogs should be 32 inches and 120 lbs; of bitches, 30 inches and 105 lbs; these to apply only to hounds over 18 months of age. Anything below this should be debarred from competition. Great size, including height at shoulder and proportionate length of body, is the desideratum to be aimed at, and it is desired to firmly establish a race that shall average from 32 to 34 inches in dogs, showing the requisite power, activity, courage and symmetry.

Head. Long, the frontal bones of the forehead very slightly raised and very little indentation between the eyes. Skull, not too broad. Muzzle, long and moderately pointed. Ears, small and Greyhoundlike in carriage.

Neck. Rather long, very strong and muscular, well arched, without dewlap or loose skin about the throat.

Chest. Very deep. Breast, wide.

Back. Rather long than short. Loins arched.

Tail. Long and slightly curved, of moderate thickness, and well covered with hair.

Belly. Well drawn up.

Forequarters. Shoulders, muscular, giving breadth of chest, set sloping. Elbows well under, neither turned inwards nor outwards.

Leg. Forearm muscular, and the whole leg strong and quite straight.

Hindquarters. Muscular thighs and second thigh long and strong as in the Greyhound, and hocks well let down and turning neither in nor out.

Feet. Moderately large and round, neither turned inwards nor outwards. Toes, well arched and closed. Nails, very strong and curved.

Hair. Rough and hard on body, legs and head; especially wiry and long over eyes and underjaw.

Color and Markings. The recognized colors are gray, brindle, red, black, pure white, fawn, or any other color that appears in the Deerhound.

Faults. Too light or heavy a head, too highly arched frontal bone; large ears and hanging flat to the face; short neck; full dewlap; too narrow or too broad a chest; sunken or hollow or quite straight back; bent forelegs; overbent fetlocks; twisted feet; spreading toes, too curly a tail; weak hindquarters and a general want of muscle; too short in body. Lips or nose liver-colored or lacking pigmentation.

LIST OF POINTS IN ORDER OF MERIT

1. *Typical.* The Irish Wolfhound is a rough-coated Greyhoundlike breed, the tallest of the coursing hounds and remarkable in combining power and swiftness. 2. *Great* size and commanding appearance. 3. Movements easy and active. 4. Head, long and level, carried high. 5. Forelegs, heavily boned, quite straight; elbows well set under. 6. Thighs long and muscular; second thighs, well muscled, stifles nicely bent. 7. Coat, rough and hard, specially wiry and long over eyes and under jaw. 8. Body, long, well ribbed up, with ribs well sprung, and great breadth across hips. 9. Loins arched, belly well drawn up. 10. Ears, small, with Greyhoundlike carriage. 11. Feet, moderately large and round; toes, close, well arched. 12. Neck, long, well arched and very strong. 13. Chest, very deep, moderately broad. 14. Shoulders, muscular, set sloping. 15. Tail, long and slightly curved. 16. Eyes, dark.

Note: The above in no way alters the 'Standard of Excellence,' which must in all cases be rigidly adhered to; they simply give the various points in order of merit. If in any case they appear at variance with Standard of Excellence, it is the latter which is correct.

Approved September 12, 1950

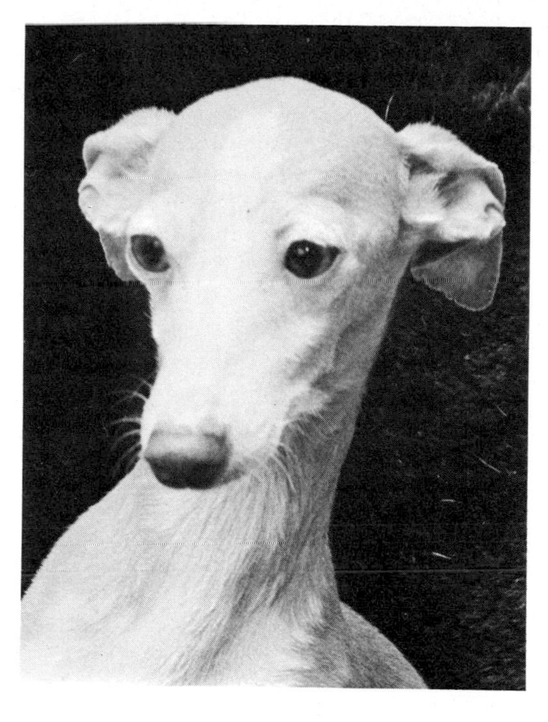

ITALIAN GREYHOUND

(THE KENNEL CLUB—TOY GROUP)

Characteristics. High stepping and free action.
General Appearance. A miniature Greyhound, more slender in all proportions, and of ideal elegance and grace in shape, symmetry and action.
Head and Skull. Skull long, flat and narrow. Muzzle very fine. Nose dark in colour.
Eyes. Rather large, bright, and full of expression.
Ears. Rose-shaped, placed well back, soft and delicate.
Mouth. Teeth level.
Neck. Should be long and gracefully arched.
Forequarters. Shoulders long and sloping. Legs straight, well set under the shoulders; fine pasterns; small delicate bones.
Body. Chest deep and narrow. Back curved, and drooping at the hindquarters.
Hindquarters. Hocks well let down. Thighs muscular.
Feet. Long, hare-feet.
Tail. Rather long, fine, with low carriage.
Coat. Skin fine and supple. Hair, thin and glossy, like satin.
Colour. Recognized colours, all shades of fawn, white cream, blue, black and fawn and white pied.
Weight and Size. The most desirable weight is from 6 to 8 lbs, and not exceeding 10 lbs.
Faults. Black or blue with tan markings, brindle.

ITALIAN GREYHOUND

(AMERICAN KENNEL CLUB—GROUP V: TOYS)

Description. The Italian Greyhound is very similar to the Greyhound, but much smaller and more slender in all proportions and of ideal elegance and grace.
Head. Narrow and long, tapering to nose, with a slight suggestion of stop.
Skull. Rather long, almost flat.
Muzzle. Long and fine.
Nose. Dark. It may be black or brown or in keeping with the color of the dog. A light or partly pigmented nose is a fault.
Teeth. Scissors bite. A badly undershot or overshot mouth is a fault.
Eyes. Dark, bright, intelligent, medium in size. Very light eyes are a fault.
Ears. Small, fine in texture; thrown back and folded except when alerted, then carried folded at right angles to the head. Erect or button ears severely penalized.
Neck. Long, slender and gracefully arched.
Body. Of medium length, short coupled; high at withers, back curved and drooping at hindquarters, the highest point of curve at start of loin, creating a definite tuck-up at flanks.
Shoulders. Long and sloping.
Chest. Deep and narrow.
Forelegs. Long, straight, set well under shoulder; strong pasterns, fine bone.
Hindquarters. Long, well muscled thigh; hindlegs parallel when viewed from behind, hocks well let down, well bent stifle.
Feet. Hare foot with well arched toes. Removal of dewclaws optional.
Tail. Slender and tapering to a curved end, long enough to reach the hock; set low, carried low. Ring tail a serious fault, gay tail a fault.
Coat. Skin fine and supple, hair short, glossy like satin and soft to the touch.
Color. Any color and markings are acceptable except that a dog with the tan markings normally found on black and tan dogs of other breeds must be disqualified.

Action. High stepping and free, front and hind legs to move forward in a straight line.
Size. Height at withers, ideally 13 inches to 15 inches.

Approved April 13, 1971

JAPANESE AKITA

(THE KENNEL CLUB—UTILITY GROUP)

AKITA

(AMERICAN KENNEL CLUB—GROUP III: WORKING DOGS)

General Appearance. Large, powerful, alert, with much substance and heavy bone. The broad head, forming a blunt triangle, with deep muzzle, small eyes and erect ears carried forward in line with back of neck, is characteristic of the breed. The large, curled tail, balancing the broad head, is also characteristic of the breed.
Head. Massive but in balance with body; free of wrinkle when at ease. Skull flat between ears and broad; jaws square and powerful with minimal dewlap. Head forms a blunt triangle when viewed from above.
Fault. Narrow or snipy nose.
Muzzle. Broad and full. Distance from nose to stop is to distance from stop to occiput as 2 is to 3.
Stop. Well defined, but not too abrupt. A shallow furrow extends well up forehead.
Nose. Broad and black. Liver permitted on white Akitas, but black always preferred.
Disqualification. Butterfly nose or total lack of pigmentation on nose.
Ears. The ears of the Akita are characteristic of the breed. They are strongly erect and small in relation to rest of head. If ear is folded forward for measuring length, tip will touch upper eye rim. Ears are triangular, slightly rounded at tip, wide at base, set wide on head but not too low, and carried slightly forward over eyes in line with back of neck.
Disqualification. Drop or broken ears.
Eyes. Dark brown, small, deep-set and triangular in shape. Eye rims black and tight.
Lips and Tongue. Lips black and not pendulous; tongue pink.
Teeth. Strong with scissors bite preferred, but level bite acceptable.
Disqualification. Noticeably undershot or overshot.
Neck and Body. Neck. Thick and muscular; comparatively short, widening gradually toward shoulders. A pronounced crest blends in with base of skull.
Body. Longer than high, as 10 is to 9 in males; 11 to 9 in bitches. Chest wide and deep; depth of chest is one-half height of dog at shoulder. Ribs well sprung, brisket well developed. Level back with firmly-muscled loin and moderate tuck-up. Skin pliant but not loose.
Serious Faults. Light bone, rangy body.
Tail. Large and full, set high and carried over back or against flank in a three-quarter, full, or double curl, always dipping to or below level of back. On a three-quarter curl, tip drops well down flank. Root large and strong. Tail bone reaches hock when let down. Hair coarse, straight and full, with no appearance of a plume.
Disqualification. Sickle or uncurled tail.
Forequarters and Hindquarters. Forequarters. Shoulders strong and powerful with moderate layback. Forelegs heavy-boned and straight as viewed from front. Angle of pastern 15 degrees forward from vertical.
Faults. Elbows in or out, loose shoulders.
Hindquarters. Width, muscular development and comparable to forequarters. Upper thighs well developed. Stifle moderately bent and hocks well let down, turning neither in nor out.
Dewclaws. On front legs generally not removed; dewclaws on hindlegs generally removed.
Feet. Cat feet, well knuckled up with thick pads. Feet straight ahead.
Coat. Double-coated. Undercoat thick, soft, dense and shorter than outer coat. Outer coat straight, harsh and standing somewhat off body. Hair on head, legs and ears short. Length of hair at withers and rump approximately two inches, which is slightly longer than on rest of body, except tail, where coat is longest and most profuse.
Fault. Any indication of ruff or feathering.
Color. Any color including white; brindle; or pinto. Colors are brilliant and clear and markings are well balanced, with or without mask or blaze. White Akitas have no mask. Pinto has a white background with large, evenly placed patches covering head and more than one-third of body. Undercoat may be a different color from outer coat.
Gait. Brisk and powerful with strides of moderate length. Back remains strong, firm and level. Rear legs move in line with front legs.
Size. Males 26 to 28 inches at the withers; bitches 24 to 26 inches.
Disqualification. Dogs under 25 inches; bitches under 23 inches.
Temperament. Alert and responsive, dignified and courageous. Aggressive toward other dogs.

DISQUALIFICATIONS

Butterfly nose or total lack of pigmentation on nose. Drop or broken ears. Noticeably undershot or overshot. Sickle or uncurled tail. Dogs under 25 inches; bitches under 23 inches.

Approved December 12, 1972

JAPANESE CHIN

(THE KENNEL CLUB—TOY GROUP)

General Appearance. That of a lively, highly-bred little dog, of dainty appearance, smart, compact carriage, and profuse coat. These dogs should be essentially stylish in movement, lifting the feet high when in motion, carrying the tail (which is heavily feathered) proudly, curved or plumed over the back.

Head and Skull. Head should be large for size of dog, with broad skull, rounded in front; muzzle very short and wide and well-cushioned, i.e., the upper lips rounded on each side of the nostrils, which should be large and black, except in the case of red and white dogs, in which brown-coloured noses are as common as black ones.

Eyes. Should be large, dark, set far apart. It is desirable that the white shows in the inner corners, this gives the Japanese that characteristic look of astonishment (wrongly called 'squint') which should on no account be lost.

Ears. Should be small, set wide apart, and high on the dog's head, and carried slightly forward, V-shaped.

Mouth. Should be wide, neither undershot nor overshot.

Neck. Should not be too long.

Forequarters. The legs should be straight and the bone fine; well feathered to the feet.

Body. Should be squarely and compactly built, wide in chest, 'cobby' in shape. The length of the dog's body should be about its height.

Hindquarters. The legs should be straight and the bone fine; well feathered to the thighs behind.

Feet. Should be long and hare-shaped, also feathered.

Tail. Should be well plumed—carried proudly over the back.

Coat. Should be long, profuse and straight, free from curl or wave, and not too flat; it should have a tendency to stand out, more particularly at the frill, with profuse feathering on the tail and thighs.

Colour. The dogs should be either black and white or red and white, i.e., parti-coloured. The term red includes all shades of sable, brindle, lemon and orange, but the brighter and clearer the red the better. The white should be clear and the colour, whether black or red, should be evenly distributed as patches over the body, cheek and ears.

Weight and Size. When divided by weight, classes should be for under and over 7 lbs. In size they vary considerably, but the smaller they are the better, provided type and quality are not sacrificed.

Faults. 'Flying' ears. Narrow muzzle. Too long a nose. Tongue showing. Light eyes. Long back. Dog being too near the ground through short legs. Drooping tail. Uneven markings. Rounded short feet. Wavy or curly coat. Narrow chest. Mouth undershot or overshot. Weakness in hindquarters.

JAPANESE SPANIEL

(AMERICAN KENNEL CLUB—GROUP V: TOYS)

General Appearance. That of a lively, high-bred little dog with dainty appearance, smart, compact carriage and profuse coat. These dogs should be essentially stylish in movement, lifting the feet high when in action, carrying the tail (which is heavily feathered, proudly curved or plumed) over the back. In size they vary considerably, but the smaller they are the better, provided type and quality are not sacrificed. When divided by weight, classes should be under and over 7 lbs.

Head. Should be large for the size of the dog, with broad skull, rounded in front.

Eyes. Large, dark, lustrous, rather prominent and set wide apart.

Ears. Small and V-shaped, nicely feathered, set wide apart and high on the head and carried slightly forward.

Nose. Very short in the muzzle part. The end or nose proper should be wide, with open nostrils, and must be the color of the dog's markings, *i.e.* black in black-marked dogs, and red or deep flesh color in red or lemon-marked dogs. It shall be a disqualification for a black and white Japanese Spaniel to have a nose any other color than black.

Neck. Should be short and moderately thick.

Body. Should be squarely and compactly built, wide in chest, 'cobby' in shape. The length of the dog's body should be about its height.

Tail. Must be well twisted to either right or left from root and carried up over back and flow on opposite side; it should be profusely covered with long hair (ring tails not desirable).

Legs. The bones of the legs should be small, giving them a slender appearance, and they should be well feathered.

Feet. Small and shaped somewhat long; the dog stands up on its toes somewhat. If feathered, the tufts should never increase in width of the foot, but only its length a trifle.

Coat. Profuse, long, straight, rather silky. It should be absolutely free from wave or curl, and not lie too flat, but have a tendency to stand out, especially at the neck, so as to give a thick mane or ruff, which with profuse feathering on thighs and tail gives a very showy appearance.

Color. The dogs should be either black and white or red and white, *i.e.* parti-colored. The term red includes all shades of sable, brindle, lemon and orange, but the brighter and clearer the red the better. The white should be clear white, and the color, whether black or red, should be evenly distributed patches over the body, cheek and ears.

SCALE OF POINTS

Head and neck	10	Tail	10
Eyes	10	Feet and legs	5
Ears	5	Coat and markings	15
Muzzle	10	Action	5
Nose	5	Size	10
Body	15	Total	100

DISQUALIFICATION

In black and whites, a nose any other color than black.

KEESHOND

(THE KENNEL CLUB—UTILITY GROUP)

General Appearance. A short, compact body; alert carriage, foxlike head; small pointed ears; a well-feathered, curling tail, carried over the back; hair very thick on the neck, forming a large ruff; head, ears and legs covered with short thick hair. Dogs should move cleanly and briskly (not lope like an Alsatian) but movement should be straight and sharp. Dogs should show boldly.

Head and Skull. Head well proportioned to the body, wedge-shaped when seen from above; from the side showing definite stop. Muzzle should be of medium length, neither coarse nor snipy.

Eyes. Dark with well-defined spectacles.

Ears. Small and well set on head, not wide and yet not meeting.

Mouth. Should be neither over not undershot, upper teeth should just overlap under teeth and should be white, sound and strong (but discoloration from distemper not to penalize severely).

Forequarters. Forelegs feathered, straight, with good bone and cream in colour.

Hindquarters. Hind legs should be straight, showing very little hock and not feathered below the hock. Cream in colour.

Feet. Round and cat-like with black nails.

Tail. Tightly curled, a double curl at the end is desirable. Plume to be white on the top where curled, with black tip.

Coat. Dense, and harsh (off-standing), dense ruff and well feathered, profuse trousers; a soft, thick, light-coloured undercoat. Coat should not be silky, wavy or woolly, nor should it form a parting on the back.

Colour. Should be wolf, ash-grey; not all black or all white, and markings should be definite.

Weight and Size. The ideal height is 18 inches for Dogs and 17 inches for Bitches, but type is of more importance.

Faults. Light eyes, prominent eyes. Curly or wavy tendency in coat. Silky coat. Absence of spectacles. Nervous demeanour. Drop ears. Whole white foot or feet. Black marks below the knee, pencilling excepted. White chest. Apple head or absence of stop.

KEESHOND

(AMERICAN KENNEL CLUB—GROUP VI: NON-SPORTING DOGS)

General Appearance and Conformation. The Keeshond is a handsome dog, of well-balanced, short-coupled body, attracting attention not only by his alert carriage and intelligent expression, but also by his luxurious coat, his richly plumed tail, well curled over his back, and by his foxlike face and head with small pointed ears. His coat is very thick round the neck, fore part of the shoulders and chest, forming a lionlike mane. His rump and hind legs, down to the hocks, are also thickly coated forming the characteristic 'trousers.' His head, ears and lower legs are covered with thick short hair. The ideal height of fully matured dogs (over 2 years old), measured from top of withers to the ground, is: for males, 18 inches; bitches, 17 inches. However, size consideration should not outweigh that of type. When dogs are judged equal in type, the dog nearest the ideal height is to be preferred. Length of back from withers to rump should equal height as measured above.

Head—Expression. Expression is largely dependent on the distinctive characteristic called 'spectacles'—a delicately pencilled line slanting slightly upward from the outer corner of each eye to the lower corner of the ear, coupled with distinct markings and shadings forming short but expressive eyebrows. Markings (or shadings) on face and head must present a pleasing appearance, imparting to the dog an alert and intelligent expression.

Fault. Absence of 'spectacles.'

Skull. The head should be well proportioned to the body, wedge-shaped when viewed from above. Not only in muzzle, but the whole head should give this impression when the ears are drawn back by covering the nape of the neck and the ears with one hand. Head in profile should exhibit a definite stop.

Fault. Apple head, or absence of stop.

Muzzle. The muzzle should be dark in color and of medium length, neither coarse nor snipy, and well proportioned to the skull

Mouth. The mouth should be neither overshot nor undershot. Lips should be black and closely meeting, not thick, coarse or sagging; and with no wrinkle at the corner of the mouth.

Fault. Overshot or undershot.

Teeth. The teeth should be white, sound and strong (but discoloration from distemper not to penalize severely); upper teeth should just overlap the lower teeth.

Eyes. Eyes should be dark brown in color, of medium size, rather oblique in shape and not set too wide apart.

Fault. Protruding round eyes or eyes light of color.

Ears. Ears should be small, triangular in shape, mounted high on head and carried erect; dark in color and covered with thick, velvety, short hair. Size should be proportionate to the head—length approximating the distance from outer corner of the eye to the nearest edge of the ear.

Fault. Ears not carried erect when at attention.

Body—Neck and Shoulders.
The neck should be moderately long, well shaped and well set on shoulders; covered with a profuse mane, sweeping from under the jaw and covering the whole of the front part of the shoulders and chest, as well as the top part of the shoulders.

Chest, Back and Loin. The body should be compact with a short straight back sloping slightly downward toward the hindquarters; well ribbed, barrel well rounded, belly moderately tucked up, deep and strong of chest.

Legs. Forelegs should be straight seen from any angle and well feathered. Hind legs should be profusely feathered down to the hocks—not below, with hocks only slightly bent. Legs must be of good bone and cream in color.

Fault Black markings below the knee, pencilling excepted.

Feet. The feet should be compact, well rounded, catlike, and cream in color. Toes are nicely arched, with black nails.

Fault. White foot or feet.

Tail. The tail should be set on high, moderately long, and well feathered, tightly curled over back. It should lie flat and close to the body with a very light gray plume on top where curled, but the tip of the tail should be black. The tail should form a part of the 'silhouette' of the dog's body, rather than give the appearance of an appendage.

Fault. Tail not lying close to the back.

Action. Dogs should show boldly and keep tails curled over the back. They should move cleanly and briskly; and the movement should be straight and sharp (not lope like a German Shepherd).

Fault. Tail not carried over back when moving.

Coat. The body should be abundantly covered with long, straight harsh hair; standing well out from a thick, downy undercoat. The hair on the legs should be smooth and short, except for a feathering on the front legs and 'trousers,' as previously described, on the hind legs. The hair on the tail should be profuse, forming a rich plume. Head, including muzzle, skull and ears, should be covered with smooth, soft, short hair—velvety in texture on the ears. Coat must not part down the back.

Fault. Silky, wavy or curly coats. Part in coat down the back.

Color and Markings. A mixture of gray and black. The undercoat should be very pale gray or cream (not tawny). The hair of the outer coat is black tipped, the length of the black tips producing the characteristic shading of color. The color may vary from light to dark, but any pronounced deviation from the gray color is not permissible. The plume of the tail should be very light gray when curled on back, and the tip of the tail should be black. Legs and feet should be cream. Ears should be very dark—almost black. Shoulder line markings (light gray) should be well defined. The color of the ruff and 'trousers' is generally lighter than that of the body. 'Spectacles' and shadings, as previously described, are characteristics of the breed and must be present to some degree. There should be no pronounced white markings.

Very Serious Faults. Entirely black or white or any other solid color; any pronounced deviation from the gray color.

SCALE OF POINTS

General conformation and appearance		20
Head		
Shape	6	
Eyes	5	
Ears	5	
Teeth	4	20
Body		
Chest, back and loin	10	
Tail	10	
Neck and shoulders	8	
Legs	4	
Feet	3	35
Coat		15
Color and markings		10
Total		100

Approved July 12, 1949

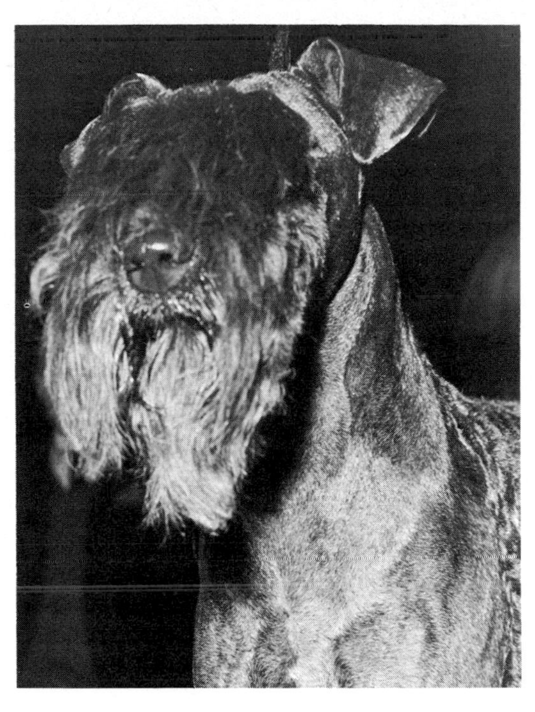

KERRY BLUE TERRIER

(THE KENNEL CLUB—TERRIER GROUP)

Characteristics. Disciplined gameness. The Kerry Blue Terrier is a compact, powerful Terrier, showing gracefulness and an attitude of alert determination, with definite Terrier style and character throughout.

General Appearance. The typical Kerry Blue Terrier should be upstanding, well knit and well proportioned, showing a well-developed and muscular body.

Head and Skull. Well balanced, long, proportionately lean, with slight stop and flat over the skull. Foreface and jaw very strong, deep and punishing; nose black; nostrils of due proportion.

Eyes. Dark as possible. Small to medium with keen Terrier expression.

Ears. Small to medium and V-shaped, carried forward but not as high as in some Terrier breeds.

Mouth. Teeth level with upper teeth just closing over the lower; dark gums and roof.

Neck. Strong and reachy, running into sloping shoulders.

Forequarters. Shoulders flat as possible with elbows carried close to the body while the dog is standing or in action. Legs straight, bone powerful. Front straight, neither too wide nor too narrow.

Body. Short coupled with good depth of brisket and well sprung ribs. Chest to be deep. Topline level.

Hindquarters. Large and well developed, stifle bent and hocks close to the ground giving perfect freedom of hind action.

Feet. Round and small. Toe nails black.

Tail. Set on high to complete a perfectly straight back and carried erect.

Coat. Soft and silky, plentiful and wavy.

Colour. Any shade of blue, with or without black points. A shade of tan is permissible in puppies, as is also a dark colour up to the age of 18 months. A small white patch on chest should not be penalized.

Weight and Size. The most desirable weight for a fully-developed dog is from 33 to 37 lbs, and bitches should weigh proportionately less, but 35 lbs is the most desirable weight to aim for. Ideal height: dogs 18 to 19 inches at shoulder; bitches slightly less.

Faults. Hard or woolly coat. Solid black after 18 months. In excess of 19 inches in height. Bumpy cheek bones, teeth undershot or very overshot. Rose ears. Snipy foreface. Light-coloured or full eyes. Roach or hollowback. Close, stilted or cow-hocked hind action.

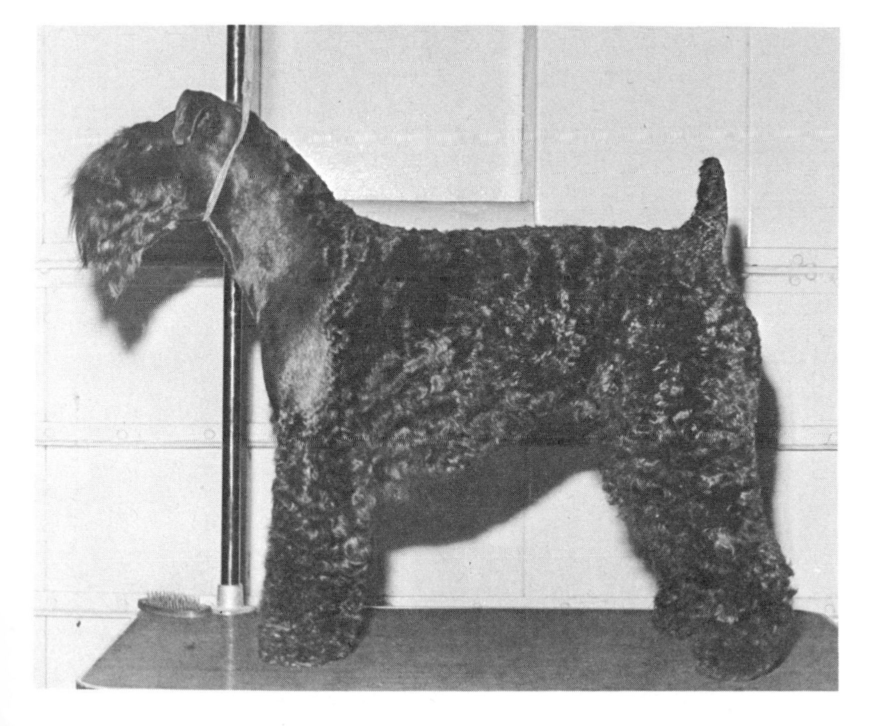

KERRY BLUE TERRIER

(AMERICAN KENNEL CLUB—GROUP IV: TERRIERS)

Head. Long, but not exaggerated and in good proportion to the rest of the body. Well balanced, with little apparent difference between the length of the skull and foreface. (20 points)

Skull. Flat, with very slight stop, of but moderate breadth between the ears, and narrowing very slightly to the eyes.

Cheeks. Clean and level, free from bumpiness.

Ears. V-shaped, small but not out of proportion to the size of the dog, of moderate thickness, carried forward close to the cheeks with the top of the folded ear slightly above the level of the skull. A 'dead' ear houndlike in appearance is very undesirable.

Foreface. Jaws deep, strong and muscular. Foreface full and well made up, not falling away appreciably below the eyes but moderately chiseled out to relieve the foreface from wedginess.

Nose. Black, nostrils large and wide.

Teeth. Strong, white and either level or with the upper (incisors) teeth slightly overlapping the lower teeth. An undershot mouth should be strictly penalized.

Eyes. Dark, small, not prominent, well placed and with a keen terrier expression. Anything approaching a yellow eye is very undesirable.

Neck. Clean and moderately long, gradually widening to the shoulders upon which it should be well set and carried proudly. (5 points)

Shoulders and Chest. Shoulders fine, long and sloping, well laid back and well knit. Chest deep and of but moderate breadth. (10 points)

Legs and Feet. Legs moderately long with plenty of bone and muscle. The forelegs should be straight from both front and side view, with the elbows hanging perpendicularly to the body and working clear of the sides in movement, the pasterns short, straight and hardly noticeable. Both forelegs and hind legs should move straight forward when travelling, the stifles turning neither in nor out. (10 points) Feet should be strong, compact, fairly round and moderately small, with good depth of pad free from cracks, the toes arched, turned neither in nor out, with black toenails.

Body. Back short, strong and straight (i.e. level), with no appearance of slackness. Loin short and powerful with a slight tuck-up, the ribs fairly well sprung, deep rather than round. (10 points)

Hindquarters and Stern. Hindquarters strong and muscular with full freedom of action, free from droop or crouch, the thighs long and powerful, stifles well bent and turned neither in nor out, hocks near the ground and, when viewed from behind, upright and parallel with each other, the dog standing well up on them. Tail should be set on high, of moderate length and carried gaily erect, the straighter the tail the better. (10 points)

Color. The correct mature color is any shade of blue gray or gray blue from deep slate to light blue gray, of a fairly uniform color throughout except that distinctly darker to black parts may appear on the muzzle, head, ears, tail and feet. (10 points) Kerry color, in its process of 'clearing' from an apparent black at birth to the mature gray blue or blue gray, passes through one or more transitions—involving a very dark blue (darker than deep slate), shades or tinges of brown, and mixtures of these, together with a progressive infiltration of the correct mature color. Up to 18 months such deviations from the correct mature color are permissible without preference and without regard for uniformity. Thereafter, deviation from it to any significant extent must be severely penalized. Solid black is never permissible in the show ring. Up to 18 months any doubt as to whether a dog is black or a very dark blue should be resolved in favor of the dog, particularly in the case of a puppy. Black on the muzzle, head, ears, tail and feet is permissible at any age.

Coat. Soft, dense and wavy. A harsh, wire or bristle coat should be severely penalized. In show trim the body should be well covered but tidy, with the head (except for the whiskers) and the ears and cheeks clear. (15 points)

General Conformation and Character. The typical Kerry Blue Terrier should be upstanding, well knit and in good balance, showing a well developed and muscular body with definite terrier style and character throughout. A low-slung Kerry is not typical. (10 points)

Height. The ideal Kerry should be 18½ inches at the withers for a dog, slightly less for a bitch. In judging Kerries, a height of 18–19½ inches for a dog, and 17½–19 inches for a bitch should be given primary preference. Only where the comparative superiority of a specimen outside of the ranges noted clearly justifies it, should greater latitude be taken. In no case should it extend to a dog over 20 inches or under 17½ inches, or to a bitch over 19½ inches or under 17 inches. The minimum limits do not apply to puppies.

Weight. The most desirable weight for a fully developed dog is from 33–40 pounds, bitches weighing proportionately less.

DISQUALIFICATIONS

Solid black. Dewclaws on hind legs.

Approved September 15, 1959

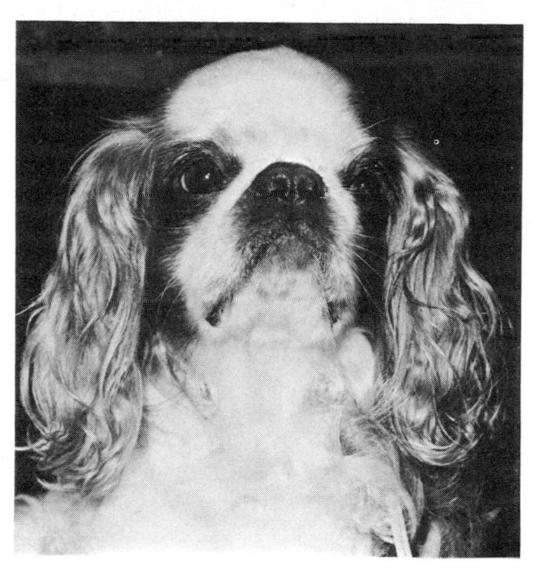

KING CHARLES SPANIEL

(THE KENNEL CLUB—TOY GROUP)

General Appearance. Compact and cobby, on refined lines, chest wide and deep, legs short and straight, back short and level. Tail well flagged, and not carried over the level of the back. Movement free, active and elegant.

Head and Skull. Skull massive in comparison to size, well domed, and full over the eyes. Nose black with large wide open nostrils, very short and turned up to meet the skull. The stop between skull and nose should be well defined. Jaw; muzzle square, wide, and deep and well turned up, lower jaw wide, lips exactly meeting, giving a nice finish. The cheeks should not fall away under the eyes, but be well cushioned up. A protruding tongue is objectionable, but does not disqualify.

Eyes. Very large and dark, set wide apart, with eyelids block square to face line, and with pleasing expression.

Ears. Set on low, and to hang quite flat to cheeks, very long and well feathered.

Coat. Long, silky and straight, a slight wave allowed, not curly. The legs, ears and tail should be profusely feathered.

Colour. Black and Tan: A rich glossy black, with bright, mahogany tan markings, on muzzle, legs, chest, linings of ears, under tail, and spots over eyes. Tri-colour; Ground pearly white and well distributed black patches, brilliant tan markings on cheeks, linings of ears, under tail, and spots over the eyes. A wide white blaze between the eyes, and up the forehead. Blenheim: A ground of pearly white with well distributed chestnut red patches. A wide clear blaze with the 'spot' in centre of skull. The 'spot' should be a clear chestnut red mark about the size of a six-pence in centre of skull. Ruby: Whole coloured, a rich chestnut red.

Weight and Size. The most desirable size is 8 to 14 lbs.

Faults. The presence of a few white hairs on the chest of a Black and Tan or Ruby is undesirable, but a white patch is a major fault.

ENGLISH TOY SPANIELS

(AMERICAN KENNEL CLUB—GROUP V: TOYS)

KING CHARLES, PRINCE CHARLES, RUBY AND BLENHEIM

Head. Should be well domed, and in good specimens is absolutely semiglobular, sometimes even extending beyond the half-circle, and absolutely projecting over the eyes, so as nearly to meet the upturned nose.

Eyes. The eyes are set wide apart, with the eyelids square to the line of the face—not oblique or foxlike. The eyes themselves are large and dark as possible, so as to be generally considered black, their enormous pupils, which are absolutely of that color, increasing the description.

Stop. The stop, or hollow between the eyes, is well marked, as in the Bulldog, or even more so; some good specimens exhibit a hollow deep enough to bury a small marble in it.

Nose. The nose must be short and well turned up between the eyes, and without any indication of artificial displacement afforded by a deviation to either side. The color of the end should be black, and it should be both deep and wide with open nostrils. A light-colored nose is objectionable, but shall not disqualify.

Jaw. The muzzle must be square and deep, and the lower jaw wide between the branches, leaving plenty of space for the tongue, and for the attachment of the lower lips, which should completely conceal the teeth. It should also be turned up or 'finished,' so as to allow of its meeting the end of the upper jaw, turned up in a similar way as above described. A protruding tongue is objectionable, but does not disqualify

Ears. The ears must be long, so as to approach the ground. In an average-sized dog they measure 20 inches from tip to tip, and some reach 22 inches or even a trifle more. They should be set low down on the head and hang flat to the side of the cheeks, and be heavy-feathered.

Size. The most desirable size is from 9 pounds to 12 pounds.

Shape. In compactness of shape these Spaniels almost rival the Pug, but the length of coat adds greatly to the apparent bulk, as the body, when the coat is wetted, looks small in comparison with that dog. Still, it ought to be decidedly 'cobby', with strong, stout legs, short broad back and wide chest.

Coat. The coat should be long, silky, soft and wavy, but not curly. There should be a profuse mane, extending well down in the front of the chest. The feather should be well displayed on the ears and feet, and in the latter case so thickly as to give the appearance of being webbed. It is also carried well up the backs of the legs. In the Black and Tan the feather on the ears is very long and profuse, exceeding that of the Blenheim by an inch or more. The feather on the tail (which is cut to the length of about $1\frac{1}{2}$ inches) should be silky, and from 3 to 4 inches in length, constituting a marked 'flag' of a square shape, and not carried above the level of the back.

COLORS OF THE TWO VARIETIES

King Charles and Ruby. The King Charles and Ruby types which comprise one show variety are solid-colored dogs. The King Charles are black and tan (considered a solid color), the black rich and glossy with deep mahogany tan markings over the eyes and on the muzzle, chest and legs. The presence of a few white hairs intermixed with the black on the chest is to be faulted, but a white patch on the chest or white appearing elsewhere disqualifies. The Ruby is a rich chestnut red and is whole-colored. The presence of a few white hairs intermixed with the red on the chest is to be faulted, but a white patch on the chest or white appearing elsewhere disqualifies.

Blenheim and Prince Charles. The Blenheim and Prince Charles types which comprise the other show variety are broken-colored dogs. The Blenheim is red and white. The ground color is a pearly white which has bright red chestnut or ruby red markings evenly distributed in large patches. The ears and cheeks should be red, with a blaze of white extending from the nose up the forehead and ending between the ears in a crescentic curve. In the center of the blaze at the top of the forehead, there should be a clear 'spot' of red, the size of a dime. The Prince Charles, a tri-colored dog, is white, black and tan. The ground color is a pearly white. The black consists of markings which should be evenly distributed in large patches. The tan appears as spots over the eyes, on the muzzle, chest and legs; the ears and vent should also be lined with tan. The Prince Charles has no 'spot,' that being a particular feature of the Blenheim.

SCALE OF POINTS

KING CHARLES, OR BLACK AND TAN. PRINCE CHARLES, WHITE, WITH BLACK AND TAN MARKINGS. RUBY, OR RED.

Symmetry, condition, size and soundness of limb	20	Eyes	10
Head	15	Ears	15
Stop	5	Coat and feathering	15
Muzzle	10	Color	10
		Total	100

BLENHEIM, OR WHITE WITH RED MARKINGS

Symmetry, condition, size and soundness of limb	15	Eyes	10
Head	15	Ears	10
Stop	5	Coat and feathering	15
Muzzle	10	Color and markings	15
		Spot	5
		Total	100

DISQUALIFICATIONS

King Charles and Ruby: A white patch on the chest, or white on any other part.

Approved July 14, 1959

KOMONDOR

(THE KENNEL CLUB—WORKING GROUP)

KOMONDOR

(AMERICAN KENNEL CLUB—GROUP III: WORKING DOGS)

General Appearance. The Komondor is characterized by imposing strength, courageous demeanor and pleasing conformation. In general, it is a big muscular dog with plenty of bone and substance, covered with an unusual, heavy, white coat.

Nature and Characteristics. An excellent house-guard. It is wary of strangers. As a guardian of herds, it is, when grown, an earnest, courageous, and very faithful dog. The young dog, however, is as playful as any other puppy. It is devoted to its master and will defend him against attack by any stranger. Because of this trait, it is not used for driving the herds, but only for guarding them. The Komondor's special task is to protect the animals. It lives during the greater part of the year in the open without protection against strange dogs and beasts of prey.

Head. The head looks somewhat short in comparison to the seemingly wide forehead. The skull is somewhat arched when viewed from the side. Stop is moderate. The muzzle somewhat shorter than the length of the skull. The top of the muzzle is straight and about parallel with the line of the top of the skull. The muzzle is powerful, bite is scissors; level bite is acceptable. Any missing teeth is a serious fault. Distinctly undershot or overshot bite is a serious fault.

Ears. Medium set, hanging and V-shaped. Erect ears or ears that move toward an erect position are faults.

Eyes. Medium-sized and almond-shaped, not too deeply set. The edges of the eyelids are gray. The iris of the eyes is dark brown, light color is not desirable. Blue-white eyes are disqualifying.

Muzzle. In comparison to the length given in the head description, the muzzle is wide, coarse and not pointed. Nostrils are wide. Color of the nose is black. A dark gray or dark brown nose is not desirable but is acceptable. Flesh-colored noses are disqualifying.

Neck. Muscular, of medium length, moderately arched. The head erect. Any dewlap is a fault.

Body. Characterized chiefly by the powerful, deep chest which is muscular and proportionately wide. Shoulders are moderately sloping. The back is level. Rump is wide, muscular, slightly sloping towards the root of the tail. The body is rectangular, only slightly longer than the height at the withers. The belly is somewhat drawn up at the rear.

Tail. A straight continuation of the rump-line, and reaches down to the hocks. Slightly curved upwards at its end. When the dog is excited, the tail is raised up to the level of the back. The tail is not to be docked. A short or curly tail is a fault. Bobtails are disqualifying.

Forelegs. Straight, well-boned and muscular. Viewed from any side, the legs are like vertical columns. The upper arms join the body closely, without loose elbows.

Hindquarters and Legs. The steely, strong bone structure is covered with highly developed muscles. The legs are straight as viewed from the rear. Stifles well bent. Dewclaws must be removed.

Feet. Strong, rather large and with close, well-arched toes. Nails are black or gray. Pads are hard, elastic and dark.

Movement. Light, leisurely and balanced. Takes long strides.

Coat. Characteristic of the breed is the dense weather-resisting double coat. The puppy coat is relatively soft, but it shows a tendency to fall into cords. In the mature dog the coat consists of a dense, soft, woolly undercoat, much like the puppy coat, and a coarser outer coat that is wavy or curly. The coarser hairs of the outer coat trap the softer undercoat forming permanent strong cords that are felty to the touch. A grown dog is covered with a heavy coat of these tassel-like cords, which form themselves naturally, and once formed, require no care other than washing. Too curly a coat is not desired. Straight or silky coat is a serious fault. Short, smooth hair on the head and legs is a disqualification. Failure of the coat to cord by two years of age is a disqualification.

The coat is longest at the rump, loins and tail. It is of medium length on the back, shoulders and chest. Shorter on the cheeks, around the eyes, ears, neck, and on the extremities. It is shortest around the mouth and lower part of the legs up to the hocks.

Color. Color of the coat is white. Any color other than white is disqualifying.

In the ideal specimen the skin is gray. Pink skin is less desirable but is acceptable if no evidence of albinism. The nose, lips, outlines of eyelids and pads are dark or gray. It is good if the gums and palate are also dark.

Size. Dogs, 25½ inches and upward at the withers; bitches 23½ inches and upward at withers. While size is important, type, character, symmetry, movement and ruggedness are of the greatest importance, and are on no account to be sacrificed for size alone.

Faults. Size below limit. Short or too curly coat; Straight or silky coat. Any missing teeth. Looseness or slackness. Short or curly tail. Light colored eyes. Erect ears or ears that move toward an erect position. Dewlaps on the neck.

DISQUALIFICATIONS

Blue-white eyes. Color other than white. Bobtails. Flesh-colored nose. Short, smooth hair on head and legs. Failure of the coat to cord by two years of age.

Revised February 13, 1973

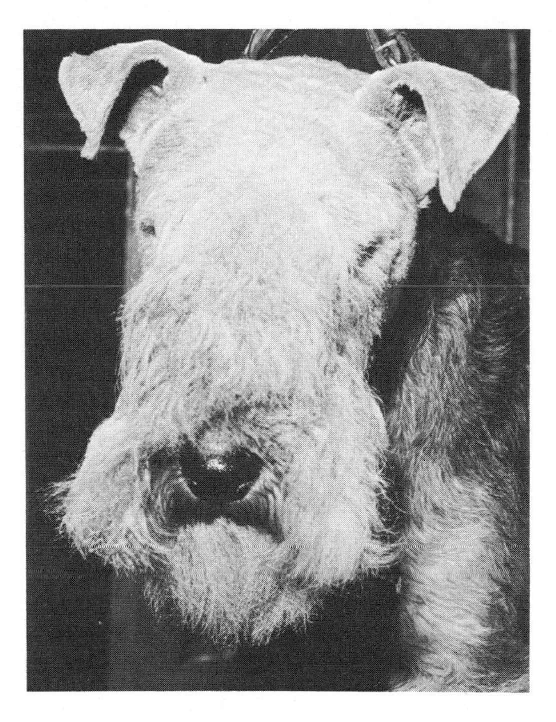

LAKELAND TERRIER

(THE KENNEL CLUB—TERRIER GROUP)

General Appearance. Smart and workman-like, with gay fearless demeanour.
Head and Skull. Well balanced. Skull flat and refined. The jaws powerful and the muzzle should be broad but not too long. The length of the head from the stop to the tip of the nose should not exceed that from the occiput to the stop. Nose black.
Eyes. Should be dark or hazel.
Ears. Moderately small, V-shaped and carried alertly. They should not be placed too high or too low on the head.
Mouth. Teeth even, closing scissor fashion, i.e., top teeth fitting closely over lower.
Neck. Reachy.
Forequarters. Shoulders well laid back. Forelegs straight, well boned.
Body. Chest reasonably narrow. Back strong, moderately short, well coupled.
Hindquarters. Strong and muscular, thighs long and powerful, well turned stifles, hocks low to ground and straight.
Feet. Small, compact, round and well padded.
Tail. Well set on, carried gaily but not to curl over the back.
Coat. Dense and weather resisting, harsh with good undercoat.
Colour. Black and tan, blue and tan, red, wheaten, red grizzle, liver, blue or black. Small tips of white on feet and chest not to debar. Mahogany or deep tan is not typical.
Weight and Size. The average weight of dogs is 17 lbs, bitches 15 lbs. The height should not exceed $14\frac{1}{2}$ inches at the shoulder.
Faults. A true Lakeland Terrier expression is determined by head, ears and eyes. Too long a head, ears set on the top of the head, and slanting eyes are faults.

LAKELAND TERRIER

(AMERICAN KENNEL CLUB—GROUP IV: TERRIERS)

General Appearance. The Lakeland Terrier is a small, workman-like dog of square, sturdy build and gay, friendly, self-confident demeanor. He stands on his toes as if ready to go, and he moves, lithe and graceful, with a straight-ahead, free stride of good length. His head is rectangular in contour, ears V-shaped, and wiry coat finished off with fairly long furnishings on muzzle and legs.
Head. Well balanced, rectangular, the length of skull equaling the length of the muzzle when measured from occiput to stop, and from stop to nose-tip.
The Skull is flat on top and moderately broad, the cheeks almost straight-sided, and the stop barely perceptible.

The Muzzle is broad with straight nose bridge and good fill-in beneath the eyes.

The nose is black, except that liver-colored noses shall be permissible on liver-coated dogs.

Jaws are powerful.

The Teeth, which are comparatively large, may meet in either a level, edge-to-edge bite, or a slightly overlapping scissors bite. Specimens with teeth overshot or undershot are to be disqualified.

The Ears are small, V-shaped, their fold just above the top of the skull, the inner edge close to the cheeks, and the flap pointed down.

The Eyes, moderately small and somewhat oval in outline, are set squarely in the skull, fairly wide apart. Their normally dark color may be a warm brown or black.

The Expression depends upon the dog's mood of the moment; although typically alert, it may be intense and determined, or gay and even impish.

Neck. Reachy and of good length; refined but strong; clean at the throat, slightly arched, and widening gradually into the shoulders. The withers, that point at the back of the neck where neck and body meet, are noticeably higher than the level of the back.

Body. In over-all length-to-height proportion, the dog is approximately square. The moderately narrow *chest* is deep; it extends to elbows which are held close to the body. Shoulder blades are sloping, that is, well laid back, their musculature lean and almost flat in outline.

The ribs are well sprung and moderately rounded.

The Back is short and level in topline. Loins are taught and short, although they may be a trifle longer in bitches than in dogs. *Quarters* are strong, broad, and muscular.

Legs and Feet—Forelegs are strongly boned, clean, and absolutely straight as viewed from the front or side, and devoid of appreciable bend at the pasterns.

Hindlegs too are strong and sturdy, the second thighs long and nicely angulated at the stifles and the hocks.

Hocks are well let down, with the bone from hock to toes straight and parallel to each other. The small *feet* are round, the toes compact and well padded, the nails strong. Dewclaws, if any, are to be removed.

Tail. Set high on the body, the tail is customarily docked so that when the dog is set up in show position, the tip of the docked tail is on an approximate level with the skull. In carriage it is gay or upright, although a slight curve in the direction of the head is considered desirable. The tail curled over the back is faulty.

Coat and Color. Two-ply or double, the outer coat is hard and wiry in texture, the undercoat soft. Furnishings on muzzle and legs are plentiful as opposed to profuse. *The color* may be blue, black, liver, black and tan, blue and tan, red, red grizzle, grizzle and tan, or wheaten. Tan as desirable in the Lakeland Terrier, is a light wheaten or straw color, with rich red or mahogany tan to be penalized. Otherwise, colors, as specified, are equally acceptable. Dark-saddled specimens (whether black, grizzle or blue) are nearly solid black at birth, with tan points on muzzle and feet. The black recedes and usually turns grayish or grizzle at maturity, while the tan also lightens.

Size. The ideal *height* of the mature dog is 14½ inches from the withers to the ground, with up to a ½-inch deviation either way permissible. Bitches may measure as much as one inch less than dogs. The *weight* of the well-balanced, mature specimen in hard, show condition, averages approximately 17 lbs, those of other heights proportionately more or less.

Size is to be considered of lesser importance than other qualities, that is, when judging dogs of equal merit, the one nearest the ideal size is to be preferred. Symmetry and proportion, however, are paramount in the appraisal, since all qualities together must be considered in visualizing the ideal.

Movement. Straight and free, with good length of stride. Paddling, moving close, and toeing-in are faulty.

Temperament. The typical Lakeland Terrier is bold, gay, and friendly, with a self-confident, cock-of-the-walk attitude. Shyness, especially shy-sharpness, in the mature specimen is to be heavily penalized.

SCALE OF POINTS

Head	15	Legs and feet	10
Eyes, ears, expression	15	Size and symmetry	10
Neck	5	Movement	10
Body	10	Temperament	10
Coat	15	Total	100

DISQUALIFICATION

The front teeth overshot or undershot.

Approved May 14, 1963

LARGE MUNSTERLANDER

(THE KENNEL CLUB—GUNDOG GROUP)

Characteristics. The Munsterlander is a multi-purpose Pointer Retriever, ideal for the rough shooter. He has an excellent nose, staying power, and works equally well on land and in water. He is a keen worker, easily taught, loyal, affectionate and trustworthy.

General Appearance. A noble, intelligent, long-haired black and white dog, with a strong muscular body, and of impressive appearance. Medium size, alert and energetic, having good movement with drive.

Head and Skull. Well proportioned to the body, elongated, with a noble intelligent expression. Skull sufficiently broad, slightly rounded, with no pronounced occiput. Strong jaw muscles, well-formed black nose, wide soft nostrils, slight rise of the nasal bone to the forehead but no pronounced stop. Lips slightly rounded, dry and should not overhang excessively.

Eyes. Intelligent, medium size, dark brown, not deep set or protruding. Eyelids must close properly.

Ears. Broad and set high, lying flat and close to the head, with a rounded tip. Hair on the ears is long, extending below the bottom tip.

Mouth. Strong and sound, with well-developed fangs, faultless scissor bite and molars meeting exactly.

Neck. Strong muscular, slightly arched, joining the shoulder and chest in a neat line.

Forequarters. Chest white and deep in proportion with the body. Muscular sloping shoulders. Shoulder-blades should not stick out from the line of the back, must be close together at the top and lie well against the ribs. Shoulder-blade, upper and lower foreleg and bones of the feet should be vertical when viewed from the front. Shoulder-blades and upper foreleg form almost a right angle when in correct standing position. Upper foreleg bones between shoulder long. Both forelegs should be lean and parallel. Pasterns slightly sloping. Dewclaws should not be removed. The muscles of the forequarters should be strong and taut.

Body. Firm strong back, short coupled, slightly higher at the shoulders sloping smoothly towards the croup and tail. Wide loin, well protected by strong muscles. Wide croup. Ribs well sprung, deep and reaching well up to the loins. Taut abdomen, slightly tucked-up.

Hindquarters. Broad hips, strong well-muscled thighs, well-bent stiffles. Both hindlegs parallel to each other. Hocks slightly bent and square with the body. Pasterns nearly straight. Dewclaws to be removed.

Feet. Well closed, moderately rounded, arched with dense hair between the toes, well padded. Nails black and strong.

Tail. Well set on, in a straight line from the back. Base thick, tapering evenly towards the tip, well feathered. It should be carried gaily, horizontally, or slightly bent upwards. The tip of the tail is usually docked, according to the length of the dog, by about 1 cm to 2 cm.

Coat. Hair long and dense, but not curly or coarse. Well feathered on front and hindlegs and on tail, more so in dogs than in bitches. The hair must lie short and smooth on the head.

Colour. Head solid black, white blaze snip or star allowed. Body white with black patches, flecked, ticked, or combination of these.

Weight and Size. Dogs, height about 24 inches (60 cm), weight about 55 to 65 lbs (23 to 30 kg). Bitches, slightly lighter and smaller: weight about 55 lbs (25 kg), height about 22 inches (55 cm).

Faults. Light-coloured nose. Over or undershot mouth. Pincer bite. Very light coloured eyes. Open eyes with haw visible. Pronounced stop and pronounced occiput. Ears too fleshy, in large folds or leathery. Pointed tips. Weak neck, narrow chested, loose or straight shoulders. Arched or sway back. Flat or barrel ribs. Coarse bones. Splayed feet, hare or cat paws. Tail high or low set. Kinked or curled. Nervous temperament. Feminine looking dogs, and masculine looking bitches.

LHASA APSO

(THE KENNEL CLUB—UTILITY GROUP)

Characteristics. The Apso should give the appearance of a well-balanced, solid dog. Gay and assertive, but chary of strangers. Free and jaunty in movement.

Head and Skull. Heavy head furnishings with good fall over the eyes, good whiskers and beard.

Skull moderately narrow, falling away behind the eyes in a marked degree; not quite flat, but not domed or apple shaped.

Straight foreface, with medium stop. Nose black. Muzzle about $1\frac{1}{2}$ inches long, but not square; the length from tip of nose to be roughly one-third the total length from nose to back of skull.

Eyes. Dark. Medium sized eyes to be frontally placed, not large or full, or small and sunk. No white showing at base or top of eye.

Ears. Pendant, heavily feathered. Dark tips an asset.

Mouth. Upper incisors should close just inside the lower, i.e., reverse scissor bite. Incisors should be nearly in a straight line. Full dentition is desirable.

Neck. Strong, well covered with a dense mane which is more pronounced in dogs than in bitches.

Forequarters. Shoulders should be well laid back. Forelegs straight, heavily furnished with hair.

Body. The length from point of shoulders to point of buttocks greater than height at withers. Well ribbed up. Level top-line. Strong loin. Well balanced and compact.

Hindquarters. Well developed with good muscle. Good angulation. Heavily furnished. The hocks when viewed from behind should be parallel and not too close together.

Feet. Round and cat-like, with good pads. Well feathered.

Tail. High set, carried well over back and not like a pot-hook. There is often a kink at the end. Well feathered.

Coat. Top coat heavy, straight and hard, not woolly or silky, of good length. Dense under-coat.

Colours. Golden, sandy, honey, dark grizzle, slate, smoke, particolour, black, white or brown.

Size. Ideal height: 10 inches at shoulder for dogs: bitches slightly smaller.

Note. Male animals should have two apparently normal testicles fully descended into the scrotum.

LHASA APSO

(AMERICAN KENNEL CLUB—GROUP VI:
NON-SPORTING DOGS)

Character. Gay and assertive, but chary of strangers.
Size. Variable, but about 10 inches or 11 inches at shoulder for dogs, bitches slightly smaller.
Color. Golden, sandy, honey, dark grizzle, slate, smoke, parti-color, black, white or brown. This being the true Tibetan Lion-dog, golden or lion-like colors are preferred. Other colors in order as above. Dark tips to ears and beard are an asset.
Body Shape. The length from point of shoulders to point of buttocks longer than height at withers, well ribbed up, strong loin, well-developed quarters and thighs.
Coat. Heavy, straight, hard, not woolly nor silky, of good length, and very dense.
Mouth and Muzzle. Mouth level, otherwise slightly undershot preferable. Muzzle of medium length; a square muzzle is objectionable.
Head. Heavy head furnishings with good fall over eyes, good whiskers and beard; skull narrow, falling away behind the eyes in a marked degree, not quite flat, but not domed or apple-shaped; straight foreface of fair length. Nose black, about $1\frac{1}{2}$ inches long, or the length from tip of nose to eye to be roughly about one-third of the total length from nose to back of skull.
Eyes. Dark brown, neither very large and full, nor very small and sunk.
Ears. Pendant, heavily feathered.
Legs. Forelegs straight; both forelegs and hind-legs heavily furnished with hair.
Feet. Well feathered, should be round and cat-like, with good pads.
Tail and Carriage. Well feathered, should be carried well over back in a screw; there may be a kink at the end. A low carriage of stern is a serious fault.

Approved April 9, 1935

LÖWCHEN

(THE KENNEL CLUB—TOY GROUP)

General Appearance. Small intelligent dog, affectionate and lively disposition combining all the good qualities of a companion dog. The body is clipped in classical Poodle fashion and the tail, also clipped, is topped with a pom pom which gives it the appearance of a little lion.
Head. Short, fairly broad skull.
Faults. Too long, skull not broad enough.
Nose. Black and well at the extension of the muzzle.
Faults. Snipy or any other colour than black, turned up.
Eyes. Round, large and intelligent, dark colour.
Faults. Small, almond shaped, bulbous and bright, wild and wicked.
Ears. Hanging, long and well fringed.
Faults. Fringe insufficiently long.
Body. Short and well proportioned.
Faults. Too long, stringy, badly knit.
Pasterns. Straight and delicate.
Faults. Weak and coarse.
Feet. Small and round.
Faults. Flat, long and splayed.
Tail. Of medium length, clipped but leaving a tuft of hair forming a beautiful pom pom.
Faults. Too long, or too short.
Coat. Fairly long and wavy but not curly.
Colour. Any colour permissible, be it solid or patched. The most sought after colours are white, black and yellow.
Height. 8 to 14 inches. 20 to 35 cm.
Weight. 4 to 9 lbs.

MALTESE

(THE KENNEL CLUB—TOY GROUP)

Characteristics. Sweet tempered and very intelligent.

General Appearance. Should be smart, lively and alert. The action must be free, without extended weaving.

Head and Skull. From stop to centre of skull (centre between forepart of ears) and stop to tip of nose should be equally balanced. Stop should be defined. Nose should be pure black.

Eyes. Should be dark brown, with black eyerims, set in centre cheeks and not bulging.

Ears. Should be long and well feathered and hanging close to the side of the head, the hair to be mingled with the coat at the shoulders.

Mouth. Level or scissor bite with teeth even.

Neck. Of medium length—set on well-sloped shoulders.

Forequarters. Legs should be short and straight. Shoulders well sloped.

Body. Should be in every way well balanced and essentially short and cobby, with good rib spring and the back should be straight from the tip of the shoulders to the tail.

Hindquarters. Legs should be short and nicely angulated.

Feet. Should be round and the pads of the feet should bc black.

Tail. Should be well arched over the back and feathered.

Coat. Should be good length, but not impeding action, of silky texture, not in any way woolly and should be straight. It should not be crimped and there should be no woolly undercoat.

Colour. Pure white, but slight lemon markings should not penalize.

Size. Not over 10 inches from ground to top of shoulder.

Faults. Bad mouth, over or undershot. Gay tail. Curly or woolly coat. Brown nose. Pink eye rims. Unsound in any way.

MALTESE

(AMERICAN KENNEL CLUB—GROUP V: TOYS)

General Appearance. The Maltese is a toy dog covered from head to foot with a mantle of long, silky, white hair. He is gentle-mannered and affectionate, eager and sprightly in action, and, despite his size, possessed of the vigor needed for the satisfactory companion.

Head. Of medium length and in proportion to the size of the dog.

The Skull is slightly rounded on top, the stop moderate.

The Drop Ears are rather low set and heavily feathered with long hair that hangs close to the head.

Eyes are set not too far apart; they are very dark

and round, their black rims enhancing the gentle yet alert expression.

The Muzzle is of medium length, fine and tapered but not snipy.

The Nose is black.

The Teeth meet in an even, edge-to-edge bite, or in a scissors bite.

Neck. Sufficient length of neck is desirable as promoting a high carriage of the head.

Body. Compact, the height from the withers to the ground equaling the length from the withers to the root of the tail. Shoulder blades are sloping, the elbows well knit and held close to the body. The back is level in topline, the ribs well sprung. The chest is fairly deep, the loins taut, strong, and just slightly tucked up underneath.

Tail. A long-haired plume carried gracefully over the back, its tip lying to the side over the quarter.

Legs and Feet. Legs are fine-boned and nicely feathered. Forelegs are straight, their pastern joints well knit and devoid of appreciable bend. Hind legs are strong and moderately angulated at stifles and hocks. The feet are small and round, with toe pads black. Scraggly hairs on the feet may be trimmed to give a neater appearance.

Coat and Color. The coat is single, that is, without undercoat. It hangs long, flat, and silky over the sides of the body almost, if not quite, to the ground. The long head-hair may be tied up in a topknot or it may be left hanging. Any suggestion of kinkiness, curliness, or woolly texture is objectionable. Color, pure white. Light tan or lemon on the ears is permissible, but not desirable.

Size. Weight under 7 lbs, with from 4 to 6 lbs preferred. Over-all quality is to be favored over size.

Gait. The Maltese moves with a jaunty, smooth, flowing gait. Viewed from the side, he gives an impression of rapid movement, size considered. In the stride, the forelegs reach straight and free from the shoulders, with elbows close. Hind legs to move in a straight line. Cowhocks or any suggestion of hindleg toeing-in or out are faults.

Temperament. For all his diminutive size, the Maltese seems to be without fear. His trust and affectionate responsiveness are very appealing. He is among the gentlest mannered of all little dogs, yet he is lively and playful as well as vigorous.

Approved November 12, 1963

MANCHESTER TERRIER

(THE KENNEL CLUB—TERRIER GROUP)

General Appearance. The dog shall be compact in appearance with good bone and free from any resemblance to the Whippet.

Head and Skull. Long, flat in skull and narrow, level and wedge-shaped, without showing cheek muscles; well-filled up under the eyes, with tapering, tight lipped jaws.

Eyes. Small, dark and sparkling, oblong in shape, set close in head, not prominent.

Ears. Small and V-shaped, carried well above the top line of the head and hanging close to the head above the eyes.

Mouth. Should be level.

Neck. The neck should be fairly long and tapering from the shoulder to the head and slightly arched at the crest, free from throatiness.

Forequarters. The shoulders should be clean and well sloped. The chest narrow and deep. The forelegs must be quite straight, set on well under the dog; and of proportionate length to the body.

Body. Short with well-sprung ribs, slightly roached and well cut up behind the ribs.

Hindquarters. The hindlegs should be neither cow-hocked nor with the feet turned in and well bent at the stifle.

Feet. Small, semi-harefooted, and strong with well-arched toes.

Tail. Short and set on where the arch of the back ends, thick where it joins the body and tapering to a point, carried not higher than the level of The back.

Coat. Close, smooth, short and glossy, of a firm texture.

Colour. Jet black and rich mahogany tan distributed as follows: on the head, the muzzle to be tanned to the nose, the nose and nasal bone to be jet black. There shall be a small tan spot on each cheek and above each eye, the under-jaw and throat to be tanned with a distinct tan V. The legs from the knee downward to be tanned with the exception of the toes which shall be pencilled with black, and a distinct black mark (thumb mark) immediately above the feet. Inside the hindlegs tanned but divided with black at the stifle joint. Under the tail tanned, the vent tanned but as narrow as possible so that it is covered by the tail. A slight tan mark on each side of the chest. Tan outside the hindlegs, commonly called breeching, a defect. In all cases the black should not run into the tan or vice versa, but the division between the colours shall be clearly defined.

Weight and Size. Desired height at shoulders 16 inches dogs, 15 inches bitches.

MANCHESTER TERRIER

(AMERICAN KENNEL CLUB—GROUP IV: TERRIERS)

Head. Long, narrow, tight-skinned, almost flat, with a slight indentation up the forehead; slightly wedge-shaped, tapering to the nose, with no visible cheek muscles, and well filled up under the eyes; tight-lipped jaws, level in mouth, and functionally level teeth, or the incisors of the upper jaw may make a close, slightly overlapping contact with the incisors of the lower jaw.

Eyes. Small, bright, sparkling and as near black as possible; set moderately close together; oblong in shape, slanting upwards on the outside; they should neither protrude nor sink in the skull.

Nose. Black.

Ears (Toy Variety). Of moderate size; set well up on the skull and rather close together; thin, moderately narrow at base; with pointed tips; naturally erect carriage. Wide, flaring, blunt-tipped or 'bell' ears are a serious fault; cropped or cut ears shall disqualify.

Ears (Standard Variety). Erect, or button, small and thin; smaller at the root and set as close together as possible at the top of the head. If cropped, to a point, long and carried erect.

Neck and Shoulders. The neck should be a moderate length, slim and graceful; gradually becoming larger as it approaches, and blend smoothly with the sloping shoulders; free from throatiness; slightly arched from the occiput.

Chest. Narrow between the legs; deep in the brisket.

Body. Moderately short, with robust loins; ribs well sprung out behind the shoulders; back slightly arched at the loin, and falling again to the tail to the same height as the shoulder.

Legs. Forelegs straight, of proportionate length, and well under body. Hindlegs should not turn in or out as viewed from the rear; carried back; hocks well let down.

Feet. Compact, well arched, with jet black nails; the two middle toes in the front feet rather longer than the others; the hind feet shaped like those of a cat.

Tail. Moderately short, and set on where the arch of the back ends; thick where it joins the body, tapering to a point, not carried higher than the back.

Coat. Smooth, short, thick, dense, close and glossy; not soft.

Color. Jet black and rich mahogany tan, which should not run or blend into each other but abruptly forming clear, well-defined lines of color division. A small tan spot over each eye; a very small tan spot on each cheek; the lips of the upper and lower jaws should be tanned, extending under the throat, ending in the shape of the letter V; the inside of the ears partly tanned. Tan spots, called rosettes, on each side of the chest above the front legs, more pronounced in puppies than in adults. There should be a black 'thumb mark' patch on the front of each foreleg between the pastern and the knee. There should be a distinct black 'pencil mark' line running lengthwise on the top of each toe on all four feet. The remainder of the forelegs to be tan to the knee. Tan on the hindlegs should continue from the penciling on the feet up the inside of the legs to a little below the stifle joint; the outside of the hindlegs to be black. There should be tan under the tail, and on the vent, but only of such size as to be covered by the tail. White in any part of the coat is a serious fault, and shall disqualify whenever the white shall form a patch or stripe measuring as much as one-half inch in its longest dimension.

Weight (Toy Variety). Not exceeding 12 lbs. It is suggested that clubs consider dividing the American-bred and open classes by weight as follows: 7 lbs and under, over 7 lbs and not exceeding 12 lbs.

Weight (Standard Variety). Over 12 lbs and not exceeding 22 lbs. Dogs weighing over 22 lbs shall be disqualified. It is suggested that clubs consider dividing the American-bred and open classes by weight as follows: over 12 lbs and not exceeding 16 lbs, over 16 lbs and not exceeding 22 lbs.

DISQUALIFICATIONS

Color. White in any part of the coat, forming a patch or stripe measuring as much as $\frac{1}{2}$ inch in its longest dimension.

Weight (Standard Variety) Over 22 pounds.

Ears (Toy Variety). Cropped or cut ears.

Approved June 12, 1962

MAREMMA ITALIAN SHEEPDOGS

(THE KENNEL CLUB—WORKING GROUP)

General Appearance and Characteristics. The Sheepdog of Central Italy is of large size, lithe, strongly built, of 'outdoor' appearance, and, at the same time, majestic, distinguished, sturdy, courageous without being aggressive, lively and intelligent. Any tendency to nervousness should be heavily penalized. Movement should be free and active, giving the impression of a nimble dog, able to move easily over rough ground and to turn quickly.

Head and Skull. The head appears large and of conical shape, but proportional to the size of the body. The skull is rather wide between the ears, and narrows towards the facial area.

The occipital ridge is little emphasized and there is a medium stop. The area under the eyes is somewhat chiselled.

The length of the muzzle is very slightly less than that of the cranial area. The side faces of the muzzle tend to converge without showing snipiness.

The jaws should be powerful and there should be plenty of substance in the foreface.

The lips are little developed.

Pigmentation of the lips and nose is black.

Eyes. The Maremma Sheepdog should have a bold eye, neither large nor small, the ball neither sunk nor protruding. The aperture is almond-shaped.

The iris should be brown, the pigment of the eyelids black.

Ears. The ears should be small in relation to the size of the dog, V-shaped, set high on the head, and covered with short hair. They should hang flat to the side of the head in repose, but should be moved forward when alert.

Mouth. The teeth should be white, strong, regularly spaced and set in a level jaw. The inner faces of the upper incisors should close on the outer faces of the lower incisors.

Neck. The neck should be strong, of medium length, and devoid of dewlap.

Forequarters. The shoulders should be long, sloping, well muscled and free moving: the forelegs well boned and muscled without heaviness, straight when viewed from the front, the elbows held close to the rib cage but not turned in or out. The pasterns should show a very slight angle in profile.

Body. The body is strong, the muscles well developed, the shoulders slightly above the level of the back, which is broad and straight, rising to a slight arch on the loins and falling to a broad, strong rump. The length of the body, measured from the point of the shoulder to the point of the buttocks, is slightly longer than the height at the shoulder.

The rib cage is full, descending down to the level of the elbows, with well sprung ribs, not barrel-chested.

The sternum is long, gradually curving up to the abdomen which shows a waist without tucking up.

Hindquarters. The hindquarters should be wide and powerful, with strongly muscled thighs, legs straight when viewed from behind, and with hocks well let down and strong with a moderately acute angle.

Feet. The dog should have large, oval feet, the toes close together and well arched.

Tail. The tail is set low, is carried low in repose, but curls into the horizontal at hock level in normal carriage. It may be carried above the level of the back in excitement. It is well provided with thick hair.

Coat. The coat should be long, plentiful, rather harsh, clinging well to the body. A slight waviness, but not curliness, is permitted. It forms a thick collar on the neck.

The hair is short on the muzzle, the cranium, ears, feet and front of limbs, but forms a slight feathering on the rear edges of the limbs.

There is a thick, close undercoat, especially in winter.

The colour of the coat is white, ivory, or pale fawn, with or without slightly darker shadings.

Weight and Size. Dogs 75 to 95 lbs. 25 to 28 inches (at the shoulder). Bitches 65 to 85 lbs. 23 to 26 inches (at the shoulder).

MUNSTERLANDER

(THE KENNEL CLUB—GUNDOG GROUP)

Characteristics. The Munsterlander Setter is a multi-purpose Pointer Retriever, ideal for the Rough Shooter. He has an excellent nose, staying power and works equally well on land and in water. He is a very keen worker, easily taught, very loyal, affectionate and trustworthy.

General Appearance. A noble, intelligent, long-haired, black and white dog, with a strong muscular body, and of impressive appearance. A medium sized dog with good movement, alert and energetic, but without nervousness.

Head and Skull. Well proportioned to the body, elongated, with a noble intelligent expression, skull sufficiently broad, slightly rounded, with no pronounced occiput. Strong jaw muscles; well-formed black nose, wide soft nostrils; slight rise of the nasal bone to the forehead, but no pronounced stop. Lips slightly rounded, dry, and should not overhang excessively.

Eyes. Intelligent, medium size, brown, the darker brown the better. Equally placed, not deep set or protruding. Eyelids must close properly.

Ears. Broad and set high, equal on both sides, lying flat and close to the head, with a rounded tip. Hair on the ears is long, extending below the bottom tip.

Mouth. Strong and sound, with well developed fangs, faultless scissor bite and molars meeting exactly. Never overshot, undershot or pincerbite.

Neck. Strong, muscular, slightly arched, joining the shoulder and the chest in a neat line.

Forequarters. Chest in proportion with the body. Seen from the front: wide, seen from the side: deep. Muscular sloping shoulders. Shoulder blades should not stick out from the line of the back, must be close together on the top and lie well against the ribs. Shoulder blade, upper and lower foreleg and bones of the feet should be vertical when viewed from the front. Shoulder blades and upper foreleg form almost a right angle when in correct standing position. Upper foreleg bones between shoulder and elbow long. Elbows pointing neither in nor out. Both forelegs should be lean and parallel. Pasterns slightly sloping, almost straight. Dewclaws should not be removed. The muscles of the forequarters should be strong and taut.

Body. Strong firm back, slightly higher at the shoulders, sloping smoothly towards the croup and tail. Wide loin, well protected by strong muscles. Wide croup. Ribs well sprung, deep and reaching well up to the loins. Chest measurement directly behind the elbows should be smaller than that about a hand's breadth behind the elbow, allowing for freedom of movement. Taut abdomen, slightly tucked up without protruding navel.

Hindquarters. Broad hips, slightly sloping towards the tail. Viewed from behind, strong well-muscled thighs, well-bent stifles should form a vertical line between hindlegs parallel to each other, hocks neither turned in nor out, slightly bent and square with the body. Pasterns nearly straight. Dewclaws to be removed. Muscles on the hindquarters should be strong and taut.

Feet. Well closed, moderately long and rounded, arched with dense hair, also between the toes, and well padded. Must not turn in nor out. Nails black and strong.

Tail. Well set on in a straight line from the back. Starts thick, tapering evenly towards the tip, well feathered, the longest hair being in the middle of the length, tapering up towards the tip. It should be carried gaily, horizontally or slightly bent upwards, never sideways, high over the back or curled over the back. The tip of the tail is usually docked according to the length of the dog, by about 1 cm to 2 cm (½ to 1 inch).

Hair. Skin should be firm without folds, but must not lie tight on the body. It should be long and dense, but not curly or coarse. Well feathered on front and hindlegs and on tail, more so in dogs than in bitches. The hair must lie short and smooth on the head.

Colour. White with black patches; white with black patches and flecks; white with black patches; black flecks, and black and white ticked; or any of the above without black patches. Head solid black; or black with white blaze or snip, stripe or star.

Weight and Size. Weight around 25 to 30 kg (55 to 65 lbs), height about 60 cm (24 in). Dogs are slightly taller and heavier than bitches.

Faults. Oddly placed or oddly-shaped eyes, ears, legs or feet, light-coloured nose. Over or undershot mouth, pincer bite. Light coloured eyes. Eyelids not closing properly, open eyes with red skin visible, pronounced stop and pronounced occiput. Ears too fleshy, in large folds or leathery, pointed tips. Head too large or too long, with wrinkles. Weak neck, narrow chest, loose shoulders, straight shoulders, long back, arched back or sway back. Flat or barrel-shaped ribs. Elbows, legs, or feet turning in or out. Cow-hocks, straight hindlegs. Heavy clumsy bones. Soft splayed toes, round catpaws, long hare paws. Tail not starting in a straight line from the back, kink in the tail. Tail held too high, sideways or curled up. Tight skin, curly or coarse coat. Any other colour than black and white. Nervous temperament. Feminine looking dogs and masculine looking bitches.

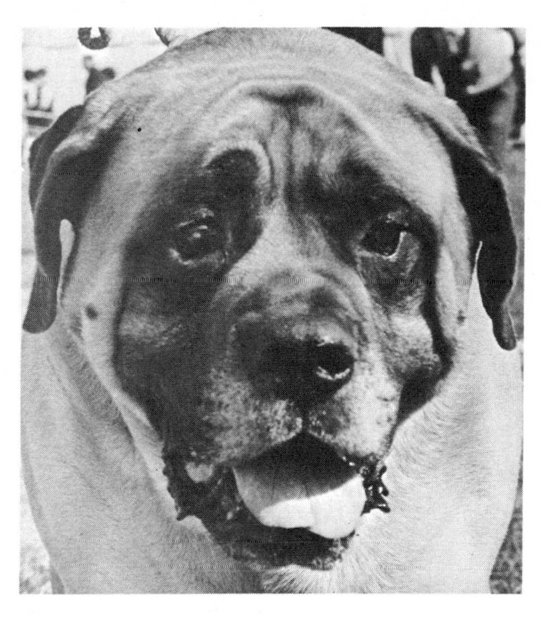

MASTIFF

(THE KENNEL CLUB—WORKING GROUP)

General Appearance. Large, massive, powerful, symmetrical and well-knit frame. A combination of grandeur and good nature, courage and docility. The head, in general outline giving a square appearance when viewed from any point. Breadth greatly to be desired, and should be in ratio to length of the whole head and face as 2 to 3. Body, massive, broad, deep, long, powerfully built, on legs wide apart and squarely set. Muscles sharply defined. Size a great desideratum, if combined with quality. Height and substance important if both points are proportionately combined.

Head and Skull. Skull broad between the ears, forehead flat, but wrinkled when attention is excited. Brows (superciliary ridges) slightly raised. Muscles of the temples and cheeks (temporal and masseter) well developed. Arch across the skull of a rounded, flattened curve, with a depression up the centre of the forehead from the median line between the eyes, to half-way up the sagittal suture. Face or muzzle, short, broad under the eyes, and keeping nearly parallel in width to the end of the nose; truncated, i.e., blunt and cut off squarely, thus forming a right-angle with the upper line of the face, of great depth from the point of the nose to under jaw. Under jaw broad to the end. Nose broad, with widely spreading nostrils when viewed from the front, flat (not pointed or turned up) in profile. Lips diverging at obtuse angles with the septum, and slightly pendulous so as to show a square profile. Length of muzzle to whole head and face as 1 to 3. Circumference of muzzle (measured mid-way between the eyes and nose) to that of the head (measured before the ears) as 3 to 5.

Eyes. Small, wide apart, divided by at least the space of two eyes. The stop between the eyes well marked but not too abrupt. Colour hazel brown, the darker the better, showing no haw.

Ears. Small, thin to the touch, wide apart, set on at the highest points of the sides of the skull, so as to continue the outline across the summit, and lying flat and close to the cheeks when in repose.

Mouth. Canine teeth healthy; powerful and wide apart; incisors level, or the lower projecting beyond the upper but never so much as to become visible when the mouth is closed.

Neck. Slightly arched, moderately long, very muscular, and measuring in circumference about one or two inches less than the skull before the ears.

Forequarters. Shoulder and arm slightly sloping, heavy and muscular. Legs straight, strong, and set wide apart; bones being large. Elbows square. Pasterns upright.

Body. Chest wide, deep and well let down between the forelegs. Ribs arched and well rounded. False ribs deep and well set back to the hips. Girth should be one-third more than the height at the shoulder. Back and loins wide and muscular; flat and very wide in a bitch, slightly arched in a dog. Great depth of flanks.

Hindquarters. Broad, wide and muscular, with well-developed second thighs, hocks bent, wide apart, and quite squarely set when standing or walking.

Feet. Large and round. Toes well arched up. Nails black.

Tail. Put on high up, and reaching to the hocks, or a little below them, wide at its root and tapering to the end, hanging straight in repose, but forming a curve with the end pointing upwards, but not over the back, when the dog is excited.

Coat. Short and close-lying, but not too fine over the shoulders, neck and back.

Colour. Apricot or silver, fawn, or dark fawn-brindle. In any case, muzzle, ears and nose should be black with black round the orbits, and extending upwards between them.

MASTIFF

(AMERICAN KENNEL CLUB—GROUP III: WORKING DOGS)

General Character and Symmetry. Large, massive, symmetrical and well-knit frame. A combination of grandeur and good nature, courage and docility.

General Description of Head. In general outline giving a massive appearance when viewed from any angle. Breadth greatly to be desired.

Skull. Broad and somewhat rounded between the ears, forehead slightly curved, showing marked wrinkles which are particularly distinctive when at attention. Brows (superciliary ridges) moderately raised. Muscles of the temples well developed, those of the cheeks extremely powerful. Arch across the skull a flattened curve with a furrow up the center of the forehead. This extends from between the eyes to halfway up the skull.

Ears. Small, V-shaped, rounded at the tips. Leather moderately thin, set widely apart at the highest points on the sides of the skull continuing the outline across the summit. They should lie close to the cheeks when in repose. Ears dark in color, the blacker the better, conforming to the color of the muzzle.

Eyes. Set wide apart, medium in size, never too prominent. Expression alert but kindly. The stop between the eyes well marked but not too abrupt. Color of eyes brown, the darker the better and showing no haw.

Face and Muzzle. Short, broad under the eyes and running nearly equal in width to the end of the nose. Truncated, *i.e.* blunt and cut off square, thus forming a right angle with the upper line of the face. Of great depth from the point of the nose to underjaw. Underjaw broad to the end and slightly rounded. Canine teeth healthy, powerful and wide apart. Scissors bite preferred but a moderately undershot jaw permissible providing the teeth are not visible when the mouth is closed. Lips diverging at obtuse angles with the septum and sufficiently pendulous so as to show a modified square profile. Nose broad and always dark in color, the blacker the better, with spread flat nostrils (not pointed or turned up) in profile. Muzzle dark in color, the blacker the better. Muzzle should be half the length of the skull, thus dividing the head into three parts—one for the foreface and two for the skull. In other words, the distance from tip of nose to stop is equal to one-half the distance between the stop and the occiput. Circumference of muzzle (measured midway between the eyes and nose) to that of the head (measured before the ears) as 3 is to 5.

Neck. Powerful and very muscular, slightly arched, and of medium length. The neck gradually increases in circumference as it approaches the shoulder. Neck moderately 'dry' (not showing an excess of loose skin).

Chest and Flanks. Wide, deep, rounded and well let down between the forelegs, extending at least to the elbow. Forechest should be deep and well defined. Ribs extremely well rounded. False ribs deep and well set back. There should be a reasonable, but not exaggerated, cut-up.

Shoulder and Arm. Slightly sloping, heavy and muscular. No tendency to looseness of shoulders.

Forelegs and Feet. Legs straight, strong and set wide apart, heavy-boned. Elbows parallel to body. Feet heavy, round and compact with well-arched toes. Pasterns strong and bent only slightly. Black nails preferred.

Hind Legs. Hindquarters broad, wide and muscular. Second thighs well developed, hocks set back, wide apart and parallel when viewed from the rear.

Back and Loins. Back muscular, powerful and straight. Loins wide and muscular, slightly rounded over the rump.

Tail. Set on moderately high and reaching to the hocks or a little below. Wide at the root, tapering to the end, hanging straight in repose, forming a slight curve but never over the back when dog is in action.

Coat. Outer coat moderately coarse. Undercoat, dense, short and close lying.

Color. Apricot, silver fawn or dark fawn-brindle. Fawn-brindle should have fawn as a background color which should be completely covered with very dark stripes. In any case muzzle, ears and nose must be dark in color, the blacker the better, with similar color tone around the orbits, extending upwards between them.

Size. Dogs, minimum, 30 inches at the shoulder; bitches, minimum, $27\frac{1}{2}$ inches at the shoulder.

SCALE OF POINTS

General character and symmetry	10	Chest and ribs	10
Height and substance	10	Forelegs and feet	10
Skull	10	Back, loins and flanks	10
Face and muzzle	12	Hind legs and feet	10
Ears	5	Tail	3
Eyes	5	Coat and color	5
		Total	100

Approved July 8, 1941

MINIATURE PINSCHER

(THE KENNEL CLUB—TOY GROUP)

General Appearance. The Miniature Pinscher is structurally a well balanced, sturdy, compact, elegant, short-coupled, smooth-coated toy dog. He is naturally well groomed, proud, vigorous and alert. The natural characteristic traits which identify him from other toy dogs are his precise Hackney gait, his fearless animation, complete self-possession and his spirited presence.

Head and Skull. Rather more elongated than short and round. Narrow and without conspicuous cheek formation. In correct proportion to the body. The skull should appear flat when viewed from the front. The muzzle must be rather strong and proportionate to the skull. The nose well formed, black only with the exception of livers and blues, which may have a self-coloured nose.

Eyes. Fitting well into the face. Neither too full nor round, neither too little nor slanting. Black or nearly black.

Ears. Must be set on high, as small as possible, erect or dropped.

Mouth. Scissors bite.

Neck. Strong yet graceful. Slightly arched. Well fitted into the shoulders. Free from throatiness.

Forequarters. Forechest well developed and full, moderately broad, shoulders clean, sloping with moderate angulation. Coordinated to permit the true action of the Hackney pony.

Body. To be square, back line straight, sloping slightly towards the rear. Belly moderately tucked up. Ribs well sprung, deep rather than barrelled. Viewed from the top slightly wedge-shaped.

Hindquarters. Should be parallel to each other and wide enough apart to fit in with a properly built body. The hindquarters should be well developed and muscular with a good sweep of stifle and their hocks turning neither in nor out.

Feet. Legs straight, medium bone. Feet cat-like, elbows close to body. Nails, dark.

Tail. A continuation of the top-line carried a little high and docked short.

Coat. Smooth, hard and short. Straight and lustrous. Closely adhering to and uniformly covering the body.

Colour. Black, blue, chocolate with sharply defined tan markings on cheeks, lips, lower jaw, throat, twin spots above eyes and chest, lower half of forelegs, inside of hindlegs and vent region, lower portion of hocks and feet. All the above colours should have black pencilling on toes with no thumb marks. Solid red of various shades. Slight white on chest is permissible but undesirable.

Height. The height is to range from 10 to 12 inches at the withers.

MINIATURE PINSCHER

(AMERICAN KENNEL CLUB—GROUP V: TOYS)

General Appearance. The Miniature Pinscher was originated in Germany and named the 'Reh Pinscher' due to his resemblance in structure and animation to a very small specie of deer found in the forests. This breed is structurally a well-balanced, sturdy, compact, short-coupled, smooth-coated toy dog. He is naturally well groomed, proud, vigorous and alert. The natural characteristic traits which identify him from other toy dogs are his precise Hackney gait, his fearless animation, complete self-possession, and his spirited presence.

Faults. Structurally lacking in balance, too long- or short-coupled, too coarse or too refined (lacking in bone development causing poor feet and legs), too large or too small, lethargic, timid or dull, shy or vicious, low in tail placement and poor in action (action not typical of the breed requirements). Knotty overdeveloped muscles.

Head. In correct proportion with the body. *From Top:* Tapering, narrow with well-fitted but not too prominent foreface which should balance with the skull. No indication of coarseness. *From Front:* Skull appears flat, tapering forward toward the muzzle. Muzzle itself strong rather than fine and delicate, and in proportion to the head as a whole; cheeks and lips small, taut and closely adherent to each other. Teeth in perfect alignment and apposition. *From Side:* Well-balanced with only a slight drop to the muzzle, which should be parallel to the top of the skull.

Eyes. Full, slightly oval, almost round, clear, bright and dark even to a true black; set wide apart and fitted well into the sockets.

Ears. Well-set and firmly placed, upstanding (when cropped, pointed and carried erect in balance with the head).

Nose. Black only (with the exception of chocolates, which may have a self-colored nose).

Faults. Too large or too small for the body, too coarse or too refined, pinched and weak in foreface, domed in skull, too flat and lacking in chiseling, giving a vapid expression. *Jaws and teeth* overshot or undershot. *Eyes* too round and full, too large, bulging, too deep-set or set too far apart; or too small, set too close (pig eyes). Light-colored eyes not desirable. *Ears* poorly placed, low-set hanging ears (lacking in cartilage) which detract from head conformation. (Poorly cropped ears if set on the head properly and having sufficient cartilage should not detract from head points, as this would be a man-made fault and automatically would detract from general appearance.) *Nose* any color other than black (with the exception of chocolates which may have a self-colored nose).

Neck. Proportioned to head and body. Slightly arched, gracefully curved, clean and firm, blending into shoulders, length well-balanced, muscular and free from a suggestion of dewlap or throatiness.

Faults. Too straight or too curved; too thick or too thin; too long or short; knotty muscles; loose, flabby or wrinkled skin.

Body. *From Top:* Compact, slightly wedge-shaped, muscular with well-sprung ribs. *From Side:* Depth of brisket, the base line of which is level with the points of the elbows; short and strong in loin with belly moderately tucked up to denote grace in structural form. Back level or slightly sloping toward the rear. Length of males equals height at withers. Females may be slightly longer. *From Rear:* High tail-set; strong, sturdy upper shanks, with croup slope at about 30 degrees; vent opening not barreled.

Forequarters. Forechest well-developed and full, moderately broad, shoulders clean, sloping with moderate angulation, co-ordinated to permit the true action of the Hackney pony.

Hindquarters. Well-knit muscular quarters set wide enough apart to fit into a properly balanced body.

Faults. *From Top:* Too long, too barreled, lacking in body development. *From Side:* Too long, too short, too thin or too fat, hips higher or considerably lower than the withers, lacking depth of chest, too full in loin, sway back, roach back or wry back. *From Rear.* Quarters too wide or too close to each other, overdeveloped, barreled vent, underdeveloped vent, too sloping croup, tail set low. *Forequarters*—forechest and spring of rib too narrow (or too shallow and underdeveloped), shoulders too straight, too loose, or too short and overloaded with muscles. *Hindquarters*—too narrow, undermuscled or overmuscled, too steep in croup.

Legs and Feet. Strong bone development and small clean joints; feet catlike, toes strong, well-arched and closely knit with deep pads and thick, blunt nails.

Forelegs and Feet. Viewed from the front straight and upstanding, elbows close to body, well-knit, flexible yet strong with perpendicular pasterns.

Hindlegs. All adjacent bones should appear well-angulated with well-muscled thighs or upper shanks, with clearly well-defined stifles, hocks short, set well apart turning neither in nor out, while at rest should stand perpendicular to the ground and upper shanks, lower shanks and hocks parallel to each other.

Faults. Too thick or thin bone development, large joints, spreading flat feet.

Forelegs and Feet. Bowed or crooked, weak pasterns, feet turning in or out, loose elbows.

Hindlegs. Thin undeveloped stifles, large or crooked hocks, loose stifle joints.

Tail. Set high, held erect, docked to $\frac{1}{2}$ to 1 inch.

Faults. Set too low, too thin, drooping, hanging or poorly docked.

Coat. Smooth, hard and short, straight and lustrous, closely adhering to and uniformly covering the body.

Faults. Thin, too long, dull; upstanding; curly; dry; area of various thickness or bald spots.

Color. 1. Solid red or stag red. 2. Lustrous black with sharply defined tan, rust-red markings on cheeks, lips, lower jaw, throat, twin spots above eyes and chest, lower half of forelegs, inside of hindlegs and vent region, lower portion of hocks and feet. Black pencil stripes on toes. 3. Solid brown or chocolate with rust or yellow markings. **Faults.** Any color other than listed; very dark or sooty spots.
Disqualifications. Thumb marks or any area of white on feet or forechest exceeding one-half (½) inch in its longest dimension.
Size. Desired height 11 inches to 11½ inches at the withers. A dog of either sex measuring under 10 inches or over 12½ inches shall be disqualified. **Faults.** Oversize; undersize; too fat; too lean.

SCALE OF POINTS

General appearance and movement—(*very important*)	30	Body	15
Skull	5	Feet	5
Muzzle	5	Legs	5
Mouth	5	Color	5
Eyes	5	Coat	5
Ears	5	Tail	5
Neck	5	Total	100

DISQUALIFICATIONS

Color. Thumb marks or any area of white on feet or forechest exceeding one-half (½) inch in its longest dimension. Size. A dog of either sex measuring under 10 or over 12½ inches.

Approved May 13, 1958

MINIATURE SCHNAUZER

(THE KENNEL CLUB—UTILITY GROUP)

General Appearance. The Miniature Schnauzer is a powerfully built, robust, sinewy, nearly square, dog (length of body equal to height at shoulders). His temperament combines high spirits, reliability, strength, endurance and vigour. Expression keen and attitude alert. Correct conformation is of more importance than colour or other purely 'beauty' points.

Head and Skull. Head strong and elongated, gradually narrowing from the ears to the eyes and thence forward toward the tip of the nose. Upper part of the head (occiput to the base of the forehead) moderately broad between the ears—with flat, creaseless, forehead and well muscled, but not too strongly developed cheeks. Medium stop to accentuate prominent eyebrows. The powerful muzzle formed by the upper and lower jaws (base of forehead to the tip of the nose) should end in a moderately blunt line, with bristly, stubby moustache and chin whiskers. Ridge of the nose straight and running almost parallel to the extension of the forehead. The nose is black and full. Lips tight and not overlapping.

Eyes. Medium sized, dark, oval, set forward, with arched bushy eyebrows.

Ears. Neat and V-shaped, set high and dropping forward to temple.

Mouth. Scissor teeth, slightly overlapping from the top; with strongly developed fangs; healthy and pure white.

Neck. Moderately long, nape strong and slightly arched, skin close to throat, neck set cleanly on shoulders.

Forequarters. Shoulders flat and sloping. Forelegs straight viewed from any position. Muscles smooth and lithe rather than prominent; bone strong, straight and carried well down to the feet; elbows set close to the body and pointing directly backward.

Body. Chest moderately broad, deep, with visible strong breast bone reaching down to at least the height of elbow and slightly rising backward to loins. Back strong and straight, slightly higher at the shoulder than at the hindquarters, with short, well developed loins. Ribs well sprung. Length of body equal to height from top of withers to ground.

Hindquarters. Thighs slanting and flat, but strongly muscled. Hindlegs (upper and lower thighs) at first vertical to the stifle, from stifle to hock, in line with the extension of the upper neck line, from hock, vertical to ground.

Feet. Short, round, extremely compact with close-arched toes (cat's paws), dark nails and hard soles. The feet also deep or thickly padded, pointing forward.

Tail. Set on and carried high, cut down to three joints.

Coat. Hard and wiry and just short enough for smartness, clean on neck, shoulder, ears and skull, plenty of good hard hair on front legs. Good undercoat is essential.

Colour. All pepper and salt colours in even proportions, or pure black.

Height. The ideal height for bitches shall be 13 inches and for dogs 14 inches. Too small, toyish-appearing dogs are not typical and should be penalised.

Faults. Too heavy or too light; too low or high on the leg. Head too heavy or round, creased forehead, sticking-out, or badly carried, ears; light eye, with yellow or light grey rings; strongly protruding cheek-bones; flabby throat skin; undershot or overshot jaw. Muzzle too pointed or too small. Back too long, sunken or roached; barrel-shaped ribs; slanting crupper; elbows turned out; heels turned in, hindpart overbuilt (too steep). Toes spread open; paws long and flat (hare). Coat too short and sleek, or too long, soft or curled. All white, spotty, tigered or red colours. Small white breast spot or marking is not a fault. Among other serious faults are cow-hocks, sunken pasterns, or any weakness of joint, bones or muscular development.

MINIATURE SCHNAUZER

(AMERICAN KENNEL CLUB—GROUP IV: TERRIERS)

General Appearance. The Miniature Schnauzer is a robust, active dog of terrier type, resembling his larger cousin, the Standard Schnauzer in general appearance, and of an alert, active disposition. He is sturdily built, nearly square in proportion of body length to height, with plenty of bone, and without any suggestion of toyishness.
Head. Strong and rectangular, its width diminishing slightly from ears to eyes, and again to the tip of the nose. The forehead is unwrinkled. The topskull is flat and fairly long. The foreface is parallel to the topskull, with a slight stop, and is at least as long as the topskull. The muzzle is strong in proportion to the skull; it ends in a moderately blunt manner, with thick whiskers which accentuate the rectangular shape of the head.
Teeth. The teeth meet in a scissors bite. That is, the upper front teeth overlap the lower front teeth in such a manner that the inner surface of the upper incisors barely touches the outer surface of the lower incisors when the mouth is closed.
Eyes. Small, dark brown and deep-set. They are oval in appearance and keen in expression.
Ears. When cropped the ears are identical in shape and length, with pointed tips. They are in balance with the head and not exaggerated in length. They are set high on the skull and carried perpendicularly at the inner edges, with as little bell as possible along the outer edges. When uncropped, the ears are small and V-shaped, folding close to the skull.
Neck. Strong and well arched, blending into the shoulders, and with the skin fitting tightly at the throat.
Body. Short and deep, with the brisket extending at least to the elbows. Ribs are well sprung and deep, extending well back to a short loin. The underbody does not present a tucked-up appearance at the flank. The topline is straight; it declines slightly from the withers to the base of the tail. The over-all length from chest to stern bone equals the height at the withers.
Forequarters. The forequarters have flat, somewhat sloping shoulders and high withers. Forelegs are straight and parallel when viewed from all sides. They have strong pasterns and good bone. They are separated by a fairly deep brisket which precludes a pinched front. The elbows are close, and the ribs spread gradually from the first rib so as to allow space for the elbows to move close to the body.
Hindquarters. The hindquarters have strong-muscled, slanting thighs: they are well bent at the stifles and straight from hock to so-called heel. There is sufficient angulation so that, in stance, the hocks extend beyond the tail. The hindquarters never appear overbuilt or higher than the shoulders.
Feet. Short and round (cat-feet) with thick, black pads. The toes are arched and compact.
Action. The trot is the gait at which movement is judged. The dog must gait in a straight line. Coming on, the forelegs are parallel, with the elbows close to the body. The feet turn neither inward nor outward. Going away, the hind legs are parallel from the hocks down, and travel wide. Viewed from the side, the forelegs have a good reach, while the hing legs have a strong drive with good pick-up of hocks.
Tail. Set high and carried erect. It is docked only long enough to be clearly visible over the topline of the body when the dog is in proper length of coat.
Coat. Double, with a hard, wiry outer coat and a close undercoat. The body coat should be plucked. When in show condition, the proper length is not less than three-quarters of an inch except on neck, ears and skull. Furnishings are fairly thick but not silky.
Size. From 12 to 14 inches. Ideal size 13½ inches. (*See disqualifications.*)
Color. The recognized colors are salt and pepper, black and silver, and solid black. The typical color is salt and pepper in shades of gray; tan shading is permissible. The salt and pepper mixture fades out to light gray or silver white in the eyebrows, whiskers, cheeks, under throat, across chest, under tail, leg furnishings, under body, and inside legs. The light under-body hair is not to rise higher on the sides of the body than the front elbows.

The black and silvers follow the same pattern as the salt and peppers. The entire salt-and-pepper section must be black.

Black is the only solid color allowed. It must be a true black with no gray hairs and no brown tinge except where the whiskers may have become discolored. A small white spot on the chest is permitted.

FAULTS

Type. Toyishness, raciness, or coarseness. **Structure.** Head coarse and cheeky. Chest too broad or shallow in brisket. Tail set low. Sway or roach back. Bowed or cowhocked hindquarters. Loose elbows. **Action.** Sidegaiting. Paddling in front, or high hackney knee action. Weak hind action. **Coat.** Too soft or too smooth and slick in appearance. **Temperament.** Shyness or viciousness. **Bit.** Undershot or overshot jaw. Level bite. **Eyes.** Light and/or large and prominent in appearance.

DISQUALIFICATIONS

Dogs or bitches under 12 inches or over 14 inches. Color solid white or white patches on the body.

Approved May 13, 1958

NEWFOUNDLAND

(THE KENNEL CLUB—WORKING GROUP)

Characteristics. A water dog, used for life-saving; he should have an exceptionally gentle and docile nature.

General Appearance. The dog should impress the eye with strength and great activity. He should move freely on his legs with the body swung loosely between them, so that a slight roll in gait should not be objectionable. Bone massive throughout, but not to give a heavy, inactive appearance.

Head and Skull. Head should be broad and massive, the occipital bone well developed; there should be no decided stop; the muzzle should be short, clean cut and rather square in shape and covered with short, fine hair.

Eyes. Should be small, of a dark brown colour; rather deeply set, but not showing any haw; should be set rather wide apart.

Ears. Should be small, set well back, square with the skull, lie close to the head, and covered with short hair without a fringe.

Mouth. Should be soft and well covered by the lips, should be neither undershot nor overshot but teeth should be level or scissor bite.

Neck. Should be strong, well set on to shoulders and back.

Forequarters. Legs should be perfectly straight, well covered with muscle, elbows in but well let down; feathered all down.

Body. Should be well ribbed up with broad back and strong muscular loins. Chest should be deep and fairly broad; well covered with hair, but not to such an extent as to form a frill.

Hindquarters. Should be very strong. The legs should have great freedom of action; slightly feathered. Slackness of loin and cow-hocks are a defect. Dewclaws are objectionable and should be removed.

Feet. Should be large and well shaped. Splayed or turned out feet are objectionable.

Tail. Should be of moderate length, reaching down a little below the hocks. It should be of fair thickness and well covered with hair, but not to form a flag. When the dog is standing still and not excited it should hang downwards with a slight curve at the end; but when the dog is in motion it should be carried up, and when he is excited straight out with only a slight curve at the end. Tails with a kink or curled over the back are very objectionable.

Coat. Should be flat and dense, of a coarsish texture and oily nature, and capable of resisting water. If brushed the wrong way it should fall back into its place naturally.

Colour. (*a*) Dull jet black. A slight tinge of bronze or white on chest and toes is not objectionable. (*b*) Other than black. Should in all respects follow the black except in colour, which may be almost any, but the colours most to be encouraged are white and black or bronze. Beauty in markings is important. Black dogs that have only white toes and white breasts and white to tip of tail must be exhibited in the classes provided for 'black'.

Weight and Size. Size and weight are very desirable so long as symmetry is maintained. A fair average height at the shoulders is 28 inches for a dog and 26 inches for a bitch, and a fair average weight is, respectively: Dogs, 140 to 150 lbs, bitches, 110 to 120 lbs.

Faults. Weak or hollow back, slackness of the loins or cow-hocks. Dewclaws. Splayed or turned-out feet. Tails with a kink in them or curled over the back.

NEWFOUNDLAND

(AMERICAN KENNEL CLUB—GROUP III: WORKING DOGS)

General Appearance. The Newfoundland is large, strong, and active, at home in water and on land, and has natural life-saving instincts. He is a multipurpose dog capable of heavy work as well as of being a devoted companion for child and man. To fulfil its purposes the Newfoundland is deep bodied, well muscled, and well coordinated. A good specimen of the breed has dignity and proud head carriage. The length of the dog's body, from withers to base of tail, is approximately equal to the height of the dog at the withers. However, a bitch is not to be faulted if the length of her body is slightly greater than her height. The dog's appearance is more massive throughout than the bitch's, with larger frame and heavier bone. The Newfoundland is free moving with a loosely slung body. When he moves, a slight roll is perceptible. Complete webbing between the toes is always present. Large size is desirable but never at the expense of gait, symmetry, balance, or conformation to the Standard herein described.

Head. The head is massive with a broad skull, slightly arched crown, and strongly developed occipital bone. The slope from the top of the skull to the tip of the muzzle has a definite but not steep stop. The forehead and face is smooth and free of wrinkles; the muzzle is clean cut and covered with short, fine hair. The muzzle is square, deep, and fairly short; its length from stop to tip of nose is less than from stop to occiput. The nostrils are well developed. The bitch's head follows the same general conformation as the dog's but is feminine and less massive. A narrow head and a snipey or long muzzle are to be faulted.

Eyes are dark brown, relatively small, and deep-set; they are spaced wide apart and have no haw showing. Round, protruding, or yellow eyes are objectionable.

Ears are relatively small and triangular with rounded tips. They are set well back on the skull and lie close to the head. When the ear is brought forward it reaches to the inner corner of the eye on the same side.

Teeth meet in a scissors or level bite.

The Newfoundland's expression is soft and reflects the character of the breed; benevolent, intelligent, dignified, and of sweet disposition. The dog never looks or acts either dull or ill-tempered.

Neck. The neck is strong and well set on the shoulders. It is long enough for proud head carriage.

Body. The Newfoundland's chest is full and deep with the brisket reaching at least down to the elbows. The back is broad, and the topline is level from the withers to the croup, never roached, slack, or swayed. He is broad at the croup, is well muscled, and has very strong loins. The croup slopes at an angle of about 30 degrees. Bone structure is massive throughout but does not give a heavy, sluggish appearance.

Forequarters. When the dog is not in motion, the forelegs are perfectly straight and parallel with the elbows close to the chest. The layback of the shoulders is about 45 degrees, and the upper arm meets the shoulder blade at an angle of about 90 degrees. The shoulders are well muscled. The pasterns are slightly sloping.

Hindquarters. Because driving power for swimming, pulling loads, or covering ground efficiently is dependent on the hindquarters, the rear assembly of the Newfoundland is of prime importance. It is well muscled, the thighs are fairly long, the stifles well bent, and the hocks wide and straight. Cowhocks, barrel legs, or pigeon toes are to be seriously faulted.

Feet. The feet are proportionate to the body in size, cat-foot in type, well-rounded and tight with firm, arched toes, and with webbing present. Dewclaws on the rear legs are to be removed.

Tail. The tail of the Newfoundland acts as a rudder when he is swimming. Therefore, it is broad and strong at the base. The tail reaches down a little below the hocks. When the dog is standing the tail hangs straight down, possibly a little bent at the tip; when the dog is in motion or excited, the tail is carried straight out or slightly curved, but it never curls over the back. A tail with a kink is a serious fault.

Gait. The Newfoundland in motion gives the impression of effortless power, has good reach and strong drive. A dog may appear symmetrical and well balanced when standing, but, if he is not structurally sound, he will lose that symmetry and balance when he moves. In motion, the legs move straight forward; they do not swing in an arc nor do the hocks move in or out in relation to the line of travel. A slight roll is present. As the dog's speed increases from a walk to a trot, the feet move in under the center line of the body to maintain balance. Mincing, shuffling, crabbing, too close moving, weaving, hackney action, and pacing are all faults.

Size. The average height for dogs is 28 inches,

for bitches 26 inches. The average weight for dogs is 150 lbs, for bitches, 120 lbs. Large size is desirable but is not to be favored over correct gait, symmetry, and structure.

Coat. The Newfoundland has a water-resistant double coat. The outer coat is moderately long and full but not shaggy. It is straight and flat with no curl, although it may have a slight wave. The coat, when rubbed the wrong way, tends to fall back into place. The undercoat, which is soft and dense, is often less dense during summer months or in tropical climates but is always found to some extent on the rump and chest. An open coat is to be seriously faulted. The hair on the head, muzzle, and ears is short and fine, and the legs are feathered all the way down. The tail is covered with long dense hair, but it does not form a flag.

Color. Black. A slight tinge of bronze or a splash of white on chest and toes is not objectionable. Black dogs that have only white toes and white chest and white tip to tail should be exhibited in the classes provided for 'black.'

Other than black. Should in all respects follow the black except in color, which may be almost any, so long as it disqualifies for the black class, but the colors most to be encouraged are bronze or white and black (Landseer) with black head marked with narrow blaze, even marked saddle and black rump extending on to tail. Beauty in markings to be taken greatly into consideration.

Disqualifications. Markings other than white on a solid-colored dog.

Approved June 9, 1970

NORFOLK TERRIER

(THE KENNEL CLUB—TERRIER GROUP)

Characteristics. The Norfolk Terrier is one of the smallest of the Terriers, but a 'demon' for its size. Of a lovable disposition, not quarrelsome, with a hardy constitution. Temperament: Alert and fearless.

General Appearance. A small low keen dog, compact and strong with short back, good substance and bone.

Head and Skull. Skull wide and slightly rounded with good width between the ears. Muzzle wedge-shaped and strong; length of muzzle slightly less than half the length of skull. Stop should be well defined.

Eyes. Oval shaped and deep set, in colour dark brown or black. Expression alert, keen and intelligent.

Ears. Size medium 'V' shaped but slightly rounded at tip, dropping forward close to the cheek.

Mouth. Tight lipped, jaw strong; teeth strong and rather large; scissor bite.

Neck. Medium length and strong.

Forequarters. Clean and powerful shoulders with short, powerful and straight legs.

Body. Compact with short back and well sprung ribs.

Hindquarters. Well muscled, good turn of stifle, hocks well let down and straight when viewed from rear; with great powers of propulsion.

Feet. Round with thick pads.

Tail. Medium docked, not excessively gay.

Coat. Hard, wiry and straight, lying close to the body. It is longer and rougher on the neck and shoulders. Hair on the head, ears and muzzle short and smooth.

Colour. All shades of red, red wheaten, black and tan or grizzle. White marks or patches are undesirable but shall not disqualify.

Size. Ideal height 10 in at withers.

Faults. Excessive trimming is not desirable. Honourable scars from fair wear and tear shall not count against.

The Norfolk Terrier is known by the American Kennel Club as the Norwich Terrier. For the American Kennel Club standard of the Norwich Terrier, see page 427.

NORWEGIAN BUHUND

(THE KENNEL CLUB—WORKING GROUP)

Characteristics. The Norwegian Buhund should be fearless and brave.

General Appearance. The Norwegian Buhund is a typical Spitz dog of under middle size, lightly built, with a short compact body, fairly smooth-lying coat, erect pointed ears, tail carried curled over the back, and with an energetic character.

It is of prime importance that the Buhund should be a well balanced dog, free from all exaggeration and should be capable of the arduous work for which it is bred.

Head and Skull. Head—lean, light, rather broad between the ears, wedge-shaped, narrowing towards the point of the nose. Skull and back of head almost flat; marked but not sharp stop; muzzle of medium length, tapering evenly from above and side, with straight bridge; lips tightly closed.

Eyes. Not protruding, colour dark brown, lively with a fearless expression.

Ears. Placed high, erect, the height greater than the base; sharply pointed and very mobile.

Neck. Medium length, lean without loose skin, good carriage.

Forequarters. Legs lean, straight and strong, elbows tightly placed.

Body. Strong and short, but light; chest deep with good ribs; straight line of back, good loins, strong couplings, slightly drawn up.

Hindquarters. Only a little angulated, straight when seen from behind.

Feet. Rather small, oval in shape, with tightly closed toes.

Tail. Placed high on, short, thick and hairy, but without long hair, tightly curled.

Coat. Close and harsh, but smooth; on head and front legs—short close and smooth; longer on chest, neck and shoulders and back of legs and inside of tail curl. The coat is made up of a harsh top hair, with soft wool undercoat.

Colour. Wheaten (biscuit), black, red (if the red is not too dark), wolf-sable. Preferably self-coloured but small symmetric markings such as white on chest and legs, blaize on head and narrow ring on neck, black masks and ears and black tips to the tail are permissible.

Size. Dogs not more than 45 cms ($17\frac{3}{4}$ inches); bitches somewhat less.

Faults. White dogs. Light eyes. Light nose. Undershot or overshot mouth. Drop ear.

NORWICH TERRIER

(THE KENNEL CLUB—TERRIER GROUP)

Characteristics. The Norwich Terrier is one of the smallest of the Terriers. Of a lovable disposition, not quarrelsome and with a hardy constitution. Temperament—gay and fearless.

General Appearance. A small, low, keen dog, compact and strong with good substance and bone. Excessive trimming is not desirable. Honourable scars from fair wear and tear should not count against.

Head and Skull. Muzzle 'foxy' and strong; length about one third less than a measurement from the occiput to the bottom of the stop, which should be well defined. Skull wide (good width between the ears) and slightly rounded.

Eyes. Dark, full of expression, bright and keen.

Ears. To be erect.

Mouth. Tight lipped. Jaws clean and strong. Teeth strong, rather large, scissor bite.

Neck. Strong, of good length, commensurate with correct overall balance.

Forequarters. Well laid back shoulders, with short powerful and straight legs; not out at elbow. Legs should be moving straight forward when travelling.

Body. Compact with good depth. Rib cage should be long and well sprung with short loin. Level topline.

Hindquarters. Strong and muscular with well-turned stifle and low set hock and with great powers of propulsion.

Feet. Round with thick pads.

Tail. Medium docked, set on high to complete a perfectly level back and carried erect.

Coat. Hard, wiry and straight, lying close to the body. It is longer and rougher on the neck and chest, forming a ruff to frame the face. Hair on the head, ears and muzzle short and smooth, except for eyebrows and whiskers.

Colour. All shades of red, wheaten, black and tan and grizzle. White marks or patches are undesirable.

Size. Ideal height 10 inches at the withers, this ideal height shall not be attained by excessive length of leg.

Faults. Light bone; long weak back; a mouth over or under-shot; a long narrow head; cow hocks; feet turned in; yellow or pale eyes; soft, wavy, curly or silky coat.

NORWICH TERRIER

(AMERICAN KENNEL CLUB—GROUP IV: TERRIERS)

Head. Skull wide, slightly rounded with good width between the ears. Muzzle strong but not long or heavy, with slightly 'foxy' appearance. Length about one-third less than the measurement from the occiput to the bottom of the stop, which should be well defined.

Faults. A long narrow head; over square muzzle; highly rounded dome.

Ears. Prick or drop. If pricked, small, pointed, erect and set well apart. If dropped, neat, small, with break just above the skull line, front edge close to cheek, and not falling lower than the outer corner of the eye.

Faults. Oversize; poor carriage.

Eyes. Very bright, dark and keen. Full of expression.

Faults. Light or protruding eyes.

Jaw. Clean, strong, tight lipped, with strong, large, closely-fitting teeth; scissors bite.

Faults. A bite over- or undershot.

Neck. Short and strong, well set on clean shoulders.

Body. Moderately short, compact and deep with level topline, ribs well sprung.

Faults. Long weak back, loaded shoulders.

Legs. Short and powerful and as straight as is consistent with the short legs for which we aim. Sound bone, round feet, thick pads.

Faults. Out at elbow, badly bowed, knuckled over. Too light in bone.

Quarters. Strong, rounded, with great powers of propulsion.

Faults. Cowhocks.

Tail. Medium docked, carriage not excessively gay.

Color. All shades of red, wheaten, black and tan and grizzle. White markings on the chest, though allowable, are not desirable.

Faults. White markings elsewhere or to any great extent on the chest.

Coat. As hard and wiry as possible, lying close to the body, with a definite undercoat. Top coat absolutely straight; in full coat longer and rougher forming almost a mane on shoulders and neck. Hair on head, ears and muzzle, except for slight eyebrows and slight whiskers, is absolutely short and smooth. These dogs should be shown with as nearly a natural coat as possible. A minimum amount of tidying is permissible but excessive trimming, shaping and clipping shall be heavily penalized by the judge.

Faults. Silky or curly coat.

Weight. Ideal, 11 to 12 lbs.

Height. Ideal, 10 inches at the withers.

General Appearance. A small, low rugged terrier, tremendously active. A perfect demon, yet not quarrelsome, and of a lovable disposition, and a very hardy constitution. Honorable scars from fair wear and tear shall not count against.

DISQUALIFICATION

Cropped ears shall disqualify.

Approved June 10, 1969

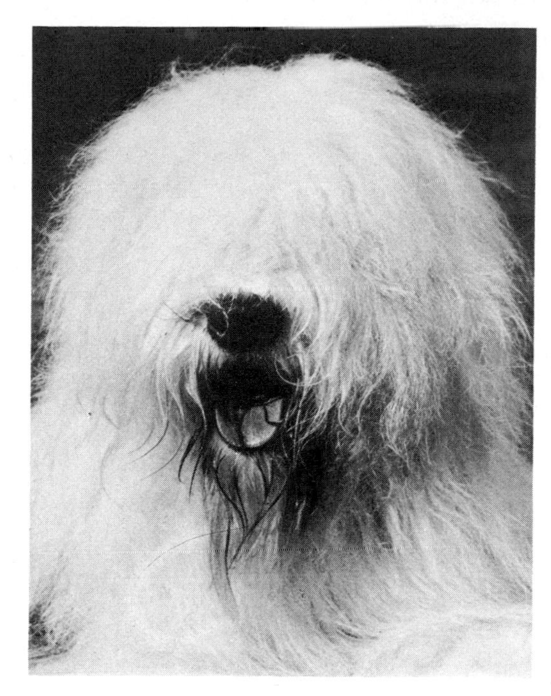

OLD ENGLISH SHEEPDOG

(THE KENNEL CLUB—WORKING GROUP)

General Appearance. A strong, compact-looking dog of great symmetry; absolutely free of legginess; profusely coated all over; very elastic in a gallop but in walking or trotting has a characteristic ambling or pacing movement; and his bark should be loud, with a peculiar 'pot casse' ring in it. All round he is a thick-set, muscular, able-bodied dog, with a most intelligent expression, free of all Poodle or Deerhound character.

Head and Skull. Skull capacious and rather squarely formed, giving plenty of room for brain power. The parts over the eyes should be well arched and the whole well-covered with hair. Jaw fairly long, strong, square, and truncated; the stop should be defined to avoid a Deerhound face.

Nose. Always black, large, and capacious.

Eyes. Dark or wall eyes are to be preferred.

Ears. Small and carried flat to side of head, coated moderately.

Mouth. Teeth strong and large, evenly placed and level.

Neck. The neck should be fairly long, arched gracefully, and well coated with hair.

Forequarters. The forelegs should be dead straight, with plenty of bone, holding the body well from the ground, without approaching legginess; well coated all round. The shoulders sloping and narrow at the points, the dog standing lower at the shoulders than at the loin.

Body. Rather short and very compact, ribs well sprung, and brisket deep and capacious. The loin should be very stout and gently arched.

Hindquarters. The hindquarters should be round and muscular, hocks well let down and the hams densely coated with a thick, long jacket in excess of that of any other part of the body.

Feet. Small, round; toes well arched, and pads thick and round.

Tail. Puppies requiring docking should have the operation performed within a week from birth, preferably within four days.

Coat. Profuse, and of good hard texture; not straight, but shaggy and free from curl. The undercoat should be a waterproof pile when not removed by grooming.

Colour. Any shade of grey, grizzle, blue or blue merle, with or without white markings; any shade of brown or sable to be considered distinctly objectionable and not to be encouraged.

Weight and Size. Twenty-two inches and upwards for dogs, slightly less for bitches. Type, symmetry and character of the greatest importance, and on no account to be sacrificed to size alone.

Faults. A long, narrow head.

OLD ENGLISH SHEEPDOG

(AMERICAN KENNEL CLUB—GROUP III: WORKING DOGS)

Skull. Capacious and rather squarely formed, giving plenty of room for brain power. The parts over the eyes should be well arched and the whole well covered with hair.
Jaw. Fairly long, strong, square and truncated. The top should be well defined to avoid a Deerhound face. (The attention of judges is particularly called to the above properties, as a long, narrow head is a deformity.)
Eyes. Vary according to the color of the dog. Very dark preferred, but in the glaucous or blue dogs a pearl, walleye or china eye is considered typical. (A light eye is most objectionable.)
Nose. Always black, large and capacious.
Teeth. Strong and large, evenly placed and level in opposition.
Ears. Medium-sized, and carried flat to side of head, coated moderately.
Legs. The forelegs should be dead straight, with plenty of bone, removing the body a medium height from the ground, without approaching legginess, and well coated all around.
Feet. Small, round; toes well arched, and pads thick and hard.
Tail. It is preferable that there should be none. Should never, however, exceed $1\frac{1}{2}$ or 2 inches in grown dogs. When not natural-born bobtails however, puppies should be docked at the first joint from the body and the operation performed when they are from three to four days old.
Neck and Shoulders. The neck should be fairly long, arched gracefully and well coated with hair. The shoulders sloping and narrow at the points, the dog standing lower at the shoulder than at the loin.
Body. Rather short and very compact, ribs well sprung and brisket deep and capacious. *Slab-sidedness highly undesirable.* The loin should be very stout and gently arched, while the hindquarters should be round and muscular and with well-let-down hocks, and the hams densely coated with a thick, long jacket in excess of any other part.
Coat. Profuse, but not so excessive as to give the impression of the dog being overfat, and of a good hard texture; not straight, but shaggy and free from curl. *Quality and texture of coat to be considered above mere profuseness.* Softness or flatness of coat to be considered a fault. The undercoat should be a waterproof pile, when not removed by grooming or season.
Color. Any shade of gray, grizzle, blue or blue-merled with or without white markings or in reverse. *Any shade of brown or fawn to be considered distinctly objectionable and not to be encouraged.*
Size. Twenty-two inches and upwards for dogs and slightly less for bitches. Type, character and symmetry are of the greatest importance and are on no account to be sacrificed to size alone.
General Appearance and Characteristics. A strong, compact-looking dog of great symmetry, practically the same in measurement from shoulder to stern as in height, absolutely free from legginess or weaselness, very elastic in his gallop, but in walking or trotting he has a characteristic ambling or pacing movement, and his bark should be loud, with a peculiar 'pot-casse' ring in it. Taking him all round, he is a profusely, but not *excessively* coated, thick-set, muscular, able-bodied dog with a most intelligent expression, free from all Poodle or Deerhound character. *Soundness should be considered of greatest importance.*

SCALE OF POINTS

Skull	5	Body and loins	10
Eyes	5	Hindquarters	10
Ears	5	Legs	10
Teeth	5	Coat (texture, quality and condition)	15
Nose	5		
Jaw	5	General appearance and movement	15
Foreface	5		
Neck and shoulders	5	Total	100

Approved October 13, 1953

OTTER HOUND

(THE KENNEL CLUB—HOUND GROUP)

OTTER HOUNDS

(AMERICAN KENNEL CLUB—GROUP II: HOUNDS)

General Appearance. The Otter Hound is a large, rough-coated, squarely symmetrical hound. The length of a dog's body from withers to base of tail is approximately equal to its height at the withers. However, a bitch is not to be faulted if her length of body is slightly greater than her height. The Otter Hound is amiable and boisterous. It has an extremely sensitive nose, and is inquisitive and persevering in investigating scents. The Otter Hound should be shown on a loose lead. The Otter Hound hunts its quarry on land and water and requires a combination of characteristics unique among hounds—most notably a rough, double coat and webbed feet.

Head. The head is large, fairly narrow, and well covered with hair. The length from tip of nose to occiput is 11 to 12 inches in a hound 26 inches at the withers. This proportion should be maintained in larger and smaller hounds.

The skull (cranium) is long, fairly harrow under the hair, and only slightly domed. The muzzle is long and square in cross-section with powerful jaws and deep flews.

The stop is not pronounced.

The nose is large, dark, and completely pigmented.

The ears are long, pendulous, and folded. They are set low and hang close to the head. They are well covered and fringed with hair. The tips of the *ear* leather reach at least to the tip of the nose.

The eyes are deeply set. The haw shows only slightly. The ears are dark, but may vary with the color of the hound.

The jaws are powerful and capable of a crushing grip. A scissors bite is preferred.

Faults. Bite grossly undershot or overshot.

Neck and Body. The neck looks shorter than it really is because of the abundance of hair on it. The neck blends smoothly into the trunk.

The chest is deep; the ribs extend well toward the rear of the trunk.

The topline is level.

The tail is fairly long, reaching at least to the hock. It is well feathered (covered and fringed hair). It is carried sickle-fashion (not over the back) when a dog is moving or alert, but may droop when the dog is at rest.

Forequarters: Shoulders clean, powerful, and well-sloped.

Legs heavy-boned and straight.

Hindquarters. Thighs large and well-muscled.

Legs Moderately angulated. Legs parallel when viewed from the rear.

Feet large, broad, compact, and well padded, with membranes connecting the toes (web-footed).

Dewclaws, if any, on the hind legs are generally removed; dewclaws on the forelegs may be removed.

Coat. The rough outer coat is three to six inches long on the back, shorter on the extremities. It must be hard (coarse and crisp). A water-resistant inner coat of short woolly hair is an essential feature of the breed. A naturally stripped coat lacking length and fringes is correct for an Otter Hound that is being worked. A proper hunting coat will show the hard outer coat and woolly undercoat.

Faults. A soft outer coat is a very serious fault as is a woolly-textured top coat. Lack of undercoat is a serious fault. An outer coat much longer than six inches becomes heavy when wet and is a fault.

Color. Any color or combination of colors is acceptable. The nose should be darkly pigmented, black or liver, depending on the color of the hound.

Gait. The Otter Hound moves freely with forward reach and drive. The gait is smooth and effortless and capable of being maintained for many miles. Otter Hounds single-track at slower speed than light-bodied hounds. Because they do not lift their feet high off the ground, Otter Hounds may shuffle when they walk or move at a slow trot.

Size. Males range from 24 to 27 inches at the withers, and weigh from 75 to 115 pounds, depending on the height and condition of the hound. Bitches are 22 to 26 inches at the withers and 65 to 100 pounds. A hound in hard working condition may weigh as much as 15 pounds less than one of the same height that is not being worked. Otter Hounds should not be penalized for being shown in working condition (lean, well-muscled, naturally stripped coat).

Approved October 12, 1971

PAPILLON

(THE KENNEL CLUB—TOY GROUP)

General Appearance. This dainty, balanced little toy dog should have an attractive head, an alert bearing and an intelligent and lively expression. Movement should be sound, light and free and not cramped or restricted in any way.

Head and Skull. The skull slightly rounded between the ears, the muzzle finely pointed and abruptly thinner than the skull accentuating the stop which should be well defined. Length from tip of the nose to the stop approximately a third length of the head. Nose should be black.

Faults. Muzzle over long or coarse. Skull flat or apple shaped. Nose other than black.

Eyes. Of medium size, rounded, dark in colour, placed rather low in the head and should not bulge.

Faults. Eyes light in colour, too small or too large or protruding.

Ears. The ears should be large with rounded tips, heavily fringed, set towards the back of the head far enough apart to show the slightly rounded shape of the skull. The ears must be completely erect or dropped. When the ears are erect they must be carried obliquely like the spread wings of a butterfly, therefore the name, Papillon. When the ears are dropped they must be completely dropped, and thus type is known as the Phalene (moth).

Faults. semi-erect or not fully dropped, small, sharply pointed or set too close together.

Mouth. Scissor bite, upper teeth fitting close over lower. The lips thin and tight.

Faults. Over or undershot to the extent that the incisors do not touch at all. Wry mouth.

Neck. Of medium length.

Forequarters. Shoulders well developed and sloping back. Chest rather deep. Forelegs straight and slender and fine boned.

Faults. Shoulders straight. Out at elbow.

Body. Level topline. The body should have plenty of length, well formed with well sprung ribs, good length of loin which must not be weak, with slightly arched belly.

Faults. Topline roached, dipped or cobby. Legs malformed and crooked, cow-hocked, too long or too short. Stifles straight, coupled with weak hindquarters.

Hindquarters. Well developed, good turn of stifle. Legs when viewed from behind, should be parallel. Dew claws on the hind legs must be removed.

Feet. Fine and fairly long as in the hare. The tufts of hair between the toes extending far beyond them.

Tail. Long and well fringed, set on high, arched over the back with the fringes falling to the side to form the plume.

Faults. Tail unduly short, too low set.

Coat. Should be abundant, (flowing) but without undercoat, long, fine, silky, falling flat on back

and sides forming a profuse frill on the chest, short and close on the skull, muzzle and front part of the legs. Back part of the front legs to pasterns, tail and thighs covered with long hair.
Faults. Harsh, curly or stand-off coat.
Colour. White with patches which may be any colour except liver. A tricolour must be black and white with tan spots over the eyes, tan inside ears and under root of tail and on cheeks. The head marking should be symmetrical about a white, narrow, clearly defined blaze.
Size. The ideal height at the withers from 8 to 11 ins. The dog will appear to be slightly longer than high when properly furnished with ruff and hind fringes.
Faults. Muzzle over long or coarse. Skull flat or apple shaped. Nose other than black. Eyes light in colour, too small or too large or protruding. Ears semi-erect or not fully dropped, small, sharply pointed or set too close together. Mouth over or undershot to the extent that the incisors do not touch at all. Wry mouth. Shoulders straight. Out at elbow. Topline roached, dipped or cobby. Legs malformed and crooked, cow-hocked, too long or too short. Stifles straight, coupled with weak hindquarters. Tail unduly short, too low set. Harsh, curly or stand-off coat.

PAPILLON

(AMERICAN KENNEL CLUB—GROUP V: TOYS)

General Appearance. The Papillon is a small, friendly, elegant toy dog of fine-boned structure, light, dainty and of lively action; distinguished from other breeds by its beautiful butterfly-like ears.
Head. Small. The skull of medium width, and slightly rounded between the ears. A well-defined stop is formed where the muzzle joins the skull. The muzzle is fine, abruptly thinner than the head, tapering to the nose. The length of the muzzle from the tip of nose to stop is approximately one third the length of the head from tip of nose to occiput.
Nose. Black, small, rounded and slightly flat on top.
Disqualification. Pink, spotted or liver-colored.
Eyes. Dark, round, not bulging, of medium size and alert in expression. The inner corner of the eyes is on a line with the stop. Eye rims black.
Mouth. Lips are tight, thin and black. Teeth meet in a scissors bite. Tongue must not be visible when jaws are closed.
Fault. Overshot or undershot.
Ears. The ears of either the erect or drop type should be large with rounded tips and set on the sides and toward the back of the head. (1) Ears of the erect type are carried obliquely and move like the spread wings of a butterfly. When alert, each ear forms an angle of approximately 45 degrees to the head. The leather should be of sufficient strength to maintain the erect position. (2) Ears of the drop type, known as Phalene, are similar to the erect type, but are carried drooping and must be completely down.
Fault. Ears small, pointed, set too high, one ear up or ears partly down.
Neck. Of medium length.
Body. Must be slightly longer than the height at withers. It is not a cobby dog. Topline straight and level. The chest is of medium depth with well-sprung ribs. The belly is tucked up.
Forequarters. Shoulders well developed and laid back to allow freedom of movement. Forelegs slender, fine-boned and must be straight. Removal of dewclaws on forelegs optional.
Hindquarters. Well developed and well angulated. Hocks inclined neither in nor out. The hind legs are slender, fine-boned and parallel when viewed from behind. Dewclaws, if any, must be removed from hindlegs.
Feet. Thin and elongated (hare-like), pointing neither in nor out.
Tail. Long, set high and carried well arched over the body. The plume may hang to either side of the body.
Fault. Low-set tail, one not arched over back or too short.
Coat. Abundant, long, fine, silky, flowing, straight with resilient quality, flat on back and sides of body. A profuse frill on chest. There is no undercoat. Hair short and close on skull, muzzle, front of forelegs and from hind feet to hocks. Ears well fringed with the inside covered with silken hair of medium length. Backs of the forelegs are covered with feathers diminishing to the pasterns. Hindlegs are covered to the hocks with abundant breeches (culottes). Tail is covered with a long flowing plume. Hair on feet is short but fine tufts may appear over toes and grow beyond them, forming a point.
Size. Height at highest point of shoulder blades 8 to 11 inches. Weight is in proportion to height.
Fault. Over 11 inches. Over 12 inches disqualifies.
Gait. Free, quick, easy, graceful, not paddle-footed or stiff in hip movements.
Color. White predominates, with patches which may be any color except liver. Also tri-color (black and white with tan spots over the eyes, on the cheeks, in the ears and under the tail). Color must cover both ears and extend over both eyes. A clearly defined white blaze and noseband, together with symmetrical head markings, are preferable but not essential. The size, shape and placement of the patches on the body are without importance. A saddle is permissible. Among the allowable colors there is no preference.
Disqualifications. Liver color, coat of solid color, all white, or one with no white, white patches on ears or around eyes.

DISQUALIFICATIONS

Nose. Pink, spotted or liver-colored. Height. Over 12 inches. Color. Liver color, coat of solid color, all white, or one with no white, white patches on ears or around eyes.

Approved June 8, 1965

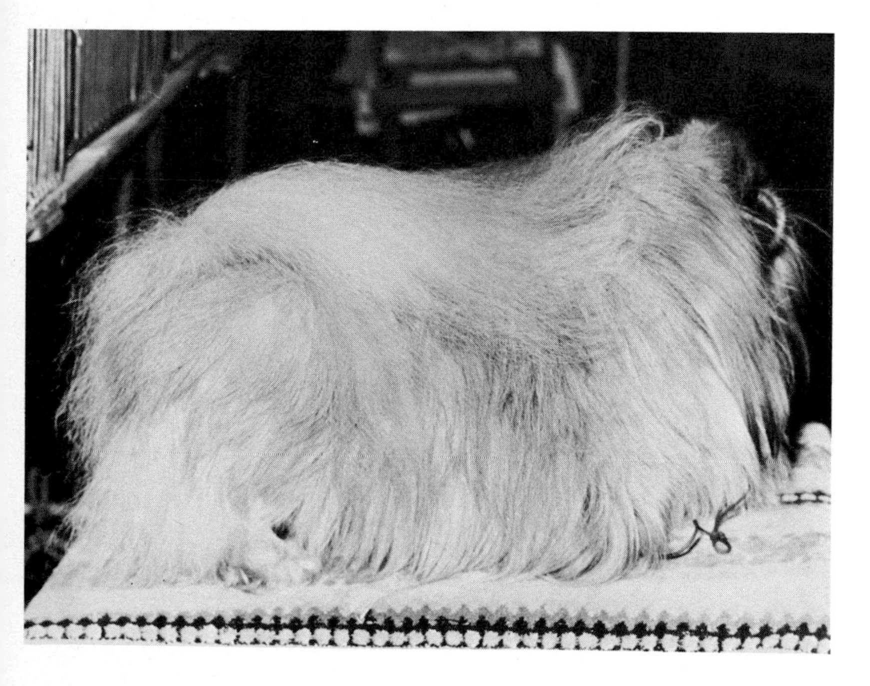

PEKINGESE

(THE KENNEL CLUB—TOY GROUP)

General Appearance. Should be a small, well-balanced, thickset dog of great dignity and quality. He should carry himself fearlessly in the ring with an alert, intelligent expression.
Head and Skull. Head massive, skull broad, wide and flat between the ears, not domed; wide between eyes. Nose very short and broad, nostrils large, open, and black; muzzle wide, well wrinkled, with firm underjaw. Profile should look quite flat with nose well up between the eyes. Deep stop.
Eyes. Large, clear, dark and lustrous. Prominent but not bolting.
Ears. Heart-shaped, set level with the skull and carried close to the head. Long profuse feathering on ears. Leather not to come below the muzzle.
Mouth. Level lips, must not show teeth or tongue.
Neck. Very short and thick.
Forequarters. Short, thick, heavily-boned forelegs; bones of forelegs bowed but firm at shoulder. Absolute soundness essential.
Body. Short but with broad chest and good spring of rib, falling away lighter behind; lion-like with distinct waist, level back; well slung between the legs, not on top of them.
Hindquarters. Hindlegs lighter but firm and well shaped. Close behind but not cow-hocked. Absolute soundness essential.
Feet. Large and flat, not round. The dog should stand well up on feet, not on pasterns. Front feet turned slightly out. Absolute soundness essential.
Tail. Set high, carried tightly, slightly curved over back to either side. Long feathering.
Coat. Long and straight with profuse mane extending beyond the shoulders forming a cape or frill round the neck; top coat rather coarse, with thick undercoat. Profuse feathering on ears, legs, thighs, tail and toes.
Colour. All colours and markings are permissible and equally good, except albino or liver. Parti-colours should be evenly broken.
Weight and Size. As a guide the ideal weight to be 7 to 11 lbs for dogs, 8 to 12 lbs for bitches. The dog should look small but be surprisingly heavy when picked up; heavy bone and a sturdy well-built body are essentials of the breed.

PEKINGESE

(AMERICAN KENNEL CLUB—GROUP V: TOYS)

Expression. Must suggest the Chinese origin of the Pekingese in its quaintness and individuality, resemblance to the lion in directions and independence and should imply courage, boldness, self-esteem and combativeness rather than prettiness, daintiness or delicacy.
Skull. Massive, broad, wide and flat between the ears (not dome-shaped), wide between the eyes.
Nose. Black, broad, very short and flat.

Eyes. Large, dark, prominent, round, lustrous.
Stop. Deep.
Ears. Heart-shaped, not set too high, leather never long enough to come below the muzzle, nor carried erect, but rather drooping, long feather.
Muzzle. Wrinkled, very short and broad, not overshot nor pointed. Strong, broad underjaw, teeth not to show.
Shape of Body. Heavy in front, well-sprung ribs, broad chest, falling away lighter behind, lionlike. Back level. Not too long in body; allowance made for longer body in bitch.
Legs. Short forelegs, bones of forearm bowed, firm at shoulder; hind legs lighter but firm and well shaped.
Feet. Flat, toes turned out, not round, should stand well up on feet, not on ankles.
Action. Fearless, free and strong, with slight roll.
Coat, Feather and Condition. Long, with thick undercoat, straight and flat, not curly nor wavy, rather coarse, but soft; feather on thighs, legs, tail and toes long and profuse.
Mane. Profuse, extending beyond the shoulder blades, forming ruff or frill round the neck.
Color. All colors are allowable. Red, fawn, black, black and tan, sable, brindle, white and parti-color well defined: black masks and spectacles around the eyes, with lines to ears are desirable.
Definition of a Parti-Color Pekingese. The coloring of a parti-colored dog must be broken on the body. No large portion of any one color should exist. White should be shown on the saddle. A dog of any solid color with white feet and chest is *not* a parti-color.
Tail. Set high; lying well over back to either side; long, profuse, straight feather.
Size. Being a toy dog, medium size preferred, providing type and points are not sacrificed; extreme limit 14 pounds.
Faults. Protruding tongue, badly blemished eye, overshot, wry mouth.

SCALE OF POINTS

Expression	5	Shape of body	15
Skull	10	Legs and feet	15
Nose	5	Coat, feather and condition	15
Eyes	5	Tail	5
Stop	5	Action	10
Ears	5		
Muzzle	5	Total	100

DISQUALIFICATIONS

Weight. Over 14 pounds; Dudley nose.

Approved April 10, 1956

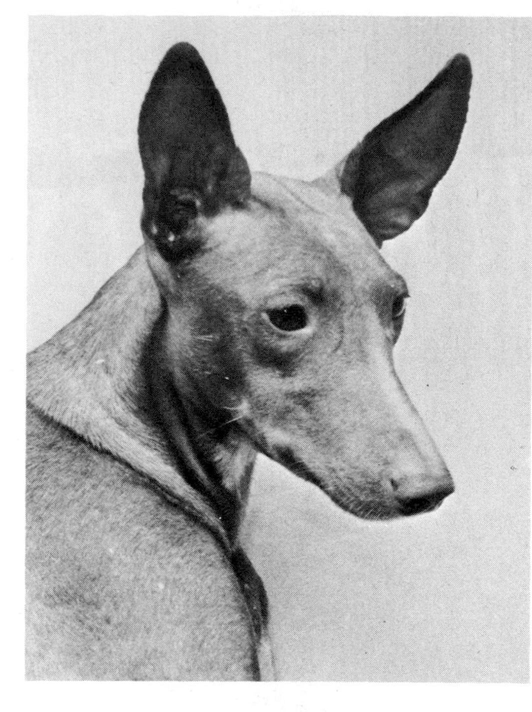

PHARAOH HOUND

(THE KENNEL CLUB—HOUND GROUP)

General Appearance. The Pharaoh Hound belongs to the original species of greyhound and bears a striking resemblance to the greyhounds with erect ears seen in the ancient Egyptian drawings.

The structure of the body is tall and slender with clean lines and flat elongated muscles, the outline almost forming a square.

The Pharaoh Hound is extraordinarily lithe and is noted for it's great speed and jumping powers.

The characteristics are: a triangular shaped head, large erect ears, a tail which is frequently curved; short, smooth, glossy coat which is white or red/tan.

The more perfect form of Pharaoh Hound is found in the Balearic Islands.

Head. Seen in profile and from above is triangular with a flat and relatively broad skull and powerful jaws, almost without a stop. The commencement of the nose is slightly raised, the jaws forming an angle tapering to the tip of the nose. The skull and jawbone are of equal length.

Nose. A fawn colour, dotted with pinkish spots.

Ears. Large, wide, high-set, erect, a soft fawn colour with divergent tips.

Eyes. Rather small, deep set with amber or light brown iris.

Jaws. Powerful and scissor-shaped.

Neck. Lean, rather long and elegantly muscled.

Body. Slim and flat muscled.

Thorax. Narrow, with flat ribs and slightly arched sides, sloping but not as deep as in the Greyhound.

Back. A straight clean line, with the curve of the loins, well muscled but not arched.

Hindquarters. Fairly long, gently sloping.

Tail. Curved, reaching down to the hind limbs. Can be carried high in case of excitement.

Abdomen. Slim rather in-drawn but not as pronounced as in other breeds of greyhound.

Fore-arm. Long, lean with fairly angular muscle structure.

Withers and the Forelegs. Long and joining the chest in a nice curve.

Hind Limbs. Exceptionally long, well let down and straight.

Hock. Relatively short.

Paws. Strong with well clenched toes. The under-side a pale colour.

Hindquarters. Equal length, lean and well-formed muscle structure.

Thighs. Long and strong, but less muscled than in the greyhound.

Hindlegs. Exactly parallel, strong and well-formed.

Paws. The same as the front paws.

Skin and Coat. The skin itself is soft and the hair short, glossy and fine.

Colour. White with red/tan or amber spots or dots, unevenly spaced. There are also entirely red/tan dogs. Other shades are excluded.

Height. Dogs: 23¾ inches to 28½ inches. Bitches: 22½ inches to 26 inches.

Character. In general a friendly, easy, playful dog and has marked keenness for hunting. Very active and needs exercise.

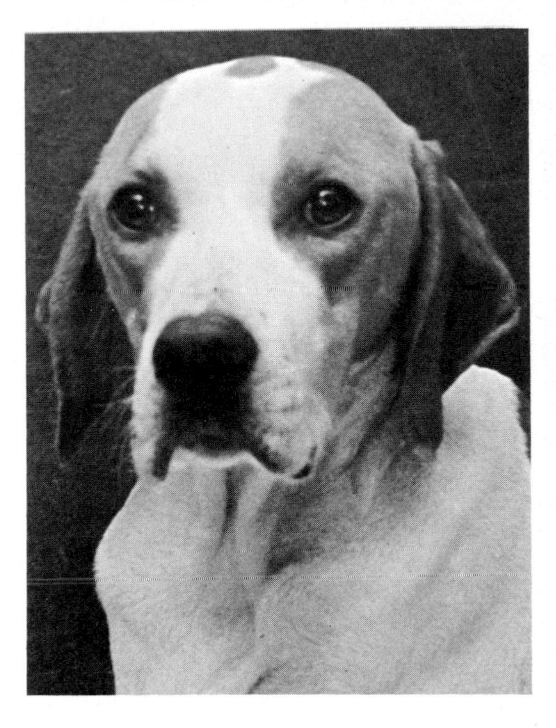

POINTER

(THE KENNEL CLUB—GUNDOG GROUP)

Characteristics. The Pointers should be symmetrical and well built all over. Alert, with the appearance of strength, endurance and speed.

Head and Skull. The skull should be medium breadth and in proportion to the length of fore-face; the stop well defined, pronounced occipital bone. Nose and eyerims dark, but may be lighter in the case of a lemon and white-coloured dog. The nostrils wide, soft and moist. The muzzle somewhat concave, and ending on a level with the nostrils, giving a slightly dish-faced appearance. The cheek-bones should not be prominent. Well developed soft lip.

Eyes. The same distance from the occiput as from the nostrils. A slight depression under the eyes, which should be bright and kindly in expression, not bold or staring, and not looking down the nose. The colour of the eyes either hazel or brown according to the colour of the coat.

Mouth. Scissors bite, neither under nor overshot.

Neck. Long, muscular, slightly arched, springing cleanly from the shoulders and free from throatiness.

Ears. The ears should be set on fairly high, and lie close to the head, they should be of medium length, and inclined to be pointed at the tips.

Forequarters. The shoulders long, sloping, and well-laid back. The chest just wide enough for plenty of heart room. The brisket well let down, to a level with the elbows. The forelegs straight and firm, of good oval bone, with the back sinews strong and visible. The knee joint should be flat with the front of the leg, and protrude very little on the inside. Pasterns lengthy, strong and resilient.

Body. Well-sprung ribs, gradually falling away at the loin, which should be strong, muscular and slightly arched. The couplings short. The haunch bones well spaced and prominent, but not above the level of the back. The general outline from head to tail being a series of graceful curves, giving a strong but lissom appearance.

Hindquarters. Well turned stifles. The hock should be well let down, and close to the ground. A good expanse of thigh, which should be very muscular, as should also the second-thighs.

Feet. The feet oval, with well-knit, arched toes, well cushioned underneath.

Gait. Smooth, covering plenty of ground with each stride. Driving hind action, elbows neither turning in nor out. Definitely not a hackney action.

Tail. The tail of medium length, thick at the root, growing gradually thinner to the point. It should be well covered with close hair, and carried on a level with the back, with no upward curl. With the dog in movement the tail should lash from side to side.

Coat. The coat should be fine, short, hard and evenly distributed, perfectly smooth and straight, with a decided sheen.

Colour. The usual colours are lemon and white, orange and white, liver and white, and black and white. Self colours and tricolours are also correct.
Size. Desirable heights. Dogs 25 to 27 inches, bitches 24 to 26 inches.

POINTER

(AMERICAN KENNEL CLUB—GROUP I: SPORTING DOGS)

General Appearance. The Pointer is bred primarily for sport afield; he should unmistakably look and act the part. The ideal specimen gives the immediate impression of compact power and agile grace; the head noble, proudly carried; the expression intelligent and alert; the muscular body bespeaking both staying power and dash. Here is an animal whose every movement shows him to be a wide-awake, hard-driving hunting dog possessing stamina, courage, and the desire to go. And in his expression are the loyalty and devotion of a true friend of man.
Temperament. The Pointer's even temperament and alert good sense make him a congenial companion both in the field and in the home. He should be dignified and should never show timidity toward man or dog.
Head. The skull of medium width approximately as wide as the length of the muzzle, resulting in an impression of length rather than width. Slight furrow between the eyes, cheeks cleanly chiseled. There should be a pronounced stop. From this point forward the muzzle is of good length with the nasal bone so formed that the nose is slightly higher at the tip than the muzzle at the stop. Parallel planes of the skull and muzzle are equally acceptable. The muzzle should be deep without pendulous flews. Jaws ending square and level, should bite evenly or as scissors. Nostrils well developed and wide open.
Ears. Set on at eye level. When hanging naturally, they should reach just below the lower jaw, close to the head, with little or no folding. They should be somewhat pointed at the tip—never round—and soft and thin in leather.
Eyes. Of ample size, rounded and intense. The eye color should be dark in contrast with the color of the markings, the darker the better.
Neck. Long, dry, muscular and slightly arched, springing cleanly from the shoulders.
Shoulders. Long, thin, and sloping. The top of blades close together.
Front. Elbows well let down, directly under the withers and truly parallel so as to work just clear of the body. Forelegs straight and with oval bone. Knee joint never to buckle over. Pasterns of moderate length, perceptibly finer in bone than the leg, and slightly slanting. Chest, deep and rather wide, must not hinder free action of forelegs. The breastbone bold, without being unduly prominent. The ribs well sprung, descending as low as the elbow-point.
Back. Strong and solid with only a slight rise from croup to top of shoulders. Loin of moderate length, powerful and slightly arched. Croup falling only slightly to base of tail. Tuck-up should be apparent, but not exaggerated.
Tail. Heavier at the root, tapering to a fine point. Length no greater than to hock. A tail longer than this or docked must be penalized. Carried without curl, and not more than 20 degrees above the line of the back; never carried between the legs.
Hindquarters. Muscular and powerful with great propelling leverage. Thighs long and well developed. Stifles well bent. The hocks clean; the legs straight as viewed from behind. Decided angulation is the mark of power and endurance.
Feet. Oval, with long, closely-set, arched toes, well padded, and deep. Cat-foot is a fault. Dewclaws on the forelegs may be removed.
Coat. Short, dense, smooth with a sheen.
Color. Liver, lemon, black, orange; either in combination with white or solid-colored. A good Pointer cannot be a bad color. In the darker colors, the nose should be black or brown; in the lighter shades it may be lighter or flesh-colored.
Gait. Smooth, frictionless, with a powerful hindquarters' drive. The head should be carried high, the nostrils wide, the tail moving from side to side rhythmically with the pace, giving the impression of a well-balanced, strongly-built hunting dog capable of top speed combined with great stamina. Hackney gait must be faulted.
Balance and Size. Balance and over-all symmetry are more important in the Pointer than size. A smooth, balanced dog is to be more desired than a dog with strongly contrasting good points and faults. Hound or terrier characteristics are most undesirable. Because a sporting dog must have both endurance and power, great variations in size are undesirable, the desirable height and weight being within the following limits:

Dogs, height—25–28 inches; weight—55–75 pounds. Bitches, height—23–26 inches; weight—45–65 pounds.

Approved November 12, 1968

POINTER (GERMAN SHORTHAIRED)

(AMERICAN KENNEL CLUB—GROUP I: SPORTING DOGS)

General Appearance. The over-all picture which is created in the observer's eye should be that of an artistocratic, well-balanced, symmetrical animal with conformation indicating power, endurance and agility and a look of intelligence and animation. The dog should be neither unduly small or conspicuously large. It should rather give the impression of medium size, but be like the proper hunter, 'with a short back, but standing over plenty of ground.' Tall, leggy individuals seldom possess endurance or sound movement.

Dogs which are ponderous or unbalanced because of excess substance should be definitely rejected. The first impression should be that of a keenness which denotes full enthusiasm for work without indication of nervous or flighty character. Movement should be alertly co-ordinated without wasted motion. Grace of outline, clean-cut head, sloping shoulders, deep breast, powerful back, strong quarters, good bone composition, adequate muscle, well-carried tail and taut coat, all of which should combine to produce a look of nobility and an indication of anatomical structure essential to correct gait which must indicate a heritage of purposefully conducted breeding.

Head. Clean-cut, neither too light nor too heavy, in proper proportion to the body. Skull should be reasonably broad, arched on side and slightly round on top. Scissura (median line between the eyes at the forehead) not too deep, occipital bone not as conspicuous as in the case of the Pointer. The foreface should rise gradually from nose to forehead—not resembling the Roman nose. This is more strongly pronounced in the dog than in the bitch, as befitting his sex. The chops should fall away from the somewhat projecting nose. Lips should be full and deep, never flewy. The chops should not fall over too much, but form a proper fold in the angle. The jaw should be powerful and the muscles well developed. The line to the forehead should rise gradually and should never possess a definite stop as in the case of the Pointer, but rather a stop-effect when viewed from the side, due to the position of the eyebrows. The muzzle should be sufficiently long to enable the dog to seize properly and to facilitate his carrying game a long time. A pointed muzzle is not desirable. The entire head should never give the impression of tapering to a point. The depth should be in the right proportion to the length, both in the muzzle and in the skull proper.

Ears. Ears should be broad and set fairly high, lie flat and never hang away from the head. Placement should be above eye level. The ears, when laid in front without being pulled, should about meet the lip angle. In the case of heavier dogs, they should be correspondingly longer.

Eyes. The eyes should be of medium size, full of intelligence and expressive, good-humored, and yet radiating energy, neither protruding nor sunk. The eyelids should close well. The best color is a dark shade of brown. Light yellow, china or wall (bird of prey) eyes are not desirable.

Nose. Brown, the larger the better; nostrils well opened and broad. Flesh-colored and spotted noses are not desirable.

Teeth. The teeth should be strong and healthy. The molars should intermesh properly. Incisors should fit close in a true scissors bite. Jaws should be neither overshot or undershot.

Neck. Of adequate length to permit the jaws reaching game to be retrieved, sloping downwards on beautifully curving lines. The nape should be rather muscular, becoming gradually larger towards the shoulders. Moderate houndlike throatiness permitted.

Breast and Thorax. The breast in general should give the impression of depth rather than breadth; for all that, it should be in correct proportion to the other parts of the body with fair depth of chest. The ribs forming the thorax should be well-curved and not flat; they should not be absolutely round or barrel-shaped. Ribs that are entirely round prevent the necessary expansion of the chest when taking breath. The back ribs should reach well down. The circumference of the breast immediately behind the elbows should be smaller than that of the breast about a hands-breadth behind elbows, so that the upper arm has room for movement.

Back and Loins. Back should be short, strong and straight with slight rise from root of tail to withers. Excessively long or hog-backed should be penalized. Loin strong, of moderate length and slightly arched. Tuck-up should be apparent.

Assembly of Back Members. The hips should be broad with hip sockets wide apart and fall slightly toward the tail in a graceful curve. Thighs strong and well muscled. Stifles well bent. Hock joints should be well angulated with strong, straight bone structure from hock to pad. Angulation of both stifle and hock joints should be such as to combine maximum combination of both drive and traction. Hocks should turn neither in nor out.

Assembly of Front Members. The shoulders should be sloping, movable, well covered with muscle. The shoulder blades should lie flat. The upper arm (also called the cross bar, i.e. the bones between the shoulder and elbow joints) should be as long as possible, standing away somewhat from the trunk so that the straight and closely muscled legs, when viewed from in front, should appear to be parallel. Elbows which stand away from the body or are pressed right into same indicate toes turning inwards or outwards, which should be regarded as faults. Pasterns should be strong, short and nearly vertical.

Feet. Should be compact, close-knit and round to spoon-shaped. The toes sufficiently arched and heavily nailed. The pad should be strong and hard.

Coat and Skin. The skin should look close and tight. The hair should be short and thick and feel tough and hard to the hand; it is somewhat longer on the underside of the tail and the back edge of the haunches. It is softer, thinner and shorter on the ears and the head.

Tail. Is set high and firm, and must be docked, leaving approximately two-fifths of length. The tail hangs down when the dog is quiet, is held horizontally when he is walking, never turned over the back or considerably bent but violently wagged when he is on the search.

Bones. Thin and fine bones are by no means desirable in a dog which should be able to work over any and every country and should possess strength. The main importance accordingly is laid not so much on the size as being in proper proportion to the body. Dogs with coarse bones are handicapped in agility of movement and speed.

Desirable Weight and Height. Dogs—55 to 70 pounds. Bitches—45 to 60 pounds. Dogs—23 to 25 inches. Bitches—21 to 23 inches at the shoulders.

Color. Solid liver, liver and white spotted, liver and white spotted and ticked, liver and white ticked, liver roan. Any colors other than liver and white (gray white) are not permitted.

Symmetry and field quality are most essential. A dog well balanced in all points is preferable to one with outstanding good qualities and defects. A smooth, lithe gait is most desirable.

Faults. Bone structure too clumsy or too light, head too large, too many wrinkles in forehead, dish-faced, snipy muzzle, ears too long, pointy or fleshy; flesh-colored nose, eyes too light, too round or too closely set together, excessive throatiness, cowhocks, feet or elbows turned inward or outward, down on pasterns, loose shoulders, sway-back, black coat or tri-colored, any colors except liver or some combination of liver and white.

Approved May 7, 1946

POINTER (GERMAN WIREHAIRED)

(THE KENNEL CLUB—GUNDOG GROUP)

POINTER (GERMAN WIREHAIRED)

(AMERICAN KENNEL CLUB—GROUP I: SPORTING DOGS)

The German Wirehaired Pointer is a dog that is essentially Pointer in type, of sturdy build, lively manner, and an intelligent, determined expression. In disposition the dog has been described as energetic, rather aloof but not unfriendly.

Head. The head is moderately long, the skull broad, the occipital bone not too prominent. The stop is medium, the muzzle fairly long with nasal bone straight and broad, the lips a trifle pendulous but close and bearded. The nose is dark brown with nostrils wide open, and the teeth are strong with scissors bite. The ears, rounded but not too broad, hang close to the sides of the head. Eyes are brown, medium in size, oval in contour, bright and clear and overhung with bushy eyebrows. Yellow eyes are not desirable. The neck is of medium length, slightly arched and devoid of dewlap, in fact, the skin throughout is notably tight to the body.

Body and Tail. The body is a little longer than it is high, as ten is to nine, with the back short, straight and strong, the entire back line showing a perceptible slope-down from withers to croup. The chest is deep and capacious, the ribs well sprung, loins taught and slender, the tuck-up apparent. Hips are broad, with croup nicely rounded and the tail docked, approximately two-fifths of original length.

Legs and Feet. Forelegs are straight, with shoulders obliquely set and elbows close. The thighs are strong and muscular. The hind legs are moderately angulated at stifle and hock and as viewed from behind, parallel to each other. Round in outline, the feet are webbed, high arched with toes close, their pads thick and hard, and their nails strong and quite heavy. Leg bones are flat rather than round, and strong, but not so heavy or coarse as to militate against the dog's natural agility.

Coat. The coat is weather resisting and to some extent water repellent. The undercoat is dense enough in winter to insulate against the cold but so thin in summer as to be almost invisible. The distinctive outer coat is straight, harsh, wiry and rather flat-lying, from one and one-half to two inches in length, it is long enough to protect against the punishment of rough cover but not so long as to hide the outline. On the lower legs it is shorter and between the toes of softer texture. On the skull it is naturally short and close fitting, while over the shoulders and around the tail it is very dense and heavy. The tail is nicely coated particularly on the underside, but devoid of feather. These dogs have bushy eyebrows of strong, straight hair and beards and whiskers of medium length.

A short smooth coat, a soft woolly coat, or an excessively long coat is to be severely penalized.

Color. The coat is liver and white, usually either liver and white spotted, liver roan, liver and white spotted with ticking and roaning or sometimes solid liver. The nose is dark brown. The head is brown, sometimes with a white blaze, the ears brown. Any black in the coat is to be severely penalized. Spotted and flesh-colored noses are undesirable and are to be penalized.

Size. Height of males should be from 24 to 26 inches at the withers, bitches smaller but not under 22 inches.

Approved February 7, 1959

POMERANIAN

(THE KENNEL CLUB—TOY GROUP)

General Appearance. The Pomeranian in build and appearance should be a compact, short-coupled dog, well knit in frame. He should exhibit great intelligence in his expression, activity and bouyancy in his deportment.

Head and Skull. The head and nose should be foxy in outline, or wedge-shaped. The skull being slightly flat, large in proportion to the muzzle, which should finish rather fine and be free from lippiness. The hair on the head and face should be smooth and short-coated. The nose should be black in white, orange, and shaded-sable dogs; brown in chocolate tipped sable dogs, but in other colours may be 'self-coloured', but never parti-coloured or white.

Eyes. Should be medium in size, slightly oval in shape, not full, not set too wide apart, bright and dark in colour, and showing great intelligence. In white, orange, shaded-sable and cream dogs the rims round the eyes should be black.

Ears. Should be small, not set too far apart, nor too low down, but carried perfectly erect like those of a fox.

Mouth. Teeth should be level, and should on no account be undershot, or overshot.

Neck. Should be rather short and well set in.

Forequarters. The shoulders should be clean and well laid back. The legs must be well feathered and perfectly straight, of medium length and not such as would be termed 'leggy' or 'low on leg', but in length and strength in due proportion to a well-balanced frame.

Body. The back must be short and the body compact, being well ribbed up and the barrel well rounded. The chest must be fairly deep and not too wide but in proportion to the size of the dog.

Hindquarters. The legs and thighs must be well feathered down to the hocks and must be neither cow-hocked nor wide behind. They must be fine in bone and free in action.

Feet. The feet should be small and compact in shape.

Tail. The tail is one of the characteristics of the breed, and should be turned over the back and carried flat and straight, being profusely covered with long, harsh, spreading hair.

Coat. There should be two coats, an undercoat and an overcoat, the one a soft, fluffy undercoat, the other a long, perfectly straight coat, harsh in texture and covering the whole of the body, being very abundant round the neck and fore-part of the shoulders and chest, where it shall form a frill of profuse off-standing straight hair, extending over the shoulders. The hindquarters should be clad with long hair or feathering from the top of the rump to the hocks.

Colour. All whole colours are admissible, but they should be free from black or white shadings. At present the whole-coloured dogs are: white, black, brown, light or dark, blue, as pale as

possible. Orange, which should be as self-coloured and bright as possible. Beaver. Cream dogs should have black noses and black rims around the eyes. Whites must be quite free from lemon or any other colour. A few white hairs, in any of the self-coloured dogs, shall not heavily penalize. Dogs (other than white) with white or tan markings, are decidedly objectionable and should be discouraged. They cannot compete as whole coloured specimens. In parti-coloured dogs, the colours should be evenly distributed on the body in patches; a dog with white or tan feet or chest would not be a parti-coloured dog. Shaded-sables should be shaded throughout with three or more colours, the hair to be as uniformly shaded as possible, and with no patches of self-colour. In mixed classes, where whole-coloured and parti-coloured Pomeranians compete together, the preference should, if in other points they are equal, be given to the whole-coloured specimens.

Weight and Size. 4 to 4½ lbs for a dog and 4½ to 5½ lbs for bitches.

Faults. Undershot or overshot mouths; double jointed; light eyes; off-coloured nose; a tail carried to the side; 'hare' feet.

POMERANIAN

(AMERICAN KENNEL CLUB—GROUP V: TOYS)

Appearance. The Pomeranian in build and appearance is a cobby, balanced, short-coupled dog. He exhibits great intelligence in his expression, and is alert in character and deportment.

Head. Well-proportioned to the body, wedge-shaped but not domed in outline, with a fox-like expression. There is a pronounced stop with a rather fine but not snipey muzzle, with no lippiness. The pigmentation around the eyes, lips, and on the nose must be black, except self-colored in brown and blue.

Teeth. The teeth meet in a scissors bite, in which part of the inner surface of the upper teeth meets and engages part of the outer surface of the lower teeth. One tooth out of line does not mean an undershot or overshot mouth.

Eyes. Bright, dark in color, and medium in size, almond-shaped and not set too wide apart nor too close together.

Ears. Small, carried erect and mounted high on the head, and placed not too far apart.

Neck and Shoulders. The neck is rather short, its base set well back on the shoulders. The Pom is not straight-in-shoulder, but has sufficient lay-back of shoulders to carry the neck proudly and high.

Body. The back must be short and the top-line level. The body is cobby, being well ribbed and rounded. The brisket is fairly deep and not too wide.

Legs. The forelegs are straight and parallel, of medium length in proportion to a well balanced frame. The hocks are perpendicular to the ground, parallel to each other from hock to heel, and turning neither in nor out. The Pomeranian stands well-up on toes.

Tail. The tail is characteristic of the breed. It turns over the back and is carried flat, set high. It is profusely covered with hair.

Coat. Double-coated; a short, soft, thick undercoat, with longer, coarse, glistening outercoat consisting of guard hairs which must be harsh to the touch in order to give the proper texture for the coat to form a frill of profuse, standing-off straight hair. The front legs are well feathered and the hindquarters are clad with long hair or feathering from the top of the rump to the hocks.

Color. Acceptable colors to be judged on an equal basis; any solid color, any solid color with lighter or darker shadings of the same color, any solid color with sable or black shadings, parti-color, sable and black and tan. Black and Tan is black with tan or rust, sharply defined, appearing above each eye and on muzzle, throat, and fore-chest, on all legs and feet and below the tail. Parti-color is white with any other color distributed in even patches on the body and a white blaze on head.

Movement. The Pomeranian moves with a smooth, free, but not loose action. He does not elbow out in front nor move excessively wide nor cow-hocked behind. He is sound in action.

Size. The weight of a Pomeranian for exhibition is 3 to 7 pounds. The ideal size for show specimens is from 4 to 5 pounds.

Trimming and Dewclaws. Trimming for neatness is permissible around the feet and up the back of the legs to the first joint; trimming of unruly hairs on the edges of the ears and around the anus is also permitted. Dewclaws, if any, on the hind legs are generally removed. Dewclaws on the forelegs may be removed.

Classifications. The Open Classes at Specialty shows may be divided by color as follows: Open Red, Orange, Cream & Sable; Open Black, Brown and Blue: Open Any Other Allowed Color.

Approved March 9, 1971

POODLE (STANDARD)

(THE KENNEL CLUB—UTILITY GROUP)

Characteristics and General Appearance. That of a very active, intelligent, well balanced and elegant looking dog with good temperament, carrying himself very proudly.
Gait. Sound, free movement and light gait are essential.
Head and Skull. Long and fine with slight peak at the back. The skull not broad and with a moderate stop. Foreface strong and well chiselled, not falling away under the eyes; bones and muscle flat. Lips tight fitting. Chin well defined, but not protruding. The whole head must be in proportion to the size of the dog.
Eyes. Almond shaped, dark, not set too close together, full of fire and intelligence.
Ears. The leather long and wide, low set on, hanging close to the face.
Mouth. Teeth—white, strong, even, with scissor bite. A full set of 42 teeth is desirable.
Neck. Well proportioned, of good length and strong to admit of the head being carried high and with dignity. Skin fitting tightly at the throat.
Forequarters. Shoulders—strong and muscular, sloping well to the back, legs set straight from the shoulders, well muscled.
Body. Chest—deep and moderately wide. Ribs—well sprung and rounded. Back—short, strong, slightly hollowed, loins broad and muscular.
Hindquarters. Thighs well developed and muscular, well bent stifles, well let down hocks, hindlegs turning neither in nor out.
Feet. Pasterns strong, tight feet proportionately small, oval in shape, turning neither in nor out, toes arched, pads thick and hard, well cushioned.
Tail. Set on rather high, well carried at a slight angle away from the body, never curled or carried over the back, thick at the root.
Coat. Very profuse and dense of good harsh texture without knots or tangles. All short hair close, thick and curly. It is strongly recommended that the traditional lion clip be adhered to.
Colour. All solid colours. White and cream poodles to have black nose, lips and eyerims, black toe-nails desirable, brown poodles to have dark amber eyes, dark liver nose, lips, eyerims and toe-nails. Apricot poodles to have dark eyes with black points or deep amber eyes with liver points. Black, silver and blue poodles to have black nose, lips, eyerims and toe-nails. Cream, apricot, brown, silver and blue poodles may show varying shades of the same colour up to 18 months. Clear colours preferred.
Size. 15 inches and over.
Faults. Heavy build, clumsiness, long back, snipy in foreface, light or round or prominent eyes, lippiness, bad carriage, heavy gait, coarse head, over or undershot or pincer mouth, flesh coloured nose, coarse legs and feet, long flat toes, open soft coats with no curl, parti-colours—white markings on black or coloured poodles, lemon or other markings on white poodles, vicious temperament.

POODLE

(AMERICAN KENNEL CLUB—GROUP VI: NON-SPORTING DOGS)

General Appearance, Carriage and Condition. That of a very active, intelligent and elegant-appearing dog, squarely built, well proportioned, moving soundly and carrying himself proudly. Properly clipped in the traditional fashion and carefully groomed, the Poodle has about him an air of distinction and dignity peculiar to himself.

Head and Expression—Skull. Moderately rounded, with a slight but definite stop. Cheekbones and muscles flat.

Muzzle. Long, straight and fine, with slight chiseling under the eyes. Strong without lippiness. The chin definite enough to preclude snipiness. Teeth white, strong and with a scissors bite.

Eyes. Set far apart, very dark, oval in appearance and showing alert intelligence.

Ears. Hanging close to the head, set at or slightly below eye level. The ear leather is long, wide, and thickly feathered, but the ear fringe should not be of excessive length.

Neck and Shoulders. Neck well proportioned, strong and long enough to permit the head to be carried high and with dignity. Skin snug at throat. The neck rises from strong, smoothly muscled shoulders. The shoulder blade is well laid back and approximately the same length as the upper foreleg.

Body. The chest deep and moderately wide with well sprung ribs. The back short, strong and slightly hollowed; the loins short, broad and muscular. Length of body and height at shoulder are in such proportion as to insure the desirable squarely built appearance.

Tail. Straight, set on high and carried up, docked, but sufficient in length to insure a balanced outline.

Legs. The forelegs are straight and parallel when viewed from the front. When viewed from the side with the leg vertical, the elbow is directly below the highest point of the shoulder blade. The hindlegs are muscular with width in the region of the stifles. The pasterns are strong and the stifles well bent. The length of the leg from the stifle joint to the hock joint is considerably greater than the length from the hock joint to the foot.

Feet. The feet are rather small, oval in shape with toes well arched and cushioned on thick firm pads. Nails short but not excessively shortened. The feet turn neither in nor out. Dewclaws may be removed.

Coat—Quality. Of naturally harsh texture, profuse and dense throughout.

Clip. A Poodle may be shown in the 'Puppy' clip or the 'English Saddle' clip or the traditional 'Continental' clip. A Poodle shown in any other type of clip shall be disqualified.

A Poodle under a year old may be shown in the 'Puppy' clip with the coat long. The face, throat, feet and base of the tail are shaved. The entire shaven foot is visible. There is a pompon on the end of the tail. In order to give a neat appearance, a slight shaping of the coat is permissible; however, a Poodle in 'Puppy' clip that is excessively scissored shall be dismissed.

Dogs one year old or older must be shown in either the 'English Saddle' clip or the 'Continental' clip.

In the 'English Saddle' clip the face, throat, feet, forelegs and base of the tail are shaved, leaving puffs on the forelegs and a pompon on the end of the tail. The hindquarters are covered with a short blanket of hair except for a curved shaved area on each flank and two shaved bands on each hindleg. The entire shaven foot and a portion of the shaven leg above the puff are visible. The rest of the body is left in full coat but may be shaped in order to insure overall balance.

In the 'Continental' clip the face, throat, feet and base of the tail are shaved. The hindquarters are shaved with pompons (optional) on the hips. The legs are shaved, leaving bracelets on the hindlegs and puffs on the forelegs. There is a pompon on the end of the tail. The entire shaven foot and portion of the shaven foreleg above the puff are visible. The rest of the body is left in full coat but may be shaped in order to insure overall balance.

In all clips the hair of the topknot may be held in place by an elastic band or barrette. The hair is only of sufficient length to present a smooth outline.

Color. The coat is an even and solid color at the skin. In blues, grays, silvers, browns, cafe-au-laits, apricots, and creams the coat may show varying shades of the same color. This is frequently present in the somewhat darker feathering of the ears and in the tipping of the ruff. While clear colors are definitely preferred, such natural variation in the shading of the coat is not to be considered a fault. Brown and cafe-au-lait Poodles have liver-colored noses, eye-rims and lips, dark toenails and dark amber eyes. Black, blue, gray, silver, cream and white Poodles have black noses, eye-rims and lips, black or self-colored toenails and very dark eyes. In the apricots while the foregoing coloring is preferred, liver-colored noses, eye-rims and lips, and amber eyes are permitted but are not desirable.

Parti-colored dogs shall be disqualified. The coat of a parti-colored dog is not an even solid color at the skin but is of two or more colors.

Gait. A straightforward trot with light springy action and strong hindquarter drive. Head and tail carried high. Forelegs and hindlegs move parallel turning neither in nor out. Sound movement is essential.

SIZE

Standard. The Standard Poodle is over 15 inches at the highest point of the shoulders. Any

Poodle which is 15 inches or less in height shall be disqualified from competition as a Standard Poodle.

Miniature. The Miniature Poodle is 15 inches or under at the highest point of the shoulders, with a minimum height in excess of 10 inches. Any Poodle which is over 15 inches or 10 inches or less at the highest point of the shoulders shall be disqualified from competition as a Miniature Poodle.

Toy. The Toy Poodle is 10 inches or under at the highest point of the shoulders. Any Poodle which is more than 10 inches at the highest point of the shoulders shall be disqualified from competition as a Toy Poodle.

VALUE OF POINTS

General appearance, temperament, carriage and condition	30
Head, expression, ears, eyes and teeth	20
Body, neck, legs, feet and tail	20
Gait	20
Coat, color and texture	10

MAJOR FAULTS

Eyes: round in appearance, protruding, large or very light.

Jaws: undershot, overshot or wry mouth.

Feet: flat or spread.

Tail: set low, curled or carried over the back.

Hindquarters: cow hocks.

Temperament: shyness or sharpness.

DISQUALIFICATIONS

Clip: A dog in any type of clip other than those listed under 'Coat' shall be disqualified.

Parti-colors: The coat of a parti-colored dog is not an even solid color at the skin but is of two or more colors. Parti-colored dogs shall be disqualified.

Size: A dog over or under the height limits specified under 'Size' shall be disqualified.

Approved November 10, 1970

POODLE (MINIATURE)

(THE KENNEL CLUB—UTILITY GROUP)

The Poodle (Miniature) should be in every respect a replica, in miniature, of the Poodle (Standard). Height at shoulder should be under 15 inches but not under 11 inches.

POODLE

(AMERICAN KENNEL CLUB—GROUP VI: NON-SPORTING DOGS)

POODLE (TOY)

(THE KENNEL CLUB—UTILITY GROUP)

The standard of the Poodle (Toy) is the same as that of the Poodle (Standard) and Poodle (Miniature) except that the height at shoulder should be under 11 inches.

PORTUGUESE RABBIT DOG (Podengo Português Pequeno)

(THE KENNEL CLUB—GUNDOG GROUP)

Characteristics. A tough, perky, intelligent and affectionate compact little dog, used for hunting rabbits in warrens and rock crevices.

General Appearance. Small, very typical, short-coated, with erect ears and rather short legs. A quick mover, always alert.

Head and Skull. The skull may be either flat or rounded, with slightly protruding superciliary arches and a moderate stop. The muzzle, which is shorter than the skull, narrows to the nose from a fairly broad base. Lips tight, neat and firm. The nose projects well forward above the mouth. Nose and visible membrane of the lips need not be black, but should be darker than the darkest colour of the coat.

Eyes. Very lively in expression. Rather small, obliquely set and not too prominent. Colour may vary from light honey to dark chestnut, but must always be at least as dark as the darkest brown of the coat. Pigmentation of the eyelids should also be dark in comparison with the coat colour.

Ears. Triangular in shape, moderately spaced and obliquely set. Delicate in texture, well balanced and of moderate length, the height being greater than the considerable width at the base. Very mobile. When alerted to the erect position, they are gracefully hooded, and may stand vertically or incline slightly forward.

Mouth. Level, with scissor bite.

Neck. Long, straight or slightly arched and well-muscled. Without dewlap.

Forequarters. Lean and muscular. Angulation at the shoulder-joint moderate. Upper arms short and sturdy, the elbows standing comfortably free from the ribs. Forearms short, they may be straight or slightly bowed, curving in from elbow to pastern. Pasterns short and gently sloping.

Body. Length from breast to rump is greater than the height at the withers. Breast rather broad and muscular, with moderately prominent breast-bone. Chest long and of medium width, well let down in front. The brisket rises gently to the slightly tucked up belly. Ribs arched, their curve like that of a barrel. The topline may be straight or delicately curved, the long back being level, or falling gradually to the loins. Loins and croup are broad, muscular and of a medium length; they may either be level or fall slightly away.

Hindquarters. Lean and muscular. Hips of medium width. Thighs and second thighs moderate in length and angulation. The hocks are short and strong, without dewclaws.

Feet. Round, compact, with strong, arched toes and hard pads. Nails short and strong; preferably dark.

Tail. Set on rather high. Strong, thick, of medium length and pointed at the tip. It may be carried in any position from low to vertical. The shape of its curve may vary from slight to sickle-like, but it should never turn over into a curl.

Coat. Short, smooth and dense.

Colour. Any fawn or yellow shade, from cream to deep chestnut. Faded black, anthracite shaded, but not grey. May be whole-coloured, with or without white markings.

Size and Weight. Height: 8 inches to 12 inches. Weight: 9 lbs to 11 lbs.

PUG

(THE KENNEL CLUB—TOY GROUP)

General Appearance. A decidedly square and cobby dog. The Pug should be 'multum in parvo', but this condensation should be shown by compactness of form, well-knit proportions, and hardness of developed muscle.

Head and Skull. Head large, massive, round—not apple-headed, with no indentation of the skull. Muzzle short, blunt, square but not upfaced. Wrinkles large and deep.

Eyes. Dark in colour, very large, bold and prominent, globular in shape, soft and solicitious in expression, very lustrous, and when excited, full of fire.

Ears. Thin, small, soft, like black velvet. There are two kinds—the 'rose' and the 'button'. Preference should be given to the latter.

Forequarters. Legs very strong, straight, of moderate length, and well under the body.

Body. Short and cobby, wide in chest and well-ribbed.

Hindquarters. Legs very strong, straight, of moderate length, and well under.

Feet. Neither so long as the foot of the hare, nor so round as that of the cat; well-split-up toes; the nails black.

Tail. (Twist). Curled tightly as possible over the hip. The double curl is perfection.

Coat. Fine, smooth, soft, short and glossy, neither hard nor woolly.

Colour. Silver, apricot fawn or black. Each should be clearly decided, to make the contrast complete between the colour, the trace and the mask. Markings: Clearly defined. The muzzle or mask, ears, moles on cheeks, thumbmark or diamond on forehead and the trace should be as black as possible. Mask: The mask should be black, the more intense and well defined, the better. Trace: A black line extending from the occiput to the twist.

Weight and Size. Desirable weight from 14 to 18 lbs (dog or bitch).

Faults. Lean, leggy. Short legs and long body.

PUG

(AMERICAN KENNEL CLUB—GROUP V: TOYS)

Symmetry. Symmetry and general appearance, decidedly square and cobby. A lean, leggy Pug and a dog with short legs and a long body are equally objectionable.

Size and Condition. The Pug should be *multum in parvo*, but this condensation (if the word may be used) should be shown by compactness of form, well-knit proportions, and hardness of developed muscle. Weight from 14 to 18 lbs (dog or bitch) desirable.

Body. Short and cobby, wide in chest and well ribbed up.

Legs. Very strong, straight, of moderate length and well under.

Feet. Neither so long as the foot of the hare, nor so round as that of the cat; well-split-up toes, and the nails black.

Muzzle. Short, blunt, square, but not up-faced.

Head. Large, massive, round—not appleheaded, with no indentation of the skull.

Eyes. Dark in color, very large, bold and prominent, globular in shape, soft and solicitous in expression, very lustrous, and, when excited, full of fire.

Ears. Thin, small, soft, like black velvet. There are two kinds—the 'rose' and 'button.' Preference is given to the latter.

Markings. Clearly defined. The muzzle or mask, ears, moles on cheeks, thumb mark or diamond on forehead, back-trace should be as black as possible.

Mask. The mask should be black. The more intense and well defined it is the better.

Wrinkles. Large and deep.

Trace. A black line extending from the occiput to the tail.

Tail. Curled tightly as possible over the hip. The double curl is perfection.

Coat. Fine, smooth, soft, short and glossy, neither hard nor woolly.

Color. Silver or apricot-fawn. Each should be decided, to make the contrast complete between the color and the trace and the mask. Black.

SCALE OF POINTS

	Fawn	Black
Symmetry	10	10
Size	5	10
Condition	5	5
Body	10	10
Legs and feet	5	5
Head	5	5
Muzzle	10	10
Ears	5	5
Eyes	10	10
Mask	5	. . .
Wrinkles	5	5
Tail	10	10
Trace	5	. . .
Coat	5	5
Color	5	10
Total	100	100

PYRENEAN MOUNTAIN DOG

(THE KENNEL CLUB—WORKING GROUP)

Characteristics. In addition to his original age-old position in the scheme of pastoral life as protector of the shepherd and his flock, the Pyrenean has been used for centuries as a guard and watch dog on the large estates of his native France, and for this he has proven ideal. He is as serious in play as he is in work, adapting and moulding himself to the moods, desires, and even the very life of his human companions, through fair weather and foul, in leisure or in danger, responsibility, and extreme exertion; he is the exemplification of gentleness and docility, of faithfulness and devotion for his master even to the point of self-sacrifice; and of courage in the protection of anything placed in his care.

General Appearance. A dog of immense size, great majesty, keen intelligence, and kindly expression; of unsurpassed beauty and a certain elegance. In the rolling, ambling gait it shows unmistakably the purpose for which it has been bred, the strenuous work of guarding the flocks in all kinds of weather on the steep mountain slopes of the Pyrenees. Hence soundness is of the greatest importance and absolutely necessary for the proper fulfilment of his centuries-old task.

Head and Skull. Head large and wedge-shaped, measuring 10 to 11 inches from dome to point of nose, with rounding crown, furrow only slightly developed and with no apparent stop. Cheeks flat. Lips close fitting, edged with black. Dewlaps developed but little. The head is, in brief, that of a brown bear, but with the ears falling down.

Eyes. Of medium size, set slightly obliquely, dark rich brown in colour with close eyelids, well pigmented.

Ears. V-shaped, but rounded at the tips, of medium size, set parallel with the eyes, carried low and close to the head except when raised at attention.

Neck. Short, stout and strongly muscular.

Forequarters. Well-placed shoulders set obliquely, close to the body.

Body. Back and loin well coupled, straight and broad. Ribs flat sided. Chest deep.

Hindquarters. Haunches fairly prominent, rump sloping slightly. Double dewclaws on hindlegs.

Feet. Close cupped.

Tail. Of sufficient length to hang below the hocks, well plumed, carried low in repose, and curled high over the back 'making the wheel' when alert.

Coat. Created to withstand severe weather, with fine white undercoat and long, flat, thick outer-coat of coarser hair, straight or slightly undulating.

Colour. All white or principally white with markings of badger, grey, or varying shades of tan.

Weight and Size. The average height at the shoulder varies between 27 and 32 inches for dogs and 25 to 29 inches for bitches. The average length from shoulder blades to root of tail should be the same as the height in any given specimen. The girth is 36 to 42 inches for dogs and 32 to 36 inches for bitches. The weight for dogs runs 100 to 125 lbs and 90 to 115 lbs for bitches.

Faults. Lack of double dewclaws; hocks too straight or cow-hocked; light eyes, eyes too round, loose eyelids; solid black markings; ears too heavy and big; too much stop; bad pigmentation; bad temperament; splay feet; undersized; barrel-ribbed; dipping back.

GREAT PYRENEES

(AMERICAN KENNEL CLUB—GROUP III: WORKING DOGS)

General Appearance. A dog of immense size, great majesty, keen intelligence, and kindly expression; of unsurpassed beauty and a certain elegance, all white or principally white with markings of badger, gray, or varying shades of tan. In the rolling, ambling gait it shows unmistakably the purpose for which it has been bred, the strenuous work of guarding the flocks in all kinds of weather on the steep mountain slopes of the Pyrenees. Hence soundness is of the greatest importance and absolutely necessary for the proper fulfillment of his centuries' old task.

Size. The average height at the shoulder is 27 to 32 inches for dogs, and 25 to 29 inches for bitches. The average length from shoulder blades to root of tail should be the same as the height in any given specimen. The average girth is 36 to 42 inches for dogs and 32 to 36 inches for bitches. The weight for dogs runs 100 to 125 lbs and 90 to 115 lbs for bitches. A dog heavily boned; with close cupped feet; double dewclaws behind and single dewclaws in front.

Head. Large and wedge-shaped, measuring 10 inches to 11 inches from dome to point of nose, with rounding crown, furrow only slightly developed and with no apparent stop.

Cheeks. Flat.

Ears. V-shaped, but rounded at the tips, of medium size, set parallel with the eyes, carried low and close to the head except when raised at attention.

Eyes. Of medium size set slightly obliquely, dark rich brown in color with close eyelids, well pigmented.

Lips. Close fitting, edged with black.

Dewlaps. Developed but little. The head is in brief that of a brown bear, but with the ears falling down.

Neck. Short, stout and strongly muscular.

Body. Well-placed shoulders set obliquely, close to the body.

Back and Loin. Well coupled, straight and broad.

Haunches. Fairly prominent.

Rump. Sloping slightly.

Ribs. Flat-sided.

Chest. Deep.

Tail. Of sufficient length to hang below the hocks, well plumed, carried low in repose, and curled high over the back, 'making the wheel' when alert.

Coat. Created to withstand severe weather, with heavy fine white undercoat and long flat thick outer coat of coarser hair, straight or slightly undulating.

Qualities. In addition to his original age-old position in the scheme of pastoral life as protector of the shepherd and his flock, the Great Pyrenees has been used for centuries as a guard and watchdog on the large estates of his native France, and for this he has proven ideal. He is as serious in play as he is in work, adapting and molding himself to the moods, desires and even the very life of his human companions, through fair weather and foul, through leisure hours and hours fraught with danger, responsibility and extreme exertion; he is the exemplification of gentleness and docility with those he knows, of faithfulness and devotion for his master even to the point of self-sacrifice; and of courage in the protection of the flock placed in his care and of the ones he loves.

SCALE OF POINTS

Head		
Shape of skull	5	
Ears	5	
Eyes	5	
Muzzle	5	
Teeth	5	25
General Conformation		
Neck	5	
Chest	5	
Back	5	
Loins	5	
Feet	5	25
Coat		10
Size and Soundness		25
Expression and General Appearance		15
Total		100

Approved February 13, 1935

RETRIEVERS, CHESAPEAKE BAY

(THE KENNEL CLUB—GUNDOG GROUP)

RETRIEVER, CHESAPEAKE BAY

(AMERICAN KENNEL CLUB—GROUP I: SPORTING DOGS)

Head. Skull broad and round with medium stop, nose medium short-muzzle, pointed but not sharp. Lips thin, not pendulous. Ears small, set well up on head, hanging loosely and of medium leather. Eyes medium large, very clear, of yellowish color and wide apart.

Neck. Of medium length with a strong muscular appearance, tapering to shoulders.

Shoulder, Chest and Body. Shoulders, sloping and should have full liberty of action with plenty of power without any restrictions of movement. Chest strong, deep and wide. Barrel round and deep. Body of medium length, neither cobby nor roached, but rather approching hollowness, flanks well tucked up.

Back Quarters and Stifles. Back quarters should be as high or a trifle higher than the shoulders. They should show fully as much power as the forequarters. There should be no tendency to weakness in either fore or hindquarters. Hindquarters should be especially powerful to supply the driving power for swimming. Back should be short, well-coupled and powerful. Good hindquarters are essential.

Legs, Elbows, Hocks and Feet. Legs should be medium length and straight, showing good bone and muscle, with well-webbed hare feet of good size. The toes well rounded and close, pasterns slightly bent and both pasterns and hocks medium length—the straighter the legs the better. Dewclaws, if any, must be removed from the hind legs. Dewclaws on the forelegs may be removed. A dog with dewclaws on the hind legs must be disqualified.

Stern. Tail should be medium length—varying from: males, 12 inches to 15 inches, and females from 11 inches to 14 inches; medium heavy at base, moderate feathering on stern and tail permissible.

Coat and Texture. Coat should be thick and short, nowhere over $1\frac{1}{2}$ inches long, with a dense fine woolly undercoat. Hair on face and legs should be very short and straight with tendency to wave on the shoulders, neck, back and loins only. The curly coat or coat with a tendency to curl not permissible.

Color. Any color varying from a dark brown to a faded tan or deadgrass. Deadgrass takes in any shade of deadgrass, varying from a tan to a dull straw color. White spot on breast and toes permissible, but the smaller the spot the better, solid color being preferred.

Weight. Males, 65 to 75 lbs; females, 55 to 65 lbs.

Height. Males, 23 inches to 26 inches; females, 21 inches to 24 inches.

Symmetry and Quality. The Chesapeake dog should show a bright and happy disposition and an intelligent expression, with general outlines impressive and denoting a good worker. The dog should be well proportioned, a dog with a good coat and well balanced in other points being preferable to the dog excelling in some but weak in others

The texture of the dog's coat is very important, as the dog is used for hunting under all sorts of adverse weather conditions, often working in ice and snow. The oil in the harsh outer coat and woolly undercoat is of extreme value in preventing the cold water from reaching the dog's skin and aids in quick drying. A Chesapeake's coat should resist the water in the same way that a duck's feathers do. When he leaves the water and shakes himself, his coat should not hold the water at all, being merely moist. Color and coat are extremely important, as the dog is used for duck hunting. The color must be as nearly that of his surroundings as possible and with the fact that dogs are exposed to all kinds of adverse weather conditions, often working in ice and snow, the color of coat and its texture must be given every consideration when judging on the bench or in the ring.

Courage, willingness to work, alertness, nose, intelligence, love of water, general quality, and, most of all, disposition should be given primary consideration in the selection and breeding of the Chesapeake Bay dog.

POSITIVE SCALE OF POINTS

Head, inc. lips, ears & eyes	16
Neck	4
Shoulders and body	12
Back quarters and stifles	12
Elbows, legs and feet	12
Color	4
Stern and tail	10
Coat and texture	18
General conformation	12
Total	100

Note:—The question of coat and general type of balance takes precedence over any scoring table which could be drawn up.

APPROXIMATE MEASUREMENTS

	Inches
Length head, nose to occiput	$9\frac{1}{2}$ to 10
Girth at ears	20 to 21
Muzzle below eyes	10 to $10\frac{1}{2}$
Length of ears	$4\frac{1}{2}$ to 5
Width between eyes	$2\frac{1}{2}$ to $2\frac{3}{4}$
Girth neck close to shoulder	20 to 22
Girth of chest to elbows	35 to 36
Girth at flank	24 to 25
Length from occiput to tail base	34 to 35
Girth forearms at shoulders	10 to $10\frac{1}{2}$
Girth upper thigh	19 to 20
From root to root of ear, over skull	5 to 6
Occiput to top shoulder blades	9 to $9\frac{1}{2}$
From elbow to elbow over the shoulders	25 to 26

DISQUALIFICATIONS

Black or liver colored. Dewclaws on hind legs, white on any part of body, except breast, belly or spots on feet. Feathering on tail or legs over $1\frac{3}{4}$ inches long. Undershot, overshot or any deformity. Coat curly or tendency to curl all over body. Specimens unworthy or lacking in breed characteristics.

Approved July 9, 1963

RETRIEVER (CURLY-COATED)

(THE KENNEL CLUB—GUNDOG GROUP)

General appearance. A strong smart upstanding dog showing activity, endurance and intelligence.
Head and Skull. Long, well proportioned flat skull, jaws strong and long but not inclined to snipiness. Nose black in the black-coated variety with wide nostrils, coarseness of head to be deprecated.
Eyes. Black or brown but not 'gooseberry' coloured, rather large but not too prominent.

Ears. Rather small, set on low, lying close to the head and covered with short curls.
Mouth. Teeth strong and level.
Neck. Should be moderately long, free from throatiness.
Forequarters. Shoulders should be very deep, muscular and well laid back.
Hindquarters. Strong and muscular, hock low to the ground with good bend to stifle and hock.
Body. Well-sprung ribs, good depth of brisket, not too long in the loin, as little tucked-up in flank as possible.
Feet. Round and compact with well-arched toes.
Tail. Moderately short, carried fairly straight and covered with curls, tapering towards the point, gay tail not desirable.
Coat. Should be one mass of crisp small curls all over. This being the main characteristic of the breed should be given great consideration when making judging awards.
Colour. Black or liver.
Weight and Size. 70 to 80 lbs. Approx. 25 to 27 inches.
Faults. Wide skull, light eyes, curled tail and bad movement.

RETRIEVER, CURLY COATED

(AMERICAN KENNEL CLUB—GROUP I: SPORTING DOGS)

General Appearance. A strong smart upstanding dog, showing activity, endurance and intelligence.
Head. Long and well proportioned, skull not too flat, jaws long and strong but not inclined to snipiness, nose black, in the black coated variety, with wide nostrils. Teeth strong and level.
Eyes. Rather small, set on low, lying close to the head, and covered with short curls.
Coat. Should be one mass of crisp curls all over. A slightly more open coat not to be severely penalized, but a saddle back or patch of uncurled hair behind the shoulder should be penalized, and a prominent white patch on breast is undesirable, but a few white hairs allowed in an otherwise good dog. Color, black or liver.
Shoulders, Chest, Body and Loins. Shoulders should be very deep, muscular and obliquely placed. Chest, not too wide, but decidedly deep. Body, rather short, muscular and well ribbed up. Loin, powerful, deep and firm to the grasp.
Legs and Feet. Legs should be of moderate length, forelegs straight and set well under the body. Quarters strong and muscular, hocks low to the ground with moderate bend to stifle and hock. Feet round and compact with well-arched toes.
Tail. Should be moderately short, carried fairly straight and covered with curls, slightly tapering towards the point.

RETRIEVER (FLAT-COATED)

(THE KENNEL CLUB—GUNDOG GROUP)

General Appearance. A bright, active dog of medium size with an intelligent expression, showing power without lumber, and raciness without weediness.

Head and Skull. The head should be long and nicely moulded. The skull flat and moderately broad. There should be a depression or stop between the eyes, slight and in no way accentuated, so as to avoid giving either a down or a dish-faced appearance. The nose of a good size, with open nostrils. The jaws should be long and strong, with a capacity of carrying a hare or pheasant.

Eyes. Should be of medium size, dark-brown or hazel, with a very intelligent expression (a round, prominent eye is a disfigurement) and they should not be obliquely placed.

Ears. Should be small and well set-on, close to the side of the head.

Neck. The head should be well set in the neck, which latter should be long and free from throatiness, symmetrically set and obliquely placed in shoulders running well into the back to allow of easily seeking for the trail.

Forequarters. The chest should be deep and fairly broad, with a well-defined brisket, on which the elbows should work cleanly and evenly. The legs are of the greatest importance, the forelegs should be perfectly straight, with bone of good quality carried right down to the feet and when the dog is in full coat the legs should be well feathered.

Body. The fore-ribs should be fairly flat, showing a gradual spring and well-arched in the centre of the body, but rather lighter towards the quarters. Open couplings are to be ruthlessly condemned. The back should be short, square and well ribbed up.

Hindquarters. Should be muscular. The stifle should not be too straight or too bent, and the dog must neither be cow-hocked nor move too widely behind; in fact he must stand and move true on legs and feet all round. The legs should be well feathered.

Feet. Should be round and strong with toes close and well arched, the soles being thick and strong.

Tail. Short, straight and well set on, carried gaily, but never much above the level of the back.

Coat. Should be dense, of fine quality and texture, flat as possible.

Colour. Black or liver.

Weight and Size. Should be between 60 and 70 lbs.

RETRIEVER (FLAT-COATED)

(AMERICAN KENNEL CLUB—GROUP I: SPORTING DOGS)

General Appearance. A bright, active dog of medium size (weighing from 60 pounds to 70 pounds) with an intelligent expression, showing power without lumber and raciness without weediness.

Head. This should be long and nicely molded. The skull flat and moderately broad. There should be a depression or stop between the eyes, slight and in no way accentuated, so as to avoid giving either a down or a dish-faced appearance. The nose of good size with open nostrils. The eyes, of medium size, should be dark brown or hazel, with a very intelligent expression (a round prominent eye is a disfigurement), and they should

Back and Quarters. The back should be short, square and well ribbed up, with muscular quarters. The stern short, straight and well set on, carried gaily but never much above the level of the back.
Legs and Feet. These are of the greatest importance. The forelegs should be perfectly straight, with bone of good quality carried right down to the feet which should be round and strong. The stifle should not be too straight or too bent and the dog must neither be cowhocked nor move too wide behind, in fact he must stand and move true all round on legs and feet, with toes close and well arched, the soles being thick and strong, and when the dog is in full coat the limbs should be well feathered.
Coat. Should be dense, of fine quality and texture, flat as possible.
Color. Black or liver.

not be obliquely placed. The jaws should be long and strong, with a capacity of carrying a hare or pheasant. The ears small and well set on close to the side of the head.
Neck, Shoulders and Chest. The head should be well set in the neck, which latter should be long and free from throatiness, symmetrically set and obliquely placed in shoulders running well into the back to allow of easily seeking for the trail. The chest should be deep and fairly broad, with a well-defined brisket, on which the elbows should work cleanly and evenly. The fore ribs should be fairly flat showing a gradual spring and well arched in the center of the body but rather lighter towards the quarters. Open couplings are to be ruthlessly condemned.

RETRIEVER (GOLDEN)

(THE KENNEL CLUB—GUNDOG GROUP)

General Appearance. Should be of a symmetrical, active, powerful dog, a good level mover, sound and well put together, with a kindly expression, not clumsy nor long in the leg.
Head and Skull. Broad skull, well set on a clean and muscular neck, muzzle powerful and wide, not weak-jawed, good stop.
Eyes. Dark and set well apart, very kindly in expression, with dark rims.
Ears. Well proportioned, of moderate size, and well set on.
Mouth. Teeth should be sound and strong. Neither overshot nor undershot, the lower teeth just behind but touching the upper.
Neck. The neck should be clean and muscular.
Forequarters. The forelegs should be straight with good bone. Shoulders should be well laid back and long in the blade.
Body. Well-balanced, short coupled, and deep through the heart. Ribs deep and well sprung.
Hindquarters. The loins and legs should be strong and muscular, with good second thighs and well bent stifles. Hocks well let down, not cow-hocked.
Feet. Round and cat-like, not open nor splay.
Tail. Should not be carried too gay nor curled at the tip.
Coat. Should be flat or wavy with good feathering, and dense, water-resisting undercoat.
Colour. Any shade of gold or cream, but neither red nor mahogany. The presence of a few white hairs on chest permissible. White collar, feet, toes or blaze should be penalized. Nose should be black.
Weight and Size. The average weight for dogs in good hard condition should be: dogs, 65 to 70 lbs; bitches, 55 to 60 lbs. Height at shoulder: dogs, 22 to 24 inches; bitches, 20 to 22 inches.

RETRIEVER, GOLDEN

(AMERICAN KENNEL CLUB—GROUP I: SPORTING DOGS)

A symmetrical, powerful, active dog, sound and well put together, not clumsy or long in the leg, displaying a kindly expression and possessing a personality that is eager, alert and self-confident. Primarily a hunting dog, he should be shown in hard working condition. Over-all appearance, balance, gait and purpose to be given more emphasis than any of his component parts.

Size. Males 23–24 inches in height at withers; females 21½–22½. Length from breastbone to buttocks slightly greater than height at withers in ratio of 12–11. Weight for dogs 65–75 lbs; bitches 60–70 lbs.

Head. Broad in skull, slightly arched laterally and longitudinally without prominence of frontal or occipital bones. Good stop. Foreface deep and wide, nearly as long as skull. Muzzle, when viewed in profile, slightly deeper at stop than at tip; when viewed from above, slightly wider at stop than at tip. No heaviness in flews. Removal of whiskers for show purposes optional.

Eyes. Friendly and intelligent, medium large with dark rims, set well apart and reasonably deep in sockets. Color preferably dark brown, never lighter than color of coat. No white or haw visible when looking straight ahead.

Teeth. Scissors bite with lower incisors touching inside of upper incisors.

Nose. Black or dark brown, though lighter shade in cold weather not serious. Dudley nose (pink without pigmentation) to be faulted.

Ears. Rather short, hanging flat against head with rounded tips slightly below jaw. Forward edge attached well behind and just above eye with rear edge slightly below eye. Low, houndlike ear-set to be faulted.

Neck. Medium long, sloping well back into shoulders, giving sturdy muscular appearance with untrimmed natural ruff. No throatiness.

Body. Well balanced, short-coupled, deep through the heart. Chest at least as wide as a man's hand, including thumb. Brisket extends to elbows. Ribs long and well sprung but not barrel shaped, extending well to rear of body. Loin short, muscular, wide and deep, with very little tuck-up. Topline level from withers to croup, whether standing or moving. Croup slopes gently. Slabsidedness, narrow chest, lack of depth in brisket, excessive tuck-up, roach or sway back to be faulted.

Forequarters. Forequarters well co-ordinated with hindquarters and capable of free movement. Shoulder blades wide, long and muscular, showing angulation with upper arm of approximately 90 degrees. Legs straight with good bone. Pastern short and strong, sloping slightly forward with no suggestion of weakness.

Hindquarters. Well-bent stifles (angulation between femur and pelvis approximately 90 degrees) with hocks well let down. Legs straight when viewed from rear. Cowhocks and sickle hocks to be faulted.

Feet. Medium size, round and compact with thick pads. Excess hair may be trimmed to show natural size and contour. Open or played feet to be faulted.

Tail. Well set on, neither too high nor too low, following natural line of croup. Length extends to hock. Carried with merry action with some upward curve but never curled over back nor between legs.

Coat and Color. Dense and water repellent with good undercoat. Texture not as hard as that of a shorthaired dog nor silky as that of a setter. Lies flat against body and may be straight or wavy. Moderate feathering on back of forelegs and heavier feathering on front of neck, back of thighs and underside of tail. Feathering may be lighter than rest of coat. Color lustrous golden of various shades. A few white hairs on chest permissible but not desirable. Further white markings to be faulted.

Gait. When trotting, gait is free, smooth, powerful and well coordinated. Viewed from front or rear, legs turn neither in nor out, nor do feet cross or interfere with each other. Increased speed causes tendency of feet to converge toward center line of gravity.

DISQUALIFICATIONS

Deviation in height of more than one inch from standard either way. Undershot or overshot bite. This condition not to be confused with misalignment of teeth. Trichiasis (abnormal position or direction of the eyelashes).

Approved September 10, 1963

RETRIEVER (LABRADOR)

(THE KENNEL CLUB—GUNDOG GROUP)

General Appearance. The general appearance of the Labrador should be that of a strongly-built, short-coupled, very active dog, broad in the skull, broad and deep through the chest and ribs, broad and strong over the loins and hindquarters. The coat close, short with dense undercoat and free from feather. The dog must move neither too wide nor too close in front or behind, he must stand and move true all round on legs and feet.

Head and Skull. The skull should be broad with a pronounced stop so that the skull is not in a straight line with the nose. The head should be clean cut without fleshy cheeks. The jaws should be medium length and powerful and free from snipiness. The nose wide and the nostrils well developed.

Eyes. The eyes of medium size expressing intelligence and good temper, should be brown or hazel.

Ears. Should not be large and heavy and should hang close to the head, and set rather far back.

Mouth. Teeth should be sound and strong. The lower teeth just behind but touching the upper.

Neck. Should be clean, strong and powerful and set into well placed shoulders.

Forequarters. The shoulders should be long and sloping. The forelegs well boned and straight from the shoulder to the ground when viewed from either the front or side. The dog must move neither too wide nor too close in front.

Body. The chest must be of good width and depth with well-sprung ribs. The back should be short coupled.

Hindquarters. The loins must be wide and strong with well-turned stifles; hindquarters well developed and not sloping to the tail. The hocks should be slightly bent and the dog must neither be cow-hocked nor move too wide or too close behind.

Feet. Should be round and compact with well-arched and well-developed pads.

Tail. The tail is a distinctive feature of the breed; it should be very thick towards the base, gradually tapering towards the tip, of medium length and practically free from any feathering, but clothed thickly all round with the Labrador's short, thick, dense coat, thus giving that peculiar 'rounded' appearance which has been described as the 'Otter' tail. The tail may be carried gaily, but should not curl over the back.

Coat. The coat is another distinctive feature of the breed, it should be short and dense and without wave with a weather-resisting undercoat and should give a fairly hard feeling to the hand.

Colour. The colour is generally black or yellow—but other whole colours are permitted. The coat should be free from any white markings but a small white spot on the chest is allowable. The coat should be of a whole colour and not of a flecked appearance.

Weight and Size. Desired height for dogs, 22 to $22\frac{1}{2}$ inches; bitches, $21\frac{1}{2}$–22 inches.

Faults. Under or overshot mouth; no undercoat; bad action; feathering; snipiness on the head; large or heavy ears; cow-hocked; tail curled over back.

RETRIEVER, LABRADOR

(AMERICAN KENNEL CLUB—GROUP IT SPORTING DOGS)

General Appearance. The general appearance of the Labrador should be that of a strongly built, short-coupled, very active dog. He should be fairly wide over the loins, and strong and muscular in the hindquarters. The coat should be close, short, dense and free from feather.

Head. The skull should be wide, giving brain room; there should be a slight stop, *i.e.* the brow should be slightly pronounced, so that the skull is not absolutely in a straight line with the nose. The head should be clean-cut and free from fleshy cheeks. The jaws should be long and powerful and free from snipiness; the nose should be wide and the nostrils well developed. Teeth should be strong and regular, with a level mouth. The ears should hang moderately close to the head, rather far back, should be set somewhat low and not be large and heavy. The eyes should be of a medium size, expressing great intelligence and good temper, and can be brown, yellow or black, but brown or black is preferred.

Neck and Chest. The neck should be medium length, powerful and not throaty. The shoulders should be long and sloping. The chest must be of good width and depth, the ribs well sprung and the loins wide and strong, stifles well turned, and the hindquarters well developed and of great power.

Legs and feet. The legs must be straight from the shoulder to ground, and the feet compact with toes well arched, and pads well developed; the hocks should be well bent, and the dog must neither be cowhocked nor be too wide behind; in fact, he must stand and move true all round on legs and feet. Legs should be of medium length, showing good bone and muscle, but not so short as to be out of balance with rest of body. In fact, a dog well balanced in all points is preferable to one with outstanding good qualities and defects.

Tail. The tail is a distinctive feature of the breed; it should be very thick towards the base, gradually tapering towards the tip, of medium length, should be free from any feathering, and should be clothed thickly all round with the Labrador's short, thick, dense coat, thus giving that peculiar 'rounded' appearance which has been described as the 'otter' tail. The tail may be carried gaily but should not curl over the back.

Coat. The coat is another very distinctive feature; it should be short, very dense and without wave, and should give a fairly hard feeling to the hand.

Color. The colors are black, yellow, or chocolate and are evaluated as follows:

(a) Blacks: All black, with a small white spot on chest permissible. Eyes to be of medium size, expressing intelligence and good temper, preferably brown or hazel, although black or yellow is permissible.

(b) Yellows: Yellows may vary in color from fox-red to light cream with variations in the shading of the coat on ears, the underparts of the dog, or beneath the tail. A small white spot on chest is permissible. Eye coloring and expression should be the same as that of the blacks, with black or dark brown eye rims. The nose should also be black or dark brown, although 'fading' to pink in winter weather is not serious. A 'Dudley' nose, (pink without pigmentation) should be penalized.

(c) Chocolates: Shades ranging from light sedge to chocolate. A small white spot on chest is permissible. Eyes to be light brown to clear yellow. Nose and eye-rim pigmentation dark brown or liver colored. 'Fading' to pink in winter weather not serious. 'Dudley' nose should be penalized.

Movement. Movement should be free and effortless. The forelegs should be strong, straight and true, and correctly placed. Watching a dog move towards one, there should be no signs of elbows being out in front, but neatly held to the body with legs not too close together, but moving straight forward without pacing or weaving. Upon viewing the dog from the rear, one should get the impression that the hind legs, which should be well muscled and not cowhocked, move as nearly parallel as possible, with hocks doing their full Share of work and flexing well, thus giving the appearance of power and strength.

Approximate weights of dogs and bitches in working condition. Dogs—60 to 75 lbs; bitches—55 to 70 lbs.

Height at shoulders. Dogs $22\frac{1}{2}$ inches to $24\frac{1}{2}$ inches; bitches—$21\frac{1}{2}$ inches to $23\frac{1}{2}$ inches.

Approved April 9, 1957

RHODESIAN RIDGEBACK

(THE KENNEL CLUB—HOUND GROUP)

Characteristics. The peculiarity of the breed is the ridge on the back which is formed by the hair growing in the opposite direction to the rest of the coat; the ridge must be regarded as the escutcheon of the breed. The ridge must be clearly defined, tapering and symmetrical. It must start immediately behind the shoulders and continue up to the hip (haunch) bones, and must contain two identical crowns only opposite each other. The lower edges of the crowns must not extend further down the ridge than one-third of the length of the ridge. Up to two inches is a good average for the width of the ridge.

General Appearance. The Ridgeback should represent a strong, muscular and active dog, symmetrical in outline, and capable of great endurance, with a fair amount of speed. Movement should be similar to the Foxhound's gait.

Head and Skull. Should be of a fair length, the skull flat and rather broad between the ears and should be free from wrinkles when in repose. The stop should be reasonably well defined, and not in one straight line from the nose to the occiput bone as required in a Bull Terrier. The nose should be black or brown, in keeping with the colour of the dog. No other coloured nose is permissible. A black nose should be accompanied by dark eyes; a brown nose by amber eyes.

Eyes. Should be moderately well apart, and should be round, bright and sparkling, with intelligent expression, their colour harmonizing with the colour of the dog.

Ears. Should be set up rather high, of medium size, rather wide at base, and gradually tapering to a rounded point. They should be carried close to the head.

Mouth. The muzzle should be long, deep and powerful, jaws level and strong, with well developed teeth, especially the canines or holders. The lips should be clean, closely fitting the jaws.

Neck. Should be fairly long, strong and free from throatiness.

Forequarters. The shoulders should be sloping, clean and muscular, denoting speed. The forelegs should be perfectly straight, strong and heavy in bone; elbows close to the body.

Body. The chest should not be too wide but very deep and capacious; ribs moderately well sprung, never rounded like barrel-hoops (which would indicate want of speed). The back powerful, and loins strong, muscular and slightly arched.

Hindquarters. In the hindlegs the muscles should be clean, well defined and hocks well down.

Feet. The feet should be compact with well-arched toes, round, tough elastic pads, protected by hair between the toes and pads.

Tail. Should be strong at the insertion and generally tapering towards the end, free from coarseness. It should not be inserted too high or too low, and should be carried with a slight curve upwards, never curled.

Coat. Should be short and dense, sleek and glossy in appearance but neither woolly nor silky.
Colour. Light wheaten to red wheaten. Head, body, legs and tail should be of a uniform colour. A little white on the chest is permissible but excessive white hairs here, on belly, or above paws should be penalized. White toes are undesirable. Dark muzzle and ears are permissible.
Weight and Size. The desirable weight is dogs 80 lb and bitches 70 lb with a permissible variation of 5 lb above and below these weights. A mature Ridgeback should be a handsome, upstanding dog; dogs should be of a height of 25 to 27 inches and bitches 24 to 26 inches. Minimum bench standard: dogs 25 inches and bitches 24 inches.

RHODESIAN RIDGEBACK

(AMERICAN KENNEL CLUB—GROUP II: HOUNDS)

The peculiarity of this breed is the *ridge* on the back, which is formed by the hair growing in the opposite direction to the rest of the coat. The ridge must be regarded as the characteristic feature of the breed. The ridge should be clearly defined, tapering and symmetrical. It should start immediately behind the shoulders and continue to a point between the prominence of the hips, and should contain two identical crowns opposite each other. The lower edges of the crown should not extend further down the ridge than one third of the ridge.
General Appearance. The Ridgeback should represent a strong muscular and active dog, symmetrical in outline, and capable of great endurance with a fair amount of speed.
Head. Should be of a fair length, the skull flat and rather broad between the ears and should be free from wrinkles when in repose. The stop should be reasonably well defined.
Muzzle. Should be long, deep and powerful, jaws level and strong with well-developed teeth, especially the canines or holders. The lips clean, closely fitting the jaws.
Eyes. Should be moderately well apart, and should be round, bright and sparkling, with intelligent expression, their color harmonizing with the color of the dog.
Ears. Should be set rather high, of medium size, rather wide at base, and tapering to a rounded point. They should be carried close to the head.
Nose. Should be black, or brown, in keeping with the color of the dog. No other colored nose is permissible. A black nose should be accompanied by dark eyes, a brown nose by amber eyes.
Neck and Shoulders. The neck should be fairly strong and free from thoatiness. The shoulders should be sloping, clean and muscular, denoting speed.
Body, Back, Chest and Loins. The chest should not be too wide, but very deep and capacious; ribs moderately well sprung, never rounded like barrel hoops (which would indicate want of speed), the back powerful, the loins strong, muscular and slightly arched.
Legs and Feet. The forelegs should be perfectly straight, strong and heavy in bone; elbows close to the body. The feet should be compact, with well-arched toes, round, tough, elastic pads, protected by hair between the toes and pads. In the hind legs the muscles should be clean, well defined, and hocks well down.
Tail. Should be strong at the insertion, and generally tapering towards the end, free from coarseness. It should not be inserted too high or too low, and should be carried with a slight curve upwards, never curled.
Coat. Should be short and dense, sleek and glossy in appearance, but neither woolly nor silky.
Color. Light wheaten to red wheaten. A little white on the chest and toes permissible but excessive white there and any white on the belly or above the toes is undesirable.
Size. A mature Ridgeback should be a handsome, upstanding dog; dogs should be of a height of 25 to 27 inches, and bitches 24 to 26 inches.
Weight. (Desirable) dogs 75 pounds, bitches 65 pounds.

SCALE OF POINTS

Ridge	20	Coat	5
Head	15	Tail	5
Neck and shoulders	10	Size, symmetry, general appearance	20
Body, back, chest, loins	10	Total	100
Legs and feet	15		

Approved November, 1955

ROTTWEILER

(THE KENNEL CLUB—WORKING GROUP)

General Appearance. The Rottweiler is an above average sized stalwart dog. His correctly proportioned, compact and powerful form permits of great strength, manoeuverability and endurance. His bearing displays boldness and courage; his tranquil gaze manifests good nature and devotion.

Head and Skull. The head is of medium length, the skull between the ears is broad. The forehead line is moderately arched as seen from the side. Occipital bone well developed but not conspicuous. Cheeks well muscled but not prominent, with the zygomatic arch well formed. The skin on the head should not be loose although it is allowed to form moderate wrinkle when the dog is attentive. Muzzle fairly deep with topline level and length not longer than the length from stop to occiput.

Nose. The nose is well developed with proportionately large nostrils and is always black.

Eyes. The eyes should be of medium size, almond shaped and dark brown in colour; eyelids close lying.

Ears. The ears are pendant, small in proportion rather than large, set high and wide apart on the head, lying flat and close to the cheek.

Mouth. The teeth are strong and the incisors of the lower jaw must touch the inner surface of the upper incisors. The flews are black and firm; they fall gradually away towards the corners of the mouth, which do not protrude excessively.

Neck. The neck should be of fair length, strong, round and very muscular. It should be slightly arched and free from throatiness.

Forequarters. The shoulders should be well placed on the body, long and sloping with the elbows well let down, but not loose. The legs should be muscular with plenty of bone and substance. The pasterns should be bent slightly forward and not be completely vertical. The front legs seen from all sides must be straight and not placed too closely to one another.

Body. The chest should be roomy, broad and deep with the ribs well sprung. The depth of brisket will not be more, and not much less than 50% of the shoulder height. The back should be straight, strong and not too large; ratio of shoulder height to length of body should be as 9 is to 10; the loins short strong and deep, the flanks should not be tucked up. The croup should be broad, of proportionate length, and very slightly sloping.

Hindquarters. The upper thigh not too short, broad and strongly muscled. The lower thigh well muscled at the top and strong and sinewy lower down. Stifles fairly well bent. Hocks well angulated without exaggeration and not completely vertical.

Feet. The feet should be strong, round and compact with the toes well arched. The hind feet are somewhat longer than the front. The pads should be very hard and the toe-nails short, dark and strong. Rear dewclaws removed.

Gait. In movement the Rottweiler should convey an impression of supple strength, endurance and purpose. While the back remains firm and stable there is a powerful hind thrust and good stride. First and foremost, movement should be harmonious, positive and unrestricted.

Tail. Carried horizontally. It is short, strong and not set too low. It should be docked at the first joint.

Coat. The coat, which consists of top coat and undercoat, should be of medium length, coarse and flat. The undercoat, which is essential on the neck and thighs, should not show through the outer coat. The hair may also be a little longer on the back of the forelegs and breachings.

Colour. The colour is black with clearly defined markings on the cheeks, muzzle, chest and legs, as well as over both eyes and the area beneath the tail. Colour of markings ranges from rich tan to mahogany brown.

Size. For males the height at the shoulder should be between 25 and 27 inches and for females between 23 and 25 inches. However, height should always be considered in relation to the general appearance of the dog.

Faults. The following faults are noted for the clarification of the Standard.

Too lightly or too heavily built. Sway backed or roach backed. Cow-hocked, bow hocked, or weak hocked. Long or excessively wavy coat. Any white markings. Nervousness and viciousness are highly undesirable.

ROTTWEILER

(AMERICAN KENNEL CLUB—GROUP III: WORKING DOGS)

General Appearance and Character. The Rottweiler is a good-sized, strongly built, active dog. He is affectionate, intelligent, easily trained to work, naturally obedient and extremely faithful. While not quarrelsome, he possesses great courage and makes a splendid guard. His demeanor is dignified and he is not excitable.

Head. Is of medium length, the skull broad between the ears. Stop well pronounced as is also the occiput. Muzzle is not very long. It should not be longer than the distance from the stop to the occiput. Nose is well developed, with relatively large nostrils and is always black. Flews which should not be too pronounced are also black. Jaws should be strong and muscular; teeth strong—incisors of lower jaw must touch the inner surface of the upper incisors. Eyes are of medium size, dark brown in color and should express faithfulness, good humor and confidence. The ears are comparatively small, set high and wide and hang over about on a level with top of head. The skin on head should not be loose. The neck should be of fair length, strong, round and very muscular, slightly arched and free from throatiness.

Forequarters. Shoulders should be well placed, long and sloping, elbows well let down, but not loose. Legs muscular and with plenty of bone and substance, pasterns straight and strong. Feet strong, round and close, with toes well arched. Soles very hard, toe nails dark, short and strong.

Body. The chest is roomy, broad and deep. Ribs well sprung. Back straight, strong and rather short. Loins strong and deep, and flanks should not be tucked up. Croup short, broad, but not sloping.

Hindquarters. Upper thigh is short, broad and very muscular. Lower thigh very muscular at top and strong and sinewy at the bottom. Stifles fairly well bent, hocks strong. The hind feet are somewhat longer than the front ones, but should be close and strong with toes well arched. There should be no dewclaws. Tail should be short, placed high (on level with back) and carried horizontally. Dogs are frequently born with a short stump tail and when tail is too long it must be docked close to body.

Coat. Hair should be short, coarse and flat. The undercoat which is absolutely required on neck and thighs should not show through outer coat. The hair should be a little longer on the back of front and hind legs and on tail.

Color. Black, with clearly defined markings on cheeks, muzzle, chest and legs, as well as over both eyes. Color of markings: tan to mahogany brown. A small spot of white on chest and belly is permissible but not desirable.

Height. Shoulder height for males is $23\frac{3}{4}$ to 27 inches, for females, $21\frac{3}{4}$ to $25\frac{3}{4}$ inches, but height should always be considered in relation to the general appearance and conformation of the dog.

Faults. Too lightly built or too heavily built, sway-back, roach back, too long body, lack of spring of ribs. Head too long and narrow or too short and plump. Lack of occiput, snipy muzzle, cheekiness, top line of muzzle not straight, light or flesh colored nose, hanging flews, overshot or undershot, loose skin on head, ears set too low, or ears too heavy, long or narrow or rose ear, or ears uneven in size. Light, small or slanting eyes, or lack of expression, neck too long, thin or weak, or very noticeable throatiness. Lack of bone and muscle, short or straight shoulders, front legs too close together or not straight, weak pasterns, splay feet, light nails, weak toes. Flat ribs, sloping croup. Too heavy or plump body. Flanks drawn up. Flat thighs, cowhocks or weak hocks, dewclaws. Tail set too high or too low or that is too long or too thin. Soft, too short, too long or too open coat, wavy coat or lack of undercoat. White markings on toes, legs, or other parts of body, markings not well defined or smudgy. The one-color tan Rottweiler with either black or light mask or with black streak on back as well as other colors such as brown or blue are not recognized and are believed to be cross bred, as is also a longhaired Rottweiler. Timid or stupid-appearing animals are to be positively rejected.

Approved April 9, 1935

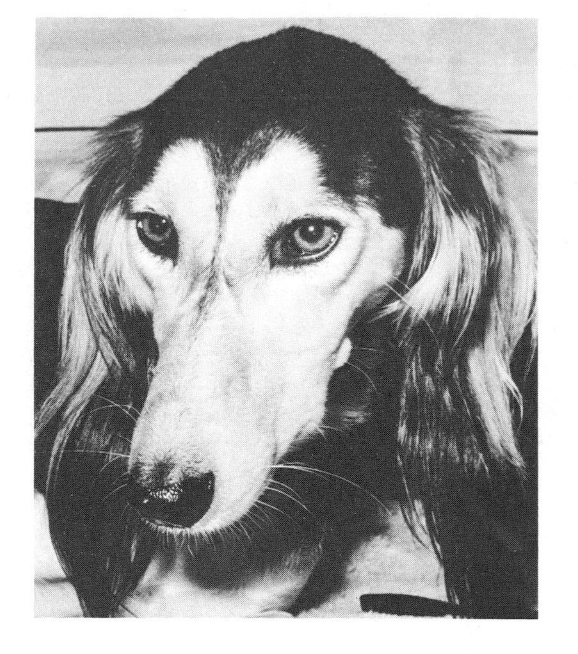

SALUKI OR GAZELLE HOUND

(THE KENNEL CLUB—HOUND GROUP)

General Appearance. The whole appearance of this breed should give an impression of grace and symmetry and of great speed and endurance coupled with strength and activity to enable it to kill gazelle or other quarry over deep sand or rocky mountain. The expression should be dignified and gentle with deep, faithful, farseeing eyes.
Head and Skull. Head long and narrow; skull moderately wide between ears, not domed, the stop not pronounced, the whole showing great quality. Nose black or liver.
Eyes. Dark to hazel and bright, large and oval, but not prominent.
Ears. Long and mobile, covered with long silky hair; hanging close to the skull.
Mouth. Teeth strong and level.
Neck. Long, supple and well muscled.
Forequarters. Shoulders sloping and set well back, well muscled without being coarse. The chest deep and moderately narrow. The forelegs straight and long from the elbow to the knee.
Body. Back fairly broad, muscles slightly arched over the loin.
Hindquarters. Strong, hip bones set wide apart, and stifle moderately bent, hocks low to the ground, showing galloping and jumping power.
Feet. Of moderate length, toes long, and well arched, not splayed out, but at the same time not cat footed; the whole being strong and supple and well feathered between the toes.
Tail. Long, set on low and carried naturally in a curve, well feathered on the underside with long silky hair, not bushy.
Coat. Smooth and of a soft silky texture; slight feather on the legs; feather at the back of the thighs; sometimes with slight woolly feather on thigh and shoulders. (In the Smooth variety the points should be the same with the exception of the coat which has no feathering.)
Colour. White, cream, fawn, golden, red, grizzle and tan, tricolour (white, black and tan), and black and tan, or variations of these colours.
Weight and Size. Height should average 23 to 28 inches, bitches proportionately smaller.

SALUKI

(AMERICAN KENNEL CLUB—GROUP II: HOUNDS)

Head. Long and narrow, skull moderately wide between the ears, not domed, stop not pronounced, the whole showing great quality. Nose black or liver.
Ears. Long and covered with long silky hair hanging close to the skull and mobile.
Eyes. Dark to hazel and bright; large and oval, but not prominent.
Teeth. Strong and level
Neck. Long, supple and well muscled.

Chest. Deep and moderately narrow.

Forequarters. Shoulders sloping and set well back, well muscled without being coarse.

Forelegs. Straight and long from the elbow to the knee.

Hindquarters. Strong, hipbones set well apart and stifle moderately bent, hocks low to the ground, showing galloping and jumping power.

Loin and Back. Back fairly broad, muscles slightly arched over loin.

Feet. Of moderate length, toes long and well arched, not splayed out, but at the same time not cat-footed; the whole being strong and supple and well feathered between the toes.

Tail. Long, set on low and carried naturally in a curve, well feathered on the underside with long silky hair, not bushy.

Coat. Smooth and of a soft silky texture, slight feather on the legs, feather at the back of the thighs and sometimes with slight woolly feather on the thigh and shoulder.

Colors. White, cream, fawn, golden, red, grizzle and tan, tricolor (white, black and tan) and black and tan.

General Appearance. The whole appearance of this breed should give an impression of grace and symmetry and of great speed and endurance coupled with strength and activity to enable it to kill gazelle or other quarry over deep sand or rocky mountains. The expression should be dignified and gentle with deep, faithful, far-seeing eyes. Dogs should average in height from 23 to 28 inches and bitches may be considerably smaller, this being very typical of the breed.

The Smooth Variety. In this variety the points should be the same with the exception of the coat, which has no feathering.

SAMOYED

(THE KENNEL CLUB—WORKING GROUP)

Characteristics. The Samoyed is intelligent, alert, full of action but above all displaying affection towards all mankind.

General Appearance. The Samoyed being essentially a working dog should be strong and active and graceful, and as his work lies in cold climates his coat should be heavy and weather-resisting. He should not be too long in back, as a weak back would make him practically useless for his legitimate work; but at the same time a cobby body, such as a Chow's, would also place him at a great disadvantage as a draught dog. Breeders should aim for the happy medium, viz., a body not long, but muscular, allowing liberty, with a deep chest and well sprung ribs, strong neck proudly arched, straight front and exceptionally strong loins. Both dogs and bitches should give the appearance of being capable of great endurance but should be free from coarseness. A full grown dog should stand about 21 inches at the shoulder. On account of the depth of chest required the legs should be moderately long, a very short-legged dog is to be deprecated. Hindquarters should be particularly well developed, stifles well angulated, and any suggestion of unsound stifles or cow-hocks severely penalized.

Head and Skull. Head powerful and wedge-shaped with a broad, flat skull, muzzle of medium length, a tapering foreface not too sharply defined. Lips black. Hair short and smooth before the ears. Nose black for preference, but may be brown or flesh-coloured. Strong jaws.

Eyes. Almond shaped, medium to dark brown in colour, set well apart with alert and intelligent expression. Eyerims should be black and unbroken.

Ears. Thick, not too long and slightly rounded at the tips, set well apart and well covered inside with hair. The ears should be fully erect in the grown dog.

Mouth. Upper teeth should just overlap the underteeth in a scissor bite.

Neck. Proudly arched.

Forequarters. Legs straight and muscular with good bone.

Body. Back medium in length, broad and very muscular. Chest broad and deep ribs well sprung, giving plenty of heart and lung room.

Hindquarters. Very muscular, stifles well angulated; cow-hocks or straight stifles very objectionable.

Feet. Long, flattish and slightly spread out. Soles well cushioned with hair.

Gait. Should move freely with a strong agile drive showing power and elegance.

Tail. Long and profuse, carried over the back when alert; sometimes dropped when at rest.

Coat. The body should be well covered with a thick, close, soft and short undercoat, with harsh hair growing through it, forming the outer coat,

which should stand straight away from the body and be free from curl.
Colour. Pure white; white and biscuit; cream.
Weight and Size. Dogs 20 to 22 inches at the shoulder. Bitches 18 to 20 inches at the shoulder. Weight in proportion to size.
Faults. Big ears with little feathering. Drop ears. Narrow width between ears. Long foreface. Blue or very light eyes. A bull neck. A long body. A soft coat; a wavy coat; absence of undercoat. Slack tail carriage; should be carried well over the back, though it may drop when the dog is at rest. Absence of feathering. Round, cat-like feet. Black or black spots. Severe unprovoked aggressiveness. Any sign of unsound movement.

SAMOYED

(AMERICAN KENNEL CLUB—GROUP III: WORKING DOGS)

General Conformation—(a) General Appearance. The Samoyed, being essentially a working dog, should present a picture of beauty, alertness and strength, with agility, dignity and grace. As his work lies in cold climates, his coat should be heavy and weather resistant, well groomed, and of good quality rather than quantity. The male carried more of a 'ruff' than the female. He should not be long in the back as a weak back would make him practically useless for his legitimate work, but at the same time, a close-coupled body would also place him at a great disadvantage as a draft dog. Breeders should aim for the happy medium, a body not long but muscular, allowing liberty, with a deep chest and well-sprung ribs, strong neck, straight front and especially strong loins. Males should be masculine in appearance and deportment without unwarranted aggressiveness; bitches feminine without weakness of structure or apparent softness of temperament. Bitches may be slightly longer in back than males. They should both give the appearance of being capable of great endurance but be free from coarseness. Because of the depth of chest required, the legs should be moderately long. A very short-legged dog is to be deprecated. Hindquarters should be particularly well developed, stifles well bent and any suggestion of unsound stifles or cowhocks severely penalized. General appearance should include movement and general conformation, indicating balance and good substance.
(b) Substance. Substance is that sufficiency of bone and muscle which rounds out a balance with the frame. The bone is heavier than would be expected in a dog of this size but not so massive as to prevent the speed and agility most desirable in a Samoyed. In all builds, bone should be in proportion to body size. The Samoyed should never be so heavy as to appear clumsy nor so light as to appear racy. The weight should be in proportion to the height.
(c) Height. Males—21 to 23½ inches; females—19 to 21 inches at the withers. An oversized or undersized Samoyed is to be penalized according to the extent of the deviation.
(d) Coat (Texture & Condition). The Samoyed is a double-coated dog. The body should bc well covered with an undercoat of soft, short, thick, close wool with longer and harsh hair growing through it to form the outer coat, which stands straight out from the body and should be free from curl. The coat should form a ruff around the neck and shoulders, framing the head (more on males than on females). Quality of coat should be weather resistant and considered more than quantity. A droopy coat is undesirable. The coat should glisten with a silver sheen. The female does not usually carry as long a coat as most males and it is softer in texture.
(e) Color. Samoyeds should be pure white, white and biscuit, cream, or all biscuit. Any other colors
Movement—(a) Gait. The Samoyed should trot, not pace. He should move with a quick agile stride that is well timed. The gait should be free, balanced and vigorous, with good reach in the forequarters and good driving power in the hindquarters. When trotting, there should be a strong rear action drive. Moving at a slow walk or trot, they will not single track, but as speed increases the legs gradually angle inward until the pads are finally falling on a line directly under the longitudinal center of the body. As the pad marks converge the forelegs and hindlegs are carried straight forward in traveling, the stifles not turned in nor out. The back should remain strong, firm and level. A choppy or stilted gait should be penalized.
(b) Rear End. Upper thighs should be well developed. Stifles well bent—approximately 45 degrees to the ground. Hocks should be well developed, sharply defined and set at approximately 30 per cent of hip height. The hindlegs should be parallel when viewed from the rear in a natural stance, strong, well developed, turning neither in nor out. Straight stifles are objectionable. Double jointedness or cowhocks are a fault. Cowhocks should only be determined if the dog has had an opportunity to move properly.
(c) Front End. Legs should be parallel and straight to the pasterns. The pasterns should be strong, sturdy and straight, but flexible with some spring for proper let-down of feet. Because of the depth of chest, legs should be moderately long. Length of leg from the ground to the elbow should be approximately 55 per cent of the total height at the withers—a very short-legged dog is to be deprecated. Shoulders should be long and sloping, with a layback of 45 degrees and be firmly set. Out at the shoulders or out at the elbows should be penalized. The withers separation should be approximately 1–1½ inches.
(d) Feet. Large, long, flattish—a hare-foot, slightly spread but not splayed; toes arched; pads thick and tough, with protective growth of hair

between the toes. Feet should turn neither in nor out in a natural stance but may turn in slightly in the act of pulling. Turning out, pigeon-toed, round or cat-footed or splayed are faults. Feathers on feet are not too essential but are more profuse on females than on males.

Head—(a) Conformation. Skull is wedge-shaped, broad, slightly crowned, not round or apple-headed, and should form an equilateral triangle on lines between the inner base of the ears and the center point of the stop.

Muzzle. Muzzle of medium length and medium width, neither coarse nor snipy; should taper toward the nose and be in proportion to the size of the dog and the width of skull. The muzzle must have depth.

Stop. Not too abrupt, nevertheless well defined.

Lips. Should be black for preference and slightly curved up at the corners of the mouth, giving the 'Samoyed smile.' Lip lines should not have the appearance of being coarse nor should the flews drop predominately at corners of the mouth.

Ears. Strong and thick, erect, triangular and slightly rounded at the tips; should not be large or pointed, not should they be small and 'bear-eared.' Ears should conform to head size and the size of the dog; they should be set well apart but be within the border of the outer edge of the head; they should be mobile and well covered inside with hair; hair full and stand-off before the ears. Length of ear should be the same measurement as the distance from inner base of ear to outer corner of eye.

Eyes. Should be dark for preference; should be placed well apart and deep-set; almond shaped with lower lid slanting toward an imaginary point approximating the base of ears. Dark eye rims for preference. Round or protruding eyes penalized. Blue eyes disqualifying.

Nose. Black for preference but brown, liver, or Dudley nose not penalized. Color of nose sometimes changes with age and weather.

Jaws and Teeth. Strong, well set teeth, snugly overlapping with scissors bite. Undershot or overshot should be penalized.

(b) Expression. The expression, referred to as 'Samoyed expression,' is very important and is indicated by sparkle of the eyes, animation and lighting up of the face when alert or intent on anything. Expression is made up of a combination of eyes, ears and mouth. The ears should be erect when alert; the mouth should be slightly curved up at the corners to form the 'Samoyed smile.'

Torso—(a) Neck. Strong, well muscled, carried proudly erect, set on sloping shoulders to carry head with dignity when at attention. Neck should blend into shoulders with a graceful arch.

(b) Chest. Should be deep, with ribs well sprung out from the spine and flattened at the sides to allow proper movement of the shoulders and freedom for the front legs. Should not be barrel-chested. Perfect depth of chest approximates the point of elbows, and the deepest part of the chest should be back of the forelegs—near the ninth rib. Heart and lung room are secured more by body depth than width.

(c) Loin and Back. The withers forms the highest part of the back. Loins strong and slightly arched. The back should be straight to the loin, medium in length, very muscular and neither long nor short-coupled. The dog should be 'just off square'—the length being approximately 5 per cent more than the height. Females allowed to be slightly longer than males. The belly should be well shaped and tightly muscled and, with the rear of the thorax, should swing up in a pleasing curve (tuck-up). Croup must be full, slightly sloping, and must continue imperceptibly to the tail root.

Tail. The tail should be moderately long with the tail bone terminating approximately at the hock when down. It should be profusely covered with long hair and carried forward over the back or side when alert, but sometimes dropped when at rest. It should not be high or low set and should be mobile and loose—not tight over the back. A double hook is a fault. A judge should see the tail over the back once when judging.

Disposition. Intelligent, gentle, loyal, adaptable, alert, full of action, eager to serve, friendly but conservative, not distrustful or shy, not overly aggressive. Unprovoked aggressiveness to be severely penalized.

DISQUALIFICATIONS

Any color other than pure white, cream, biscuit, or white and biscuit. Blue eyes.

Approved April 9, 1963

SCHNAUZER

(THE KENNEL CLUB—UTILITY GROUP)

General Appearance. The Schnauzer is a powerfully built, robust, sinewy, nearly square, dog (length of body equal to height at shoulders). His temperament combines high spirits, reliability, strength, endurance and vigour. Expression keen and attitude alert. Correct conformation is of more importance than colour or other purely 'beauty' points.

Head and Skull. Head strong and elongated, gradually narrowing from the ears to the eyes and thence forward toward the tip of the nose. Upper part of the head (occiput to the base of the forehead) moderately broad between the ears—with flat, creaseless, forehead and well muscled, but not too strongly developed cheeks. Medium stop to accentuate prominent eyebrows. The powerful muzzle formed by the upper and lower jaws (base of forehead to the tip of the nose) should end in a moderately blunt line, with bristly, stubby moustache and chin whiskers. Ridge of the nose straight and running almost parallel to the extension of the forehead. The nose is black and full. Lips tight and not overlapping.

Eyes. Medium sized, dark, oval, set forward, with arched bushy eyebrows.

Ears. Neat and V-shaped, set high and dropping forward to temple.

Mouth. Scissor teeth, slightly overlapping from the top; with strongly developed fangs; healthy and pure white.

Neck. Moderately long, nape strong and slightly arched, skin close to throat, neck set cleanly on shoulders.

Forequarters. Shoulders flat and sloping. Forelegs straight viewed from any position. Muscles smooth and lithe rather than prominent; bone strong, straight and carried well down to the feet; elbows set close to the body and pointing directly backward.

Body. Chest moderately broad, deep, with visible strong breast bone reaching down to at least the height of elbow and slightly rising backward to loins. Back strong and straight, slightly higher at the shoulder than at the hindquarters, with short, well developed loins. Ribs well sprung. Length of body equal to height from top of withers to ground.

Hindquarters. Thighs slanting and flat, but strongly muscled. Hindlegs (upper and lower thighs) at first vertical to the stifle, from stifle to hock, in line with the extension of the upper neck line, from hock, vertical to ground.

Feet. Short, round, extremely compact with close-arched toes (cat's paws), dark nails and hard soles. The feet also deep or thickly padded, pointing forward.

Tail. Set on and carried high, cut down to three joints.

Coat. Hard and wiry and just short enough for smartness, clean on neck, shoulder, ears and skull, plenty of good hair on front legs. Good undercoat is essential.

Colour. All pepper and salt colours in even proportions, or pure black.

Height. The ideal height for bitches shall be 18 inches and for dogs 19 inches. Any variation of more than 1 inch in these heights should be penalized.

Faults. Too heavy or too light; too low or high on the leg. Head too heavy or round, creased forehead, sticking-out, or badly carried, ears; light eye, with yellow or light grey rings; strongly protruding cheek-bones; flabby throat skin; undershot or overshot jaw. Muzzle too pointed or too small. Back too long, sunken or roached; barrel-shaped ribs; slanting crupper; elbows turned out; heels turned in, hindpart overbuilt (too steep). Toes spread open; paws long and flat (hare). Coat too short and sleek, or too long, soft or curled. All white, spotty, tigered or red colours. Small white breast spot or marking is not a fault. Among other serious faults are cow-hocks, sunken pasterns, or any weakness of joint, bones or muscular development.

STANDARD SCHNAUZER

(AMERICAN KENNEL CLUB—GROUP III: WORKING DOGS)

General Appearance. The Standard Schnauzer is a robust, heavy-set dog, sturdily built with good muscle and plenty of bone; square-built in proportion of body-length to height. His nature combines high-spirited temperament with extreme reliability. His rugged build and dense harsh coat are accentuated by the hallmark of the breed, the arched eyebrows, bristly mustache, and luxuriant whiskers.

Head. Strong, rectangular, and elongated; narrowing slightly from the ears to the eyes and again to the tip of the nose. The total length of the head is about one half the length of the back measured from the withers to the set-on of the tail. The head matches the sex and substance of the dog. The top line of the muzzle is parallel with the top line of the skull. There is a slight stop which is accentuated by the wiry brows.

Skull (Occiput to Stop). Moderately broad between the ears with the width of the skull not exceeding two thirds the length of the skull. The skull must be flat; neither domed nor bumpy; skin unwrinkled.

Cheeks. Well-developed chewing muscles, but not so much that 'cheekiness' disturbs the rectangular head form.

Muzzle. Strong, and both parallel and equal in length to the topskull; it ends in a moderately blunt wedge with wiry whiskers accenting the rectangular shape of the head. Nose is large, black and full. The lips should be black, tight and not overlapping.

Eyes. Medium size; dark brown; oval in shape and turned forward; neither round nor protruding. The brow is arched and wiry, but vision is not impaired nor eyes hidden by too long an eyebrow.

Bite. A full complement of white teeth, with a strong, sound scissors bite. The canine teeth are strong and well developed with the upper incisors slightly overlapping and engaging the lower. The upper and lower jaws are powerful and neither overshot nor undershot.

Faults. A level bite is considered undesirable but a lesser fault than an overshot or undershot mouth.

Ears. Evenly shaped, set high and carried erect when cropped. If uncropped, they are small, V-shaped button ears of moderate thickness and carried rather high and close to the head.

Neck. Strong, of moderate thickness and length, elegantly arched and blending cleanly into the shoulders. The skin is tight, fitting closely to the dry throat with no wrinkles or dewlaps.

Shoulders. The sloping shoulder blades are strongly muscled yet flat and well laid back so that the rounded upper ends are in a nearly vertical line above the elbows. They slope well forward to the point where they join the upper arm, forming as nearly as possible a right angle when seen from the side. Such an angulation permits the maximum forward extension of the forelegs without binding or effort.

Chest. Of medium width with well-sprung ribs, and if it could be seen in cross-section would be oval. The breastbone is plainly discernible. The brisket must descend at least to the elbows and ascend gradually to the rear with the belly moderately drawn up.

Body. Compact, strong, short-coupled and substantial so as to permit great flexibility and agility. The height at the highest point of the withers equals the length from breastbone to point of rump.

Faults. Too slender or shelly; too bulky or coarse; excessive tuck-up.

Back. Strong, stiff, straight and short, with a well-developed loin section; the distance from the last rib to the hips as short as possible. The top line of the back should not be absolutely horizontal, but should have a slightly descending slope from the first vertebra of the withers to the faintly curved croup and set-on of the tail.

Forelegs. Straight, vertical, and without any curvature when seen from all sides; set moderately far apart; with heavy bone; elbows set close to the body and pointing directly to the rear.

Hindquarters. Strongly muscled, in balance with the forequarters, never appearing higher than the shoulders. Croup full and slightly rounded. Thighs broad with well-bent stifles. The second thigh, from knee to hock, is approximately parallel with an extension of the upper-neck line. The legs, from the clearly defined hock joint to the feet, are short and perpendicular to the

ground and when viewed from the rear are parallel to each other.
Feet. Small and compact, round with thick pads and strong black nails. The toes are well closed and arched (cat's paws) and pointing straight ahead.
Dewclaws. Dewclaws, if any, on the hind legs are generally removed. Dewclaws on the forelegs may be removed.
Tail. Set moderately high and carried erect. It is docked to not less than 1 inch nor more than 2 inches.
Faults. Squirrel tail.
Height. Ideal height at the highest point of the shoulder blades, $18\frac{1}{2}$ to $19\frac{1}{2}$ inches for males and $17\frac{1}{2}$ inches to $18\frac{1}{2}$ inches for females. Dogs measuring over or under these limits must be faulted in proportion to the extent of the deviation. Dogs measuring more than one half inch over or under these limits must be disqualified.
Coat. Tight, hard, wiry and as thick as possible, composed of a soft close undercoat and a harsh outer coat which, when seen against the grain, stands up off the back, lying neither smooth nor flat. The outer coat (body coat) is trimmed (by plucking) only to accent the body outline. When in show condition, the outer coat's proper length is approximately $1\frac{1}{2}$ inches, except on the ears, head, neck, chest, belly and under the tail where it may be closely trimmed to give the desired typical appearance of the breed.

On the muzzle and over the eyes the coat lengthens to form luxuriant beard and eyebrows; the hair on the legs is longer than that on the body. These 'furnishings' should be of harsh texture and should not be so profuse so as to detract from the neat appearance or working capabilities of the dog.
Faults. Soft, smooth, curly, wavy or shaggy; too long or too short; too sparse or lacking undercoat; excessive furnishings; lack of furnishings.
Color. Pepper and salt or pure black.
Pepper and Salt. The typical pepper and salt color of the topcoat results from the combination of black and white hairs, and white hairs banded with black. Acceptable are all shades of pepper and salt from dark iron-gray to silver gray. Ideally, pepper and salt Standard Schnauzers have a gray undercoat, but a tan or fawn undercoat is not to be penalized. It is desirable to have a darker facial mask that harmonizes with the particular shade of coat color. Also, in pepper and salt dogs, the pepper and salt mixture may fade out to light gray or silver white in the eyebrows, whiskers, cheeks, under throat, across chest, under tail, leg furnishings, under body, and inside legs.
Black. Ideally the black Standard Schnauzer should be a true rich color, free from any fading or discoloration or any admixture of gray or tan hairs. The undercoat should also be solid black. However, increased age or continued exposure to the sun may cause a certain amount of fading and burning. A small white smudge on the chest is not a fault. Loss of color as a result of scars from cuts and bites is not a fault.
Faults. Any colors other than specified, and any shadings or mixtures thereof in the topcoat such as rust, brown, red, yellow or tan; absence of peppering; spotting or striping; a black streak down the back; or a black saddle without typical salt and pepper coloring—and gray hairs in the coat of a black; in blacks, any undercoat color other than black.
Gait. Sound, strong, quick, free, true and level gait with powerful, well-angulated hindquarters that reach out and cover ground. The forelegs reach out in a stride balancing that of the hindquarters. At a trot, the back remains firm and level, without swaying, rolling or roaching. When viewed from the rear, the feet, though they may appear to travel close when trotting, must not cross or strike. Increased speed causes feet to converge toward the center line of gravity.
Faults. Crabbing or weaving; paddling, rolling, swaying; short, choppy, stiff, stilted rear action; front legs that throw out or in (East and West movers); hackney gait, crossing over, or striking in front or rear.
Faults. Any deviation from the specifications in the Standard is to be considered a fault and should be penalized in proportion to the extent of the deviation. In weighing the seriousness of a fault, greatest consideration should be given to deviation from the desired alert, highly intelligent, spirited, reliable character of the Standard Schnauzer, and secondly to any deviation that detracts from the Standard Schnauzer's desired general appearance of a robust, active, square-built, wire-coated dog. Dogs that are shy or appear to be highly nervous should be seriously faulted and dismissed from the ring. Vicious dogs shall be disqualified.

DISQUALIFICATIONS

Vicious dogs. Males under 18 inches or over 20 inches in height. Females under 17 inches or over 19 inches in height.

Approved May 14, 1968

SCHIPPERKE

(THE KENNEL CLUB—UTILITY GROUP)

General Appearance. A small cobby animal, with sharp expression, intensely lively, presenting the appearance of being always on the alert.
Head and Skull. Head foxy in type, skull not round, but fairly broad, flat and with little stop. The muzzle should be moderate in length, fine but not weak, should be well filled out under the eyes. Nose black and small.
Eyes. Dark brown, small, more oval than round and not full; bright and full of expression.
Ears. Sharp, of moderate length, not too broad at the base, tapering to a point. Carried stiffly erect and strong enough not to be bent other than lengthways.
Mouth. Teeth strong and level.
Neck. Strong and full, rather short set, broad on the shoulders, and slightly arched.
Forequarters. Shoulders muscular and sloping. Legs perfectly straight, well under the body, with bone in proportion to the body.
Body. Chest broad and deep in brisket. Back short, straight and strong. Loins powerful, well drawn up from brisket.
Hindquarters. Fine compared to the foreparts, muscular and well-developed thighs; tail-less rump well rounded. Legs strong, muscular, hocks well let down.
Feet. Should be small, cat-like, and standing well on the toes.
Coat. Abundant, dense and harsh, smooth on the head, ears and legs, lying close on the back and sides, but erect and thick round the neck, forming a mane and frill and with a good culotte on the back of the thighs.
Colour. Should be black but other whole colours are permissible.
Weight and Size. Weight about 12 to 16 lbs.
Faults. Drop or semi-erect ears, Dudley noses in the coloured variety. A light-coloured eye. Head narrow and elongated, or too short. Coat sparse, wavy or silky. Absence of the mane and 'culotte'. Coat too long, and white spots. Undershot or overshot mouth.

SCHIPPERKE

(AMERICAN KENNEL CLUB—GROUP VI: NON-SPORTING DOGS)

Appearance and General Characteristics. Excellent and faithful little watchdog, suspicious of strangers. Active, agile, indefatigable, continually occupied with what is going on around him, careful of things that are given him to guard, very kind with children, knows the ways of the household; always curious to know what is going on behind closed doors or about any object that that has been moved, betraying his impressions by his sharp bark and upstanding ruff, seeking the company of horses, a hunter of moles and other

vermin; can be used to hunt, a good rabbit dog.
Color. Solid black.
Head. Foxlike, fairly wide, narrowing at the eyes, seen in profile slightly rounded, tapering muzzle not too elongated nor too blunt, not too much stop.
Nose. Small and black.
Eyes. Dark brown, small, oval rather than round, neither sunken nor prominent.
Expression. Should have a questioning expression: sharp and lively, not mean or wild.
Ears. Very erect, small, triangular, placed high, strong enough not to be capable of being lowered except in line with the body.
Teeth. Meeting evenly. A tight scissors bite is acceptable.
Neck. Strong and full, slightly arched, rather short.
Shoulders. Muscular and sloping.
Chest. Broad and deep in brisket.
Body. Short, thick-set and cobby. Broad behind the shoulders, seeming higher in front because of ruff. Back strong, short, straight and level or slightly sloping down toward rump. Ribs well sprung.
Loins. Muscular and well drawn up from the brisket but not to such an extent as to cause a weak and leggy appearance of the hindquarters.
Forelegs. Straight under body, with bone in proportion, but not coarse.
Hindquarters. Somewhat lighter than the foreparts, but muscular, powerful, with rump well rounded, tail docked to no more than 1 inch in length.
Feet. Small, round and tight (not splayed), nails straight, strong and short.
Coat. Abundant and slightly harsh to the touch, short on the ears and on the front of legs and on the hocks, fairly short on the body, but longer around neck beginning back of the ears, and forming a ruff and a cape; a jabot extending down between the front legs, also longer on rear where it forms a culotte, the points turning inward. Undercoat dense and short on body, very dense around neck making ruff stand out. Culotte should be as long as the ruff.
Weight. Up to 18 lbs.
Faults. Light eyes, large round prominent eyes, ears too long or too rounded, narrow head and elongated muzzle, too blunt muzzle, domed skull, smooth short coat with short ruff and culotte, lack of undercoat, curly or silky coat, body coat more than three (3) inches long, slightly overshot or undershot, sway-back, Bull Terrier shaped head, straight hocks. Straight stifles and shoulders, cowhocks, feet turning in or out, legs not straight when viewed from front. Lack of distinction between length of coat, ruff and culotte.

DISQUALIFICATIONS

Any color other than solid black. Drop or semi-erect ears. Badly overshot or undershot.

Approved May 12, 1959

SCOTTISH TERRIER

(THE KENNEL CLUB—TERRIER GROUP)

General Appearance. A Scottish Terrier is a sturdy thick-set dog of a suitable size to go to ground, placed on short legs, alert in carriage, and suggestive of great power and activity in small compass. The head gives the impression of being long for a dog of its size. The body is covered with a close-lying, broken, rough-textured coat; with its keen intelligent eyes and sharp prick ears, the dog looks willing to go anywhere and do anything. In spite of its short legs, the construction is such that it is a very agile and active dog. The movement of the dog is smooth, easy, and straight forward, with free action at shoulder, stifle and hock.

Head and Skull. Without being out of proportion to the size of the dog, it should be long, the length of skull enabling it to be fairly wide and yet retain a narrow appearance. The skull is nearly flat and the cheek-bones do not protrude. There is a slight, but distinct stop between skull and foreface just in front of the eye. The nose is large, and in profile the line from the nose towards the chin appears to slope backwards.

Eyes. Should be almond-shaped, dark brown, fairly wide apart and set deeply under the eyebrows.

Ears. Neat, of fine texture, pointed and erect.

Mouth. The teeth large, the upper incisors closely overlapping the lower.

Neck. Muscular, of moderate length.

Forequarters. The head is carried on a muscular neck of moderate length, showing quality, set into a long sloping shoulder; the brisket well in front of the forelegs, which are straight and well-boned to straight pasterns. The chest fairly broad and hung between the forelegs, which must not be out at elbows nor placed under the body.

Body. The body has well-rounded ribs, which flatten to a deep chest and are carried well back. The back is proportionately short and very muscular. In general the top line of the body should be straight; the loin muscular and deep, thus powerfully coupling the ribs to the hindquarters.

Hindquarters. Remarkably powerful for the size of the dog. Big and wide buttocks. Thighs deep and muscular, well bent at stifle. Hocks strong and well bent and turned neither inwards nor outwards.

Feet. Of good size and well padded, toes well arched and close-knit.

Tail. Of moderate length to give a general balance to the dog, thick at the root and tapering towards the tip, set on with an upright carriage or with a slight bend.

Coat. The dog has two coats, the undercoat short, dense, and soft; the outer coat harsh, dense, and wiry; the two making a weather-resisting covering to the dog.

Colour. Black, wheaten, or brindle of any colour.

Weight and Size. The ideally-made dog in hard show condition should weigh from 19 to 23 lbs. Height, 10 to 11 inches.

SCOTTISH TERRIER

(AMERICAN KENNEL CLUB—GROUP IV: TERRIERS)

Skull (5 points). Long, of medium width, slightly domed and covered with short, hard hair. It should not be quite flat, as there should be a slight stop or drop between the eyes.

Muzzle (5 points). In proportion to the length of skull, with not too much taper toward the nose. Nose should be black and of good size. The jaws should be level and square. The nose projects somewhat over the mouth, giving the impression that the upper jaw is longer than the lower. The teeth should be evenly placed, having a scissors or level bite, with the former being preferable.

Eyes (5 points). Set wide apart, small and of almond shape, not round. Color to be dark brown or nearly black. To be bright, piercing and set well under brow.

Ears (10 points). Small, prick, set well up on the skull, rather pointed but not cut. The hair on them should be short and velvety.

Neck (5 points). Moderately short, thick and muscular, strongly set on sloping shoulders, but not so short as to appear clumsy.

Chest (5 points). Broad and very deep, well let down between the forelegs.

Body (15 points). Moderately short and well ribbed up with strong loin, deep flanks and very muscular hindquarters.

Legs and Feet (10 points). Both forelegs and hind legs should be short and very heavy in bone in proportion to the size of the dog. Forelegs straight or slightly bent with elbows close to the body. Scottish Terriers should not be out at the elbows. Stifles should be well bent and legs straight from hock to heel. Thighs very muscular. Feet round and thick with strong nails, forefeet larger than the hind feet.

Note. The gait of the Scottish Terrier is peculiarly its own and is very characteristic of the breed. It is not the square trot or walk that is desirable in the long-legged breeds. The forelegs do not move in exact parallel planes—rather in reaching out incline slightly inward. This is due to the shortness of leg and width of chest. The action of the rear legs should be square and true and at the trot both the hocks and stifles should be flexed with a vigorous motion.

Tail ($2\frac{1}{2}$ points). Never cut and about 7 inches long, carried with a slight curve but not over the back.

Coat (15 points). Rather short, about 2 inches, dense undercoat with outer coat intensely hard and wiry.

Size and Weight (10 points). Equal consideration must be given to height, length of back and weight. Height at shoulder for either sex should be about 10 inches. Generally, a well-balanced Scottish Terrier dog of correct size should weigh from 19 to 22 lbs and a bitch, from 18 to 21 lbs. The principal objective must be symmetry and balance.

Color ($2\frac{1}{2}$ points). Steel or iron gray, brindled or grizzled, black, sandy or wheaten. White markings are objectionable and can be allowed only on the chest and that to a slight extent only.

General Appearance (10 points). The face should wear a keen, sharp and active expression. Both head and tail should be carried well up. The dog should look very compact, well muscled and powerful, giving the impression of immense power in a small size.

Penalties. Soft coat, round or very light eye, overshot or undershot jaw, obviously oversize or undersize, shyness, timidity or failure to show with head and tail up are faults to be penalized. No judge should put to Winners or Best of Breed any Scottish Terrier not showing real terrier character in the ring.

SCALE OF POINTS

Skull	5	Legs and feet	10
Muzzle	5	Tail	$2\frac{1}{2}$
Eyes	5	Coat	15
Ears	10	Size	10
Neck	5	Color	$2\frac{1}{2}$
Chest	5	General appearance	10
Body	15	Total	100

Approved June 10, 1947

SEALYHAM TERRIER

(THE KENNEL CLUB—TERRIER GROUP)

General Appearance. Should be that of a freely moving and active dog.
Head and Skull. The skull slightly domed and wide between the ears. Jaw powerful and long, with a punishing and square jaw. Nose black.
Eyes. Dark, well set, round and of medium size.
Ears. Size medium, slightly rounded at tip, and carried at side of cheek.
Mouth. Teeth level and square, strong, with canine teeth fitting well into each other, and long for the size of the dog.
Neck. Fairly long, thick and muscular, strongly set on sloping shoulders.
Forequarters. Forelegs short, strong and straight.
Body. Medium length, level and ribs well sprung. Body very flexible. Chest broad and deep, well let down between forelegs.
Hindquarters. Remarkably powerful for size of dog. Thighs deep and muscular, well bent at stifle. Hocks strong, well bent and neither turned inwards nor outwards.
Feet. Round and cat-like with thick pads.
Tail. Carried erect.
Coat. Long, hard and wiry.
Colour. Mostly all white, or white with lemon, brown, or badger pied markings on head and ears.
Weight and Size. Weight: dogs should not exceed 20 lbs; bitches should not exceed 18 lbs. Height should not exceed 12 inches at the shoulder.
Faults. Eyes, light in colour or small. Nose, white, cherry, or spotted to a considerable extent with either of these colours. Ears, prick, tulip or rose. Colour, much black objectionable. Teeth, defective, much undershot or overshot. Coat soft and woolly.

SEALYHAM TERRIER

(AMERICAN KENNEL CLUB—GROUP IV: TERRIERS)

The Sealyham should be the embodiment of power and determination, ever keen and alert, of extraordinary substance, yet free from clumsiness.
Height. At withers about $10\frac{1}{2}$ inches.
Weight. 21 pounds for dogs, and 20 pounds for bitches. It should be borne in mind that size is more important than weight.
Head. Long, broad and powerful, without coarseness. It should, however, be in perfect balance with the body, joining neck smoothly. Length of head roughly, three-quarters height at withers, or about an inch longer than neck. Breadth between ears a little less than one half length of head.
Skull. Very slightly domed, with a shallow indentation running down between the brows, and joining the muzzle with a moderate stop.
Cheeks. Smoothly formed and flat, without heavy jowls.

Jaws. Level, powerful and square. Overshot or undershot bad faults.
Teeth. Sound, strong and white, with canines fitting closely together.
Nose. Black, with large nostrils. White, cherry or butterfly bad faults.
Eyes. Very dark, deeply set and fairly wide apart, of medium size, oval in shape with keen terrier expression. Light, large or protruding eye bad faults.
Ears. Folded level with top of head, with forward edge close to cheek. Well rounded at tip, and of length to reach outer corner of eye. Thin, not leathery, and of sufficient thickness to avoid creases. Prick, tulip, rose or hound ears bad faults.
Neck. Length slightly less than two-thirds of height of dog at withers. Muscular without coarseness, with good reach, refinement at throat, and set firmly on shoulders.
Shoulders. Well laid back and powerful, but not over-muscled. Sufficiently wide to permit freedom of action. Upright or straight shoulder placement highly undesirable.
Legs. Forelegs strong, with good bone; and as straight as is consistent with chest being well let down between them. Down on pasterns, knuckled over, bound, and out at elbow, bad faults. Hind legs longer than forelegs and not so heavily boned.
Feet. Large but compact, round with thick pads, strong nails. Toes well arched and pointing straight ahead. Forefeet larger, though not quite so long as hind feet. Thin, spread or flat feet bad faults.
Body. Strong, short-coupled and substantial, so as to permit great flexibility. Brisket deep and well let down between forelegs. Ribs well sprung.
Back. Length from withers to set-on of tail should approximate height at withers, or $10\frac{1}{2}$ inches. Topline level, neither roached nor swayed. Any deviations from these measurements undesirable.
Hindquarters. Very powerful, and protruding well behind the set-on of tail. Strong second thighs, stifles well bent, and hocks well let down. Capped or cowhocks bad faults.
Tail. Docked and carried upright. Set on far enough forward so that spine does not slope down to it.
Coat. Weather-resisting, comprised of soft, dense undercoat and hard, wiry top coat. Silky or curly coat bad fault.
Color. All white, or with lemon, tan or badger markings on head and ears. Heavy body markings and excessive ticking should be discouraged'
Action. Sound, strong, quick, free, true and level.

SCALE OF POINTS

General character, balance and size		15	Body, ribs, & loin	10	
Head	5		Hindquarters	10	
Eyes	5		Legs and feet	10	
Mouth	5		Coat	10	50
Ears	5		Tail	5	
Neck	5	25	Color (body marking & ticking	5	10
Shoulders and brisket	10		Total		100

Approved March 12, 1935

SHETLAND SHEEPDOG

(THE KENNEL CLUB—WORKING GROUP)

Characteristics. To enable the Shetland Sheepdog to fulfil its natural bent for sheepdog work, its physical structure should be on the lines of strength and activity, free from cloddiness and without any trace of coarseness. Although the desired type is similar to that of the Rough Collie there are marked differences that must be noted. The expression, being one of the most marked characteristics of the breed, is obtained by the perfect balance and combination of skull and foreface, size, shape, colour and placement of eyes, correct position and carriage of ears, all harmoniously blended to produce that almost indefinable look of sweet, alert, gentle intelligence.

The Shetland Sheepdog should show affection and response to his owner, he may show reserve to strangers but not to the point of nervousness.

General Appearance. The Shetland Sheepdog should instantly appeal as a dog of great beauty, intelligence and alertness. Action lithe and graceful with speed and jumping power great for its size. The outline should be symmetrical so that no part appears out of proportion to the whole. An abundance of coat, mane and frill, with shapeliness of head and sweetness of expression all combine to present the ideal Shetland Sheepdog that will inspire and secure admiration.

Head and Skull. The head should be refined and its shape when viewed from the top or side is a long blunt wedge tapering from ear to nose. The width of skull necessarily depends upon the combined length of skull and muzzle and the whole must be considered in connection with the size of the dog. The skull should be flat, moderately wide between the ears, showing no prominence of the occipital bone. Cheeks should be flat and merge smoothly into a well rounded muzzle. Skull and muzzle to be of equal length, central point to be the inner corner of the eye. In profile the topline of the skull should be parallel to the topline of the muzzle, but on a higher plane due to a slight but definite stop. The jaws should be clean and strong and with a well developed underjaw. Lips should be tight. Teeth should be sound and level, with an evenly spaced scissor bite.

Eyes. A very important feature giving expression to the dog. They should be of medium size obliquely set and of almond shape. Colour dark brown except in the case of melies, where blue is permissible.

Ears. Should be small and moderately wide at the base, placed fairly close together on the top of the skull. When in repose they should be thrown back, but when on the alert brought forward and carried semi-erect with tips dropping forward

Neck. The neck should be muscular, well arched and of sufficient length to carry the head proudly.

Body and Quarters. From the withers the

shoulder blade should slope at a 45 degree angle, forward and downward to the shoulder joint. At the withers they are separated only by the vertebrae but they must slope outwards to accommodate the desired spring of ribs. The upper arm should join the shoulder blade at as nearly a right angle as possible. The elbow joint to be equidistant from the ground and the withers. The forelegs should be straight when viewed from the front, muscular and clean, with strong bone. Pasterns strong and flexible. The body is slightly longer from the withers to the root of the tail than the height at the withers, but most of the length is due to the proper angulation of the shoulder and hindquarters. The chest should be deep reaching to the point of the elbow. The ribs well sprung but tapering at their lower half to allow free play of the forelegs and shoulders. The back should be level with a graceful sweep over the loins and the croup should slope gradually to the rear. The thigh should be broad and muscular, the thigh bones to be set into the pelvis at right angles, corresponding to the angle of the shoulder blade. The stifle joint where the femur bone joins the tibia bone must have a distinct angle, hock joint to be clean cut, angular and well let down with strong bone. The hock must be straight when viewed from behind.

Tail. Set on low, tapering bone must reach at least to the hock joint, with abundant hair and slight upward sweep, raised when the dog is moving, but never over the level of the back.

Feet. Oval in shape, soles well padded, toes arched and close together.

Gait. The action of the Shetland Sheepdog should denote speed and smoothness. There should be no pacing, plaiting, rolling or stiff stilted up and down movement.

Coat. Must be double, the outer coat of long hair of harsh texture and straight, the under coat soft (resembling fur) short and close. The mane and frill should be very abundant and forelegs well feathered. Hindlegs above the hocks profusely covered with hair, but below the hocks fairly smooth. The mask or face smooth. What are commonly known as smooth coated specimens are barred.

Colour. Tricolours should be an intense black on the body with no signs of ticking, rich tan markings on a tricolour to be preferred. Sables may be clear or shaded, any colour from gold to deep mahogany but in its shade the colour should be rich in tones. Wolf sable and grey colours undesirable. Blue Merles, clear silvery blue is desired, splashed and marbled with black. Rich tan markings to be preferred, but the absence not to be counted as a fault. Heavy black markings, slate coloured or rusty tinge in either top or undercoat is high undesirable. General effect should be blue. White markings may be shown in the blaze, collar, chest frill, legs, stifle and tip of tail. All or some tan markings may be shown on eyebrows, cheeks, legs, stifles and undertail. All or some of the white markings are to be preferred whatever the colour of the dog, but the absence of these markings shall not be considered a fault. Black and White and Black and Tan are also recognized colours. Over markings of patches of white on the body are highly undesirable. The nose black whatever the colour of the dog.

Size. Ideal height measured at the withers 14 inches for bitches, 14½ inches for dogs, anything more than 1 inch above these heights to be considered a serious fault.

Faults. Domed or receding skull, lack of stop, large drooping or pricked ears, over-developed cheeks, weak jaw, snipy muzzle, not full complement of teeth, crooked forelegs, cow-hocks, tail kinked, short or carried over the back, white or white colour predominating. Pink or flesh coloured nose, blue eyes in any other colour than merles. Nervousness. Full or light eye. Under or overshot mouth.

SHETLAND SHEEPDOG

(AMERICAN KENNEL CLUB—GROUP III: WORKING DOGS)

Preamble. The Shetland Sheepdog, like the Collie, traces to the Border Collie of Scotland, which, transported to the Shetland Islands and crossed with small, intelligent, longhaired breeds, was reduced to miniature proportions. Subsequently crosses were made from time to time with Collies. This breed now bears the same relationship in size and general appearance to the Rough Collie as the Shetland Pony does to some of the larger breeds of horses. Although the resemblance between the Shetland Sheepdog and the Rough Collie is marked, there are differences which may be noted.

General Description. The Shetland Sheepdog is a small, alert, rough-coated, longhaired working dog. He must be sound, agile and sturdy. The outline should be so symmetrical that no part appears out of proportion to the whole. Dogs should appear masculine; bitches feminine.

Size. The Shetland Sheepdog should stand between 13 and 16 inches at the shoulder. Note: Height is determined by a line perpendicular to the ground from the top of the shoulder blades, the dog standing naturally, with forelegs parallel to line of measurement.

Disqualification. Heights below or above the desired size range are to be disqualified from the show ring.

Coat. The coat should be double, the outer coat consisting of long, straight, harsh hair; the undercoat short, furry, and so dense as to give the entire coat its 'stand-off' quality. The hair on face, tips of ears and feet should be smooth. Mane and frill should be abundant, and particularly impressive in males. The forelegs well feathered, the hind legs heavily so, but smooth below the hock joint. Hair on tail profuse. Note:

Excess hair on ears, feet, and on hocks may be trimmed for the show ring.

Faults. Coat short or flat, in whole or in part; wavy, curly, soft or silky. Lack of undercoat. Smooth-coated specimens.

Color. Black, blue merle, and sable (ranging from golden through mahogany); marked with varying amounts of white and/or tan.

Faults. Rustiness in a black or a blue coat. Washed out or degenerate colors, such as pale sable and faded blue. Self-color in the case of blue merle, that is, without any merling or mottling and generally appearing as a faded or dilute tri-color. Conspicuous white body spots. Specimens with more than 50 per cent white shall be so severely penalized as to effectively eliminate them from competition.

Disqualification. Brindle.

Temperament. The Shetland Sheepdog is intensely loyal, affectionate, and responsive to his owner. However, he may be reserved toward strangers but not to the point of showing fear or cringing in the ring.

Faults. Shyness, timidity, or nervousness. Stubbornness, snappiness, or ill temper.

Head. The head should be refined and its shape, when viewed from top or side, be a long, blunt wedge tapering slightly from ears to nose, which must be black.

Skull and Muzzle. Top of skull should be flat, showing no prominence at nuchal crest (the top of the occiput). Cheeks should be flat and should merge smoothly into a well-rounded muzzle. Skull and muzzle should be of equal length, balance point being inner corner of eye. In profile the top line of skull should parallel the top line of muzzle, but on a higher plane due to the presence of a slight but definite stop. Jaws clean and powerful. The deep, well-developed under-jaw, rounded at chin, should extend to base of nostrils. Lips tight. Upper and lower lips must meet and fit smoothly together all the way around. Teeth level and evenly spaced. Scissors bite.

Faults. Two-angled head. Too prominent stop, or no stop. Overfill below, between, or above eyes. Prominent nuchal crest. Domed skull. Prominent cheekbones. Snipy muzzle. Short, receding, or shallow under-jaw, lacking breadth and depth. Overshot or undershot, missing or crooked teeth. Teeth visible when mouth is closed.

Eyes. Medium size with dark, almond-shaped rims, set somewhat obliquely in skull. Color must be dark, with blue or merle eyes permissible in blue merles only.

Faults. Light, round, large or too small. Prominent haws.

Ears. Small and flexible, placed high, carried three-fourths erect, with tips breaking forward. When in repose the ears fold lengthwise and are thrown back into the frill.

Faults. Set too low. Hound, prick, bat, twisted ears. Leather too thick or too thin.

Expression. Contours and chiseling of the head, the shape, set and use of ears, the placement, shape and color of the eyes, combine to produce expression. Normally the expression should be alert, gentle, intelligent and questioning. Toward strangers the eyes should show watchfulness and reserve, but no fear.

Neck. Neck should be muscular, arched, and of sufficient length to carry the head proudly.

Faults. Too short and thick.

Body. In over-all appearance the body should appear moderately long as measured from shoulder joint to ischium (rearmost extremity of the pelvic bone), but much of this length is actually due to the proper angulation and breadth of the shoulder and hindquarter, as the back itself should be comparatively short. Back should be level and strongly muscled. Chest should be deep, the brisket reaching to point of elbow. The ribs should be well sprung, but flattened at their lower half to allow free play of the foreleg and shoulder. Abdomen moderately tucked up.

Faults. Back too long, too short, swayed or roached. Barrel ribs. Slab side. Chest narrow and/or too shallow.

Forequarters. From the withers the shoulder blades should slope at a 45-degree angle forward and downward to the shoulder joints. At the withers they are separated only by the vertebra, but they must slope outward sufficiently to accommodate the desired spring of rib. The upper arm should join the shoulder blade at as nearly as possible a right angle. Elbow joint should be equidistant from the ground or from the withers. Forelegs straight viewed from all angles, muscular and clean, and of strong bone. Pasterns very strong, sinewy and flexible. Dew-claws may be removed.

Faults. Insufficient angulation between shoulder and upper arm. Upper arm too short. Lack of outward slope of shoulders. Loose shoulders. Turning in or out of elbows. Crooked legs. Light bone.

Feet (front and hind). Feet should be oval and compact with the toes well arched and fitting tightly together. Pads deep and tough, nails hard and strong.

Faults. Feet turning in or out. Splay feet. Hare-feet. Cat-feet.

Hindquarters. There should be a slight arch at the loins, and the croup should slope gradually to the rear. The hipbone (pelvis) should be set at a 30-degree angle to the spine. The thigh should be broad and muscular. The thighbone should be set into the pelvis at a right angle corresponding to the angle of the shoulder blade and upper arm. Stifle bones join the thighbone and should be distinctly angled at the stifle joint. The over-all length of the stifle should at least equal the length of the thighbone, and preferably should slightly exceed it. Hock joint should be clean-cut, angular, sinewy, with good bone and strong ligamentation. The hock (metatarsus) should be short and straight viewed from all angles. Dewclaws should be removed. Feet (*see* Forequarters.

Faults. Croup higher than withers. Croup too straight or too steep. Narrow thighs. Cowhocks. Hocks turning out. Poorly defined hock joint. Feet (*see* Forequarters).

Tail. The tail should be sufficiently long so that when it is laid along the back edge of the hind legs the last vertebra will reach the hock joint. Carriage of tail at rest is straight down or in a slight upward curve. When the dog is alert the tail is normally lifted, but it should not be curved forward over the back.

Faults. Too short. Twisted at end.

Gait. The trotting gait of the Shetland Sheepdog should denote effortless speed and smoothness. There should be no jerkiness, nor stiff, stilted, up-and-down movement. The drive should be from the rear, true and straight, dependent upon correct angulation, musculation, and ligamentation of the entire hindquarter, thus allowing the dog to reach well under his body with his hind foot and propel himself forward. Reach of stride of the foreleg is dependent upon correct angulation, musculation and ligamentation of the forequarters, together with correct width of chest and construction of rib cage. The foot should be lifted only enough to clear the ground as the leg swings forward. Viewed from the front, both forelegs and hindlegs should move forward almost perpendicular to ground at the walk, slanting a little inward at a slow trot, until at a swift trot the feet are brought so far inward toward center line of body that the tracks left show two parallel lines of footprints actually touching a center line at their inner edges. *There should be no crossing of the feet nor throwing of the weight from side to side.*

Faults. Stiff, short steps, with a choppy, jerky movement. Mincing steps, with a hopping up and down, or a balancing of weight from side to side (often erroneously admired as a 'dancing gait' but permissible in young puppies). Lifting of front feet in hackney-like action, resulting in loss of speed and energy. Pacing gait.

SCALE OF POINTS

General Appearance			*Forequarters*		
Symmetry	10		Shoulder	10	
Temperament	10		Forelegs and feet	5	15
Coat	5	25	*Hindquarters*		
Head			Hip, thigh and stifle	10	
Skull and stop	5		Hocks and feet	5	15
Muzzle	5		*Gait*		
Eyes, ears and expression	10	20	Gait—smoothness and lack of waste motion when trotting		5
Body					
Neck and back	5				
Chest, ribs and brisket	10				
Loin, croup, and tail	5	20	Total		100

DISQUALIFICATIONS

Heights below or above the desired range, i.e. 13–16 inches. Brindle color.

Approved May 12, 1959

SHIH TZU

(THE KENNEL CLUB—UTILITY GROUP)

General Appearance. Very active, lively and alert, with a distinctly arrogant carriage. The Shih Tzu is neither a terrier nor a toy dog.
Head and Skull. Head broad and round; wide between the eyes. Shock-headed with hair falling well over the eyes. Good beard and whiskers; the hair growing upwards on the nose gives a distinctly chrysanthemum-like effect. Muzzle square and short, but not wrinkled like a Pekingese; flat and hairy. Nose black for preference and about one inch from tip to stop.
Eyes. Large, dark and round but not prominent.
Ears. Large, with long leathers, and carried drooping. Set slightly below the crown of the skull; so heavily coated that they appear to blend with the hair of the neck.
Mouth. Level or slightly underhung.
Forequarters. Legs short and muscular with ample bone. The legs should look massive on account of the wealth of hair.
Body. Body between withers and root of tail should be longer than height at withers; well-coupled and sturdy; chest broad and deep, shoulders firm, back level.
Hindquarters. Legs short and muscular with ample bone. They should look straight when viewed from the rear. Thighs well-round and muscular. Legs should look massive on account of the wealth of hair.
Feet. Firm and well-padded. They should look big on account of the wealth of hair.
Tail. Heavily plumed and curled well over back; carried gaily, set on high.
Coat. Long and dense, but not curly, with good undercoat.
Colour. All colours permissible, but a white blaze on the forehead and a white tip to the tail are highly prized. Dogs with liver markings may have dark liver noses and slightly lighter eyes. Pigmentation on muzzle as unbroken as possible.
Weight and Size. Up to 18 lb, ideal weight 9 to 16 lb, type and breed characteristics of the utmost importance and on no account to be sacrificed to size alone.
Faults. Narrow heads, pig-jaws, snipyness, pale pink noses and eyerims, small or light eyes, legginess, sparse coats.

SHIH TZU

(AMERICAN KENNEL CLUB—GROUP V: TOYS)

General Appearance. Very active, lively and alert, with a distinctly arrogant carriage. The Shih Tzu is proud of bearing as befits his noble ancestry, and walks with head well up and tail carried gaily over the back.
Head. Broad and round, wide between the eyes. Muzzle square and short, but not wrinkled, about one inch from tip of nose to stop. *Definite stop.*

Eyes. Large, dark and round but not prominent, placed well apart. Eyes should show warm expression.
Ears. Large, with long leathers, and carried drooping; set slightly below the crown of the skull; so heavily coated that they appear to blend with the hair of the neck.
Teeth. Level or slightly undershot bite.
Forequarters. Legs short, straight, well boned, muscular, and heavily coated. Legs and feet look massive on account of the wealth of hair.
Body. Body between the withers and the root of the tail is somewhat longer than the height at the withers; well coupled and sturdy. Chest broad and deep, shoulders firm, back level.
Hindquarters. Legs short, well boned and muscular, are straight when viewed from the rear. Thighs well rounded and muscular. Legs look massive on account of wealth of hair.
Feet. Of good size, firm, well padded, with hair between the pads. Dewclaws, if any, on the hind legs are generally removed. Dewclaws on the forelegs may be removed.
Tail. Heavily plumed and curved well over the back; carried gaily, set on high.
Coat. A luxurious, long, dense coat. May be slightly wavy but not curly. Good woolly undercoat. The hair on top of the head may be tied up.
Color. All colors permissible. Nose and eye rims black, except that dogs with liver markings may have liver noses and slightly lighter eyes.
Gait. Slightly rolling, smooth and flowing, with strong rear action.
Size. Height at withers—9 to 10½ inches—should be no more than 11 inches nor less than 8 inches. Weight of mature dogs—12 to 15 lbs—should be no more than 18 lbs nor less than 9 lbs. However, type and breed characteristics are of the greatest importance.
Faults. Narrow head, overshot bite, snipiness, pink on nose or eye rims, small or light eyes, legginess, sparse coat, lack of definite stop.

Approved May 13, 1969
Effective September 1, 1969

SKYE TERRIER

(THE KENNEL CLUB—TERRIER GROUP)

Characteristics. A one-man dog, distrustful of strangers but not vicious.
Head and Skull. Head long with powerful jaws. Nose black.
Eyes. Hazel, preferably dark brown, medium size, close set and full of expression.
Ears. Prick or drop. When prick, gracefully feathered, not large, erect at outer edges and slanting towards each other at inner edge, from peak to skull. When drop, larger, hanging straight, lying flat and close at front.
Mouth. Teeth closing level.
Neck. Long and slightly crested.
Forequarters. Shoulders broad and close to body, chest deep. Legs short and muscular.
Body. Long and low. Back level. Ribs well sprung, giving flattish appearance to sides.
Hindquarters. The hindquarters and flanks full and well developed. Legs short and muscular, no dew claws.
Feet. Large and pointing forward.
Tail. When hanging, upper part pendulous and lower half thrown back in a curve. When raised, a prolongation of the incline of the back, not raising higher nor curling up.
Coat. Double. Under-coat short, close, soft and woolly. Overcoat long, hard, straight, flat and free from crisp and curl. Hair on head shorter, softer, veiling forehead and eyes. On ears overhanging inside, falling down and mingling with side locks, surrounding the ears like a fringe and allowing their shape to appear. Tail gracefully feathered.
Colour. Dark or light grey, fawn, cream, black, with black points. In fact, any self colour allowing shading of the same colour and lighter undercoat, so long as the nose and ears are black. A small white spot on the chest is permissible.
Weight and Size. Height 10 inches, total length $41\frac{1}{2}$ inches, weight 25 lbs. Bitch, slightly smaller in same proportions.
Faults. Yellow eyes, tail curled over back or any deformity.

SKYE TERRIER

(AMERICAN KENNEL CLUB—GROUP IV: TERRIERS)

General Appearance. The Skye Terrier is a dog of style, elegance, and dignity; agile and strong with sturdy bone and hard muscle. Long, low, and lank—he is twice as long as he is high—he is covered with a profuse coat that falls straight down either side of the body over oval-shaped ribs. The hair well feathered on the head veils forehead and eyes to serve as protection from brush and briar as well as amid serious encounters with other animals. He stands with head high and long tail hanging, and moves with a seemingly effortless gait. Of suitable size for his hunting work, strong in body, quarters, and jaw.

Temperament. That of the typical working terrier capable of overtaking game and going to ground, displaying stamina, courage, strength, and agility. Fearless, good-tempered, loyal, and canny, he is friendly and gay with those he knows and reserved and cautious with strangers.

Head. Long and powerful, strength being deemed more important than extreme length. Moderate width at the back of the skull tapers gradually to a strong muzzle. The stop is slight. The dark muzzle is just moderately full as opposed to snipy, and the nose is always black. A Dudley flesh-colored, or brown nose shall disqualify. Powerful and absolutely true jaws and mouth with the incisor teeth closing level, or with the upper teeth slightly overlapping the lower.

Eyes. Brown, preferably dark brown, medium in size, close-set, and alight with life and intelligence.

Ears. Symmetrical and gracefully feathered. They may be carried prick or drop. When prick they are medium in size, placed high on the skull, erect at the outer edges, and slightly wider at the peak than at the skull. Drop ears, somewhat larger in size and set lower, hang flat against the skull.

Neck. Long and gracefully arched, carried high and proudly.

Body. Pre-eminently long and low. The backline is level, the chest deep, with oval-shaped ribs. The sides appear flattish due to the straight falling and profuse coat.

Legs and Feet. Forequarters. Legs short, muscular, and straight as possible. 'Straight as possible' means straight as soundness and chest will permit; it does not mean 'terrier straight.' Shoulders well laid back, with tight placement of shoulder blades at the withers, and elbows should fit closely to the sides and be neither loose nor tied. Forearm should curve slightly around the chest.

Hindquarters. Strong, full, well developed, and well angulated. Legs short, muscular, and straight when viewed from behind.

Feet. Large harefeet preferably pointing forward, the pads thick and nails strong and preferably black.

Movement. The legs proceed straight forward when traveling. When approaching, the forelegs form a continuation of the straight line of the front, the feet being the same distance apart as the elbows. The principal propelling power is furnished by the hind legs, which travel straight forward. Forelegs should move well forward, without too much lift. The whole movement may be termed free, active, and effortless and give a more or less fluid picture.

Tail. Long and well feathered. When hanging, its upper section is pendulous, following the line of the rump, its lower section thrown back in a moderate arc without twist or curl. When raised, its height makes it appear a prolongation of the backline. Though not to be preferred, the tail is sometimes carried high when the dog is excited or angry. When such carriage arises from emotion only, it is permissible. But the tail should not be constantly carried above the level of the back nor hang limp.

Coat. Double. Undercoat short, close, soft, and woolly. Outer coat hard, straight, and flat, $5\frac{1}{2}$ inches long without extra credit granted for greater length. The body coat hangs straight down each side, parting from head to tail. The head hair, which may be shorter and softer, veils forehead and eyes and forms a moderate beard and apron. The long feathering on the ears falls straight down from the tips and outer edges, surrounding the ears like a fringe and outlining their shape. The ends of the hair should mingle with the coat at the sides of the neck.

Color. The coat must be of one over-all color at the skin but may be of varying shades of the same color in the full coat, which may be black, blue, dark or light gray, silver, platinum, fawn, or cream. The dog must have no distinctive markings except for the desirable black points of ears, muzzle, and tip of tail, all of which points are preferably dark even to black. The shade of head and legs should approximate that of the body. There must be no trace of pattern, design, or clear-cut color variations, with the exception of the breed's only permissible white which occasionally exists on the chest not exceeding 2 inches in diameter.

The puppy coat may be very different in color from the adult coat. As it is growing and clearing, wide variations of color may occur; consequently this is permissible in dogs under 18 months of age. However, even in puppies there must be no trace of pattern, design, or clear-cut variations with the exception of the black band of varying width frequently seen encircling the body coat of the cream-colored dog, and the only permissible white which, as in the adult dog, occasionally exists on the chest not exceeding 2 inches in diameter.

Size. Dogs: Shoulder height, 10 inches. Length, chest bone over tail at rump, 20 inches. Head, $8\frac{1}{2}$ inches. Tail, 9 inches. Bitches: Shoulder height, $9\frac{1}{2}$ inches. Length, chest bone over tail at rump, 19 inches. Head, 8 inches. Tail, $8\frac{1}{2}$ inches. A slightly higher or lower dog of either sex is acceptable, providing body, head, and tail dimensions are proportionately longer or shorter. The ideal ratio of body length to shoulder height is 2 to 1, which is considered the correct position.

Measurements are taken with the Skye standing in natural position with feet well under. A box caliper is used vertically and horizontally. For the height, the top bar should rest on the withers. The head is measured from the tip of the nose to the back of the occipital bone, and the tail from the root to tip. Dogs 8 inches or less at the withers and bitches $7\frac{1}{2}$ inches or less at the withers are to be penalized.

Approved February 8, 1964

SIBERIAN HUSKY
(THE KENNEL CLUB—WORKING GROUP)

SIBERIAN HUSKY
(AMERICAN KENNEL CLUB—GROUP III: WORKING DOGS)

General Appearance. The Siberian Husky is a medium-sized working dog, quick and light on his feet and free and graceful in action. His moderately compact and well-furred body, erect ears and brush tail suggest his Northern heritage. His characteristic gait is smooth and seemingly effortless. He performs his original function in harness most capably, carrying a light load at moderate speed over great distances. His body proportions and form reflect this basic balance of power, speed and endurance. The males of the Siberian Husky breed are masculine but never coarse; the bitches are feminine but without weakness of structure. In proper condition, with muscle firm and well-developed, the Siberian Husky does not carry excess weight.

Head—Skull. Of medium size and in proportion to the body; slightly rounded on top and tapering gradually from the widest point to the eyes.

Faults. Head clumsy or heavy; head too finely chiseled.

Muzzle. Of medium length; that is, the distance from the tip of the nose to the stop is equal to the distance from the stop to the occiput. The stop is well-defined and the bridge of the nose is straight from the stop to the tip. The muzzle is of medium width, tapering gradually to the nose, with the tip neither pointed nor square. The lips are well-pigmented and close fitting; teeth closing in a scissors bite.

Faults. Muzzle either too snipy or too coarse; muzzle too short or too long; insufficient stop; any bite other than scissors.

Ears. Of medium size, triangular in shape, close fitting and set high on the head. They are thick, well-furred, slightly arched at the back, and strongly erect, with slightly rounded tips pointing straight up.

Faults. Ears too large in proportion to the head; too wide-set; not strongly erect.

Eyes. Almond shaped, moderately spaced and set a trifle obliquely. The expression is keen, but friendly; interested and even mischievous. Eyes may be brown or blue in color; one of each or parti-colored are acceptable.

Faults. Eyes set too obliquely; set too close together.

Nose. Black in gray, tan or black dogs; liver in copper dogs; may be flesh-colored in pure white dogs. The pink-streaked 'snow nose' is acceptable.

Body.—Neck. Medium in length, arched and carried proudly erect when dog is standing. When moving at a trot, the neck is extended so that the head is carried slightly forward.

Faults. Neck too short and thick; neck too long.

Shoulders. The shoulder blade is well laid back at an approximate angle of 45° to the ground. The upper arm angles slightly backward from point of shoulder to elbow, and is never perpendicular to the ground. The muscles and ligaments holding shoulder to rib cage are firm and well-developed.

Faults. Straight shoulders; loose shoulders.

Chest. Deep and strong, but not too broad, with the deepest point being just behind and level with the elbows. The ribs are well-sprung from the spine but flattened on the sides to allow for freedom of action.

Faults. Chest too broad; 'barrel ribs'; ribs too flat or weak.

Back. The back is straight and strong, with a level topline from withers to croup. It is of medium length, neither cobby nor slack from excessive length. The loin is taut and lean, narrower than the rib cage, and with a slight tuck-up. The croup slopes away from the spine at an angle, but never so steeply as to restrict the rearward thrust of the hind legs. In profile, the length of the body from the point of the shoulder to the rear point of the croup is slightly longer than the height of the body from the ground to the top of the withers.

Faults. Weak or slack back; roached back; sloping topline.

Legs and Feet—Forelegs. When standing and viewed from the front, the legs are moderately spaced, parallel and straight, with elbows close to the body and turned neither in nor out. Viewed from the side, pasterns are slightly slanted, with pastern joint strong, but flexible. Bone is substantial but never heavy. Length of the leg from elbow to ground is slightly more than the distance from the elbow to the top of withers. Dewclaws on forelegs may be removed.

Faults. Weak pasterns; too heavy bone; too narrow or too wide in front; out at the elbows.

Hindquarters. When standing and viewed from the rear, the hindlegs are moderately spaced and parallel. The upper thighs are well-muscled and powerful, the stifles well-bent, the hock joint well-defined and set low to the ground. Dewclaws, if any, are to be removed.

Faults. Straight stifles, cowhocks, too narrow or too wide in the rear.

Feet. Oval in shape, but not long. The paws are medium in size, compact and well-furred between the toes and pads. The pads are tough and thickly cushioned. The paws neither turn in nor out when dog is in natural stance.

Faults. Soft or splayed toes; paws too large and clumsy; too small and delicate; toeing in or out.

Tail. The well-furred tail of fox-brush shape is set on just below the level of the topline, and is usually carried over the back in a graceful sickle curve when the dog is at attention. When carried up, the tail does not curl to either side of the body, nor does it snap flat against the back. A trailing tail is normal for the dog when working or in repose. Hair on the tail is medium length, approximately the same length on top, sides and bottom, giving the appearance of a round brush.

Faults. A snapped or tightly curled tail; highly plumed tail; tail set too low or too high.

Gait. The Siberian Husky's characteristic gait is smooth and seemingly effortless. He is quick and light on his feet, and when in the show ring should be gaited, on a loose lead at a moderately fast trot, exhibiting good reach in the forequarters and good drive in the hindquarters. When viewed from the front to rear while moving at a walk, the Siberian Husky does not single-track, but as the speed increases the legs gradually angle inward until the pads are falling on a line directly under the longitudinal center of the body. As the pad marks converge, the forelegs and hindlegs are carried straight forward, with neither elbows nor stifles turned in or out. Each hind leg moves in the path of the foreleg on the same side. While the dog is gaiting, the topline remains firm and level.

Faults. Short, prancing or choppy gait, lumbering or rolling gait; crossing; crabbing.

Coat. The coat of the Siberian Husky is double and medium in length, giving a well-furred appearance, but is never so long as to obscure the clean-cut outline of the dog. The undercoat is soft and dense and of sufficient length to support the outer coat. The guard hairs of the outer coat are straight and somewhat smooth-lying, never harsh nor standing straight off from the body. It should be noted that the absence of the undercoat during the shedding season is normal. Trimming of the whiskers and fur between the toes and around the feet to present a neater appearance is permissible. Trimming on any other part is not to be condoned and should be severely penalized.

Faults. Long, rough or shaggy coat; texture too harsh or too silky; trimming of the coat, except as permitted above.

Color. All colors from black to pure white are allowed. A variety of markings on the head is common, including many striking patterns not found in other breeds.

Temperament. The characteristic temperament of the Siberian Husky is friendly and gentle, but also alert and outgoing. He does not display the possessive qualities of the guard dog, nor is he overly suspicious of strangers or aggressive with other dogs. Some measure of reserve and dignity may be expected in the mature dog. His intelligence, tractability, and eager disposition make him an agreeable companion and willing worker.

Size—Height. Dogs, 21 to 23½ inches at the withers. Bitches, 20 to 22 inches at the withers.

Weight. Dogs 45 to 60 lbs. Bitches, 35 to 50 lbs. Weight is in proportion to height. The measurements mentioned above represent the extreme height and weight limits, with no preference given to either extreme.

Disqualification. Dogs over 23½ inches and bitches over 22 inches.

Summary. The most important breed characteristics of the Siberian Husky are medium size, moderate bone, well balanced proportions, ease and freedom of movement, propr coat, pleasing head and ears, correct tail, and good disposition. Any appearance of excessive bone or weight, constricted or clumsy gait, or long, rough coat should be penalized. The Siberian Husky never appears so heavy or coarse as to suggest a freighting animal; nor is he so light and fragile as to suggest a sprint-racing animal. In both sexes the Siberian Husky gives the appearance of being capable of great endurance. In addition to the faults already noted, obvious structural faults common to all breeds are as undesirable in the Siberian Husky as in any other breed, even though they are not specifically mentioned herein.

DISQUALIFICATION: *Dogs over 23½ inches bitches over 22.*

Approved November 9, 1971

SOFT-COATED WHEATEN TERRIERS

(THE KENNEL CLUB—TERRIER GROUP)

Head. Long, in good proportion to the body, skull flat and clean between ears, not too wide. Defined stop, jaws strong and punishing. Foreface not longer than skull. Hair same colour as on body. Cheek bones not prominent. Head in general powerful without being coarse.
Teeth. Large, level or scissors, neither undershot nor overshot.
Nose. Black and well developed.
Eyes. Dark, dark hazel, not too large, not prominent, well placed.
Ears. Small to medium, carried in front, level with skull. Dark shading of ears allowed and not uncommon. 'Rose' or 'flying' ears are objectionable.
Neck. Moderately long and strong but not throaty.
Shoulders. Sloping, fine, well laid back, muscular.
Chest. Deep, ribs well sprung.
Body. Compact and not too long with powerful short loins, thighs strong and muscular, hocks well let down.
Tail. Well set, not too thick, carried gaily. To be docked at $\frac{1}{3}$ (one third) the total length, or cut after the 6th (sixth) joint assuming that this is in balance and proportion to the dog.
Forelegs. Perfectly straight viewed from any angle, good bone and muscle.
Hindlegs. Well developed with powerful muscle. Stifles bent. Hocks turned neither in nor out.
Feet. Small not spreading. Toe-nails preferably black but varying colours allowed.
Coat. Texture to be soft and silky to feel and not harsh. Young dogs to be excluded from this. Colour any shade from light wheaten to golden reddish hue. Trimming to be permitted.
Trimmed Dog. Coat to be close cut to the body at neck, chest and skull; to be especially long over eyes and under jaw. Whiskers to be encouraged. Profuse feathering on legs. Body to be trimmed to follow the outline of the dog. Tail to be trimmed close and neatly tapered.
Untrimmed Dog. The coat at its longest not to exceed five inches. Abundant and soft, wavy or loosely curled. Abundance not to be interpreted as length. UNDER NO CIRCUMSTANCES should the coat be 'fluffed out' like a Poodle or an Old English Sheepdog. Dogs shown in this condition to be heavily penalized as they give a wrong impression of TYPE and BREED.

Special attention is drawn to puppy coat development.

As pups are seldom born with the correct coat of maturity, care must be exercised when assessing this point. They go through several changes of colour and texture before developing the adult coat. This usually occurs between 18 months and $2\frac{1}{2}$ years.

Gait. Straight action fore and after going and

coming. Elbows tucked in. Side view: Free, light co-ordinated movement.

Appearance. A hardy, active, short coupled dog, well built, giving the idea of strength. Not too leggy nor too low to the ground.

Serious Faults. Undershot mouth. Excessive nervousness. Viciousness. Pale nose. White coat. Light yellow eyes. Any colour other than wheaten in body coat.

Character. Good tempered, spirited and game. Most affectionate and loyal to his owner. Most intelligent. A trusty, faithful friend, defensive without aggression.

Pups are born true to type. They come reddish, greyish and sometimes clear wheaten. The masks are generally black. Sometimes there is a black streak down the centre back or black tips to the body coat. These dark markings clear away with maturity. No black is allowed in body coat at full maturity.

Height and Weight. Dogs: 18 to 19 inches at the shoulder. Bitches somewhat less. Dogs: 35 to 40 lbs. Bitches somewhat less.

SOFT-COATED WHEATEN TERRIER

(AMERICAN KENNEL CLUB—GROUP IV: TERRIERS)

General Appearance. The Soft-Coated Wheaten Terrier is a medium-sized, hardy, well-balanced sporting terrier covered abundantly with a soft, naturally wavy coat of a good clear wheaten color. The breed requires moderation in all points and any exaggerated features are to be shunned. The head is only moderately long, is well balanced and should be free of any coarseness; the back is level with tail set on high and carried gaily; legs straight in front and muscular behind with well-laid-back shoulders and well-bent stifles to provide a long graceful stride. The dog should present an overall appearance of a hardy, active and happy animal, strong and well-coordinated.

Head. Well balanced and moderately long, profusely covered with coat which may fall forward to shade the eyes.

Skull flat and not too wide with no suggestion of coarseness. Skull and foreface about equal length.

Cheeks clean and stop well defined.

Muzzle square, powerful and strong, with no suggestion of snipiness. Lips are tight and black.

Nose is black and large for size of the dog.

Eyes. Dark hazel or brown, medium in size and well protected under a strong brow; eye rims black.

Ears. Break level with the skull and drop slightly forward close to the cheeks rather than pointing to the eyes; small to medium in size.

Teeth. Large, clean and white with either level or scissors bite.

Neck. Medium in length, strong and muscular, well covered with protective coat.

Shoulders. Well laid back, clean and smooth.

Body. Body is compact; back strong and level. Ribs are well sprung but without roundness to provide a deep chest with relatively short coupling.

Length of back from point of withers to base of tail should measure about the same as from point of withers to ground.

Tail is docked and well set on, carried gaily but never over the back.

Legs and Feet. Forelegs, straight and well boned; hindlegs well developed with well bent stifles; hocks well let down, turned neither in nor out.

Feet are round and compact with good depth of pad. Nails dark.

Dewclaws on forelegs may be removed; dewclaws on hindlegs should be removed.

Coat. Abundant, soft and wavy, of a good clear wheaten color; may be shaded on the ears and muzzle.

The Soft-Coated Wheaten Terrier is a natural dog and should so appear. Dogs that appear to be overly trimmed should be penalized.

Coat on ears may be left natural or relieved of the fringe to accent smallness.

Coat color and texture do not stabilize until about 18 to 24 months and should be given some latitude in young dogs.

For show purposes the coat may be tidied up merely to present a neat outline but may not be clipped, plucked or stylized.

Size. Dogs should measure 18 to 19 inches at the withers and should weigh between 35 to 45 lbs, bitches somewhat less.

Movement. Free; gait graceful and lively, having reach in front and good drive behind; straight action fore and aft.

Temperament. Good tempered, spirited and game; exhibits less aggressiveness than is sometimes encouraged in terriers in the show ring; alert and intelligent.

Major Faults. Overshot. Undershot. Coat texture deviation. Any color save wheaten.

Approved June 12, 1973

SPANIEL, AMERICAN WATER

(AMERICAN KENNEL CLUB—GROUP I: SPORTING DOGS)

General Appearance. Medium in size, of sturdy typical spaniel character, curly coat, an active muscular dog, with emphasis placed on proper size and conformation, correct head properties, texture of coat and color. Of amicable disposition; demeanor indicates intelligence, strength and endurance.

Head. Moderate in length, skull rather broad and full, stop moderately defined, but not too pronounced. Forehead covered with short smooth hair and without tuft or topknot. Muzzle of medium length, square and with no inclination to snipiness, jaws strong and of good length, and neither undershot nor overshot, teeth straight and well shaped. Nose sufficiently wide and with well developed nostrils to insure good scenting power.

Faults. Very flat skull, narrow across the top, long, slender or snipy muzzle.

Eyes. Hazel, brown or of dark tone to harmonize with coat; set well apart. Expression alert, attractive, intelligent.

Fault. Yellow eyes to disqualify.

Ears. Lobular, long and wide, not set too high on head, but slightly above the eyeline. Leather extending to end of nose and well covered with close curls.

Neck. Round and of medium length, strong and muscular, free of throatiness, set to carry head with dignity, but arch not accentuated.

Body Structure. Well developed, sturdily constructed but not too compactly coupled. General outline is a symmetrical relationship of parts. Shoulders sloping, clean and muscular. Strong loins, lightly arched, and well furnished, deep brisket but not excessively broad. Well-sprung ribs. Legs of medium length and well boned, but not so short as to handicap for field work.

Legs and Feet. Forelegs powerful and reasonably straight. Hind legs firm with suitably bent stifles and strong hocks well let down. Feet to harmonize with size of dog. Toes closely grouped and well padded.

Fault. Cowhocks.

Tail. Moderate in length, curved in a slightly rocker shape, carried slightly below level of back; tapered and covered with hair to tip, action lively.

Faults. Rat or shaved tail.

Coat. The coat should be closely curled or have marcel effect and should be of sufficient density to be of protection against weather, water or punishing cover, yet not coarse. Legs should have medium short, curly feather.

Faults. Coat too straight, soft, fine or tightly kinked.

Color. Solid liver or dark chocolate, a little white on toes or chest permissible.

Height. 15 to 18 inches at the shoulder.

Weight. Males, 28 to 45 lbs; females, 25 to 40 lbs.

DISQUALIFICATION

Yellow eyes.

SPANIELS, BRITTANY

(AMERICAN KENNEL CLUB—GROUP I: SPORTING DOGS)

General Description. A compact, closely knit dog of medium size, a leggy spaniel having the appearance as well as the agility of a great ground coverer. Strong, vigorous, energetic and quick of movement. Not too light in bone, yet never heavy-boned and cumbersome. Ruggedness, without clumsiness, is a characteristic of the breed. So leggy is he that his height at the withers is the same as the length of his body. He has no tail or at most, not more than 4 inches.

Weight. Should weigh between 30 and 40 lbs.

Height. $17\frac{1}{2}$ to $20\frac{1}{2}$ inches—measured from the ground at the highest point of the shoulders.

Disqualifications. Any Brittany Spaniel Measuring under $17\frac{1}{2}$ inches or over $20\frac{1}{2}$ inches shall be disqualified from bench-show competition. Any black in the coat or a nose so dark in color as to appear black shall disqualify. A tail substantially more than 4 inches in length shall disqualify.

Coat. Hair dense, flat or wavy, never curly. Not as fine as in other spaniel breeds, and never silky. Furnishings not profuse. The ears should carry little fringe. Neither the front nor hind legs should carry heavy featherings. Note: Long, curly, or silky hair is a fault. Any tendency toward excessive feathering should be severely penalized as undesirable in a sporting dog which must face burrs and heavy cover.

Skin. Fine and fairly loose. (A loose skin rolls with briars and sticks, thus diminishing punctures or tearing. But a skin so loose as to form pouches is undesirable.

Color. Dark orange and white, or liver and white. Some ticking is desirable, but not so much as to produce belton patterns. Roan patterns or factors of orange or liver shade are permissible. The orange or liver are found in standard parti-color, or piebald patterns. Washed out or faded colors are not desirable. Tri-colors (liver and white with some orange markings) are to be severely faulted. Black is a disqualification.

Skull. Medium length (approximately $4\frac{3}{4}$ inches). Rounded, very slightly wedge-shaped, but evenly made. Width, not quite as wide as the length (about $4\frac{3}{8}$ inches) and never so broad as to appear coarse, or so narrow as to appear racy. Well defined, but gently sloping stop effect. Median line rather indistinct. The occipital crest only apparent to the touch. Lateral walls well rounded. The Brittany should never be 'apple-headed' and he should never have an indented stop. (All measurements of skull are for a $19\frac{1}{2}$-inch dog.)

Muzzle. Medium length, about two thirds the length of the skull, measuring the muzzle from the tip to the stop, and the skull from the occipital crest to the stop between the eyes. Muzzle should taper gradually in both horizontal and vertical dimensions as it approaches the nostrils. Neither a Roman nose nor a concave curve (dish-face) is desirable. Never broad, heavy, or snipy.

Nose. Nostrils well open to permit deep breathing of air and adequate scenting while at top speed. Tight nostrils should be penalized. Never shiny. Color, fawn, tan, light shades of brown or deep pink. A black nose is a disqualification. A two-tone or butterfly nose should be severely penalized.

Eyes. Well set in head. Well protected from briars by a heavy, expressive eyebrow. A prominent, full or pop eye should be heavily penalized. It is a serious fault in a hunting dog that must face briars. Skull well chiseled under the eyes, so that the lower lid is not pulled back to form a pocket or haw for catching seeds, dirt and weed dust. Judges should check by forcing head down to see if lid falls away from the eye. Preference should be for darker-colored eyes, though lighter shades of amber should not be penalized. Light and mean-looking eyes to be heavily penalized.

Ears. Set high, above the level of the eyes. Short and leafy, rather than pendulous, reaching about half the length of the muzzle. Should lie flat and close to the head, with the tip rounded very slightly. Ears well covered with dense, but relatively short hair, and with little fringe.

Lips. Tight to the muzzle, with the upper lip overlapping the lower jaw only sufficiently to cover under lip. Lips dry so that feathers do not stick. Drooling to receive a heavy penalty. Flews to be penalized.

Teeth. Well joined incisors. Posterior edge of upper incisors in contact with anterior edge of lower incisors, thus giving a true scissors bite. Overshot or undershot jaw to be penalized heavily.

Neck. Medium length. Not quite permitting the dog to place his nose on the ground without bending his legs. Free from throatiness, though not a serious fault unless accompanied by dewlaps. Strong, without giving the impression of being overmuscled. Well set into sloping shoulders. Never concave or ewe-necked.

Body Length. Approximately the same as the height when measured at the withers. Body length is measured from the point of the fore-chest to the rear of the haunches. A long body should be heavily penalized.

Withers. Shoulder blades should not protrude much. Not too widely set apart with perhaps two thumbs' width or less between the blades. At the withers, the Brittany is slightly higher than at the rump.

Shoulders. Sloping and muscular. Blade and upper arm should form nearly a 90-degree angle when measured from the posterior point of the blade at the withers to the junction of the blade and upper arm, and thence to the point of the elbow nearest the ribs. Straight shoulders do not permit sufficient reach.

Back. Short and straight. Slight slope from

highest point of withers to the root of the tail. Never hollow, saddle, sway, or roach-backed. Slight drop from hips to root of tail. Distance from last rib to upper thigh short, about three to four finger widths.

Chest. Deep, reaching the level of the elbow. Neither so wide nor so rounded as to disturb the placement of the shoulder bones and elbows, which causes a paddling movement, and often causes soreness from elbow striking ribs. Ribs well sprung, but adequate heart room provided by depth as well as width. Narrow or slab-sided chests are a fault.

Flanks. Rounded. Fairly full. Not extremely tucked up, nor yet flabby and falling. Loins short and strong. Narrow and weak loins are a fault. In motion the loin should not sway sideways, giving a zigzag motion to the back, wasting energy.

Hindquarters. Broad, strong and muscular, with powerful thighs and well-bent stifles, giving a hip set well into the loin and the marked angulation necessary for a powerful drive when in motion. Fat and falling hindquarters are a fault.

Tail. Naturally tailless, or not over four inches long. Natural or docked. Set on high, actually an extension of the spine at about the same level.

Front Legs. Viewed from the front, perpendicular, but not set too wide as in the case of a dog loaded in shoulder. Elbows and feet turning neither in nor out. Viewed from the side, practically perpendicular to the pastern. Pastern slightly bent to give cushion to stride. Not so straight as in terriers. Falling pasterns, however, are a serious fault. Leg bones clean, graceful, but not too fine. An extremely heavy bone is as much a fault as spindly legs. One must look for substance and suppleness. Height to the elbows should approximately equal distance from elbow to withers.

Hind Legs. Stifles well bent. The stifle generally is the term used for knee joint. If the angle made by the upper and lower leg bone is too straight, the dog quite generally lacks drive, since his hind legs cannot drive as far forward at each stride as is desirable. However, the stifle should not be bent as to throw the hock joint far out behind the dog. Since factors not easily seen by the eye may give the dog his proper drive, a Brittany should not be condemned for straight stifle until the judge has checked the dog in motion from the side. When at a trot, the Brittany's hind foot should step into or beyond the print left by the front foot. The stifle joint should not turn out making a cowhock. (The cowhock moves the foot out to the side, thus driving out of line, and losing reach at each stride.) Thighs well feathered, but not profusely, halfway to the hocks. Hocks, that is, the back pasterns, should be moderately short, pointing neither in nor out; perpendicular when viewed from the side. They should be firm when shaken by the judge.

Feet. Should be strong, proportionately smaller than other spaniels, with close-fitting, well-arched toes and thick pads. The Brittany is not 'up on his toes'. Toes not heavily feathered. Flat feet, splayed feet, paper feet, etc., are to be heavily penalized. An ideal foot is halfway between the hare- and cat-foot.

A Guide to the Judge. The points below indicate only relative values. To be also taken into consideration are type, gait, soundness, spirit, optimum height, body length and general proportions.

SCALE OF POINTS

Head	25
Body	35
Running gear	40
Total	100

DISQUALIFICATIONS

Any Brittany Spaniel measuring under 17½ inches or over 20½ inches. Any black in the coat or a nose so dark in color as to appear black. A tail substantially more than 4 inches in length.

Approved September 13, 1966

SPANIEL (CLUMBER)

(THE KENNEL CLUB—GUNDOG GROUP)

General Appearance. Should be that of a heavy, massive but active dog, with a thoughtful expression.

Head and Skull. Head large, square and massive, of medium length, broad on top, with a decided occiput; heavy brows with a deep stop; heavy muzzle, with well-developed flew, and level jaw and mouth. Nose square and flesh-colored.

Eyes. Dark amber, slightly sunk. Full, light, very objectionable.

Ears. Large, vine-leaf shaped, and well covered with straight hair, and hanging slightly forward, the feather not to extend below the leather.

Mouth. Should be level and neither over nor undershot.

Neck. Fairly long, thick and powerful, and well feathered underneath.

Forequarters. Shoulders strong, sloping and muscular; chest deep. Legs short, straight, thick and strong.

Body. Long and heavy, and near the ground, with well-sprung ribs. Back straight, broad and long.

Hindquarters. Very powerful and well developed. Loin powerful, well let down in flank. Hocks low, stifles well bent and set straight.

Feet. Large and round, well covered with hair.

Tail. Set low, well feathered, and carried about level with the back.

Coat. Abundant, close, silky and straight; legs well feathered.

Colour. Plain white, with lemon markings; orange permissible, but not desirable; slight head markings and freckled muzzle, with white body preferred.

Weight and Size. Dogs about 55 to 70 lbs; bitches about 45 to 60 lbs.

SPANIEL, CLUMBER

(AMERICAN KENNEL CLUB—GROUP I: SPORTING DOGS)

General Appearance and Size. General appearance, a long, low, heavy-looking dog, of a very thoughtful expression, betokening great intelligence. Should have the appearance of great power. Sedate in all movements, but not clumsy. Weight of dogs averaging between 55 and 65 lbs; bitches from 35 to 50 lbs.

Head. Head large and massive in all its dimensions; round above eyes, flat on top, with a furrow running from between the eyes upon the center. A marked stop and large occipital protuberance. Jaw long, broad and deep. Lips of upper jaw overhung. Muzzle not square, but at the same time powerful-looking. Nostrils large, open and flesh-coloured, sometimes cherry-colored.

Eyes. Eyes large, soft, deep-set and showing haw.

Hazel in color, not too pale, with dignified and intelligent expression.

Ears. Ears long and broad at the top, turned over on the front edge; vine-shaped: close to the head; set on low and feathered only on the front edge, and there but slightly. Hair short and silky, without the slightest approach to wave or curl.

Neck and Shoulders. Neck long, thick and powerful, free from dewlap, with a large ruff. Shoulders immensely strong and muscular, giving a heavy appearance in front.

Body. Long, low and well ribbed up. The chest is wide and deep, the back long, broad, and level, with very slight arch over the loin.

Legs and Feet. Forelegs short, straight, and very heavy in bone; elbows close. Hind legs only slightly less heavily boned than the forelegs. They are moderately angulated, with hocks well let down. Quarters well developed and muscular. No feather above the hocks, but thick hair on the back of the legs just above the feet. Feet large, compact, and well filled with hair between the toes.

Coat and Feathers. Coat silky and straight, not too long, extremely dense; feather long and abundant.

Color and Markings. Color, lemon and white, and orange and white. Fewer markings on body the better. Perfection of markings, solid lemon or orange ears, evenly marked head and eyes, muzzle and legs ticked.

Stern. Stern set on a level and carried low.

SCALE OF POINTS

General appearance and size	10	Body and quarters	20
Head	15	Legs and feet	10
Eyes	5	Coat and feather	10
Ears	10	Color and marking	5
Neck and shoulders	15	Total	100

Approved February 6, 1960

SPANIEL (COCKER)

THE KENNEL CLUB—GUNDOG GROUP)

General Appearance. That of a merry sturdy sporting dog. The Cocker Spaniel should be well balanced and compact and should measure about the same from the withers to the ground as from the withers to the root of the tail.

Head and Skull. There should be a good square muzzle with a distinct stop which should be midway between the tip of the nose and the occiput. The skull should be well developed, cleanly chiselled, neither too fine nor too coarse. The cheek bones should not be prominent. The nose should be sufficiently wide to allow for the acute scenting power of this breed.

Eyes. The eyes should be full but not prominent, brown or dark brown in colour but never light, with a general expression of intelligence and gentleness though decidedly wide awake, bright and merry. The rims should be tight.

Ears. Lobular, set on low, on a level with the eyes, with fine leathers which extend to but not beyond the tip of the nose; well clothed with long silky hair which should be straight.

Mouth. Jaws should be strong and teeth should have a scissor bite.

Neck. Neck should be moderate in length, clean in throat, muscular and neatly set into fine sloping shoulders.

Forequarters. The shoulders should be sloping and fine, the chest well developed and the brisket deep, neither too wide nor too narrow in front. The legs must be well boned, feathered and straight and should be sufficiently short for concentrated power but not too short to interfere with the tremendous exertions expected from this grand little sporting dog.

Body. Body should be immensely strong and compact for the size and weight of the dog. The ribs should be well sprung behind the shoulder blades, the loin short wide and strong, with a firm topline gently sloping downwards to the tail.

Hindquarters. Hindquarters should be wide, well rounded and very muscular. The legs must be well boned, feathered above the hock with a good bend of stifle and short below the hock allowing for plenty of drive.

Feet. Feet should be firm, thickly padded and catlike.

Tail. Tail should be set on slightly lower than the line of the back; it must be merry, carried in line with the back and never cocked up. The tail should not be docked too long nor too short to interfere with its merry action.

Coat. Flat and silky in texture, never wiry or wavy, with sufficient feather; not too profuse and never curly.

Colour. Various. In self colours no white is allowed except on the chest.

Gait. There should be true through action both fore and aft, with great drive covering the ground well.

Weight and Size. The weight should be about 28 to 32 lbs. The height at the withers should be approximately 15 to $15\frac{1}{2}$ inches for bitches and approximately $15\frac{1}{2}$ to 16 inches for dogs.
Faults. Light bone; straight shoulder; flat ribs; unsound movement; weak hocks; weak pasterns; open or large feet; frown; small beady eyes; undershot or overshot mouth; uncertain or aggressive temperament.

SPANIEL, ENGLISH COCKER

(AMERICAN KENNEL CLUB—GROUP I: SPORTING DOGS)

General Appearance. The English Cocker Spaniel is an attractive active, merry sporting dog; with short body and strong limbs, standing well up at the withers. His movements are alive with energy; his gait powerful and frictionless. He is alert at all times, and the carriage of head and incessant action of his tail while at work give the impression that here is a dog that is not only bred for hunting but really enjoys it. He is well balanced, strongly built, full of quality and is capable of top speed combined with great stamina. His head imparts an individual stamp peculiar to him alone and has that brainy appearance expressive of the highest intelligence; and is in perfect proportion to his body. His muzzle is a most distinctive feature, being of correct conformation and in proportion to his skull.
Character. The character of the English Cocker is of extreme importance. His love and faithfulness to his master and household, his alertness and courage are characteristic. He is noted for his intelligence and merry disposition; not quarrelsome; and is a responsive and willing worker both in the field and as a companion.
Head. The skull and forehead should be well developed with no suggestion of coarseness, arched and slightly flattened on top when viewed both from the stop to the end of the skull as well as from ear to ear, and cleanly chiseled under the eyes. The proportion of the head desirable is approximately one half for the muzzle and one half for the skull. The muzzle should be square with a definite stop where it blends into the skull and in proportion with the width of the skull. As the English Cocker is primarily a sporting dog, the muzzle and jaws must be of sufficient strength and size to carry game; and the length of the muzzle should provide room for the development of the olfactory nerve to insure good scenting qualities, which require that the nose be wide and well developed. Nostrils black in color except in reds, livers, parti-colors and roans of the lighter shades, where brown is permissible, but black preferred. Lips should be square, full and free from flews. Teeth should be even and set squarely.
Faults. Muzzle too short or snipy. Jaw overshot or undershot. Lips snipy or pendulous. Skull too flat or too rounded, cheeky or coarse. Stop insufficient or exaggerated.
Eyes. The eyes should be of medium size, full and slightly oval shaped; set squarely in skull and wide apart. Eyes must be dark brown except in livers and light parti-colors where hazel is permissible, but the darker the better. The general expression should be intelligent, alert, bright and merry.
Faults. Light, round or protruding eyes. Conspicuous haw.
Ears. Lobular; set low and close to the head; leather fine and extending at least to the nose, well covered with long, silky, straight or slightly wavy hair.
Faults. Set or carried too high; too wide at the top; insufficient feathering; positive curls or ringlets.
Neck. Long, clean and muscular; arched towards the head; set cleanly into sloping shoulders.
Faults. Short; thick; with dewlap or excessive throatiness.
Body. Close coupled, compact and firmly knit, giving the impression of great strength without heaviness. Depth of brisket should reach to the elbow, sloping gradually upward to the loin. Ribs should spring gradually to middle of body, tapering to back ribs which should be of good depth and extend well back.
Faults. Too long and lacking depth; insufficient spring of rib; barrel rib.
Shoulders and Chest. Shoulders sloping and fine; chest deep and well developed but not too wide and round to interfere with the free action of the forelegs.
Faults. Straight or loaded shoulders.
Back and Loin. Back short and strong. Length of back from withers to tail-set should approximate height from ground to withers. Height of the dog at the withers should be greater than the height at the hip joint, providing a gradual slope between these points. Loin short and powerful, slightly arched.
Faults. Too low at withers; long, sway-back or roach back; flat or narrow loin; exaggerated tuck-up.
Forelegs. Straight and strong with bone nearly equal in size from elbow to heel; elbows set close to the body with free action from shoulders; pasterns short, straight, and strong.
Faults. Shoulders loose; elbows turned in or out; bowed or set too close or too wide apart; knees knuckled over; light bone.
Feet. Size in proportion to the legs; firm, round and catlike with thick pads and strong toes.
Faults. Too large, too small; spreading or splayed.
Hindquarters. The hips should be rounded; thighs broad; well developed and muscular, giving abundance of propelling power. Stifles strong and well bent. Hock to pad moderately short, strong and well let down.
Faults. Excessive angulation; lightness of bone;

stifle too short; hocks too long or turned in or out.
Tail. Set on to conform with the topline of the back. Merry in action.
Faults. Set too low; habitually carried too high; too short or too long.
Color. Various. In self colors a white shirt frill is undesirable. In parti-colors, the coloring must be broken on the body and be evenly distributed. No large portion of any one color should exist. White should be shown on the saddle. A dog of any solid color with white feet and chest is not a parti-color. In roans it is desirable that the white hair should be distributed over the body, the more evenly the better. Roans come in various colors; blue, liver, red, orange and lemon. In black and tans the coat should be black; tan spots over the eyes, tan on the sides of the muzzle, on the throat and chest, on forelegs from the knees to the toes and on the hind legs on the inside of the legs, also on the stifle and extending from the hock to the toes.
Faults. White feet are undesirable in any specimen of self color.
Coat. On head short and fine; on body flat or slightly wavy and silky in texture. Should be of medium length with enough undercoating to give protection. The English Cocker should be well feathered but not so profusely as to hide the true lines or interfere with his field work.
Faults. Lack of coat; too soft, curly or wiry. Excessive trimming to change the natural appearance and coat should be discouraged.
Height. Ideal heights at withers: Males, 16 to 17 inches; females, 15 to 16 inches. Deviations to be severely penalized but not disqualified.
Weight. The most desirable weights: Males, 28 pounds to 34 pounds; Females, 26 pounds to 32 pounds. Proper physical conformation and balance should be considered more important than weight alone.

Approved September 13, 1955

SPANIEL (COCKER, AMERICAN)

(THE KENNEL CLUB—GUNDOG GROUP)

General Appearance. A serviceable-looking dog with a refinedly chiselled head; standing on straight legs and well up at the shoulders; of compact body and wide, muscular quarters. The American Cocker Spaniel's sturdy body, powerful quarters and strong, well-boned legs show him to be a dog capable of considerable speed combined with great endurance. Above all he must be free and merry, sound, well balanced throughout, and in action show a keen inclination to work, equable in temperament with no suggestion of timidity.

Head and Skull. Well developed and rounded with no tendency towards flatness, or pronounced roundness, of the crown (dome). The forehead smooth, i.e., free from wrinkles, the eyebrows and stop clearly defined, the median line distinctly marked and gradually disappearing until lost rather more than halfway up to the crown. The bony structure surrounding the socket of the eye should be well chiselled; there should be no suggestion of fullness under the eyes nor prominence in the cheeks which, like the sides of the muzzle, should present a smooth, clean-cut appearance. To attain a well-proportioned head, which above all should be in balance with the rest of the dog, the distance from the tip of the nose to the stop at a line drawn across the top of the muzzle between the front corners of the eyes, should approximate one-half the distance from the stop at this point up over the crown to the base of the skull. The muzzle should be broad and deep, with square even jaws. The upper lip should be of sufficient depth to cover the lower jaw, presenting a square appearance. The nose of sufficient size to balance the muzzle and foreface, with well-developed nostrils and black in colour in the blacks and black and tans; in the reds, buffs, livers, and parti-colours and in the roans it may be black or bown, the darker colouring being preferable.

Mouth. The teeth should be sound and regular and set at right angles to their respective jaws. The relation of the upper teeth to the lower should be that of scissors, with the inner surface of the upper in contact with the outer surface of the lower when the jaws are closed.

Eyes. The eyeballs should be round and full and set in the surrounding tissue to look directly forward and give the eye a slightly almond-shape appearance. The eye should be neither weak nor goggled. The expression should be intelligent, alert, soft and appealing. The colour of the iris should be dark brown to black in the blacks, black and tans, buffs and creams, and in the darker shades of the parti-colours and roans. In the reds, dark hazel; in the livers, parti-colours, and roans of the lighter shades, not lighter than hazel, the darker the better.

Ears. Lobular, set on a line no higher than the lower part of the eye, the leathers fine and extending to the nostrils; well clothed with long, silky, straight or wavy hair.

Neck. The neck sufficiently long to allow the nose to reach the ground easily, muscular and free from pendulous 'throatiness'. It should rise strongly from the shoulders and arch slightly as it tapers to join the head.

Forequarters. The shoulders deep, clean-cut and sloping without protrusion and so set that the upper points of the withers are at an angle which permits a wide spring of rib. Forelegs straight, strongly boned and muscular and set close to the body well under the scapulae. The elbows well let down and turning neither in nor out. The pasterns short and strong.

Body. Its height at the withers should approximate the length from the withers to the set-on of tail. The chest deep, its lowest point no higher than the elbows, its front sufficiently wide for adequate heart and lung space, yet not so wide as to interfere with straight forward movement of the forelegs. Ribs deep and well-sprung throughout. Body short in the couplings and flank, with its depth at the flank somewhat less than at the last rib. Back strong and sloping evenly and slightly downward from the withers to the set-on of tail. Hips wide with quarters well-rounded and muscular. The body should appear short, compact and firmly knit together, giving the impression of strength.

Hindquarters. The hindlegs strongly-boned and muscled, with well-turned stifles and powerful, clearly defined thighs. The hocks strong, well let down and parallel when in motion and at rest.

Feet. Feet compact, not spreading, round and firm, with deep, strong, tough pads and hair between the toes; they should turn neither in nor out.

Tail. Set on and carried on a line with the topline of the back, and when the dog is at work, its action should be incessant.

Coat. On the head, short and fine. On the body, flat or slightly wavy (never curly), silky in texture, of medium length, with enough under-coating to give protection. The ears, chest, abdomen and posterior sides of the legs should be well feathered, but no so excessively as to hide the American Cocker Spaniel's true lines and movement or affect his appearance and function as a Sporting Dog. Excessive coat or feathering shall be penalized.

Colour. Blacks should be jet black with no tinge of brown or liver in sheen of coat. Black and tans (classified under solid colours) should have clearly defined tan markings, at specified locations, on a jet black body. The tan may be any shade of cream or red; some black hairs or pencilling permissible but brindling will be penalized. A mere semblance of tan in any one of these locations is undesirable, while a total absence or tan in any one of these locations will be penalized.

The locations of tan are as follows:

1. A clear spot over each eye.
2. On sides of muzzle; tan should not extend over and join.
3. On sides of cheeks.
4. On undersides of ears.
5. On all feet and legs, extending upwards towards knees and hocks.
6. On underside of tail.

Solid colours, other than black or black and tan, should be of sound shade.

In all the above solid colours a small amount of white on chest and throat, while not desirable, is allowed but white in any other location shall be penalized.

Parti-colours should have one or more colours appearing in clearly defined markings on a white background. Roans may be any of the accepted roaning patterns of mottled appearance or alternating colours of hairs distributed throughout the coat.

Weight and Size. Ideal height at withers for an adult dog should be 15 inches and maximum height 15½ inches. Ideal height at withers for an adult bitch should be 14 inches and maximum height 14½ inches.

Note. Height is determined by a line perpendicular to ground from top of shoulder blades, dog standing naturally with its forelegs and lower hindlegs parallel to line of measurement.

SPANIEL, COCKER

(AMERICAN KENNEL CLUB—GROUP I: SPORTING DOGS)

General Appearance. The Cocker Spaniel is the smallest member of the Sporting Group. He has a sturdy, compact body and a cleanly chiseled and refined head, with the over-all dog in complete balance and of ideal size. He stands well up at the shoulder on straight forelegs with a topline sloping slightly toward strong, muscular quarters. He is a dog capable of considerable speed, combined with great endurance. Above all he must be free and merry, sound, well balanced throughout, and in action show a keen inclination to work; equable in temperament with no suggestion of timidity.

Head. To attain a well-proportioned head, which must be in balance with the rest of the dog, it embodies the following:

Skull. Rounded but not exaggerated with no tendency toward flatness; the eyebrows are clearly defined with a pronounced stop. The bony structure beneath the eyes is well chiseled with no prominence in the cheeks.

Muzzle. Broad and deep, with square, even jaws. The upper lip is full and of sufficient depth to cover the lower jaw. To be in correct balance, the distance from the stop to the tip of the nose is one half the distance from the stop up over the crown to the base of the skull.

Teeth. Strong and sound, not too small, and meet in a scissors bite.

Nose. Of sufficient size to balance the muzzle and foreface, with well-developed nostrils typical of a sporting dog. It is black in color in the blacks and black and tans. In other colors it may be brown, liver or black, the darker the better. The color of the nose harmonizes with the color of the eye rim.

Eyes. Eyeballs are round and full and look directly forward. The shape of the eye rims gives a slightly almond-shaped appearance; the eye is not weak or goggled. The color of the iris is dark brown and in general the darker the better. The expression is intelligent, alert, soft and appealing.

Ears. Lobular, long, of fine leather, well

feathered, and placed no higher than a line to the lower part of the eye.

Neck and Shoulders. The neck is sufficiently long to allow the nose to reach the ground easily, muscular and free from pendulous 'throatiness'. It rises strongly from the shoulders and arches slightly as it tapers to join the head. The shoulders are well laid back forming an angle with the upper arm of approximately 90 degrees which permits the dog to move his forelegs in an easy manner with considerable forward reach. Shoulders are clean-cut and sloping without protrusion and so set that the upper points of the withers are at an angle which permits a wide spring of rib.

Body. The body is short, compact and firmly knit together, giving an impression of strength. The distance from the highest point of the shoulder blades to the ground is fifteen (15%) per cent or approximately two inches more than the length from this point to the set-on of the tail. Back is strong and sloping evenly and slightly downward from the shoulders to the set-on of the docked tail. Hips are wide and quarters well rounded and muscular. The chest is deep, its lowest point no higher than the elbows, its front sufficiently wide for adequate heart and lung space, yet not so wide as to interfere with the straightforward movement of the forelegs. Ribs are deep and well sprung. The Cocker Spaniel never appears long and low.

Tail. The docked tail is set on and carried on a line with the topline of the back, or slightly higher; never straight up like a terrier and never so low as to indicate timidity. When the dog is in motion the tail action is merry.

Legs and Feet. Forelegs are parallel, straight, strongly boned and muscular and set close to the body well under the scapulae. When viewed from the side with the forelegs vertical, the elbow is directly below the highest point of the shoulder blade. The pasterns are short and strong. The hind legs are strongly boned and muscled with good angulation at the stifle and powerful, clearly defined thighs. The stifle joint is strong and there is no slippage of it in motion or when standing. The hocks are strong, well let down, and when viewed from behind, the hind legs are parallel when in motion and at rest.

Feet. Compact, large, round and firm with horny pads; they turn neither in nor out. Dewclaws on hind legs and forelegs may be removed.

Coat. On the head, short and fine; on the body, medium length, with enough undercoating to give protection. The ears, chest, abdomen and legs are well feathered, but not so excessively as to hide the Cocker Spaniel's true lines and movement or affect his appearance and function as a sporting dog. The *texture* is most important. The coat is silky, flat or slightly wavy, and of a texture which permits easy care. Excessive or curly or cottony textured coat is to be penalized.

Color and Markings. Black Variety is jet black; shadings of brown or liver in the sheen of the coat is not desirable. A small amount of white on the chest and throat is to be penalized, and white in any other location shall disqualify.

Any Solid Color Other than Black shall be a uniform shade. Ligher coloring of the feathering is permissible. A small amount of white on the chest and throat is to be penalized, and while in any other location shall disqualify.

Black and Tans, shown under the Variety of Any Solid Color Other than Black, have definite tan markings on a jet black body. The tan markings are distinct and plainly visible and the color of the tan may be from the lightest cream to the darkest red color. The amount of tan markings is restricted to ten (10%) per cent or less of the color of the specimen; tan markings in excess of ten (10%) per cent shall disqualify. Tan markings which are not readily visible in the ring or the absence of tan markings in any of the specified locations shall diqualify. The markings shall be located as follows:

1. A clear spot over each eye.
2. On the sides of the muzzle and on the cheeks.
3. On the underside of the ears.
4. On all feet and legs.
5. Under the tail.
6. On the chest, optional, presence or absence not penalized.

Tan on the muzzle which extends upward, over and joins, shall be penalized. A small amount of white on the chest and throat is to be penalized, and white in any other location shall diqualify.

Parti-Color Variety. Two or more definite colors appearing in clearly defined markings, distinctly distributed over the body, are essential. Primary color which is ninety (90%) per cent or more shall disqualify; secondary color or colors which are limited solely to one location shall disqualify. Roans are classified as Parti-colors and may be of any of the usual roaning patterns. Tricolors are any of the above colors combined with tan markings. It is preferable that the tan markings be located in the same pattern as for Black and Tans.

Movement. The Cocker Spaniel, though the smallest of the sporting dogs, possesses a typical sporting dog gait. Prerequisite to good movement is balance between the front and rear assemblies. He drives with his strong, powerful rear quarters and is properly constructed in the shoulders and forelegs so that he can reach forward without constriction in a full stride to counterbalance the driving force from the rear. Above all, his gait is coordinated, smooth and effortless. The dog must cover ground with his action and excessive animation should never be mistaken for proper gait.

Height. The ideal height at the withers for an adult dog is 15 inches and for an adult bitch 14 inches. Height may vary one-half inch above or below this ideal. A dog whose height exceeds 15½ inches or a bitch whose height exceeds 14½ inches shall be disqualified. An adult dog whose height is less than 14½ inches or an adult bitch whose height is less than 13½ inches shall be penalized. **Note.** Height is determined by a line perpendicular to the ground from the top of the shoulder blades, the dog standing naturally with its forelegs and the lower hind legs parallel to the line of measurement.

DISQUALIFICATIONS

Color and Markings—
Blacks. *White markings except on chest and throat.*
Solid Colors Other Than Black. *White markings except on chest and throat.*
Blacks and Tans. *Tan markings in excess of ten (10%) per cent; tan markings not readily visible in the ring, or the absence of tan markings in any of the specified locations; white markings except on chest and throat.*
Parti-Colors. *Ninety (90%) per cent or more of primary color; secondary color or colors limited solely to one location.*
Height. *Males over 15½ inches; females over 14½ inches.*

Approved December 12, 1972

SPANIEL (FIELD)

(THE KENNEL CLUB—GUNDOG GROUP)

General Appearance. That of a well-balanced, noble, upstanding sporting dog; built for activity and endurance; a combination of beauty and utility; of unusual docility.

Head and Skull. The head should be characteristic as is that of the Bulldog or the Bloodhound; its very stamp and countenance should at once convey the impression of high breeding, character and nobility; skull well developed, with a distinct occipital protuberance, which gives the character alluded to; not too wide across the muzzle, long and lean, neither snipy nor squarely cut, and in profile curving gradually from nose to throat; lean beneath the eyes, a thickness here gives coarseness to the whole head. The great length of muzzle gives surface for the free development of the olfactory nerve, and thus secures the highest possible scenting powers. Nose, well developed, with good open nostrils.

Eyes. Not too full, but not small, receding or overhung, colour dark hazel or brown, or nearly black, according to the colour of the dog. Grave in expression and showing no haw.

Ears. Moderately long and wide, sufficiently clad with nice Setter-like feather and set low. They should fall in graceful folds, the lower parts curling inwards and backwards.

Mouth. Level and strong—neither overshot nor undershot.

Neck. Long, strong and muscular, so as to enable the dog to retrieve his game without undue fatigue.

Forequarters. The shoulders should be long and sloping and well set back, thus giving great activity and speed. The forelegs should be of fairly good length, with straight, clean, flat bone and nicely feathered. Immense bone is not desirable.

Body. Should be of moderate length, well ribbed up to a good strong loin, straight or slightly arched, never slack. The chest, deep and well developed, but not too round and wide. Back and loins very strong and muscular.

Hindquarters. Strong and muscular. The stifles should be moderately bent and not twisted either in or out.

Feet. Not too small; round with short, soft hair between the toes; good, strong pads.

Tail. Well set on and carried low, if possible below the level of the back, in a straight line or with a slight downward inclination, never elevated above the back, and in action always kept low, nicely fringed with wavy feather of silky texture.

Coat. Flat or slightly waved, and never curled. Sufficiently dense to resist the weather and not too short. Silky in texture, glossy and refined without duffelness, curliness or wiriness. On the chest, under the belly and behind the legs, there should be abundant feather, but never too much, especially below the hocks, and that of the right sort—viz., Setter-like.

Colour. The Field Spaniel should be a self-coloured dog, viz.: Black, Liver, Golden Liver, Mahogany Red, Roan; or any one of these colours with Tan over the Eyes, on the Cheeks, Feet and Pasterns. Other colours, such as Black and White, Liver and White, Red or Orange and White, etc., while not debarring a dog, is a fault.

Weight and Size. From about 35 to 50 lb. Height: about 18 inches to shoulder.

SPANIEL, FIELD

(AMERICAN KENNEL CLUB—GROUP I: SPORTING DOGS)

Head. Should be quite characteristic of this grand sporting dog, as that of the Bulldog, or the Bloodhound; its very stamp and countenance should at once convey the conviction of high breeding, character and nobility; skull well developed, with a distinctly elevated occipital tuberosity, which, above all, gives the character alluded to; not too wide across the muzzle, long and lean, never snipy or squarely cut, and in profile curving gradually from nose to throat; lean beneath the eyes—a thickness here gives coarseness to the whole head. The great length of muzzle gives surface for the free development of the olfactory nerve, and thus secures the highest possible scenting powers.

Eyes. Not too full, but not small, receding or overhung, color dark hazel or brown, or nearly black, according to the color of the dog. Grave in expression and showing no haw.

Ears. Moderately long and wide, sufficiently clad with nice setterlike feather and set low. They should fall in graceful folds, the lower parts curling inwards and backwards.

Neck. Long, strong and muscular, so as to enable the dog to retrieve his game without undue fatigue.

Body. Should be of moderate length, well ribbed up to a good strong loin, straight or slightly arched, never slack.

Nose. Well developed, with good open nostrils.

Shoulders and Chest. Former long, sloping and well set back, thus giving great activity and speed; latter deep and well developed, but not too round and wide.

Back and Loin. Very strong and muscular.

Hindquarters. Strong and muscular. The stifles should be moderately bent, and not twisted either in or out.

Stern. Well set on and carried low, if possible below the level of the back in a straight line or with a slight downward inclination, never elevated above the back, and in action always kept low, nicely fringed with wavy feather of silky texture.

Forelegs. Should be of fairly good length, with straight, clean, flat bone, and nicely feathered. Immense bone is no longer desirable.

Feet. Not too small; round, with short soft hair between the toes; good, strong pads.

Coat. Flat or slightly waved, and never curled. Sufficiently dense to resist the weather, and not too short. Silky in texture, glossy and refined in nature, with neither duffleness on the one hand, nor curl or wiriness on the other. On the chest, under belly and behind the legs, there should be abundant feather, but never too much, especially below the hocks, and that of the right sort, *viz.* setterlike. The hindquarters should be similarly adorned.

Color. Black, liver, golden liver, mahogany red, or roan; or any one of these colors with tan over the eyes and on the cheeks, feet, and pasterns. Other colors, such as black and white, liver and white, red or orange and white, while not disqualifying, will be considered less desirable since the Field Spaniel should be clearly distinguished from the Springer Spaniel.

Height. About 18 inches to shoulder.

Weight. From about 35 pounds to 50 pounds.

General Appearance. That of a well-balanced, noble, upstanding sporting dog; built for activity and endurance. A grand combination of beauty and utility, and bespeaking of unusual docility and instinct.

SCALE OF POINTS

Head and jaw	15	Hind legs	10
Eyes	5	Feet	10
Ears	5	Stern	10
Neck	5	Coat and feather	10
Body	10	General appearance	10
Forelegs	10	Total	100

Approved July 14, 1959

SPANIEL (IRISH WATER)

(THE KENNEL CLUB—GUNDOG GROUP)

Characteristics. The gait, peculiar to the breed, differs from that of any other variety of Spaniel.
General Appearance. The Irish Water Spaniel is a gundog bred for work in all types of shooting and particularly suited for wild-fowling. His fitness for this purpose should be evident in his appearance; he is a strongly built, compact dog, intelligent, enduring and eager.
Head and Skull. The head should be of good size. The skull high in dome, of good length and width sufficient to allow adequate brain capacity. The muzzle long, strong and somewhat square with a gradual stop. The face should be smooth and the skull covered with long curls in the form of a pronounced top-knot growing in a well-defined peak to a point between the eyes. Nose large and well developed, dark liver colour. Withal there should be an impression of fineness.
Eyes. Comparatively small, medium to dark-brown colour, bright and alert.
Ears. Very long and lobe-shaped in the leather, low set, hanging close to the cheeks and covered with long twisted curls of live hair.
Mouth. The teeth regular and meeting in a normal bite.
Neck. Strongly set into the shoulders, powerful, arching and long enough to carry the head well above the level of the back. The back and sides of the neck should be covered with curls similar to those on the body. The throat should be smooth, the smooth hair forming a V-shaped patch from the back of the lower jaw to the breast bone.
Forequarters. The shoulders should be powerful and sloping. The chest deep and of large girth with ribs so well sprung behind the shoulders as to give a barrel-shaped appearance to the body but with normal width and curvature between the forelegs. The forelegs should be well boned and straight, with arms well let down and carrying the forearm at elbow and knee in a straight line with the point of the shoulder.
Body. Should be of good size. The back short, broad and level, strongly coupled to the hindquarters. The ribs carried well back. The loins deep and wide. The body as a whole being so proportioned as to give a barrel-shaped appearance accentuated by the springing of the ribs.
Hindquarters. Powerful with long well-bent stifles and hocks set low.
Feet. Should be large and somewhat round and spreading; well-covered with hair over and between the toes.
Tail. Peculiar to the breed, should be short and straight, thick at the root and tapering to a fine point. It should be low set, carried straight and below the level of the back; and in length should not reach the hock joint. Three to four inches of the tail at the root should be covered by close curls which stop abruptly, the remainder should be bare or covered by straight fine hairs.

Coat. Should be composed of dense, tight, crisp ringlets free from wooliness. The hair should have a natural oiliness. The forelegs covered with feather in curls or ringlets down to the feet. The feather should be abundant all round, though shorter in front so as only to give a rough appearance. Below the hocks the hindlegs should be smooth in front, but feathered behind down to the feet.

Colour. A rich dark liver having the purplish tint or bloom peculiar to the breed and sometimes referred to as puce-liver.

Weight and Size. Height to the shoulders: Dogs about 21 to 23 inches. Bitches about 20 to 22 inches.

SPANIEL, IRISH WATER

(AMERICAN KENNEL CLUB—GROUP I: SPORTING DOGS)

Head. Skull rather large and high in dome with prominent occiput; muzzle square and rather long with deep mouth opening and lips fine in texture. Teeth strong and level. The nose should be large with open nostrils, and liver in color. The head should be cleanly chiseled, not cheeky, and should not present a short wedge-shaped appearance. Hair on face should be short and smooth.

Topknot. Topknot, a characteristic of the true breed, should consist of long loose curls growing down into a well-defined peak between the eyes and should not be in the form of a wig; *i.e.* growing straight across.

Eyes. Medium in size and set almost flush, without eyebrows. Color of eyes hazel, preferably of dark shade. Expression of the eyes should be keenly alert, intelligent, direct and quizzical.

Ears. Long, lobular, set low with leathers reaching to about the end of the nose when extended forward. The ears should be abundantly covered with curls becoming longer toward the tips and extending two or more inches below the ends of the leathers.

Neck. The neck should be long, arching, strong and muscular, smoothly set into sloping shoulders.

Shoulders and Chest. Shoulders should be sloping and clean; chest deep but not too wide between the legs. The entire front should give the impression of strength without heaviness.

Body, Ribs and Loins. Body should be of medium length, with ribs well sprung, pear-shaped at the brisket, and rounder toward the hindquarters. Ribs should be carried well back. Loins should be short, wide and muscular. The body should not present a tucked-up appearance.

Hindquarters. The hindquarters should be as high as or a trifle higher than the shoulders and should be very powerful and muscular with well-developed upper and second thighs. Hips should be wide; stifles should not be too straight; and hocks low-set and moderately bent. Tail should be set on low enough to give a rather rounded appearance to the hindquarters and should be carried nearly level with the back. Sound hindquarters are of great importance to provide swimming power and drive.

Forelegs and Feet. Forelegs medium in length, well boned, straight and muscular with elbows close set. Both fore and hind feet should be large, thick and somewhat spreading, well clothed with hair both over and between the toes, but free from superfluous feather.

Tail. The so-called 'rat tail' is a striking characteristic of the breed. At the root it is thick and covered for 2 or 3 inches with short curls. It tapers to a fine point at the end, and from the root-curls is covered with short, smooth hair so as to look as if the tail had been clipped. The tail should not be long enough to reach the hock joint.

Coat. Proper coat is of vital importance. The neck, back and sides should be densely covered with tight crisp ringlets entirely free from wooliness. Underneath the ribs the hair should be longer. The hair on lower throat should be short. The forelegs should be covered all around with abundant hair falling in curls or waves, but shorter in front than behind. The hind legs should also be abundantly covered by hair falling in curls or waves, but the hair should be short on the front of the legs below the hocks.

Color. Solid liver; white on chest objectionable.

Height and Weight. Dogs, 22 to 24 inches; bitches, 21 to 23 inches. Dogs, 55 to 65 pounds; bitches, 45 to 58 pounds.

General Appearance. That of a smart, upstanding, strongly built but not leggy dog, combining great intelligence and the rugged endurance with a bold, dashing eagerness of temperament.

Gait. Should be square, true, precise and not slurring.

SCALE OF POINTS

Head		
Skull and topknot	6	
Ears	4	
Eyes	4	
Muzzle and nose	6	20
Body		
Neck	5	
Chest, shoulders, back, loin and ribs	12	17
Driving Gear		
Feet, hips, thighs, stifles and continuity of hindquarter muscles	14	
Feet, legs, elbows and muscles of forequarters	9	23
Coat		
Tightness, denseness of curl and general texture	16	
Color	4	20
Tail		
General appearance and 'set on,' length and carriage	5	5
General Conformation and Action		
Symmetry, style, gait, weight and size	15	15
		100

Approved June 11, 1940

SPANIEL (SPRINGER, ENGLISH)

(THE KENNEL CLUB—GUNDOG GROUP)

Characteristics. The English Springer is the oldest of our Sporting Gundogs and the taproot from which all of our sporting land spaniels (Clumbers excepted) have been evolved. It was originally used for the purpose of finding and springing game for the net, falcon, or greyhound, but at the present time it is used entirely to find, flush, and retrieve game for the gun. The breed is of ancient and pure origin, and should be kept as such. The Springer's gait is strictly his own. His forelegs should swing straight forward from the shoulder, throwing the feet well forward in an easy and free manner, not a paddle nor choppied terrier-like stride. His hocks should drive well under his body, following in a line with his forelegs. At slow movements many Springers have a pacing stride typical of the breed.

General Appearance. The general appearance of the modern Springer is that of a symmetrical, compact, strong, upstanding, merry and active dog, built for endurance and activity. He is the highest on the leg and raciest in build of all British land Spaniels.

Head and Skull. The skull should be of medium length and fairly broad and slightly rounded, rising from the foreface, making a brow or stop, divided by a fluting between the eyes gradually dying away along the forehead towards the occiput bone, which should not be peaked. The cheeks should be flat, that is not rounded or full. The foreface should be of proportionate length to the skull, fairly broad and deep without being coarse, well chiselled below the eyes, fairly deep and square in flew, but not exaggerated to such an extent as would interfere with comfort when retrieving. Nostrils well developed, underjaw strong and level mouth, that is neither over nor under shot.

Eyes. The eyes should be neither too full nor too small but of medium size, not prominent nor sunken but well set in (not showing haw) of an alert, kind expression. A mouse-like eye without expression is objectionable, as also is a light eye. The colour should be dark hazel.

Ears. The ears should be lobular in shape, set close to the head, of good length and width, but not exaggerated. The correct set should be in a line with the eye.

Neck. The neck should be strong and muscular, of nice length and free from throatiness, well set in the shoulders, nicely arched and tapering towards the head—this giving great activity and speed. A ewe neck is objectionable.

Forequarters. The forelegs should be straight and nicely feathered, elbows set well to body and with proportionate substance to carry the body, strong flexible pasterns.

Body. The body should be strong and of proportionate length, neither too long nor too short, the chest deep and well developed with plenty of heart

and lung room, well sprung ribs, loins muscular and strong with slight arch and well coupled, thighs broad and muscular and well developed.
Hindquarters. The hindlegs should be well let down from hip to hocks. Stifles and hocks moderately bent, inclining neither inwards nor outwards. Coarseness of hocks objectionable.
Feet. Feet tight, compact, and well rounded with strong full pads.
Tail. The stern should be low and never carried above the level of the back, well feathered and with a lively action.
Coat. The coat should be close, straight and weather resisting without being coarse.
Colour. Any recognized Land Spaniel colour is acceptable, but liver and white, black and white, or either of these colours with tan markings preferred.
Weight and Size. The approximate height should be 20 inches. The approximate weight should be 50 lbs.

SPANIEL, ENGLISH SPRINGER

(AMERICAN KENNEL CLUB—GROUP I: SPORTING DOGS)

General Appearance and Type. The English Springer Spaniel is a medium-size sporting dog with a neat, compact body, and a docked tail. His coat is moderately long, glossy, usually liver and white or black and white, with feathering on his legs, ears, chest and brisket. His pendulous ears, soft gentle expression, sturdy build and friendly wagging tail proclaim him unmistakably a member of the ancient family of spaniels. He is above all a well proportioned dog, free from exaggeration, nicely balanced in every part. His carriage is proud and upstanding, body deep, legs strong and muscular with enough length to carry him with ease. His short level back, well developed thighs, good shoulders, excellent feet, suggest power, endurance, agility. Taken as a whole he looks the part of a dog that can go and keep going under difficult hunting conditions, and moreover he enjoys what he is doing. At his best he is endowed with style, symmetry, balance, enthusiasm and is every inch a sporting dog of distinct spaniel character, combining beauty and utility. To be penalized: Those lacking true English Springer type in conformation, expression, or behavior.
Temperament. The typical Springer is friendly, eager to please, quick to learn, willing to obey. In the show ring he should exhibit poise, attentiveness, tractability, and should permit himself to be examined by the judge without resentment or cringing. To be penalized: Excessive timidity, with due allowance for puppies and novice exhibits. But no dog to receive a ribbon if he behaves in vicious manner toward handler or judge. Aggressiveness toward other dogs in the ring *not* to be construed as viciousness.
Size and Proportion. The Springer is built to cover rough ground with agility and reasonable speed. He should be kept to medium size—neither to small nor too large and heavy to do the work for which he is intended. The ideal shoulder height for dogs is 20 inches; for bitches, 19 inches. Length of topline (the distance from top of the shoulders to the root of the tail) should be approximately equal to the dog's shoulder height —never longer than his height—and not appreciably less. The dog too long in body, especially when long in loin, tires easily and lacks the compact outline characteristic of the breed. Equally undesirable is the dog too short in body for the length of his legs, a condition that destroys his balance and restricts the gait.

Weight is dependent on the dog's other dimensions: a 20-inch dog, well proportioned, in good condition should weigh about 49–55 pounds. The resulting appearance is a well-knit, sturdy dog with good but not too heavy bone, in no way coarse or ponderous. To be penalized: Over-heavy specimens, cloddy in build. Leggy individuals, too tall for their length and substance. Oversize or undersize specimens (those more than one inch under or over the breed ideal).
Color and Coat. Color may be liver or black with white markings; liver and white (or black and white) with tan markings; blue or liver roan; or predominantly white with tan, black or liver markings. On ears, chest, legs and belly the Springer is nicely furnished with a fringe of feathering (of moderate heaviness). On his head, front or forelegs, and below hocks on front of hindlegs the hair is short and fine. The body coat is flat or wavy, of medium length, sufficiently dense to be water-proof, weather-proof and thorn-proof. The texture fine and the hair should have the clean, glossy, live appearance indicative of good health. It is legitimate to trim about head, feet, ears; to remove dead hair; to thin and shorten excess feathering particularly from the hocks to the feet and elsewhere as required to give a smart, clean appearance. To be penalized: Rough, curly coat. Over-trimming especially of the body coat. Any chopped, barbered or artificial effect. Excessive feathering that destroys the clean outline desirable in a sporting dog. Off colors such as lemon, red or orange not to place.
Head. The head is impressive without being heavy. Its beauty lies in a combination of strength and refinement. It is important that the size and proportion be in balance with the rest of the dog. Viewed in profile the head should appear approximately the same length as the neck and should blend with the body in substance. The skull (upper head) to be of medium length, fairly broad, flat on top, slightly rounded at the sides and back. The occiput bone inconspicuous, rounded rather than peaked or angular. The foreface (head in front of the eyes) approximately the same length as the skull, and in harmony as to width and general character. Looking down on the head the

muzzle to appear to be about one half the width of the skull. As the skull rises from the foreface it makes a brow or 'stop,' divided by a groove or fluting between the eyes. This groove continues upward and gradually disappears as it reaches the middle of the forehead. The amount of 'stop' can best be described as moderate. It must not be a pronounced feature as in the Clumber Spaniel. Rather it is a subtle rise where the muzzle blends into the upper head, further emphasized by the groove and by the position and shape of the eyebrows which should be well-developed. The stop, eyebrow and the chiseling of the bony structure around the eye sockets contribute to the Spinger's beautiful and characteristic expression.

Viewed in profile the topline of the skull and the muzzle lie in two approximately parallel planes. The nasal bone should be straight, with no inclination downward toward the tip of the nose which gives a downfaced look so undesirable in this breed. Neither should the nasal bone be concave resulting in a 'dish-faced' profile; nor convex giving the dog a Roman nose. The jaws to be of sufficient length to allow the dog to carry game easily; fairly square, lean, strong, and even, (neither undershot nor overshot). The upper lip to come down full and rather square to cover the line of the lower jaw, but lips not to be pendulous nor exaggerated. The nostrils, well opened and broad, liver color or black depending on the color of the coat. Flesh-colored ('Dudley noses') or spotted ('butterfly noses') are undesirable. The cheeks to be flat, (not rounded, full or thick) with nice chiseling under the eyes. To be penalized: Oval, pointed or heavy skull. Cheeks prominently rounded, thick and protruding. Too much or too little stop. Over heavy muzzle. Muzzle too short, too thin, too narrow. Pendulous slobbery lips. Under- or over-shot jaws —a very serious fault, to be heavily penalized.

Teeth. The teeth should be strong, clean, not too small; and when the mouth is closed the teeth should meet in an even bite or a close scissors bite (the lower incisors touching the inside of the upper incisors). To be penalized: Any deviation from above description. One or two teeth slightly out of line not to be considered a serious fault, but irregularities due to faulty jaw formation to be severely penalized.

Eyes. More than any other feature the eyes contribute to the Springer's appeal. Color, placement, size influence expression and attractiveness. The eyes to be of medium size, neither small, round, full and prominent, nor bold and hard in expression. Set rather well apart and fairly deep in their sockets. The color of the iris to harmonize with the color of the coat, preferably a good dark hazel in the liver dogs and black or deep brown in the black and white specimens. The expression to be alert, kindly, trusting. The lids, tight with little or no haw showing. To be penalized: Eyes yellow or brassy in color or noticeably lighter than the coat. Sharp expression indicating unfriendly or suspicious nature. Loose droopy lids. Prominent haw (the third eyelid or membrane in the inside corner of the eye).

Ears. The correct ear-set is on a level with the line of the eye; on the side of the skull and not too far back. The flaps to be long and fairly wide, hanging close to the cheeks, with no tendency to stand up or out. The leather, thin, approximately long enough to reach the tip of the nose. To be penalized: Short round ears. Ears set too high or too low or too far back on the head.

Neck. The neck to be moderately long, muscular, slightly arched at the crest gradually blending into sloping shoulders. Not noticeably upright nor coming into the body at an abrupt angle. To be penalized: Short neck, often the sequence to steep shoulders. Concave neck, sometimes called ewe neck or upside down neck (the opposite of arched). excessive throatiness.

Body. The body to be well coupled, strong, compact; the chest deep but not so wide or round as to interfere with the action of the front legs; the brisket sufficiently developed to reach to the level of the elbows. The ribs fairly long, springing gradually to the middle of the body then tapering as they approach the end of the ribbed section. The back (section between the withers and loin) to be straight and strong, with no tendency to dip or roach. The loins to be strong, short; a slight arch over loins and hip bones. Hips nicely rounded, blending smoothly into hind legs. The resulting topline slopes *very gently* from withers to tail—the line from withers to back descending without a sharp drop; the back practically level; arch over hips somewhat lower than the withers; croup sloping gently to base of tail; tail carried to follow the natural line of the body. The bottom line, starting on a level with the elbows, to continue backward with almost no up-curve until reaching the end of the ribbed section, then a more noticeable up-curve to the flank, but not enough to make the dog appear small waisted or 'tucked up.' To be penalized: Body too shallow, indicating lack of brisket. Ribs too flat sometimes due to immaturity. Ribs too round (barrel-shaped), hampering the gait. Sway-back (dip in back), indicating weakness or lack of muscular development, particularly to be seen when dog is in action and viewed from the side. Roach back (too much arch over loin and extending forward into middle section). Croup falling away too sharply; or croup too high—unsightly faults, detrimental to outline and good movement. Topline sloping sharply, indicating steep withers (straight shoulder placement) and a too low tail-set.

Tail. The Springer's tail is an index both to his temperament and his conformation. Merry tail action is characteristic. The proper set is somewhat low following the natural line of the croup. The carriage should be nearly horizontal, slightly elevated when dog is excited. Carried straight up is untypical of the breed. The tail should not be docked too short and should be well fringed with wavy feather. It is legitimate to shape and shorten the feathering but enough should be left to blend with the dog's other furnishings. To be penalized: Tail habitually upright. Tail set too high or too low. Clamped down tail (indicating timidity or undependable temperament, even less to be desired than the tail carried too gaily).

Forequarters. Efficient movement in front calls for proper shoulders. The blades sloping back to form an angle with the forearm of approximately 90 degrees which permits the dog to swing his forelegs forward in an easy manner. Shoulders (fairly close together at the tips) to lie flat and mold smoothly into the contour of the body. The forelegs to be straight with the same degree of size to the foot. The bone, strong, slightly flattened, not too heavy or round. The knee, straight, almost flat; the pasterns short, strong; elbows close to the body with free action from the shoulders. To be penalized: Shoulders set at a steep angle limiting the stride. Loaded shoulders (the blades standing out from the body by over-development of the muscles). Loose elbows, crooked legs. Bone too light or too coarse and heavy. Weak pasterns that let down the feet at a pronounced angle

Hindquarters. The Springer should be shown in hard muscular condition, well developed in hips and thighs and the whole rear assembly should suggest strength and driving power. The hip joints to be set rather wide apart and the hips nicely rounded. The thighs broad and muscular; the stifle joint strong and moderately bent. The hock joint somewhat rounded, not small and sharp in contour, and moderately angulated. Leg from hock joint to foot pad, short and strong with good bone structure. When viewed from the rear the hocks to be parallel whether the dog is standing or in motion. To be penalized: Too little or too much angulation. Narrow, undeveloped thighs. Hocks too short or too long (a proportion of one-third the distance from hip joint to foot is ideal). Flabby muscles. Weakness of joints.

Feet. The feet to be round, or slightly oval, compact, well arched, medium size with thick pads, well feathered between the toes. Excess hair to be removed to show the natural shape and size of the foot. To be penalized: Thin, open or splayed feet (flat with spreading toes). Hare foot (long, rather narrow foot).

Movement. In judging the Springer there should be emphasis on proper movement which is the final test of a dog's conformation and soundness. Prerequisite to good movement is balance of the front and rear assemblies. The two must match in angulation and muscular development if the gait is to be smooth and effortless. Good shoulders laid back at an angle that permits a long stride are just as essential as the excellent rear quarters that provide the driving power. When viewed from the front the dog's legs should appear to swing forward in a free and easy manner, with no tendency for the feet to cross over or interfere with each other. Viewed from the rear the hocks should drive well under the body following on a line with the forelegs, the rear legs parallel, neither too widely nor too closely spaced. Seen from the side the Springer should exhibit a good, long forward stride, without high-stepping or wasted motion. To be penalized: Short choppy stride, mincing steps with up and down movement, hopping. Moving with forefeet wide, giving roll or swing to body. Weaving or crossing of fore or hind feet. Cowhocks—hocks turning in toward each other.

In judging the English Springer Spaniel the over-all picture is a primary consideration. It is urged that the judge look for type which includes general appearance, outline and temperament and also for soundness especially as seen when the dog is in motion. Inasmuch as the dog with a smooth easy gait must be reasonably sound and well balanced he is to be highly regarded in the show ring, however, not to the extent of forgiving him for not looking like an English Springer Spaniel. A quite untypical dog, leggy, foreign in head and expression, may move well. But he should not be placed over a good all-round specimen that has a minor fault in movement. It should be remembered that the English Springer Spaniel is first and foremost a sporting dog of the spaniel family and he must look and behave and move in character.

Approved June 12, 1956

SPANIEL (SPRINGER, WELSH)

(THE KENNEL CLUB—GUNDOG GROUP)

Characteristics. The 'Welsh Spaniel' or 'Springer' is also known and referred to in Wales as a 'Starter.' He is of very ancient and pure origin, and is a distinct variety.

General Appearance. A symmetrical, compact, strong, merry, very active dog; not stilty; obviously built for endurance and hard work. A quick and active mover displaying plenty of push and drive.

Head and Skull. Skull proportionate, of moderate length, slightly domed, with clearly defined stop and well chiselled below the eyes. Muzzle of medium length, straight, fairly square; the nostrils well developed and flesh-coloured or dark. A short chubby head is objectionable.

Eyes. Hazel or dark, medium size, not prominent, nor sunken, nor showing haw.

Ears. Set moderately low and hanging close to the cheeks, comparatively small and gradually narrowing towards the tip and shaped somewhat like a vine leaf, covered with setter-like feathering.

Mouth. Jaw strong, neither under nor overshot.

Neck. Long and muscular, clean in throat, neatly set into long, sloping shoulders.

Forequarters. Forelegs of medium length, straight, well boned, moderately feathered.

Body. Not long; strong and muscular with deep brisket, well-sprung ribs; length of body should be proportionate to length of leg and very well balanced; muscular loin slightly arched and well coupled up.

Hindquarters. Strong and muscular, wide and fully developed with deep second thighs. Hindlegs, hocks well let down; stifles moderately bent (neither twisted in nor out), moderately feathered.

Feet. Round, with thick pads. Firm and cat-like, not too large or spreading.

Tail. Well set on and low, never carried above the level of the back; lightly feathered and lively in action.

Coat. Straight or flat, and thick, of a nice silky texture, never wiry nor wavy. A curly coat is most objectionable.

Colour. Rich red and white only.

Weight and Size. A dog not to exceed 19 inches in height at shoulder and a bitch 18 inches approximately.

Faults. Coarse skull, light bone, long or curly coat, bad shoulders, poor movement.

SPANIEL, WELSH SPRINGER

(AMERICAN KENNEL CLUB—GROUP I: SPORTING DOGS)

The 'Welsh Spaniel' or 'Springer' is also known and referred to in Wales as a 'Starter.' He is of very ancient and pure origin, and is a distinct variety which has been bred and preserved purely for working purposes.

Head—Skull. Proportionate, of moderate length, slightly domed, clearly defined stop, well chiseled below the eyes.
Muzzle. Medium length, straight, fairly square; the nostrils well developed and flesh colored or dark.
Jaw. Strong, neither undershot nor overshot.
Eyes. Hazel or dark, medium size, not prominent, nor sunken, nor showing haw.
Ears. Set moderately low and hanging close to the cheeks, comparatively small and gradually narrowing towards the tip, covered with nice setterlike feathering. A short chubby head is objectionable.
Neck and Shoulders—Neck. Long and muscular, clean in throat, neatly set into long and sloping shoulders.
Forelegs. Medium length, straight, well boned, moderately feathered.
Body. Not long; strong and muscular with deep brisket, well sprung ribs; length of body should be proportionate to length of leg, and very well balanced; with muscular loin slightly arched and well coupled up.
Quarters. Strong and muscular, wide and fully developed with deep second thighs.
Hindlegs. Hocks well let down; stifles moderately bent (neither twisted in nor out), moderately feathered.
Feet. Round with thick pads.
Stern. Well set on and low, never carried above the level of the back; lightly feathered and with lively action.
Coat. Straight or flat and thick, of a nice silky texture, never wiry nor wavy. A curly coat is most objectionable.
Color. Dark rich red and white.
General Appearance. A symmetrical, compact, strong, merry, very active dog; not stilty, obviously built for endurance and activity.

SPANIEL (SUSSEX)

(THE KENNEL CLUB—GUNDOG GROUP)

General Appearance. Massive and strongly built. An active, energetic, strong dog, whose characteristic movement is a decided roll, and unlike that of any other Spaniel.

Head and Skull. The skull should be wide and show a moderate curve from ear to ear, neither flat nor apple headed, with a centre indentation and a pronounced stop. Brows frowning—occiput decided, but not pointed. Nostrils well developed and liver colour. A well balanced head.

Eyes. Hazel colour, fairly large, not too full, but soft expression and not showing the haw over much.

Ears. Thick, fairly large and lobe shape, set moderately low but above eye level. Should lie closely, hair soft and wavy, but not too profuse.

Mouth. Strong and level, neither over nor undershot, with a scissor bite.

Neck. Long, strong and slightly arched, not carrying the head much above the level of the back. Not much throatiness, but well marked frill.

Forequarters. The shoulders should be sloping and free: arms well boned as well as muscular. Knees large and strong, pasterns short and well boned. Legs rather short and strong, moderately well feathered.

Body. Chest deep and well developed: not too round and wide. Back and loin well developed and muscular both in width and depth. The back ribs must be deep. Whole body should be strong and level with no sign of waistiness from aitches to hips.

Hindquarters. The thighs must be strongly boned as well as muscular: hocks large and strong, legs rather short and strong with good bone, moderately well feathered. The hindlegs should not appear shorter than the forelegs, or be too much bent at the hocks so as to give a settery appearance, which is objectionable. The hindlegs should be well feathered above the hocks, but not much hair below the hocks.

Feet. Circular, well padded, well feathered between toes.

Tail. Set low and not carried above level of the back. Free actioned, thickly clothed with hair, but no feather. Docked from 5 to 7 inches.

Coat. Abundant and flat with no tendency to curl and ample under coat for weather resistance.

Colour. Rich golden liver and hair shading to gold at the tips: the gold predominating. Dark liver or puce is objectionable.

Weight and Size. Ideal weight: Dogs, 45 lbs, bitches, 40 lbs. Height, 15 to 16 inches.

SPANIEL, SUSSEX

(AMERICAN KENNEL CLUB—GROUP I: SPORTING DOGS)

Head. The skull should be moderately long and also wide, with an indention in the middle and a full stop, brows fairly heavy; occiput full, but not pointed, the whole giving an appearance of heaviness without dullness.

Eyes. Hazel color, fairly large, soft and languishing, not showing the haw overmuch.

Nose. The muzzle should be about three inches long, square, and the lips somewhat pendulous. The nostrils well developed and liver color.

Ears. Thick, fairly large and lobe shaped; set moderately low, but relatively not so low as in the black Field Spaniel; carried close to the head and furnished with soft, wavy hair.

Neck. Is rather short, strong and slightly arched, but not carrying the head much above the level of the back. There should not be much throatiness about the skin, but well-marked frill in the coat.

Chest and Shoulders. The chest is round, especially behind the shoulders, deep and wide giving a good girth. The shoulders should be oblique.

Back and Back Rib. The back and loin is long and should be very muscular, both in width and depth; for this development the back ribs must be deep. The whole body is characterized as low, long and level.

Legs and Feet. The arms and thighs must be bony as well as muscular, knees and hocks large and strong; pasterns very short and bony, feet large and round, and with short hair between the toes. The legs should be very short and strong, with great bone, and may show a slight bend in the forearm, and be moderately well feathered. The hindlegs should not appear to be shorter than the forelegs, nor be too much bent at the hocks. They should be well feathered above the hocks but should not have much hair below that point. The hindlegs are short from the hock to the ground, and wide apart.

Tail. Should be docked from 5 to 7 inches, set low, and not carried above the level of the back, thickly covered with moderately long feather.

Coat. Body coat abundant, flat or slightly waved, with no tendency to curl, moderately well feathered on legs and stern, but clean below the hocks.

Color. Rich golden liver; this is a certain sign of the purity of the breed, dark liver or puce denoting unmistakably a recent cross with the black or other variety of Field Spaniel.

General Appearance. Rather massive and muscular, but with free movements and nice tail action, denoting a cheerful and tractable disposition. Weight from 35 pounds to 45 pounds.

POSITIVE POINTS

Head	10	Legs and feet	10
Eyes	5	Tail	5
Nose	5	Coat	5
Ears	10	Color	15
Neck	5	General appearance	15
Chest and shoulders	5	Total	100
Back and back ribs	10		

NEGATIVE POINTS

Light eyes	5	Color, too light or too dark	15
Narrow head	10	Legginess or light of bone	5
Weak muzzle	10	Shortness of body or flat sided	5
Curled ears or set on on high	5	General appearance—sour or crouching	10
Curled coat	15	Total	100
Carriage of stern	5		
Topknot	10		
White on chest	5		

Approved July 14, 1959

ST BERNARD

(THE KENNEL CLUB—WORKING GROUP)

General Appearance. Expression should be token benevolence, dignity, and intelligence. Movement is most important, and St Bernards have often failed in this direction, the hindlegs being especially faulty.

Head and Skull. Large and massive, circumference of skull being rather more than double the length of the head from nose to occiput. Muzzle short, full in front of the eye, and square at nose end. Cheeks flat; great depth from eye to lower jaw. Lips deep, but not too pendulous. From nose to stop perfectly straight and broad. Stop somewhat abrupt and well defined. Skull broad, slightly rounded at the top, with somewhat prominent brow. Nose large and black, with well developed nostrils.

Eyes. Rather small and deep set, dark in colour, not too close together, the lower eyelid drooping so as to show a fair amount of haw at the inner corner, the upper eyelid falling well over the eye.

Ears. Of medium size lying close to the cheeks, and not heavily feathered.

Mouth. Level.

Neck. Lengthy, thick, muscular, and slightly arched, with dewlap well developed.

Forequarters. Shoulders broad and sloping, well up at the withers. Legs perfectly straight, strong in bone and of good length.

Body. Back broad and straight, ribs well rounded. Loin wide and very muscular. Chest wide and deep. The lower part should not project below the elbows.

Hindquarters. Legs heavy in bone, hocks well bent and thighs very muscular.

Feet. Large and compact with well-arched toes. Dewclaws should be removed.

Tail. Set on rather high, long, and in long-coated variety well feathered. Carried low when in repose, and when excited or in motion should not be curled over the back.

Coat. In Rough specimens, should be dense and flat, rather fuller round the neck; thighs well feathered. In Smooth specimens it should be close and houndlike, slightly feathered on thighs and tail.

Colour. Orange, mahogany-brindle, red-brindle; white with patches on body of any of the above-named colours. The markings should be as follows: White muzzle, white blaze up face, white collar round neck, white chest, white forelegs, feet, and end of tail; black shadings on face and ears.

Weight and Size. The taller the better, provided that symmetry is maintained; thoroughly well proportioned, and of great substance. The general outline should suggest great power and capability of endurance.

Faults. Dudley, liver, flesh-coloured or split nose; over or under-shot mouth; snipy muzzle; light or staring eyes; cheek bumps; wedge head;

flat skull; badly set or carried, or heavily feathered ears; too much peak; short neck; curly coat; flat sides; hollow back; roach back; flat thighs; ring tail; open or hare feet; cow-hocks; fawn or self-coloured, straight hocks.

ST BERNARD

(AMERICAN KENNEL CLUB—GROUP III: WORKING DOGS)

SHORTHAIRED

General. Powerful, proportionately tall figure, strong and muscular in every part, with powerful head and most intelligent expression. In dogs with a dark mask the expression appears more stern, but never ill-natured.

Head. Like the whole body, very powerful and imposing. The massive skull is wide, slightly arched and the sides slope in a gentle curve into the very strongly developed, high cheek bones. Occiput only moderately developed. The supra-orbital ridge is very strongly developed and forms nearly a right angle with the horizontal axis of the head. Deeply imbedded between the eyes and starting at the root of the muzzle, a furrow runs over the whole skull. It is strongly marked in the first half, gradually disappearing toward the base of the occiput. The lines at the sides of the head diverge considerably from the outer corner of the eyes toward the back of the head. The skin of the forehead, above the eyes, forms rather noticeable wrinkles, more or less pronounced, which converge toward the furrow. Especially when the dog is in action, the wrinkles are more visible without in the least giving the impression of morosity. Too strongly developed wrinkles are not desired. The slope from the skull to the muzzle is sudden and rather steep.

The muzzle is short, does not taper, and the vertical depth at the root of the muzzle must be greater than the length of the muzzle. The bridge of the muzzle is not arched, but straight; in some dogs, occasionally, slightly broken. A rather wide, well-marked, shallow furrow runs from the root of the muzzle over the entire bridge of the muzzle to the nose. The flews of the upper jaw are strongly developed, not sharply cut, but turning in a beautiful curve into the lower edge, and slightly overhanging. The flews of the lower jaw must not be deeply pendant. The teeth should be sound and strong and should meet in either a scissors or an even bite; the scissors bite being preferable. The undershot bite, although some times found with good specimens, is not desirable. The overshot bite is a fault. A black roof to the mouth is desirable.

Nose (Schwamm). Very substantial, broad, with wide open nostrils, and, like the lips, always black.

Ears. Of medium size, rather high set, with very strongly developed burr (Muschel) at the base. They stand slightly away from the head at the base, then drop with a sharp bend to the side and cling to the head without a turn. The flap is tender and forms a rounded triangle, slightly elongated toward the point, the front edge lying firmly to the head, whereas the back edge may stand somewhat away from the head, especially when the dog is at attention. Lightly set ears, which at the base immediately cling to the head, give it an oval and too little marked exterior, whereas a strongly developed base gives the skull a squarer, broader and much more expressive appearance.

Eyes. Set more to the front than the sides, are of medium size, dark brown, with intelligent, friendly expression, set moderately deep. The lower eyelids, as a rule, do not close completely and, if that is the case, form an angular wrinkle toward the inner corner of the eye. Eyelids which are too deeply pendant and show conspicuously the lachrymal glands, or a very red, thick haw, and eyes that are too light, are objectionable.

Neck. Set high, very strong and in action is carried erect. Otherwise horizontally or slightly downward. The junction of head and neck is distinctly marked by an indentation. The nape of the neck is very muscular and rounded at the sides which makes the neck appear rather short. The dewlap of throat and neck is well pronounced: too strong development, however, is not desirable.

Shoulders. Sloping and broad, very muscular and powerful. The withers are strongly pronounced.

Chest. Very well arched, moderately deep, not reaching below the elbows.

Back. Very broad, perfectly straight as far as the haunches, from there gently sloping to the rump, and merging imperceptibly into the root of the tail.

Hindquarters. Well-developed. Legs very muscular.

Belly. Distinctly set off from the very powerful loin section, only little drawn up.

Tail. Starting broad and powerful directly from the rump is long, very heavy, ending in a powerful tip. In repose it hangs straight down, turning gently upward in the lower third only, which is not considered a fault. In a great many specimens the tail is carried with the end slightly bent and therefore hangs down in the shape of an '*f*'. In action all dogs carry the tail more or less turned upward. However it may not be carried too erect or by any means rolled over the back. A slight curling of the tip is sooner admissible.

Forearms. Very powerful and extraordinarily muscular.

Forelegs. Straight, strong.

Hindlegs. Hocks of moderate angulation. Dewclaws are not desired; if present, they must not obstruct gait.

Feet. Broad, with strong toes, moderately closed, and with rather high knuckles. The so-called dewclaws which sometimes occur on the inside of the hindlegs are imperfectly developed toes. They are of no use to the dog and are not taken into consideration in judging. They may be removed by surgery.

Coat. Very dense, short-haired (stockhaarig), lying smooth, tough, without however feeling rough to the touch. The thighs are slightly bushy. The tail at the root has longer and denser hair which gradually becomes shorter toward the tip. The tail appears bushy, not forming a flag.

Color. White with red or red with white, the red in its various shades; brindle patches with white markings. The colors red and brown-yellow are of entirely equal value. Necessary markings are: white chest, feet and tip of tail, nose band, collar or spot on the nape; the latter and blaze are very desirable. Never of one color or without white. Faulty are all other colors, except the favorite dark shadings on the head (mask) and ears. One distinguishes between mantle dogs and splash-coated dogs.

Height at Shoulder. Of the dog should be 27½ inches minimum, of the bitch 25½ inches. Female animals are of finer and more delicate build.

Considered as faults are all deviations from the Standard, as for instance a sway-back and a disproportionately long back, hocks too much bent, straight hindquarters, upward growing hair in spaces between the toes, out at elbows, cowhocks and weak pasterns.

LONGHAIRED

The longhaired type completely resembles the shorthaired type except for the coat which is not shorthaired (stockhaarig) but of medium length plain to slightly wavy, never rolled or curly and not shaggy either. Usually on the back, especially from the region of the haunches to the rump, the hair is more wavy, a condition, by the way, that is slightly indicated in the shorthaired dogs. The tail is bushy with dense hair of moderate length. Rolled or curly hair on the tail is not desirable. A tail with parted hair, or a flag tail, is faulty. Face and ears are covered with short and soft hair; longer hair at the base of the ear is permissible. Forelegs only slightly feathered; thighs very bushy.

Approved May 12, 1959

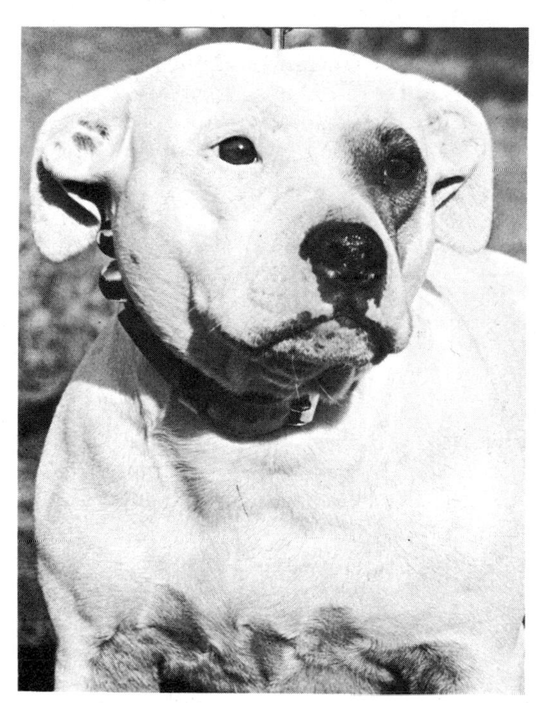

STAFFORDSHIRE BULL TERRIER

(THE KENNEL CLUB—TERRIER GROUP)

Characteristics. From the past history of the Staffordshire Bull Terrier, the modern dog draws his character of indomitable courage, high intelligence and tenacity. This coupled with his affection for his friends, and children in particular; his off-duty quietness and trustworthy stability, makes him the foremost all-purpose dog.

General Appearance. The Staffordshire Bull Terrier is a smooth-coated dog. He should be of great strength for his size and although muscular, should be active and agile.

Head and Skull. Short, deep through, broad skull, very pronounced cheek muscles, distinct stop, short foreface, black nose.

Eyes. Dark preferable but may bear some relation to coat colour. Round, of medium size, and set to look straight ahead.

Ears. Rose or half-pricked and not large. Full drop or prick to be penalized.

Mouth. The mouth should be level, i.e., the incisors of the bottom jaw should fit closely inside the incisors of the top jaw, and the lips should be tight and clean. The badly undershot or overshot mouth to be heavily penalized.

Neck. Muscular, rather short, clean in outline and gradually widening towards the shoulders.

Forequarters. Legs straight and well-boned, set rather wide apart, without looseness at the shoulders, and showing no weakness at the pasterns, from which point the feet turn out a little.

Body. The body should be close-coupled, with a level topline, wide front, deep brisket, well-sprung ribs and rather light in the loins.

Hindquarters. The hindquarters should be well muscled, hocks let down with stifles well bent. Legs should be parallel when viewed from behind.

Feet. The feet should be well padded, strong and of medium size.

Tail. The tail should be of medium length, low set, tapering to a point and carried rather low. It should not curl much and may be likened to an old-fashioned pump handle.

Coat. Smooth, short and close to the skin.

Colour. Red, fawn, white, black or blue, or any of these colours with white. Any shade of brindle or any shade of brindle with white. Black and tan or liver-colour not to be encouraged.

Weight and Size. Weight: Dogs, 28 to 38 lbs, bitches, 24 to 34 lbs. Height (at shoulder), 14 to 16 inches, these heights being related to the weights.

Faults. To be penalized in accordance with the severity of the fault: Light eyes or pink eyerims. Tail too long or badly curled. Non-conformation to the limits of weight or height. Full drop and prick ears. Undershot or overshot mouths. The following faults should debar a dog from winning any prize: Pink (Dudley) nose. Badly undershot or overshot mouth. Badly undershot—where the lower jaw protrudes to such an extent that the incisors of the lower jaw do not touch those of the upper jaw. Badly overshot—where the upper jaw protrudes to such an extent that the incisors of the upper jaw do not touch those of the lower jaw.

STAFFORDSHIRE TERRIER

(AMERICAN KENNEL CLUB—GROUP IV: TERRIERS)

General Impression. The Staffordshire Terrier should give the impression of great strength for his size, a well put together dog, muscular, but agile and graceful, keenly alive to his surroundings. He should be stocky, not long-legged or racy in outline. His courage is proverbial.

Head. Medium length, deep through, broad skull, very pronounced cheek muscles, distinct stop; and ears are set high.

Ears. Cropped or uncropped, the latter preferred. Uncropped ears should be short and held half rose or prick. Full drop to be penalized.

Eyes. Dark and round, low down in skull and set far apart. No pink eyelids.

Muzzle. Medium length, rounded on upper side to fall away abruptly below eyes. Jaws well defined. Underjaw to be strong and have biting power. Lips close and even, no looseness. Upper teeth to meet tightly outside lower teeth in front. Nose definitely black.

Neck. Heavy, slightly arched, tapering from shoulders to back of skull. No looseness of skin. Medium length.

Shoulders. Strong and muscular with blades wide and sloping.

Back. Fairly short. Slight sloping from withers to rump with gentle short slope at rump to base of tail. Loins slightly tucked.

Body. Well-sprung ribs, deep in rear. All ribs close together. Forelegs set rather wide apart to permit of chest development. Chest deep and broad.

Tail. Short in comparison to size, low set, tapering to a fine point; not curled or held over back. Not docked.

Legs. The front legs should be straight, large or round bones, pastern upright. No resemblance of bend in front. Hindquarters well-muscled, let down at hocks, turning neither in nor out. Feet of moderate size, well-arched and compact. Gait must be springy but without roll or pace.

Coat. Short, close, stiff to the touch, but all white, more than 80 per cent white, black and tan, and liver not to be encouraged.

Size. Height and weight should be in proportion. A height of about 18 to 19 inches at shoulders for the male and 17 to 18 inches for the female is to be considered preferable.

Faults. Faults to be penalized are Dudley nose, light or pink eyes, tail too long or badly carried, undershot or overshot mouths.

Approved June 10, 1936

TIBETAN SPANIEL

(THE KENNEL CLUB—UTILITY GROUP)

Characteristics. Gay and assertive, highly intelligent, and aloof with strangers.
General Appearance. Should be small, well balanced, active, alert.
Head. Should be of medium or small size in proportion to size of body.
Skull. Slightly domed, muzzle fairly short and blunt.
Nose. Black, but brown or liver coloured permissible.
Eyes. Should be dark brown in colour, bright, expressive, set fairly wide apart, not full or prominent.
Ears. Pendant, well feathered, they can have a slight 'lift' away from the side of the head.
Mouth. Slightly undershot preferable. Teeth should not show when the mouth is closed.
Neck. Short, well covered with a mane which is more pronounced in dogs than in bitches.
Forequarters. The bones of the forelegs are slightly bowed but firm at the shoulder. Well feathered at back.
Body. Longer from point of shoulder to root of tail than the height at shoulder.
Hindquarters. Hindlegs smooth, feathered at back with heavy feathering on buttocks.
Feet. Hare footed, small and neat with featherings between the toes often extending beyond the feet. White markings allowed.
Tail. Set high, richly plumed and carried in a gay curl over the back.
Coat. Double coated, silky in texture, lies rather flat with a mane on neck and shoulders.
Colours. Golden, cream, white, biscuit, fawn, brown, shaded sable, red sable, black, parti-colour or tri-colour.
Weight. Dogs from 10 to 16 lbs; bitches from 9 to 15 lbs.
Height. Dogs up to 11 inches; bitches up to $9\frac{1}{2}$ inches.
Faults. Large full eye. Broad flat face. Very domed head. Accentuated stop. Pointed muzzle.

TIBETAN TERRIER

(THE KENNEL CLUB—UTILITY GROUP)

Characteristics. Alert, intelligent and game, not fierce nor pugnacious. Chary of strangers.
General Appearance. A well-muscled medium-sized dog, in general appearance not unlike an Old English Sheepdog in miniature.
Head and Skull. Skull of medium length, not broad or coarse, narrowing slightly from ear to eye, not domed but not absolutely flat between the ears. The malar bones are curved, but should not be over developed so as to bulge. There should be a marked stop in front of the eyes, but this must not be exaggerated. The head should be well furnished with long hair, falling forward over the eyes. The lower jaw should carry a small, but not exaggerated amount of beard. The length from eye to tip of nose equal to length from eye to base of skull; not broad nor massive. Nose black.
Eyes. Large, dark, neither prominent nor sunken: should be set fairly wide apart. Eyelids dark.
Ears. Pendant, not too close to head, V-shaped, not too large, heavily feathered.
Mouth. Level by preference but if slightly undershot not to be penalized.
Forequarters. Legs parallel and heavily furnished. Pasterns slightly sloping.
Body. Compact and powerful. Length from point of shoulder to root of tail equal to height at withers. Well ribbed up. Loin slightly arched.
Hindquarters. Heavily furnished, should be slightly longer than forelegs with well bent stifles and low set hocks giving a level back.
Feet. The feet should be large, round, heavily furnished with hair between the toes and pads. The dog should stand well down on its pads. There should be no arch in the feet.
Gait. When walking or trotting the hindlegs should neither go inside nor outside the front ones but run on the same track.
Tail. Medium length, set on fairly high and carried in a gay curl over the back. Very well feathered. There is often a kink near the tip.
Coat. Double coated. The undercoat fine wool, the top coat profuse, fine but not silky or woolly; long; either straight or waved.
Colour. White, golden, cream, grey or smoke, black, parti-colour, and tri-colours; in fact any colour except chocolate or liver colour.
Size. Height at shoulders, dogs should be from 14 to 16 inches, bitches slightly smaller.
Faults. A weak snipy foreface should be penalized. Lack of double coat. Cat feet.

TIBETAN TERRIER

(AMERICAN KENNEL CLUB—GROUP VI: NON SPORTING)

Skull and Head. Skull of medium length, not broad or coarse, narrowing slightly from ear to eye, not domed but not absolutely flat between the ears. The malar bones are curved, but should not be overdeveloped so as to bulge. There should be a marked stop in front of the eyes, but this must not be exaggerated. The head should be well furnished with long hair, falling forward over the eyes. The lower jaw should carry a small but not over-exaggerated amount of beard. Jaws between the canines should form a distinct curve. The length from the eye to tip of nose should be equal to that from eye to base of skull, not broad or massive.

Nose. Black. Any color other than black shall disqualify.

Eyes. Large, dark, neither prominent nor sunken; should be set fairly wide apart. Eyelids dark.

Ears. Pendant, not too close to the head, 'V' shaped, not too large; heavily feathered.

Mouth. Level by preference but a slight undershot should not be penalized.

Forequarters. Legs straight, heavily furnished.

Body. Compact and powerful. Length from point of shoulder to root of tail equal to height at withers. Well ribbed up. Loin slightly arched.

Hindquarters. Heavily furnished, hocks well let down.

Feet. The feet should be large, round, and heavily furnished with hair between the toes and pads. The dog should stand well down on its pads.

Tail. Medium length, set on fairly high and carried in a gay curl over the back. Very well feathered. There is often a kink near the tip.

Coat. Double-coated. The undercoat fine wool, the top coat profuse, fine, but not silky or woolly; long; either straight or waved.

Color. Any color or colors including white.

Weight and Size. Average weight 22 to 23 pounds . . . but may be 18 to 30 lbs. Height from 14 to 16 inches.

Faults. Poor coat; mouth very undershot or overshot; a weak snipy foreface.

DISQUALIFICATION

Nose any color other than black.

Approved June 12, 1973

WEIMERANER

(THE KENNEL CLUB—GUNDOG GROUP)

Characteristics. In the case of the Weimaraner his hunting ability is the paramount concern and any fault of body or mind which detracts from this ability should be penalized. The dog should display a temperament that is keen, fearless and friendly, protective and obedient.

General Appearance. A medium-sized grey dog with light eyes, he should present a picture of great driving power, stamina, alertness and balance. Above all, the dog should indicate ability to work hard in the field. The walk is rather awkward. The trot should be effortless and groundcovering and should indicate smooth coordination. When seen from the rear, the hind feet should parallel the front feet. When seen from the side, the topline should remain strong and level.

Head and Skull. Moderately long and aristocratic, with moderate stop and slight median line extending back over the forehead. Rather prominent occipital bone and trumpets set well back, beginning at the back of the eye sockets. Measurement from the tip of the nose to stop to equal that from the stop to occipital bone. The flews should be moderately deep, enclosing a powerful jaw. Forehead perfectly straight, delicate at the nostrils. Skin tightly drawn. Neck clean cut and moderately long. Expression keen, kind and intelligent.

Eyes. Round, in shades of light amber and hazel, set well enough apart to indicate good disposition and intelligence. When dilated under excitement the eyes may appear almost black.

Ears. Long and lobular, slightly folded and set high. The ear when drawn alongside the jaw should end approximately one inch from the point of the nose.

Mouth. Well-set, strong and even teeth, well developed and proportionate to jaw with correct scissors bite, the upper teeth protruding slightly over the lower teeth but not more than one sixteenth of an inch. Complete dentition is greatly desired. Grey nose. Lips and gums of pinkish flesh shade.

Forequarters. Forelegs straight and strong, with measurement from elbow to the ground equalling the distance from the elbow to the top of the withers.

Body. The length of the body from the highest point of the withers to the root of the tail should equal the measurement from the highest point of the withers to the ground. The back set in a straight line should slope slightly from the withers. The chest should be well developed and deep, shoulder well laid and snug. Ribs well sprung and long. Abdomen firmly held, moderately tucked up flank. The brisket should drop to the elbow.

Hindquarters. Well angulated with short stifles and straight hocks well let down. Musculation well developed.

Feet. Firm and compact, webbed, toes well arched, pads closed and thick. Nails short and grey or amber in colour. Dewclaws allowable only on dogs whelped prior to March 1, 1950 or adult dogs imported with claws on.

Tail. Docked, at maturity it should measure approximately six inches with a tendency to be light rather than heavy and should be carried in a manner expressing confidence and sound temperament.

Coat. Short, smooth and sleek.

Colour. Shades of silver, mouse or roe grey usually blending to a lighter shade on the head and ears. Small white mark allowable on chest, but not on any other part of the body. White spots that have resulted from injuries shall not be penalized.

Weight and Size. Height at withers, dogs 23 to 25 inches, bitches 22 to 24 inches. Weight fully grown, dogs 55 to 65 lbs, bitches 45 to 55 lbs.

Faults. Very serious faults: Coat any other colour than silver, mouse or roe grey. Eyes any other colour than light amber or hazel. Black or mottled mouth. Any other coat than short and sleek. Non-docked tail. Shyness or viciousness.

Serious Faults. Poor gait. Very poor feet. Cow-hocks. Faulty back, either roached or sway. Badly overshot or undershot. Snipy muzzle. Short ears. Yellow or white markings.

Faults. Doggy bitches, bitchy dogs. Improper muscular condition. Badly affected teeth. More than four teeth missing. Back too long or too short. Faulty coat (other than seasonal). Neck too short, thick or throaty. Undersize. Low set tail. Elbows in or out, feet turned in or out.

Minor Faults. Tail too short or too long. Pink nose. Dewclaws on. Oversize should not be considered a serious fault, providing correct structure and working ability is in evidence.

WEIMARANER

(AMERICAN KENNEL CLUB—GROUP I: SPORTING DOGS)

General Appearance. A medium-sized gray dog, with fine aristocratic features. He should present a picture of grace, speed, stamina, alertness and balance. Above all, the dog's conformation must indicate the ability to work with great speed and endurance in the field.

Height. Height at the withers: dogs, 25 to 27 inches; bitches, 23 to 25 inches. One inch over or under the specified height of each sex is allowable but should be penalized. Dogs measuring less than 24 inches or more than 28 inches and bitches measuring less than 22 inches or more than 26 inches shall be disqualified.

Head. Moderately long and aristocratic, with moderate stop and slight median line extending back over the forehead. Rather prominent occipital bone and trumpets well set back, beginning at the back of the eye sockets. Measurement from tip of nose to stop equal that from stop to occipital bone. The flews should be straight, delicate at the nostrils. Skin drawn tightly. Neck clean-cut and moderately long. Expression kind, keen and intelligent.

Ears. Long and lobular, slightly folded and set high. The ear when drawn snugly alongside the jaw should end approximately 2 inches from the point of the nose.

Eyes. In shades of light amber, gray or blue-gray, set well enough apart to indicate good disposition and intelligence. When dilated under excitement the eyes may appear almost black.

Teeth. Well set, strong and even; well-developed and proportionate to jaw with correct scissors bite, the upper teeth protruding slightly over the lower teeth but not more than $\frac{1}{16}$ of an inch. Complete dentition is greatly to be desired.

Nose. Gray.

Lips and Gums. Pinkish flesh shades.

Body. The back should be moderate in length, set in a straight line, strong, and should slope slightly from the withers. The chest should be well developed and deep with shoulders well laid back. Ribs well sprung and long. Abdomen firmly held; moderately tucked-up flank. The brisket should extend to the elbow.

Coat and Color. Short, smooth and sleek, solid color, in shades of mouse-gray to silver-gray, usually blending to lighter shades on the head and ears. A small white marking on the chest is permitted, but should be penalized on any other portion of the body. White spots resulting from an injury should not be penalized. A distinctly long coat is a disqualification. A distinctly blue or black coat is a disqualification.

Forelegs straight and strong, with the measurement from the elbows to the ground approximately equalling the distance from the elbow to the top of the withers.

Hindquarters. Well-angulated stifles and straight hocks. Musculation well developed.

Feet. Firm and compact, webbed, toes well arched, pads closed and thick, nails short and gray or amber in color.

Dewclaws. Should be removed.

Tail. Docked. At maturity it should measure approximately 6 inches with a tendency to be light rather than heavy and should be carried in a manner expressing confidence and sound temperament. A non-docked tail shall be penalized.

Gait. The gait should be effortless and should indicate smooth coordination. When seen from the rear, the hind feet should be parallel to the front feet. When viewed from the side, the topline should remain strong and level.

Temperament. The temperament should be friendly, fearless, alert and obedient.

Minor Faults. Tail too short or too long. Pink nose.

Major Faults. Doggy bitches. Bitchy dogs. Improper muscular condition. Badly affected teeth. More than four teeth missing. Back too long or too short. Faulty coat. Neck too short, thick or throaty. Low-set tail. Elbows in or out. Feet east and west. Poor gait. Poor feet. Cow-hocks. Faulty backs, either roached or sway. Badly overshot, or undershot bite. Snipy muzzle. Short ears.

Very Serious Faults. White, other than a spot on the chest. Eyes other than gray, blue-gray or light amber. Black mottled mouth. Non-docked tail. Dogs exhibiting strong fear, shyness and extreme nervousness.

DISQUALIFICATIONS

Deviation in height of more than one inch from standard either way. A distinctly long coat.

Approved June 8, 1965

WELSH CORGI (CARDIGAN)

(THE KENNEL CLUB—WORKING GROUP)

General Appearance. Expression to be as foxy as possible; alertness essential; the body to measure about 36 inches from point of nose to tip of tail.

Head and Skull. Head to be foxy in shape and appearance. Skull to be fairly wide and flat between the ears, tapering towards the eyes, above which it should be slightly domed. Muzzle to measure about 3 inches in length (or in proportion to skull as three to five) and to taper towards the snout. Nose black (except in Blue Merles) slightly projecting and in no sense blunt, with nostrils of moderate size. Underjaw to be clean cut and strong but without prominence.

Eyes. To be of medium size, but giving a sharp and watchful expression, rather widely set with corners clearly defined; preferably dark in colour but clear. Silver eyes permissible in Blue Merles.

Ears. To be rather large (in proportion to size of dog) and prominent, moderately wide at the base, carried erect, set about $3\frac{1}{2}$ inches apart and well back so that they can be laid flat along neck.

Mouth. Teeth strong, level and sound.

Neck. To be muscular, well developed and in proportion to the dog's build, fitting into well-sloped shoulders.

Forequarters. Front to be slightly bowed, with strong bone. Legs short and strong. Shoulders strong and muscular.

Body. Chest to be moderately broad with prominent breast bone. Body to be fairly long and strong, with deep brisket, well-sprung ribs and clearly defined waist.

Hindquarters. To be strong with muscular thighs. Legs short and strong.

Feet. Round and well padded. All dewclaws removed. Rather large.

Tail. To be moderately long and set in line with body (not curled over back) and resembling that of a fox.

Coat. Short or medium, of hard texture.

Colour. Any colour except pure white.

Weight and Size. Height to be as near as possible to 12 inches at shoulder. Weight: Dogs 22 to 26 lbs, bitches 20 to 24 lbs.

Faults. Over or undershot mouth, high peaked occiput, prominent cheeks, low flat forehead, expressionless eyes, crooked forearms, splayed feet, tail curled over back. Silky coat.

WELSH CORGI, CARDIGAN

(AMERICAN KENNEL CLUB—GROUP III: WORKING DOGS)

General Appearance. Low-set, sturdily built, with heavy bone and deep chest. Over-all silhouette long in proportion to height, culminating in low tail-set and fox-like brush. Expression alert and foxy, watchful yet friendly.

General Impression. A handsome, powerful, small dog, capable of both speed and endurance, intelligent, sturdy, but not coarse.

Head and Skull. Skull moderately wide and flat between the ears, with definite though moderate stop.

Muzzle to measure about 3 inches in length, or in proportion to the skull as 3 to 5. Muzzle medium, *i.e.* neither too pointed nor too blunt but somewhat less fine than the Pembroke. Nose black. Nostrils of moderate size. Under-jaw clean-cut and strong.

Eyes. Medium to large, and rather widely set, with distinct corners. Color dark to dark amber but clear. Blue eyes, or one dark and one blue eye, permissible in blue merles.

Mouth. Teeth strong and regular, neither overshot nor undershot. Pincer (level) bite permissible but scissors bite preferred, *e.g.* the inner side of the front teeth resting closely over the front of the lower front teeth.

Ears. Large and prominent in proportion to size of dog. Slightly rounded at the tips, moderately wide at the base, and carried erect, set well apart and well back, sloping slightly forward when erect. Flop ears a serious fault.

Neck. Muscular, well developed, especially in males, and in proportion to dog's build; fitting into strong, well-shaped shoulders.

Forequarters. Chest broad, deep, and well let down between forelegs. Forelegs short, strong, and slightly bowed around chest, and with distinct but not exaggerated crook below the carpus. Elbows close to side. A straight, terrier-like front is a fault.

Body. Long and strong, with deep brisket, well-sprung ribs with moderate tuck-up of loin. Top-line level except for slight slope of spine above tail.

Hindquarters. Strong, with muscular thighs. Legs short and well boned.

Feet. Round and well padded. Hind dewclaws, if any, should be removed. Front dewclaws may be removed.

Tail. Long to moderately long, resembling a fox brush. Should be set fairly low on body line, carried low when standing or moving slowly, streamlining out when at a dead run, lifted when tracking or excited, but never curled over the back. A rat tail or a whip tail are faults.

Coat. Medium length but dense. Slightly harsh texture, but neither wiry nor silky. Weather-resistant. An overly short coat or a long and silky and/or curly coat are faults. Normal grooming and trimming of whiskers is permitted. Any trimming that alters the natural length of the coat is not permitted and is a serious fault. A distinctly long coat is a disqualification.

Size. Height approximately 12 inches at the highest point of the shoulder blades. Length usually between 36 and 44 inches from nose to tip of tail. In considering the height, weight, and length of a dog, over-all balance is a prime factor.

Colors. Red, sable, red-brindle, black-brindle, black, tri-color, blue merle. Usually with white flashings on chest, neck, feet, face or tip of tail. No preferences among these colors. A dog predominantly white in color should be seriously faulted. Pure white is a disqualification.

DISQUALIFICATIONS

A distinctly long coat. Pure white.

Approved February 11, 1967

WELSH CORGI (PEMBROKE)

(THE KENNEL CLUB—WORKING GROUP)

General Appearance. Low set, strong, sturdily built, alert and active, giving an impression of substance and stamina in a small space, outlook bold, expression intelligent and workmanlike. The movement should be free and active, elbows fitting closely to the sides, neither loose nor tied. Forelegs should move well forward, without too much lift, in unison with thrusting action of hindlegs.

Head and Skull. Head to be foxy in shape and appearance, with alert and intelligent expression, skull to be fairly wide and flat between the ears; moderate amount of stop. Length of foreface to be in proportion to the skull as three is to five. Muzzle slightly tapering. Nose black.

Eyes. Well set, round, medium size, hazel in colour and blending with colour of coat.

Ears. Pricked, medium sized, slightly pointed. A line drawn from the tip of the nose through the eye should, if extended, pass through, or close to, the tip of the ear.

Mouth. Teeth level, or with the inner side of the upper front teeth resting closely on the front of the under ones.

Neck. Fairly long.

Forequarters. Legs short and as straight as possible. Ample bone carried right down to the feet. Elbows should fit closely to the sides, neither loose nor tied.

Body. Of medium length, with well-sprung ribs. Not short coupled or terrier like. Level topline. Chest broad and deep, well let down between the forelegs.

Hindquarters. Strong and flexible, slightly tapering. Legs short. Ample bone carried right down to the feet. Hocks straight when viewed from behind.

Feet. Oval, the two centre toes slightly in advance of two outer ones, pads strong and well arched. Nails short.

Tail. Short, preferably natural.

Coat. Of medium length and dense; not wiry.

Colour. Self colours in red, sable, fawn, black and tan, or with white markings on legs, chest and neck. Some white on head and foreface is permissible.

Weight and Size. Dogs 20 to 24 lbs; bitches 18 to 22 lbs. Height from 10 to 12 inches at shoulder.

Faults. The following are serious faults: White on the body giving a piebald or skewbald effect, or hound like markings. Long fluffy coat, accompanied with feathering on ears and feet. Overshot or undershot mouth.

WELSH CORGI—PEMBROKE

(AMERICAN KENNEL CLUB—GROUP III: WORKING DOGS)

General Appearance. Low-set, strong, sturdily built and active, giving an impression of substance and stamina in a small space. Should not be so low and heavy-boned as to appear coarse or overdone, nor so light-boned as to appear racy. Outlook bold, but kindly. Expression intelligent and interested. Never shy nor vicious.

Size and Proportions. Moderately long and low. The distance from the withers to base of tail should be approximately 40 per cent greater than the distance from the withers to the ground.

Height (from ground to highest point on withers) should be 10 to 12 inches.

Weight is in proportion to size, not exceeding 30 lbs for dogs and 28 lbs for bitches. In show condition, the preferred medium-size dog of correct bone and substance will weigh approximately 27 lbs, with bitches approximately 25 lbs. Obvious oversized specimens and diminutive toylike individuals must be very seriously penalized.

Head and Skull. Head to be foxy in shape and appearance, but not sly in expression. Skull to be fairly wide and flat between the ears. Moderate amount of stop. Very slight rounding of cheek, and not filled in below the eyes, as foreface should be nicely chiseled to give a somewhat tapered muzzle. Distance from the occiput to center of stop to be greater than the distance from stop to nose tip. The proportion being five parts of total distance for the skull and three parts for the foreface. Muzzle should be neither dish-faced nor Roman-nosed.

Nose. Black and fully pigmented.

Eyes. Oval, medium in size, not round nor protruding, nor deep-set and piglike. Set somewhat obliquely. Variations of brown in harmony with coat color. Eye rims dark, preferably black. While dark eyes enhance the expression, true black eyes are most undesirable, as are yellow or bluish eyes.

Ears. Erect, firm, and of medium size, tapering slightly to a rounded point. Ears are mobile, and react sensitively to sounds. A line drawn from the nose tip through the eyes to the ear tips and across should form an approximate equilateral triangle. Bat ears, small cat-like ears, overly large weak ears, hooded ears, ears carried too high or too low are undesirable. Button, rose or drop ears are very serious faults.

Mouth. Scissors bite, the inner side of the upper incisors touching the outer side of the lower incisors. Level bite is acceptable. Lips should be tight, with little or no fullness, and black. Overshot or undershot bite is a very serious fault.

Neck. Fairly long, of sufficient length to provide over-all balance of the dog. Slightly arched, clean and blending well into the shoulders. A very short neck giving a stuffy appearance, and a long, thin or ewe neck, are faulty.

Body. Rib cage should be well sprung, slightly egg-shaped, and moderately long. Deep chest, well let down between forelegs. Exaggerated lowness interferes with the desired freedom of movement and should be penalized. Viewed from above, the body should taper slightly to end of the loin. Loin short. Firm level topline, neither riding up to nor falling away at the croup. A slight depression behind the shoulders caused by heavier neck coat meeting the shorter body coat is permissible. Round or flat rib cage, lack of brisket, extreme length or cobbiness are undesirable.

Forequarters. Legs short: forearms turned slightly inward, with the distance between the wrists less than between the shoulder joints, so that the front does not appear absolutely straight. Ample bone carried right down into the feet. Pasterns firm and nearly straight when viewed from the side. Weak pasterns and knuckling over are serious faults. Shoulder blades long and well laid back along the rib cage. Upper arms nearly equal in length to shoulder blades. Elbows parallel to the body, not prominent, and well set back to allow a line perpendicular to the ground to be drawn from the tip of the shoulder blade through to elbow.

Hindquarters. Ample bone, strong and flexible, moderately angulated at stifle and hock. Exaggerated angulation is as faulty as too little. Thighs should be well muscled. Hocks short, parallel, and when viewed from the side are perpendicular to the ground. Barrel hocks or cowhocks are most objectionable. Slipped or double-jointed hocks are very faulty.

Tail. Docked as short as possible without being indented. Occasionally a puppy is born with a natural dock, which if sufficiently short is acceptable. A tail up to two inches in length is allowed, but if carried high tends to spoil the contour of the topline.

Feet. Oval, with the two center toes slightly in advance of the two outer ones. Turning neither in nor out. Pads strong and feet arched. Nails short. Dewclaws on both forelegs and hind legs usually removed. Too round, long and narrow, or splayed feet are faulty.

Movement. Free and smooth. Forelegs should reach well forward, without too much lift, in unison with the driving action of hind legs. The correct shoulder assembly and well-fitted elbows allow the long, free stride in front. Viewed from the front, legs do not move in exact parallel planes, but incline slightly inward to compensate for shortness of leg and width of chest. Hind legs should drive well under the body and move on a line with the forelegs, with hocks turning neither in nor out. Feet must travel parallel to the line of motion with no tendency to swing out, cross over, or interfere with each other. Short, choppy movement, rolling or high-stepping gait, close or overly wide coming or going are incorrect. This is a herding dog which must have the agility, freedom of movement, and endurance to do the work for which he was developed.

Color. The outer coat is to be of self colors in red, sable, fawn, black and tan, with or without white markings. White is acceptable on legs, chest, neck (either in part or as a collar), muzzle, underparts, and as a narrow blaze on head.

Very Serious Faults—Whitelies. Body color white with red or dark markings.

Mismarks. Self colors with any area of white on back between withers and tail, on sides between elbows and back of hindquarters, or on ears. Black with white markings and no tan present.

Bluies. Colored portions of the coat have a distinct bluish or smoky cast. This coloring is associated with extremely light or blue eyes and liver or gray eye rims, nose and lip pigment.

Coat. Medium length; short, thick, weather-resistant undercoat with a coarser, longer outer coat. Over-all length varies, with slightly thicker and longer ruff around neck, chest and on the shoulders. The body coat lies flat. Hair is slightly longer on back of forelegs and underparts, and somewhat fuller and longer on rear of hind-quarters. The coat is preferably straight, but some waviness is permitted. This breed has a shedding coat, and seasonal lack of undercoat should not be too severely penalized, providing the hair is glossy, healthy, and well groomed. A wiry, tightly marcelled coat is very faulty, as is an overly short, smooth and thin coat.

Very Serious Fault—Fluffies. A coat of extreme length with exaggerated feathering on ears, chest, legs and feet, underparts and hind-quarters. Trimming such a coat does not make it any more acceptable.

The Corgi should be shown in its natural condition with no trimming permitted except to tidy the feet and, if desired, remove the whiskers.

Over-all Picture. Correct type, including general balance and outline, attractiveness of headpiece, intelligent outlook and correct temperament, is of primary importance. Movement is especially important, particularly as viewed from the side. A dog with smooth and free gait has to be reasonably sound and must be highly regarded. A minor fault must never take precedence over the above desired qualities.

A dog must be very seriously penalized for the following faults, regardless of whatever desirable qualities the dog may present: Whitelies, Mismarks or Bluies; Fluffies; Button, Rose or Drop Ears; Overshot or Undershot Bite; Oversize or Undersize.

The judge shall dismiss from the ring any Pembroke Welsh Corgi that is vicious or excessively shy.

Approved June 13, 1972

WELSH TERRIER

(THE KENNEL CLUB—TERRIER GROUP)

Characteristics. The Welsh Terrier is of a gay, volatile disposition and is rarely of a shy nature. He is affectionate, obedient and easily controlled, thus making him an eminently suitable dog for town life. His size and colour render him ideal as a house dog, as the former point is in his favour where accommodation is limited, whilst the latter feature precludes the necessity for frequent washing as in the case of a white terrier. He is game and fearless, but definitely not of a pugnacious disposition, although at all times able to hold his own when necessary. He is ideally constituted to be a perfect town or country companion. Welsh Terriers are normally hardy and of robust constitution, and need no pampering, whilst as working terriers they are second to none, being easily trained to all sorts of game and vermin to work with gun or ferrets, and are generally found to be capital water dogs.

Head and Skull. The skull should be flat and rather wider between the ears than the Wire-Haired Fox Terrier. The jaw should be powerful, clean cut, rather deeper, and more punishing—giving the head a more masculine appearance than that usually seen on a Fox Terrier. Stop not too defined, fair length from stop to end of nose, the latter being of a black colour.

Eyes. Should be small, well set in, of a dark colour, expressive and indicating abundant keenness. A round full eye is undesirable.

Ears. Should be V-shaped, small, not too thin, set on fairly high, carried forward and close to the cheek.

Mouth. Should be level with strong teeth.

Neck. The neck should be of moderate length and thickness, slightly arched and sloping gracefully into the shoulders.

Forequarters. The shoulders should be long, sloping and well set back. The legs should be straight and muscular, possessing ample bone, with upright and powerful pasterns.

Body. The back should be short, and well ribbed up, the loin strong, good depth, and moderate width of chest.

Hindquarters. Should be strong, thighs muscular, and of good length, with the hocks well bent, well let down and with ample bone.

Feet. The feet should be small, round and catlike.

Tail. The tail should be well set on, but not too gaily carried.

Coat. Should be wiry, hard, very close and abundant. A single coat is undesirable.

Colour. The colour should be black and tan for preference, or black grizzle and tan, free from black pencilling on toes. Black below the hocks is a fault.

Weight and Size. The height at shoulder should not exceed $15\frac{1}{2}$ inches. 20 to 21 lbs. shall be considered a fair average weight in working condition.

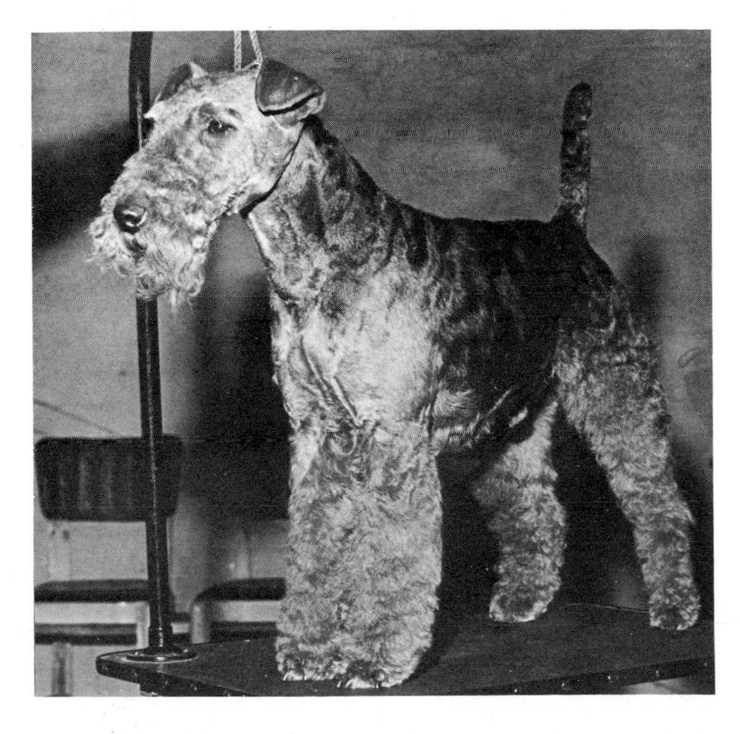

Faults. A white, cherry or spotted nose. Prick, tulip or rose ears. An appreciable amount of black below the hocks.

WELSH TERRIER

(AMERICAN KENNEL CLUB—GROUP IV: TERRIERS)

Head. The skull should be flat, and rather wider between the ears than the Wirehaired Fox Terrier. The jaw should be powerful, clean-cut, rather deeper, and more punishing—giving the head a more masculine appearance than that usually seen on a Fox Terrier. Stop not too defined, fair length from stop to end of nose, the latter being of a black colour.

Ears. The ear should be V-shaped, small, not too thin, set on fairly high, carried forward and close to the cheek.

Eyes. The eye should be small, not being too deeply set in or protruding out of skull, of a dark hazel color, expressive and indicating abundant pluck.

Neck. The neck should be of moderate length and thickness, slightly arched and sloping gracefully into the shoulders.

Body. The back should be short, and well-ribbed up, the loin strong, good depth, and moderate width of chest. The shoulders should be long, sloping, and well set back. The hindquarters should be strong, thighs muscular and of good length, with the hocks moderately straight, well let down, and fair amount of bone. The stern should be set on moderately high, but not too gaily carried.

Legs and Feet. The legs should be straight and muscular, possessing fair amount of bone, with upright and powerful pasterns. The feet should be small, round and catlike.

Coat. The coat should be wiry, hard, very close and abundant.

Color. The color should be black and tan, or black grizzle and tan, free from black penciling on toes.

Size. The height at shoulder should be 15 inches for dogs, bitches proportionately less. Twenty pounds shall be considered a fair average weight in working condition, but this may vary a pound or so either way.

SCALE OF POINTS

Head and jaws	10	Legs and feet	10
Ears	5	Coat	15
Eyes	5	Color	5
Neck and shoulders	10	Stern	5
Body	10	General appearance	15
Loins and hindquarters	10	Total	100

DISQUALIFICATIONS

Nose: White, cherry or spotted to a considerable extent with either of these colors. Ears: Prick, tulip or rose. Undershot jaw or pig-jawed mouth. Black below hocks or white to an appreciable extent.

WEST HIGHLAND WHITE TERRIER

(THE KENNEL CLUB—TERRIER GROUP)

General Appearance. The general appearance of the West Highland White Terrier is that of a small, game, hardy-looking Terrier, possessed of no small amount of self-esteem; with a varminty appearance; strongly built, deep in chest and back ribs; level back and powerful quarters on muscular legs, and exhibiting in a marked degree a great combination of strength and activity. Movement should be free, straight and easy all round. In the front the legs should be freely extended forward by the shoulder. The hind movement should be free, strong and close. The hocks should be freely flexed and drawn close in under the body, so that when moving off the foot, the body is pushed forward with some force. Stiff, stilted movement behind is very objectionable.

Head and Skull. The skull should be slightly domed and when gripped across the forehead, should present a smooth contour. There should only be a very slight tapering from the skull at the level of the ears to the eyes. The distance from the occiput to the eyes should be slightly greater than the length of the foreface. The head should be thickly coated with hair, and carried at a right-angle or less, to the axis of the neck. On no account should the head be carried in the extended position. The foreface should gradually taper from the eye to the muzzle. There should be a distinct stop formed by heavy, bony ridges, immediately above and slightly overhanging the eye, and a slight indentation between the eyes. The foreface should not dish or fall away quickly below the eyes where it should be well made up. The jaws should be strong and level. The nose must be black. Should be fairly large, and forming a smooth contour with the rest of the muzzle. The nose must not project forward giving rise to a snipy appearance.

Eyes. Should be widely set apart, medium in size, as dark as possible in colour. Slightly sunk in head, sharp and intelligent, which, looking from under the heavy eyebrows, imparts a piercing look. Full or light-coloured eyes are objectionable.

Ears. Small, erect and carried firmly, terminating in a sharp point. The hair on them should be short, smooth (velvety) and should not be cut. The ears should be free from any fringe at the top. Round pointed, broad, large or thick ears are very objectionable, also ears too heavily coated with hair.

Mouth. Should be as broad between the canine teeth as is consistent with the sharp varminty expression required. The teeth should be large for the size of the dog, and should articulate in the following manner: the lower canines should lock in front of the upper canines. There should be six teeth between the canines of the upper and lower incisors. The upper incisors should slightly overlap the lower incisors, the inner side of the upper incisors being in contact with the outer side of the lower incisors. There should be no appreciable space between the incisors when the mouth is closed ensuring a keen bite; a dead level mouth is not a fault.

Neck. Should be sufficiently long to allow the proper set on of head required, muscular and gradually thickening towards the base allowing the neck to merge into nicely sloping shoulders, thus giving freedom of movement.

Forequarters. The shoulders should be sloped backwards. The shoulder blades should be broad and lie close to the chest wall. The joint formed by the shoulder blade and the upper arm should be placed forward, on account of the obliquity of the shoulder blades, bringing the elbows well in and allowing the foreleg to move freely, parallel to the axis of the body, like the pendulum of a clock. Forelegs should be short and muscular, straight and thickly covered with short hard hair.

Body. Compact. Back level, loins broad and strong. The chest should be deep and the ribs well arched in the upper half presenting a flattish side appearance. The back ribs should be of a considerable depth and the distance from the last rib of the quarters as short as is compatible with free movement of the body.

Hindquarters. Strong, muscular and wide across the top. Legs should be short, muscular and sinewy. The thighs very muscular and not too wide apart. The hocks bent and well set in under the body so as to be fairly close to each other when standing, walking or trotting. Cow-hocks detract from the general appearance. Straight or weak hocks are undesirable and are a fault.

Feet. The forefeet are larger than the hind ones, are round, proportionate in size, strong, thickly padded and covered with short hard hair. The hind feet are smaller and thickly padded. The under-surface of the pads of feet and all nails should be preferably black.

Tail. 5 to 6 inches long, covered with hard hair, no feather, as straight as possible, carried jauntily, not gay nor carried over the back. A long tail is objectionable and on no account should tails be docked.

Coat. Colour pure white, must be doublecoated. The outer coat consists of hard hair, about 2 inches long, free from any curl. The undercoat, which resembles fur, is short, soft and close. Open coats are objectionable.

Colour. Pure white.

Weight and Size. Size about 11 inches at the withers.

WEST HIGHLAND WHITE TERRIER

(AMERICAN KENNEL CLUB—GROUP IV: TERRIERS)

General Appearance. The West Highland White Terrier is a small, game, well-balanced, hardy-looking Terrier, exhibiting good showmanship, possessed with no small amount of self-esteem, strongly built, deep in chest and back ribs, straight back and powerful hindquarters on muscular legs, and exhibiting in marked degree a great combination of strength and activity. The coat should be about 2 inches long, white in color, hard, with plenty of soft undercoat. The dog should be neatly presented. Considerable hair should be left around the head to act as a frame for the face to yield a typical Westie expression.

Color and Pigmentation. Coat should be white, as defined by the breed's name. Nose should be black. Black pigmentation is most desirable on lips, eye-rims, pads of feet, nails and skin.

Faults. Any coat color other than white and nose color other than black are serious faults.

Coat. Very important and seldom seen to perfection; must be double-coated. The outer coat consists of straight hard hair, about 2 inches long, with shorter coat on neck and shoulders, properly blended.

Faults. Any silkiness or tendency to curl is a serious fault, as is an open or single coat.

Size. Dogs should measure about 11 inches at the withers, bitches about one inch less.

Faults. Any specimens much over or under height limits are objectionable.

Skull. Should be fairly broad, being in proportion to his powerful jaw, not too long, slightly domed, and gradually tapering to the eyes. There should be a defined stop, eyebrows heavy.

Faults. A too long or too narrow skull.

Muzzle. Should be slightly shorter than the skull, powerful and gradually tapering to the nose, which should be large. The jaws should be level and powerful, the teeth well set and large for the size of the dog. There shall be 6 incisor teeth between the canines of both lower and upper jaws. A tight scissors bite with upper incisors slightly overlapping the lower incisors or level mouth are equally acceptable.

Faults. Muzzle longer than skull. Teeth much undershot or overshot are a serious fault, as are teeth defective or missing.

Ears. Small, carried tightly erect, set wide apart and terminating in a sharp point. They must never be cropped. The hair on the ears should be short, smooth and velvety, and trimmed free of fringe at the tips.

Faults. Round-pointed, drop, broad and large ears are very objectionable, as are mule-ears, ears set too closely together or not held tightly erect.

Eyes. Widely set apart, medium in size, dark in color, slightly sunk in the head, sharp and intelligent. Looking from under heavy eyebrows, they give a piercing look.

Faults. Too small, too full or light-colored eyes are very objectionable.

Neck. Muscular and nicely set on sloping shoulders.

Faults. Short neck or too long neck.

Chest. Very deep and extending at least to the elbows with breadth in proportion to size of the dog.

Fault. Shallow chest.

Body. Compact and of good substance, level back, ribs deep and well arched in the upper half of rib, presenting a flattish side appearance, loins broad and strong, hindquarters strong, muscular, and wide across the top.

Faults. Long or weak back; barrel ribs; high rump.

Legs and Feet. Both forelegs and hindlegs should be muscular and relatively short, but with sufficient length to set the dog up so as not to be too close to the ground. The shoulder blades should be well laid back and well knit at the backbone. The chest should be relatively broad and the front legs spaced apart accordingly. The front legs should be set in under the shoulder blades with definite body overhang before them. The front legs should be reasonably straight and thickly covered with short hard hair. The hind legs should be short and sinewy; the thighs very muscular and not set wide apart, with hocks well bent. The forefeet are larger than the hind ones, are round, proportionate in size, strong, thickly padded, and covered with short hard hair; they may properly be turned out a slight amount. The hind feet are smaller and thickly padded.

Faults. Steep shoulders, loaded shoulders, or out at the elbows. Too light bone, Cowhocks, weak hocks and lack of angulation. A 'fiddle-front' is a serious fault.

Tail. Relatively short, when standing erect it should never extend above the top of the skull. It should be covered with hard hairs, no feather, as straight as possible, carried gaily but not curled over the back. The tail should be set on high enough so that the spine does not slope down to it. The tail must never be docked.

Faults. Tail set too low; tail too long or carried at half mast or over back.

Movement. Should be free, straight and easy all around. In front, the leg should be freely extended forward by the shoulder. The hind movement should be free, strong and fairly close. The hocks should be freely flexed and drawn close under the body; so that when moving off the foot the body is thrown or pushed forward with some force.

Faults. Stiff, stilty or too wide movement behind. Lack of reach in front, and/or drive behind.

Temperament. Must be alert, gay, courageous and self-reliant, but friendly.

Faults. Excess timidity or excess pugnacity.

Approved December 10, 1968

WHIPPET

(THE KENNEL CLUB—HOUND GROUP)

General Appearance. Should convey an impression of beautifully balanced muscular power and strength, combined with great elegance and grace of outline. Symmetry of outline, muscular development and powerful gait are the main considerations; the dog being built for speed and work all forms of exaggeration should be avoided. The dog should possess great freedom of action, the forelegs should be thrown forward and low over the ground like a thoroughbred horse not in a Hackney-like action. Hindlegs should come well under the body giving great propelling power, general movement not to look stilted, high stepping or in a short or mincing manner.

Head and Skull. Long and lean, flat on top tapering to the muzzle, rather wide between the eyes, the jaws powerful and clean cut, nose black, in blues a bluish colour is permitted and in livers a nose of the same colour and in whites or particolour a butterfly nose is permissible.

Eyes. Bright, expression very alert.

Ears. Rose shaped, small and fine in texture.

Mouth. Level. The teeth in the top jaw fitting closely over the teeth in lower jaw.

Neck. Long and muscular, elegantly arched.

Forequarters. Shoulders oblique and muscular the blades carried up to the spine closely set together at the top. Forelegs straight and upright, front not too wide, pasterns strong with slight spring, elbows well set under the body.

Body. Chest very deep with plenty of heart-room, brisket deep and well defined, back broad, firm, somewhat long and showing definite arch over the loin but not humped, loin giving the impression of strength and power, ribs well sprung; well muscled on back.

Hindquarters. Strong and broad across thighs, stifles well bent, hocks well let down, second thighs strong, the dog then being able to stand over a lot of ground and show great driving power.

Feet. Very neat, well split up between the toes, knuckles highly arched, pads thick and strong.

Tail. No feathering. Long, tapering, when in action carried in a delicate curve upward but not over the back.

Coat. Fine, short, as close as possible in texture.

Colour. Any colour or mixture of colours.

Weight and Size. The ideal height for dogs is $18\frac{1}{2}$ inches and for bitches $17\frac{1}{2}$ inches. Judges should use their discretion and not unduly penalize an otherwise good specimen.

Faults. Front and Shoulders. Weak, sloping or too straight pasterns, pigeon toes, tied elbows, loaded or bossy shoulders wide on top and straight shoulderblades, flat sides. An exaggerated narrow front not to be encouraged.

Head and Skull. Appleskull, short fore face or down face.

Ears. Pricked or tulip.

Mouth. Over or undershot.
Neck. Throatiness at the join of neck and jaw, and at base of neck.
Body and Hindquarters. A short coupled or cramped stance, also an exaggerated arch, a Camel or Humped back (the arch starting behind the shoulderblades), a too short or overlong loin. Straight stifles, poor muscular development of thighs and second thighs.
Feet. Splayed, flat or open.
Tail. Gay, ringed or twisted, short or docked.
Coat. Wire or Broken coated; a coarse or woolly coat; coarse thick skin.

WHIPPET

(AMERICAN KENNEL CLUB—GROUP II: HOUNDS)

General Appearance. A moderate size sight-hound giving the appearance of elegance and fitness, denoting great speed, power, and balance without coarseness. A true sporting hound that covers a maximum of distance with a minimum of lost motion.
Head. Long and lean, fairly wide between the ears, scarcely perceptible stop, good length of muzzle which should be powerful without being coarse. Nose entirely black.
Ears. Small, fine in texture, thrown back and folded. Semipricked when at attention. Gay ears are incorrect and should be severely penalized.
Eyes. Large, dark, with keen intelligent alert expression. Lack of pigmentation around eyelids is undesirable. Yellow or dilute-colored eyes should be strictly penalized. Blue or china-colored eyes shall disqualify. Both eyes must be of the same color.
Muzzle. Muzzle should be long and powerful denoting great strength of 'bite' without coarseness. Teeth should be white and strong. Teeth of upper jaw should fit closely over teeth of lower jaw creating a strong scissors bite. Extremely short muzzle or lack of underjaw should be strictly penalized. An even bite is extremely undesirable. Undershot shall disqualify. Overshot one-quarter inch or more shall disqualify.
Neck. Long and muscular, well-arched and with no suggestion of throatiness, widening gradually into the shoulders. Must not have any tendency to a 'ewe' neck.
Shoulders. Long, well-laid back with long, flat muscles. Loaded shoulders are a *very* serious fault.
Brisket. Very deep and strong, reaching as nearly as possible to the point of the elbow. Ribs well sprung but with no suggestion of barrel shape. Should fill in the space between the forelegs so that there is no appearance of a hollow between them.
Forelegs. Straight and rather long, held in line with the shoulders and *not* set under the body so as to make a forechest. Elbows should turn neither in nor out and move freely with the point of the shoulder. Fair amount of bone, which should carry right down to the feet. Pasterns strong.
Feet. Must be well formed with strong, thick pads and well-knuckled-up paws. A thin, flat, open foot is a serious fault.
Hindquarters. Long and powerful, stifles well bent, hocks well let down and close to the ground. Thighs broad and muscular, the muscles should be long and flat. A steep croup is most undesirable.
Back. Strong and powerful, rather long with a good, natural arch over the loin creating a definite tuck-up of the underline but covering a lot of ground.
Tail. Long and tapering, should reach to a hip-bone when drawn through between the hind legs. Must not be carried higher than the top of the back when moving.
Coat. Close, smooth, and firm in texture.
Color. Immaterial.
Size. Ideal height for dogs 19 to 22 inches; for bitches 18 to 21 inches measured across the shoulders at the highest point. One-half inch above or below the above stated measurements will disqualify.
Gait. Low, free moving and smooth, as long as is commensurate with the size of the dog. A short, mincing gait with high knee action should be severely penalized.

DISQUALIFICATIONS

Blue or china-colored eyes. Undershot. Overshot one-quarter inch or more. A dog one-half inch above or below the measurements specified under 'Size'.

Approved October 12, 1971

WIREHAIRED POINTING GRIFFON

(AMERICAN KENNEL CLUB—GROUP I: SPORTING DOGS)

The Wirehaired Griffon is a dog of medium size, fairly short-backed, rather a little low on his legs. He is strongly limbed, everything about him indicating strength and vigor. His coat is harsh like the bristles of a wild boar and his appearance, notwithstanding his short coat, is as unkempt as that of the long-haired Griffon, but on the other hand he has a very intelligent air.

Head. Long, furnished with a harsh coat, forming a mustache and eyebrows, skull long and narrow, muzzle square.

Eyes. Large, open, full of expression, iris yellow or light brown.

Ears. Of medium size, flat or sometimes slightly curled, set rather high, very lightly furnished with hair.

Nose. Always brown.

Neck. Rather long, no dewlap.

Shoulders. Long, sloping.

Ribs. Slightly rounded.

Forelegs. Very straight, muscular, furnished with rather short wire hair.

Hind Legs. Furnished with rather short stiff hair, the thighs long and well developed.

Feet. Round, firm and well formed.

Tail. Carried straight or gaily, furnished with a hard coat without plume, generally cut to a third of its length.

Coat. Hard, dry, stiff, never curly, the undercoat downy.

Color. Steel gray with chestnut splashes, gray white with chestnut splashes, chestnut, dirty white mixed with chestnut, never black.

Height. $21\frac{1}{2}$ to $23\frac{1}{2}$ inches for males, and $19\frac{1}{2}$ to $21\frac{1}{2}$ inches for females.

YORKSHIRE TERRIER

(THE KENNEL CLUB—TOY GROUP)

General Appearance. Should be that of a long-coated toy terrier, the coat hanging quite straight and evenly down each side, a parting extending from the nose to the end of the tail. The animal should be very compact and neat, the carriage being very upright and conveying an 'important' air. The general outline should convey the impression of a vigorous and well-proportioned body.

Head and Skull. Head should be rather small and flat, not too prominent or round in the skull, nor too long in the muzzle, with a perfect black nose. The fall on the head to be long, of a rich golden tan, deeper in colour at the sides of the head about the ear roots, and on the muzzle where it should be very long. On no account must the tan on the head extend on to the neck, nor must there be any sooty or dark hair intermingled with any of the tan.

Eyes. Medium, dark and sparkling, having a sharp intelligent expression, and placed so as to look directly forward. They should not be prominent and the edge of the eyelids should be of a dark colour.

Ears. Small V-shaped, and carried erect or semi-erect, and not far apart, covered with short hair, colour to be of a very deep rich tan.

Mouth. Perfectly even, with teeth as sound as possible. An animal having lost any teeth through accident not to be faulted providing the jaws are even.

Forequarters. Legs quite straight, well covered with hair of a rich golden tan a few shades lighter at the ends than at the roots, not extending higher on the forelegs than the elbow.

Body. Very compact with a good loin. Level on the top of the back.

Hindquarters. Legs quite straight, well covered with hair of a rich golden tan, a few shades lighter at the ends than at the roots, not extending higher on the hind legs than the stifle.

Feet. As round as possible; the toe-nails black.

Tail. Cut to medium length; with plenty of hair, darker blue in colour than the rest of the body, especially at the end of the tail, and carried a little higher than the level of the back.

Coat. The hair on the body moderately long and perfectly straight (not wavy), glossy like silk, and of a fine silky texture.

Colour. A dark steel blue (not silver blue), extending from the occiput (or back of skull) to the root of tail, and on no account mingled with fawn, bronze or dark hairs. The hair on the chest a rich bright tan. All tan hair should be darker at the roots than in the middle, shading to a still lighter tan at the tips.

Weight and Size. Weight up to 7 lbs.

YORKSHIRE TERRIER

(AMERICAN KENNEL CLUB—GROUP V: TOYS)

General Appearance. That of a long-haired toy terrier whose blue and tan coat is parted on the face and from the base of the skull to the end of the tail and hangs evenly and quite straight down each side of body. The body is neat, compact and well proportioned. The dog's high head carriage and confident manner should give the appearance of vigor and self-importance.

Head. Small and rather flat on top, the skull not too prominent or round, the muzzle not too long, with the bite neither undershot nor overshot and teeth sound. Either scissors bite or level bite is acceptable. The nose is black. Eyes are medium in size and not too prominent; dark in color and sparkling with a sharp, intelligent expression. Eye rims are dark. Ears are small, V-shaped, carried erect and set not too far apart.

Body. Well proportioned and very compact. The back is rather short, the back line level, with height at shoulder the same as at the rump.

Legs and Feet—Forelegs should be straight, elbows neither in nor out.

Hind legs straight when viewed from behind, but stifles are moderately bent when viewed from the sides.

Feet are round with black toenails. Dewclaws, if any, are generally removed from the hind legs. Dewclaws on the forelegs may be removed.

Tail. Docked to a medium length and carried slightly higher than the level of the back.

Coat. Quality, texture and quantity of coat are of prime importance. Hair is glossy, fine and silky in texture. Coat on the body is moderately long and perfectly straight (not wavy). It may be trimmed to floor length to give ease of movement and a neater appearance, if desired. The fall on the head is long, tied with one bow in center of head or parted in the middle and tied with two bows. Hair on muzzle is very long. Hair should be trimmed short on tips of ears and may be trimmed on feet to give them a neat appearance.

Colors. Puppies are born black and tan and are normally darker in body color, showing an intermingling of black hair in the tan until they are matured. Color of hair on body and richness of tan on head and legs are of prime importance in *adult dogs* to which the following color requirements apply:

BLUE. Is a dark steel-blue, not a silver-blue and not mingled with fawn, bronzy or black hairs.

TAN. All tan hair is darker at the roots than in the middle, shading to still lighter tan at the tips. There should be no sooty or black hair intermingled with any of the tan.

Color on Body. The blue extends over the body from back of neck to root of tail. Hair on tail is a darker blue, especially at end of tail.

Headfall. A rich golden tan, deeper in color at sides of head, at ear roots and on the muzzle, with ears a deep rich tan. Tan color should not extend down on back of neck.

Chest and Legs. A bright, rich tan, not extending above the elbow on the forelegs nor above the stifle on the hind legs.

Weight. Must not exceed seven lbs.

Approved April 12, 1966